**This book is to be returned on or before
the last date stamped below.**

LIBREX

Minority rights in Europe

A review of the work and standards of the Council of Europe

Patrick Thornberry and María Amor Martín Estébanez

Council of Europe Publishing

This publication describes the situation as at 31 December 2002.

Cover design: Graphic Design Workshop Council of Europe
Layout: DTP unit, Council of Europe

Edited by Council of Europe Publishing
http://book.coe.int
F-67075 Strasbourg Cedex

ISBN 92-871-5366-3
© Council of Europe, March 2004
Printed in Germany by Koelblin-Fortuna-Druck

Contents

List of selected abbreviations

AC   Advisory Committee for the Framework Convention for the Protection of National Minorities

ADACS   Activities for the Development and Consolidation of Democratic Stability

CAHLR   ad hoc Committee of Experts on Regional or Minority Languages in Europe

CAHMEC ad hoc Committee of Experts [advising the CoM]

CAHMIN   ad hoc Committee of Experts for the Protection of National Minorities

CAHP   European Population Committee [formerly CDPO]

CDCC   Council for Cultural Co-operation [later replaced by GR-C]

CDCJ   European Committee on Legal Co-operation

CDDH   Steering Committee for Human Rights

CDMG   European Committee on Migration

CDMM   Steering Committee on the Mass Media

CDLR   Steering Committee on Local and Regional Democracy [later replaced by RAP-LOC]

CDPO   see CAHP

CERD   Committee on the Elimination of Racial Discrimination

CLRAE   Congress of Local and Regional Authorities of Europe (referred to as Congress throughout publication)

CoM   Committee of Ministers

CPT   European Committee for the Prevention of Torture and Inhuman or Degrading Treatment or Punishment

CSCE   Conference on Security and Co-operation in Europe [the Helsinki process, now OSCE]

DH-MIN   The Committee of Experts on Issues relating to the Protection of National Minorities

EBLUL   European Bureau for Lesser Used Languages

ECHR   European Commission on Human Rights

ECMI   European Centre for Minority Issues

ECRI   European Commission against Racism and Intolerance

EUMC   European Monitoring Centre on Racism and Xenophobia

FCNM   Framework Convention for the Protection of National Minorities

GR-C   Rapporteur Group on Education, Culture, Sport, Youth and the Environment

GR-EDS   Rapporteur Group on Democratic Stability

GR-H   Rapporteur Group on Human Rights

GT-MIN   ad hoc working party of the ministers' deputies on the implementation mechanism of the Framework Convention

GT-SAGES   ad hoc working party on follow-up action on the final report of the Committee of Wise Persons

GT-SUIVI-   CoM monitoring group for treaty obligations of states party
AGO

HCNM   High Commissioner on National Minorities

ICCPR   International Covenant on Civil and Political Rights

ILO   International Labour Organisation

OECD   Organisation for Economic Co-operation and Development

OHCHR   Office of the High Commissioner for Human Rights

OSCE   Organisation for Security and Co-operation in Europe; formerly CSCE

PCIJ   Permanent Court of International Justice

R/M   regional or minority languages

UNDM   UN Declaration on the rights of persons belonging to national or ethnic, religious and linguistic minorities

UNHCR   United Nations High Commissioner for Refugees

Introduction
Perspectives on minorities and minority rights

The new awareness

Questions concerning minorities are high on the agendas of the United Nations, the Council of Europe, the Organisation for Security and Co-operation in Europe (OSCE), the European Union, and other inter-governmental and non-governmental organisations. Events in eastern Europe and the former USSR and Yugoslavia pushed minorities to the forefront of international consciousness in the 1990s, and the fate of groups in various theatres of conflict continues to trouble the inter-national conscience.[1] Following Bosnia, we think of Kosovo, and Chechnya. Violent ethnic conflict afflicts Asia, Africa and the Americas – East Timor, Rwanda and Chiapas are only three of the many names that spring to mind. There have been other conflicts, not always violent, where ethnicity is part of the context if not the whole story. For Europe, we could name Estonia and Latvia, Greece and Turkey, the United Kingdom, Spain and Cyprus, the Caucasus and beyond, as among the corners where an ethnic or part-ethnic drama is still being played out, though some situations are less dramatic than before, and in others there are prospects of reconciliation.

Ethnic conflict is rarely "pure" and never "simple", often "mixed in" with other elements such as religion, immigration, economic stress, popular unease with government, or inter-state tensions.[2] More subtle forms of oppression such as discrimination against groups like the Europe-wide Roma,[3] appear to have a longer "shelf life" than the "merely violent":[4] the European Conference Against Racism has spoken of the "banalisation" of racism and intolerance, based less on theories of racial/ethnic supremacy and more on recognition of a range of "others".[5] Some ethnic questions appear to have deep roots,[6] others are more recently "constructed".[7] Globalisation makes its own distinctive contribution to ethnic difficulties through exacerbation of the structural, institutional and entrenched patterns of racism that exist within and between countries and regions as a result of migration flows and allied phenomena, though it can also provide networking and other benefits to marginalised groups and peoples.[8] Ethnic and nationalist issues have also increasingly preoccupied the academic world: liberals, communitarians and republicans,[9] cultural relativists and agnostics,[10] idealists and sentimentalists,[11] post-moderns who would leave it as it is, and fundamentalists who would turn it all over to Eternity, have all visited the shores of ethnicity and nationalism. Disciplines seem driven by the compulsion to speculate, theorise and inform about "ethnic/minority questions". Some of the great European thinkers of our age have been ambivalent on these issues.[12]

The conflict perspective should not be over-stressed. While the denial of minority rights has been commonplace, almost all states remain rich in ethnic groups, languages and religions – the complexity of the world is still capable of astonishing, though some have sensed that the stock is diminishing.[13] Most groups co-exist peacefully with others, interacting, socialising and participating in public and private spheres.[14] Commentators suggest that there are many "models of good practice" in the treatment of minorities.[15] As a United Nations Special Rapporteur has observed:

> much inspiration can be derived from the constructive developments that have taken place in many parts of the world, where the different groups have accommodated to each other, live peacefully side by side, preserve their own identities ... adapt to ... new conditions ... develop bonds of inter-marriage and reciprocal understanding.[16]

This positive aspect should be kept in mind as should what needs to be done in case facile pessimism of the intellect suffocates optimism of the will. The effort of international organisations in the last decade has been to support positive developments, acting more critically when necessary, under diverse mandates. Hence the emphasis on technical assistance and advisory services of all kinds, on confidence-building, on an exchange of knowledge and experience, on dissemination of international standards and good practice, and the attempt to make the standards work in reality. It is not simply a question of averting conflict, but of laying the foundations for durable and diverse democracies through the building of long-lasting peace.

From 1945 to 1989, international relations were dominated by the perspective of a bipolar world and rival utopias of development, the capitalist and the communist. Societies resolved themselves into classes and the ethnic and religious component of individual and collective identities was underplayed or ignored. Reflections on large conflicts, the rediscovery of the local,[17] the development of transnational solidarities among, for example, indigenous groups,[18] the emergence of a politics of recognition,[19] have all led to new social paradigms. Governments apologise for wrongs done to whole communities when it is too late for individuals to claim back their loss. Subaltern groups roll out their "subversive" narratives, redefining nations in pluralist terms, though many governments resist this change, especially if they represent peoples newly claiming their place in the sun. Ethno-nationalist regimes have fought their corner in recent years, with devastating results.[20]

The events and perspective shifts have particular significance for Europe, the home of nation–state ideology and the "classic" minorities question. In the European case, it is not appropriate to draw too sharp a distinction between East and West. As a former President of the European Parliament noted:

> Western Europeans are witnessing phenomena similar to those seen in eastern and central Europe in their own countries. Demagogical parties were exploiting irrational sentiment to propagate the belief that minorities were worsening the problems confronting our societies. This was generating xenophobia in countries with large migrant minorities. And worse than this, a climate of permissiveness with regard to the utterances of extreme right-wing groups seemed to be creeping in under the guise of tolerance ... Western Europe therefore faced the same challenges as central and eastern Europe. It was vital to find common solutions to these problems.[21]

The phrase "common solutions" suggests avoidance of double standards, and one of the dilemmas of intervention is the local question: why us, and not them? Why Kosovo, and not Rwanda? The enhanced activity in relation to minorities in eastern Europe can usefully direct itself to the West. Some European bodies – for example the European Commission against Racism and Intolerance (ECRI),[22] and presumptively the Advisory Committee for the Framework Convention for the Protection of National Minorities[23] – have done so and will need to display balance in addressing minority and cognate issues. The broader monitoring mechanisms initiated by the Council of Europe organs, such as the Committee of Ministers and the Parliamentary Assembly,[24] will also function best if they free themselves from limiting perspectives, and initial steps have already been taken in that direction, by the Congress of Local and Regional Authorities for example.[25] Otherwise, human rights can seem to be just another western "imposition". Hence the importance of "common standards" if we are to find "common solutions" on the basis of "common values"; hence the World Conference on Human Rights' reaffirmation of "the importance of ensuring the universality, objectivity and non-selectivity of the consideration of human rights issues".[26]

Nonetheless, while the problems relating to minorities in the European arena are broadly similar, in that no state or group of states has a monopoly on virtue, the accession of eastern European and former USSR states to the European organisations increased the dimensions of the minority question and the scale of response necessary to deal with it. The expansion in the number and range of groups following the influx of states was considerable. Wars, migrations, the historically recent collapse of the

Ottoman and Austro-Hungarian Empires, nationalist movements and totalitarian doctrine have all left their mark on the area, producing states which unavoidably resemble an ethnic, cultural and religious mosaic. The complexity of this expanded Europe is added to by the effect of intercontinental migrations, notably from Africa and Asia, which have produced populations of permanent residents in Europe that are culturally and ethnically different from majority cultures and the "traditional" minorities in those states.[27] The effect in cultural terms is to telescope time and distance, bringing diverse populations into close proximity, challenging the identity of "host" nations in the resulting interaction.

The sharpened view of the role of ethnicity and religion in underpinning social aggregations can and should lead to better normative frameworks and practice. Through the articulation of norms balancing respect for individual rights, group aspirations and the interests of states, international organisations can play a vital role in buttressing the positive achievements of states, while encouraging others to make adjustments in law and practice. Until recently, there was only a slow maturing of international norms and principles on human rights relevant to minorities. Legal paradigms have gradually moved from "undifferentiated" rights of individuals towards recognition of the collective element in human rights and the acceptance of categories of the rights holder within a universal framework.[28] International human rights bodies, including the purely intergovernmental, appear to be developing along the lines of ethnicity-sensitisation. The enhanced appreciation of ethnicity creates practical possibilities for the expansion of normative frameworks and the elaboration of monitoring mechanisms to address minority questions – both aspects of minority protection are now found within the Council of Europe.

International organisations and minority rights in Europe

Council of Europe work on minorities does not proceed in a normative or strategic vacuum. International organisations continue to develop their own systems of rule and practice in dealing with these phenomena. Co-ordination of strategy is an obvious desideratum, though each organisation and organ or body within it is ultimately responsible according to its own charter or mandate. Co-ordination of approaches – or the lack of it – is addressed in later chapters. On the co-ordination of norms, the present work deals with the regulation of the interethnic realm from the standpoint of international law and organisation. While the focus is on one regional European system, the backdrop of general standards must also be taken into account, otherwise the international corpus of rights becomes incoherent, and fails to offer guidance for the practice of states. The present section seeks only to sketch some basic principles and

mechanisms as they affect minorities. A regional system must be expected to take universal norms as a basis, adapt the standards to its particular geopolitical space, and where possible enhance them.[29]

The League of Nations

The League of Nations developed after the first world war some of the cardinal principles and strategies in dealing with minority questions. In a system largely confined to the continent of Europe,[30] the League of Nations made the protection of minorities a major part of its programme. Its method represented an extension of a long historical tradition in Europe and dealt with minority rights through treaties and declarations relating to specific groups. No universal prescription for minorities was created, though the treaties and declarations exhibited a recurring pattern of rights with variations for particular group circumstances.[31] Key points in the system were:

- Recognition of the minorities question as one with distinct parameters;
- An attempt to guarantee the rights of minorities for humanitarian and pragmatic reasons – the threat to world peace presented by the mistreatment of the groups;
- Procedures to implement the rights, including a system of petitions for individuals and groups;
- Encouragement of human rights throughout state laws and constitutions;
- Treaties and declarations providing rights for all inhabitants of the states, rights for all nationals, and nationals belonging to "racial, religious or linguistic minorities";
- Autonomy rights for groups concentrated in particular regions.

Rights were expressed as belonging to individuals but collective rights were also recognised. In terms of the philosophy of the system, and indeed of any system for the protection of minorities, the statement by the Permanent Court of International Justice (PCIJ) in the case of the minority schools in Albania remains valid for Europe. At least two principles may be extracted from its work. The object of the system of minority protection – and perhaps any such system – was to "[s]ecure for certain elements incorporated in a State, the population of which differs from them in race, language or religion, the possibility of living peaceably alongside that population and co-operating amicably with it, while at the same time preserving the characteristics which distinguish them from the majority, and satisfying the ensuing special needs". The court continued:

> In order to attain this object, two things were regarded as particularly necessary ... The first is to ensure that nationals belonging to racial,

religious or linguistic minorities shall be placed in every respect on a footing of perfect equality with the other nationals of the State. The second is to ensure for the minority elements suitable means for the preservation of their ... traditions and their national characteristics.[32]

A related principle derives from the court's pronouncement on the case of the Greco-Bulgarian communities:[33]

By tradition ... the 'community' is a group of persons living in a given country or locality, having a race, religion, language and traditions in a sentiment of solidarity, with a view to preserving their traditions, maintaining their form of worship, ensuring the instruction and upbringing of their children ... The existence of communities is a question of fact; it is not a question of law.[34]

The League of Nations system was overthrown by the second world war. A United Nations Secretariat study in 1950 concluded that the minorities regime had been terminated.[35] It is beyond the remit of the present report to discuss the UN study, though scholars have disputed the conclusions as to the termination of treaties and declarations.[36] Some of the instruments from the League of Nations continue to play a role in the contemporary administration of minority rights:[37] European Convention on Human Rights (ECHR) case-law involving Greece and Turkey has evoked the instruments of that period. The model of the bilateral or limited multilateral treaty for the protection of specific minority groups continues to prove attractive to European states.[38] The attention in the League of Nations system to issues of language, education, self-administration and discrimination also characterises contemporary instruments, as does the distinction between minority rights and self-determination: United Nations and Council of Europe instruments continue to differentiate the two principles.[39]

United Nations standards

Non-discrimination

The expansion in activity of international organisations of all kinds since 1945 has produced the result that a range of standards and mechanisms on minorities operate contemporaneously in the European space. The Charter of the United Nations sets a fundamental standard: human rights and fundamental freedoms are to be secured for all, without distinction on grounds of "race, sex, language, or religion". This principle, elaborated in the Universal Declaration of Human Rights, and various instruments on discrimination, is a cardinal principle in the protection of minorities. Its continuing significance must not be underestimated in discussions on the utility of more positive statements of rights. The UN Sub-Commission on Prevention of Discrimination and Protection of

Minorities (now known as the Sub-Commission on the Promotion and Protection of Human Rights) distinguished the concepts "prevention of discrimination" and "protection of minorities":

> Prevention of discrimination is the prevention of any action which denies to individuals or groups of peoples equality of treatment which they may wish.

> Protection of minorities is the protection of non-dominant groups which, while wishing in general for equality of treatment with the majority, wish for a measure of differential treatment in order to preserve basic characteristics which they possess and which distinguish them from the majority of the population.[40]

Interpretations of the non-discrimination principle, stressing the prohibition of indirect as well as direct discrimination,[41] and the need for special measures to remedy disadvantage, have expanded the scope of the non-discrimination principle for the benefit of national minorities and other vulnerable groups.[42] Key texts such as the UN Convention on the Elimination of All Forms of Racial Discrimination are not narrowly fixed on the notion of "race", but also explore the parameters of discrimination on grounds of colour, descent, and national or ethnic origin.[43] The broader shores of the phenomena of racism and xenophobia have been examined by the European Conference Against Racism[44] – Europe's contribution to the World Conference against Racism, Racial Discrimination, Xenophobia and Related Intolerance, and of course by the World Conference itself.

Specific minority rights

Article 27 of the International Covenant on Civil and Political Rights[45]

The Human Rights Committee, the implementing monitoring body of the International Covenant on Civil and Political Rights (ICCPR), has been solicited by this brief, weight-bearing article on many occasions:

> In those states in which ethnic, religious or linguistic minorities exist, persons belonging to such minorities shall not be denied the right, in community with the other members of their group, to enjoy their own culture, to profess and practise their own religion, or to use their own language.[46]

The opening phrase "[i]n those States in which ... minorities exist" almost invites states to declare that they have no minorities, but only France has recorded an "official" statement to that effect, declaring that "Article 27 is not applicable so far as the French Republic is concerned".[47] Following this example, reservations and declarations on Article 30 of the UN Convention on the Rights of the Child were made upon signature confirmed on ratification by France, by Venezuela, and upon signature by Turkey.[48]

However, according to General Comment No. 23 of the Human Rights Committee:[49] "[t]he existence of an ethnic, religious or linguistic minority in a given State party ... requires to be established by objective criteria".[50] In the language of the General Comment and following the line in the *Greco-Bulgarian Communities case* of the PCIJ (see above) "existence" "does not depend upon a decision by [a] State party ...".[51] Article 27 does not contain a definition of "minority" and the General Comment does not offer one. In *Ballantyne, Davidson and McIntyre v. Canada*,[52] a majority of the committee decided that members of the numerically superior Anglophone community in Canada could not be considered a minority even when they were a minority in a province (Quebec).[53] Other members of the committee dissented.[54] Confining the meaning of "minority" to exclude members of a majority in a minority situation in provinces or autonomous areas distances the approach of the committee from that found in some "European" texts and practice.[55]

Minority rights have been "admitted" into the contemporary canon of human rights as rights of individuals, not as "collective" or "group" rights. The terms are ambiguous and conceal two truisms: that "the individual" is an abstraction as much as "the group", and that all rights are "collective" in that they apply to a class of persons.[56] Of the contested conceptions, we should distinguish between collective rights of individuals by virtue of belonging to, or being perceived as a member of, a particular group (collective as adjective); and rights of a "collective" – a corporate conception implying rights for the group as such, against the world and even against its "members". Article 27 clearly eschews the corporate conception; rights are for: "persons belonging to ... minorities".[57]

However, Article 27 exhibits some collective dimension in that members of minorities "enjoy the rights in community with the other members of their group". The Human Rights Committee has indicated that in the enjoyment of rights under Article 27, the right of individuals to participate in aspects of community life may be restricted, but only if the restricting legislation reflects the legitimate aim of minority group survival and well-being, and the restriction on the right of an individual is not disproportionate to that aim.[58] If the principle of survival of minority cultures and religions in the face of assimilationist pressures is to have meaning, states should take positive measures to ensure that the disadvantages of minority status do not result in the denial of their rights. The General Comment on Article 27 insists on the positive nature of the article despite its negative language, and on its "horizontal" effect.[59] The most widely applicable "mechanism" for the ICCPR is a reporting procedure; there is also the possibility of an individual communications procedure for states party to the (first) optional protocol. Overlaps between ICCPR petitions and those under the ECHR occasionally arise.[60]

The United Nations declaration on minorities[61]

The text of the UN "Declaration on the rights of persons belonging to national or ethnic, religious and linguistic minorities" (hereafter referred to as the UNDM) is focused on individual rights – for "persons belonging to" minorities. On the other hand, Article 1.1 of the declaration explicitly describes identity and existence as fundamental attributes of groups. Article 2 replaces the "shall not be denied the right" of Article 27 of the ICCPR with the positive "have the right": the Article 27 formula suggested that a kind of "aggrieved hospitality" was at work,[62] not quite a welcome for minority rights. The declaration makes an explicit advance on Article 27 in its wide-ranging specification of participation rights – minority rights "to participate effectively in cultural, religious, social, economic and public life", and the right to participate effectively in decisions affecting them. Article 3 provides for the exercise of rights individually "as well as" collectively – in case states should be tempted to "decide" that culture, religion, etc., are to be carried on only in private. According to Article 4.2, states must facilitate the expression and development of minority culture, traditions and customs, etc., "except where specific practices are in violation of national law and international standards"[63] The qualification is necessary and meets an objection sometimes placed against minorities and indigenous people: that group traditions may incorporate practices inconsistent with human rights.

As with some European instruments, provisions on learning and instruction in the mother tongue contained in Article 4.3 are qualified and ambiguous. The intended contrast in the references to "learning" and "instruction" is between being taught one's own language as one is taught other languages, and learning through the medium of one's own language. The "philosophical" point of Article 4 – expressed in its fourth paragraph – is to promote self-knowledge on the part of minorities, and their awareness of the wider world, while informing society at large of the cultural and other contributions of minorities to the nation as a whole. Accordingly, the culture, history, traditions, etc., of minority groups should be the subject of positive valuations and not of the kind of distorted representations which produce low self-esteem in the groups and negative stereotypes in the wider community. Reciprocally, ethnic exclusiveness is discouraged.[64] Article 8 "balances" minority rights against the rights of others, implying that measures for minorities are generally compatible with equality, though this also suggests that they should not be pushed too far.

Article 8.4 expresses the fear of some states that minority rights may lead to self-determination: to the extent that a secessionist threat exists, it must be in virtue of other principles of international law. This applies equally to the converse argument that the declaration "protects" territorial integrity from valid claims to self-determination. The UN Commission on Human Rights adopted, on 3 March 1995, Resolution 1995/24, authorising the sub-commission to establish a working group on minorities to meet for the purpose of reviewing the promotion and realisation of the declaration, examining possible solutions to problems involving minorities, and recommending, where appropriate, further measures for the promotion and protection of minority rights. The working group met for the ninth time in 2003, and now enjoys an "indefinite" mandate.[65]

The ILO

In the related area of indigenous peoples, the International Labour Organisation (ILO) has produced two international treaties, the most recent of which is the 1989 Convention Concerning Indigenous and Tribal Peoples in Independent Countries, No. 169.[66] ILO standards are "backed up" by sophisticated, multilayered implementation mechanisms, and provisions for "representations" and "complaints" concerning the non-implementation of standards.[67] The Convention Concerning Indigenous and Tribal Peoples in Independent Countries provides a statement of coverage of relevant groups and extensive rights protection in the fields of land rights, recruitment and conditions of employment, vocational training, social security and health, and education.[68] There is also a specific provision on the facilitation of cross-border contacts and co-operation among indigenous groups.[69] Unlike the instruments on minorities, there is extensive citation of collective rights. Broad rights to participation in a variety of fields are another feature of the convention, which is backed up by the extensive implementation machinery of the ILO.

The convention is of interest here on account of participation by European states: Denmark, the Netherlands and Norway are parties, and other states may follow. States without indigenous groups on their territory may decide to ratify the convention as a guide to their development policies and a gesture of solidarity with indigenous peoples.[70] Indigenous groups are usually also minorities. The Saami of northern Europe figure in chapters that follow, and in particular the admission of the Russian Federation and other CIS countries to the Council of Europe brings with it numerous other indigenous peoples.[71] As noted, the European Conference Against Racism recognises the presence of indigenous peoples in Europe and the discrimination against them,[72] as does the Political Declaration adopted by ministers of member states of the Council of Europe at its concluding session.[73]

The OSCE

From the inception of the Organisation for Security and Co-operation in Europe (OSCE), as an intergovernmental conference in the mid-1970s (the Conference on Security and Co-operation in Europe – CSCE – also known as "Helsinki process"), it has been concerned with minorities.[74] The question of minority protection is already present in the 1975 Helsinki Final Act, the founding document of the CSCE process of East–West dialogue during the Cold War, and it has been an essential element of the comprehensive approach to international peace and security which has characterised the Organisation ever since. The OSCE, which constitutes a regional arrangement under Chapter VIII of the Charter of the United Nations,[75] regards human rights and the protection of human rights and the rule of law, together with political, military and economic considerations, as constituent elements of security and as closely interlinked. Normative detail on the minorities issue has developed notably since 1975.[76] Major steps in the process are the 1989 Vienna Concluding Document, the 1990 Document of the Copenhagen Conference on the Human Dimension of the CSCE (OSCE Copenhagen Document), the 1990 Charter of Paris for a New Europe, the 1991 Geneva Meeting of Experts on National Minorities, and the Concluding Document of the 1992 Helsinki Follow-up Meeting.

The Copenhagen Document in particular incorporates very broad statements on minority rights some of which remain unmatched,[77] linking their observance with the achievement of a democratic political framework and proposing respect for the rights as "an essential factor for peace, justice, stability and democracy in the participating States".[78] The OSCE participating states have affirmed that issues concerning national minorities, as well as compliance with international obligations and commitments concerning the rights of persons belonging to them are matters of international concern and they are no longer a matter for each state alone.[79] OSCE standards concerning minorities have often broken new ground,[80] both as to the areas of protection covered and the level of protection envisaged, and clearly influenced the drafting of UN and Council of Europe texts. Especially in areas such as participation rights, the relationship between official and minority languages, the inadmissibility of forced assimilation, their stance on the maintenance of organisations and associations, membership of minority groups and the like, all of which have become part of the standard repertoire of minority rights. The cautious stance on autonomy[81] – to be commended in particular circumstances if not a right of minorities – also set a standard, departures from which may provoke controversy.[82]

Most of the OSCE permanent institutions and decision-making structures as well as field presences,[83] including long-term missions,[84] deal with minority questions on a constant basis. The OSCE was innovative in introducing, during the cold war still, a general human dimension mechanism which was used on numerous occasions to address minority situations,[85] especially before the OSCE developed its more permanent structures. In 1992 the institution of the High Commissioner on National Minorities (HCNM) was created,[86] with a mandate to provide "early warning" and, as appropriate, "early action" at the earliest possible stage in regard to tensions involving national minority issues which have not yet developed beyond an early warning stage, but, in the judgement of the HCNM, have the potential to develop into a conflict within the CSCE area, affecting peace, stability or relations between participating states.[87] The HCNM operates essentially in the area of conflict prevention, including in the context of post-conflict situations.[88] The HCNM employs a low-key diplomatic approach to the resolution of difficulties and has emphasised the need for long-term approaches to the prevention of conflicts, based on the implementation of human rights and minority protection standards in particular. In practice, the High Commissioner has not been inhibited by restrictive definitions of minorities (citizens only – see below) and has investigated, *inter alia*, the situation of Russian-speakers in the Baltic states, including non-citizens. Major reports on the Roma have also been issued.[89] The HCNM has also contributed to the conceptual elaboration of minority rights and their specific implications for law and policy through sponsorship of expert "recommendations" or "guidelines" in areas such as education, language, participation, and the use of languages in the broadcast media.[90]

OSCE texts have a particular imprint: they are texts of political rather than legal commitment, though they reflect consensus and repeat customary law on certain points as well as contributing to its formation.[91] The OSCE human dimension and minority protection commitments derive their obligatory character from their being the constituent part of a broader package of "comprehensive security" measures which states have undertaken to fulfil in order to facilitate the development of peaceful relations in the OSCE region. In this sense they can be considered to have a strong binding character. It is also from this perspective that states are expected to follow the OSCE HCNM recommendations. The Vienna Summit of Heads of State and Government of the Council of Europe considered in relation to the OSCE that "the Council of Europe should apply itself to transforming, to the greatest possible extent, these political commitments into legal obligations".[92] Political approaches may lose credibility if they are understood only as a means of avoiding obligations and not as pragmatic strategies for the promotion of rights. However, as the experience of the OSCE shows, a great deal can be achieved in minority protection through methods other than the "hard law" approach.

The European Union

The European Union (EU) has not developed a specific, legally-binding instrument on "minority rights", but treaty references to culture and education, and to European cultural and linguistic diversity are significant.[93] Article 13 of the EC Treaty, as amended by the Treaty of Amsterdam, establishes EU competence "to combat discrimination" based, among other things, on racial or ethnic origin, religion or belief. Directive 2000/43/EC, implementing the principle of equal treatment between persons irrespective of racial or ethnic origin, has addressed the issue of discrimination, differentiating between "direct" and "indirect" and enshrined a right to redress through judicial or administrative procedures. It has also required the establishment of bodies for the promotion of equal treatment within states. Similarly, Directive 2000/78/EC establishing a general framework for equal treatment in employment and occupation, has interdicted discrimination in the labour market on grounds which include religion or belief.

EU institutions have often considered issues relevant for minority protection, such as the respect for different cultural and ethnic identities,[94] the respect for linguistic diversity,[95] and combating racism and xenophobia,[96] when considering internal community policy, especially in the fields of education, the media, access to the labour market and free movement of persons more generally.[97] However, a comprehensive minority policy has been lacking, and for a long time, the only allocation within the EU budget specifically devoted to minority protection has been that in support of the activities of the European Bureau for Lesser-Used Languages, largely financed by the European Commission. The Bureau watches over the autochthonous linguistic heritage of EU members.

It has been in the area of external relations that a more long-standing and solid "minority policy" has been developed: the "Europe Agreements", and "Association Agreements" with potential members have incorporated minority rights.[98] Given the limited attention to minority questions within the EU, one writer summarises the EU approach as insisting that:

> East European minority nations must be recognised as legitimate groups within their respective societies, and must be accorded group rights ... [whereas] in Western Europe, within the EU, minority nations have self-evidently not been protected through the granting of group rights.[99]

Practical "external" action on minorities has included the activities of the Pact on Stability in Europe,[100] the International Conference on the Former Yugoslavia and its Arbitration Commission (the Badinter Commission),[101] as well as the Stability Pact for south-eastern Europe. The "Guidelines on the recognition of new states in eastern Europe and in the Soviet Union" issued by the Foreign Affairs Ministers in December 1991 include "[g]uarantees for the rights of ethnic and national groups and minorities in accordance with the commitments subscribed to in the framework of the CSCE". Similarly, the Copenhagen Criteria for Membership, adopted by the European Council in 1993, refer to the need to show that the candidate country has established respect for and protection of minorities.[102]

The Charter of Fundamental Rights of the European Union omits any specific reference to minorities, though the preamble and Article 22 encapsulate some of the spirit of minority rights provisions in expressing concern for cultural, religious and linguistic diversity in Europe.[103] However, the potential for the EU to engage in an active policy in this field seems enormous, already within its present sphere of competencies. Aided by the adoption of Council Regulation (EC) No. 1035/97 of 2 June 1997 establishing a European Monitoring Centre on Racism and Xenophobia (EUMC), the EU has engaged in the development of a "comprehensive architecture to combat racism" which relies not only on the aforementioned legislation and approach by EU institutions but also on "a variety of programmes and projects that draw in civil society, transfer knowledge and experience, amongst and between governments and society and raise awareness and build capacity".[104] Co-operation on minority questions between the EU and the Council of Europe, and in particular between the EU Commission and the Council of Europe Secretariat is touched upon in the present volume.

The Council of Europe

The Council of Europe was founded in 1949 as a European organisation for intergovernmental and parliamentary co-operation. The central motive for its creation was the need to secure democracy in the light of recent and current totalitarianism and to prevent the recurrence of the gross violations of human rights which took place under Nazi instigation. According to the Council of Europe Statute, the aim of the Organisation is to "achieve a greater unity between its members for the purpose of safeguarding and realising the ideals and principles which are their common heritage and facilitating their economic and social progress".[105] The Council of Europe's statutory principles are pluralist democracy and respect for human rights and the rule of law, and every member "must accept the principles of the rule of law and of the enjoyment by all persons within its jurisdiction of human rights and fundamental freedoms".[106]

Organisational structures

Although not part of the "permanent" structures of the Council of Europe, "summits" of heads of state and government have played a notable role in advancing consciousness about minorities and minority rights in the 1990s. The Vienna Summit of 1993 in particular, and to a lesser extent the Strasbourg Summit in 1997, moved the agenda forward. Vienna "achievements" include significant developments in standards and mechanisms: the European Framework Convention for the Protection of National Minorities (hereafter referred to as the Framework Convention), and the declaration and plan of action on racism which resulted in the creation of the European Commission against Racism and Intolerance (ECRI). It also paved the way for the establishment of the Committee of Ministers monitoring procedure. The contributions of the summits are evaluated in Chapter 5.

The "regular" structures of the Organisation most closely related to the subject of this study include, firstly, the Committee of Ministers, the organ of the Council of Europe which represents the governments of the member states.[107] It operates mainly through the adoption of recommendations to the member states as well as resolutions. Its work also results in the elaboration of European conventions, declarations and agreements.[108] The committee is of a traditional character for intergovernmental organisations: each member state has one representative and one vote. The ministers' deputies are the governments' permanent representatives to the Council of Europe, and their decisions are considered to have been taken on behalf of the ministers who appointed them. The committee provides opportunities for political dialogue at ministerial and other levels on the development of European co-operation, with reference to the principles of the Organisation. Conferences of specialised ministers serve as platforms for political dialogue in specific fields of activity. The monitoring procedure stemming from the 1994 "Declaration on compliance with commitments accepted by member states of the Council of Europe" includes human rights commitments and is the subject of a detailed analysis in Chapter 6, particularly for its potential impact on minority protection.

The broad nature of the committee's activities produces analyses and comment at many points in the present work, including comment on the division of labour between the Committee of Ministers and the Advisory Committee on the Framework Convention. Proposals for activities to be conducted within the framework of the Council of Europe are usually subjected to an initial discussion within so-called steering committees which are bodies under the direct authority of the Committee of Ministers; steering committees have "programming powers" and forward their proposals to the Committee of Ministers. The Committee of

Ministers also establishes ad hoc committees charged with specific tasks. The Committee of Experts on Issues relating to the Protection of National Minorities (DH-MIN), a sub-committee of the Committee of Ministers' Steering Committee for Human Rights (CDDH), was set up in 1998 and operated between that date and 2001;[109] discussions are on-going concerning its revival.

The Parliamentary Assembly – "the deliberative organ of the Council of Europe"[110] – has consultative rather than legislative powers, and consists of representatives from the parliaments of member states, complemented since 1989 by representatives of parliaments of non-member states from eastern and central Europe with "Special Guest status". The Assembly has its own Secretary General. The conclusions of the Assembly have been the source of much Council of Europe activity and are presented to the Committee of Ministers in the form of "recommendations", "resolutions" and "opinions". Specialist committees of the Assembly include a number which have produced work on minority rights, notably the Committee on Legal Affairs and Human Rights. The Assembly provides a forum for public debate and for initiatives to promote European co-operation, lending democratic legitimacy to this co-operation. The Assembly is a major driving political force within the Council of Europe, not least in the field of the protection of minorities. The work of the Assembly in standard-setting on minority rights, monitoring of commitments relevant to minority protection, and on specific minority questions and minority groups including the Roma are all discussed in the present work.

The original "statutory" organs are complemented by the Congress of Local and Regional Authorities of Europe (CLRAE/Congress).[111] The Congress is a consultative organ consisting of national delegations of local and regional elected representatives, with the aim to promote co-operation between local and regional authorities by allowing these representatives to pool their experience and express their views and interests regarding European co-operation. Each member state has the same number of seats in the Congress as it has in the Parliamentary Assembly. The Congress may grant Special Guest status to delegations from local and regional authorities in non-member states which have such status with the Parliamentary Assembly. The Congress issues recommendations and opinions which are sent as appropriate to the Parliamentary Assembly and/or to the Committee of Ministers for possible action by these organs. Other texts adopted by the Congress, such as resolutions, are sent to them for their information. The Congress has become a motor for minority protection, including standard-setting: among others, the European Charter for Regional or Minority Languages (hereafter referred to as the Languages Charter) emerged through the

Congress. The Council of Europe organs are served by the Secretariat under the authority of a Secretary General elected by the Assembly. The Secretary General of the Council of Europe has always played a more active role in the life of the Organisation than the statute would suggest, and this is also true in the area of minority rights. The various initiatives taken throughout the Council of Europe respond to a certain power or force of "impulsion" attributable to an active Secretary General with ideas and propositions on the Organisation's role in relation to minorities. The Secretariat is divided into a number of "directorates": Directorate General II – on human rights – is a principal actor in this study, as well as the Directorates of Political Affairs and Strategic Planning. Important Secretariat activities are reviewed in succeeding chapters: they include the "Co-operation Activities", which recently replaced the ADACS (Activities for the Development and Consolidation of Democratic Stability), and especially the discontinued Joint Programme on "National minorities in Europe" between the EU Commission and the Council of Europe – described below as one of the most important multilateral enterprises on minorities undertaken by the Council of Europe.[112]

The institution of Commissioner for Human Rights was created by a resolution of the Committee of Ministers.[113] The independent and impartial[114] commissioner is mandated to promote education in and awareness of human rights[115] and, among other things, to identify shortcomings in the law and practice of member states,[116] and help promote the effective observance of human rights in the various Council of Europe instruments, while respecting the competence of the various treaty bodies.[117] The commissioner is a non-judicial institution.[118] The holder of this office has a duty to report annually to the Committee of Ministers and the Parliamentary Assembly, and may report on specific matters when he or she deems it appropriate, either to the Committee of Ministers, or to the Committee of Ministers and the Parliamentary Assembly. There is also a duty to respond to requests made by these organs in the context of their task of ensuring compliance with the human rights standards of the Council of Europe. The commissioner may issue recommendations, opinions and reports.[119]

Bodies established or proposed under specific treaties or draft treaties in the area of minority rights are also considered in this work. The powers of the European Commission of Human Rights and European Court of Human Rights are also alluded to: in the area of "hard law", they are the pre-eminent bodies, the workings of which furnish starting-points for discussions on model forms of implementation of minority rights. The Advisory Committee for the Framework Convention and the Committee of Experts under the Languages Charter are discussed in the context of their particular treaties.[120]

The creation of the European Commission for Democracy through Law (the Venice Commission) resulted from a conference held in Venice on 19 and 20 January 1990 at the invitation of the Italian Government.[121] Established in May 1990 as a partial agreement of 18 member states of the Council of Europe, the Commission in February 2002 became an enlarged agreement, comprising all member states of the Organisation and working with a number of countries from Africa, Asia and Europe.[122] The Venice Commission is composed of "independent experts who have achieved eminence through their experience in democratic institutions or by their contribution to the enhancement of law and political science."[123] Most of the members are senior academics, particularly in the fields of constitutional or international law, supreme or constitutional court judges or members of national parliaments. Although the members are appointed – for four years – by member states of the enlarged agreement, they serve in their individual capacity.

The field of action of the Venice Commission is "the guarantees offered by law in the service of democracy."[124] In particular, it may supply opinions further to requests made through the Committee of Ministers, the Parliamentary Assembly, the Congress of Local and Regional Authorities, the Secretary General or a state, international organisation or body participating in the work of the commission. Other states may request opinions with the consent of the Committee of Ministers.[125] The Venice Commission is active throughout the constitutional domain, and covers a wide range of issues beyond constitutions as such. The commission has covered such areas as legislation on political parties and elections, national minorities, constitutional courts, and other legislation with implications for national democratic institutions. It monitors closely the European integration process, and above all its constitutional implications. It is concerned with dissemination of the European constitutional heritage and fundamental legal values, a process assisted by the Bulletin on Constitutional Case-Law, comparative studies and seminars, in particular UniDem (Universities for Democracy) seminars, organised in co-operation with universities and constitutional courts.

Constitutional assistance remains a major focus, moving from "emergency constitutional engineering" towards a more enduring approach. Within this framework, the Venice Commission pays particular attention to countries which are going through or have gone through ethno-political conflicts. Thus the commission has played an important role in developing and interpreting the constitutional law of Bosnia and Herzegovina, and has taken part in the drafting of the Rambouillet Agreement, the Constitutional Framework for Kosovo, the Ohrid Framework Agreement on "the Former Yugoslav Republic of Macedonia", and the Constitutional Charter of Serbia and Montenegro. It has also been involved in efforts to settle the conflicts on the status of Abkhazia in Georgia and Transnistria in Moldova.

Among matters of particular interest to minorities, the Venice Commission drafted a European Framework Convention for the Protection of National Minorities in 1991,[126] the legacy of which is discussed at various points in the present work. The controversies ensuing from the adoption by Hungary, in June 2001, of the Act on Hungarians living in Neighbouring Countries suggested that not enough attention had been paid until then by the international community to the relationship between minorities and kin-states. In this context, the commission undertook a study in 2001, and organised a colloquy in Athens in 2002, on preferential treatment of national minorities by their kin-state.[127] It also dealt with draft legislation on minority protection in Croatia and Bosnia Herzegovina,[128] and with the question of ratification of the Framework Convention on National Minorities by Belgium.[129] Reports on "Electoral law and national minorities",[130] and on "Self-determination and secession in constitutional law"[131] are highly pertinent for minority questions, though this brief list does not exhaust the potential relevance of the Venice Commission's in-depth exploration of issues of international and constitutional law.

The decision to set up the European Commission against Racism and Intolerance (ECRI) was taken by the 1st Summit of Heads of State and Government of the Council of Europe in Vienna on 8 and 9 October 1993 (the Vienna Summit).[132] At the summit, the heads of state and government expressed their alarm at the rise of racism, xenophobia,[133] anti-semitism and intolerance across Europe, and adopted a plan of action to be implemented by the Council of Europe to combat these phenomena.[134] The mandate given to ECRI by this summit was to:

- review member states' legislation, policies and other measures to combat racism and the like, and their effectiveness;

- propose further action at local, national and European level;

- formulate general policy recommendations to member states;

- study international legal instruments applicable in the matter with a view to their reinforcement where appropriate.[135]

Further modalities of the functioning of this new mechanism were to be decided by the Committee of Ministers. In due course, the Committee of Ministers outlined the membership and working methods of ECRI,[136] agreeing that it should be composed of members chosen for their moral authority in their countries as well as their recognised expertise in dealing with racism, xenophobia, etc.[137] The European Conference against Racism, held in Strasbourg on 11-13 October 2000, called for the strengthening of ECRI's action. On 13 June 2002, the Committee of Ministers adopted a new Statute for ECRI, consolidating its role as an independent, human-rights monitoring body on issues related to racism and racial discrimination.

The role of non-governmental organisations (NGOs) as partners in the Council of Europe should also be noted: in most cases, the relations between NGOs and the Council of Europe are governed by a consultative-status system.[138] The Council of Europe has also engaged in direct contacts with NGOs, especially through the implementation of its co-operation programmes and the programme of confidence-building measures in civil society. The latter programme has facilitated the engagement of civil society in promoting mutual knowledge and peaceful co-existence between minority and majority communities.[139] In the present work, further points on the role of NGOs are made particularly in the context of the Framework Convention, notably on the presentation of "alternative reports",[140] and in connection with the work of the Commissioner for Human Rights.[141]

Minorities

Reflections are extended because of basic complexities in the concept of "minority". Even in a limited, conservative reading of "minority", a range of groups is to be considered. Europe knows many group varieties, including minorities within traditional, relatively well-defined areas of settlement, groups dispersed throughout the whole or most of a state (see further, Chapter 7) or across state frontiers, nomadic groups, and so on. They may be defined in national legislation as "minorities", "nationalities", "ethnic groups", "national communities", and others.[142] These are often citizens of the states they inhabit. A cluster of definitions of minority adopted by various bodies in and outside the Council of Europe can be cited to demonstrate that frequently the term "national minority" incorporates the idea that minorities must also be citizens/nationals of the state in question.[143] It is not clear whether the asserted restriction on the scope of "national minority" results from the word "national" or "minority" or the two in combination: some definitions of "minority" alone (unaccompanied by "national") incorporate the same restriction.[144] On the other hand, as noted above, general international law does not present a definitive view.[145]

Within the Council of Europe, the OSCE and the UN, there has not been an acceptance of such a restriction, as illustrated by the definitional elements of minority/ies in international legal instruments and in their preparatory work, as well as in the views expressed by the various monitoring bodies responsible to monitor these instruments. As a working hypothesis or heuristic for the present work, the definition offered by UN Rapporteur Eide may be utilised:

> a minority is any group of persons resident within a sovereign state which constitutes less than half the population of the national society and whose members share common characteristics of an ethnic, religious or linguistic nature that distinguish them from the rest of the population.[146]

The definition does not distinguish between citizens and non-citizens, traditional groups and immigrants, "old" immigrants and "new" arrivals.[147] It is offered as a working definition, not as a scientific resolution of a difficult conceptual and practical issue. Further "refinements" are offered in succeeding chapters, keeping in mind the Council of Europe's frequent use of the term "national minority" rather than "minority" *simpliciter*. State reports – under the Framework Convention for the Protection of National Minorities, for example – display wide variation in their understanding of the term "national minority".

Scope of the present work

Minority rights texts exhibit a "deep structure", refining principles on group existence and membership; individual and collective rights; provisions on assimilation and integration; non-discrimination; rights in the fields of culture, language, religion and education, and limitations thereon; participation in decision-making; and protection of the integrity of minority areas. Minority rights also express a multicultural and intercultural "philosophy". As observed, the texts strain to distinguish minority rights issues from self-determination, mainly by not mentioning the latter; they (usually) also eschew specific reference to "autonomy". Much of the present work is focused on analysis of instruments in the specific field of minority rights: the contemporary standards of the Council of Europe. The range of texts appraised goes beyond this remit to include areas where aspects of ethnicity are relevant: hence the chapter on ECRI, and reference to instruments on local government, migration, etc.

The first substantive chapter is devoted to an analysis of the European Convention on Human Rights – still the flagship of the Council of Europe's commitment to human rights – taking as the framework "typical" minority rights issues rather than the structure of the Convention as such. The chapters on the Framework Convention and the Languages Charter (Chapters 2 and 3) present the main substance of the work of the Council of Europe on minority and minority-related standards. Chapter 4 on the Roma was written by Alexandra Xanthaki at the invitation of the authors and hardly needs justification, though the presentation goes beyond a consideration of relevant standards to identification of difficulties, and attempts to address them, implicating the "work" of the Council of Europe in a broader sense. Chapters 5, 6 and 7 on intergovernmental co-operation and minority protection, concentrate on high-level political decisions, including those on monitoring, the work of subsidiary political committees and the activities of the Secretariat.

Chapters 8 to 12 address the role of the Parliamentary Assembly in the field of minority protection, including its monitoring procedures, the role of the Congress (and its monitoring procedures) as well as that of ECRI and of the Commissioner for Human Rights, respectively. The broader procedures have been concerned with various groups, and have general significance for minorities in their vocation to protect and promote human rights or specific aspects of democratic performance; ECRI has conceptually the closest relationship with minority questions as such. The concluding reflections appraise the work of the Council of Europe as a whole in this highly sensitive field of minorities

The present work does not penetrate every "corner" of the work of the Council of Europe on minorities, nor does it promise details of the complex labours of the council over the half-century and more of its existence. In particular, the authors do not address Council of Europe responses to conflict in any detailed way: this would be a complete study on its own and falls beyond the scope of the present work.[148] However, references to these responses are made throughout, in the light of the proposition that attention to minority rights is a crucial modality of conflict prevention and resolution in the modern world. This work, which reviews developments until the end of 2002, including later information on a selective basis whenever possible, seeks to present an account and a substantive critique of the principal minority-related standards mechanisms, as well as their work and potential for development. The critical standpoint centres on the challenge presented by the "ethnic question" to an intergovernmental organisation – the Council of Europe – devoted to human rights, democracy and the rule of law, and the substance, quality and appropriateness of the Council of Europe's response.

Notes

1.   A broad spectrum of minorities and minority questions throughout the world is set out in *World Directory of Minorities* (London: Minority Rights Group, 1997).

2.   For a classification, see T.R. Gurr and B. Harff, *Ethnic Conflict in World Politics* (Boulder/San Francisco/Oxford: Westview Press, 1994).

3.   Roma populations also exist outside Europe: "The Human Rights Problems of the Roma", Working Paper prepared by Y.K.J. Yeung Sik Yuen pursuant to Sub-Commission Resolution 1999/109, UN Doc. E/CN.4/Sub.2/2000, 23 June 2000. The present work contains numerous references to the Roma. See, in particular, Chapter 4.

4.   T. Gurr, *Peoples versus States: Minorities at Risk in the New Century* (Washington: United States Institute of Peace Press, 2000). Consult also the Minorities at Risk Data Generation and Management Program (MARGene) of the Minorities at Risk (MAR) Project of the University of Maryland on the Internet, free of charge, at http://www.cidcm.umd.edu/inscr/mar/home.htm.

5.   "General conclusions of the European Conference Against Racism", EUROCONF (2000), p. 4.

6.   Samuel Huntington, "The clash of civilisations", *Foreign Affairs*, Vol. 72, No. 3, 1993.

7.   J. Hutchinson and A.D. Smith (eds), *Ethnicity* (Oxford: Oxford University Press, 1996) is a valuable repository of essays.

8.   For a development of these views, see the *Bellagio Consultation*, 24-28 January 2000, for the World Conference against Racism, UN Doc. A/CONF.189/PC.1/10, paragraphs 18-25, paragraph 23.

9.   For a spectrum of "philosophy", see W. Kymlicka (ed.), *The Rights of Minority Cultures* (Oxford: Oxford University Press, 1995). The term "republicans" is employed in P. Pettit, *Republicanism: A Theory of Freedom and Government* (Oxford University Press, 1997).

10.   A distinction made by Makau wa Mutua, "Politics and human rights: an essential symbiosis", in M. Byers (ed.), *The Role of Law in International Politics* (Oxford University Press, 2000), pp. 149-75.

11.   The implied reference is to that "sentimental education" which Richard Rorty urges as a non-foundationalist basis of human rights: "Human rights, rationality and sentimentality", in S. Shute and S. Hurley (eds), *On Human Rights: The Oxford Amnesty Lectures, 1993* (New York: Basik Books, 1994).

12.   W. Bowring, "New nations and national minorities: Ukraine and the question of citizenship", in P. Cumper and S. Wheatley (eds), *Minority Rights in the "New" Europe* (The Hague: Martinus Nijhoff, 1999), pp. 233-50.

13.   For an impression of this complexity, and an impassioned plea for diversity, see T. Skutnabb-Kangas, *Linguistic Genocide in Education – or Worldwide Diversity and Human Rights?* (Mahwah, New Jersey and London: Lawrence Erlbaum Associates, 2000).

14.   P. Thornberry, *Minorities and Human Rights Law* (London: Minority Rights Group, 1991). See also the many situations reviewed in H. Hannum, *Autonomy, Sovereignty, and Self-Determination* (Philadelphia: University of Pennsylvania Press, 1990); and Minority Rights Group (ed.), *Minorities and Autonomy in Western Europe* (London: Minority Rights Group, 1991). For detailed texts on the legal regulation of minority rights in a range of states, consult H. Hannum (ed.), *Documents on Autonomy and Minority Rights* (Dordrecht: Martinus Nijhoff, 1993).

15.   See comments in Chapter 11 on "good practices" identified by the European Commission against Racism and Intolerance (ECRI).

16.   Study of "Possible ways and means of facilitating the peaceful and constructive solution of problems involving minorities", report submitted by Special Rapporteur A. Eide, UN Doc. E/CN.4/Sub.2/1993/34, paragraph 9.

17.   In the conceptualisation of which the anthropologist Clifford Geertz has played a significant part: C. Geertz, *Local Knowledge* (London: Fontana Press, 1993).

18.   P. Thornberry, *Indigenous Peoples and Human Rights* (Manchester: Manchester University Press, 2002); C.P. Cohen (ed.), *Human Rights of Indigenous Peoples* (Ardsley, New York: Transnational Publishers, 1998).

19.   C. Taylor, "The politics of recognition", in A. Gutmann (ed.), *Multiculturalism and the "Politics of Recognition"* (Princeton, New Jersey: Princeton University Press, 1992), pp. 25-73.

20.   "Ethno-nationalism" is described by UN Special Rapporteur Eide as incorporating the following propositions: "firstly, nations should be defined in ethnic terms, referring to a common past history, tradition, preferably also common language; secondly, nations should as far as possible have their own States, so that the society composing a State should as far as possible be congruent with the nation as defined in ethnic terms; thirdly, the loyalty of members of nations to that nation should override all other loyalties": Study of "Possible ways and means of facilitating the peaceful and constructive solution of problems involving minorities", UN Doc. E/CN.4/Sub.2/1992/27, paragraph 16.

21.   Parliamentary Assembly, Report on the Colloquy on the "Rights of minorities", held at the French Senate, 13-14 November 1991, Doc. AS/Jur (43) 38, p. 6.

22.   Discussed in Chapter 11.

23.   Chapter 2.

24.   See Chapters 6 and 9, respectively.

25.   Chapter 10.

26.   UN Doc. A/CONF.157/24 (part I), Vienna Declaration and Programme of Action, paragraph 32.

27.   For reflections on this, see P. Thornberry, "Human rights and the shaping of loyalties", in M. Waller and A. Linklater (eds.), *Political Loyalty and the Nation-State* (London and New York: Routledge, 2003), pp. 91-104.

28.   Among a wide range of writing on this subject, see P. Thornberry, *International Law and the Rights of Minorities* (Oxford: Clarendon Press, 1991 and 1992); N. Lerner, *Group Rights and Discrimination in International Law* (Dordrecht: Martinus Nijhoff, 1991); essays by N. Lerner and M. Nowak in C. Brolmann, R. Lefeber and M Zieck (eds.), *Peoples and Minorities in International Law* (Dordrecht: Martinus Nijhoff, 1993); D. Sanders, "Collective rights", *Human Rights Quarterly*, No. 13, 1991, pp. 368-86.

29.   Consider the thoughts and citations of Nowak et al. in T. van Boven, "General Course on Human Rights", *Collected Courses of the Academy of European Law*, Vol. IV, No. 2, 1993, pp. 1-106. The van Boven criteria for appraising the "performance" of a regional organisation are considered in the concluding chapter of the present work.

30.   The system of minority protection concerned minorities in Albania, Austria, Bulgaria, Czechoslovakia, the Free City of Danzig, Estonia, Finland, Greece, Hungary, Latvia, Lithuania, Romania, the Serb-Croat-Slovene State and Turkey; but the League of Nations also extended its protection to minorities in Iraq.

31.   Among many general reviews of the system, consult C.A. Macartney, *National States and National Minorities* (London: Oxford University Press, 1934); P. de Azcarate, The League of Nations and National Minorities (Washington: The Carnegie Endowment, 1945); J. Robinson et al., *Were the Minorities Treaties a Failure?* (New York: Institute of Jewish Affairs, 1943); P. Thornberry, *International Law and the Rights of Minorities* (Oxford: Clarendon Press, 1991 and 1992).

32.	Advisory Opinion of 1935, PCIJ Ser. A/B, No. 64, p. 17.

33.	The treaty, the subject of the Advisory Opinion, was the convention of 27 November 1919 between Bulgaria and Greece.

34.	PCIJ Ser. B, Nos. 17, 19, 21, 22 (present authors' emphasis).

35.	"Study of the legal validity of the undertakings concerning minorities", UN Doc. E/CN.4/367 (1950).

36.	N. Feinberg, "The legal validity of the undertakings concerning minorities and the *Clausula Rebus Sic Stantibus*", *Scripta Hierosolymitana*, Vol. 5, (1958), p. 95; S. Rosenne, "Minorities and human rights", in Y. Dinstein and M. Tabory (eds.), *The Protection of Minorities and Human Rights* (Dordrecht: Martinus Nijhoff, 1992). See also the statement submitted by the International Fellowship of Reconciliation, an NGO in consultative status with the UN Economic and Social Council, to the UN Sub-Commission on Prevention of Discrimination and Protection of Minorities, UN Doc. E/CN.4/Sub.2/1992/NGO/27.

37.	The arrangements between Finland and Sweden concerning the Åland Islands are a case in point. For a very interesting study of these arrangements in the light of the requirements of modern human rights law, see L. Hannikainen, *Cultural, Linguistic and Educational Rights in the Åland Islands: An Analysis in International Law* (Helsinki; Advisory Board for International Human Rights Affairs, 1993).

38.	Examples of minority protection in bilateral arrangements in Europe and else-where are listed in *Protection of Minorities*, UN Sales No. 67.XIV.3. There is an updated account of the position in Europe in A. Bloed and P. van Dijk (eds.), *Protection of Minority Rights Through Bilateral Treaties: The case of Central and Eastern Europe* (The Hague: Kluwer Law International, 1999). For reflections on the League of Nations model, see J. Mertus, "The Dayton Peace Accords: lessons from the past and for the future", in Cumper and Wheatley, op. cit., pp. 261-83.

39.	See T. Franck, "Postmodern tribalism and the right to secession" and R. Higgins, "Postmodern tribalism and the right to secession, comments" in C. Brölmann, R. Lefeber and M. Zieck, op. cit., pp. 3-27 and 29-35.

40.	UN Doc. E/CN.4/ 52, Section V.

41.	For an elaboration of the distinction between direct and indirect discrimination, see the discussion of ECRI General Policy Recommendation No. 7 in Chapter 11; see also Chapter 2.

42.	The primary vehicle for this normative expansion in the UN system has been the International Convention on the Elimination of All Forms of Racial Discrimination [ICEARD], and its "treaty-body", the Committee on the Elimination of Racial Discrimination [CERD]. For a study, see M. Banton, *International Action against Racial Discrimination* (Oxford: Clarendon Press, 1996); see also K. Boyle and A. Baldaccini, "A critical evaluation of international human rights approaches to racism", in S. Fredman (ed.), *Discrimination and Human Rights: the Case of Racism* (Oxford: Oxford University Press, 2001), pp. 135-91.

43.	Article 1.1.

44.	See above.

45.	For recent appraisals of Article 27, see G. Pentassuglia, op. cit., Chapter V; P. Thornberry, *Indigenous Peoples and Human Rights*, Chapter 6.

46.	Cf. Article 30 of the Convention on the Rights of the Child, which adapts Article 27 to provide for rights of minority and indigenous children.

47. *Human Rights: Status of International Instruments* (New York: United Nations, 1987), p. 35. The Federal Republic of Germany has interpreted the declaration by France (ibid., p. 88) to mean that "the Constitution of the French Republic already fully guarantees the individual rights protected by Article 27." France has reaffirmed this position on many occasions. For its reiteration before a European human rights body, see the European Commission against Racism and Intolerance [ECRI], "Second Report on France", Council of Europe Doc. CRI (2000) 31, Adopted 10 December 1999. "Observations" on the report by the French authorities reaffirm the validity of France's "Republican principles" – see Chapter 11 of the present work.

48. UN Doc. CRC/C/2 (22 August 1991), pp. 10, 16, 17.

49. 26 April 1994.

50. General Comment, paragraph 5.2. While general international law has still not adopted a "conclusive" definition of minorities, criteria for the existence of minorities has frequently been the subject of elaboration – criteria utilised by the European Commission for Democracy through Law (the Venice Commission) in the case of Belgium are discussed in the concluding chapter of the present work.

51. Paragraph 5.2.

52. UN Doc. CCPR/C/47/D/359/1989 and 385/1989/Rev.1 (31 March 1993).

53. Paragraph 11.2.

54. Individual opinion by Mrs E. Evatt, co-signed by Messrs. Ando, Bruni Celli and Dimitrijevic, 23.

55. For example, Recommendation 1201 (1993) of the Parliamentary Assembly of the Council of Europe (Article 1) defines "national minority" to include groups "smaller in number than the rest of the population of that State or of a region of that State". For the practice of the Advisory Committee under the Framework Convention on National Minorities, see Chapter 3. Further preliminary reflections on the concept of minority are offered in the present chapter. See further, Chapters 8, 9 and 12.

56. W. Barbieri, "Group Rights and the Muslim Diaspora", *Human Rights Quarterly*, No. 21, 1999, pp. 907-26 and 916-18.

57. Compare the repetition of the formula "persons belonging to national minorities" in the Framework Convention for the Protection of National Minorities – see later, Chapter 2.

58. *Kitok v. Sweden*, UN Doc. CCPR/C/33/D/197/1985; Views of the Committee adopted on 27 July 1988.

59. Where the state is held responsible for violations of rights by other individuals, not just by the state authorities.

60. See references to *Coeriel and Aurik v. Netherlands*, subject to decisions under both instruments.

61. Contained in General Assembly Resolution 47/135, 18 December 1992. Two relevant commentaries are: P. Thornberry, "The UN Declaration on the Rights of ... Minorities: Background, Analysis, Observations, and an Update", in A. Phillips and A. Rosas (eds.), *Universal Minority Rights* (London and Åbo: Minority Rights Group and Åbo Akademi University, 1995), pp. 13-76; A. Eide, Commentary to the Declaration, UN Doc. E/CN.4/Sub.2/AC.5/2001/2.

62. Barbieri, op. cit., p. 910.

63. In the drafting of the text, a number of governments were exercised by issues such as female genital mutilation. Less obvious issues included ritual slaughter of animals: cf. discussion of *Cha'Are Shalom Ve Tsedek v. France* in Chapter 1 on the ECHR, and also Chapter 2 on the Framework Convention.

64. European instruments express the same moral.

65. The background to the establishment of the Working Group and its mandate are set out in "Report of the Fifth Session", UN Doc. E/CN.4/Sub.2/1999/21, 24 June 1999. The eighth report of the Working Group is contained in UN Doc. E/CN.4/Sub.2/2002/19, 14 June 2002.

66. Adopted at the 76th Session of the ILO, 1989.

67. A succinct account of the mechanisms is provided in A.H. Robertson and J. Merrills, *Human Rights in the World* (Manchester University Press, fourth edition 1996), pp. 282-88.

68. M. Tomei and L. Swepston, *Indigenous and Tribal Peoples: A Guide to ILO Convention No. 169* (Geneva: International Labour Office, 1996); and *ILO Convention on Indigenous and Tribal Peoples, 1899 [No. 169]: A Manual* (Geneva: International Labour Organisation, Project to Promote ILO Policy on Indigenous and Tribal Peoples, 2000).

69. On the application of ILO Convention No. 169 to, for example, travellers of Jenisch, Roma or Gypsy origin, see International Labour Office, "Opinion relative to the Decisions of the International Labour Conference", in *Report of the Director-General*, ILO Doc. GB.280/18, Geneva, March 2001, pp. 8-13.

70. This appears to be true of the ratification of ILO Convention No. 169 by the Netherlands.

71. See the chapter by N. Vakhtin in Minority Rights Group (ed.), *Polar Peoples: Self-Determination and Development* (London: Minority Rights Group 1994).

72. See above on "targeted groups".

73. EUROCONF (2000) 1 final, 13 October 2000, p. 4.

74. See J. Helgesen, "Protecting Minorities in the Conference on Security and Co-operation in Europe (CSCE) Process" in A. Rosas and J. Helgesen (eds.), *The Strength of Diversity* (Dordrecht/London: Kluwer Academic 1992), pp. 159-86.

75. See Charter for European Security, Istambul, 19 November 1999, paragraph 7.

76. V.-Y. Ghebali, "The Protection of Minorities at the CSCE – a Greater European Approach", paper presented to the Athens Colloquy on the Rights of Minorities and Peoples, December 1992. By the same author, see "La CSCE et la question des minorités nationales" in A. Liebich and A. Regler (eds.), *L'Europe Centrale et ses Minorités: vers une solution Européenne?* (Paris: Presses Universitaires de France, 1993), pp. 51-72.

77. See M.A. Martín Estébanez, "Minority Protection and the Organisation for Security and Co-operation in Europe" in P. Cumper and S. Wheatley, *Minority Rights in the New Europe* (The Hague/London/Boston: Martinus Nijhoff, 1999), pp. 33-34.

78. Paragraph 30.

79. Report of the OSCE Meeting of Experts on National Minorities, Geneva 1991, Chapter II, paragraph 2.

80. See A. Heraclides, "The CSCE and Minorities – the Negotiations behind the Commitments, 1972-1992", *Helsinki Monitor*, No. 3, 1992, pp. 5-18.

81. Document of the Copenhagen Meeting of the Conference on the Human Dimension of the OSCE, 1990, paragraph 35.

82. Notably the reception accorded in some states to Parliamentary Assembly Recommendation 1201 (1993), Article 11 of which set out such a right in highly qualified form: see the discussion by P. Thornberry, "Images of Autonomy and Individual and Collective Rights in International Instruments on the Rights of Minorities" in M. Suksi (ed.), *Autonomy: Applications and Implications* (The Hague: Kluwer Law International, 1998), pp. 97-124.

83. OSCE handbook (Vienna: OSCE, 2000), pp. 45-82.

84.   A. Rosas and T. Lahelma, "OSCE Long-Term Missions", in M. Bothe, N. Ronzitti and A. Rosas (eds.), *The OSCE in the Maintenance of Peace and Security* (The Hague/London/Boston: Kluwer Law International, 1997, pp. 167-90.

85.   See R. Brecht, "Is More Better? – An Explanation of the CSCE Human Dimension Mechanism and its relationship to other systems for the promotion and protection of Human Rights", *Papers on the Theory and Practice of Human Rights*, No. 9, 1994.

86.   OSCE Helsinki Document, 1992, The Challenges of Change, II (3). For the antecedents of the mandate of the HCNM and details on his establishment, see R. Zaagman and H. Zaal, "The CSCE High Commissioner on National Minorities, Prehistory and Negotiations", in A. Bloed (ed.), *The Challenges of Change: The Helsinki Summit of the CSCE and its Aftermath* (Dordrecht, Martinus Nijhoff, 1994), p. 95. See also K.J. Huber, "The CSCE and Ethnic Conflict in the East", *RFE/RL Research Report*, Vol. 2, No. 31, July 1993, pp. 30-36; K.J. Huber and R. Zaagman, "Towards the Prevention of Ethnic Conflict in CSCE: the High Commissioner on National Minorities and Other Developments", *International Journal of Group Rights*, No. 1, 1993, pp. 51-58; H. Zaal, "The CSCE High Commissioner on National Minorities", *Helsinki Monitor*, Vol. 3, No. 4, 1992, pp. 33-37.

87.   On how the mandate of the HCNM has been interpreted and implemented, see M.A. Martín Estébanez, "The High Commissioner on National Minorities, Development of the Mandate", in M. Bothe, N. Ronzitti and A. Rosas (eds.), *The OSCE in the Maintenance of Peace and Security* (The Hague/London/Boston: Kluwer Law International, 1997), pp. 123-166.

88.   For a recent review of the HCNM's work, see W.A. Kemp (ed.), *Quiet Diplomacy in Action: the OSCE High Commissioner on National Minorities* (The Hague/London/Boston: Kluwer Law International, 2001). See also J. Packer, "The Role of the OSCE High Commissioner on National Minorities in the Former Yugoslavia", *XII Cambridge Review of International Affairs*, No. 2, 1999, pp. 169-184.

89.   See High Commissioner on National Minorities, "Report on the Situation of the Roma and Sinti in the OSCE Area", March 2000. See below, Chapter 4 on Roma/Gypsies. For information on the HCNM approach and interpretation of the national minority concept and some references on his involvement in the Baltic states, as well as previous reporting on the Roma question, see M.A. Martín Estébanez, "The High Commissioner on National Minorities, Development of the Mandate", in M. Bothe, N. Ronzitti and A. Rosas (eds.), *The OSCE in the Maintenance of Peace and Security*, pp. 130-31 and 143. For notes on the current work of the High Commissioner, consult the monthly issue of the *OSCE Newsletter*, published by the OSCE Secretariat on OSCE website http//:www.osce.org. The Foundation on Inter-Ethnic Relations has issued bibliographies on the HCNM (to 1997); copies of his speeches and recommendations may be obtained from the website: http://www.hcnm.org.

90.   The Hague Recommendations Regarding the Education Rights of National Minorities (1996); the OSLO Recommendations Regarding the Linguistic Rights of National Minorities (1998); the Lund Recommendations on the Effective Participation of National Minorities in Public Life (1999); Guidelines on the Use of Minority Languages in the Broadcast Media (forthcoming).

91.   See M. Pentikäinen, "Human Rights Commitments within the CSCE Process: Nature, Contents and Application in Finland", *Publications of the Advisory Board for International Human Rights Affairs*, No. 3, 1994, pp. 48-72. Further comments in G. Pentassuglia, op. cit., Chapter VII.

92.   Appendix II, National Minorities.

93. R. Hofmann, "National Minorities and European Community Law", in *Baltic Yearbook of International Law*, Vol. 2, 2002, pp. 159-74. See also B. de Witte, "Politics versus Law in the EU's approach to Ethnic Minorities", *European University Institute Working Paper* No. 4, 2000, and G. Toggenburg, "A Rough Orientation through a Delicate Relationship: The European Union's Endeavours for (its) Minorities" in *European Integration Online Papers* Vol. 4, No. 16, 2000. For earlier studies see B. de Witte, "The European Communities and its Minorities" in C. Brölman, R. Lefeber and M. Zieck (eds.), op. cit., and M.A. Martín Estébanez, "The Protection of National or Ethnic, Religious and Linguistic Minorities" in N. Neuwahl and A. Rosas (eds.), *The European Union and Human Rights* (The Hague/London/Boston: Kluwer Law International, 1995), pp. 133-64. See also references in P. Alston, M. Bustelo and J. Heenan (eds.), *The EU and Human Rights* (Oxford University Press, 1999).

94. For example the resolution on linguistic and cultural minorities in the European Community adopted by the European Parliament on 9 February 1994, OJ No C 61, 29.2.1994, pp. 110-13.

95. As in Council Directive 89/552/EEC of 3 October 1989 on the co-ordination of certain provisions laid down by law, regulation or administrative action in member states concerning the pursuit of television broadcasting activities, OJ No. L298, 17.10.1989, p. 23. On the EU and linguistic diversity generally see N. Shuibhne, *EC Law and Minority Language Policy: Culture, Citizenship and Fundamental Rights* (The Hague: Kluwer 2002).

96. For example, the communication of the European Commission on countering racism, xenophobia and anti-semitism in the candidate countries presented to the European Council meeting in Cologne on 3 and 4 June 1999 and the Council Resolution on the fight against racism and xenophobia (OJ 1999 No. C 157, p. 1).

97. For discussions on recent relevant ECJ jurisprudence see B. de Witte (ed.), *Linguistic Diversity and European Law* (Antwerp: Intersentia, forthcoming).

98. See generally B. Brandtner and A. Rosas, "Human Rights and the External Relations of the European Community: an Analysis of Doctrine and Practice", *European Journal of International Law*, Vol. 9, No. 3 (1998).

99. A. Biscoe, "The European Union and Minority Nations", in Wheatley and Cumper, op. cit., pp. 89-103, p. 98.

100. F. Benoît-Rohmer and H. Hardeman, "The Pact on Stability in Europe, a Joint Action of the Twelve in the Framework of their Common Foreign and Security Policy", *Helsinki Monitor*, Vol. 5, 1994, pp. 39-53. See also F. Benoît-Rohmer, *The Minority Question in Europe, Texts and Commentary* (Strasbourg: Council of Europe, 1996), pp. 30-36. See further, E. Greco, *L'Europa Senza Muri: La Sfide della Pace Freda* (Milano: Stampa Tipomonza, 1995), pp. 94-98.

101. See A. Pellet, "The Opinions of the Badinter Arbitration Committee – A Second Breath for the Self-Determination of Peoples", *European Journal of International Law*, Vol. 3, 1992, pp. 178-81.

102. See discussion by M. Nowak of "The Copenhagen Political Criteria for Accession to the EU", in P. Alston, M. Bustelo and J. Heenan (eds.), op. cit., pp. 687-98, at pp. 691-92.

103. Adopted at the Nice European Council, December 2000. The preamble recites that the European Union contributes to the preservation of common values "while respecting the diversity of the cultures and traditions of the peoples of Europe"; Article 22 provides simply that "The Union shall respect cultural, religious and linguistic diversity". Earlier drafts had omitted any such references. EU action in the field of minorities is assessed also in G. Pentassuglia, op. cit., Chapter VII.

104. Statement by B. Winkler, EUMC Director at the OSCE-Conference on Racism, Vienna, 4-5 September 2003. Doc. PC.DEL/984/03, p. 3. The EUMC has established an information network, "RAXEN", to collect data on the situation of racism and racial discrimination at the level of EU states, provided by member organisations operating at the domestic level. It publishes a monthly periodical: *Equal Voices.* For further information consult the website http://eumc.eu.int.

105. Article 1.a.

106. Article 3.

107. See G. de Vel, *The Committee of Ministers of the Council of Europe* (Strasbourg: Council of Europe, 1995).

108. See J. Polakiewicz, *Treaty Making in the Council of Europe* (Strasbourg: Council of Europe, 1999).

109. See also references below (especially in Chapter 7) to the European Committee on Migration (CDMG), the European Population Committee (CAHP – formerly CDPO), the Steering Committee on Local and Regional Democracy (CDLR), and the Council for Cultural Co-operation (CDCC, recently replaced by the Rapporteur Group on Education, Culture, Sport, Youth and the Environment: GR-C).

110. Article 22 of the Statute.

111. See Chapter 10.

112. See later, Chapter 7.

113. Resolution (99) 50, adopted by the Committee of Ministers at its 104th session, 7 May 1999.

114. Ibid., Article 2. The Commissioner is elected by the Parliamentary Assembly from a list of three candidates drawn up by the Committee of Ministers. The issue of impartiality is touched upon in Chapter 12.

115. Ibid., Article 1.

116. Article 3.

117. Article 1.2.

118. Article 1. However, Article 5.1 of Resolution (99) 50 provides that the commissioner may act on any information including that from, among others, "individuals and organisations".

119. The Commissioner's role is discussed in Chapter 12.

120. In Chapters 2 and 3 of the present work, respectively.

121. See [DAJ.SC.DEMOCRACY] FACTSHEET.A, 17.01.1991; Council of Europe leaflet *Democracy through Law*, The Venice Commission.

122. European states which have not yet joined the Council of Europe are associate members, while Argentina, Canada, the Holy See, Israel, Japan, Kazakhstan, the Republic of Korea, Kyrgyzstan, Mexico, the United States and Uruguay are observers. South Africa enjoys a special co-operation status.

123. See Article 2, paragraphs 1-3, of the Statute of the European Commission for Democracy through Law, adopted by Resolution of the Committee of Ministers Res(2002)3.

124. Ibid., Article 1, paragraph 1.

125. Ibid., Article 3, paragraph 3.

126. Discussed in detail in P. Thornberry and M.A. Martín Estébanez, op. cit., Chapter 5.

127. See issue No. 32 of the Venice Commission, Science and Technique of Democracy series entitled *The protection of minorities by their kin-state* (Strasbourg: Council of Europe, 2002). This volume contains the Commission's report of October 2001, as well as a collection of existing national legislation on kin-minorities.

128. For Bosnia and Herzegovina, and Croatia, see *Opinion on the Constitutional Law on the Rights of National Minorities in Croatia*, CDL-INF (2001) 014, 7 July 2001; *Opinion on the Draft Law on the Rights of Ethnic and National Communities and Minorities in Bosnia and Herzegovina*, CDL-INF (2001) 013, 7 July 2001; *Opinion on the Draft Law on Rights of National Minorities of Bosnia and Herzegovina*, CDL-INF (2001) 012, 7 July 2001.

129. The Commission's opinion "On possible groups of persons to which the Framework Convention for the Protection of National Minorities could be applied in Belgium" has, besides its specific uses in the context of Belgium, a broader application to the vexed question of the definition of minorities – see conclusions to the present work.

130. Doc. CDL-INF (2000) 4, 25 January 2000.

131. Doc. CDL-INF (2000) 2, 12 January 2000.

132. See later, Chapters 5 and 11.

133. According to the summit, "the development of aggressive nationalism and ethnocentrism ... constitute new expressions of xenophobia".

134. The plan of action is complex, with elements pertaining to a European Youth Campaign, an invitation to member states to reinforce guarantees against discrimination, support for research programmes to study causes of intolerance, eliminating prejudices in the teaching of history, and requests for the media to report factually and with responsibility on issues of racism and intolerance. The final declaration of the second summit (11 October 1997) called for "the intensification of the fight against, racism, xenophobia, etc., through, among others, intensification of the work of ECRI": see Chapter 5.

135. *ECRI Procedural Documents*, Doc. CRI (98) 18, 25 February 1998, p. 9.

136. January 1994, 506th meeting of ministers' deputies. The current terms of reference of the Commission were due to expire on 31 December 2002.

137. ECRI's terms of reference, internal organisation and working methods are set out in Procedural Documents, Doc. CRI (98) 18, 23 February 1998.

138. See *Activities of the Council of Europe, 1991 Report* (Strasbourg: Council of Europe, 1993), pp. 37-38.

139. Discussed principally in Chapter 7.

140. Chapter 2.

141. Chapter 12.

142. For comments on the variety of terminology and groups, see the report by Professor Asbjørn Eide, op. cit., and its Addenda 1, 2 and 3. Also F. Capotorti, *Study on the Rights of Persons belonging to Ethnic, Religious and Linguistic Minorities*, UN Sales No. E.91.XIV.2.

143. In the previous report prepared by the present authors, the definitions of "national minority" offered in the various additional protocols to the European Convention on Human Rights may be consulted, as well as that put forward by the Venice Commission in its draft convention on minorities. The most well-known definition in general international law is probably that of UN Special Rapporteur F. Capotorti in relation to Article 27 of the Covenant on Civil and Political Rights: "A group numerically inferior to the rest of the population of a State, in a non-dominant position, whose members – being nationals of the State – possess ethnic, religious or linguistic characteristics differing from those of the rest of the population, and show, if only implicitly, a sense of solidarity, directed towards preserving their culture, traditions, religion or language."

144. Capotorti, ibid.

145. R. Wolfrum, "The Emergence of 'New Minorities' as a Result of Migration", in C. Brolmann, R. Lefeber and M. Zieck (eds.), *Peoples and Minorities in International Law* (Dordrecht: Martinus Nijhoff, 1993), pp. 153-66.

146. UN Doc. E/CN.4/Sub.2/1993/34, paragraph 29.

147. Neither does it incorporate the Capotorti criterion of "non-dominance": i.e., that dominant or "co-dominant" groups are not to be regarded as requiring minority rights protection under international law.

148. For a work on this topic, see J. Manas, "The Democracy Ideal and the Challenge of Ethno-National Diversity: An Evaluation of the Council of Europe's Democracy Mission in Situations of Ethno-National Conflict", European Law Research Centre, Harvard Law School, Working Paper No. 1 (New York: The Project on Conflict Prevention in Eastern Europe and the Former Soviet Union, supported by The Carnegie Corporation of New York, 1994).

Chapter 1

The European Convention on Human Rights (ECHR) and "ethnic" questions

Introduction

Despite the absence of "positive" minority rights provisions (the European Convention on Human Rights – hereafter referred to as the ECHR or the Convention – "does not provide for any rights of a ... minority as such"),[1] the ECHR nevertheless sets out a rights agenda which interfaces with essential concerns of minorities. The present outline does not follow the sequence of ECHR articles, but connects with the standard set of issues reflected in instruments on minority rights.[2] After a brief glance at the history of efforts to insert a "minority clause" in the Convention, this chapter reflects on the Convention's account of the following issues pertaining to minorities:

- existence, pluralism, self-definition;
- self-determination;
- the norm of non-discrimination;
- human dignity;
- identity issues including private life/ways of life, expression and promotion of identity, language, education, participation, religion, property;
- the question of loyalty; and
- implementation.

The chapter concludes with a brief assessment of the style, substance and limits of the Convention in the minorities area, and its relevance to developing a human rights agenda for the benefit of minorities. Illustrative cases are necessarily selective in view of the vast jurisprudence of the (former) European Commission of Human Rights (the Commission) and ("old" and "new") European Court of Human Rights (the Court); where possible, recent jurisprudence is highlighted. The text commented upon is the Convention as amended by Protocol No. 11, in force from 11 November 1998.

Shaping the Convention

Article 14 of the Convention prohibits discrimination on grounds of "sex, race, colour, language, religion, political or other opinion, national or social origin, association with a national minority, property, birth or other status".[3] The parameters of Article 14 are explored later, but in the reference to a "national minority", the ECHR parts company with the Charter of the United Nations, the Universal Declaration of Human Rights and the American Convention on Human Rights. Early proposals to include minority rights in the embryonic ECHR are largely associated with H. Lannung, Danish representative to the Consultative Assembly,[4] whose motivations related in part to anxiety concerning the Danish minority in Schleswig.[5]

In general debate on the proposed human rights convention,[6] Lannung observed that while fundamental human rights are important, "it is necessary to extend, supplement and elaborate [them] in order that national minorities may secure the right to a free national life and protection against persecution and encroachment on account of their national convictions, aspirations and activities".[7] The minority question in his view was "of general European interest", the neglect of which might lead to serious disputes among members of the Council of Europe. Work on the Convention was undertaken by the Assembly's Committee on Legal and Administrative Questions for the purposes of which Lannung made the proposal that "national minorities should be assured a free life with a free enjoyment of their own cultural development".[8] This did not find support and was withdrawn.

The committee instead outlined a draft article similar to the present Article 14, which included "affiliation to a national minority" among prohibited grounds of discrimination.[9] The Consultative Assembly passed to the Committee of Ministers its approval of the committee's report with its draft convention. In turn, the Committee of Ministers set up its own committee of experts to draw up a convention. The records of the committee contain an instructive debate prompted by Turkish concerns on territorial integrity and related matters. Commenting on the grounds for restriction of rights – on the basis of "just requirements of ... national security and territorial integrity"[10] – in the Parliamentary Assembly's draft the committee of experts observed, in a comment which is still pertinent to the interpretation of the ECHR,[11] that:

> permission [for] the imposition of certain restrictions in the interests of territorial integrity, was accepted by the Committee on the clear understanding that it did not permit a restriction on the rights of national minorities to express their views by democratic means.[12]

The committee of experts prepared alternative drafts, which were further processed by a Conference of High/Senior Officials. A notable development was the widening of the circle of petitioners from individuals and legal entities to include non-governmental organisations and groups of individuals.[13] Lannung continued to press his points on the necessity for a minority clause, but to no avail. Some members of the Consultative Assembly considered that the inclusion of "association with a national minority" in the anti-discrimination clause had already gone too far,[14] while others besides Lannung reflected that the draft did not go far enough.[15]

Following the adoption of the Convention, the Consultative Assembly continued to remind the Committee of Ministers of the limits of the ECHR. Studies were undertaken, and a sub-committee of the Assembly's Legal Committee examined the possibility of an additional protocol to the ECHR, preparing a draft article:

> Persons belonging to a national minority shall not be denied the right, in community with the other members of their group, and as far as compatible with public order, to enjoy their own culture, to use their own language, to establish their own schools and receive teaching in the language of their choice, or to profess and practise their own religion.[16]

Work in standard-setting on minority rights was temporarily halted at the time of the *Belgian Linguistic case*.[17] A committee of experts reported to the Committee of Ministers that, from the strictly legal point of view, there was no need for an additional protocol.[18] Further work was effectively stalled until dramatic changes in global politics, including upheavals in eastern Europe, forced reconsideration of the question. Substantive work undertaken by the Parliamentary Assembly, the Steering Committee for Human Rights (CDDH), and the DH-MIN again advanced the idea of an additional protocol to the ECHR.[19] The 1993 Vienna Summit, of Heads of State and Government, of the Council of Europe – in addition to authorising work on a Framework Convention for the Protection of National Minorities – instructed the Committee of Ministers "to begin work on drafting a protocol complementing the European Convention on Human Rights in the cultural field, in particular for persons belonging to national minorities".[20]

Work on the project of drafting the additional protocol was suspended by the Committee of Ministers in January 1996,[21] which subsequently noted that "its decision to suspend the work does not imply a final decision on an additional protocol, but ... leaves open the possibility of re-examining the question in the light of subsequent experience with the implementation of existing standards".[22] In this respect, the Committee of Ministers endorsed an opinion of the CDDH to the effect that "the experience drawn from the implementation of the Framework Convention, may reveal a need to consider further standard-setting".[23] Additional to developments in the area of minority-related rights, work has been under way in the Council of Europe to widen the scope of Article 14;[24] The Committee of Ministers adopted Protocol No. 12 on 26 June 2000 – the new protocol is discussed later in this chapter.

i. *Existence, pluralism, self-definition*

International law insists that the existence of minorities is a question of fact, not law.[25] What this means is that the state does not have the last word in deciding if minorities exist on its territory or not – this is to be decided on the basis of the factual situation. Little guidance can be found on the meaning of "national minority" in Article 14 – the Court's jurisprudence (discussed below) is described by one author as "evasive"[26] although "undeveloped" is perhaps a better term.

On the other hand, Commission and Court have frequently spoken of and dealt with minorities. The Kurds of Turkey figure in a stream of cases emanating from the continuing conflict in south-eastern Turkey, cases in which questions of minority identity are central. Roma, various Greek minorities, the Saami, East African Asians, various "racial" groups, minorities of west, east and central Europe, and so on, have all litigated, and more judgments may be expected from "old" and "newer" members of the Council of Europe. General norms of minority rights insist on the fundamental principle of self-identification as a member of a minority or otherwise. In the privileged sphere of privacy, self-identification must be regarded as an absolute right; in other cases the notion of minority "existence" may be predicated on a combination of "objective" and "subjective" characteristics.[27] The acceptance of minority existence by state authorities results in a certain "pluralism of communities" and thus perhaps to a "re-imagining" of the national community.[28]

Questions of self-identification came to the fore in *Ahmet Sadik v. Greece*,[29] where the applicant was imprisoned following an election campaign in which he published a series of communiqués referring, among other things, to the "Turkish community of western Thrace" and the "Turkish minority" instead of "the Greek minority of Muslim faith" – the terminology of the Treaty of Lausanne 1923.[30] The Greek Court of Cassation averred that "there was no Turkish minority in western Thrace".[31] The case was lost before the European Court on the grounds of non-exhaustion of domestic remedies. In a strong dissent, Judge Martens, joined by Judge Foighel, considered that the essence of the case was the extent of the rights of ethnic minorities in a democratic society[32] questioning whether "the mere fact of repeatedly referring to the Muslim minority as 'Turkish' justified the applicant's conviction and sentence".[33]

Dissenting judges counselled extreme vigilance – the criticism of Greek policy advanced by the applicant "concerned the government's attitude towards the minority ... and more especially its policy of denying that the minority is not only a religious but also an ethnic one".[34] Their final suggestion that in such cases "there is no room for relying on the judgments of the national courts nor for a margin of appreciation" leads the way to ECHR recognition of the principle that minority "existence" is not simply the gift of the state.

Analogous questions inform *Sidiropoulos and Others v. Greece*,[35] where the applicants, who claimed to be of "Macedonian" ethnic origin and to have a "Macedonian national consciousness", applied to register a non-profit-making association under the name of "Home of Macedonian Civilisation".[36] The application for registration was refused on the basis of a spectrum of evidence including reports of assertions by the applicants before a meeting of the Organisation on Security and Co-operation in Europe (OSCE) that there was a Macedonian minority in Greece.[37] The Court found a violation of Article 11 (freedom of association), casting doubt on the legitimacy of restricting the right on the basis of "upholding ... Greece's cultural traditions and historical and cultural symbols".[38] The Court also observed that mention of "the consciousness of belonging to a minority and development of a minority's culture" could not be said to constitute a threat to "democratic society",[39] adding that "the existence of minorities and different cultures in a country was a historical fact that a 'democratic society' had to tolerate and even protect and support according to the principles of international law".[40] This last statement brings the ECHR closer to legal texts which mandate positive action to promote minority identity and are more explicit on the existence of groups. Analogous "Turkish cases" are considered below.

Questions of naming, self-identification and their limits continue to engage the attention of the Court. In *Gorzelik and Others v. Poland*,[41] the rejection by the state authorities of the registration of "The Union of People of Silesian Nationality" on the ground, *inter alia*, that the Silesians were not a "nation" or a "national minority", was not deemed by the European Court to constitute a violation of Article 11. While the Court was at least prepared to review the process by which Poland had denied national minority status to the group concerned, it recognised a considerable margin of appreciation as to whether there was a "pressing social need" legitimating the restriction on Convention rights. The Court did not attempt a definition of "minority"[42] and, *inter alia*, pointed out the value of concessions by individuals and groups of individuals "so as to ensure the greater stability of the country as a whole".[43] The concession in this case would have been to compromise on the name of the association because it raised particularly sensitive issues for the state.

ii. *Self-determination*

The recognition of a "pluralism of communities" does not necessarily lead to the affirmation of a right of self-determination, a right of international law which is not explicitly mentioned in the Convention.[44] Accordingly, claims to self-determination by Germans formerly living in Czechoslovakia[45] and by indigenous ethnic groups of Surinam,[46] have been declared inadmissible. Self-determination – with potential effects on territorial integrity[47] – underlies a number of the Turkish and Greek cases. As noted, freedom of expression may be restricted on grounds, among others, of protecting "territorial integrity". The issue has been carefully handled by the Commission and the Court on the basis of a distinction (roughly) between argument and advocacy on the one hand, and incitement to violence on the other.[48]

In *United Communist Party of Turkey (TBKP) and Others v. Turkey,*[49] the applicant party (the TBKP) contested the party's dissolution by the Turkish Constitutional Court. The state's application to the Constitutional Court claimed that the TBKP sought to establish the domination of one social class over the others, had included the word "communist" in its name, and had carried on activities likely to undermine the territorial integrity of the state and the unity of the nation. The Constitutional Court rejected the state prosecutor's submissions on the first issue, but upheld the others on the grounds that Turkey was unitary, indivisible and there was only one nation. The Constitutional Court stated that by asserting the existence of "two nations" in Turkey, Turks and Kurds, the TBKP's programme "was intended to create minorities, to the detriment of the unity of the Turkish nation." "Nationals of Kurdish origin" were precluded from forming a nation or a minority distinct from the Turkish nation. The Commission decided unanimously that there had been a violation of Article 11.

Before the European Court of Human Rights, the applicants claimed violations of Article 11 and Article 1 and 3 of Protocol No. 1. The Court unanimously upheld the claim under Article 11, agreeing with the Commission that political parties were within its protection, even if their activities "are regarded by the national authorities as undermining the constitutional structures of the state".[50] The European Court was impressed by the TBKP's commitment to peaceful and democratic debate on the "national" question, as expressed through its documentation. One of the "principal characteristics" of democracy is "the possibility it offers of resolving a country's problems through dialogue".[51] On the other hand, the Court observed that the TBKP's programme referred to a Kurdish people and Kurdish citizens, "it neither describes them as a 'minority' nor makes any claim – other than for recognition of their existence – for them to enjoy special treatment or rights, still less a right to secede".[52] This sends out an uncertain message. What if the TBKP had used the term "minority", or had advocated secession?

This last question is clarified by other cases. In *Freedom and Democracy Party (OZDEP) v. Turkey*,[53] the applicant party was dissolved for allegedly promoting terrorism and advocating the creation of a Kurdish state. The programme of the party made a number of references to the right of "our peoples" (Turks and Kurds) to self-determination, to "oppressed peoples", and so on, stating that it "will fully respect the Kurdish people's right to self-determination so that a democratic solution [to Turkey's difficulties] based on the self-determination and equality of peoples can be found".[54] In finding a violation of Article 11, the Court read OZDEP's programme to reflect something like a concept of "internal self-determination",[55] in line with developments elsewhere in international law:

> the passages in issue present a political project whose aim is in essence the establishment – in accordance with democratic rules – of 'a social order encompassing the Turkish and Kurdish peoples' ... It is true that in its programme OZDEP also refers to the right of self-determination of the 'national or religious minorities'; however, taken in context, these words do not encourage people to seek separation from Turkey but are intended instead to emphasise that the proposed political project must be underpinned by the freely given, democratically expressed, consent of the Kurds.[56]

It is probably not accurate to read the Court's pronouncement as critical of separationist projects, in view of the sentence following the above, that "it is of the essence of democracy to allow diverse political projects to be proposed and debated ... provided that they do not harm democracy itself".

In *Stankov and the United Macedonian Organisation Ilinden v. Bulgaria*, the Court (First Section) offered the robust statement that "the fact that a group of persons calls for autonomy or even requests secession of part of the country's territory ... cannot automatically justify a prohibition of its assemblies ... In a democratic society based on the rule of law political ideas which challenge the existing order and whose resolution is advocated by peaceful means must be afforded a proper opportunity of expression through the exercise of the right of assembly as well as by other lawful means".[57] It is clear from the cases that the overriding principle preferred by the Court is the protection and advancement of democracy, and that the preferred form of democracy is that which offers participatory structures to relevant groups or peoples. Elsewhere the Court has stated that democracy is "the only political model contemplated by the Convention",[58] and that the preferred form of democracy is pluralistic,[59] and deliberative.[60]

This pluralism suffuses a range of rights, assuming the form of a general Convention characteristic. The importance of pluralism – or at least a certain form of pluralism (democratic pluralism) – is strongly asserted by the European Court of Human Rights in *Refah Partisi (the Welfare Party) and Others v. Turkey,*[61] in a judgment that raises perplexing questions on religion and culture. The essence of the case was that the Welfare Party, which had been dissolved by the Turkish Constitutional Court, had – through its leader Erbakan and others – proposed the abolition of secularism in Turkey and its replacement by a plurality of jurisdiction-exercising religious communities (legal systems) and the introduction of Sharia (Islamic) Law for Muslims.

The Court made wide-ranging remarks in finding that Turkey had not violated Article 11 of the Convention. The multiple legal systems approach of the Welfare Party would be incompatible with the Convention because firstly, it would substitute the static rules of law imposed by religion for the guarantor role of the state for individual freedoms,[62] and secondly, would violate the principle of non-discrimination.[63] In a sweeping statement on Sharia Law, the Court (Third Section) asserted that:

> It is difficult to declare one's respect for democracy and human rights while at the same time supporting a regime based on sharia, which clearly diverges from Convention values, particularly with regard to its criminal law and criminal procedure, its rules on the legal status of women and the way it intervenes in all spheres of private and public life in accordance with religious precepts … In the Court's view, a political party whose actions seem to be aimed at introducing sharia in a State party … can hardly be regarded as an association complying with the democratic ideal that underlies the whole of the Convention.[64]

While this is a clear statement of Convention values on the facts of the case, it is perhaps unnecessarily wide as a general claim concerning Sharia Law, a legal system which, in some cases, co-exists with and is modified in practice by non-religious, secular systems.[65] The judgment was confirmed by the Grand Chamber, specifically quoting key points made by the Third Section on the Sharia.[66] In a concurring opinion, Judge Kovler expressed concern about some of the Court's findings, describing them as "unmodulated" particularly insofar as they imported terms from "politico-ideological discourse" such as "Islamic Fundamentalism". He regretted that the Court missed the opportunity to examine the concept of a plurality of legal systems, a concept understood not only in anthropology but in some modern constitutions, where it was accepted "that under certain conditions members of minorities of all kinds may have more than one type of personal status".

iii. *Non-discrimination*

The full text of Article 14 of the Convention is:

> The enjoyment of the rights and freedoms set forth in this Convention shall be secured without discrimination on any ground such as sex, race, colour, language, religion, political or other opinion, national or social origin, association with a national minority, property, birth or other status.

This principle concerns discrimination and not equal protection of the law,[67] and looks to the promotion of equality through the elimination of discrimination. Article 14 limits itself to the rights in the Convention and is not "open" to dealing with rights which are not in the Convention.[68] On the other hand, the description of prohibited grounds of discrimination is illustrative and open-ended, including the phrases: "any ground such as" and "other status".

In the jurisprudence, the Belgian linguistic case[69] retains much of its interest. In the language legislation of 1963, the national territory of Belgium was divided into four regions: the Flemish, the French, the German, and Greater Brussels. The regime incorporated rules mandating teaching in the regional language in public schools, with no subsidies offered to private schools which use another language. Parents who did not want to use the regional language were free to teach at home or send the children to an unsubsidised school. They could also send children across the linguistic border or to Greater Brussels where the language of instruction would be in Dutch or French according to the child's home language. There were additional problems with school certificates which did not conform to the language regime – the state would refuse to confirm the certificates.

A special regime deviating from the territorial principle existed in six communes on the outskirts of Brussels. In this regime, French classes were restricted to children whose parents resided in the communes; on the other hand, the Dutch classes accepted children from outside. The case was brought by French-speaking applicants residing in the Dutch unilingual region who asserted that the principles of immutable linguistic boundaries and territorial unilingualism violated Articles 8 and 14 of the ECHR and Article 2 of Protocol No. 1.[70] The chief ground of complaint was that language laws forced the families to move, since they had no access to public, subsidised education in French.

The Commission found the Belgian system incompatible with Article 2 of Protocol No. 1 in conjunction with Article 14 in relation to the limitations on access to the French language schools in the special status communes, as well as a violation in regard to the school certificates. The Court disagreed in that it did not find a violation on the subsidy and school certificate regulations. The Court held that the Convention did not recognise a right to be educated through a particular language – Article 2 of Protocol No. 1 did not specify the language in which instruction had to be provided, though it would be meaningless if it did not imply the right of the holder to receive an education in a national (possibly understood as "official") language. The education article in essence safeguarded access to the then existing school institutions.[71] Equally, the judgment did not call into question the pursuit of linguistic unity within the regions.

The Court did however find a violation of Article 2 of Protocol No. 1 in conjunction with Article 14 on the access to education in the special communes: the law prevented children, solely on the basis of residence of their parents, from having access to the French schools in the six communes. The violation was found on the ground of residence in relation to language (a prohibited ground of discrimination), not on the specific ground of "association with a national minority". Not all distinctions are prohibited by Article 14:[72] however, the principle of equality of treatment is violated if the distinction has no objective and reasonable justification, and: "The existence of such a justification must be assessed in relation to the aim and effects of the measure under consideration, regard being had to the principles which normally prevail in democratic societies. A difference in treatment ... must not only pursue a legitimate aim: Article 14 is likewise violated when it is clearly established that there is no reasonable relationship of proportionality between the means employed and the aim sought to be realised."[73]

While the Court's exposition of the non-discrimination principle represents a significant and persuasive determination of a norm, the decision in the case is more ambivalent as regards general minority issues. For the Commission, the Belgian policy amounted to the assimilation of minorities against their will into the regional language bloc, whereas for the Court, the Belgian legislation was in the defensible realm of pursuing the public interest through the attainment of linguistic unity.[74] One important point for minority protection is that language maintenance and development constitute legitimate aims within the Convention, consistent with Article 14. Another positive point is the understanding that official recognition of diplomas attained is indispensable to the completion of the education process;[75] otherwise there would be only limited economic benefit to be derived from establishing private schools.[76] On the other hand, the refusal to interpret the right to education to include the right to education in one's own language is limiting. The Court argued that, if it were otherwise, anyone would be free to claim any language of instruction in the territories of the contracting states – an unnecessary *reductio ad absurdum* argument.[77] The question of the language of education is addressed in later instruments of minority rights and minority languages.[78]

It may be observed that the organs of the ECHR have displayed some reluctance to find discrimination relevant and proven, dealing with discrimination only when "a clear inequality of treatment in the enjoyment of the right in question is a fundamental aspect of the case".[79] Thus in the Turkish cases the Court finds regular violations by the state of rights to life, liberty and property of Kurds, without the further step of identifying the reason for violations as the Kurdish ethnicity of victims.[80] In *Tanrikulu v. Turkey*, the Court discussed the claim of the applicant, under Article 14, who alleged that her husband had been killed because of his Kurdish origins,[81] dismissing it for want of evidence. An Article 14 point is often not pursued because it is covered by another article.[82] However, in *Ozgur Gundem v. Turkey*,[83] where the applicants had argued that "any expression of Kurdish identity was treated by the authorities as advocacy of separatism and PKK propaganda",[84] a phenomenon which "could only be explained by prohibited discrimination",[85] the Court decided affirmatively that there had been no discrimination.[86]

Decisions finding discrimination also seem to require a high standard of proof before it can be said to have occurred. In *Cyprus v. Turkey*, the European Commission of Human Rights made reference to the conditions of the Roma/Gypsy community in northern Cyprus. Despite finding that living conditions were poor, that houses were demolished, and Roma/Gypsy children were humiliated at school, and so on, the Commission decided on the ground of non-exhaustion of domestic remedies that there had been no violation of a spectrum of rights,[87] including the right to education and to be free from discrimination and degrading treatment. It was added that, moreover, "the Commission does not find it established beyond reasonable doubt that there is a deliberate practice of the authorities ... to discriminate against Gypsies".[88] The Commission's findings in this respect were supported by the Court of Human Rights.[89]

The practice of the authorities concerning Roma/Gypsies suggests indirect discrimination, a concept which appeared only fleetingly in the jurisprudence of the ECHR.[90] The notion of indirect discrimination gains strength from *Shanaghan and Kelly v. the United Kingdom*,[91] cases alleging killings of disproportionately large numbers of Catholics in Northern Ireland. In *Shanaghan*, the Court stated that where "a general policy or measure has disproportionately prejudicial effects on a particular group, it is not excluded that this may be considered as discriminatory notwithstanding that it is not specifically aimed or directed at that group".[92]

Whereas discrimination on grounds of race or sex is regarded as particularly "suspect" in the ECHR canon,[93] there has also been reluctance to utilise "national minority" as a ground of discrimination, although "ethnic origin" and "race" may function as near equivalents. In *Velikova v. Bulgaria*,[94] a case involving the death of an individual of Roma/Gypsy ethnicity, in assessing the application of Article 14 the Court discussed the issues under "ethnic origin", "ethnicity" and "racial prejudice" without employing the phrase "national minority". Previous Commission findings on Cyprus were based on "ethnic origin, race and religion".[95] The applicant in *Chapman v. UK* alleged discrimination on the assorted grounds of "race, national or social origin, association with a national minority and birth or other status ... such discrimination is caused by popular prejudice against gypsies and a failure by local and national government to act despite that prejudice".[96] Although Article 14 is not explicit on the question, it may be argued that states are obliged to ensure effective enjoyment of protection from discrimination on the basis of the Belgian linguistic case and Airey. The problem is that positive readings of Article 14 tend to be "submerged" in positive readings of substantive articles in view of the subsidiary role of non-discrimination in the ECHR.[97] This applies equally to suggestions that the ECHR sanctions special measures for disadvantaged groups.[98]

Protocol No. 12[99]

The preamble to the protocol declares the resolve of states party "to take further steps to promote the equality of all persons through the collective enforcement of a general prohibition of discrimination", reaffirming that the principle "does not prevent ... measures in order to promote full and effective equality, provided that there is an objective and reasonable justification for these measures". Article 1 of the protocol reads:

> 1. The enjoyment of any right set forth by law shall be secured without discrimination on any ground such as sex, race, colour, language, religion, political or other opinion, national or social origin, association with a national minority, property, birth or other status.
>
> 2. No one shall be discriminated against by any public authority on any ground such as those mentioned in paragraph 1.[100]

The explanatory report to the protocol traces the history of the project, and recognises the influence of work in the field of sexual equality and in combating racism and intolerance – the role of ECRI is regarded as of special significance.[101] The explanatory report summarises the need for the protocol in view of the fact that "Article 14 is clearly accessory to the other, substantive guarantees in the Convention".[102] The principle of equality is described as "a fundamental and well-established principle of international law",[103] requiring "that equal situations are treated equally and unequal situations differently".[104] The explanatory report compares Article 14 with a range of texts, including those which permit or mandate "special measures" to ameliorate disadvantage, observing that "the present Protocol does not impose any obligation to adopt such measures".[105]

This judgment is reached in terms of a questionable contrast between the "programmatic" nature of such an obligation, and the specific "justiciable" nature of the ECHR. On the other hand, the opinion opens up juridical space between the ECHR and the Framework Convention, one of the conventions cited as including "special measures".[106] Rights "set forth by law" includes cases where there is discrimination in relation to specific rights under national law, or in rights to be inferred from a clear obligation of a public authority under national law, or in the exercise of a discretion by a public authority, or by any other act or omission of a public authority.[107] The explanatory report admits that "law" may also cover international law, but this does not mean that the provision "entails jurisdiction for the European Court of Human Rights to examine compliance with rules of law in other international instruments".[108] On possible horizontal effects (relations between private persons), the position in the explanatory report is nuanced. First, it includes the observation that "while such positive obligations cannot be excluded altogether",[109] the protocol "is not intended to impose a general positive obligation on the parties ... to prevent or remedy all instances of discrimination in relations between private persons".[110] It then concedes that "it cannot totally be excluded that the duty to 'secure' ... might entail positive obligations",[111] observing further that such positive obligations are likely to be limited.[112]

iv. *Dignity*

In the case of *Kalderas Gypsies v. the Federal Republic of Germany and the Netherlands,*[113] forty-eight Kalderas Roma/Gypsies in the Federal Republic of Germany and the Netherlands claimed violations of Articles 3 and 14 of the Convention because of the refusal by the authorities to issue identification papers. The Commission observed that refusing identification documents to a nomadic group might amount to a violation of Article 3, as degrading treatment, and Article 14, as discrimination. On birth certificates, refusal may amount to a violation of Article 8. The applications were rejected for non-exhaustion of domestic remedies.

In *Assenov and Others v. Bulgaria,*[114] the applicants were a Roma/Gypsy family of Bulgarian nationality who claimed that Assenov had been ill-treated by police in connection with and subsequent to his arrest. Among others, Article 3 and Article 5 issues were raised. Article 3 was violated by the failure of the Bulgarian authorities to carry out an official investigation into the allegations.[115] The Court observed that if "this were not the case, the general legal prohibition on torture and inhuman and degrading treatment and punishment ... would be ineffective in practice and it would be possible in some cases for agents of the state to abuse the rights of those within their control with virtual impunity".[116] Additionally, it was decided that Article 13 (right to an effective remedy) had been violated.[117] The Court ruled on the latter article that, where there is an arguable claim that the applicant has been ill-treated under Article 3, the notion of an effective remedy includes – "in addition to a thorough and effective investigation of the kind also required by Article 3"[118] – effective access of the complainant to an investigatory procedure and to the payment of compensation where appropriate.

While such principles have an impact on others besides minorities, their utility in cases of generalised official "prejudice" against specific groups is obvious – authorities can less easily hide behind evidential and pro-cedural smokescreens. In *Sevtap Veznedaroglu v. Turkey*,[119] the applicant, a research student in public law, was arrested by the authorities on sus-picion of being a member of the Kurdistan Workers Party (PKK), a charge which eventually failed for lack of evidence. She alleged severe torture during interrogation by the police, in violation of Article 3.[120] The Court found that it was impossible to establish on the evidence whether or not the applicant's injuries were caused by the police. Citing Assenov, the Court nevertheless found a violation of Article 3 "on account of the fail-ure of the authorities of the respondent state to investigate the appli-cant's complaint of torture".[121]

In the Commission decision in *Cyprus v. Turkey*, the consequences of the Turkish policy of ethnic separation for the Greek community in the north of Cyprus was assessed in terms of Article 3 and human dignity:

> This policy has led to the confinement of the Greek Cypriot population ... within a small area of the Karpas peninsula. There is a steady decrease of their numbers as a result of specific measures which prevent the renewal of the population ... their property is confiscated if they die or leave the area ... the restrictions imposed on them have the effect of ensuring that "inexorably with the passage of time, these communities [will] cease to exist ...".[122] The Commission considers that ... the hardships to which the Greek Cypriots living in the Karpas area of northern Cyprus were subjected ... still affected their daily life to such an extent that it is justified to conclude that the discriminatory treatment com-plained of attained a level of severity which constitutes an affront to their human dignity.[123]

v. *Identity issues*
Private life/ways of life

a. *Names*[124]

Other international treaties,[125] and texts on minority rights, make specific reference to names of persons and places.[126] A person's choice of name on the basis of language, religion and/or ethnic appurtenance is widely understood as an essential aspect of personal identity. The naming of a place may have profound historical significance for national groups. While the ECHR is silent on this issue, the Commission and the Court have held that regulation of names falls within the sphere of family and private life.[127] In the Burghartz case (the first "names" case to reach the Court),[128] the Court ruled that a person's name as a means of identification concerns family and private life, but that the state has an interest in regulating the use of names. Accordingly, in the case of Swiss nationals married in Germany, the application to use a wife's name – Burghartz – as the family name in Switzerland succeeded, but not a claim by the husband to use his family name – Schnyder – before Burghartz. The Court ruled that there had been a violation of Article 8 taken with Article 14.

On the other hand, in the case of *Stjerna v. Finland*,[129] the applicant was refused permission to change his last name from Stjerna to Tawasterjna, a name last used by ancestors in 1773. The Court distinguished the situation where permission to change is refused from that where a name is "imposed" by the state, but accepted that legal restrictions on a change of name may be justified in the public interest – for purposes of population registration, linking the bearer to a family, and so on. In the absence of legal common ground among member states of the Council of Europe, states enjoy a wide margin of appreciation in such cases. [130] As elsewhere, the Court attempts to balance individual choice and the public interest.[131] Self-identification is not an absolute principle here because "names retain a crucial role in the identification of people" (presumably the identification of people by others).[132] In the case of minorities, names have sometimes been forcibly changed by the authorities – this clearly violates the right to a private life.

On the other hand, there appears to be no special sensitivity in the ECHR to the adoption of a name to express an "ethnic" or "national" sentiment. In a case such as Stjerna for example, if the "ancestor" were less remote and the name more clearly tied to the usage of a particular community, a different result can be imagined. In the words of the UN Human Rights Committee, "a person's surname constitutes an important component of one's identity and ... the protection against arbitrary or unlawful interference with one's privacy includes protection against arbitrary or unlawful interference with the right to choose and change one's name".[133]

b. *Ways of life*

Key Article 8 cases have dealt with characteristic ways of life of certain communities. *G. and E. v. Norway*[134] concerned the effects of the construction of a dam and a hydro-electric plant in the Alta Valley. The applicants were members of the Saami community that had traditionally used the lands for reindeer herding, fishing and hunting. The case was declared inadmissible by the Commission, but aspects of the reasoning under Article 8 of the Convention are significant. The Commission noted the statements of the applicants:

> that by birth they belong to a minority group, the Lapps. For hundreds of years their kinsfolk have been working with reindeer, fishing and hunting. Every year they move their herd of deer around, and, therefore, there is a great demand for space. The Lapps have their own culture and language, far apart from the other Scandinavian languages ... [The applicants] maintain that they will not only lose their land, but also their identity.[135]

The Commission observed that "under Article 8, a minority group is, in principle, entitled to claim the right to respect for the particular lifestyle it may lead as being 'private life', 'family life', or 'home'".[136] It was also stated that the traditional use of vast territories for grazing, hunting and fishing is not a property right within the meaning of Article 1 of Protocol No. 1,[137] but that the consequences of the plant on traditional Saami economic activities may entitle them to compensation. Nonetheless, the applicants could continue their traditional way of life. Therefore, the measure complained of could properly be regarded as an interference in accordance with law and:

> necessary in a democratic society for one of the purposes enumerated ... the economic well-being of the country. The Commission finds that, without ascertaining the exact extent and nature of the interference with the applicants' rights ... after the careful consideration of the necessity of the project by the national organs, the interference could reasonably be considered as justified.[138]

It is notable that the Commission's assessment of the effects of the projects on the Saami is measured primarily in spatial and economic rather than cultural terms.[139] The Commission also uses a "generalist" criterion of "economic well-being" to justify the interference, and as Scheinin observes, a reference to "majority decision-making as a proper justification for interfering with a minority culture"[140] – the adequacy of decision by the "national organs". The Commission rebutted any allegation of discrimination by noting that the ECHR does not guarantee specific rights to minorities and that the authors had, as other Norwegian citizens, the right to vote and stand for election to the Norwegian Parliament.[141]

Buckley v. UK[142] was the first Roma/Gypsy case to reach the European Court of Human Rights. The applicant was a Gypsy by birth whose family had for generations been based in the area of South Cambridgeshire near Willingham.[143] The case concerned the refusal of planning permission by UK local authorities and the Secretary of State for the Environment for the applicant to station caravans on her own land.[144] Permission was refused because of the unsightly nature of the caravans,[145] the concentration of Gypsy caravans in the area and the availability of an official Gypsy site.[146] Following an inspector's report, the Secretary of State found, among other things, that "the concentration of Gypsy sites in the area had reached the desirable maximum and the need for additional sites for Gypsies should not outweigh the planning and highway objections".[147] The Commission concluded by seven votes to five that there had been a violation of Article 8 of the Convention. The applicant had a right to a home – an autonomous concept which did not depend on classification by domestic law.[148] It was accepted that planning measures pursued, among other legitimate aims, "the economic well-being of the country".[149]

However, the Commission expressed doubts concerning the nature of the planning restrictions and the limited alternatives available to Ms Buckley in the choice of a home[150] in view of her traditional lifestyle as a Roma/Gypsy. Rights under Article 8 were "an intrinsic part of [the applicant's] security and well-being".[151] Disagreement among Commission members in part concerned the relevance of considering traditional lifestyle in the context of the Convention.[152] The Commission concluded[153] that the interference with rights was not "necessary in a democratic society" – the burdens upon the applicant were excessive and disproportionate, and "the interests of the applicant in this case outweigh the general interest ... Special considerations arise in the planning sphere regarding the needs of Roma/Gypsies which are acknowledged in the Government's own policies".[154] Whether the correct balance has been struck between the rights of an individual Gypsy or Gypsy family and the interests of the general community will always depend on the particular facts of the case.[155]

The Court[156] took a different view, finding that there had been no violation of Article 8,[157] particularly in the light of the doctrine of the "margin of appreciation" allowed to national authorities in the application of the Convention. The process of weighing the interest of the applicant against the general interest had been done responsibly by the national authorities.[158] In the Court's view, the "special needs of the applicant as a Gypsy following a traditional lifestyle were taken into account".[159] On this last issue the Court cited the report of the inspector which included the statement "... I consider it important to keep concentrations of sites for Gypsies small, because this way they are more readily accepted by the local community".[160] In relation to the applicant's refusal to accept alternative accommodation on the official caravan site, the Court simply stated that "Article 8 does not go so far as to allow individuals' preferences as to their place of residence to override the general interest".[161] Neither was there any violation using Article 8 in conjunction with

Article 14. The Court did not find that the applicant had at any time been penalised or subjected to any detrimental treatment for attempting to follow a traditional Roma/Gypsy lifestyle. On the contrary, the Court charitably interpreted UK law as "aimed at enabling Gypsies to cater for their own needs".[162]

Dissenting opinions appended to the judgment forcefully articulated aspects of the case concerned with minority culture and group oppression. Judge Repik was concerned "about how the Court's first judgment on this subject will be interpreted and how it will be received by the Gypsy community". He could not find the "pressing social need" implied in the concept of "necessity", and argued that the interests of the applicant were only taken into account "in abstract, general terms", and not her financial situation or the possible consequences of eviction. The cultural aspect was delineated by Judge Repik in terms of the psychological rootedness of the travelling imperative of Gypsies, which in this case presupposed a secure site to which to return.[163] Judge Lohmus set out a basic theorem of minority rights:

> It has been stated before the Court that the applicant as a Gypsy has the same rights and duties as all the other members of the community. I think that this is an oversimplification of the question of minority rights. It may not be enough to prevent discrimination so that members of minority groups receive equal treatment under the law. In order to establish equality in fact, different treatment may be necessary to preserve their special cultural heritage.

He observed that the factors weighing in favour of the public interest in planning controls are of "a slight and general nature".

The longest dissent was offered by Judge Pettiti, who recalled the "special responsibility" of Europe towards Roma/Gypsies and the opportunity offered by the European Convention to address the discrimination, rejection and exclusion practised against them. He pointed to the unreasonable combinations of rules from different government departments that apply to Roma/Gypsies, which make it difficult to avoid contraventions. He believed that British policy was discriminatory, and that if the Buckley case "was transposed to a family of ecologists or adherents of a religion instead of Gypsies, the harassment ... would not have occurred". Specifically, he argued that the obstacles to free movement placed in the way of Gypsies go beyond the general law. In relation to the right to family property, there is a breach of family life; the requirement that an owner move because of the concentration of Gypsy sites is unacceptable interference, "since the owner is not liable for the acts or omissions of others". On the landscape issue, the authorities:

> rely on this argument only against Gypsy families [which] amounts to a disproportionate interference ... in the hierarchy of the state's positive

obligations, the survival of families must come before bucolic or aesthetic concerns.

Judge Pettiti added that respect for family life should not be subordinated "to the greater convenience of the local community and its greater willingness to accept others". His concluding paragraph delivers a tangible note of regret that the Court had lost the opportunity for a legal critique of national law "transposable to the rest of Europe" in partial compensation for injustices suffered by the Gypsy community.

The issue will not go away. Following Buckley, the Commission considered seven applications from Roma/Gypsies under Article 8 and Article 1 of Protocol No. 1, and all but one were declared admissible as raising serious issues of fact and law under the Convention.[164] The same question arose in each case – the purchase of land and the stationing of a caravan on the land without planning permission, followed by the failure of planning appeals and some prosecutions. Thus for example, in *Joseph and Mary Varey v. the UK*,[165] the government submitted that their refusal to grant planning permission to station caravans was in order to defend the "green belt" policy, and that interference with applicants' rights was "proportionate to the legitimate aim of protecting the environment".

Expression/promotion of identity

The thirteen cases

On 8 July 1999, the Court found violations of human rights in thirteen cases against Turkey,[166] in eleven of which Article 10 was violated.[167] The cases raise essentially the same points with minor variations. Accordingly, the President of the Court decided that a single Grand Chamber should be constituted to hear the thirteen cases. The first named of the cases, *Arslan v. Turkey*, serves to introduce the issues on Article 10. The proceedings concerned the conviction of the applicant on two occasions by the Turkish courts for publishing in 1989 and republishing in 1991 a book dealing with the historical and contemporary oppression of the Kurds in Turkey entitled *History in Mourning: 33 Bullets*. The author was charged in the first case with dissemination of separatist propaganda[168] and in the second with publishing propaganda against the indivisible unity of the state.[169]

The first conviction was declared null and void by the National Security Court, which held in the second case that the applicant had intended to incite citizens of Kurdish origin to rebel against the state.[170] On Article 10,[171] the Court accepted that the restriction on freedom of expression connected with legitimate aims, namely the protection of national security and territorial integrity, and the prevention of disorder and crime.[172] Exceptions to a principle must be construed narrowly. The Court assessed whether the restrictions were necessary in a democratic society on the basis of linked considerations: firstly, was the interference proportionate to legitimate aims pursued?; secondly, were the reasons for it relevant and sufficient? – bearing in mind that thirdly, the limits of permissible criticism are wider with regard to governments than with private individuals, but that fourthly where remarks incite to violence "against an individual or a public official or a sector of the population" the state enjoys a wider margin of appreciation.[173] The Court observed, among other things, that:

> although certain particularly acerbic passages in the book paint an extremely negative picture of the population of Turkish origin and give the narrative a hostile tone, they do not constitute an incitement to violence, armed resistance or an uprising.[174]

One of the two concurring opinions to the decision that Article 10 had been violated[175] suggested that the Court should look to the "contextual setting" in which words were uttered rather than just the words themselves.[176] The second opinion[177] challenged the view that incitement to violence cancelled out the protection of Article 10. It should not have this effect unless the incitement was such as to create a "clear and present danger" of violence ensuing, a question of "proximity and degree".[178] In *Surek v. Turkey Nos. 1 and 3*, the restrictions on freedom of expression were justified because there was incitement to violence and individuals were identified exposing them to a risk of violence.[179] These cases have since been followed by a series of others on essentially the same points.[180]

Freedom of expression for members of minorities may be compared with freedom from hate speech. In a number of cases, the Commission "gave scant protection" to intentional propagation of racial hatred.[181] However, in *Jersild v. Denmark*,[182] where the media assisted in the dissemination of racial insults, the Court found that a journalist's conviction for aiding and abetting was a violation of his freedom of expression. The Court considered the position of the press as a watchdog and regarded the programme in question as a responsible and dispassionate presentation of information on views held by others.[183]

Language

"Linguistic freedom" has been treated in a very limited fashion in the Convention.[184] In Article 6.3.e, which provides for the free assistance of an interpreter if an accused person cannot understand or speak the language of the court,[185] the provision has been treated as an aspect of the administration of justice and not as incorporating a right to use a language of choice. In *Isop v. Austria*[186] the applicant claimed that the Austrian State Treaty of 1955 gave him a right to use the Slovene language in criminal proceedings in the area where he lived. He claimed a violation of Article 6 in conjunction with Article 14. It was observed that he understood and spoke German. The Commission pointed out that Article 6 guaranteed the right to present a case to court; it did not include a right to be heard in one's own language. Equally, the Convention does not give a right to witnesses in a court case to speak a language of their choice.[187] Similarly, according to *Fryske Nasjonale Partij v. Netherlands*,[188] the Convention does not guarantee a right to use a language of choice in dealings with the authorities – a matter latterly addressed by the Framework Convention.

The case of *Mathieu-Mohin v. Clerfayt*[189] concerned the system in Belgium, which uses the language of the Parliamentary Oath of Office to determine membership of language groups. The language of the parliamentary oath also produces effects at the level of the councils responsible for Flanders and Wallonia. The case arose from a complaint by Wallonians in Flanders that if they elected a French-speaking delegate to Parliament, they would not be represented in the Flemish Council, which had authority in their election district. The Commission ruled that Article 3 of Protocol No. 1 had been violated in that it forced the Wallonian voters in the district in question to vote against their conscience for a Flemish speaker in order to secure local representation. However, drawing heavily upon the concept of the margin of appreciation, the Court found no violation of the protocol nor of Article 14. The Court accepted linguistic decentralisation as a legitimate aim and noted the existence of analogous systems elsewhere. Dissenting judges questioned whether in fact the representation of French speakers at the regional level ensured "the free expression of the opinion of the people" as required by the article.[190]

In *Podkolzina v. Latvia*,[191] the applicant's name had been struck from the list of candidates for election to the Latvian Parliament on grounds of a finding by the State Language Centre that her command of the Latvian language was insufficient. The European Court found that the decision to strike the applicant off the electoral list amounted to a violation of Article 3 of Protocol 1. In point of fact, her linguistic competence had already been certificated as satisfactory before the later "impromptu" examination by the Language Board which, in the view of the Court, did not meet standards of objectivity and procedural fairness. In passing, the Court observed that the choice of the working language of a national parliament is one which "is determined by historical and political considerations specific to each country [and] is in principle one which the State alone has the power to make".[192]

All of the above deal with the use of language in the public realm. In such cases, requirements of bureaucratic efficiency, costs of providing language services, and the existence of official or state languages, weigh along with individual preferences. In the private sphere, recalling that Article 8 safeguards the right to respect for "private and family life ... home and correspondence", the situation is different. In essence, the reservoir of potential restrictions on the right to privacy in Article 8 can have little relevance to the private use of languages of choice. Stjerna implies that the bearing of a name in a minority language is a matter for the individual; it is only when considerations of public interest invest the situation that limited restrictions can be demanded. The principle applies also to the use of minority languages. ECHR case-law does not make the matter abundantly clear, but assistance may be found in the lapidary statement of the UN Human Rights Committee that a state "may choose one or more official languages, but it may not exclude, outside the spheres of public life, the freedom to express oneself in a language of one's choice".[193]

Education

The right to education is referred to in Article 2 of Protocol No. 1:

> No person shall be denied the right to education. In the exercise of any functions which it assumes in relation to education and to teaching, the state shall respect the right of parents to ensure such education and teaching in conformity with their own religious and philosophical convictions.

The provision was interpreted restrictively in the Belgian Linguistic case. According to the Court, the states party are not obliged by Article 2 to establish at their own expense, or to subsidise, education of any particular type or at any particular level. Rather, the case safeguards the question of access to schools once established. One authority comments that "the exercise of the right to education, even if understood in this way, requires by implication the existence and the maintenance of a minimum of education provided by the state, since otherwise the right would be illusory, in particular for those who have insufficient means".[194] In any case, the parties to the ECHR will also be parties to the International Covenant on Economic, Social and Cultural Rights (ICESCR),[195] where the right to education is spelled out in more explicit terms and has been given a positive interpretation.[196]

In the Belgian linguistic case, the applicants argued that "philosophical convictions" should be interpreted to include the cultural and linguistic preferences of the parents. However, the Commission, followed by the Court, was unanimous that the second sentence of Article 2 was not intended to guarantee respect for preferences or opinions in cultural or linguistic matters. In *Kjeldsen, Busk Madsen and Pedersen v. Denmark*,[197] the European Court of Human Rights emphasised the role played by education in a democratic society, observing that the Protocol "aims ... at safeguarding the possibility of pluralism in education ... essential for the preservation of the 'democratic society' as conceived by the Convention ...". This implies that the state must take care that information or knowledge included in the curriculum is conveyed in an objective, critical and pluralistic manner. The state is forbidden to pursue an aim of indoctrination – which might be considered as not respecting parents' religious and philosophical convictions. The term "philosophical convictions" was explained by the European Court of Human Rights in *Campbell and Cosans v. the United Kingdom*[198] as relating to "such convictions as are worthy of respect in a democratic society ... and are not incompatible with human dignity".[199] The views of the applicant on the practice of corporal punishment in schools related to "a weighty and substantial aspect of human life and behaviour".[200]

On the basis of the reading of "philosophical convictions" in *Campbell and Cosans*, one author comments that "the desire of parents, based on cultural and linguistic association with an ethnic group, to have their children educated in their mother tongue also has to be recognised as such a conviction".[201] Other authors have commented on the "muddled" case-law of the ECHR. Taking together Belgian linguistic, Kjeldsen et al., and Campbell and Cosans, they observe that:

> One possible explanation is that corporal punishment involves the physical integrity of the individual, whereas sex education reflects the duty of the state to provide children with information and language education arouses great political and constitutional sensitivities in some regions of Europe.[202]

These assertions do not offer a complete answer to the propriety of variations in jurisprudence. There is potential in the ECHR to address the education issues again, in view of the openness of the criterion of "philosophical convictions" – this is implicit in the authors' critique.[203] It would be inappropriate if the existence of the newer texts on minority rights were to act as a "reason" for not developing ECHR jurisprudence further.

The opinion of the European Commission of Human Rights in the case of *Cyprus v. Turkey*[204] points to further potential in the ECHR. On schools in northern Cyprus that offered teaching in English or Turkish, but were also open to Greek Cypriots, the Commission observed that:

> education in such schools does not correspond to the needs of the persons concerned who have the legitimate wish to preserve their own ethnic and cultural identity. While it is true that Article 2 of Protocol No. 1 guarantees access only to existing educational facilities, it must be noted that ... such educational facilities have in fact existed in the past and have been abolished by the Turkish Cypriot authorities ... In the Commission's opinion, the total absence of appropriate secondary

schools for Greek Cypriots living in northern Cyprus cannot be compensated for either by the authorities' allowing the pupils concerned to attend such schools in southern Cyprus. In fact, this permission is not unconditional in that until recently all pupils were not allowed to return after completion of their studies and even now male students beyond the age of sixteen are not allowed to do so. In these circumstances the practice of the Turkish authorities amounts to a denial of the substance of the right to education.[205]

The Commission's opinion is heavily conditioned by the facts of the case, including the previous existence of schools, latterly abolished. The decision brings to mind the principle that human rights instruments should be interpreted as far as possible to preserve and augment the existing stock of international and domestic rights. The Court supported the finding by the Commission of a violation of Article 2 of Protocol No. 1:

> the option available to Greek-Cypriot parents to continue their children's education in the north is unrealistic in view of the fact that the children in question have already received their primary education in a Greek-Cypriot school there. The authorities must no doubt be aware that it is the wish of Greek-Cypriot parents that the schooling of the children be completed through the medium of the Greek language. Having assumed responsibility for the provision of Greek-language primary schooling, the failure of the TRNC authorities to make continuing provision for it must be considered in effect a denial of the substance of the right at issue. It cannot be maintained that the provision of secondary education in the south in keeping with the linguistic tradition of the enclaved Greek Cypriots suffices to fulfil the obligation ... in Article 2 of the First Protocol, having regard to the impact of that option on family life.[206]

Participation

The right to participation is dealt with in the major instruments of human rights and minority rights. In the former, the paradigm case is that of political participation;[207] in minority rights the concept is wider and includes minority participation in decisions which affect them.[208] In the ECHR, Article 3 of Protocol No. 1 requires the parties to undertake to hold free elections at reasonable intervals by secret ballot, "under conditions which will ensure the free expression of the opinion of the people in the choice of the legislature". Exclusion of a minority group from political participation is clearly in violation of this provision.[209] On the positive side, proportional voting systems are adopted in many countries, partly in order to increase minority representation.

In the case of *Lindsay et al. v. the UK*,[210] the issue concerned the voting system in Northern Ireland for elections to the European Parliament which, in contrast to other regions of the UK, took place under a system of proportional representation and not "first past the post". The

Commission observed that the system chosen for Northern Ireland would better ensure that the minority was represented in the legislature. Far from being in disharmony with the article, a system which took into account the special position of majority and minority made it easier for the people to freely express their opinion. Neither was the differential system a breach of Article 14 since it was based on reasonable and objective criteria.

While the protocol does not make any particular system mandatory, the Lindsay rule means that minorities can legitimately be favoured by a system: the substance of the equality/non-discrimination rule is to be assessed in relation to particular systems. On the matter of favouring minorities in terms of the effect on votes, the Commission case of *X v. Iceland*[211] suggests that even a fluctuation in the value of the vote between 1 and 4.8 does not validate the conclusion that the weighting is too great. In view of the margin of appreciation[212] and the diversity of electoral systems within the Council of Europe, Article 3 does not mandate any particular electoral system. The system of "first past the post", which may have the effect of reducing minority representation, is as valid as others.[213]

Religion

The Convention outlines a basic freedom of religious provision, not specific to minorities, in Article 9:

> 1. Everyone has the right to freedom of thought, conscience and religion; this right includes freedom to change his religion or belief and freedom, either alone or in community with others and in public or private, to manifest his religion or belief, in worship, teaching, practice and observance.

The right assumes high relevance for minorities where religion is at least partly constitutive of minority identity, especially where that identity supplements a "national" identity which has religious overtones. As elsewhere in the human rights canon, the basic freedom of religion is not subject to restrictions, though its manifestation is open to limitations if prescribed by law and necessary in a democratic society "in the interests of public safety, for the protection of public order, health or morals, or for the protection of the rights and freedoms of others".[214] This "individual" right nevertheless incorporates "communal" dimensions – the right is to be exercised "either alone or in community with others", phraseology which compares with minority rights instruments – indicating that the state may not "reduce" the exercise of religion to a purely private activity, to the detriment of its communal dimension.[215] Additionally, ECHR jurisprudence establishes that the church as a whole and not just individual members can be protected by Article 9.[216]

In the light of Article 9, the state may need to address the consequences where a plurality of religious communities seek to enjoy a degree of autonomy. In *Serif v. Greece,*[217] following the death of the Mufti of Rodopi, the Greek authorities appointed MT as Mufti of Rodopi, having changed the method of selection from community election to appointment by presidential decree. Serif, on the other hand, was elected Mufti after Friday prayers at the Mosque. Serif proceeded to dress and act as Mufti, challenging the credentials of MT, and was fined for usurping the functions of a minister of a "known religion". The Court side-stepped complex questions of treaty law in favour of finding a violation of Article 9 (freedom of religion), rejecting the government justification that it was unifying the leadership of the community in order to ease communal tensions. The Court recalled that:

> freedom of thought, conscience and religion is one of the foundations of a 'democratic society' within the meaning of the Convention ... Although the Court recognises that it is possible that tension is created in situations where a religious or any other community becomes divided, it considers that this is one of the unavoidable consequences of pluralism. The role of the authorities in such circumstances is not to remove the cause of tension by eliminating pluralism, but to ensure that the competing groups tolerate each other.[218]

The Court did not decide explicitly between the claims of the state and the community, but the judgment suggests that states should be cautious in interfering with the autonomy of religious groups.[219] With stronger reason, governmental authorities should not make religious freedom unavailable in practice through requiring that permission be obtained from authorities before religious worship can take place.[220]

In a broad statement of principle, the Court considered that freedom of religion under the Convention excluded "any discretion on the part of the state to determine whether religious beliefs or the means used to express such beliefs are legitimate".[221] This is a very wide proposition, bearing in mind the variety of practices that potentially cluster under the umbrella of religion. In *Cha'Are Shalom Ve Tsedek v. France,*[222] the applicant Jewish organisation contested the prohibition by the French authorities of its method of ritual slaughter of animals on the grounds of public order and considerations of public morals as understood in modern societies.[223] Whereas the Commission decided that Article 9 taken with Article 14 had been violated, the Court disagreed.[224]

The issue of public acceptability of religious practices played only a minor role in the case, which hinged rather on the means employed by the government to permit the exercise of religion and whether the Liturgical Association was a religious body.[225] On the facts, the Court observed that "there would be an interference with freedom to manifest one's religion only if the illegality of performing religious slaughter made it impossible for ultra-orthodox Jews to eat meat from animals slaughtered in accordance with the religious prescriptions they considered applicable",[226] which was found not to be the case. A strong dissent by a group of judges claimed that the case was essentially about religious pluralism.[227] The issue of "cultural" limits can be important in the sphere of minority rights – international law promotes cultural (and religious) diversity but will not validate all cultural practices.[228] The Court recognises another kind of limitation in distinguishing between "evangelical witness", and "improper proselytism" on the part of religions or their activists. While the business of securing the continuing existence of a religion by persuading outsiders to convert/join must demonstrate respect for the rights of others, minority religions are entitled to seek converts.[229]

Article 9 has enjoyed only limited development, and its import – like Article 14 – is often submerged in violations of other articles.[230] None the less, the Convention evinces strong respect for religious beliefs and practices. Religious susceptibilities were regarded as worthy of protection in *Otto Preminger Institut v. Austria*,[231] where the Court justified the seizure by the authorities of a film which offended the sensibilities of Catholics (a majority in the region in question), on grounds of protection of the rights and freedoms of "others". Accordingly the manner in which religious beliefs are opposed or denied can engage the responsibility of the state, and individuals must "avoid as far as possible expressions which are gratuitously offensive to others".[232]

This solicitude for "others" can be extended to minority sensibilities; religious sentiment is not confined to large majoritarian or state-supported religions.[233] The Court's espousal of the responsibility of contracting states to ensure the peaceful enjoyment by holders of religious beliefs of their rights under Article 9 approximates to the protection expected for minorities under Article 27 of the ICCPR.[234] However, minority religious sensibilities have not always fared well. In *Choudhury v. UK*,[235] the Commission decided that the absence of a criminal sanction in English law for publications which offended the religious beliefs of non-Christians was not a violation of Article 9. In a number of cases, the Commission has dealt with complaints from prisoners concerning restrictions on religious observance. The cases, which justify restrictions on worship and dietary practices,[236] access to literature,[237] and refusal to wear prison clothing,[238] by invoking a broad margin of appreciation for the benefit of state authorities, now appear dated. The Commission has also ruled that domestic laws requiring everyone, including Sikhs, to wear crash helmets, are justified in the interests of public safety[239] – national laws may be more "liberal" in respect of Sikhs.

Property

Article 1 of Protocol No. 1

Article 1 of Protocol No. 1 to the Convention states a basic property right, styled as the right of every natural or legal person to the "peaceful enjoyment of ... possessions", and that "[n]o one shall be deprived of ... possessions except in the public interest and subject to the conditions provided by law and by the general principles of international law". These provisions are stated not to impair the right of the state to enforce laws controlling the use of property "in accordance with the general interest ...". The Court has taken a broad view of what constitutes "possessions", which, besides chattels and land, include items having an economic value such as business goodwill[240] and patents.[241]

In the *Konkama* case,[242] the applicant Saami villages[243] claimed that national and regional regulations on small game hunting and fishing constituted an infringement of exclusive Saami hunting and fishing rights in the area in question[244] and thus of Article 1 of the protocol. One purpose in the Swedish legislative design was "to give the general public wider access to hunting and fishing in the mountain region".[245] The Commission observed that reindeer herding, hunting and fishing "are fundamental elements of the Saami culture", and considered that "the exclusive hunting and fishing rights claimed by the applicant Saami villages ... can be regarded as possessions" within the meaning of Article 1 of the protocol.[246] The Commission considered that the central issue in the dispute was whether the Saami villages were holders of exclusive hunting and fishing rights, noting, however, that this was a matter of dispute. While the issues were not resolved by the Commission in the light of its finding that the claims were inadmissible, the decision recognises that such specific indigenous rights fall within the ambit of the protocol. The Commission also agreed that Article 6 of the Convention was applicable in as far as the Saami claims raised an issue of "civil rights".[247]

vi. *Loyalty*

The issue of minority "loyalty" to the state occasionally surfaces in legal and political debates. Contemporary standards on minority rights usually omit such a requirement, though "functional equivalents" include the guarantee that the provisions on minority rights are not to call into question the territorial integrity of the state. In the case of the ECHR, the injunction in Article 17 against destroying or limiting rights and freedoms, incorporates an aspect of "loyalty" provisions, as does the restriction on freedom of expression on grounds of territorial integrity. Domestic law loyalty requirements in some cases involve oaths of fidelity to government or state.

In *McGuinness v. the UK*,[248] the applicant, a newly elected member of the British Parliament belonging to the Sinn Fein party, refused to swear an oath of allegiance to the queen. On being denied access to House of Commons facilities, he claimed violation of a number of Convention rights, including Article 9 (oath contrary to his Roman Catholic religion) and Article 10 (oath in violation of his political principles). In declaring the application inadmissible, the Court observed that Article 10 could be restricted in order to protect effective democracy,[249] and that the swearing of the oath "can be reasonably viewed as an affirmation of loyalty to the constitutional principles which support, among other things, the workings of representative democracy ...".[250] The Court attached importance to the fact that the applicant was not required to swear allegiance to a particular religion,[251] and that he could continue to pursue his republican principles.

vii. *Implementation*

Apart from the inter-state procedure,[252] Article 34 (formerly Article 25) of the Convention provides that petitions may be received from "any person, non-governmental organisation or group of individuals claiming to be a victim of a violation". Broad categories of applicant have been held not to include local government institutions or semi-state bodies.[253] On the other hand, besides individuals, applications have been accepted from building societies,[254] churches,[255] companies,[256] political parties,[257] professional associations[258] and trades unions.[259] Each "victim" claims a violation of their own rights, and in the case of joint claims, each claimant must be a victim. Since "minorities" are not owed rights, they are not victims as such. On the other hand, political parties, NGOs or other entities which reflect the interests of minorities can be victims of violations of the organisations' own rights. The concept of indirect victim can extend the range of effective claimants. Limitations for the vindication of minority rights may not be great in practice; the absence of substantive minority rights norms is more important.

The manner in which a minority is "organised" can assist petition procedures, and domestic legal arrangements are not decisive. In the Konkama case, the Swedish government agreed that the applicant Saami villages[260] were "non-governmental organisations" for the purpose of the Convention, but denied that the villages could be "victims" of alleged violations as the rights under the relevant legislation were not afforded to the villages but to their members. This was rejected by the Commission on the grounds that the rights could be exercised by an individual Saami only as a member of a Saami village. Accordingly, the applicant villages could claim to be "victims"[261] – this subject is discussed further in other cases.[262]

In *Stankov and United Macedonian Organisation "ILINDEN" v. Bulgaria*,[263] the government disputed the recognised position of the applicant organisation on the grounds that it had been refused registration in Bulgaria and thus could not be considered a "non-governmental organisation" under Article 34. This was rejected by the Commission in the light of jurisprudence establishing that dissolution or refusal of registration of NGOs did not necessarily lead to questions about recognised position.[264] The Commission observed that "any other solution would to a substantial degree restrict the right of non-governmental organisations to petition". The issue is roughly analogous to a question about the "existence" of a minority which, equally, depends on accepting the realities of association, and not on the constructions of domestic law.[265]

Brief assessment

This snapshot of ECHR principles and cases underlines the great strengths of the Convention and its limitations from the viewpoint of national minorities. For minorities, the broad strengths of the Convention, apart from the much-lauded implementation mechanisms, include the pluralist ambience which extends to forms of association, ideas and ways of life, and the commitment to pluralist democracy of which the Convention is itself an expression. The Court has observed many times that "there can be no democracy without pluralism",[266] and that although:

> individual interests should on occasion be subordinated to those of a group, democracy does not simply mean that the views of the majority must always prevail: a balance must be achieved which ensures the fair and proper treatment of minorities and avoids abuse of a dominant position.[267]

In the face of assimilationist ideologies, the insistence on the vitality of difference (and opposition to systems which would destroy the possibility of difference) is fundamental. As with other "generalist" conventions on human rights, it seems clear that the ECHR is in the process of sharpening its sensitivity to "ethnic" issues, transcending at least some of the assumptions which prevailed at the time of drafting. It should not be forgotten that the inclusion of the term "national minority" in Article 14 was outstanding for its time in the immediate post-war period,[268] so that the potential for regulating minority concerns was always part of the ECHR project. Nevertheless, it is not a text on minority rights and deals with some if not all concerns. It does not recognise the group as such as a bearer of rights, nor deal in categories of individual (the rights are for "everyone"), so that minorities pass through the text formally disregarded by the principles. However, the politics of minority group recognition and geopolitical changes have pressed on the Convention, as they have on other areas of the Council of Europe, and the implementation mechanism has been obliged to respond.

Among specific principles, that of non-discrimination continues to occupy a vital space. While the notion of "national minority" has not been the subject of great development by Commission and Court, other prohibited grounds of discrimination can be adapted to address most of the discrimination against minorities.[269] However, the development of Article 14 has been hampered by a subordinate position relative to the substantive rights. Practice under the Convention does not produce results as clear as those emerging from comparable instruments on the question of special measures,[270] and it appears difficult to encourage the Court to focus on discrimination as a vital aspect of cases. The limits of Convention practice under Article 14 of the Convention in the light of widened perceptions of who can be the subject of discrimination produces the following comment from Wildhaber:

> The perception of discrimination as, primarily, intentional unfavourable treatment of a section of the community has given way to a broader notion embracing unintentional or even traditional differentiation and more recently recognition that discrimination may be indirect, where identical treatment had disproportionately adverse effects on members of a particular group.[271]

A striking (partly) dissenting opinion by Judge Bonello in *Anguelova v. Bulgaria*[272] further illustrates the nature of the jurisprudential and social issues in Roma and other racial and ethnic cases stemming from the limited employment of Article 14. In the opinion, Judge Bonello identifies the inappropriateness of the standard of proof "beyond reasonable doubt" in Roma and other cases, and urges to Court to use its arsenal of legal weapons "to break the stalemate that has not allowed it, throughout fifty years of activity, to censure one single act of racial discrimination in areas of deprivation of life or inhuman treatment. Ideally it should reconsider whether the standards of proof should not be the more juridically justifiable ones of preponderance of evidence or of a balance of probabilities. Alternatively it should, in my view, hold that when a member of a disadvantaged minority group suffers harm in an environment where racial tensions are high and impunity of State officials epidemic, the burden to prove that the event was not ethnically induced, shifts to the government".[273] The approach of the Convention organs is in effect to write a fifty-year narrative of Europe as "an exemplary haven of ethnic fraternity, in which peoples of the most diverse origin coalesce without distress, prejudice or recrimination. The present case energises that delusion".[274]

While it is clear from the above that questions of discrimination – including those linked to minorities – continue to cause stress to the jurisprudence of the Court, the differentiated approach to discrimination expressed in Thlimmenos (see above) is capable of encouraging fresh developments in the direction of reading the principle to validate the adoption of positive measures and recognition of group differences. While not introducing a new substantive minority right, the "opening out" of the Convention under Protocol No. 12 has the potential to ameliorate the position of minorities. The explanatory report is hesitant on "positive" readings of the Protocol in the areas of "special measures" and discrimination between private persons, distinguishing the ECHR from more "programmatic" endeavours elsewhere in the international canon. The narrow view taken of the "justiciability" of special measures is out of step with broader developments on minority rights. However, the implied inclusion of international law in the prohibition of discrimination on any ground "set forth by law" opens up possibilities of linkage with developments in comparable human rights instruments. The ECHR does not swallow up the juridical space inhabited by the Framework Convention for the Protection of National Minorities.

Provisions on respect for private and family life, home and ways of life are also fundamental to the Convention. It may be questioned if cultural arguments have been treated as having sufficient weight. Lifestyle in the Roma/Gypsy and Saami cases is not the best description for cultural characteristics.[275] It suggests that individuals choose a way of life, and does not adequately address those who were born into the folkways of specific communities. The fact of being a member of such a community is the result of choice only in a very limited sense – perhaps to stay or leave, though the latter could do considerable violence to a sense of self-nurture within a particular people.[276] In this sense, the notion of choice of lifestyle is not comparable to the seriousness of minority membership and may influence readings of the interests to be served by particular regulations.

Further, qualitative assessments of the weight of a minority right are to be preferred to quantitative (as in *G. and E. v. Norway*), otherwise minorities lose out by weight of numbers. Analogously, differentiated concepts of "the nation" are to be preferred to reductionist notions: the national interest need not be set against that of the minority, because minorities contribute to an inclusive and enriched concept of the nation and thus redefine that interest. In the light of these and other considerations, the results of Roma/Gypsy litigation against the UK in the Buckley (see above) and other cases is frankly disappointing.

Upbeat assessments of the potential of the Convention in minority issues need to take account of the results of Roma/Gypsy litigation in *Chapman v. UK, Coster v. UK, Beard v. UK, Lee v. UK, and Jane Smith v. UK* (see above), where allegations of violations of Articles 6, 8, 10, 14, and Articles 1 and 2 of Protocol No. 1 were all rejected, although the Grand Chamber judgments on Article 8 were narrowly decided by ten votes to seven. As noted, all the cases concerned the situation where Roma/Gypsy individuals bought land on which they proposed to station caravans, but fell foul of planning regulations. Besides the jurisprudence of the Convention, extensive evidence of developments in minority rights was presented: reference to the Framework Convention, Recommendation 1203 (1993) of the Parliamentary Assembly on Gypsies in Europe, ECRI General Policy Recommendation 3 on combating racism and intolerance against Roma/Gypsies, and the report of the OSCE High Commissioner on National Minorities on the situation of Roma and Sinti in the OSCE area (7 April 2000).

The significance of this ensemble of minority rights instruments was appraised by the Court,[277] which observed that:

> there may be said to be an emerging international consensus amongst the contracting states ... recognising the special needs of minorities and an obligation to protect their security, identity and lifestyle ... not only for the purpose of safeguarding the interests of the minorities themselves but to preserve a cultural diversity of value to the whole community ... However, the Court is not persuaded that the consensus is sufficiently concrete for it to derive any guidance as to the conduct or standards which contracting states consider desirable in any particular situation.

The Court referred to the Framework Convention as incorporating general principles and goals, which indicated that "the complex sensitivity of the issues involved in policies balancing the interests of the general population, in particular with regard to environmental protection and the interests of a minority with possibly conflicting requirements, renders the Court's role a strictly supervisory one". This seems a remarkably conservative approach to the developments in the Council of Europe and elsewhere in international law particularly – throughout the 1990s – in the field of minority rights. When would a consensus be deemed to have finally emerged? Equally remarkable is the suggestion (paragraph 106 in Beard) that according different treatment to Roma/Gypsies unlawfully establishing caravans compared to non-Gypsies establishing houses would raise substantial problems under Article 14, especially since the Court also cited the Thlimmenos case in its conclusions.

The reading of obligations under Article 8 was more positive for Gypsy applicants in the future, the Court observing that "although the fact of belonging to a minority with a traditional lifestyle different from that of the majority does not confer an immunity from general laws intended to safeguard the assets of the community as a whole ... it may have an incidence on the manner in which such laws are to be implemented" –

71

accordingly, the Court averred that, to the extent of such considerations, "there is ... a positive obligation ... by virtue of Article 8 to facilitate the Gypsy way of life".[278] It is clear nevertheless that the issue of minority rights – including that of Roma rights – continues to cause considerable pain to the Court: a vigorous joint dissent by Judges Pastor Ridruejo, Bonello, Tulkens, Strážnická, Lorenzen, Fischbach and Casadevall contradicted the majority on the essence of Article 8. The narrowness of the vote and the strength of the dissent may point to future jurisprudential directions when questions affecting vulnerable communities come before the Court.[279]

The paucity of ECHR jurisprudence in the linguistic and education fields suggests that state policy, economics, the requirements of homogenising and centralising bureaucracies, and margin of appreciation, are primary considerations which sometimes outweigh rights to the promotion of identity through mother tongue. The textual boundaries of the ECHR appear to set limits on what can be achieved. Other areas of concern relate to loyalty requirements in the light of McGuinness. Minorities have often been tarred with the brush of disloyalty, and there is a lengthy political history of attempts to insert loyalty clauses into international legal instruments. Fortunately, these have been avoided.[280] It is clear from the "Turkish cases" that sentiments of disloyalty have protection provided they do not incite to hatred. Political programmes are not required to cohere with the ideology of the state. Rights are not a reward for good (officially-approved) behaviour; they are inherent in human beings. In this instance, there should not be a special rule for minorities and another rule for the rest.

As far as can be judged, and in the absence of a formal definition by Commission or Court, the recognition of minorities by the organs of the Convention appears to be relatively undemanding in conceptual terms and would not disbar groups such as the Roma/Gypsy from national minority "status", nor would it be refused recognition because of disloyalty to its home state, and longstanding ties with the state are probably not required.[281] In *Gorzelik and Others v. Poland*, the Court stated that it was prepared to review the legal process by which the States had denied the status of national minority to a group, even in the absence of a definition of national minority, which not even the Framework Convention had achieved.[282]

The ECHR recognises further important elements of a minority policy. The Convention's appreciation of self-identification is potentially important in minority matters, and is crucial in underpinning of the dignity and importance of cultures. In some cases, the linkage between ethnicity and economy has been recognised, as well as the linkage between land and identity.[283] The promotion of intercultural toleration (as well as intra-cultural toleration) is another plus, as well as the Convention's structural reminder that rights do not exist in a vacuum – rights define the boundaries of other rights. The ECHR promotes rights, not rights-egotism. The boundaries and toleration aspects of rights oppose one of the besetting sins of the age – that "we" matter and "they" do not. Texts of minority rights encourage this mutuality of respect in a more direct manner, but the message of the ECHR is implicitly the same. It only remains for the potential of the ECHR in minority matters to be realised: to date institutional practice is somewhat equivocal.

Notes

1.   *X v. Austria*, No. 8142/78, D.R. 18 (1980), p. 88 at pp. 92-93.

2.   See later, Chapters 2 and 3 on the Framework Convention and the Languages Charter, respectively.

3.   Present author's emphasis.

4.   The history of proposals is set out briefly in P. Thornberry, *International Law and the Rights of Minorities* (Oxford: Clarendon Press, 1991), pp. 304-06, and more extensively in C. Hillgruber and M. Jestaedt, *The European Convention on Human Rights and the Protection of National Minorities* (Cologne: Verlag Wissenschaft und Politik, 1994), pp. 13-21; and A. Spiliopoulou-Åkermark, *Justifications of Minority Protection in International Law* (Uppsala: Iustus Forlag, 1997), Chapter 8.

5.   For Lannung's own account, see "The Rights of Minorities", in *Mélanges offerts à Polys Modinos* (Paris: Editions A. Pedone, 1968), pp. 181-95. For a brief account of Danish-German arrangements concerning Schleswig, see J. Kuhl, *The Schleswig Experience: The National Minorities in the Danish-German Border Area* (Åbenrå: Institut for Graenseregionsforskning, 1998).

6.   Debate of 19 August 1949.

7.   *Collected Edition of the Travaux Preparatoires [Travaux]*, Vol. 1 (The Hague: Martinus Nijhoff, 1975-85), p. 54.

8.   Ibid., pp. 180-182.

9.   The committee, in the so-called Teitgen Report, asserted that the proposed regime of freedoms would prevent discrimination based on membership of a national minority. The report, while stressing the importance of the minority "problem", proposed to include in the Convention only those rights suitable for inclusion in an immediate international guarantee. According to Teitgen, only rights which imposed negative obligations were to be included – so minority rights were in effect to suffer the same exclusion as economic and social rights: P.-H. Teitgen, "Introduction to the European Convention on Human Rights", in R.St.J. McDonald et al. (eds.), *The European System for the Protection of Human Rights* (Dordrecht: Kluwer, 1993), p. 10. For further reflection on the reasons for non-inclusion, see Spiliopoulou-Åkermark, op. cit., pp. 200-204.

10.   *Travaux*, op. cit., Vol. 4, p. 54.

11.   See Article 10.2.

12.   *Travaux*, op. cit., Vol. 4, p. 24. See also the observations of Lannung, cited by Hillgruber and Jestaedt, op. cit., p. 19.

13.   *Travaux*, Vol. 4, p. 68.

14.   Sixth Sitting of the Second Session of the Consultative Assembly, p. 256.

15.   Hillgruber and Jestaedt, op. cit., pp. 20-21.

16.   Parliamentary Assembly Doc. 1299, 26 April 1961. The draft is commented on in P. Thornberry, *International Law and the Rights of Minorities* (Oxford: Clarendon Press, 1991), p. 306.

17.   See below. See also P. Thornberry and M.A. Martín Estébanez, *The Council of Europe and Minorities* (Strasbourg: COEMIN, 1994), Chapter 3.

18.   Report of the committee of experts to the Committee of Ministers, 9 November 1973, Doc. DH/Exo (73).

19.   Thornberry and Estébanez, op. cit., Chapter 7.

20.   Appendix II, final (unnumbered) paragraph. The fate of this project is considered further in this chapter.

21.   See CAHMIN (95) 22, 24 January 1996 – work was suspended at the 544th meeting of Ministers' Deputies, 8-10 and 15 January 1996.

22. Decision 656/4.1 of the Ministers' Deputies (19 January 1999).

23. Committee of Ministers Decision 656/4.1 – CDDH opinion appended to the reply of the Committee of Ministers to Parliamentary Assembly Recommendation 1345 (1997) on the protection of national minorities, paragraph 9. See further, Chapter 5 of the present work.

24. At its 47th meeting (30 November-3 December 1999) the CDDH adopted for the attention of the Committee of Ministers its final activity report on the elaboration of a draft protocol (No. 12) to the ECHR, broadening in general the field of application of Article 14 and containing a non-exhaustive list of discrimination grounds: *Human Rights Information Bulletin* No. 47 (July-October 1999), p. 56.

25. See Chapter 2 on the Framework Convention. For a statement of principle, see General Comment 23 of the Human Rights Committee under the ICCPR – UN Doc. A/49/40, pp. 107-10.

26. Spiliopoulou-Åkermark, op. cit., p. 217.

27. Cf. the reference to "objective criteria" in ICCPR General Comment 23, paragraph 5.2.

28. B. Anderson, *Imagined Communities* (London: Verso, 1991).

29. No. 18877/91, judgment of 15 November 1996.

30. Which "recognised only the existence in that region of a Muslim (religious) minority, not a Turkish minority": Court of Cassation, cited in judgment, paragraph 18.

31. Ibid.

32. Dissenting opinion, paragraph 1.

33. Ibid., paragraph 17.

34. Ibid., paragraph 19.

35. No. 26695/95, judgment of 10 July 1998.

36. Judgment, paragraphs 8 and 9.

37. Judgment, paragraph 10.

38. Ibid., paragraph 37.

39. Judgment, paragraph 41.

40. Ibid.

41. No. 44158/98, judgment of 20 December 2001, Fourth Section. At the time of writing, the judgment awaits consideration by the Grand Chamber.

42. "The Court observes that it is not its task to express an opinion on whether or not the Silesians are a 'national minority', let alone to formulate a definition of that concept ... no international treaty – not even the Council of Europe's Framework Convention for the Protection of National Minorities – defines the notion of 'national minority'": judgment, paragraph 62.

43. Ibid., paragraph 66.

44. For an attempt to link self-determination with the ECHR, constructed on the basis of Article 53 of the ECHR, see G. Gilbert, "Jurisprudence of the European Court and Commission of Human Rights in 1999 and Minority Groups", UN Doc. E/CN.4.Sub.2/AC.5/2000/CRP.1; the author submitted papers to the Working Group on this topic for subsequent years. See also G. Gilbert, "The Burgeoning Minority Rights Jurisprudence of the European Court of Human Rights", *Human Rights Quarterly*, Vol. 24 (2002), pp. 736-80.

45. *X v. Federal Republic of Germany*, No. 6742/74, D.R. 3 (1975), p. 98.

46. *X v. Netherlands*, No. 7230/75, D.R. 7 (1976), p. 109.

47.   As self-determination is outside the explicit scope of the ECHR, litigation has not served to elicit nuances in the legal concept of self-determination. In a vast literature, see C. Tomuschat (ed.), *Modern Law of Self-Determination* (The Hague: Martinus Nijhoff, 1993).

48.   See the "Turkish cases" below, notably *Surek and Ozdemir v. Turkey*, Nos. 23927/94 and 24277/94, 3 March, 8 July 1999, especially paragraph 60 and the dissent by President Wildhaber et al. Inflammatory remarks can legitimately be subject to restrictions "where such remarks incite to violence against an individual, a public official or a sector of the population ... [in such cases] the national authorities enjoy a wider margin of appreciation ..." – *Ozturk v. Turkey*, No. 22479/93, judgment of 28 September 1999, paragraph 66. Cf. *Zana v. Turkey*, No. 18954/91, judgment of 25 November 1997, paragraphs 58-60.

49.   No. 19392/92, judgment of 30 January 1998.

50.   Judgment, paragraph 27.

51.   Ibid., paragraph 57.

52.   Judgment, paragraph 56.

53.   No. 23885/94, judgment of 8 December 1999.

54.   Judgment, paragraph 8. The Constitutional Court, in dissolving OZDEP, made the interesting observation (judgment, paragraph 14) that the Turkish Constitution "did not preclude the 'celebration of difference' but forbade propaganda based on racial difference ... aimed at destroying the constitutional order" (present authors' emphasis).

55.   A. Cassese, *Self-Determination of Peoples: A Legal Reappraisal* (Cambridge University Press, 1995).

56.   Judgment, paragraph 41.

57.   Nos. 29221/95 and 29225/95, judgment of 2 October 2001, paragraph 97.

58.   United Communist Party, paragraph 45.

59.   Ibid., paragraph 43. The forms of "pluralism" generally referred to are pluralism in the realm of ideas and opinions, and in political parties.

60.   See H.H. Koh and R.C. Shue, *Deliberative Democracy and Human Rights* (New Haven and London: Yale University Press, 1999).

61.   Nos. 41340/98, 41342/98, 41343/98, and 41344/98, judgment of 31 July 2002.

62.   Paragraph 70.

63.   Ibid. Compare the nuanced approach to the principle of non-discrimination in *Thlimmenos v. Greece*, discussed later in the present chapter.

64.   Paragraph 72. The strong joint dissenting opinion of Judges Fuhrmann, Loucaides and Sir Nicholas Bratza expressed disagreement with the Turkish action in dissolving the party, while agreeing that "[t]he example provided by States governed by fundamentalist regimes underlines the risk to democracy posed by a departure from the secular ideal".

65.   A range of examples is provided in K. Boyle and J. Sheen (eds.), *Freedom of Religion and Belief: A World Report* (London and New York: Routledge, 1997).

66.   Nos. 41340/98, 41342/98, 41343/98 and 41344/98, judgment of 13 February 2003.

67.   Compare Article 26 of the International Covenant on Civil and Political Rights.

68.   Protocol No. 12 would open this out to discrimination in respect of "any right set forth by law". See discussion later in this chapter.

69.   Judgment of 23 July 1968, Series A, No. 6.

70.   Respectively, rights to respect for family life, non-discrimination, and education.

71.   The Court considered that the second sentence of Article 2 of Protocol No. 1 (the right to education and teaching in accordance with religious and philosophical convictions) was not relevant. It did not entail a right to language instruction in a language other than that of the country in question (possibly again understood as the official language/s of the state).

72.   The interpretation of discrimination in the ECHR implies also that where individuals are different in material ways, it can be discrimination to treat them as if they were the same – *Christians against Racism and Fascism v. the UK*, No. 8440/78, 21 D.R. (1980), p. 138 at 152. For a more detailed discussion of this issue, see further below.

73.   Judgment, section I B, paragraph 10. The Court concluded that the means employed by the Belgian legislation pursuant to its linguistic policy objectives were not disproportionate.

74.   For instructive commentary, see B. de Witte, "Surviving in Babel: Language Rights and European Integration", in Y. Dinstein and M. Tabory (eds.), *The Protection of Minorities and Human Rights* (Dordrecht/Boston/London: Martinus Nijhoff, 1992), pp. 277-300.

75.   The laws did not block this access to careers, etc., but only made access dependent on a further examination.

76.   The OSCE Hague Recommendations, which subsume and restate the provisions of the ECHR along with minority rights instruments, do not deal explicitly with the certificates issue. However, Recommendation 9 states that, in the matter of private schools, states may not hinder the enjoyment of the right "by imposing unduly burdensome legal and administrative requirements regulating the establishment and management of such schools": *The Hague Recommendations Regarding the Education Rights of National Minorities and Explanatory Note* (The Hague: Foundation on Inter-Ethnic Relations, 1996), p. 6.

77.   Comment in de Witte, op. cit., p. 287.

78.   Compare Article 14 of the Framework Convention, and Article 8 of the Languages Charter.

79.   *Airey v. Ireland*, Series A, No. 32 (1980), paragraph 30. See also *Ireland v. the United Kingdom*, Series A, No. 25 (1978), paragraphs 225-30.

80.   Comment by F. Hampson, "Recent Turkish Cases: Their Contribution to the Case-Law of the European Court of Human Rights", *Human Rights Law Review*, Vol. 4, No. 3 (December 1999), pp. 9-16. On the question of whether Article 14, as employed by the European Court, amounted only to a 'second-class guarantee', see L. Wildhaber, "Protection against Discrimination under the European Convention on Human Rights – A Second-Class Guarantee?", *Baltic Yearbook of International Law*, Vol. 2 (2002), pp. 71-82.

81.   No. 23763/94, judgment of 8 July 1999.

82.   See, for example, *Association Ekin v. France*, No. 39288/98, judgment of 17 July 2001, Third Section.

83.   No. 23144/93, judgment of 16 March 2000, Fourth Section.

84.   Ibid., paragraph 73.

85.   Ibid.

86.   Judgment, paragraph 75.

87.   No. 24781/94, European Commission of Human Rights, 4 June 1999, paragraph 577.

88.   Ibid., paragraph 576.

89.   No. 24781/94, *Cyprus v. Turkey*, judgment of 10 May 2001, paragraph 353.

90.   Indirect discrimination is suggested by the above cited passage in the Belgian Linguistic case on "aim and *effects*" (author's emphasis). See also *Abdulaziz, Cabales and Balkandali v. UK*, Series A 92 (1985). An element of indirect discrimination is also associated with the case of *Thlimmenos* – see below.

91.   Nos. 37715/97; 30054/96, judgments of 4 May 2001, Third Section. On the facts, the Court found no violation of Article 14.

92.   Judgment, paragraph 129.

93.   *East African Asians*, Nos. 4403/70-419/70, 4422/70, 4423/70, 4434/70, 4443/70, 4476/70-4478/70, 4486/70, 4501/70 and 4526/70-4530/70, 3 EHRR 76 (1976), where the European Commission of Human Rights took the view that publicly to single out persons for differential treatment on the basis of race may amount to degrading treatment when differential treatment on other grounds would not; *Abdulaziz, Cabales and Balkandali v. UK*, Ser. A, No. 94 (1985). The "suspect categories" make it particularly difficult for the state to defend on the basis of a margin of appreciation. Authors point to the possible identification of such categories on the basis of "clear evidence of a European consensus": D.J. Harris, M. O'Boyle and C. Warbrick, *Law of the European Convention on Human Rights* (London, Dublin, Edinburgh: Butterworths, 1995), p. 482. On this basis, it may be possible to argue that discrimination on grounds of ethnic origin and association with a national minority could be added – the "European consensus" has advanced enormously over the last decade with the emergence of key texts such as the Framework Convention – see, however, the remarks in *Beard v. UK* in the concluding part of the present chapter.

94.   No. 41488/98, judgment of 18 May 2000, Fourth Section. See further, Chapter 4 on the Roma in the present work.

95.   Nos. 6780/74 and 6950/75, Commission Report of 1976, p. 156, paragraph 502.

96.   No. 27238/95, Commission admissibility decision, 4 March 1998. In the Roma cases against the UK, violations of Article 14 were widely alleged but uniformly rejected by the Court.

97.   Harris et al., op. cit., pp. 483-85. In *M. v. UK*, No. 10316/83, D.R. 37 (1984), p. 134, it was said that "Article 14 has no independent existence, but plays an important role by completing the other normative provisions ... It is as if Article 14 formed an integral part of each of the provisions laying down specific rights and freedoms".

98.   Harris et al., op. cit., pp. 485-88. The Court's understanding of the principle of non-discrimination has been renovated in *Thlimennos v. Greece*, No. 34369/97, judgment of 6 April 2000, where, in a case concerning discrimination against a Jehovah's Witness, the Court observed (paragraph 44) that it had "so far considered that the right under Article 14 not to be discriminated against ... is violated when states treat differently persons in analogous situations without providing an objective and reasonable justification ... However, the Court considers that this is not the only facet of prohibition of discrimination in Article 14. 'The right not to be discriminated against in the enjoyment of the rights guaranteed under the Convention is *also violated when states without an objective and reasonable justification fail to treat differently persons whose situations are significantly different*" (emphasis added). The statement is of considerable potential significance for minority rights – that is, rights which are "differentiated" to address the claims and interests of specific groups. The case also reiterated the point (paragraph 40) that the application of Article 14 does not presuppose a breach of other provisions of the Convention: "For Article 14 to become applicable it suffices that the facts of a case fall within the ambit of another substantive provision of the Convention or its Protocols."

99.   The protocol was opened for signature on 4 November 2000, the date of the 50th Anniversary of the Convention. The text of the protocol can be found on the Council of Europe Human Rights website: http://www.echr.coe.int/

100. The protocol requires expressions of consent from ten states and a subsequent period of three months to bring it into force – Article 5. By May 2003, the protocol had been signed by thirty-two states, of which four had deposited ratifications: Croatia, Cyprus, Georgia and San Marino.

101. Explanatory report, paragraphs 1-12.

102. Explanatory report, paragraph 3.

103. Ibid., paragraph 14.

104. Ibid., paragraph 15. See comment, above, on *Thlimennos v. Greece.*

105. Explanatory report, paragraph 16.

106. The UN Convention on the Elimination of All Forms of Racial Discrimination, and the Convention on the Elimination of Discrimination against Women are also cited for provisions on special measures.

107. Explanatory report, paragraph 22.

108. Ibid., paragraph 29. The report (paragraph 25) makes clear however that the protocol "may not be construed as limiting or derogating from domestic or treaty provisions which provide further protection from discrimination".

109. Ibid., paragraph 24.

110. Ibid., paragraph 25.

111. Ibid., paragraph 26.

112. Ibid., paragraph 27.

113. No. 7823/77 and 7824/77, 11 D.R. (1977), p. 221.

114. No. 24760/94, judgment of 28 October 1998.

115. Article 3 was read in conjunction with the general duty of the state under Article 1 to "secure to everyone within their jurisdiction" the rights and freedoms defined in the Convention, which thus "requires by implication that there should be an effective official investigation" – judgment, paragraph 102. The Court instanced the application of this principle in cases on the right to life (Article 2).

116. Judgment, paragraph 102.

117. Judgment, paragraph 118.

118. Ibid., paragraph 117.

119. No. 32357/96, judgment of 11 April 2000, Second Section.

120. Judgment, paragraphs 11-13.

121. Judgment, paragraph 35.

122. The Commission is citing a UN Humanitarian Review of the situation – see paragraph 387 of the Commission report.

123. Paragraph 498. For Article 3 issues in the Court's judgment in *Cyprus v. Turkey,* see paragraphs 153, 158, 311, and 315.

124. Further issues are explored in H. Mickiewicz, "A Human Right to the Native Spelling of a Personal Name?", *Journal of International Relations,* Vol. 4, Nos. 1-4 (1977), pp. 49-69.

125. Article 24 (2) of the ICCPR; Articles 7 and 8 of the Convention on the Rights of the Child; Article 18 of the American Convention on Human Rights.

126. Council of Europe instruments include Article 7.2. of Assembly Recommendation 1201 (1993), and Article 11.1 of the Framework Convention, which also carries a provision on place names in minority languages – Article 11.3. In the latter context, see the admissibility decision of the *Courtin Raif Oglu v. Greece*, No. 33738/96, decision of 16 March 1999, which was declared admissible in as far as it concerned the possibility of discrimination on grounds of religious beliefs and ethnic origin. Part of Oglu's offence under Greek law was to distribute a document containing the "old Turkish names of villages". See also the judgment of 27 June 2000, where the Third Section of the Court decided to strike the case off its list, as the applicant could no longer claim to be a victim following his re-hiring as a teacher and the payment of compensation.

127. See also *Coeriel and Aurik v. Netherlands*, UN Doc. A/50/40, Vol. I (1994), pp. 21-31 – refusal by the Dutch authorities to allow a change of name by a convert to Hinduism violated Article 17 (right to privacy) of the ICCPR. The application had previously been rejected by the Commission as manifestly ill-founded under Article 9 of the ECHR: No. 18050/91, published in *Human Rights Law Journal*, Vol. 15 (1994), pp. 448-49.

128. *Burghartz v. Switzerland*, judgment of 22 February 1994, Series A, No. 280B.

129. Judgment of 25 November 1994, Series A. No. 299B.

130. Stjerna, paragraph 39.

131. Ibid., paragraph 38.

132. Ibid., paragraph 39.

133. *Coeriel and Aurik*, op. cit., paragraph 10.2. See also Harris et al., op. cit., p. 307: "The fundamental interest within the sphere of private life is the capacity of the individual to determine ... identity ... Within the individual's power are matters like ... choice of name ... dress and ... sexual identity".

134. Nos. 9278/81 and 9415/81, D.R. 35 (1983), pp. 30-45.

135. Ibid., pp. 32-33.

136. Ibid., p. 35.

137. Compare *Konkama v. Sweden*, below.

138. Ibid., p. 36.

139. M. Scheinin, op. cit, styles this as the distinction between "quantitative" and "qualitative" assessments. K. Henrard, *Devising an Adequate System of Minority Protection* (London: Kluwer, 2000), p. 102.

140. M. Scheinin, op. cit, p. 13 (emphasis in the original).

141. D.R. 35, p. 35.

142. No. 20348/92. The report of the Commission was adopted on 11 January 1995. Judgment of the Court was delivered on 25 September 1996.

143. Report of the Commission, paragraph 21.

144. For the UK legal background, see report of the Commission, paragraphs 46-57.

145. Which would, according to the local District Council, "detract from the rural and open quality of the landscape": Report of the Commission, paragraph 24.

146. Described by an official of the Romani Union as subject to disorder, and not suitable for a single mother (the applicant): Report, paragraph 41.

147. Ibid., paragraph 27.

148. Ibid., paragraph 63.

149. Ibid., paragraph 72.

150. "Given that there are insufficient places for gypsies on official sites, it is unreasonable ... to expect the applicant ... to apply for a site which offers distinct disadvantages compared to her present location on her own land, close to other members of her family": Report, paragraph 82.

151. Ibid., paragraph 76.

152. The dissent of Conforti et al. was insensitive to the "ethnic" dimensions of the case. The opinion insisted on the irrelevance of "lifestyle", and equated Buckley's actions with those who construct buildings abusively and are then confronted with a demolition order.

153. By seven votes to five.

154. See in particular Circular 1/94 from the Department of the Environment, intended "to provide that the planning system recognises the need for accommodation consistent with the Gypsies' nomadic lifestyle" – Report, paragraph 56.

155. Ibid., paragraph 84.

156. *Buckley v. the United Kingdom,* judgment of 25 September 1996.

157. Agreeing with the Commission that the case concerned the applicant's right to respect for her "home": judgment, paragraph 54.

158. In the submission of the government, national law "was designed to achieve a fair balance between interests of individuals and those of the community as a whole": judgment, paragraph 68. The government also offered the view (ibid.) that, in any event, "it was unacceptable to exempt any section of the community from planning controls, or to allow any group the benefit of more lenient standards than those to which the general population is subject" – a claim which would deny the right of a minority to differential standards in cases backed up by international standards.

159. Judgment, paragraph 80.

160. Ibid.

161. Ibid., paragraph 81.

162. Ibid., paragraph 88.

163. And not the precariously available official site.

164. *Coster v. UK,* No. 24876/94; *Beard v. UK,* No. 24882/94; *Smith v. UK,* No. 2154/94; *Lee v. UK,* No. 25289/94; *Varey v. UK,* No. 26662/95; *Smith v. UK* (1998), 25 EHRR, C.D., 52; *Chapman v. UK,* No. 27238. The second Smith case – 25 EHRR, C.D., 52 – was declared inadmissible. Since writing this chapter, all the cases have been rejected by the Court (judgments of 18.1.2001) – a short account of developments is given in the conclusion to the present chapter. The Commission also concluded that the cases did not disclose violations of the Convention.

165. The case has been settled by payment by the UK government of a substantial sum of money plus legal costs: *Varey v. UK,* judgment, 21 December 2000. See below on the outcomes of the litigation before the Court.

166. *Arslan v. Turkey,* No. 23462/94; *Başkaya and Okcuoglu v. Turkey,* Nos. 23536/94 and 24408/94; *Ceylan v. Turkey,* No. 23556/94; *Erdoğdu and İnce v. Turkey,* Nos. 25067/94 and 25068/94; *Gerger v. Turkey,* No. 24919/94; *Karatas v. Turkey,* No. 23168/94; *Okcuoglu v. Turkey,* No. 24146/94; *Polat v. Turkey,* No. 23500/94; *Sürek and Özdemir v. Turkey,* Nos. 23927/94 and 24277/94; *Sürek v. Turkey* No. 1, No. 26682/95; *Sürek v. Turkey* No. 2, No. 24122/94; *Sürek v. Turkey* No. 3, No. 24735/94, and *Sürek v. Turkey* No. 4, No. 24762/94.

167. No violation of Article 10 was found in *Sürek* No. 1 and *Sürek* No. 3 – though a violation of Article 6.1 was found in these cases.

168. Under paragraphs 3 and 6 of the Criminal Code: paragraph 3 reads "A person who, prompted by racial considerations, by any means whatsoever spreads propaganda aimed at abolishing in whole or in part public law rights guaranteed by the Constitution or undermining or destroying patriotic sentiment shall, on conviction, be liable to a term of imprisonment of from five to ten years"; by paragraph 6, the penalties were increased by half if the offence was committed through publication: judgment, paragraph 22.

169. Law 3713, section 8 (1) "Written and spoken propaganda, meetings, assemblies and demonstrations aimed at undermining the territorial integrity of the Republic of Turkey or the indivisible unity of the nation are prohibited, irrespective of the methods used and the intention ...": judgment, paragraph 23.

170. Judgment, paragraph 19.

171. The issue was narrowed down by agreement of the parties to Article 10: judgment, paragraph 30; the Court decided that no separate issue arose under Article 14: ibid., paragraphs 51-54.

172. Article 10.2.

173. Judgment, paragraphs 44-50.

174. Ibid., paragraph 48.

175. "Mr Arslan's conviction was disproportionate to the aims pursued" and accordingly "not necessary in a democratic society": judgment, paragraph 50.

176. Judges Palm, Tulkens, Fischbach, Casadevall and Greve.

177. Judge Bonello.

178. It is not "manifest to me that instant suppression of those [Arslan's] expressions was indispensable for the salvation of Turkey": Bonello.

179. See also *Sener v. Turkey*, No. 26680/95, judgment of 18 July 2000, Third Section; *Castells v. Spain* (1992), Series A, No. 236.

180. See G. Gilbert, above, n.44, pp. 755-61.

181. Harris et al., op. cit., p. 374.

182. *Jersild v. Denmark* (1994), Series A, No. 298.

183. In the television programme, self-confessed racist youths ("Greenjackets") were heard to make derogatory remarks about black people. In relation to the youths, the European Court, in paragraph 35 of the judgment, stated that: "There can be no doubt that the remarks in respect of which the Greenjackets were convicted were ... insulting to members of the targeted groups and did not enjoy the protection of Article 10".

184. See remarks above on the *Belgian Linguistic case.*

185. See also Article 5.2 and 6.3.*a.*

186. No.808/60, 5 YBECHR (1962), p. 108.

187. *Bideaut v. France*, No. 11261/84, D.R. 48 (1986), 232 – concerning the use of the Breton language. The claim was manifestly ill-founded: the claimant did not argue that he was unable to speak French. For the continuing relevance of the basic right to interpretation in criminal proceedings, see *Twalib v. Greece*, No. 24294/94, judgment of 9 June 1998.

188. No.11100/84, D.R. 45 (1985), p. 240.

189. *Mathieu-Mohin and Clerfayt v. Belgium*, Series A, No. 113 (1987).

190. Discussion in Spiliopoulou-Åkermark, op. cit., p. 209.

191. No. 46726/99, judgment of 9 April 2002, Fourth Section.

192. *Podkolzina*, para. 34.

193. *Ballantyne et al. v. Canada*, UN Doc. A/48/40 (1993), paragraph 11.4. For a nuanced view of the ECHR jurisprudence, see de Witte, op. cit., pp. 280-83, who concludes (p. 281) that "the question whether freedom of expression might have an implicit linguistic component" has never been openly confronted, but if it were raised again the "institutions might well find that freedom of expression includes the freedom of linguistic expression".

194. Van Dijk and van Hoof, *Theory and Practice of the European Convention*, p. 467.

195. See Article 53 of the ECHR.

196. General Comment No. 13, The Right to Education (Article 13), UN Doc. E/C.12/1999/10, 8 December 1999.

197. Judgment of 7 December 1976, Series A, No. 23 (1979-80).

198. Judgment of 25 February, 1982, Series A, No. 48.

199. Ibid., p. 16.

200. Ibid.

201. Blum, cited in C. Hillgruber and M. Jestaedt, *The European Convention on Human Rights and the Protection of National Minorities* (Cologne: Verlag Wissenschaft und Politik, 1994), p. 26, No. 64.

202. F.G. Jacobs and R.C.A. White, *The European Convention on Human Rights* (Oxford: Clarendon Press, 2nd edition 1996), pp. 266-67.

203. Ibid., p. 264. This approach to the meaning of "philosophical convictions" was doubted in the admissibility decision in *Skender v. the Former Yugoslav Republic of Macedonia*, where the Third Section of the Court revisited the Belgian Linguistic case, and stated that to interpret "religious" and "philosophical" as covering linguistic preferences "would amount to a distortion of their ordinary and usual meaning and read into the Convention something which is not there" – No. 6205900, decision of 22 November 2001.

204. No. 25781/94, report adopted on 4 June 1999.

205. Ibid., paragraph 478.

206. Ibid., paragraph 278. See also, ibid., paragraphs 273-77 and 279-80.

207. As in, for example, Article 21 of the UDHR and Article 25 of the ICCPR.

208. For discussion of Article 15 of the Framework Convention, see Chapter 2.

209. Admissibility decision in *Grande Oriente D'Italia di Palazzo Giustiniani v. Italy*, No. 35972/97, 21 October 1999.

210. No. 8364/78, Commission decision of 8 March 1979.

211. No. 8941/80, D.R. 27 (1981), p. 145.

212. *Mathieu-Mohin and Clerfayt*, paragraph 54.

213. *Liberal Party v. UK*, D.R. 21 (1981), p. 211.

214. See comments on this by the European Court in *Kalac v. Turkey*, No. 20704/92, judgment of 23 June 1997, paragraphs 21-31.

215. *X v. UK*, No. 8169/78, D.R. 22 (1981), p. 27.

216. For example, *X and Church of Scientology v. Sweden*, No. 7805/77, D.R. 16 (1979), p. 68.

217. No. 38178/97, judgment of 14 December 1999, Second Section. See also *Agga v. Greece*, Nos. 50776/99 and 52912/99, judgment of 17 October 2002, First Section.

218. Judgment, paragraphs 49 and 53. Cf. Harris, O'Boyle and Warbrick, op. cit., p. 357: "Article 9 embraces another manifestation of tolerance and pluralism which runs through its conception of the values protected by the Convention".

219. Cf. *Hasan and Chaus v. Bulgaria*, No. 30985/96, judgment of 26 October 2000, where the First Section of the Court said (paragraph 62) that "Where the organisation of the religious community is at issue, Article 9 must be interpreted in the light of Article 11 ... which safeguards associative life against unjustified State interference ... the believer's right to freedom of religion encompasses the expectation that the community will be allowed to function peacefully free from arbitrary State intervention ... the autonomous existence of religious communities is indispensable for pluralism in a democratic society and is thus an issue at the very heart of the protection which Article 9 affords". See also *Metropolitan Church of Bessarabia and others v. Moldova*, No. 45701/99, judgment of 13 December 2001, First Section.

220. *Manoussakis et al. v. Greece*, No. 18748/91, judgment of 26 February 1996.

221. Ibid., paragraph 47.

222. No. 27417/95, *Cha'Are Shalom Ve Tsedek v. France*, declared admissible by the Commission, 7 April 1997.

223. The Convention organs have investigated whether a particular belief is in fact an element of, or required by, the religion – Harris, O'Boyle and Warbrick, op. cit., p. 358.

224. *Case of the Jewish Liturgical Association Cha'Are Shalom Ve Tsedek v. France*, judgment of the Grand Chamber, 27 June 2000.

225. Religious methods of slaughtering are permitted to Jews and Muslims in France, though the government emphasised the exceptional nature of the permissions in legislation for animal protection and public hygiene: judgment, paragraphs 68-69. Cf. the European Convention for the Slaughter of Animals 1979, Articles 13, 17 and 19; Recommendation No. R (91) 7 of the Committee of Ministers of the Council of Europe, 17 June 1991.

226. Ibid., paragraph 80.

227. Judges Bratza, Fischbach, Thomassen, Tsatsa-Nikolovska, Pantiru, Levits and Traja.

228. Cf. *Hoffmann v. Austria*, judgment of 23 June 1993, Series A No. 255-C (1993), paragraph 33.

229. *Kokkinakis v. Greece*, judgment of 25 May 1993, Series A 260-A.

230. *Hoffmann v. Austria*, Series A 255-C (1993).

231. Judgment of 20 September 1994, Series A, No. 295-A.

232. Ibid., paragraph 49.

233. Ibid., paragraph 47 of the judgment referred to members of a religious majority or minority.

234. Human Rights Committee General Comment No. 23.

235. No. 17439/90, *Human Rights Law Journal*, Vol. 12, (1991), p. 172.

236. No. 5442/72, *X v. UK*, D.R. 1 (1975), p. 41.

237. No. 6886/75, *X v. UK*, D.R. 5 (1976), p. 100.

238. No. 8121/78, *X v. UK*, D.R. 28 (1982), p. 5.

239. No. 7992/77, *X v. UK*, D.R. 14 (1978), p. 234.

240. *Van Marle and Others v. the Netherlands* (1986), Series A., No. 101, paragraph 41.

241. No. 12633/87, *Smith Kline and French Laboratories v. the Netherlands*, D.R. 66 (1990), p. 70.

242. No. 27033/95, *Konkama and twenty-eight other Saami Villages v. Sweden*, admissibility decision of 25 November 1996.

243. Thirty-nine villages in total.

244. The relevant Bill (1992/93: 32) applied to state property above the cultivation line and in the reindeer grazing mountains. Relevant provisions on hunting and fishing were enacted in a reindeer-herding ordinance.

245. Admissibility decision, "Particular circumstances of the Case".

246. The Saami claimed immemorial rights of reindeer herding, hunting and fishing on certain land, as confirmed by a 1993 Amendment to the Reindeer Herding Act. They also claimed ownership of the land and waters in the area. The Commission noted the "so-called Taxed Mountains Case" of 1981, where the Supreme Court of Sweden rejected ownership and related claims, while acknowledging that there existed a strongly protected right of usage *(bruskratt)*.

247. Article 6.1.

248. No. 39511/98, Court of Human Rights, Third Section, 8 June 1999.

249. The Court cited *Ahmed v. the UK*, judgment of 2 September 1998.

250. *Vogt v. Germany*, judgment of 26 September 1995, Series A No. 323, 28, paragraph 59.

251. See *Buscarini et al. v. San Marino*, No. 24645/94, judgment of 18 February 1999. In the McGuinness case, the Court reiterated that "it would be contradictory to make the exercise of a mandate intended to represent different views of society within Parliament subject to a declaration of commitment to a particular set of beliefs".

252. Comments in Hillgruber and Jestaedt, op. cit. (see No. 201), pp. 77-78.

253. *Rothenthurm Commune v. Switzerland*, D.R. 59 (1988), 251; *Ayuntamiento de M v. Spain*, D.R. 68 (1991), p. 209.

254. *National and Provincial Building Society et al. v. UK*, Nos. 21319/93, 21449/93 and 21675/93, judgment of 23 October 1997.

255. *Church of Scientology v. Sweden*, D.R. 21 (1980), 109; *Canea Catholic Church v. Greece*, No. 25528/94, judgment of 16 December 1997.

256. *Pine Valley Developments Ltd. and Others v. Ireland* (1991), Series A, No. 222.

257. Including cases cited in the present chapter – for example, *United Communist Party of Turkey v. Turkey*, *OZDEP v. Turkey*.

258. *Asociación de Aviadores de la República v. Spain*, D.R. 41 (1988), p. 211.

259. *CCSU v. UK*, D.R. 50 (1987), p. 228. *National Union of Belgian Police v. Belgium*, judgment of 22 October 1975, Series A, No. 19; *Swedish Engine Drivers Union v. Sweden*, judgment of 6 February 1976, Series A, No. 20.

260. Emphasis added.

261. Gilbert comments – "that a community might have standing opens up various possibilities for protecting minority groups ... since groups can claim to be victims, discrimination in the enjoyment of rights as between the minority group and the majority or as between different minority groups might well give rise to a violation by the State justiciable before the Court": G. Gilbert, *Jurisprudence of the European Court and Commission of Human Rights in 2000 and Minority Groups*, UN Doc. E/CN.4/Sub.2/AC.5/2001/CRP.4, text following fn. 9.

262. Compare *Muonio Saami Village v. Sweden*, No. 28222/95, admissibility decision of 15 February 2000; also *Noack v. Germany*, No. 46346/99, admissibility decision 25 May 2000 – DOMOWINA, an organisation defending the interests of Sorbs had no standing to lodge an application contesting a measure that affects its members since it could not claim to be a victim for the purposes of Article 34 of the Convention.

263. Nos. 29221/95 and 29225/95, Commission admissibility decision, 29 June 1998. The Court (see above) found a violation by Bulgaria of Article 11 of the Convention. The applicant organisation had been founded in order, *inter alia*, to gain recognition for the Macedonian minority in Bulgaria. The Court decided that demands for autonomy or even secession did not automatically justify banning assemblies, and made the observation (paragraph 107) that "[t]he fact that what was at issue touched on national symbols and national identity cannot be seen in itself – contrary to the Government's view – as calling for a wider margin of appreciation to be left to the authorities. The national authorities must display particular vigilance to ensure that national public opinion is not protected at the expense of the assertion of minority views no matter how unpopular they may be".

264. On the other hand, the refusal of registration does not amount to interference with freedom of assembly if the association can still carry out its functions without registration: No 18874/91, D.R. 76, p. 44.

265. For further contemporary reflection, see J. Bengoa, "Existence and Recognition of Minorities", UN Doc. E/CN.4/Sub.2/AC.5/2000/WP.2, 3 April 2000.

266. *Socialist Party and Others v. Turkey*, No. 21237/93, judgment of 25 May 1998, paragraph 41.

267. *Young, James and Webster v. the UK* (1981), Series A, No. 44, paragraph 64.

268. See Introduction, above.

269. For argument that "national minority" can be substituted by other terms, see K.J. Partsch, "Discrimination" in R.St J. McDonald et al. (eds.), *The European System for the Protection of Human Rights* (Dordrecht: Kluwer, 1993), pp. 571-92, at p. 576. This is an imperfect assessment: "race", "religion" and "national origin" are not identical with "national minority" – none of those terms connotes non-dominance, numerical inferiority, etc. The concept of "minority" in the ECHR is explored in Hillgruber and Jestaedt, op. cit., pp. 87-89.

270. Developments in the *Shanaghan and Kelly* cases (above), and elsewhere in the oeuvre of the Court on indirect discrimination, bring the European Convention closer to the explicit provisions against this form of discrimination in such instruments as the International Convention on the Elimination of All Forms of Racial Discrimination.

271. Wildhaber, above No. 80, pp. 71-72. The author (p. 82) highlights *Thlimmenos* and Additional Protocol 12 as possibly heralding "a new lease of life" in Convention practice.

272. No. 38361/97, judgment of 13 June 2002, First Section.

273. Opinion, paragraph 18.

274. Ibid., paragraph 2. The case concerned the death of a young man of Roma origin who died following ill-treatment by police. The Court (First Section) found violations of Articles 2, 3, 5 and 13 of the Convention, but found no violation of Article 14 – Judge Bonello dissented only on the finding in relation to Article 14.

275. See the remarks of the Ploiesti round table cited in Chapter 4 on the Roma, text following No. 65.

276. See W. Kymlicka, *Multicultural Citizenship: A Liberal Theory of Minority Rights* (Oxford: Clarendon Press, 1995). On the potential strength of community ties, see the dramatic article by S. Saharso, "Female Autonomy and Cultural Imperative: Two Hearts Beating Together", in W. Kymlicka and W. Norman (eds.), *Citizenship in Diverse Societies* (Oxford University Press, 2000), pp. 224-42.

277. *Beard v. UK*, paragraphs 104-05.

278. Judgment in *Chapman*, paragraph 96. See also *Noack v. Germany*, where, although the application was declared inadmissible, the Court nevertheless recognized that "a minority's way of life is, in principle, entitled to the protection guaranteed for an individual's private life, family and home". Accordingly, the displacement of the Sorb minority to a village some twenty kilometres away was a serious matter in terms of the Convention. Hoewever, in its decision, the Court took into account legal guarantees of continued enjoyment of culture in the new area that the Sorb identity would not be destroyed.

279. But see the above remarks of Judge Bonello in Anguelova. In a number of cases subsequent to those of January 2001, other, similar applications by Gypsies from the UK concerning planning regulations have been declared inadmissible: *Smith v. UK*, No. 34334/96; *Harrison v. UK*, No. 32263/96; *Smith v. UK*, No. 40435/98; *Eatson v. UK*, No. 39664/98; *Porter v. UK*, No. 47953/99, and *Clark and Others v. UK*, No. 28575/95. The Court concluded, *inter alia*, that preservation of the environment and highway safety validated the proportionate interference with the rights of the applicants under Article 8.

280. Cf. discussion of Article 20 of the Framework Convention.

281. Article 1 of Parliamentary Assembly Recommendation 1201. In the UK Gypsy cases of January 2001 (above), the Court noted (see *Beard v. UK*, paragraph 68) without commenting that the UK report of 1999 under the Framework Convention included Roma/Gypsies as within the definition of a national minority.

282. Cited above.

283. In particular, in *G. and E. v. Norway*.

Chapter 2

The Framework Convention for the Protection of National Minorities

Introduction

The Framework Convention for the Protection of National Minorities is the most comprehensive of the Council of Europe instruments touching on minority rights.[1] The text was adopted by the Committee of Ministers on 10 November 1994, and opened for signature on 1 February 1995. The Convention entered into force on 1 February 1998,[2] and as of 31 December 2002 had been signed by forty-one member states of the Council of Europe and one non-member state, Serbia and Montenegro,[3] and ratified by thirty-five states.[4] Twenty-five states had submitted reports under the Convention.[5]

The explanatory report to the Framework Convention for the Protection of National Minorities describes the Convention as the first ever legally binding multilateral instrument devoted to the protection of national minorities in general,[6] and as a text which makes clear that this protection is an integral part of the protection of human rights.[7] The latter proposition emerges from Article 1, which declares that:

> The protection of national minorities and of the rights and freedoms of persons belonging to those minorities forms an integral part of the protection of human rights, and as such falls within the scope of international co-operation.

The immediate origins of the Convention lie in the instruction given to the Committee of Ministers by the Vienna Summit, held on 8 and 9 October 1993, to draft "with minimum delay a framework convention specifying the principles which contracting states commit themselves to respect, in order to assure the protection of national minorities".[8] As noted, the Vienna Summit also proposed work on an additional protocol to the European Convention on Human Rights.[9]

Appendix II to the Declaration essays a number of observations on minority rights.[10] National minorities, the summit agreed, "should be protected and respected so that they can contribute to stability and peace";

the challenge for Europe is to assure "the protection of the rights of persons belonging to national minorities within the rule of law, respecting the territorial integrity and the national sovereignty of states". States should:

> create the conditions necessary for persons belonging to national minorities to develop their culture, while preserving their religion, traditions and customs. These persons must be able to use their language, both in private and in public and should be able to use it, under certain conditions, in their relations with the public authorities.

These observations go to the substance of the eventual convention.

The summit also posited a relationship between the Council of Europe and the OSCE: while the heads of state and government confirmed their determination to implement fully the commitments concerning protection of national minorities in the OSCE Copenhagen Document, and the like, the Council of Europe "should apply itself to transforming, to the greatest possible extent, these political commitments into legal obligations". It would seem that the aim of the Council of Europe was not to dilute but to reaffirm the – largely parallel – obligations towards minorities set out in the overall code of the OSCE. Instruments such as the Copenhagen Document were very much part of the normative context in which the Council of Europe moved.[11]

The summit appendix also suggests a formula which contributes to an understanding of "national minority" with its reference to "national minorities which the upheavals of history have established in Europe". This is taken by one author as pointing to the exclusion of recent immigrants.[12] However, there is more than one kind of historical upheaval. Immigrant communities of various kinds are part of the rich tapestry of European history, and many are "established" in different ways.[13] It would appear doubtful that the restrictive stance suggested by the author was intended, especially in advance of serious negotiating on the text.

The drafting of the Framework Convention was entrusted by the Committee of Ministers to an Ad hoc Committee for the Protection of National Minorities (CAHMIN), appointed on 4 November 1993.[14] CAHMIN commenced work in January 1994 and completed the draft of the Convention and the explanatory report in October 1994. The work was substantially completed even more quickly: apart from the convention's control system,[15] the main elements were in place by the Committee's deadline of 30 June 1994.[16] The final text of the Convention sets out that it shall be monitored by the Committee of Ministers,[17] assisted by an Advisory Committee, "the members of which shall have recognised expertise in the field of protection of minorities".[18]

The composition and procedure of the Advisory Committee were to be determined by the Committee of Ministers within one year of the entry into force of the Convention.[19] The question of the composition/procedures of the Advisory Committee was crucial; the text of the Convention is not transparent on the nature of the expertise and the provenance and mandate of potential members. The Committee of Ministers adopted rules on the monitoring arrangements for the Framework Convention in 1997,[20] going some way to appeasing critics who feared that too much would be left to the discretion of governments in naming and controlling members.[21] The Advisory Committee has since proceeded with considerable thoroughness, amassing a considerable amount of documentation in the process – in view of the volume of material, references to and extracts from the documentation in this chapter are necessarily selective.

General aspects

A "framework"

The incorporation of the notion of a "framework" into the title of a legally binding convention has attracted critical comment, to the general effect that the terminology represents a considerable softening of legal obligations on states party from what would be the case if the term were absent.[22] The nature of state obligation takes colour from two paragraphs in the preamble, the first of which expresses the resolution of the signatories "to define the principles to be respected and the obligations which flow from them, in order to ensure ... the effective protection of national minorities";[23] and the second, describing the signatories as "[b]eing determined to implement the principles set out in this Framework Convention through national legislation and appropriate government policies".[24]

One author notes that the term "framework", "to which legal theorists have given little attention, is essentially employed in environmental matters",[25] an observation which is coupled with the suggestion that the convention somehow has a "less binding nature".[26] Another considers that the framework idea "seems to impose upon states only an obligation to endeavour to put ... vague and imprecise descriptions of rights into effect",[27] which, along with other defects, renders the convention "almost worthless".[28] This last remark assumes too much. All human rights instruments are in essence open and developmental, only imprecisely accommodating disagreements, so that the task of discovering meanings in the human rights canon is a constant in the work of the implementing "treaty-bodies" of various denominations. Furthermore, irrespective of its precise form, the Framework Convention creates obligations in international law; it cannot be treated as less binding on account of its structure.[29]

The explanatory report on the Framework Convention observes that the convention "contains mostly programme-type provisions setting out objectives which the parties undertake to pursue", and that these provisions "will not be directly applicable".[30] However, international supervisory organs have translated undertakings into the language of rights in appropriate cases. Two random examples are the right to medical and social assistance under Article 13 of the European Social Charter,[31] and the rights constructed from the parties undertakings in Article 3 of Protocol No. 1 to the ECHR,[32] though the translation of "undertaking" to "right" in the latter case takes colour from the overall rights context of the ECHR. In any case, certain provisions of the Framework Convention appear to be appropriate for direct application. This applies to, but is not necessarily limited to, articles which track or parallel the obligations under the ECHR.[33] Among others, Article 3 would also be a strong candidate.

Some states already appear to have committed themselves to something like a programme of direct application,[34] and to understand obligations as rights.[35] However, human rights treaties employ different mechanisms to ensure their implementation, and the most important issue is that the rights are secured to individuals through the mechanism appropriate to the treaty in question. If the essence of the Framework Convention is the international law obligation to secure the rights in domestic law and practice, then "law and practice" must be adequate to the task and reformed as necessary in order to meet the international standard.

The language of obligation

None of the above lessens the task of the Committee of Ministers, assisted by the Advisory Committee, to achieve tangible human rights gains through substantively awkward provisions. International bodies have struggled with some success to make sense of vague obligations.[36] The principle of effectiveness in the interpretation of treaties[37] suggests that the treaty should be interpreted as far as possible to achieve its objectives. The expressed determination to "implement",[38] and the obligations to undertake to "guarantee",[39] "promote",[40] "recognise",[41] "respect" and "implement",[42] "not to interfere",[43] and so on, cannot be treated as if they are meaningless, even if they do not immediately disclose a set of preordained outcomes. Flexibility has its own value in the face of varying situations.[44] In time, it is foreseeable that the practice of the Advisory Committee will lead to a substantive lexicon of result-orientated recommendations to state action.[45] Some Convention vocabulary, such as "shall ensure respect",[46] "shall recognise",[47] "shall create",[48] "shall refrain",[49] is already hard-edged.

Definition, existence, recognition

While UN instruments generally avoid definitions of national or other minorities, definitions abound in the scientific literature,[50] and are found in some European instruments.[51] Case-law has also made a contribution at the UN level, notably in *Ballantyne, Davidson and McIntyre v. Canada*,[52] and the elaboration by the Venice Commission of the question of minorities in Belgium has clarified aspects of the debate.[53] The explanatory report on the Framework Convention comments on the absence of a definition in the convention. In the course of drafting "it was decided to adopt a pragmatic approach, based on the recognition that at this stage, it is impossible to arrive at a definition capable of mustering general support of all Council of Europe member states". Thus we are left with the unelaborated descriptor – "national minority" in the convention – as elsewhere in the context of the Council of Europe and the OSCE,[54] coupled with the preamble's citation of the resolve of the parties "to protect within their respective territories the existence of national minorities". Klebes none the less finds in the absence of a definition, constitutive elements of a definition in the preamble and elsewhere.[55]

In this respect, the Vienna Summit's notion of the "upheavals of European history"[56] figures in the preamble, which also refers to respecting the "ethnic, cultural, linguistic and religious identity" of each person belonging to a minority, and makes a positive valuation of cultural diversity. Article 5 refers to the "religion, language, traditions and cultural heritage" as essential elements of minority identity, whereas the preferred phrase in Article 6 is "ethnic, cultural, linguistic or religious identity". These descriptors outline a silhouette of the groups in the gaze of the convention.

The explanatory report comments on Article 5 that the provision "does not imply that all ethnic, cultural, linguistic differences necessarily lead to the creation of national minorities".[57] The comment appears superfluous except to the extent that it suggests that "community" or "solidarity", and the desire to sustain a culture, are elements of a national minority. Enhanced rights are envisaged in Articles 10, 11 and 14 for members of minorities who inhabit (unspecified) areas "traditionally or in substantial numbers",[58] or areas "traditionally inhabited by substantial numbers" of persons belonging to minorities.[59] In some cases, a measure of stable habitation appears to be implied by the descriptors; in others not.

It cannot be contended, without more detail, that the term national minority implies only those with state citizenship. Even less can it be maintained that the Framework Convention applies only to minorities with a so-called kin-state – there is no scope for such a limitation in the text, which would disable groups without such a protector or point of reference.[60] In assessing which groups are covered by the convention, the preamble's reference to minority rights commitments pertaining to Framework Convention parties would include the ICCPR, where Article 27 has been interpreted by the Human Rights Committee as meaning not to require citizenship of the state in question,[61] and the Convention on the Rights of the Child, Article 30 of which appears to distil similar principles.[62]

The preamble refers to "UN conventions and declarations" as "commitments concerning the protection of national minorities". The explanatory report observes that the implied reference in the preamble to Article 27 of the ICCPR and to the UN declaration on minorities (UNDM) "does not extend to any definition of a national minority which may be contained in those texts".[63] This comment is oblique. Neither text defines a minority and only the declaration employs the phrase "national minority". But while neither contains a definition, a role as a baseline for rights is relevant to the interpretation of the convention. This must surely extend to the question of who benefits from norms as well as the norms themselves.[64] The UN texts also suggest an approach based on open-minded assessment of situations based on objective criteria, a practice which would appear to be mandated by the good faith requirement of Article 2.

It is instructive to set the relative openness of the text on what may constitute a national minority against the restrictive assertions of some states offered in connection with ratification and signature, and in the reports. A number of states have made reservations or declarations to the effect that they have no minorities,[65] or that minorities are confined to citizens of the state.[66] Some states have further insisted on the necessity of a territorial element for a national minority – raising a question on the approach to dispersed or nomadic groups.[67]

It should be stressed at the outset that the Framework Convention applies in principle to all parts of ratifying states, unless a particular article carries an "area" designation.[68] Germany makes a distinction between the national minority and "ethnic groups traditionally resident in Germany" who include Roma/Gypsy and Sinti;[69] Slovenia makes an analogous distinction between the national autochthonous minorities and the Roma/Gypsy community.[70] Sweden distinguishes between recent immigrants and others:

> The ethnic groups who in recent times have immigrated to Sweden are ... not regarded as national minorities as they do not satisfy the criteria

for national minorities established by the government, concerning, among other things, a long historic bond with Sweden.[71]

Restrictive claims and the rest will be explicated further in state reports. Denmark applies the convention only to the German minority in South Jutland, and explains that home-rule arrangements in the case of the Faroe Islands and Greenland "are not based on ethnic or linguistic criteria" and accordingly, "the populations of these territories are not under international conventions defined as minorities of Denmark".[72] The Danish view is not accepted by the Advisory Committee, which observed that:

> the reasoning [of Denmark] appears to assume that the recognition of a group of persons as constituting an indigenous people or a people excludes the possibility of at the same time benefiting from protection as a national minority. The ... Committee does not share this view. The fact that a group of persons may be entitled to a different form of protection, cannot by itself justify their exclusion from other forms of protection.[73]

Critical remarks were essayed by some members of the UN Human Rights Committee in the face of similar claims by Denmark under Article 27 of the ICCPR, but not in the Committee's concluding observations.[74]

Against such restrictive views may be set the liberal approach of most states, in terms of the absence of any definition of national minority, willingness to extend the notion of national minority to regional minorities – even if a majority in the state as a whole,[75] statements to the effect that the existence of a minority depends simply "on the factual situation in the country",[76] statements that all ethnic groups in the country can be regarded as national minorities,[77] and willingness to accept that the emergence of new national minorities may be a consequence of social developments.[78] A number of states have also reported that their domestic law attempts neither to define nor to recognise national minorities,[79] to which may be added, on the exemption of non-citizens from the national minority, the objection of the Russian Federation, which considers "that none is entitled to include unilaterally in reservations or declarations ... a definition of the term 'national minority'".[80] Furthermore:

> attempts to exclude from the scope of the ... Convention ... persons who permanently reside in the territory of state parties ... and previously had a citizenship but have been arbitrarily deprived of it, contradict the purpose of the ... Convention.[81]

The Russian declaration raises an issue of the validity of the various readings of the term "national minority", particularly the narrower versions.[82] The Russian statement is close to claiming that the restrictions contradict, in the language of the Vienna Convention on the Law of

Treaties, the object and purpose of the convention.[83] Such objections are capable of raising delicate legal issues between objector and the state on the application of the treaty.[84] The Human Rights Committee offers the helpful advice in such situations that "an objection to a reservation made by states may provide some guidance ... in ... interpretation as to ... compatibility with the object and purpose" of the treaty in question.[85]

It may be noted that, unlike the European Convention on Human Rights, the Framework Convention makes no provision for reservations. In view of the alleged flexibility of the convention for the contracting states, further clawbacks would hardly seem to be necessary. Most of the statements are styled "declarations", but this is not decisive. Statements which purport to exclude or modify the legal effect of a treaty constitute reservations, irrespective of what they are called.[86] In the case of the national minority, much will depend upon whether there is a standard from which the state in question is purporting to close down. While this may not be crystal clear in the absence of definition, the object and purpose of the treaty will be gravely impaired if genuine minorities are excluded from its purview. Exclusion also raises issues of discrimination.[87]

International law determines that the existence of minorities is a question of fact not of law.[88] This lapidary statement does not resolve the issue of definition, but signifies a relationship between international law and state prerogatives. It suggests that states will not be able to justify every restrictive claim, and makes it clear that, in dialogues on the existence of groups, the state does not necessarily have the final word. On the contrary, by engaging in treaty relationship, the state submits itself to judgments based on international standards: as the Human Rights Committee has stated, the existence of a minority "does not depend upon a decision by that state party but requires to be established by objective criteria".[89] The flexibility of the Framework Convention does not displace this basic standard.[90]

Membership and belonging

While the question of membership of a community is logically separate from that of the existence of a minority, there is the obvious connection that a group without members is a phantom.[91] There are two basic polarities in any purported relationship: one attributes membership on the basis of characteristics, typically set out in a definition; the other places primary emphasis on individual choice. These correspond to notions of identity as given or primordial and identity as constructed or chosen.[92] A third element, the role of the group, can also enter the equation and this element has been strongly emphasised by indigenous groups.[93] The questions are interwoven with issues of individual and collective rights as they affect the notion of "belonging" rather than the nature of the rights to be exercised. Article 3.1 attempts to deal with this issue:

> Every person belonging to a national minority shall have the right freely to choose to be treated or not to be treated as such and no disadvantage shall result from this choice or from the exercise of the rights which are connected to that choice.

The provision propels choice in the direction of individual preferences. On the other hand its inherent individualism does not bite as deeply as, for example, paragraph 32 of the OSCE Copenhagen Document, which states that "[t]o belong to a national minority is a matter of a person's individual choice and no disadvantage may arise from the exercise of such choice".[94]

So while it is clear that in the Framework Convention no one belonging to a minority may be denied, or compelled to accept, minority rights – both of which are issues of free choice – "membership" is not entirely subject to self-identification.[95] As the explanatory report puts it, the paragraph "does not imply a right for an individual to choose arbitrarily to belong to any national minority. The individual's choice is inseparably linked to objective criteria relevant to the person's identity".[96] The point in paragraph 3.1 on "rights connected to that choice" is, according to the explanatory report intended to secure that "enjoyment of the freedom to choose shall ... not be impaired indirectly".[97]

Article 3.1 coheres with some other references to self-identification in international law which attempt to balance subjective choice against the reality of the "givens" of social existence,[98] though the criteria of minority identity in a particular case may be fluid and leave considerable room for assertions of individual preference. How the balance is to be struck is important. The UN Committee on the Elimination of Racial Discrimination takes the view that membership of a group "shall, if no justification exists to the contrary, be based on self-identification by the individual concerned".[99] Such an approach places the issue in the realm of justification and argument, and effectively places the burden of justifying denial of membership on the state authorities. Issues of privacy may be raised in cases where individuals identify with a group despite the lack of obvious connection with it perhaps in order to avoid persecution, or to benefit positively from social programmes directed towards that group.[100]

States have reported varying degrees of generosity on this issue. Denmark states that the Copenhagen Declaration of 1955 "establishes that it shall be possible to profess one's loyalty to the German people and German culture and that such a profession of loyalty shall not be contested or verified by an official authority".[101] Romania reports that the provisions of the Framework Convention apply to "all persons who as a result of their freely expressed choice belong to a national minority".[102] Hungary observes that an individual's identity and right to choose to belong to a minority "do not exclude acknowledgement of two or more affiliations".[103] Hungary also notes that its citizens can acknowledge membership in the national census in confidential and anonymous terms.[104] The question of membership will often be difficult. Hungary also reports the concerns of minority organisations that, following elections to self-government bodies in 1998, "people who do not belong to the minority communities nominated themselves to several bodies and were elected".[105]

It seems clear that international law generally does not privilege extravagant assertions of belonging, but places individual preferences in the context of reason and argument while discouraging interference with private choices. In some contexts, notably in connection with indigenous peoples, the continued viability or coherence of the group is a pertinent consideration, and may also be here. Group coherence may be equally affected by individuals claiming rights of entry or rights of exit. The Hungarian statement also implies that international standards should be understood in the light of contemporary perceptions of the fluidity of identity, to which may be added the possibility of changes in individual self-perception. Considerable violence to liberal principles would be done by attempting to lock individuals permanently into ethnic boxes, even when these are the result of initial choices.[106]

Persons and communities

The Framework Convention's title and preamble outline the object of the convention as the protection and the effective protection of national minorities, affirming the value of cultural diversity.[107] The object of protection is conceived in holistic terms – protection of national minorities; this is also the case with the references to protection in Articles 1 and 5.1. On the other hand, the language of rights is strongly personalist: rights of persons are the medium through which the objective of protection is to be achieved. On Article 1, the explanatory report observes that "no collective rights of minorities are envisaged".[108] The dichotomy between the beneficiaries of protection and the ascription of rights is a commonplace of contemporary texts of minority rights,[109] while instruments on indigenous peoples exhibit a stronger preference for the collective in the ascription of rights.[110]

On the other hand, Article 3.2 provides that "persons belonging to national minorities may exercise the rights ... in the present Framework Convention individually as well as in community with others". This is analogous to, for example, the International Covenant on Civil and Political Rights (ICCPR), the UNDM and the Copenhagen Document, with one subtle difference: whereas Article 27 of the ICCPR describes an exercise of rights "in community with the other members of their group", and the UNDM and Copenhagen Document refer to exercising rights "in community with other members of their group", the Convention refers only to exercise along with "others".[111] The explanatory report interprets Article 3.2 as recognising "the possibility of joint exercise of these rights and freedoms, which is distinct from the notion of collective rights", adding that "others" shall be understood in the widest possible sense and shall include persons belonging to the same national minority, to another national minority, or to the majority.[112]

The phrase "in community with others" appears, for example in Article 9 of the ECHR and Article 18 of the ICCPR in connection with the general human right of freedom of religion. If minority rights are designed to empower vulnerable communities – an objective recognised as valid by the Framework Convention – and individuals belonging to minorities may not be compelled to exercise minority rights, it is difficult to see why and how "others" enter into the exercise of minority rights. Whether one accepts collective rights or not, the community envisaged in the convention is not an entirely amorphous assembly of individuals; it is not the whole society, and it is not another national minority.

The joint exercise referred to in the report implies that there is no minority collective with a separate moral status that would exercise rights over and against individuals. But it is not necessary for convention purposes to build in safeguards against strong corporate conceptions of the community. The joint exercise of rights is consistent with the notion of a group bound together by a common identity and common interests in safeguarding a culture, and jointly exercising rights "in community".[113] Thus the Convention arguably seeks an unnecessary individualisation of the social dimension of existence which underpins the basic notions of minority rights.[114] On the other hand, it should be noted that "in community with others" is permissive, not mandatory. The Convention also opens a window on the helpful possibility that others can assist the exercise of minority rights through multiple forms of empathetic social action.

Human rights

Article 1 of the Framework Convention states that minority protection and rights form "an integral part of the international protection of human rights, and as such falls within the scope of international co-operation". The message, according to the explanatory report, is that the protection of national minorities "does not fall within the reserved domain of states".[115] There are other messages in Article 1. One is that minority rights do not exist in a parallel universe to human rights, but are integrated with basic conceptions of human rights. This implies that interpretations of convention rights should be integrated with the general corpus of human rights. This suggests balance between convention norms for members of minorities and non-members, bearing in mind the objectives of the Framework Convention.

The effect of the article is also to discourage unduly corporatist notions of minority rights, at least where the "incorporation" of communities would destroy basic choices associated with human rights. On the other hand, the integration with human rights should also alert to possible changes in the canon of human rights which, in some areas, notably that of indigenous peoples, is not averse to an amplification of collective dimensions where these approximate to collective conceptions current in particular modes of social organisation. Hungary has already indicated that it sees no incompatibility between collective minority rights and human rights.[116]

Substantive provisions

Section II of the Convention – Articles 4 to 19 – sets out a broad range of specific provisions. The provisions will be discussed under the following headings:

- non-discrimination and positive measures;
- culture and its limitations;
- ECHR-related freedoms;
- education and language;
- participation;
- cross-border contacts; and
- obligations of minorities.

i. *Non-discrimination and positive measures*

In accordance with a fundamental principle of contemporary human rights law, Article 4.1 guarantees equality and non-discrimination to members of minorities.[117] Equality is defined in terms of "equality before the law and equal protection of the law", and the Framework Convention prohibits any discrimination based on belonging to a national minority, which appears wide enough to catch discrimination even in matters not explicitly covered by the convention. The prohibition of discrimination thus goes beyond the ECHR, which is limited, according to Article 14, to discrimination in respect of "the rights and freedoms set forth in this Convention".[118]

The Framework Convention formula allies itself with the practice of the Human Rights Committee under Article 26 of the ICCPR, which does not limit the prohibition of discrimination to the rights expressed therein.[119] Additionally, paragraph 2 of Article 4 recites that the parties undertake "to adopt, where necessary, adequate measures" to promote "full and effective equality" between (members of) minorities and majority, taking "due account" of the specific conditions of persons belonging to a national minority. Such measures shall not be considered to be an act of discrimination.[120] The provision is appropriate to remedy the consequences of historical discrimination against minority groups.[121] The explanatory report interprets "adequate" by connecting it with proportionality. The measures envisaged in the convention are not specifically limited in time/scope, in the manner of general anti-discrimination provisions in international law.[122] However, the explanatory report reads in the requirement that any special measures "do not extend, in time or in scope, beyond what is necessary in order to achieve the aim of full and effective equality".[123]

The argument about general-versus-special rights for groups such as minorities has moved on since the early postwar standards of international law. In a regime which recognised only general rights, plus special measures of a limited nature, the situation of specific rights for members of minority groups appeared precarious, though the difference between the vocabulary of "special measures" and "special rights" should be noted. However, when minority rights are clearly inscribed as human rights, the function of the non-discrimination principle is subtly clarified: it does not hint at doubts on the justification of rights of minorities, nor suggest that such rights are temporary. The function is rather to ensure that, as between different minorities, a policy of non-discrimination is applied (as it is between any other holders of human rights), and that these rights do not overbear other human rights – the general rights of individuals who are not members of minority groups. The position is set out carefully in General Comment No. 23 of the UN Human Rights Committee.[124] The essence of the measures in Article 4.2 of the Framework Convention is thus the correcting of conditions which impair the enjoyment of the rights in the Convention. This should not be taken to suggest that the rights themselves are not permanent.

The differential minority rights will be required indefinitely as long as the minority status/condition persists. They are rights "to accommodate enduring cultural differences, rather than remedy historical discrimination".[125] In the Framework Convention, the differential rights are those set out in the text. McKean reminds us that special rights for minority groups are designed to produce an equilibrium between different situations, and "should be maintained as long as the groups concerned wish".[126] Dimitrov suggests that the absence from a legal system of differential rights means the absence of conditions for the maintenance of minority distinctiveness.[127] Such a situation would, he argues, leave no choice but to assimilate into the majority, an assimilation (involuntary by definition), violating the prohibition of "policies or practices aimed at assimilation of persons belonging to minorities against their will".[128] Accordingly, the minority rights instrument turns a common argument on its head: that differential rights are the problem from a human rights perspective. On the contrary, from the Convention viewpoint, the problem would be their absence.

ii. *Culture and its limitations*

The preamble to the Convention refers to respecting the ethnic, cultural (and similar) identity of each person and to creating conditions for the expression of this identity. The text implies that identity may have multiple aspects, so that the nuances of expressing identity will vary with the person. According to Article 5.1, the parties undertake to promote the conditions necessary for persons belonging to minorities "to maintain and develop their culture, and to preserve the essential elements of their identity, namely their religion, language, traditions and cultural heritage".[129] The reference to "essential elements of their identity" appears to be a narrower formulation than that in the UNDM, which speaks simply of "identity".[130] The OSCE Copenhagen Document also uses "identity", and describes a right to maintain and develop culture in all its aspects.[131]

Unlike the Framework Convention, the UNDM limits cultural self-expression in cases where specific practices run contrary to national and international standards,[132] a limitation that brings in a raft of reflections in the academic literature on "cultural relativism", which cannot be explored here.[133] The applicability of an analogous limitation is suggested in the explanatory report, which comments that "reference to 'traditions' is not an endorsement or acceptance of practices which are contrary to national law or international standards. Traditional practices remain subject to limitations arising from the requirements of public order".[134] Interpreted in the light of this explanation, the limits of cultural expression in the convention are narrower than in either of the instruments quoted above. The UNDM implies, in careful language, that cultural practices must not violate international human rights standards and national law. The report would allow wider scope for restrictive national legislation.[135] In this instance, the provisions of Article 19 of the Framework Convention become relevant, allowing only for limitations, or other restrictions, "which are provided for in international legal instruments", in particular the ECHR.[136]

International human rights law does not in general view cultures and cultural self-expression as static phenomena.[137] The Convention also recognises that culture and identities are mutable, by employing terms such as "express, preserve and develop", and "maintain and develop". There is no question within its terms of locking-in minorities to an unchangeable corpus of traditional lifestyles and practices before allowing access to the norms of international law. The detailed parameters of cultural rights and traditions are explored below in relation to language, education and similar issues.

iii. *ECHR-related freedoms*

The Framework Convention structures a number of links with the ECHR.[138] In the preamble the signatories introduce the Framework Convention "having regard" to the ECHR; Articles 7, 8 and 9 mirror the ECHR and elaborate some provisions therein; Article 19 relates limitations of rights to the ECHR; and Article 23 provides that the provisions of the Convention "in so far as they are the subject of a corresponding provision ... [in the ECHR] ... shall be understood so as to conform to the latter provisions". In the Convention, Article 7 bundles together freedom of peaceful assembly, freedom of association, freedom of expression, and freedom of thought, conscience and religion – the subject of three separate articles in the ECHR. In the light of the references in the Framework Convention to religious identity,[139] Article 8 elaborates the religious dimension, adding the "right to ... establish religious institutions, organisations and associations" to the basic freedom in Article 9 of the ECHR, in language which echoes the Copenhagen Document.[140] The explanatory report comments that, given "the importance of this freedom in the present context,[141] it was felt particularly appropriate to give it special attention".[142]

Freedom of expression is given further elaboration in Article 9, building on Article 10 of the ECHR. The provision differs from the ECHR in making specific reference to information and ideas imparted in the minority language. Article 9 develops points on minorities and the media: firstly, there is to be no discrimination in access to the media; but secondly, states may license sound radio,[143] television and cinema "without discrimination and based on objective criteria";[144] thirdly, the creation and use of printed media is not to be obstructed; and fourthly, in broadcast media, the state should grant the possibility of the minority's own media. The article also provides that adequate measures are to be taken to facilitate minority access to media and "in order to promote tolerance and permit cultural pluralism".[145] All this represents a considerable elaboration of Article 10 of the ECHR.[146] In Article 9.3, the Convention adopts a differential approach to the printed media on the one hand, and broadcast media on the other. In the former case, states are obliged not to hinder its creation and use by minority members; in the latter, states are required to take positive measures. The report explains the different requirements for print as opposed to radio and TV, in terms of "the relative scarcity of available frequencies and the need for regulation in the latter field".[147]

The basic ECHR freedom of association is amplified by the Framework Convention in terms of a right of persons belonging to minorities to "free and peaceful contacts across frontiers" with persons in other states, in particular those with whom they share ethnic, etc., identity. There is no analogous provision in the ECHR, but the right of contact is a staple of international instruments on minority rights, and of indigenous peoples.[148] The question is of particular importance in Europe, in the many cases where international frontiers divide ethnic and religious groups. The contacts must be free and peaceful, and are not confined to contacts with citizens of other states,[149] only with persons lawfully staying in other states. It follows, even more so, that intra-state minority contacts are similarly privileged.

iv. *Language and education*

For many minority groups, the provisions on language and education represent core issues in the Framework Convention. This was the case even in the time of the League of Nations, when such provisions were the subject of frequent polemics.[150] Language and education are also at the centre of more recent exercises in minority rights law-making at the UN and elsewhere, though it should be recalled that not all minorities (or larger cultural formations) define themselves in linguistic terms.[151]

Language

The language provisions are brief compared to the European Charter for Regional or Minority Languages, but more extensive than the UNDM and the OSCE Copenhagen instrument. They are also somewhat convoluted, and replete with qualifiers of various kinds. The provisions also introduce the concept of a minority area, within the (indeterminate but protected)[152] boundaries of which some enhanced minority rights are envisaged.[153] Article 10 commences (paragraph 1) with a recognition of the right to use a minority language freely and without interference, in public or in private.

The right to use a minority language perfects the freedom of expression set out in Articles 7 and 9.[154] The explanatory report indicates that "in public" means in a public place, "but is not concerned ... with relations with public authorities".[155] Paragraph 2 of Article 10 is directed towards ensuring the possibility of using minority languages in dealings with administrative authorities. Not all relations with public authorities are dealt with in Article 10.2 of the convention, which extends only to administrative authorities, though the latter should be broadly interpreted. The explanatory report specifically mentions ombudsmen in this context.[156]

The right to engage administrative authorities through a minority language (set out in Article 10.2) is subjected to a dense network of qualifiers. The area where it applies is an area inhabited by minority members "traditionally or in substantial numbers". For the right to be activated, there must be a request and the minority request should correspond to a "real need". If this is the case, the parties are only committed to the thin obligation "to endeavour to ensure, as far as possible, the conditions which would make it possible" to use the minority language in relations with administrative authorities. The provision imports a lexicon of qualifiers – traditional or substantial inhabitation, real need, and sundry vocabularies of possibility.

The right struggles to escape its chains, and is gripped even more tightly by the explanatory report, which suggests that the existence of a real need "is to be assessed by the state on the basis of objective criteria",[157] and that the financial resources of the state must also be taken into consideration in applying the article. The issue of need can hardly be in the exclusive domain of the state – simply to be assessed by state agencies. If need is subject to objective criteria, as the report suggests, the question of a minority input to the assessment cannot be discounted.[158] If the criteria are to be objective, then the good faith provisions of Article 2 are highly relevant. In as far as resources are concerned, all human rights consume resources. Even the elimination of official torture requires education (re-education) and training for aberrant officials, as well as continuous vigilance against recurrence. Bodies charged with the implementation of economic, social and cultural rights offer lessons in this respect. Lack of resources is not an excuse for inaction.[159]

The first paragraph of Article 11 sets out a right to use names in the minority language "and the right to official recognition of them, according to modalities provided for in their legal system".[160] This is followed by the right to display minority language "signs, inscriptions and other information of a private nature visible to the public";[161] and the second "minority area" provision,[162] whereby the state "shall endeavour" "to display traditional local names, street names and other topographical indications intended for the public also in the minority language".[163]

There are difficult issues in Article 11. According to the explanatory report, the first paragraph, providing for official recognition of minority names, allows these to be transcribed into the alphabet of the official language in their phonetic forms.[164] Relying largely on Article 11, the Oslo recommendations interpret this requirement to mean that the phonetic rendering "must be done in accordance with the language system and tradition of the national minority".[165] This will be the case even if the minority linguistic system sits uneasily with the forms of the official language.[166]

Paragraph 68 of the explanatory report also states that Article 11 means that persons who have been forced to change their names – perhaps under policies of forced assimilation – should have the right to revert to them.[167] It must be supposed that in such cases any costs incurred in securing a reversion will fall on the authorities and not on the victims. The question of minority language signs visible to the public draws the comment from the explanatory report that the right does not prevent the individual being required to use the official language in addition to the minority language.[168] As a blanket proposition, this cannot be right. While particular issues may be raised under health and safety, or signs using offensive language, these can be addressed by specific state legislation. On the other hand, many private signs (the name of a house, a poster in the window) are visible to the public, and there are clearly cases where there is no conceivable state interest in adding the official or other language. Some states reporting on this article indicate that the freedom to display is not subject to restriction.[169]

Different issues are raised by paragraph 3, where the question is the public allocation of street names and the like, if there is sufficient demand. In this case, it is appropriate that the official or state language enters the equation. What is "sufficient" will vary with the case;[170] questions of visibility of the respective language components of any signage will also be raised. Size matters.[171] Erasing minority footprints through changing names of towns, villages and historical sites can be part of a process of assimilation against the will of a minority.

Education

Article 6 of the Convention provides that the parties shall encourage "a spirit of tolerance and intercultural dialogue and take effective measures to promote mutual respect and understanding and co-operation among all persons living on their territory ... in particular in the fields of education, culture and the media". The tolerance theme is developed by Article 12, which makes the important provision for general education that parties "shall, where appropriate, take measures in the fields of education and research to foster knowledge of the culture, history, language and religion of their national minorities and of the majority". This is the Framework Convention's account of intercultural education, implying that the general population should be aware of minority presence, history, culture, and so on, and equally that minorities should not retreat into ghettoes where they take no interest in fellow citizens.[172]

Analogous provisions are found in the human rights canon.[173] The aim, in the words of the explanatory report is to "create a climate of tolerance and dialogue".[174] Accordingly, the Advisory Committee has taken the view that history taught in schools should reflect a country's ethnic diversity,[175] and that education materials that contain negative stereotypes of minorities should be revised.[176] In cases where states report that they provide multicultural education in minority areas, but not elsewhere, the Committee recommends the authorities to extend the content of such curricula to areas other than those inhabited by national minorities.[177]

Provisions on intercultural education require balancing with provisions to strengthen the minority's sense of itself. Accordingly, the convention makes provision in Article 13 for the setting up of private educational establishments, and, in Article 14, for learning minority languages. Apart from the general right "to learn his or her minority language",[178] the parties shall endeavour to ensure, in minority areas and within the framework of their education systems, that minorities "have adequate opportunities for being taught the minority language or for receiving instruction in this language", without prejudice to learning or teaching in the official language.[179] The linguistic education provision in Article 14.2 is prefaced by the qualification "if there is sufficient demand". The Advisory Committee criticises states that do not set out clear "demand" thresholds to trigger the introduction of minority language education,[180] as well as taking a view on appropriate and inappropriate numbers of pupils to justify classes.[181] In cases like the UK, where there is less demand from the large immigrant population, the Committee encouraged a more proactive approach to minority language education, particularly in areas "where there are substantial numbers of ethnic minorities".[182]

The education provisions look tentative and ambiguous. The draconian statement in Article 13.2 that the right to set up private institutions "shall not entail any financial obligation" for the parties may be incorrect for many practical situations. As the explanatory report notes in respect of paragraph 1, the principle of non-discrimination enters the equation when considering minority education.[183] It can be argued that, in conformity with this principle, if states subsidise the education of some groups, they would be obliged to consider subsidising others.[184] The wording of the language-learning provisions appears to visualise either being taught the minority language in the same way as any other language; or being taught through the medium of the minority language.

In this case it is inexpertly drafted, since the provision for learning through the minority language comes across as a vague injunction concerning "instruction".[185] Assuming that both alternatives are indicated, there appears to be no obligation to support education through the medium of a minority language. The explanatory report observes in paragraph 77 that there is nothing to prevent a state from implementing both alternatives, perhaps through the medium of bilingual instruction.[186] The learning of minority languages may be for some groups an essential aspect of strengthening the culture.

The assumption of the convention seems to be that minority and official languages stand opposed; that capabilities in one diminish the standards of the other. The Hague recommendations attempt to countermand this perception by suggesting a scheme whereby a solid base in the minority language leads to confidence in approaching the state language. The Hague approach is only partly grounded in an interpretation of the Framework Convention, but reaches out to "relevant international norms" interpreted in the light of educational research.[187] The Framework Convention makes no comment on levels of education.[188] Nor does it comment on the drafting of curricula which particularly concern minorities, including the general curriculum to the extent that minority cultures are represented therein. However, the participation provisions of Article 15 suggest, at least, that minorities should have input into curricula, making education more responsive to their interests and concerns.

In minority affairs, education issues are often delicately balanced between integration and separation.[189] If integration is pushed too far, the result is assimilation and the disappearance of the minority as a distinct culture; a policy of separation, on the other hand, can lead to a ghetto culture of withdrawal from society.[190] Education is a powerful instrument for the achievement of social engineering. The convention suggests ways and means through which a balance is to be achieved between the separate domain reserved for the flourishing of minority culture, and the common domain of shared rights and responsibilities.[191] The convention's premises are that identity is shaped through interaction with others and that identity is multiple or hybrid:[192] that each person may be touched by a complex of influences, from family to neighbourhood, through ethnic group, religion and the wider society of the state, as well as the cosmopolitan ideals of human rights.[193] The education (and other) provisions should be seen as opening up possibilities of individual self-authorship in conjunction with community survival and the aspirations of states to a coherent and functioning democratic polity.

v. *Participation*

Article 15 tersely provides that the parties "shall create the conditions necessary for the effective participation of persons belonging to national minorities in cultural, social and economic life and in public affairs, in particular those affecting them". The provision may be compared with

Article 2 (paragraphs 2 and 3) of the UNDM, and paragraph 35 of the OSCE Copenhagen Document. Unlike Article 15, these documents specify participation as a right. Additionally, the UNDM describes a general right of participation, and a right to participate effectively in decisions affecting the minority; the omission of the latter blunts the edge of the convention. However, the emphasis on effective participation in Article 15 is a strong indication that minority input into decision-making is a legitimate demand. Interpretative assistance may be derived from the increasing insistence of the Human Rights Committee under the ICCPR that populations affected by government projects in cultural and other spheres should have an input into decision-making processes.[194] Article 17.2 makes provision for non-interference with minority participation in national and international NGOs.[195]

Participation is not confined to the political sphere, but implicates wide areas of public and social life.[196] In education processes, for example, it would not be in accordance with the convention to allow decisions on educational curricula that affected minority interests to go ahead without appropriate minority participation.[197] Article 15 does not specify precise modalities of participation, and in principle the convention does not seek to model national approaches, which may be expected to show wide variations. The explanatory report offers suggestions which borrow heavily from OSCE practice;[198] parties could promote the participation of persons belonging to minorities through, "among others", the following measures:

- consultation ... when parties are contemplating legislation or administrative measures likely to affect them directly;[199]

- involving these persons in the preparation, implementation and assessment of national and regional development plans and programmes likely to affect them directly;

- undertaking studies, in conjunction with these persons, to assess the possible impact on them of projected development activities;

- effective participation ... in ... decision-making processes and elected bodies both at national and local levels;

- decentralised or local forms of government.[200]

States report a variety of methods for securing the participation of minorities.[201] At the political level, systems of reserved seats in parliament are reported by, among others, Croatia[202] and Romania,[203] with Finland making an exception to the general situation (no special representation) for the benefit of Åland.[204] Denmark states that proportional representation benefits minorities.[205] There are many examples of special commissions, round-tables, and the like, with minority participation.[206] The UK makes a complex statement itemising various forms of participation including its approach to the problem of social exclusion.[207] Other states – notably Hungary – set out the benefits of a system of minority local and national self-government.[208] Hungary has instituted the position of Ombudsman (National Assembly Commissioner) for the Rights of National Minorities.[209] If a general criticism may be essayed on the reports, it is that they concentrate largely on public affairs participation, particularly with respect to political life, while the concept in the Framework Convention is more general. The UK report is a good reflection of the potential scope of participation as set out in the convention.

The multiple institutional forms make it difficult to judge their contribution to the principle of effective participation, though some of the systems appear insufficient in themselves to achieve the purposes of the convention.[210] In the context of minority rights, effectiveness must be assessed in line with the overall purposes of the instruments in question – facilitating the survival and flourishing of minorities, and enabling them to make a purposeful contribution to society as a whole, thus "promoting the good governance and integrity of the state".[211] Participation is a key aspect of the contemporary politics of recognition pursued by many groups, suggesting the importance of group-differentiated rights as a characteristic route to fulfilling their aspirations.

The OSCE Lund recommendations develop this point in observing that experience in Europe and elsewhere "has shown that, in order to promote ... participation, governments often need to establish specific arrangements for national minorities".[212] This view receives implicit support from Finland, whose report makes the critical observation that:

> The existing electoral system does not make a full political participation of small ethnic and other groups possible, because it is in practice difficult for persons representing such groups to be elected. Thus for example Saami people do not have their own member of Parliament ... nor has a person representing the Roma ever been elected to Parliament.[213]

The Lund principles also suggest that effective participation moves along with principles of decentralisation and subsidiarity – that effective participation is facilitated by devolved structures.[214]

vi. *Cross-border contacts*

Article 17.1 recites the commitment of the parties "not to interfere with the right of persons belonging to national minorities to establish and maintain free and peaceful contacts across frontiers with persons lawfully staying in other states, in particular those with whom they share an ethnic, cultural, linguistic or religious identity". The provision draws only the brief observation in the explanatory report that it was unnecessary to include an explicit provision on contacts within the state, as this was adequately covered by other provisions, notably Article 7.[215] A number of states have reported substantively on this provision.[216]

The observations of the UK on the relationship between Article 17 and legislation on terrorism appear over-cautious in view of the article's emphasis on free and peaceful contacts. The contacts right may also be linked with the consideration in the preamble that the realisation of a tolerant and prosperous Europe does not depend solely on co-operation between states "but also requires transfrontier co-operation between local and regional authorities without prejudice to the constitution and territorial integrity of each state".[217]

vii. *Obligations of minorities*

While it does not elaborate a special principle to promote the loyalty of minority members to their host state, the convention approaches the question of duties in Article 20:

> In the exercise of the rights and freedoms ... in the present Framework Convention, any person belonging to a national minority shall respect the national legislation and the rights of others, in particular those of persons belonging to the majority or to other national minorities.

The loyalty of members of minorities has not been an explicit demand of international human rights law.[218] Duties of members of minorities are expressed in general phrases in the Universal Declaration of Human Rights – Article 29 of which states that "everyone has duties to the community" – and in general citizenship legislation. In the UNDM[219] and the Copenhagen Document[220] there are only broad references to refraining from actions contrary to the purposes and principles of the Charter of the United Nations. This is also the case with Article 21 of the Framework Convention with respect to the fundamental principles of international law "and in particular of the sovereign equality, territorial integrity and political independence of States". Such provisions tend to appear in instruments on minority rights because of sensitivities about self-determination, secession, and so on, despite the often explicit separation of the issues in international discourse.[221]

While no objection may be taken to members of minorities respecting the rights of others, respect for national legislation as a treaty demand raises questions. Is this the equivalent of a loyalty clause? What if the national legislation does not respect the rights of members of minorities? Are minorities placed under an obligation to "respect" when others are not? Does the article carry the implicit message that minority rights are a kind of privilege? One thing must be absolutely clear: the rights in the Framework Convention are in no sense conditional on respecting the national legislation. It would be contrary to their stated essence as human rights to suppose such conditionality. The explanatory report offers limited guidance to the application of the provision, noting that "this reference to national legislation clearly does not entitle Parties to ignore the provisions of the ... Convention".[222] The report indicates that the provision is directed at "situations where persons belonging to national minorities are in a minority nationally but form a majority within one area of the State".[223] In which case, a formula similar to that in the UNDM would have been greatly preferable – "The exercise of the rights set forth ... shall not prejudice the enjoyment by all persons of universally recognised human rights and fundamental freedoms".[224]

Thus far, few states have reported explicitly on Article 20, which perhaps indicates that they do not perceive any pressing problems. Among these states, Ukraine reports that its "citizens of all nationalities ... are obliged to observe the Constitution and laws of Ukraine, to defend its state sovereignty and territorial integrity, to respect languages, cultures, traditions, customs, religious originality of the Ukrainian people and all national minorities"[225] – a provision not directed specifically at minorities. Croatia merely recites the intention of its laws "to enable less numerous ethnic and national communities or minorities ... a free development of their distinctive characteristics" – a provision in keeping with the above-cited provision in the UNDM.[226] Romania makes a similar observation on Article 20.[227]

The Advisory Committee (AC)

Personnel and methodology[228]

As indicated above, the Framework Convention sketches little more than an outline of an implementation mechanism.[229] Article 25.1 provides that, within one year from the convention coming into force for the contracting party, state reports are to be transmitted to the Secretary General of the Council of Europe, who will transmit them to the Committee of Ministers (CoM). Further information of relevance to the implementation of the convention will be transmitted "on a periodical basis" and "whenever the Committee of Ministers so requests".[230] The CoM is assisted by an Advisory Committee (AC), "the members of which shall have recognised expertise in the field of protection of national minorities".[231]

The supervision of the convention is thus entrusted to the political wisdom of the CoM, with the AC playing a subordinate but substantive role. These heavily criticised arrangements were developed in less ostensibly political directions through a set of rules adopted by the CoM in 1997 on the basis of preparatory work by an ad hoc committee of experts (CAHMEC) with a significant input from the Parliamentary Assembly and expert opinion.[232] While the rules augment the transparency and impartiality of the mechanism, its success will be assessed on the basis of its eventual track record.[233]

The rules are set out in Resolution (97) 10 of the CoM. They can be summarised – firstly in relation to the Advisory Committee:

- the ordinary membership of the AC is between twelve and eighteen[234] – this is less than the number of parties;
- in addition to their expertise in minority protection, the members serve in their individual capacity and are to be "independent and impartial";[235]
- the CoM elected a list of experts from which it appointed eighteen ordinary members of the AC;
- vacancies will be filled with priority given to experts from states from which no expert has been appointed;[236]
- rule 16 provides that the term of office is four years, renewable once (drawing of lots two years after the commencement of the committee's work will decide which half of the ordinary members gain a further two years of the initial term).

On the monitoring functions, the following rules were adopted:

- the country reports shall be made public by the Council of Europe on receipt by the Secretary General;[237]
- the state concerned can publicise them earlier;[238]
- rule 21 envisages a five-year reporting cycle;
- under rule 22, the CoM transmits reports to the AC;
- according to rule 23, the AC shall consider the reports and transmit "opinions" to the CoM;
- rule 24 provides that the CoM can adopt conclusions and recommendations, and set a time-limit for the submission of information on their implementation;
- CoM conclusions and recommendations shall be made public upon adoption (rule 25);
- according to rule 26, the AC opinion is made public at the same time as conclusions/recommendations of the CoM, unless the CoM decides otherwise;[239]
- rule 27 provides that the comments of the parties shall be made public alongside the CoM conclusions and recommendations, and the opinion of the AC;[240]
- the rules raise important questions on sources of information for utilisation by the AC – rule 30 provides that the AC may receive information from other sources than state reports, and rule 31 provides

that the AC can invite information from other sources unless otherwise directed by the CoM;

- rule 32 provides that the AC can meet with the government concerned and must do so if the government requests;

- however, the AC must obtain a specific mandate if it wishes to
hold meetings with other sources for purposes of ascertaining
information;[241]

- according to rule 35, the AC can call on the CoM to mandate an ad
hoc report;

- rule 36 provides that the AC can be involved in monitoring follow-up
to the conclusions and recommendations as instructed by the CoM.

The rules also gave the Advisory Committee the responsibility of drawing up its own rules of procedure. These were adopted by the committee
in October 1998.[242] The committee has a president and a first and second
vice-president. It meets in camera unless it decides otherwise, with decisions ordinarily taken by majority vote. A majority of ordinary members
is also required to support an opinion of the committee. The rules of procedure also envisage the setting up of working parties and other subsidiary bodies, as well as rapporteurs on specific questions. The
committee may seek the assistance of outside experts and consultants,
and co-operate with other Council of Europe bodies. The AC is to be kept
aware of cases of non-submission of reports, and can propose measures.

Practice

The first year of operation of the Advisory Committee saw the setting
up of various procedures and processes. In general, the AC observes that
in almost all cases additional information has been sought from the
country concerned, data mainly relating to the application of norms in
practice.[243] In-country meetings have been held.[244] The committee argued
the usefulness of involving NGOs and minority groups in processes leading to state reports, and decided that contacts with independent sources
should be a regular feature of its work. Information is sought from non-
governmental sources as well as official reports, and meetings have been
held with concerned groups.[245] "Parallel" or "alternative" reports from
various NGOs have been submitted to the Advisory Committee.[246]
Initially at least, and in the interests of consistency, the AC decided to
group together a set of opinions on the country reports, rather than
submit separate single opinions.[247]

The President of the Advisory Committee has argued that the committee is under-resourced: a secretariat of three administrators "is clearly

inadequate and needs to be augmented as a matter of urgency".[248] He issued the following warning:

> The recent events in Kosovo and elsewhere demonstrate all too clearly the high costs that result from ignoring minority protection. If we do not provide consistent, vigorous monitoring, a human rights problem may develop into a full-blown crisis, and by then it is already too late for the monitoring mechanism ... to intervene effectively.

The second activity report notes that the examination of the implementation of the Framework Convention benefits from written exchanges with state representatives and has established the methodology of addressing a questionnaire to parties, notably concerning the implementation of the convention in practice. Responses have, in the AC's view, been commendable and facilitate a constructive dialogue. The report also logs the country visits, observing that the meetings "are not only useful for the purposes of preparing its own opinions but also that such exchanges may in themselves contribute to the protection of national minorities in the countries concerned".[249] The AC also declared an intention to "devote a significant portion of its visits to states parties to contacts with NGOs and other independent sources".[250] Efforts made by the AC and the convention Secretariat to publicise the convention are outlined, and the issue of resources again raised.

Concise assessment of the Framework Convention

The Framework Convention is one of the most important texts of the Council of Europe, and is destined to carry much of the burden of putting into effect minority rights in European space for the foreseeable future. As the President of the Advisory Committee has indicated, adequate resourcing of this instrument is vital for future success. The convention may appear to incorporate only limited standards compared to other texts on minority rights, and the notion of a framework appears to some to dilute its potential impact, but this is a binding treaty in international law and takes its strength from that fact, as well as from the clear integration of minority rights concepts into the mainstream of human rights. The Framework Convention is no less binding because it sets out a framework for action: its language of international obligation is clear.

On specifics, the absence of definition of "national minority" is in line with other international law texts. The understanding of the basic concept is left to be worked out in practice. This too is broadly in line with practice elsewhere. Implementation of the provisions will call up a host of issues around their application to specific groups. The effectiveness of implementation will be enhanced if the Advisory Committee takes a robust view of what constitutes a minority in particular cases, as have the UN Human Rights Committee and the OSCE High Commissioner on National Minorities.[251] Analogously, the lack of explicit collective rights is not fatal to the success of the Framework Convention; on the other hand, excessive individualisation of rights would undermine community benefits to be gained from the norms. The convention deploys broader notions of equality and non-discrimination than the ECHR and is clear on the legitimacy and necessity of special measures to benefit minorities.[252]

The language provisions also represent a tentative advance from the ECHR, pushing minority rights into the public realm so jealously guarded by states. The confinement of the enhanced rights to minority areas is not equivalent to mandating autonomy but is capable of acting as its functional substitute, recognising the reality of complex population mixes in most states ratifying the convention.[253] In line with other texts on minority rights, the provisions on participation distil a broader concept than the essentially political notion of participation in the ECHR.[254]

The implementation mechanism is more diffuse than that of the ECHR. We note the absence of an individual claims mechanism and its related bodies. On the other hand, minority rights texts in particular may benefit from the type of broad overview procedure envisaged in the Framework Convention. In this way, systemic and structural issues can be critically appraised for the benefit of the communities as a whole. It is excessive legalism to imagine that all human rights texts must ideally specify an individual rights mechanism. The attention of the supervisory bodies should rightly focus on avoidance of violation by states through positive legislative and other strategies, and not confine themselves to matters of redress. The expertise of the Advisory Committee, where possible integrating its work with the human rights agendas of civil society, will be a crucial factor in making impartial judgements of what is to be done in general and in particular states.

Further, the employment by the Committee of Ministers of the Council of Europe of its various restraining and other powers on the basis of objective criteria will facilitate the success of the whole. The balance between Advisory Committee and Committee of Ministers is vital; where possible, the balance should favour the former specialist treaty-body.[255] This is not simply a matter of the political body versus the experts: all human rights instruments are politicised to the extent that human rights decisions affect the lives of citizens and the interests of state. What human rights instruments do is reduce the politics to a definitive code; what matters is that the code is implemented by responsible bodies assigned to that duty within their respective spheres of competence.

Notes

1. European Treaty Series No. 157.

2. In accordance with Article 28.1 of the convention, twelve ratifications were required to bring it into force.

3. The non-signatory member states of the Council of Europe are Andorra, Belgium, France and Turkey.

4. The thirty-five states parties are: Albania, Armenia, Austria, Azerbaijan, Bosnia and Herzegovina, Bulgaria, Croatia, Cyprus, Czech Republic, Denmark, Estonia, Finland, Germany, Hungary, Ireland, Italy, Liechtenstein, Lithuania, Malta, Moldova, Norway, Poland, Portugal, Romania, the Russian Federation, San Marino, Slovakia, Slovenia, Spain, Sweden, Switzerland, "the former Yugoslav Republic of Macedonia", Ukraine, the United Kingdom and Serbia and Montenegro.

5. The number has subsequently risen to thirty-one with the receipt of the reports of Albania, Azerbaijan, Lithuania, Serbia and Montenegro, and Ireland.

6. Explanatory report, paragraph 10.

7. Ibid., paragraph 30.

8. The instruction is contained in Appendix II to the Declaration – SUM (93) 2, 9 October 1993.

9. See above, Chapter 1.

10. In the main text of the Vienna Declaration, the heads express their "awareness that the protection of national minorities is an essential element of stability and democratic security in our continent".

11. For a more critical view, based on the author's impression that in the Summit Declaration, "the Council of Europe tries to minimise the value of the OSCE documents by reminding us of their 'political' nature", etc., see Spiliopoulou-Åkermark, *Justifications of Minority Protection in International Law* (Uppsala: Iustus Forlag, 1997), p. 227.

12. Ibid., p. 226.

13. Note the employment of "historical reasons" as the rationale for defining the Germans in Denmark as a national minority – Initial Report of Denmark under the Framework Convention, p. 13. In expressing its disagreement with comments of the Advisory Committee on the Framework Convention (below) on which minorities are covered by the convention, the government of Denmark again cites "historical upheavals" as justification for reporting only on the German minority in South Jutland as a "national minority" – opinion of the Advisory Committee, ACFC/INF/OP/I(2001) 005; comments of the Government of Denmark, GVT/COM/INF/OP/I(2002) 005.
    Editing note: a slightly different documentary reference is now used for the initial reports – page references to initial reports in the present chapter are based on the first hard copies of the reports received by the authors. The current documentation references may be found in the list of State reports on the national minorities pages of the Council of Europe website: http://www.coe.int. In the case of opinions of the Convention's Advisory Committee, the full reference is given in this chapter on first mention only.

14. The membership of CAHMIN consisted of experts designated from each member state of the Council of Europe – thirty-two at that time. The Committee was assisted by the participation of representatives of the CDDH, the Council for Cultural Co-operation (CDCC), the Steering Committee on the Mass Media (CDMM), and the European Commission for Democracy through Law. The OSCE High Commissioner on National Minorities and the Commission of the European Communities also took part as observers – Explanatory report, paragraph 6.

15. See "Control of the Implementation of the Framework Convention for the Protection of National Minorities" – outline of several options prepared by the Secretariat, CAHMIN (94) 17, 20 June 1994.

16. See CAHMIN (94) 19, Report of the 5th Meeting 27 June-1 July 1994. During its sixth meeting for 12-16 September 1994, CAHMIN carried out the final drafting of the preamble and of Articles 1-16.

17. Article 24.

18. Article 26.1.

19. Article 26.2.

20. Committee of Ministers Resolution (97) 10, adopted on 17 December 1997 at the 601st meeting of the ministers' deputies. See also Rules of Procedure of the Advisory Committee on the Framework Convention for the Protection of National Minorities, adopted by the Advisory Committee on 29 October 1998, ACFC/INF (98) 2. These basic sets of rules have been supplemented – see later on the Advisory Committee.

21. See the critical remarks prepared by Rapporteur Bindig for the Parliamentary Assembly of the Council of Europe, Doc. 7442, 20 December 1995, and Parliamentary Assembly Recommendations 1255 (1995), 1285 (1996), and 1300 (1996). Stimulating contributions to the debate on the nature of the proposed body were made by A. Phillips – AS/Jur/DH (1996) 2 – and G. Alfredsson – AS/Jur/DH (1996) 3 – before the Parliamentary Assembly's Committee on Legal Affairs and Human Rights. For a set of ideas and recommendations on the monitoring mechanism, see M.A. Martín Estébanez and K. Gal, *Implementing the Framework Convention for the Protection of National Minorities* (Flensburg: European Centre for Minority Issues, 1998). See also C. Barnes and M. Olsthoorn, *The Framework Convention for the Protection of National Minorities: A Guide for Non-Governmental Organisations* (London: Minority Rights Group, 1999).

22. Strong language emanated from the Parliamentary Assembly of the Council of Europe in their overall assessment that the Convention "is weakly worded", and "formulates a number of vaguely defined objectives and principles, the observation of which will be an obligation of the contracting states but not a right which individuals may invoke. Its implementation machinery is feeble and there is a danger that, in fact, the monitoring procedure will be left entirely to governments" – Recommendation 1255 (1995), text adopted by the Assembly on 31 January 1995. The force of this criticism is now somewhat abated, especially in view of developments in the monitoring mechanism (see later).

23. 12th preambular paragraph.

24. 13th preambular paragraph.

25. F. Benoît-Rohmer, *The Minority Question in Europe: Texts and Commentary* (Strasbourg: Council of Europe, 1996), p. 39.

26. Ibid.

27. G. Gilbert, "Minority Rights under the Council of Europe", in P. Cumper and S. Wheatley (eds.), *Minority Rights in the "New" Europe* (The Hague: Martinus Nijhoff, 1999), pp. 53-70, at p. 63.

28. Ibid. For more nuanced views, see Gilbert's "The Council of Europe and Minority Rights", *Human Rights Quarterly*, Vol. 18 (1996), pp. 160-89.

29. The point is rightly made by Spiliopoulou-Åkermark, op. cit., p. 229, No. 114. Note also her remark that "the contracting parties cannot avoid the legal implementation of a treaty by calling it 'framework convention' or 'convention specifying principles'" – ibid., p. 227.

30. Explanatory report, paragraph 11.

31. Discussed by M. Scheinin, "Women's Economic and Social Rights as Human Rights", in L. Hannikainen and E. Nykanen (eds.), *New Trends in Discrimination Law: International Perspectives* (Publications of Turku Law School, Vol. 3, No. 1/1999), pp. 1-28.

32. European Court of Human Rights in *Mathieu-Mohin and Clerfayt v. Belgium*, judgment of 2 March 1987, Ser. A, No. 113 – discussed in F.G. Jacobs and R.C.A. White, *The European Convention on Human Rights*, Chapter 16, and Chapter 1 of the present work. The translation from undertakings to rights is discussed by S. Lewis-Anthony, "Autonomy and the Council of Europe – with Special Reference to the Application of Article 3 of the First Protocol, etc.", in M. Suksi (ed.), *Autonomy: Applications and Implications* (The Hague: Kluwer Law International, 1998), pp. 317-42.

33. A general and detailed review of internal effects – questions of self-execution, justiciability, etc. in the area of human rights, is provided in B. Conforti and F. Francioni (eds.), *Enforcing International Human Rights in Domestic Courts* (The Hague: Martinus Nijhoff, 1997).

34. Consider Article 15.4.a of the Hungarian-Slovak Treaty on Good-Neighbourliness, etc., wherein the parties declare "that as regards the rights and obligations of persons belonging to minorities living within their respective territories they shall apply the Framework Convention ... unless their domestic legal systems provide for broader protection of rights of persons belonging to national minorities" – treaty in force 6 May 1996, text in A. Bloed and P. van Dijk (eds.), *Protection of Minority Rights through Bilateral Treaties* (The Hague: Kluwer Law International, 1999), pp. 370-75.

35. This may be inferred negatively from the reservation made by Malta against Article 15 to the extent that it involved "the right to vote or stand for election" – reservation deposited on 10 February 1998, Council of Europe Information, 21.01.2000.

36. M. Craven, "The Justiciability of Economic, Social and Cultural Rights", in R. Burchill, D. Harris and A. Owers (eds.), *Economic, Social and Cultural Rights: Their Implementation in United Kingdom Law* (University of Nottingham Human Rights Law Centre, 1999), pp. 1-13.

37. The principle was deemed by the International Law Commission [ILC] to be inherent in Article 31 of the Vienna Convention on the Law of Treaties: "A treaty shall be interpreted in good faith in accordance with the ordinary meaning to be given to the terms of the treaty in their context and in the light of their object and purpose". The ILC comments that "[w]hen a treaty is open to two interpretations one of which does and the other does not enable the treaty to have appropriate effects, good faith and the objects and purposes of the treaty demand that the former interpretation should be adopted" – *Year Book of the ILC*, 1966, II, p. 219. For an earlier appreciation, see D.P. O'Connell, *International Law* (London: Stevens and Sons, 1965), Vol. I, pp. 273-74. O'Connell describes the principle as pertaining to matters intrinsic to the treaty.

38. Preamble.

39. Articles 4 and 10.

40. Articles 5 and 12.

41. Articles 8, 9, 10, 11, 14.

42. Article 19.

43. Article 17.

44. For an appreciation of this point, see N. Dimitrov, *The Framework Convention for the Protection of National Minorities: Historical Background and Theoretical Implications* (Skopje and Melbourne: Matica Makedonska, 1999), pp. 145-48.

45.   In its second activity report, ACFC/INF(2000) 0011 June 1999 – 31 October 2000, the Advisory Committee observed (paragraph 11) that "many of the state reports still focus too heavily on the legislative framework and provide only a limited amount of information on the relevant practice", implying that the committee will look for results as well as appropriate legal structures. A third activity report, ACFC/INF(2002) 001 covers the period from 1 November 2000 to 31 May 2002.

46.   Article 7.

47.   Article 13.

48.   Article 15.

49.   Article 16.

50.   For a strong argument in favour of definition, consult J. Packer, "On the Definition of Minorities", in J. Packer and J. Myntti (eds.), *The Protection of Ethnic and Linguistic Minorities in Europe* (Åbo/Turku: Åbo Akademi University, 1993), pp. 23-65; and "Problems in Defining Minorities", in D. Fottrell and B. Bowring (eds.), *Minority and Group Rights in the New Millennium* (The Hague: Kluwer Law International, 1999), pp. 223-73, and G. Pentassuglia, *Minorities in International Law* (Strasbourg: Council of Europe, 2002), pp. 55-75. See also E. Gayim, *The Concept of Minority in International Law: a Critical Study of the Vital Elements* (Rovaniemi: University of Lapland, 2001).

51.   The definition in Parliamentary Assembly Recommendation 1201 (1993) will be recalled. See also Article 1 of the CEI Instrument on Minority Rights 1994, and Article 1 of the CIS Convention on Minority Rights 1994.

52.   Communications nos. 359/1989 and 385/1989, views of the Human Rights Committee adopted 31 March 1993. In this case, the Anglophone community of Quebec were not regarded as a minority because in Canada as a whole they were a majority – the decision was subject to strong dissents from members of the committee. In the declaration made on ratification of the Framework Convention by Switzerland, "national minority" is understood as "groups of individuals numerically inferior to the rest of the population of the country 'or of a canton'" (emphasis added) – Council of Europe Information 21.01.2000. This extends the meaning of minority beyond the Ballantyne formula. Compare Article 1 of Recommendation 1201 (1993) of the Parliamentary Assembly of the Council of Europe, and see later comments of the government of Finland and the Advisory Committee on Finnish-speakers in Åland.

53.   *Opinion on Possible Groups of Persons to which the Framework Convention for the Protection of National Minorities Could be Applied in Belgium*, CDL-AD (2002) 1. The Commission concludes (paragraph 40) that "A group of persons that is numerically inferior to the rest of the population, shares common ethnic, cultural, linguistic or religious features and wishes to preserve them is not to be considered as a minority in the sense of the Framework Convention if and to the extent that it finds itself in a dominant or co-dominant position." Further (paragraph 41), "the question of whether a group is dominant or co-dominant must be assessed at both the State and the sub-State levels."

54.   Recall that there is also a reference to the national minority along with others in the UN canon – in the UN Declaration on the Rights of Persons belonging to National or Ethnic, Religious and Linguistic Minorities, contained in UN General Assembly Resolution 47/135, 18 December 1992.

55.   H. Klebes, "The Framework Convention", *Human Rights Law Journal*, Vol. 16, No. 1-3, (1995), pp. 92-98, at p. 93.

56.   See above on the use made of this concept by Denmark.

57.   Paragraph 43. This nostrum was borrowed from the Geneva Meeting of CSCE Experts 1991, section II, paragraph 4. The government of Denmark cites paragraph 43 of the explanatory report in support of its view "that immigrants and refugees cannot be considered to be covered by the notion of national minority" (comments of the government of Denmark on the opinion of the Advisory Committee, GVT/COM/INF/OP/I(2001) 005).

58.   Articles 10 and 14.

59.   Article 11.

60.   N. Dimitrov, op. cit., pp. 134-39.

61.   UN Doc. A/49/40, pp. 107-10.

62.   See R. Hodgkin and P. Newell, *Implementation Handbook for the Convention on the Rights of the Child* (Geneva: UNICEF, 1998), pp. 407-14.

63.   Explanatory report, paragraph. 26.

64.   In this respect, Article 22 of the Convention has a role in inclining interpretation towards consistency with existing standards of minority rights: "Nothing in the present Framework Convention shall be construed as limiting or derogating from any of the human rights and fundamental freedoms which may be ensured under the laws of any Contracting Party or under any other agreement to which it is a Party." While the task of the implementing organs of the Framework Convention is to interpret this specific text, an awareness of the general human rights context will help to ensure consistency between the convention and related instruments.

65.   Statements on ratification by Liechtenstein and Malta; declaration of Luxembourg made on signature. The statements by Malta and Liechtenstein include the claim that ratification "is an act of solidarity in the view of the objectives of the Convention". The opinion on Liechtenstein, ACFC/INF/OP/I(2001) 003, adopted by the Advisory Committee on 30 November 2000, suggests nonetheless (paragraph 13) that the application of the convention on an article-by-article basis for the benefit of some religious groups and foreigners could be considered; Liechtenstein disagrees (Comments of the Government of Liechtenstein, GVT/COM/INF/OP/I (2001) 003).
         Although Spain has not made a declaration or analogous statement on signature or ratification, the initial report deals in effect with only one minority – the Roma. Some understanding of the position may be gathered from this report (p. 4) which, *inter alia*, recites the preamble to the Constitution of 1978: "The Constitution is founded on the indissoluble unity of the Spanish nation, etc.", adding (ibid.) that "[t]he Constitution does not formally recognise or define ethnic minorities. As stated in the preamble, it recognises and protects all the peoples of Spain and their cultures, traditions, languages and institutions".

66.   Explicit references were made at the time of ratification and/or signature by Austria, Estonia, Germany, Luxembourg (leading to the proposition that there is no national minority in Luxembourg), Poland and Switzerland. Denmark and "the former Yugoslav Republic of Macedonia" refer either to specific groups or to internal law definitions. If states claim that the meaning of the international term (national minority) and thus the international obligation is "conditioned" by domestic law, this carries the unacceptable logic that, if domestic law changes, so must the international obligation.

67.   See the ratification statements by Austria and Denmark – Council of Europe website.

68.   See Articles 10, 11 and 14; reference may also be made to Article 30 of the convention, allowing a state party to specify "the territory or territories for whose international relations it is responsible" to which the Convention applies. In its opinion (paragraph 17) on Denmark, the Advisory Committee noted that "[a]lthough the ... Convention attaches importance in a number of its provisions to the criterion of traditional inhabitation of certain areas for protection, the majority of its provisions are designed to apply throughout the territory of the state concerned ... taking into account all relevant circumstances".

69.   On signature, 11 May 1995, and ratification, 10 September 1997.

70.   On ratification, 25 March 1998.

71.   Initial report, p. 6. Sweden couples this statement with an account of criteria for the recognition of minorities set out in a government bill – Initial report, p. 5. Appendix 1 to the report of Sweden lists the Saami, the Swedish Finns, the Tornedalers, the Roma and the Jews, as the minorities relevant to the convention. Compare the approach set out in the initial report of Norway (pp. 11ff): "In Norway, the term 'national minorities' is understood to mean minorities with a long-term connection with the country. Minority groups must be in the minority and must hold a non-dominant position in society. Furthermore, they must have distinctive ethnic, linguistic, cultural and/or religious characteristics which make them substantially different from the rest of the population of Norway. The persons concerned must also have a common will to maintain and develop their own identity. The term 'long-term connection' has not been defined, but the Norwegian authorities have taken into consideration a criterion suggested internationally to the effect that groups must be able to claim a minimum of 100 years of connection with the state in question. Thus more recent immigrant groups are not deemed to be national minorities in Norway. However, the situation is more nuanced in the case of immigrants to Norway with backgrounds from the same groups that have been granted the status of national minorities in Norway. These immigrants will be eligible for measures designed for the national minority (such as language training) even if the individual immigrant does not have a long-term connection with Norway."

72.   Initial report, p. 14. On the other hand, the report goes on to describe the distinct languages of these territories, and their "culture and language" – ibid., p. 15. So even if the home-rule arrangements are not defined in ethnic or linguistic terms, these cover ethnic groups which have minority characteristics.

73.   Opinion, paragraph 17. Compare the statement of Sweden – listing the Saami, "who are also an indigenous people" among the minorities in Sweden: Initial report, pp. 5-6. However, in the case of Norway, the initial report (p. 2) contains the following statement: "The Saami people in Norway are also a national minority in the terms of international law. However, the *Sámediggi* (the Saami Assembly) has declared that it does not consider the Framework Convention to be applicable to the Saami people, since as an indigenous people the Saami have legal and political rights that exceed those covered by the provisions of the Convention. In keeping with the wish of the *Sámediggi*, therefore, the Saami people will not be discussed in this report. Instead, Norway's reports on the implementation of ILO Convention No.169 concerning Indigenous and Tribal Peoples in Independent Countries are appended hereto." This does not appear to be a case of "exclusion" practised by a state party, but an acceptance of the principle in Article 3.1 discussed below.
     In its opinion on Norway, ACFC/INF/OP/I (2003) 003, the Committee takes a similar line to that for Denmark, pointing out (paragraph 19) that recognition as an indigenous people does not exclude persons from the group concerned from benefiting under the Framework Convention, and that protection under the latter convention is available should such persons wish to rely on it. Comments on the Committee opinion by the government of Norway (GVT/COM/INF/OP/I (2003) 003) note the

government will continue its dialogue with the Saami Parliament with a view to ensuring that the Framework Convention and the treaties designed for indigenous peoples are not construed as mutually exclusive regimes. See also the opinion on Ukraine, ACFC/INF/OP/I (2002) 010, paragraph 19 concerning preferred self-descriptions of the Crimean Tatars as "indigenous people".

74.   The text of Article 27 is set out above. In Human Rights Committee discussions (CCPR/C/SR.1533), members considered that "minority status is not dependent on residence in certain regions" (Mavromattis, paragraph 42), and asked why the favourable treatment of the German minority is not considered as discrimination (Evatt, paragraph 63). A question was asked on what were the criteria for minority status (Bhagwati, paragraph 77), and another committee member (Evatt) suggested that Denmark needed to develop greater understanding of the principles of Article 27 (CCPR/C/SR.1534, paragraph 62). The concluding observations did not carry through these remarks.

75.   See remarks above on the initial report of Switzerland. References were made to "minorities within minorities" in the initial report of Finland, 16 February 1999, p. 5. In its opinion (paragraph 17) of 22 September 2000 on Finland, ACFC/INF/OP/I (2001) 002, the Advisory Committee commented "Taking into account the level of autonomy enjoyed and/or the nature of the powers exercised by the Province of Åland, the … Committee is of the opinion that the Finnish-speaking population there could also be given the possibility to rely on the protection provided by the … Convention as far as the issues concerned are within the competence of the Province of Åland". However, reference should also be made to the comments by the Finnish Government (p. 3) on the opinion of the Committee which seem to nuance the governmental approach of the notion of "minority within a minority" with respect to the Finnish-speaking people of the Province of Åland.

76.   Ibid., p. 7.

77.   For example in the initial report of Lithuania p. 13, "Lithuanian legislation does not contain any definition of the concept of a national minority or a group of persons recognised to be a national minority. In Lithuania there are no linguistic or ethnic groups which are not considered national minorities."

78.   See remarks on the "newly developing Russian minority" in the initial report of the Slovak Republic, p. 11. The statement made by Ireland in its initial report is instructive: "Ireland … recognises that the definition of what constitutes a national minority is not fixed in international law or in the Framework Convention. The definition of what constitutes a national minority is therefore dynamic. Ireland recognises that the number and composition of national minorities in a State may change and develop over time, *always being subject to the individual's right to consider him or herself as a member of a national minority*" – Initial report, p. 3 (emphasis added). A flexible approach is also adumbrated concerning the traveller community of Ireland, apropos of which the report states that "The government fully accepts the right of travellers to their cultural identity, regardless of whether they may be described as an ethnic group or national minority" – ibid., p. 12.

79.   Romanian initial report, p. 15.

80.   Declaration made on ratification, 21 August 1998 – Council of Europe website, 21.01.2000.

81.   Ibid.

82.   The Advisory Committee has intimated that constitutional designations and nomenclature are not decisive for the purposes of the Convention. Thus, in the case of the Maronite community in Cyprus, described in the state report as a religious group, despite their specific ethnic origin and language in addition to religion, the

Committee invited the state (opinion on Cyprus, ACFC/INF/OP/I (2002) 004, paragraph 19) "to re-examine the question of the designation of the Maronites as simply a religious group".

83. Article 19.*c.*

84. See in general, F.G. Jacobs and R.C.A. White, *The European Convention on Human Rights* (Oxford: Clarendon Press, second edition, 1996), Chapter 22.

85. General Comment No. 24 (52), CCPR/C/21/Rev.1/Add.6, 11 November 1994, paragraph 17. See also Council of Europe Committee of Ministers Recommendation No. R (99) 13, on responses to inadmissible reservations to international treaties, 18 May 1999: the recommendation charts models of response by states to reservations of dubious legality.

86. Article 2.1.*d* of the Vienna Convention.

87. Remarks of Evatt in the Human Rights Committee, above.

88. Greco-Bulgarian Communities case, above, Introduction.

89. General Comment No. 23 (50), UN Doc. A/49/40, pp. 107-110, paragraph 5.2.

90. "Nor should interpretative declarations or reservations seek to remove an autonomous meaning to Covenant obligations" – Human Rights Committee, General Comment No. 24, paragraph 19.

91. The state reports identify many minority groups whose numbers are small and whose existence is precarious. In the case of the Maronites of Cyprus, the Advisory Committee recommended that the government pay particular attention to them in view of their low numbers and dispersed population – Opinion on Cyprus, paragraph 29. In its opinion on Armenia, ACFC/INF/OP/I (2002) 001, the Committee took the view, in paragraph 21, that in the case of some ethnic groups, "the mere fact that the individuals belonging to these groups have no representative organisations should not lead to their exclusion from the right to benefit from the protection of the Framework Convention".

92. For a short account of controversies, see Robin Cohen, "The Making of Ethnicity: A Modest Defence of Primordialism", in E. Mortimer with R. Fine (eds.), *People, Nation and State: The Meaning of Ethnicity and Nationalism* (London and New York: I.B. Tauris, 1999), pp. 3-11. See also the extracts from Geertz, Eller and Couglan, and Grosby, in J. Hutchinson and A.D. Smith (eds.), *Ethnicity* (Oxford and New York: Oxford University Press, 1996), pp. 40-56.

93. The role of the group in deciding membership is captured in the definition of indigenous peoples of UN Special Rapporteur J. Martinez-Cobo, UN Doc. E/CN.4/Sub.2/1986/7/Add.4, paragraphs 378-80. See also J.J. Corntassel and T.H. Primeau, "The Paradox of Indigenous Identity: A Levels-of-Analysis Approach", *Global Governance*, Vol. 4, No. 2 (1998), pp. 139-56. Compare the statement by Sweden – under the heading of "Self-identification", the initial report (p. 5) states that for purposes of Swedish law on national minorities, "The individual *and also the group* should have a desire and ambition to retain their identity" (emphasis added).

94. Document of the Copenhagen Meeting of the Conference on the Human Dimension of the CSCE 1990, emphasis added.

95. In its opinion on Slovakia (ACFC/INF/OP/I (2001) 001, paragraph 16), the Advisory Committee expressed concern about reports suggesting that non-voluntary collection of ethnic data is carried out, stating that "collection of personal data on individuals' affiliation with a particular national minority without their consent and without adequate legal safeguards would not be in compliance with Article 3 of the Convention, which also contains the right not to be treated as a person belonging to a national minority". The Committee has been much exercised by the phenomenon of compulsory registration of individuals in censuses, etc., as members of particular ethnic groups, pointing out that the right not to be treated as a member of a minority is protected in the Convention. See also the opinions on Croatia, ACFC/INF/OP/I (2002) 003, paragraph 18; on Estonia, ACFC/INF/OP/I (2002) 005, paragraph 19; Germany, ACFC/INF/OP/I (2002) 008; paragraph 21; and Ukraine, paragraphs 22-23. In a number of instances the opinions invoke Committee of Ministers Recommendation No. (97) 18 concerning the protection of personal data collected and processed for statistical purposes.

96. Ibid., paragraph 35.

97. Ibid., paragraph 36. In the case of Cyprus, the Advisory Committee criticised the position whereby members of religious groups (Latins, Maronites, Armenians) which had opted to join the larger "communities" (Greek and Turkish) of Cyprus, were, as individuals, permitted to leave that "community" but only if they joined the other "community" – opinion on Cyprus, paragraph 18.

98. Compare the views of the Human Rights Committee in *Lovelace v. Canada* in UN Doc. A/36/40 (1981), 166-75, paragraph 14. One of the present authors commented on the case that, while "a certain threshold weight may be accorded to 'self-definition as a member of a minority' by ... [the Human Rights Committee's] statement, that criterion is not absolute" – P. Thornberry, "The UN Declaration on the Rights of Persons belonging to Minorities, etc.", in A. Phillips and A. Rosas (eds.), *Universal Minority Rights* (Turku/Åbo and London: Åbo Akademi and Minority Rights Group, 1995), pp. 13-76, at p. 23.

99. General Recommendation VIII 1990; text in UN Doc. CERD/C/365, 11 February 1999, p. 7.

100. The attitude of the Permanent Court of International Justice to such questions was that it "would not be in conformity with the true construction of the provisions of the Minorities Treaties to consider as excluded the extension of the advantage of protection stipulated on behalf of minorities to persons who in fact do not belong to a minority ... on the other hand, such an extension cannot be presumed" – PCIJ Ser A/B No. 29, 33.

101. ACFC/SR (99) 9, p. 13.

102. Initial report, p. 15.

103. Initial report, ACFC/SR (99) 10, p. 33.

104. Ibid.

105. Ibid., p. 35. On this "cuckoo-problem", the Advisory Committee stated in its opinion on Hungary (ACFC/INF/OP/I (2001) 004, paragraph 52) that it shared the Hungarian concern, noting that a number of creative solutions had been proposed which, "whilst not going so far as to introduce a form of ethnic registration, would allow for this risk to be reduced. The ... Committee considers that the Hungarian authorities should actively pursue such remedies in order to avoid the credibility of the system as a whole being undermined".

106. Compare statements on cultures and the "right of exit" by C. Kukathas, "Are there any Cultural Rights?", and L. Green, "Internal Minorities and their Rights", in W. Kymlicka (ed.), *The Rights of Minority Cultures* (Oxford: Oxford University Press, 1995), pp. 228-56 and pp. 257-72.

107. Described in the preamble as "a source ... of enrichment for each society".

108. Explanatory report, paragraph. 31.

109. Compare the wording of the UN Declaration on the Rights of Persons Belonging to Minorities.

110. Compare ILO Convention No. 169 on Indigenous and Tribal Peoples in Independent Countries 1989 with the Framework Convention.

111. The formulation is close to Parliamentary Assembly Recommendation 1201, which refers in Article 3.2 to enjoying rights "individually or in association with others".

112. Explanatory report, paragraph. 37.

113. This issue is explored in P. Jones, "Human Rights, Group Rights, and Peoples' Rights", *Human Rights Quarterly*, Vol. 21 (1999), pp. 80-107.

114. Dimitrov describes the Convention approach as "an attempt to impair the collective dimension" of the rights of members of minorities – ibid., p .150.

115. Explanatory report, paragraph 30.

116. "The Hungarian Parliament declared ... that it considers the right to national and ethnic identity to be a universal human right and that the special individual and collective rights of the national and ethnic minorities are fundamental freedoms ... the right to national and ethnic identity is a fundamental human right to which both individuals and communities are entitled" – Hungary, Initial report, p. 35.

117. W.A. McKean, *Equality and Discrimination under International Law* (Oxford University Press, 1983).

118. This observation is subject to the widening of the ECHR in consequence of Protocol No. 12, discussed in Chapter 1.

119. See Human Rights Committee, General Comment 18 (37), text in UN Doc. HRI/GEN/1/Rev.3, pp. 26-29, especially paragraph 12. It is clear from its extensive practice that the Advisory Committee looks at discrimination in all areas of life, including economic, social and cultural life, encompassing the private as well as the public sphere, and that de facto discrimination is accounted for as well as discrimination in law. We may observe that in the implementation of Article 4 of the Convention, taking together the state reports, the opinions of the Committee and resolutions of the Committee of Ministers, the shapes and forms of discrimination encountered are drearily familiar, focusing heavily on Roma in virtually all aspects of existence, though reporting states also outline strenuous efforts to combat the widespread discrimination against this community. See also Chapter 4 of the present work. See the various entries under Article 4 in: Secretariat of Framework Convention, *Compilation of ACFC Opinions Article by Article*, ACFC/I/Secr (03) 001, March 2003. The Committee has indicated to a number of countries that it favours widening of the scope of anti-discrimination legislation, and that there should be effective monitoring of legislation in this field: see as examples, the Opinions on Croatia, paragraphs 23 and 24; Estonia, paragraphs 21-23.

120. Article 4.3.

121. Cf. The comment in the initial report of Norway (p. 3): "In its Report to the Storting, the Government strongly condemns the abuses committed against the Romani people/Travellers. Moreover, the Government regrets the Norwegianisation policy to which all the national minorities have been subjected, and apologises on behalf of the state for the way in which the minorities have been treated."

122. Compare Articles 1.4 and 2.2 of the International Convention on the Elimination of All Forms of Racial Discrimination.

123. Explanatory report, paragraph 39.

124. UN Doc. A/49/40, Vol. 1, Annex V.

125. W. Kymlicka, *Multicultural Citizenship: A Liberal Theory of Minority Rights* (Oxford: Clarendon Press, 1995), p. 4.

126. McKean, op. cit., p. 288.

127. Dimitrov, op. cit., p. 157.

128. Article 5.2. Hence for example the warning by the Advisory Committee in the case of Estonia, where the amount of instruction in Russian was drastically reduced, that "the implementation of the reform must be carried out in a manner that contributes to the integration of persons belonging to national minorities but not their assimilation" – opinion on Estonia, paragraph 50.

129. The identity of some indigenous groups may be intimately bound up with rights over lands, an aspect which has been recognised by the Advisory Committee – opinion on Norway, paragraph 79. The Committee has encouraged greater financial and other support for cultural development. See, for example, the opinions on Armenia, paragraph 36; Austria, paragraph 27; Cyprus, paragraph 29; Italy, paragraphs 28-34. In the case of Germany, deep concern was expressed (Committee opinion, paragraph 32) on the effects on the Sorb population of displacement resulting from the dissolution of a municipality, leading to the observation that: "As the forced dissolution of municipalities in which minorities reside is undeniably likely to make the preservation of their identity more difficult, it is essential, for such action to be compatible with Article 5 of the ... Convention, that it is taken only as a last resort, when there is no alternative." The comments of the government of Germany, GVT/COM/INF/OP/I (2002) 009, insisted that conditions had been created to enable the inhabitants to maintain their cultural identity. See references in Chapter 1 to *Noack v. Germany*.

130. Article 1.1.

131. Copenhagen Document, paragraph 32.

132. Article 4.2.

133. For a selection of authors, see H.J. Steiner and P. Alston (eds.), *International Human Rights in Context: Law, Politics, Morals* (Oxford: Clarendon Press, second edition 2000), pp. 323-402.

134. Explanatory report, paragraph 44. In 1994, the CAHMIN promised an elaboration of the fundamental elements of cultural identity – CAHMIN (94) 9, Report of the 2nd Meeting, p. 3.

135. See remarks in the report of Slovakia on "value modification" in relation to Roma through education – Initial report, p. 27.

136. See Jacobs and White, op. cit., Chapter 19.

137. See the views of the Human Rights Committee in *Ilmari Lansman v. Finland*, UN Doc. A/50/40 (1995), 66-76, paragraph 9.3.

138. See above.

139. Preamble, Article 5, Article 6 and Article 17.

140. Copenhagen Document, paragraph. 32.2, 32.3 and 32.6.

141. For a restrictive reading of Article 8 on religion, see Czech Republic Initial report, ACFC/SR (99) 6, p. 27. In the case of the UK, the Advisory Committee commented on the absence of legislation against religious discrimination and on the limitations of the blasphemy laws, which extend only to Christians and not to other religions – opinion on the UK, ACFC/INF/OP/I (2002) 006, especially paragraphs 116, 117 and 135. In resolution RESCMN (2002) 9, the Committee of Ministers recommended further consideration to the development of comprehensive legislation against religious discrimination and reform of the blasphemy laws.

142. Explanatory report, paragraph 54. The Advisory Committee has taken the view that where states choose to teach about the dominant or state-recognised religion, the curriculum should ensure that the classes "adequately reflect [the] various religious backgrounds of the pupils" – opinion on Norway, paragraph 40.

143. On the words "sound radio" – they "do not imply any material difference in meaning from Article 10 ECHR" – ibid., paragraph 60.

144. The explanatory report notes that the inclusion of these requirements, which are not expressly mentioned in Article 10 ECHR, "was considered important for an instrument designed to protect persons belonging to a national minority" – paragraph 59.

145. Paragraph 62 of the explanatory report alludes to some helpful possibilities – the envisaged measures "could ... consist of funding for minority broadcasting or for programme productions dealing with minority issues and/or offering a dialogue between groups, or of encouraging, subject to editorial independence, editors and broadcasters to allow national minorities access to their media".

146. It may be observed that, particularly in connection with Article 6 of the Framework Convention, the Advisory Committee has pointed out the negative contribution of media outlets in fomenting intolerance against Roma, refugees and asylum-seekers, and other groups.
We may note in this connection that restrictive readings of the scope of the Convention cannot extend to such media "activities": the Convention's proscriptions of discrimination and promotion of tolerance must necessarily include protection for such groups, whether or not they are citizens of the state concerned. Hence the statement in respect of Austria that "the personal scope of Article 6 ... is wide and ... includes asylum-seekers and persons belonging to other groups that have not been traditionally residing in the country concerned" – Opinion on Austria, ACFC/INF/OP/ I (2002) 009, paragraph 32. See also the point on "Islamophobia" in the opinion on the UK, paragraph 51.

147. Explanatory report, paragraph 61. The paragraph also contains the observation that the right of persons belonging to minorities to seek funds for the establishment of media is not referred to specifically because it was considered self-evident.

148. Article 32 ILO Convention No. 169 on indigenous and tribal peoples.

149. Compare Article 2.5 of the UN declaration on the rights of persons belonging to minorities, which uses the term "citizens" of other states.

150. J. Robinson et al., *Were the Minorities Treaties a Failure?* (New York: Institute of Jewish Affairs, 1943), various references therein.

151. The Hague and Oslo recommendations – on minority education and language rights respectively – usefully subsume global and European standards in these areas (Foundation on Inter-Ethnic Relations, 1996 and 1998). Texts may be found on http://www.hcnm.org.

152. Article 16 imparts a measure of integrity to minority areas – see below.

153. Finland refers to Åland and the Saami homeland as relevant areas: initial report, pp. 19-20.

154. Paragraph 3 of Article 10 – which provides a right to be informed of reasons for arrest, etc., – adds little or nothing to the body of minority rights. The paragraph is satisfied by proceedings in the language understood by a person arrested, etc., not necessarily a minority language. Compare Articles 5 and 6 ECHR, and Article 9 of the Charter for Regional or Minority Languages. On the relationship between freedom of expression and the use of language, see Introduction on the ECHR.

155. Explanatory report, paragraph 63.

156. Ibid., paragraph 64.

128

157. Ibid., paragraph. 65.

158. Article 15 supports this view.

159. UN Committee on Economic, Social and Cultural Rights, General Comment 3 (Fifth session, 1990), *Compilation of General Comments and General Recommendations adopted by Human Rights Treaty Bodies*, UN Doc. HRI/GEN/1/Rev.3, 15 August 1997, pp. 61-65.

160. For comment on provisions in Danish law requiring registration of names with the state church, see the Advisory Committee opinion on Denmark, paragraph 32. According to the Committee of Ministers, the situation merited review: RESCMN (2002) 2.

161. Article 11, paragraph 2.

162. In this case dependent on being traditionally inhabited by substantial numbers of persons belonging to minorities – unlike Article 10.2, inhabitation and numbers are cumulative requirements.

163. Ibid., paragraph 3. Hence the welcome for an interpretation by the Austrian Constitutional Court that a threshold of 10% minority inhabitation of an area over a long period was sufficient to entitle the inhabitants to bilingual topographical indications as "entirely in keeping with Article 11, paragraph 3 of the Convention": Committee opinion on Austria, paragraph 50. The Committee observed, however, (paragraph 49) that Article 11, paragraph 3, was a flexible provision, which did not set minimum percentages.

164. Explanatory report, paragraph 68. See also R. Hofmann, "A Presentation of the Framework Convention ... and its Contribution to the Protection of Minority Languages", in *Implementation of the European Charter for Regional or Minority Languages* (Strasbourg: Council of Europe, 1999), pp. 21-24, at p. 23.

165. Oslo Recommendation 1 and explanatory report.

166. This applies for example to non-Slovak female suffixes. Thus, the "female surname of a person other than Slovak nationality is written without the grammatical ending of Slovak declination" – in the event of various requests to that effect: initial report of Slovakia, p. 23. This is a question relating to linguistic systems. The Advisory Committee referred, in its opinion on Slovakia (paragraph 37), to "disturbing reports that the Slovak form of a surname is still imposed in some instances on women belonging to national minorities", advising the government to review the situation and take appropriate measures. In its comments (GVT/COM/INF/OP/I (2001) 004), the government of Slovakia requested concrete references to the cases highlighted in the Advisory Committee's opinion.

167. See the opinion of the Advisory Committee on Norway, paragraph 48 – the possibility of reverting to original names changed under policies of "Norwegianisation" should apply "not only to situations where the person at issue was himself/herself directly the subject of a forced change of surname but also to cases where the ancestors of the person were forced to change their name." The initial report of Sweden (p. 22) outlines the unusual case whereby, despite a regime of "names" legislation and the origin of claimants, "Assyrians/Syrians have been granted permission to adopt Assyrian/Syrian family names of which they were deprived in Turkey around the year 1917".

168. Explanatory report, paragraph 69.

169. See initial report of Finland, p. 22; initial report of Hungary, p. 99. In the case of Estonia, the Advisory Committee was concerned with a provision of the Language Act which provided that public signs, signposts, announcements, notices and advertisements were to be in Estonian, commenting that the provision appeared to be very wide. In the view of the Committee (opinion on Estonia, paragraph 43): "Bearing in mind that the expression "of a private nature" in Article 11 ... refers to all that is not official, there should not be a prohibition to use a minority language ... in a sign, poster or an advertisement of a private enterprise by a person belonging to a national minority". The government responded that there was no interference with minority language signs unless a public interest was involved. In RESCMN (2002) 8, the Committee of Ministers observed that "Despite certain recent improvements in the relevant legislation, there remain shortcomings with respect to the use of minority languages, including as regards private signs visible to the public".

170. Estonia requires place names in Estonian, unless an exception is "justified historically" – initial report, p. 50; Finland adopts the lowest percentage rule for a minority population in a municipality to trigger bilingual signage rules – 8% minority inhabitation – as well as all municipalities where over 3 000 inhabitants speak the other official language – initial report, pp. 22-23; Romania opts for 20% habitation – initial report, p. 38; Slovakia also operates a 20% minority settlement rule for road signs – initial report, p. 24; Ukraine appears to require a majority in a locality of members of a national minority – initial report, p. 26; UK rules are generally permissive and devolve to local bodies (in Northern Ireland, adding a language implicates the agreement of the occupiers of a street) – initial report, p. 37.

171. Among reporting states, Denmark (initial report, p. 37) uniquely raises the issue of road safety for bilingual signs – a novel and highly questionable claim. The Advisory Committee (Opinion, paragraph 34) states that it "is dismayed by and rejects" the Danish view.

172. The issue of Roma education in particular has been addressed by the Committee of Ministers in Recommendation No. R (2000) 4, 3 February 2000. Among others, the Ministers recommend (paragraph 8) that educational policies in favour of Roma/Gypsy children "should be implemented in the framework of broader intercultural objectives, taking into account the particular features of the Romani culture and the disadvantaged position of many Roma/Gypsies in the member states".

173. See for example Article 4 of the UN Declaration on the Rights of Persons belonging to Minorities, paragraph 34 of the OSCE Copenhagen Document, and Articles 27 and 31 of ILO Convention No. 169 on Indigenous and Tribal Peoples.

174. Explanatory report, paragraph. 71. The Advisory Committee recommended that Albania consider including the teaching of tolerance in schools as a means of reducing discrimination against Roma and Egyptians in the country: opinion on Albania, ACFC/INF/OP/I(2003) 004, paragraphs 39-40.

175. Opinion on Finland, paragraph 36; on Norway, paragraph 53; on Romania, paragraph 54.

176. Opinion on Albania, paragraph 57; on Croatia, paragraph 47.

177. Opinion on Austria, paragraph 56; on Germany, paragraph 55.

178. Article 14.1.

179. Article 14.2 and 14.3. The explanatory report (paragraph 78) observes that "knowledge of the official language is a factor of social cohesion and integration". The Advisory Committee has made it clear that adequate resources must be dedicated by the State to the teaching of the State language for national minorities – opinion on Armenia, paragraph 74.

180. Opinion on Croatia, paragraph 51; opinion on Armenia, paragraph 71.

181. In one case, the Committee considered that a minimum requirement of 20 pupils to run a class offering minority language teaching was very high – opinion on Germany, paragraph 60.

182. Opinion on the UK, paragraph 91.

183. Explanatory report, paragraph 72.

184. Here, the Hague recommendations make two pertinent points: i. the setting up of private schools should not be inhibited by unduly burdensome regulations (Recommendation 9); ii. minority education institutions (or promoters) are entitled to seek funding from the state or elsewhere (Recommendation 10). A number of states report that they subsidise private minority education – Czech Republic, initial report, pp. 35-36; Denmark, initial report, p. 40; Hungary, initial report, pp. 120-22; Slovakia, initial report, p. 29; UK, initial report, p. 32. The Advisory Committee has encouraged states that subsidise the schools of some minorities to expand the practice to include other groups – opinion on Germany, paragraph 56. For a broad review, see *Report on the Linguistic Rights of Persons belonging to National Minorities in the OSCE Area* (The Hague: OSCE High Commissioner on National Minorities, March 1999).

185. The UN Declaration on Minorities is also ambiguous on this point; the Copenhagen Document is clearer.

186. The fact that there is a general provision on language learning in paragraph 1 of Article 14 suggests that the provisions in paragraphs 2 and 3 of that article, which are restricted to minority areas, must add something significant to the basic right in paragraph 1. This should mean the right to have education (instruction) through the medium of the minority language, subject to the conditions in paragraphs 2 and 3. We may call this the strong conclusion. The distinction between paragraphs cannot imply, as the explanatory report appears to suggest (paragraph 74), that the state under paragraph 1 is in effect obliged to do nothing. The explanatory report does not draw the strong conclusion in respect of paragraphs 2 and 3, though it concedes (paragraph 77) that bilingual education may be a means of fulfilling convention requirements.

187. The Hague Recommendations 11-18 and explanatory report.

188. In which respect, see Parliamentary Assembly Recommendation 1353 (1998), 27 January 1998, on access of minorities to higher education – see further, Chapter 8. In practice, the Advisory Committee appears to consider any under-representation of minorities in institutions of higher education to be contrary to the right to equal opportunities in access to education at all levels as set out in Article 12 (3) – opinion on the UK, paragraph 85. Under certain circumstances the Convention may require the creation of multicultural universities where languages other than the state language are used as the medium of instruction; initiatives to set up such institutions should be pursued through consultation with the groups concerned – opinion on Romania, paragraph 55; on Ukraine, paragraph 61. For approval of reserving places for Roma students at institutions of higher education, see opinion on Romania, ACFC/INF/OP/I (2002) 001, paragraph 57; and on Moldova, ACFC/IJNF/OP/I (2003) 002, paragraph 72.

189. Dimitrov, op. cit., p. 173.

190. The anxieties of governments – and the need for balance – are reflected in the Romanian Law on Education (1995, as amended), Article 12.2 of which provides that the "organisation and content of education shall not be structured according to exclusivist and discriminatory criteria of an ideological, political, religious or ethnic nature". Such provisions can result in the disablement of institutions of minority education. Accordingly, the provision (necessarily) adds that "[e]ducational units and institutions established for religious or linguistic reasons in which education is provided in accordance with the choice of pupils' parents or legal guardians shall not be regarded as structured according to exclusivist or discriminatory criteria" – initial report, p. 42.

The Advisory Committee has been particularly critical of "special schools" for Roma – the placing of minority students in special schools designed for mentally handicapped students is, according to the Committee, an unacceptable phenomenon incompatible with the Convention. It may occur only when absolutely necessary and always on the basis of consistent, objective and comprehensive tests: opinion on Hungary, paragraph 41; on Croatia, paragraph 49; on Czech Republic, ACFC/INF/OP/I (2002) 002, paragraph 61; on Finland, paragraph 37; and on Albania, paragraph 39. The Committee, while respecting principles of parental choice, urges states to find ways of combating de facto segregation.

191. A. Eide, *Possible Ways and Means of Facilitating the Peaceful and Constructive Solution of Problems involving Minorities*, UN Doc. E/CN.4/Sub.2/1993/34, section II.

192. C. Taylor, *The Ethics of Authenticity* (Cambridge, Mass. and London: Harvard University Press, 1991).

193. Cf. Article 26.2 of the Universal Declaration of Human Rights: "Education shall be directed to the full development of the human personality and to the strengthening of respect for human rights and fundamental freedoms. It shall promote tolerance and friendship among all nations, racial or religious groups".

194. Human Rights Committee General Comment No. 23 (on Article 27 ICCPR), paragraph 7.

195. Compare paragraph 32.6 of the OSCE Copenhagen Document.

196. The Advisory Committee has frequently referred in its practice to participation in economic, cultural and social life, in addition to participation in the political sphere. See following footnote.

197. For example in the Roma context, "involvement of all parties concerned (ministry of education, school authorities, Roma families and organisations) in the design, implementation and monitoring of education policies for Roma/Gypsies should be promoted by the state": Committee of Ministers Recommendation No. R (2000) 4, paragraph 19. For expressions of concern over the limited participation of Roma in many spheres of life, including economic and cultural life, see, among others, Committee opinions on Albania, paragraph 75; on Austria, paragraph 71; on Croatia, paragraph 65; on Czech Republic, paragraph 71 and paragraphs on Articles 4, 5 and 6; on Finland, paragraph 48; on Italy, ACFC/INF/OP/I (2002) 007, paragraph 65 – see also Committee of Ministers resolution RESCMN (2002)10; on Norway, paragraph 63; on Romania, paragraph 69.

198. See particularly the report of the OSCE Meeting of Experts on National Minorities, Geneva, 1991. See also Eide, op. cit., paragraphs 206-09, and his 1992 progress report – UN Doc. E/CN.4/Sub.2/1992/37, paragraphs 124-26 and paragraphs 140-45.

199. Consultation may not necessarily amount to the "effective participation" referred to in Article 15: see for example the opinion of the Advisory Committee on Cyprus, paragraph 41.

200. Explanatory report, paragraph 80.

201. See also "Overview of forms of participation of national minorities in decision-making processes in seventeen countries", prepared by the Minorities Unit of the Council of Europe Directorate of Human Rights, February 1998.

202. Report, pp. 153ff.

203. Report, p. 54.

204. Report, p. 28.

205. Report, p. 45.

206. See for example, the reports of Croatia, Czech Republic, Estonia, Hungary, Romania, Slovakia and Ukraine.

207. Report, pp. 45-62.

208. Report, pp. 126-41.

209. Report, pp. 40-41.

210. Initial Report of Cyprus, pp. 59-61.

211. OSCE *Lund Recommendations on the Effective Participation of National Minorities in Public Life* (Foundation on Inter-Ethnic Relations, September 1999), Recommendation 1.

212. Ibid.

213. Ibid., p. 28.

214. Hence the bifurcation of the Lund Principles into "participation in decision-making" and "self-governance". The nostrum that exercise of powers at the local and regional levels is a positive good for minorities is not always borne out in practice. For example, in the field of education, the Advisory Committee has observed that local bodies do not always contribute to the achievement of national minority rights policies: see for example the opinion on Estonia, paragraph 51; on Austria, paragraph 64.

215. Explanatory report, paragraph 84. Compare paragraph 32.4 of the Copenhagen Document, and Article 2.5 of the UNDM.

216. Initial reports of: Croatia, pp. 165-67; Czech Republic, p. 43; Denmark, pp. 49-50; Estonia, p. 64; Finland, p. 29; Hungary, pp. 143-47; Italy, pp. 152-53; Romania, pp. 62-63; Slovak Republic, pp. 40-41; Ukraine, pp. 33-34; and the UK, p. 65.

217. This has been addressed in the Council of Europe through the adoption of the European Convention on Transfrontier Co-operation between Territorial Communities or Authorities and its two Additional Protocols: see further, Chapter 10.

218. For an appreciation of the issues, see various references in J. Jackson Preece, *National Minorities and the European Nation-States System* (Oxford: Clarendon Press, 1998).

219. UNDM, Article 8.4.

220. Copenhagen Document, paragraph 37.

221. See, for example, the opening paragraphs of General Comment 23 of the Human Rights Committee, above.

222. Explanatory report, paragraph 89.

223. Ibid.

224. Article 8.2.

225. Report, p. 35.

226. Report, p. 171.

227. Report, p. 64.

228. For a review of the initial working of the convention mechanism, consult the first, second and third activity reports of the Advisory Committee.

229. The convention and associated documents are brought together in *Framework Convention for the Protection of National Minorities: Collected Texts* (Strasbourg: Council of Europe, 1999).

230. Article 25.2.

231. Article 26.1.

232. See text above pertaining to note 21.

233. The Committee of Ministers also adopted an outline for reports to be submitted, etc. on 30 September 1998: op. cit., pp. 44-63. The outline pertains only to first reports, which are to contain part I on state policy, etc., and a part II which will provide a detailed article-by-article breakdown of state activity. In part II, information is to be presented in five categories: 1. narrative – a short description of government activity, potential developments, difficulties encountered, etc.; 2. legal – containing all relevant laws, regulations, etc.; 3. state infrastructure – an account of national, local and regional level authorities with relevant competences; 4. policy – policies, measures, statements, including public expenditure; and 5. factual – an evaluation of the effectiveness of measures through statistical survey and their scientific methods of assessment.

234. The question of additional members is dealt with in rule 19 – cases where a country report is examined and the committee has no member from that country.

235. Rule 6. The rule appears to be taken seriously – two members of the committee resigned following appointment to posts within the executive branch of their home countries, "arguing that their new positions would hurt their independence and impartiality": speech by the President of the Committee, Prof. Hofmann, to the Committee on Legal Affairs and Human Rights of the Parliamentary Assembly, 6 April 2000.

236. Rule 15.

237. Rule 20.

238. Ibid.

239. A complete list of resolutions of the Committee of Ministers concerning the Framework Convention is available on the Council of Europe website, under "national minorities".

240. The ministers' deputies, at their meetings on 7 February 2001 and 12-14 June 2001, took a number of procedural decisions, including setting a time-limit of four months for submission of state comments on the opinions of the AC, agreeing that the AC may be invited to be represented at meetings held for monitoring purposes under the convention in order to introduce the opinions and answer questions, and permitting the possible publication of an opinion and related state comments before the adoption of conclusions and recommendations by the CoM, "without prejudice" to the CoM's consideration of the opinion.

241. Rule 32. Such meetings shall be held in closed session. Ministers' deputies subsequently (3 May 2000) authorised the AC to hold meetings with NGOs and independent institutions in the context of visits conducted on the invitation of states party. The authorisation was granted for the entire monitoring cycle and relieves the AC of the need to request a separate mandate for each such meeting as required by rule 32.2. See comment in the second activity report, paragraph 25.

242. Rules of Procedure, op. cit. (see note 20 above), pp. 64-71.

243. Ibid., paragraph 17.

244. Ibid., paragraphs 19-20. "The custom and practice has gradually developed of states parties inviting the AC to visit ... every state to date has invited the AC when a visit has been thought to be valuable. These visits have become central in monitoring the FCNM and have transformed the methodology into a process of engagement of government and civil society, including national minorities": A. Phillips, *The Framework Convention for the Protection of National Minorities: A Policy Analysis* (London: Minority Rights Group, 2002), pp. 6-7. The author comments further (p. 7) that, at its meeting in February 2002, the AC considered an evaluation paper and concluded that country visits had become one of the most valuable parts of monitoring the implementation of the FCNM. See also the Third Activity Report, paragraph 18.

245. First Activity Report, paragraph 20.

246. Hofmann speech, 6 April 2000 (see note 235).

247. First activity report, paragraph 21.

248. Hofmann speech, 6 April 2000 (see note 235).

249. Second activity report, paragraph 22.

250. Ibid., paragraph 25.

251. See Introduction to the present work.

252. Article 4 in particular. For the broadening out of the ECHR, see the references to ECHR Additional Protocol No. 12. For the implications of differential treatment on the context of the ECHR, see references in the ECHR chapter to the Thlimmenos case.

253. For a development of this point, see P. Thornberry, "Images of autonomy and collective rights in international instruments on the rights of minorities", in M. Suksi (ed.), *Autonomy: Applications and Implications* (The Hague: Kluwer, 1998), pp. 97-124.

254. The European Court of Human Rights has stated that it is willing in principle to assume an interpretative role in the field of minority protection in the context of a draft additional protocol to the Framework Convention: opinion of the European Court, Appendix 6 to Decision of the Committee of Minsters at their 799th meeting – on 13 June 2002 – concerning Parliamentary Assembly Recommendation 1492 (2001). The various appendices to the Decision – from the CDDH, the Advisory Committee, the Committee of Experts of the European Charter for Regional or Minority Languages, the Committee on the rehabilitation and integration of people with disabilities, the Commissioner for Human Rights and the European Court – strongly suggest that the way forward in the implementation of the Framework Convention is through the consolidation of existing work, an increase in human and financial resources, stepping up international co-operation, and dovetailing the work of various bodies associated with the protection of national minorities, rather than through the development of new instruments – at least for the time being.

255. In its second activity report, the AC notes that "a spirit of trust and co-operation has continued to guide the relations between the two bodies involved in the monitoring of the Framework Convention". For a more elaborate assessment of a generally very fruitful co-operation, see Phillips, op. cit. (in note 244), pp. 5, 7 and 8.

Chapter 3

The European Charter for Regional or Minority Languages[1]

Language is the perfect instrument of Empire
Antonio de Nebrija[2]

Genesis of the Languages Charter

The situation of regional or minority languages (R/M languages) has been a matter of concern to the Council of Europe for many years.[3] The Standing Conference of Local and Regional Authorities of Europe (now the Congress of Local and Regional Authorities of Europe) decided to take up the question and, following a survey of the actual situation of regional and minority languages in Europe, and a public hearing involving representatives of some forty language-speaking groups, began the process of drafting an instrument.[4] In Resolution 192 (1988), the Standing Conference proposed the text of a charter designed to have the status of a convention.[5]

The Standing Conference's initiative was supported by the Parliamentary Assembly in Opinion No. 142 (1988) which, among other things, expressed the belief that the charter appended to Resolution 192:

> *a.* is sufficiently flexible to be applied to the widely different situations throughout Europe without interfering with the territorial integrity or official languages of contracting states;

> *b.* contains basic conditions for protecting and initiating a revival of these languages and represents a practical and necessary first step in this direction.[6]

The opinion also stressed the fact that the draft charter concerns languages and not linguistic minorities.[6] The explanatory report elaborates that the charter:

> sets out to protect and promote regional or minority languages, not linguistic minorities ... emphasis is placed on the cultural dimension and the use of a regional or minority language in all the aspects of the life of its speakers. The Charter does not establish any individual or

collective rights ... Nevertheless, the obligation of the parties with regard to the status of these languages and the domestic legislation which will have to be introduced ... will have an obvious effect on the situation of the communities concerned and their individual members.[8]

The Committee of Ministers subsequently established an Ad hoc Committee of Experts on Regional or Minority Languages in Europe (CAHLR) with responsibility for drafting a charter, bearing the Standing Conference's text in mind. The CAHLR began work in 1989 and submitted the final text in 1992.

The European Charter for Regional or Minority Languages (the Languages Charter) was adopted as a convention by the Committee of Ministers at the 478th meeting of the ministers' deputies on 25 June 1992 and opened for signature on 5 November 1992. The Charter requires ratifications by five member states of the Council of Europe to bring it into force;[9] slow progress in ratifying meant that it came into force only on 1 March 1998. The Charter has received seventeen ratifications: Armenia, Austria, Croatia, Cyprus, Denmark, Finland, Germany, Hungary, Liechtenstein, the Netherlands, Norway, Slovakia, Slovenia, Spain, Sweden, Switzerland and the United Kingdom; twelve other states have signed but not yet ratified.[10]

In their initial reports under the charter,[11] a number of states have explained their reasons for ratifying. Switzerland refers to national and international considerations. From the national aspect, the preservation of "quadrilingualism" is key; internationally, ratification flows from the fact that "the Charter constitutes a fundamental building block in the construction of a Europe based on respect for cultural diversity".[12] The declaration contained in the instrument of ratification of Liechtenstein states that there are no regional or minority languages in Liechtenstein in the sense of the charter; the initial report of Liechtenstein explains that ratification expresses the importance Liechtenstein attaches to the Charter "as an instrument for the protection and promotion of regional or minority languages as a threatened part of the European cultural heritage".[13]

Philosophy and basic concepts

The explanatory report provides an illuminating discussion of the basic orientations of the Languages Charter. The report's point concerning the omission of individual and collective rights has proved encouraging to the government of France, which made the following statement on signature:

> In so far as the aim of the Charter is not to recognise or protect minorities but to promote the European language heritage, and as the use of the

term 'groups' of speakers does not grant collective rights, the French government interprets the instrument in a manner compatible with the Preamble to the Constitution which ... recognises only the French people, composed of all citizens, without distinction as to origin, race or religion.[14]

The explanatory report explains that the Charter does not conceive of regional, minority and official languages "in terms of competition or antagonism", but deliberately adopts an intercultural and multilingual approach "in which each category of language has its proper place".[15] The references to "intercultural"[16] and "multilingual" approaches echo the preamble to the Charter[16] – "stressing the value of interculturalism and multilingualism, and considering that the protection and encouragement of regional or minority languages should not be to the detriment of the official languages and the need to learn them".[17]

It is not entirely clear from this if "interculturalism and multilingualism" represent general values for whole societies including persons who are not users of regional or minority languages, though the syntax of the preambular paragraph suggests that general values are intimated.[18] To suggest less than this would indicate a "falling away" from the values of the Council of Europe, which cannot have been the drafting intention. Thus, a later paragraph in the preamble looks forward to the building of a Europe "based on the principles of democracy and cultural diversity" – an inclusive phraseology.

It is important that the Charter is not read as detracting from general values in its focus on the particular case (R/M languages). The value of intercultural principles as guidelines for integration processes, in a rapidly globalising age producing massive population flows, cannot be overestimated. This caveat is necessary because, as the explanatory report observes, the Charter "does not deal with the situation of new, often non-European languages which may have appeared in the signatory states as a result of recent migration flows"[19] – a limitation reflected in Article 1 on the definition of "regional or minority languages" (though Article 1 excludes "the languages of migrants",[20] whereas the report refers to "recent" migration flows).[21] That the narrower focus of the Charter is not to detract from greater values such as interculturalism should also follow from the Charter's "value-added" statement in Article 4: the Charter is not intended to detract from "existing regimes", domestic or international, which go further than the Charter.[22] The Charter's endorsement of a broad approach to interculturalism receives its clearest expression in Article 7.[23]

The terms "regional" and "minority" in relation to languages were used in the Charter in reference to less widespread languages. According to the explanatory report, "regional" denotes a language spoken in a limited part of the territory of a state, within which it may well be spoken by a majority of persons; "minority" languages are those spoken by persons dispersed throughout the state, or by "a group of persons, which, though concentrated on part of the territory of a state, is numerically smaller than the population in this region which speaks the majority language of the state". More importantly, "regional" and "minority" refer to factual criteria, and not to legal notions,[24] an affirmation of the parallel principle in the field of minority rights that the existence of minorities is a question of fact, not law. The Charter does not provide examples of regional or minority languages.[25]

Concise analysis

1. *Structure of the Charter*

The Languages Charter is a lengthy instrument. It comprises twenty-three articles, some of which are subdivided into paragraphs and sub-paragraphs. The text incorporates a preamble and five parts: I. General provisions; II. Objectives and principles; III. Measures to promote the use of regional or minority languages in public life; IV. Application of the Charter; V. Final provisions. As is normally the case in international instruments, the preamble explains the basic underpinnings of the Charter. The essential elements are: linguistic diversity is an important element of the European cultural heritage; this diversity needs special support; respect for diversity does not imply a policy of linguistic segregation – knowledge of official languages is necessary; the protection and promotion of R/M languages is carried out within the framework of the national unity and territorial integrity of European states.

While the Charter as a whole is not structured to recognise the linguistic rights of individuals, the preamble recalls that "the right to use a regional or minority language in private and public life is an inalienable right" conforming to the principles embodied in the ICCPR, and according to the spirit of the ECHR.[26] Pre-eminent in the case-law of the ICCPR is the case of *Ballantyne, Davidson and McIntyre v. Canada* (1993),[27] where the UN Human Rights Committee made the lapidary statement that a state "may choose one or more official languages, but it may not exclude, outside the spheres of public life, the freedom to express oneself in a language of one's choice".[28] The case-law of the ECHR does not distil this principle with equal clarity. The preamble to the Charter may be taken to suggest that the principle is latent in the ECHR and will emerge in due course.[29] The preamble also refers to the CSCE (OSCE), recalling the Final Act and the Copenhagen Document, both of which are concerned with minority issues in different ways.[30]

The Languages Charter is essentially concerned with the use of languages in public life "as it is self-evident that in the sphere of private life ... linguistic freedom is complete".[31] However, as a French observer noted:

> The Charter stresses the right to use languages in private and public life ... 'public life' automatically suggests the relations between individuals and the authorities (the justice system, public administration, etc). However, this is not all that is meant ... With the term 'public life', the Charter actually means the whole range of contacts people have outside their own homes, not only with the authorities ... but also in the fields of education, the media, business, banking and so on.[32]

2. *Definition and scope*

Article 1 sets out basic definitions for the purposes of the Charter:

a. 'regional or minority languages' means languages that are:

- traditionally used within a given territory of a state by nationals of that state who form a group numerically smaller than the rest of the state's population; and
- different from the official language(s) of that state;
- it does not include either dialects of the official language(s) of the state or the languages of migrants;

b. 'territory in which the regional or minority language is used' means the geographical area in which the said language is the mode of expression of a number of people justifying the adoption of the various protective and promotional measures provided for in this charter;

c. 'non-territorial languages' means languages used by nationals of the state which differ from the language or languages used by the rest of the state's population but which, although traditionally used within the territory of the state, cannot be identified with a particular area thereof.

The definition of relevant languages contains traces of earlier definition efforts, such as those by Capotorti in the field of minority rights, which emphasised numerical inferiority and nationality or citizenship of the state party.[33] The Charter does not give separate definitions of "regional" and "minority" languages – these are discussed in the explanatory report.

i. *Traditional use*

The term "traditionally used within a given territory", together with other indications in the Charter, is intended to distinguish between historical European languages and the languages of immigrants.[34] Little clarification is forthcoming from the report, which notes simply that the Charter is about historical languages, spoken over a long period in the state in question.[35] This is a somewhat open-ended criterion – there are no bright

141

white lines between the traditional and the recent. And what if a language was traditional, but has ceased to be used in a given territory?

Despite the use of the present tense, the term "traditionally occupied" in the ILO Convention concerning Indigenous and Tribal Peoples in Independent Countries (No. 169) – applying to lands – is interpreted to apply also to groups recently dispossessed from such lands.[36] By analogy, languages subject to recent processes of assimilation should not be ruled out of consideration under the charter: the right under the Framework Convention of persons deprived of traditional names to recover those names is another relevant comparator.[37] Any line between traditional and recent must logically be modified over a period of time in the life of the charter. To apply the Charter otherwise would be a futile exercise in attempting to freeze linguistic situations existing at the time of ratification.

ii. *Migrants*

Following the endorsement of traditional languages, Article 1 is explicit on its non-application to "the languages of migrants".[38] Since the general definition of R/M languages in Article 1 refers to "nationals of the State", it might be assumed that "migrants" in the same article refers to "non-nationals". However the explanatory report states that:

> The purpose of the Charter is not to resolve the problems arising out of recent immigration phenomena ... In particular, the Charter is not concerned with the phenomenon of non-European groups who have immigrated recently into Europe and acquired the nationality of a European state.

On the one hand, this is less restrictive than the text of the Charter, excluding only "recent" immigrants"; on the other, it is possibly more restrictive, since it excludes those acquiring the nationality of the host state. There are other problems with the explanation. For clarity, one might ask, if "non-Europeans" are excluded, what of "European" groups (such as migrating Roma) recently acquiring the nationality of a state party to the charter? And who are the "Europeans" and the "non-Europeans"?

Again, following the discussion above, there is no indication as to when – or if – a language can cease to be regarded as a language of migrants. Should we distinguish – as is the case elsewhere in the Council of Europe – "recent" immigration from "long-term immigration"? It is possible that the report introduces distinctions which are not present in the charter.[39] However if the exclusion of (some) languages of nationals reflects the true import of the charter, we arrive at the point where norms of non-discrimination on grounds of language affect the argument, bearing in mind that non-discrimination principles do not forbid all distinctions but only indefensible ones. One must presume therefore that the drafters of the Charter thought the distinctions it introduces defensible in the instant case.

iii. *Official language(s)*

The exclusion of official languages is not complete. According to Article 3, states can specify – besides regional or minority languages – an "official language which is less widely used on the whole or part of its territory" in applying Part III. Finland has recognised Swedish as such a language in its instrument of ratification.[40] In Switzerland, where "all the national languages are official languages",[41] the two official languages that meet the description "less widely used" are Romansh and Italian.[42] The position of official languages in European countries shows considerable variation. While many states have one or more official languages, some states have none.[44] In others, official status may be implicit.[45] In some cases, a language may be official only in a certain region of the state.[46] Although it is not crystal clear from Article 3 of the Charter whether the provision on less widely used official languages enjoys the benefits of Part II as well as Part III, the committee of experts in evaluating the report of Finland make extensive references to Swedish (a lesser-used official language) in presenting their account of Part II, observing specifically that it is covered by both Parts II and III.[47]

iv. *Dialects*

Article 1.*a* excludes from consideration "dialects of the official language(s) of the State". The explanatory report does not offer a set of criteria for distinguishing between languages and dialects,[48] insisting that the Charter "does not concern local variants or different dialects of one and the same language", while observing that the question "depends not only on strictly linguistic considerations, but also on psycho-sociological and political phenomena".[49] The report opts for a process point, noting that the application of the distinction "will be left to the authorities concerned within each state, in accordance with its own democratic processes, to determine at what point a form of expression constitutes a separate language".[50]

Such statements offer a wide margin of appreciation to state authorities. And how does the determination of the dialect/language distinction depend on "political phenomena"? What phenomena?[51] Confusion can arise at many levels – witness the debates on the differences between regional languages in France and "regional variations of French".[52] Additionally, the report appears to go beyond the text of the Charter in excluding dialects in general, not just dialects of the official language. This path has not been followed by the committee of experts, which digressed on the vulnerable situation of Inari and Skolt Saami in the case of the Saami language in Finland,[53] which is not "official", an urgency taken up by the Committee of Ministers, which recommended *inter alia* that "[s]pecial efforts should be devoted to pre-school and primary education and to making available the necessary teacher training and teaching materials for Skolt and Inari Saami which seem to be in danger of extinction".[54]

The above "determination" – like others in the Charter – does not operate outside a framework of rights. For example, when the language/dialect determination limits opportunities for language speakers to take advantage of the Charter, minority rights law provides that members of linguistic minorities have the right to participate in democratic processes attendant on such "determinations". The report's reference to "own democratic processes" must include the application of international standards, in line with Articles 4 and 5 of the charter.[55] In some cases, consultation processes to determine the status of a dialect/language have been fairly broad.[56] The committee of experts has advised that the state has a duty to inform R/M speakers of possibilities under the Charter and to give them the possibility of being consulted, even in cases where, according to the state report, speakers have not requested linguistic support.[57]

v. *Territory*

The Charter is heavily territorialised: "most of the measures which it advocates necessitate the definition of a geographical field of application other than the state as a whole".[58] There are two spatial concepts at work in the definition. In the first, the basic notion of territory in Article 1 is defined by the people, not the people by the territory – demography, not geography. If the focus is on the demography of language, then the application of the Charter may require action across state administrative or self-government boundaries. Speakers of an R/M language are not always neatly concentrated into a particular administrative area. If it were otherwise, a state could avoid the application of the Charter by splitting linguistic groups into fractions through administrative gerrymandering, in such a way that none of the groups would be sufficiently large to justify application.[59]

The second spatial concept, an area "justifying" the application of the charter, introduces a contrasting element. This space is normative, not demographic. No minimum number of people is required, only enough to justify the application of the Charter. In the latter case, the report observes that "the authors of the Charter avoided establishing a fixed percentage of speakers ... at or above which the measures ... should apply". Clearly, the two spatial concepts intersect, and the Charter should be applied in such a way as to maximise the range of application.[60] To act otherwise would not do justice to the Charter's mission to conserve and develop the European linguistic heritage.

vi. *Non-territorial languages*

As is evident from the definition in Article 1.*c*, the phrase "non-territorial" is essentially used in relation to languages where the speakers are not regionally identified. The Charter suggests limits on its applicability to such languages.[61] The explanatory report mentions Yiddish and Romany as examples,[62] pointing out that only a limited part of the charter can be applied to such languages.[63] Romani and Romanes are stated by Norway to be non-territorial languages.[64] In Finland, the term is applied to Roma/Gypsy, Russian and Tatar.[65] The "languages of the Gypsies and Yiddish" are the non-territorial languages of Switzerland.[66] Croatia recognises the existence of such languages (German, Hebrew, and Roma/Gypsy languages) but did not wish them to be included in the charter, making a reservation to Article 7.5.[67] The specifying of Romany in a number of reports shows beyond doubt that the language is part of the linguistic heritage of Europe. Despite the potential charter limitations on Romany deriving from its description as non-territorial, it is not inconceivable that much of the Charter could be applied to some Roma/Gypsy concentrations. The language is traditional in many countries, and the flexibility of the concept of territory in Article 1.*b* (above) allows elements of justice and need to enter calculations on whether Charter measures should be applied.[68]

3. *Basic undertakings*

In virtue of Article 2, each state party undertakes to apply Part II of the Charter to all the languages on its territory which come under the definition in Article 1. In essence, this is a question of fact. The report makes it clear that Part II "is general in scope and applies in its entirety to all regional or minority languages spoken on the territory".[69] One author comments that the state must apply Part II even if the regional or minority languages "are not mentioned in its ratification instrument; thus, a state may not refuse minimum protection ... by not recognising a ... language".[70] In this respect, the Article 1 definition of the relevant languages has paramount force.

On the languages specified at ratification, or at some other time, the obligation is to apply a minimum of thirty-five paragraphs (or subparagraphs) from Part III, including at least three each from Articles 8 and 12, and one each from Articles 9, 10, 11 and 13.[71] While such a system makes for a reasonable distribution of undertakings across a spectrum of language arenas, it implies a certain privileging of the articles on education (Article 8) and cultural activities and facilities (Article 12).

All specifying states appear to have accepted levels of commitment above the basic quota. As examples, Finland accepted sixty-five Part III provisions on behalf of Swedish, and fifty-nine provisions for Saami;[72] France specified thirty-nine provisions on signature;[73] The Netherlands accepts forty-eight.[74] In a careful note, the explanatory report admits the possibility that a state, without offending the spirit of the Charter, can recognise the existence of a relevant language, but decide not to extend to it the provisions of Part III, cautioning however that "the reasons which prompt a state to exclude a recognised ... language completely from ... Part III must be reasons compatible with the spirit, objectives and principles of the Charter".[75] Nevertheless, a number of states have taken this course.

As noted, Finland relates Part III to Swedish and Saami, and not to Russian, Romany and Tatar.[76] Hungary reports that, under the terms of its domestic legislation, some thirteen languages are spoken by minorities; Hungary has undertaken commitments in respect of six.[77] The selection of languages by Hungary is said to be based on languages with sufficient concentration in well-defined regions (Romanian, Slovene), or scattered languages which nevertheless have, "because of their numbers, a developed structure for native language education and cultural life".[78] The Part III commitments of Norway relate only to Saami, and not to the regional or minority Kven or Finnish.

4. *Existing regimes and obligations*

The Charter should not be construed as limiting or derogating from rights in the ECHR, nor should it affect more favourable provisions on regional or minority languages or the rights of persons belonging to minorities found in domestic law or relevant agreements.[79] In the words of the explanatory report, "the protection afforded by the Charter is additional to the rights and guarantees granted by other instruments".[80] Where competing provisions exist on the same subject, the most favourable should apply.[81] Neither is the Charter to be interpreted as implying a right to engage in action contrary to the Charter of the United Nations "or other obligations under international law, including the principle of the sovereignty and territorial integrity of states".[82] The explanatory report links this principle to sovereignty-threatening actions by other states with a special interest in the language, or action by users of the language. It is difficult in principle to see the relevance of the limitation to speakers of a language as speakers. Threats to sovereignty would come, if at all, from the content of speech, not its linguistic medium. If it were otherwise, linguistic freedoms could be negated on the basis of vague assertions of sovereignty.

5. *Objectives and principles*

Part II of the Charter consists of Article 7 on the "Objectives and principles" which constitute the necessary framework for the preservation of regional or minority languages. In view of its broad application – to all languages satisfying the definition in Article 1 – Article 7 is "of fundamental importance for understanding 'the spirit' and ideological basis of the whole instrument".[83] The basic principles are: recognition of the language(s) as an expression of cultural wealth;[84] respect for the geographical area of each regional or minority language – the Charter is against devising administrative divisions which would constitute an obstacle to the survival of the languages;[85] the need for positive action for the benefit of these languages;[86] guarantee of the teaching and study of the languages;[87] facilities for non-speakers of these languages to gain a knowledge of them;[88] relations between groups speaking a regional or minority language;[89] elimination of discrimination – the application of special measures for regional or minority languages is not an act of discrimination against users of other languages;[90] promotion of respect and understanding between linguistic groups;[91] establishment of bodies to represent the interests of regional or minority languages;[92] and application of the Charter to non-territorial languages – Article 7 can be applied to them "in a flexible manner, bearing in mind the needs and wishes, and respecting the traditions and characteristics, of the groups which use the languages concerned".[93]

Article 7 principles stand by themselves and inform and complement other provisions in the Charter. The principles also echo some parallel provisions in minority rights instruments. Linking with the spatial concepts discussed above, the report elaborates – in relation to Article 7 – that, while administrative divisions may not be congruent with linguistic territory, the Charter condemns:

> practices which devise territorial divisions so as to render the use or survival of a language more difficult or to fragment a language community among a number of ... units. If ... units cannot be adapted to the ... language, they must at least remain neutral and not have a negative effect on the language.[94]

While Article 8 deals in detail with education in relation to languages specified by the ratifying state, Article 7 requires that regional or minority languages be present "at all appropriate stages" in the education system, a principle which opens up a broad range of possibilities, depending upon what is appropriate for the language in question.[95] The article also promotes intercultural education, not just for minorities but

147

for all linguistic groups – the wider society – and encourages mass media to pursue the same objective.[96] The point on provision of facilities for speakers of languages other than minority languages implicitly carries an important intercultural component – the purpose is "to ensure greater mutual permeability between language groups".[97]

Article 7 further implies that linguistic minorities (the users/speakers as such) have a role. States shall take into consideration their "needs and wishes". This effectively suggests the right of members of minorities to "participation in decisions affecting them", elaborated in minority rights instruments.[98] As one commentator observes:

> Peaceful co-existence within civil society can be achieved only if all the participants are involved in decision-making and can thus assume responsibility for the results. This may be the charter's central element.[99]

The initial report of Hungary states that, in drawing up the report, the National and Ethnic Minorities Office involved, among others, the national self-governments of the Croats, Germans, Romanians, Serbs, Slovaks and Slovenes living in Hungary.[100]

The Charter objective of facilitating intra-country contacts between linguistic groups is recognised, with the necessary changes, in texts of minority rights.[100] This is also true of the pronouncement on discrimination – that the special measures are not in themselves discriminatory. As elsewhere, the question of what is or is not discriminatory boils down to a question of justification of differences in treatment.[102] The Committee of Experts made a pertinent observation on the changing face of the non-discrimination principle, noting in relation to Hungary that "the traditional conception of anti-discrimination policy as entailing assimilation" as applied to Roma/Gypsies "seems to have been only partly successful. Discrimination persists, but the majority of Roma people have lost their traditional culture and language, without becoming really integrated".[103]

Non-territorial languages

Article 7 suggests that despite the overall territorialisation of the Charter, the article's principles can be applied, with the necessary changes, to non-territorial languages. The question arises as to what measures can be so applied; what Article 7 principles do not presuppose a territorial base? Of the list in Article 7.1, it would appear that only 7.1.*b* suggests a case for exclusion in virtue of references to "geographical area" and "administrative divisions". But even this exclusion cannot be taken for granted in view of the flexibility of the geographical concepts in the charter.

In principle, therefore, with the possible exception of 7.1.*b*, all provisions of Article 7 can be applied to non-territorial languages. In the case of

Roma/Gypsy languages, recognition of their contribution to cultural wealth, access to culturally appropriate education, and incentives to understand and respect the Roma people are strongly indicated by the article, and the need for "resolute action" on the part of the authorities.[104] Finland provides an extensive account of Article 7 initiatives on the Roma under Article 7.1.*c*, to 7.1.*i*.[105]

6. *Measures to promote the use of regional or minority languages in public life*

This is the subject of a complex of provisions in Part III. Detailed provisions apply to the use of the languages in or with regard to: education;[106] the administration of justice;[107] administrative authorities and public services;[108] the media;[109] cultural activities and facilities;[110] economic and social life;[111] and transfrontier exchanges.[112] The provisions are complex, and not every aspect will be commented upon in detail. As noted above, the articles are patterned to offer a wide range of alternatives to the ratifying states – "a protection method consisting of a differentiated series of measures, ranging from maximal solutions to minimal solutions".[113] On the choice of languages and provisions for inclusion, the committee of experts observed in relation to Croatia:

> The instrument of ratification has been drawn up in such a manner as to provide exactly the same level of protection for all the seven languages under Part III ... The Charter, however, is constructed in such a way that the State can adapt the protection of the various languages to the real situation of each language ... The instrument of ratification indicates on the other hand that all the languages chosen should receive equal protection. This is however contrary to the actual situation of the languages.[114]

i. *Education – Article 8*

The provisions on languages in education in Article 8.1 are to be implemented "within the territory in which such languages are used, according to the situation of each of these languages", and "without prejudice to the teaching of the official language(s) of the State".[115] Article 8.1 sets out a pattern of choices for education at various levels – primary, secondary, technical and vocational education (TVE), higher education, and adult and continuing education. In the case of education at pre-school, the "menu" offers choices from:

 i. "making available" education in the relevant languages;

 ii. making available a "substantial part" of the education in the languages;

 iii. applying one of the measures in i and ii "to those pupils whose families request and whose number is considered sufficient";

149

    iv. if the public authorities have no direct competence in the field, "to favour and/or encourage the application of the measures in i to iii above".

This general pattern applies, with the necessary changes, to the various levels of education. The reference to sufficient numbers to validate a particular option "recognises that the public authorities cannot be required to take the measures concerned where the situation of the linguistic group makes it difficult to obtain the minimum number of pupils required to form a class", a requirement which "may be applied flexibly".[116] For primary, secondary and TVE levels, point iii above is replaced with a reference to the teaching of the language(s) "as an integral part of the curriculum". Changes are made to the basic scheme at secondary and TVE level, on the question of whose choice for language education is to be respected: the choice of the pupils concerned is posited as an alternative to parental choice, "where appropriate".[117] At university level, emphasis is placed on "providing facilities" for language study. The explanatory report notes that in certain states where numbers may be insufficient to justify university education in a particular language, agreements on recognition of diplomas are a possible practice.[118]

Article 8.1.*g* introduces a choice that stands alone, by which parties undertake "to make arrangements to ensure the teaching of the history and culture which is reflected by the regional or minority language". The report comments that "languages are often related to a separate history and specific traditions. This history and ... culture constitutes a component of Europe's heritage. It is ... desirable that non-speakers of the language should have access to it too".[119] The various choices in Article 8.1 are linked to the necessity for teacher training by Article 8.1.*h*, and the creation of a supervisory body to monitor progress in the language teaching area. The characteristics of such a body are not specified, though the kind of body envisaged in Article 7.4 would be appropriate, especially if it included representatives of language groups. The findings of such a body must be made public.[120]

Finally, Article 7 is echoed in 8.2 which envisages the possibility of language teaching outside areas where the language is traditionally used "at all the appropriate stages of education". The provision was drafted in the light of modern phenomena of social mobility including the migration of language speakers to large cities. Language teaching in such a case would apply only where numbers justify it.[121] The importance of the education component of the Charter has been emphasised:

> The more aware speakers of the majority language are of their country's language diversity, and the more freely and fully information on this question circulates, the more easily mutual respect and ... tolerance take root. It is education above all which enables people to develop these

qualities. It can institutionalise dialogue and transmit the knowledge which gives peoples a better understanding of linguistic and cultural diversity, helping them to see it, not as something to be feared, but as something which enriches.[122]

Patterns of specification of paragraphs and sub-paragraphs show considerable variation.[123] In relation to Article 8.1, weaker options predominate, except in relation to university education. Excluding the case of Liechtenstein, all states accepted 8.1.*g* and 8.1.*h* on the teaching of history and teacher training; states except Croatia, Slovakia and Switzerland accepted 8.2.

ii. *Judicial authorities – Article 9*

The pattern of possibilities in this case is predicated upon the number of residents of judicial districts justifying the measures,[124] the situation of the languages, "and on condition that the use of facilities afforded by the present paragraph is not considered by the judge to hamper the proper administration of justice". The latter appears to allow great discretion to state officials. It is placed in a favourable light by the report, which refers to possible misuse of the language facility – a concern which does not justify general restrictions, hence the role of the judge in specific cases. There is no reference in the Charter or the report to any duty to give reasons for making an exclusion, though this could be implied. It is important that the scope and possibilities of such an article are not nullified by restrictive judicial practice.

Article 9 applies to proceedings before criminal, civil and administrative courts, as well as to legal documents and statutes.[125] The article goes considerably beyond the provisions in general human rights instruments on the need for an accused person in a criminal case to understand the language of the court.[126] Such provisions are aspects of due process of law rather than minority rights. Even minority rights provisions typically do not extend beyond the criminal process,[127] although Parliamentary Assembly Recommendation 1201 (1993) is broader, as are the Oslo recommendations adopted under the sponsorship of the OSCE High Commissioner on National Minorities.[128] The justification for the facility is that, even if parties to a case can understand the language of the court, they may be better able to express themselves in their own language and thus serve better the administration of justice. This has implications for criminal cases, but also for other types of proceeding.

The options in Article 9 in the case of criminal proceedings are that, at the request of one party, the proceedings shall be conducted in the regional or minority language: to guarantee the accused the right to use the language, to provide that evidence, or other presentation, shall not be rejected because it is in a regional or minority language, and to produce documents in the language and interpretation without extra expense to the accused. Similar provisions are found, with the necessary changes, for other types of proceedings. Parties may also undertake not to deny the validity of legal documents drawn up in minority languages, and to make available in regional or minority languages "the most important national statutory texts", and "those particularly relating to users of these languages".

Article 9.*a*, 9.*b* and 9.*c* use the phrase "conduct the proceedings" in the minority language. The explanatory report observes that it is up to each state, "in the light of the particular characteristics of its judicial system, to determine the precise scope of the expression".[129] The provision on the validity of legal documents drawn up in minority languages "does not preclude a State from providing for additional formalities ... for example the need for a particular formula ... to be added in the official language".[130]

iii. *Administrative authorities and public services – Article 10*

The question of contact with administrative or self-governing authorities in minority languages is dealt with by, among others, the Framework Convention. The issue can be very controversial in some countries. From the viewpoint of bringing government closer to the citizen, localising or patriating the offices of state can engender feelings of belonging on the part of minorities. Conversely, obliging individuals always to respect only the language of the bureaucracy can have alienating effects. From the linguistic point of view, other justifications may be relevant:

> The integration of regional or minority languages in the work of admin-
> istrative or judicial authorities is an essential means of stimulating and
> modernising these languages, enabling them to display and develop
> their terminological range and full expressive potential.[131]

Article 10.1 applies to administrative districts where the number of minority language users justifies the measures. Parties undertake, as far as this is reasonably possible, to ensure that the administrative author-ities may use the language, ensure that officers use it, ensure that users of regional or minority languages receive a reply in that language, ensure that users may submit applications in the language, or ensure that users may validly submit documents in that language. The second set of options relates to local and regional authorities.[132] The third set of options relates to "public services provided by the administrative author-ities or other persons acting on their behalf".[133] These provisions are supplemented by undertakings relating to supplying translation or inter-pretation, and recruitment, training and deployment of officials to the particular language territory.[134]

Article 10.5 introduces another aspect, which has received separate treatment in minority rights instruments: the parties undertake "to allow the use or adoption of family names in ... regional or minority languages, at the request of those concerned". Article 10.5 should be construed as an additional encouragement to states to adopt a names regime – the right to a name in the minority language and to official recognition of the name is inscribed in the Framework Convention.[135] All ratifying states have exceeded their minima in relation to Article 10 and agreed to a relatively large number of undertakings. The names provision is one of the least controversial provisions and has been accepted by most ratifying states concerned for minority languages.[136]

iv. *Media – Article 11*

Provisions on the media apply to the extent that "the public authorities, directly or indirectly, are competent, have power or play a role in this field" and will respect "the principle of the independence and autonomy of the media".[137] The first set of options is qualified by the phrase "to the extent that radio and television carry out a public service mission".[138] The explanatory report explains that where there is such a mission, the state can make provision for the broadcasting of programmes in regional or minority languages; where there is no such mission, "the State can do no more than encourage and/or facilitate".[139] Accordingly, in the case of public service broadcasting, while there are lesser options (encourage/facilitate the station or channel; "make adequate provision" for programmes), the strongest option is to ensure the creation of at least one radio station and one television channel in the regional or minority languages. In the case of the private operators, the maximum option is to encourage/facilitate the setting up of such institutions.

Additional provisions apply to newspapers,[140] audiovisual productions and the training of journalists,[141] and there is recognition of the problem of additional costs to media using regional or minority languages.[142] Article 11.2 is drafted to recognise the importance of cross-border transmissions, and the like, to minority language speakers, and is subjected to a lengthy spectrum of possible restrictions on the grounds of national security, territorial integrity, public safety, and so on – safeguards adapted from Article 10.2 of the ECHR.[143]

On the other hand, Article 11.2 does not contain any proviso on the competence of the public authorities. It is explained that the undertaking to guarantee freedom of reception "relates not only to obstacles placed in the way of the reception of programmes broadcast from neighbouring countries but also to passive obstacles resulting from the failure of the competent authorities to make any such reception possible". Article 11.3 is another participation point – recognising the importance of representation of the interests of the users of minority languages in bodies which are supposed to guarantee "the freedom and pluralism of the media".[144]

v. *Cultural activities and facilities – Article 12*

The term "cultural activities and facilities" is not the subject of an exhaustive definition by the Charter, but there is a lengthy illustrative list of such activities, including:

> libraries, video libraries, cultural centres, museums, archives, academies, theatres and cinemas, as well as literary work and film production, festivals and the culture industries, including ... new technologies.[145]

The objective of the provisions is to ensure that R/M languages have an appropriate place in the functioning of a wide range of activities. In Article 12.1.*a*, states are asked to encourage initiatives typical of the modes of cultural expression specific to R/M languages. Because R/M languages may not have the same cultural productivity as more widely-spoken languages, the Charter seeks to foster access to such wider cultural domains through "translation, dubbing, post-synchronisation and subtitling activities".[146] The avoidance of cultural barriers is a two-way process, hence the provision in Article 12.1.*b* that important works produced in R/M languages should become available to a wider public.

On the functioning of cultural institutions, states are asked to see to it that R/M languages and their encompassing cultures are accorded sufficient importance in their programmes:[147] they should make "sufficient allowance" for them. In this respect, the report observes that the role of states "is generally one of guidance and supervision; they are not asked to further this objective themselves, but merely to 'ensure' that it is pursued".[148] Article 12.1.g envisages a degree of system in encouraging/facilitating the creation of a body to collect and conserve works in a particular language; the detail of the organisation of such a body is left to states.[149] Finally, the parties can undertake to make appropriate provision to reflect R/M languages and cultures in their "cultural policy abroad", in order, as the report recognises, "to give a complete and faithful picture of that culture".[150] Patterns of ratification indicate widespread support for all provisions of Article 12. Paragraph 2 is accepted by all states except Croatia, and paragraph 3 by all states except Croatia and Sweden.[151]

vi. *Economic and social life – Article 13*

In assessing the possibilities of state intervention in economic and social life, the basic purpose of the public-life focus of Part III of the Charter should be borne in mind. This is also true to a large extent of language regulation in the sphere of economic life, particularly in the light of the waves of privatisation which have swept over countries inside and outside the Council of Europe in recent decades. In that process, many publicly-owned corporations and other bodies have passed over to private ownership. The phenomenon serves to remind us that boundaries of the public and the private are not set in stone. The limitations of state intervention in economic and social spheres are recognised in the report.[152]

The provisions of Article 13 might therefore be expected to be "light" rather than "heavy" in terms of undertakings generated. This is not completely the case, particularly in the economic sphere where the Charter incorporates a particularly strong effort to legitimate the use of R/M languages. Article 13.1.a provides for the elimination from legislation of provisions prohibiting or limiting the use of R/M language in relation to a range of documentation, including particularly contracts of employment. Paragraph 1.*b* is an undertaking to prohibit the insertion of restrictive language clauses in company and private documents. Softer options appear in the remaining sub-paragraphs – "opposing" restrictive practices, and the more positive undertaking to facilitate/encourage R/M language use by (unspecified) means other than the above.

The explanatory report interprets the provisions of Article 13.1 as a concrete application of the principle of non-discrimination. The paragraph therefore applies throughout the state in question – within the whole country – and cannot be territorialised as other provisions can. By contrast, Article 13.2 contains a list of territorialised measures to be undertaken, "in so far as the public authorities are competent ... and as far as ... reasonably possible". There follows a list of sectors – banking regulations, public sector activities, social care, health and safety, and consumer protection – where the parties are encouraged to support R/M languages. Ratifying states have been reluctant to endorse the provisions in 13.1.*b* – only Croatia, Slovakia, Slovenia and Spain have done so. Norway does not apply any of Article 13.1.

vii. *Transfrontier exchanges – Article 14*

This article develops a notion in Article 7.1.i concerning "the promotion of appropriate types of transnational exchanges". The general issue of transfrontier co-operation between states of the Council of Europe at the local and regional level is the subject of a dedicated outline convention of the Council of Europe. The Languages Charter attempts to sharpen co-operation in the field of language, particularly in the case of R/M languages spoken on either side of a border. The Charter looks to the application of existing agreements,[153] and to general facilitation/promotion of co-operation across borders "in particular between regional or local authorities in whose territory the same language is used in identical or similar form".[154] Article 14 receives almost universal acceptance by ratifying states, though not all states have relevant agreements for the application of paragraph *a.* Hungary highlights a significant number of relevant agreements emerging in consequence of its recent diplomacy.[155]

7. Application of the Languages Charter

The Charter requires that the parties shall "periodically" present a report on their Part II policy and Part III measures to the Secretary General of the Council of Europe. The first report is to be presented within the year following entry into force for the state, and then at three-yearly intervals.[156] Parties shall make their reports public.[157] Examination of the reports is entrusted to a committee of independent experts, the members of which are nominated by states party and appointed by the Committee of Ministers "from a list of individuals of the highest integrity and recognised competence in the matters dealt with by the Charter".[158] Members enjoy six-year terms.[159] The committee of experts, comprising experts in law, linguistics, minority and languages issues, historians, and so on, held its first constitutive meeting from 29 to 30 June 1998.

The Charter makes specific provision in Article 16.2 for bodies legally established in a state party to draw the attention of the committee of experts to Part III matters and to submit statements or comments on Part II policies. The "legally established" requirement is designed "to prevent groups whose headquarters is outside the Party concerned ... from using the monitoring system ... to generate discord among the parties".[160] The bodies "can be variously cultural, political, or any other association which has an interest in the promotion of regional or minority languages in their country".[161] The facilitation of information from non-governmental sources does not convert the procedure into any kind of judicial or quasi-judicial system:

> The Committee is not a judicial body; it is not authorized to bring judgments on State Parties. It is authorised, however, to monitor the implementation of the Charter and receive information to that end. Naturally, it is entitled to form an opinion on the performance by [a] particular party.[162]

On the basis of country reports and information, the experts prepare a report for the Committee of Ministers, accompanied by any comments the parties make and this "may be made public" by the Committee of Ministers.[163] The report shall contain proposals for recommendations by the Committee of Ministers to one or more of the parties.[164] The Committee of Ministers takes note of the report without changing the content, but discusses and adapts the suggestions for recommendations. Article 16.5 of the Charter provides that the Secretary General of the Council of Europe shall make a two-yearly detailed report to the Parliamentary Assembly on the application of the Charter – a unique provision in Council of Europe treaties.[165]

Article 17 provides that the number of experts is the same as the number of parties to the charter. Rules of procedure have been drawn up by the experts in accordance with Article 17.3.[166] In addition to detailing how to handle information and advice received from non-governmental sources,[167] the rules envisage on-the-spot missions for the "evaluation of any situation which might be relevant to the implementation of the Charter".[168] An outline for periodical reports was adopted by the experts in June 1998 and approved by the Committee of Ministers.[169] In addition to requiring information on the specifics of each article, the outline asks for "the general considerations which have guided your country in the ratification process, statistics of R/M language speakers, the names and addresses of any organisation consulted in the preparation of the report, and any future measures which are envisaged".[170]

In this last respect, the committee of experts, according to one member, "will encourage the parties to gradually reach a higher level of commitment in accordance with the Charter".[171] A revised outline for three-yearly reports was issued in February 2002[172] which, *inter alia*, includes guidance on incorporating information on changes in legislation and other significant changes since the first report, as well as information on measures taken to implement the recommendations of the Committee of Ministers – the states are invited to provide full details of these follow-up measures and summarise them for each recommendation.[173]

The committee of experts has issued a number of country reports on the application of the Charter. At the time of writing, eight reports (referred to in the body of the present chapter) have been made public – those for Croatia, Finland, Germany, Hungary, Liechtenstein, the Netherlands, Norway and Switzerland.[174] The reports follow a standard pattern: background information; the committee's evaluation of Part II and Part III of the charter; findings of the committee; with the instrument of ratification or acceptance of the Charter provided as an appendix. The comments of the state authorities on the experts' report are also included as an appendix.

The report is that of the committee of experts, and is submitted to the Committee of Ministers together with suggestions for recommendations that the latter could decide to address to the parties as required.[175] The reports are very detailed – for example, the report on the Netherlands runs to forty-eight pages, with an additional three pages of comments by the state party. Specific comments are inserted by the committee throughout its evaluation, in addition to the chapter on the findings of the committee. The committee finds particular Charter provisions "fulfilled", "generally fulfilled", "partially fulfilled", "formally fulfilled", or "not fulfilled".

The Languages Charter, like the Framework Convention, is an open convention, to which non-members of the Council of Europe may be invited to accede. As noted, reservations may only be made in respect of Article 7, paragraphs 2 to 5. This is a considerable concession in view of the latitude already given by the Charter to ratifying states. Paragraphs 2 to 5 contain basic principles relating to non-discrimination, promotion of mutual understanding between groups, participation by R/M language groups, and non-territorial languages. States purporting to reserve against such provisions may well infringe other provisions of international law – the ECHR and those other regimes of protection endorsed by Article 4.

8. *Concise assessment*

The Languages Charter is now part of the corpus of European standards and candidates for membership of the Council of Europe have been expected to conform to its provisions.[176] The purposes of the instrument are primarily cultural – the protection of cultural diversity is a fundamental aim.[177] The Charter does not operate explicitly through the ascription of individual or collective minority rights but seeks a route to endpoints analogous to rights-based instruments through a complex of undertakings by states. According to the appraisal by one of the initiators of the Charter project:

> It may seem strange that a language is a beneficiary of an international conventional instrument. Normally, the subject of an arrangement carrying legal protection ... is a State, an institution or a person. The situation appears less strange if we consider that the Charter does not attribute rights and that its objective is to encourage states to take concrete measures of internal law applicable to regional or minority languages.[178]

Despite this, the implementation of the Charter cannot be entirely detached from that of the rights instruments, since its prescriptions are capable of having profound affects on the lives of language speakers throughout Europe and of leading to the creation of individual and collective entitlements. In this respect, the same speaker noted the necessity of co-ordination between the organs of the Framework Convention and the Charter: complementary instruments whereby states party may through the Charter achieve the objectives of the Framework Convention in the linguistic sphere.[179]

The prescription for a positive synergy could be extended to other instruments which touch on language – including the ECHR – and those which touch on local government or transfrontier co-operation. There is therefore room for inter-institutional co-operation and mutual learning in key respects. It is noteworthy for example that "problem areas" identified in the second biennial report of the Secretary-General to the

Parliamentary Assembly[180] – education, the use of languages before the courts, relations with administrative authorities, the timidity of users of minority languages in standing out for fear of being seen to be "different" – echo through other institutional arrangements for minorities, global, regional and national.

The stance of the Charter is broadly comparable with that of minority rights texts, in that it seeks an improving relationship between the public and official languages, and the living languages of European minorities. While the Charter may be commended for its technical and non-confrontational approach to minority language issues, reservations about minority rights which may have existed in the early 1990s, impelling the focus on language and not persons, are less pressing now. On the other hand, while some states remain resolutely opposed to minority rights, ratification of the Charter may represent an avenue to realise some minority rights objectives. From its own perspective, the Charter goes beyond other instruments in interlacing the public space with a complex of language requirements. The implementation of its requirements will require serious and sustained work on the part of state bureaucracies.

The complex of procedures under the Charter – the initial reports, the questionnaires, the on-the-spot visits, the reports adopted and made public, and the adoption of the recommendations by the Committee of Ministers – add up to what is in essence an unbroken multiparty dialogue on the Charter's requirements. The charter's flexibility is capable of meeting the resource constraints on human rights programmes, though it is important that the application of the Charter should not be unduly minimalist. Perhaps the principal concern for civil society is that the Languages Charter should be worked through in as transparent a manner as possible, with as much engagement with civil society as the structures can tolerate. The other is broadly philosophical – migrants are a part of European society, and the Charter's focus on languages traditionally used may appear divisive. However, in conceptual terms there are possibilities of "slippage" between the traditional and the new. Conceptions of languages of European tradition to be safeguarded are subject to change: further exploration of this point by the committee of experts over the life of the instrument will be welcome.

Notes

1.   *European Treaty Series* No. 148. The convention was opened for signature on 5 November 1992 by the Committee of Ministers. 'Languages Charter' is used in the present chapter merely for purposes of exposition.

2.   Antonio de Nebrija's reply to a question from Queen Isabella of Castile on his *Gramatica* (presented to her in 1492). Recalled in R.A. Williams Jr., *The American Indian in Western Legal Thought: The Discourses of Conquest* (New York and Oxford: Oxford University Press, 1990), p. 74.

3.   European Charter for Regional or Minority Languages, explanatory report (Strasbourg: Council of Europe Publishing, 1993). Key texts include Resolution 136 (1957) of the Consultative Assembly; Recommendation 285 (1961) of the Parliamentary Assembly; and Recommendation 928 (1981) of the Parliamentary Assembly – Explanatory report, pp. 3-5. On the activities of the Assembly, see further, Chapters 8 and 9.

4.   Explanatory report, paragraphs 5 and 6. Experts from the Parliamentary Assembly of the Council of Europe and the Congress of Local and Regional Authorities participated in the drafting process; contacts were maintained with experts from the European Parliament.

5.   Standing Conference of Local and Regional Authorities of Europe, 23rd Session, 15-17 March 1988, resolution adopted on 16 March.

6.   Opinion, paragraph 6, Parliamentary Assembly, Fortieth Ordinary Session, Assembly debate and adoption of text on 4 October 1988. See also Doc. 5933, report of the Committee on Culture and Education, Rapporteur: de Puig.

7.   Ibid., paragraph 7.

8.   Ibid., paragraph 11.

9.   Article 19.1 of the charter.

10.   The twelve states which have signed the charter, but not yet ratified it, are: Azerbaijan, – Czech Republic, France, Iceland, Italy, Luxembourg, Malta, Moldova, Romania, the Russian Federation, "the former Yugoslav Republic of Macedonia" and Ukraine. Situation as at 7 June 2002.

11.   See below, Article 15.

12.   MIN-LANG/PR (99) 7, 30 November 1999, p. 8.

13.   MIN-LANG/PR (99) 1, 15 March 1999, p. 9. See also report of the committee of experts under the charter, ECRML (2001) 5 (Liechtenstein), p. 6. The role of the committee of experts on the charter is appraised later in the present chapter.

14.   Council of Europe website, 1 February 2000. In June 1999, the Constitutional Council of France ruled that some aspects of the charter ran contrary to fundamental principles in the French constitution: references to groups of language speakers, and the notion of a right to use a language other than French in public life. On the other hand, the paragraphs specified in the French signature were not unconstitutional. According to ECRI, "the French authorities have ... confirmed that, without ratifying the Charter, France will apply, or in some cases is already applying, these paragraphs in practice": second ECRI report on France, 27 June 2000, p. 5.

15.   Explanatory report, paragraph 14.

16.   See ibid., paragraphs 25-29 for comment on the preamble to the charter.

17.   The explanatory report adds (paragraph 14) that this intercultural, etc., approach "corresponds fully to the values traditionally upheld by the Council of Europe and its efforts to promote closer relations between peoples ... and a better understanding between different population groups within the state on an intercultural basis".

18. See further, M.A. Martín Estebanez, 'Linguistic Diversity and the Council of Europe: the European Charter for Regional or Minority Languages and Council of Europe Policies', Workshop on Linguistic Diversity and European Law (Florence: European University Institute, RSCAS-Law, 12-13 November 2000), pp. 10-25; B. de Witte (ed.), *Linguistic Diversity and European Law* (Antwerp: Intersentia, forthcoming).

19. Explanatory report, paragraph 15.

20. See below.

21. Commented on further below.

22. See the brief comments in the explanatory report, paragraph 16, and paragraphs 52-54.

23. Discussed below.

24. Ibid., paragraph 18.

25. Ibid., paragraph 21.

26. See observations in the initial report of Finland, MIN-LANG/PR (99) 4, 12 April 1999, p. 1.

27. UN Doc. CCPR/C/47/D/359/1989 and 385/1989, 1 November 1993.

28. Ibid., paragraph 11.4.

29. See Chapter 1.

30. See Introduction.

31. A. Spiliopoulou-Åkermark, *Justifications of Minority Protection in International Law* (Uppsala: Iustus Forlag, 1997), p. 235. The charter does stray to a limited extent into the private sphere – see particularly Article 13 on economic and social life.

32. B. Poignant, "Prospects for ratification of the charter by France", in *Implementation of the European Charter for Regional or Minority Languages, Regional or Minority Languages No. 2* (Strasbourg: Council of Europe Publishing, 1999) [Implementation], pp. 45-49, at p. 48 – citing G. Carcassone, report of 7 October 1998. The Committee of Experts on the charter have endeavoured to clarify the term "public life" in their published opinions. For example, in their report on Croatia – ECRML (2001) 2, p. 13, they observe that "[t]he term 'public life' as understood by the Charter, is fairly wide and can include the use of the language in education, justice, administration, economic and social life, cultural life, the media and in transfrontier exchanges".

33. F. Capotorti, *Study on the Rights of Persons Belonging to Ethnic, Religious and Linguistic Minorities* (New York: United Nations, 1991), paragraph 568. Compare the formula defining "national minority" in Article 1 of Parliamentary Assembly Recommendation 1201 (1993).

34. Explanatory report, paragraph 31.

35. Ibid.

36. Article 14.1. Commentary by L. Swepston in *Oklahoma City University Law Review*, Vol. 15, No. 3 (1990), pp. 677-714.

37. Article 11.1, discussed in Chapter 13.

38. Cf. A. van der Goot, "The experience of the Netherlands in implementing the charter", op. cit. *[Implementation]*, pp. 30-37, at p. 32.

39.   The Committee of Experts in the case of Finland chose to deal with the Russian language without making a distinction between "Old Russians" and "New Russians" – the latter group is significantly larger than the former – ECRML (2001) 3, paragraph 14. The comments of the government of Finland do not take issue with the committee's approach. Although at the time of writing Baltic states such as Estonia and Latvia are not parties to the charter (and have also not signed it), it is interesting to speculate how the committee of experts would address their significant Russian-speaking populations, only some of which have acquired Estonian and Latvian citizenship.

40.   See also Spiliopoulou-Åkermark, op. cit., p. 236.

41.   Initial report, MIN-LANG/PR (99) 7, 30 November 1999, p. 9.

42.   Ibid. For comments by the committee of experts, see ECRML (2001) 7, 23 November 2001.

43.   *Report on the Linguistic Rights of Persons belonging to National Minorities in the OSCE Area* (OSCE, High Commissioner on National Minorities, 1999), pp. 10-11. Cf. "The situation of regional or minority languages in Europe" (DELA (94) 1 Rev., Strasbourg: 1995) – "a compilation of national contributions established under the sole responsibility of the governments concerned".

44.   Response to OSCE questionnaire from Hungary and Sweden.

45.   Czech Republic.

46.   Responses to OSCE from, among others, Croatia, Denmark, Italy, Slovenia and Spain.

47.   ECRML (2001) 3, paragraph 26. Part II is evaluated in paragraphs 27-61.

48.   Explanatory report, paragraph 32.

49.   Ibid.

50.   Ibid. See report of the committee of experts under the charter on the Netherlands concerning Limburger – ECRML (2001) 1, pp. 27-28. In its findings (E), the committee of experts observes that "[t]here seems to be uncertainty as regards the position of the Limburger language. It is recognised as a language under the Charter by the Dutch authorities, but is not so far recognised by the Dutch Language Union ... this in no way affects the obligations of the Dutch Government under Part II of the Charter".

51.   See comments on the choice of languages made by Hungary in M.A. Martín Estébanez, "Linguistic diversity and the Council of Europe" (cited above in note 18), pp. 16 and 17.

52.   J.-L. Fauconnier, "Statement from CROMBEL on the Poignant Report", *Contact Bulletin*, Vol. 15, No. 2 (European Bureau for Lesser Used Languages, 1999), p. 7.

53.   In finding C of its report on Finland (ECRML (2001) 3), the committee of experts observed that "[o]wing to the assimilation policy of the past, a rapid decline of social and economic status and the widespread stigmatisation of Saami-speakers, the number of Saami-speaking population in general and the size of the Inari and Skolt Saami-speakers in particular, has considerably decreased. As a result of these factors, Skolt and Inari Saami are in danger of extinction and need ... immediate positive action".

54.   Committee of Ministers Recommendation RecChL (2001) 3, adopted by the Committee of Ministers on 19 September 2001, paragraph 1.

55.   For a contemporary account of such standards, see Yash Ghai, *Public Participation and Minorities* (London: Minority Rights Group, 2001). See also Article 7.4. of the charter.

56.   See A. van der Goot, op. cit. *[Implementation]*, p. 32.

57. ECRML (2001) 3 (Finland), Findings and recommendations, paragraph D. The remarks in the instant cases were directed to the cases of the Yiddish and Tatar languages, though they have wider repercussions.

58. Explanatory report, paragraph 33.

59. By way of analogy, consider the protection accorded to minority "areas" by Article 16 of the Framework Convention.

60. See below on Article 7.

61. See for example Article 7.5.

62. Cf. Parliamentary Assembly Recommendation 1291 (1996) on Yiddish culture, and Resolution 885 (1987) on the Jewish contribution to European culture.

63. Ibid., paragraphs 36 and 37.

64. Initial report, MIN-LANG/PR (99) 5, 31 May 1999, 2. Parliamentary Assembly Recommendation 1203 (1993) (discussed elsewhere in the present work) envisaged the initiation of a European programme for the study of Romanis, and that the provisions of the Charter on Regional or Minority Languages "should be applied to Gypsy minorities" – paragraph 11.ii and 11.iii respectively.

65. Initial report, MIN-LANG/PR, 12 April 1999, 6. The report of the committee of experts (ECRML (2001) 3) also discusses Yiddish as a non-territorial language.

66. Initial report, p. 11. See also the initial report of the Netherlands, p. 3.

67. See observation by the committee of experts on Croatia, ECRML (2001) 2, paragraphs 27-28, and the comment in paragraph 46; "The Croatian authorities have made a reservation to this paragraph, thereby excluding all protection and promotion of non-territorial languages under the Charter. The Committee hopes that the Croatian authorities will nevertheless strengthen efforts to promote these languages, and will especially take into consideration the needs of the Romany language".

68. And see below on Article 7.

69. Initial report, paragraph 39.

70. Spiliopoulou-Åkermark, op. cit. (in note 31), p. 235.

71. For a clear explanation of the convoluted terminology of paragraphs and sub-paragraphs, see paragraph 45 of the explanatory report. In essence, the terms refer to distinct provisions of the charter which stand on their own.

72. Initial report, p. 1.

73. Council of Europe information, signature of 7 May 1999.

74. Initial report, p. 4.

75. Explanatory report, paragraph 42.

76. Initial report, pp. 1 and 6.

77. Initial report, p. 17.

78. Ibid.

79. Article 4.

80. Explanatory report, paragraph 53.

81. Ibid.

82. Article 5.

83. Spiliopoulou-Åkermark, op. cit., p. 235.

84. Article 7.1.*a*.

85. Article 7.1.*b*.

86. Article 7.1.*c*. and *d*.

87. Article 7.1.*f* and *h*.

88. Article 7.1.*g*.

89. Article 7.1.*e* and *i*.

90. Article 7.2. See remarks of the committee of experts on Hungary in relation to the Romani and Beas languages: "there have been few efforts to develop a systematic language policy in favour of these two languages. Admittedly, *it is not always easy to reconcile classical goals of anti-discrimination policy and modern approaches directed towards the preservation of linguistic identity*" – ECRML (2001) 4, Finding D [*emphasis* added].

91. Article 7.1.*e* and 7.3.

92. Article 7.4.

93. Article 7.5. It may be noted that, according to Article 21.1, paragraphs 2 to 5 of Article 7 are the only paragraphs in the charter on which reservations can be made.

94. Explanatory report, paragraph 60.

95. The explanatory report observes that, in some cases, "provision will have to be made for teaching 'in' the regional or minority language and in others only for teaching 'of' the language" – paragraph 63. If this is the case, the charter may be stronger in effect than the Framework Convention – compare paragraph 63 above with paragraph 77 of the explanatory report on the Framework Convention.

96. Article 7.3. See explanatory report, paragraph 74.

97. Ibid., paragraph 66.

98. In its opinion of 22 March 1996, the Venice Commission argued that states' freedom of choice in the matter of which languages to specify is only relative because of Article 7.4, and because of the requirement that the selection must relate to the characteristics and state of development of the particular language: "Opinion on the provisions of the European Charter ... which should be accepted by all the Contracting States", CDL-INF (1996) 003e, paragraph 3.2. See remarks and citations on participation, above.

99. R. Arquint, "Regional or minority languages and education problems", in *International Conference on the European Charter for Regional or Minority Languages 1 [International Conference]* (Strasbourg: Council of Europe Publishing, 1998), pp. 18-23, at p. 21.

100. MIN-LANG/PR (99) 6, 7 September 1999, p. 21.

101. Article 2.5 of the UNDM.

102. See Chapters 1 and 2.

103. ECRML (2001) 4, paragraph 34.

104. Article 7.1.*c*.

105. Initial report, pp. 9-14.

106. Article 8.

107. Article 9.

108. Article 10, the purpose of which "is to allow the speakers of regional or minority languages to exercise their rights as citizens and fulfil their civic duties in conditions that respect their mode of expression": Explanatory report, paragraph 100.

109. Article 11.

110. Article 12.

111. Article 13.

112. Article 14.

113. F. Albanese, "The position of the ... Charter ... in the general context of the protection of minorities", in op. cit. *[Implementation]*, pp. 25-29, at p. 27.

114. ECRML (2001) 2, paragraph 17. See also paragraph 43 of the explanatory report.

115. The last phrase "is intended to avert any possibility of interpreting the provisions of Article 8, paragraph 1 – and in particular the first option in each of sub-paragraphs a to f – as excluding the teaching of the language(s) spoken by the majority". The exclusion is justified by the desire to avoid the formation of "linguistic ghettoes". In cases where the charter applies to less widely used official languages, the exclusion on 8.1 should be interpreted/rewritten as "without prejudice to the teaching of *other* official languages" – Explanatory report, paragraph 80 *[emphasis* added].

116. Explanatory report, paragraph 82.

117. See Explanatory report, paragraph 83.

118. Explanatory report, paragraph 85. The report does not label such arrangements as "good practice", although that may be the implication.

119. Explanatory report, paragraph 86. Cf. The project of the Council of Cultural Co-operation entitled "Democracy, human rights, minorities: educational and cultural aspects", within which a pilot project on "history and identity" was initiated: see among other things, "History and identity: final seminar", DECS/SE/DHRM (96), p. 26. Also "Local history and minorities (with special reference to the Gypsy minority)", DECS/SE/BS/Sem (94), p. 17. See further, Chapter 7.

120. The possibility is adverted to in paragraph 88 of the explanatory report.

121. Ibid., paragraph 89.

122. R. Arquint, op. cit. (in note 99), p. 19.

123. See S. Gramstad, "The adaptability of the charter to national situations", in op. cit., *[Implementation]*, pp. 59-62, at p. 61 – a table of paragraphs and sub-paragraphs ratified in relation to Article 8.1, focusing on at least one of the languages in a state which has specified more than one. Information is taken from the ratification patterns of Croatia, Finland, Germany, Hungary, Netherlands, Norway and Switzerland.

124. For higher courts located outside the language territory, it is a matter for the state concerned "to take account of the special nature of the judicial system and its hierarchy of instances" – Explanatory report, paragraph 90.

125. According to the explanatory report, "the term 'courts' should, where appropriate, be understood as covering other bodies exercising a judicial function" – paragraph 93.

126. Cf. Articles 6.3.e and 5.2 of the ECHR; Article 14.3 of the ICCPR. On the charter provisions in relation to languages, the committee of experts observed in its report on Croatia that the measure goes further than Article 6.3.e of the ECHR "in the sense that the speakers of a regional or minority language may use that language before a court of law, *even if they are capable of communicating in the official language,* thereby creating or enlarging the space for the use of these languages in the public sphere": ECRML (2991) 2, paragraph 62 *[emphasis* added].

127. Cf. Article 10.3 of the Framework Convention.

128. Article 7.3. See also paragraphs 17, 18 and 19 of the Oslo recommendations regarding the linguistic rights of national minorities (Foundation on Inter-Ethnic Relations, 1998).

129. Explanatory report, paragraph 94.

130. Explanatory report, paragraph 97.

131. J.-M. Woehrling, "Problems raised by the use of regional or minority languages before public and judicial authorities", *International Conference*, pp. 24-33, at p. 26.

132. Article 10.2.

133. Article 10.3.

134. Article 10.4.

135. Article 11.1.

136. The provision for Low German – described as a regional language in the German ratification – is an exception. France has not specified Article 10.5 in its declaration made on signature.

137. Article 11.1. The media "constitute a field where public intervention is limited and action by means of regulations in not very effective"; public authorities "act in this field essentially by encouragement and provision of aid" – Explanatory report, paragraph 107.

138. Such a mission "involves the provision of a broad range of programmes including the consideration of minority tastes and interests" – ibid., paragraph 110.

139. Where there is a mission, Article 11.1.*a* applies; where there are purely private-sector media, sub-paragraphs 11.1.*b* and 11.1.*c* apply – ibid.

140. Article 11.1.*e*.

141. Article 11.1.*d*, 11.1.*g*.

142. Article 11.1.*f*.

143. The report notes that in respect of those states which are parties to the European Convention on Transfrontier Television, the restrictions will be determined by that convention – paragraph 112.

144. Explanatory report, paragraph 113.

145. Article 12.1.

146. Article 12.1.

147. Article 12, paragraph 1.*d* to *f*.

148. Explanatory report, paragraph 117.

149. The position in territories outside the traditional reach of the R/M language is again addressed in Article 12.2, which provides that states can encourage and/or provide appropriate cultural facilities for the languages.

150. Article 12.3, and report paragraph 120.

151. In the case of Croatia, the committee of experts observed in relation to media and culture that the "major drawback to the application of the Charter in these two fields is the lack of participation by the users or representatives of the regional or minority languages in the organisation, planning and funding of activities": ECRML (2001) 2, Finding E.

152. Explanatory report, paragraph 121.

153. Article 14.*a*.

154. Article 14.*b*.

155. Initial report, MIN-LANG/PR (99) 6, pp. 65-68.

156. Article 15.1.

157. Article 15.2.

158. Article 17.1.

159. Article 17.2.

160. Explanatory report, paragraph 128.

161. V. Crnic-Grotic, "The committee of experts", in op. cit. *[Implementation]*, pp. 73-75, at p. 74.

162. Ibid.

163. Article 16.3.

164. The Committee of Ministers decides on a case-by-case basis which reports are to be published – for justification of this modus operandi, see the explanatory report, paragraph 130.

165. The first report by the Secretary General was presented on 18 October 2000. On the procedure, the Secretary-General commented that, "[a]s for the Parliamentary Assembly, the role assigned to it by the charter is exceptional for a Council of Europe convention. Few conventions provide for reports to be submitted to the Assembly and no other convention requires the Secretary General to present his own report on its application. The significance of this role of the Assembly should not be under-estimated. The debate on the biennial report gives a regular opportunity to Europe's parliamentarians to review the state of implementation of the charter and exert political pressure to improve it". For pertinent Assembly observations on the charter, see Recommendation 1492 (2001), adopted on 23 January 2001, and Recommendation 1539 (2001) on the European Year of Languages, adopted on 28 September 2001. The second report of the Secretary-General was presented on 11 September 2002 – references are made to it in the concluding part of this chapter.

166. MIN-LANG (98) 6, 9 December 1998 – the rules were adopted on 29 June 1998.

167. See rules 12 and 17.

168. To be decided by a two-thirds majority of votes cast. Fact-finding visits have become a regular aspect of the committee's working methods. The Council of Europe website lists the dates of on-the-spot visits of the committee of experts to the countries concerned.

169. MIN-LANG (98) 7, 23 November 1998. The outline was adopted on 29 June 1998, and approved in revised form by the Committee of Ministers on 10 November 1998.

170. Outline for Part I and Part II of the charter.

171. V. Crnic-Grotic [member of the committee of experts for Croatia], "The committee of experts", op. cit. *[Implementation]*, pp. 73-75, at p. 74.

172. MIN-LANG (2002) 1, 7 February 2002.

173. By the end of 2002, second periodical reports had been submitted by Norway, MIN-LANG/PR (2002) 3; Liechtenstein, MIN-LANG/PR (2002) 4; and Hungary, MIN-LANG/PR (2002) 6.

174. ECRML (2001) 1 (Netherlands), ECRML (2001) 2 (Croatia), ECRML (2001) 3 (Finland), ECRML (2002) 1 (Germany), ECRML (2001) 4 (Hungary), ECRML (2001) 5 (Liechtenstein), ECRML (2001) 6 (Norway), ECRML (2001) 7 (Switzerland). See subsequently, the report on Sweden, ECRML (2003) 1; and on Norway, ECRML (2003) 2 - the first report of the second monitoring cycle.

175. Recommendations were adopted by the Committee of Ministers at the 765th and 766th meetings of ministers' deputies (19 September and 4 October 2001) in respect of Croatia, Finland, Hungary, Liechtenstein and the Netherlands. The ministers also authorised automatic declassification of each report after it had been examined by the Committee of Ministers, unless the state concerned objected to its publication. Recommendations have subsequently been adopted in respect of Croatia, RecChL (2001) 2; Finland, RecChL (2001) 3; Hungary, RecChL (2001) 4; the Netherlands, RecChL (2001) 1, Norway, RecChL (2001) 5; Switzerland, RecChL (2001) 6; and Germany, RecChL (2002) 1 – Council of Europe website http://www.coe.int/local/

176. See Chapter 9.

177. Cf. Spiliopoulou-Åkermark, op. cit., pp. 237-38.

178. F. Albanese, op. cit. *[Implementation]*, p. 26.

179. Ibid., p. 29.

180. Doc. 9540, 11 September 2002.

Chapter 4

Protection of a specific minority: the case of Roma/Gypsies[1]

by Dr Alexandra Xanthaki, Liverpool Law School, UK

Introduction

At least eight million Roma/Gypsies live in Europe today.[2] The 2000 Central and Eastern European preparatory meeting for the World Conference against Racism noted that:

> Despite their lasting presence in Europe, the Roma remained the least integrated and most persecuted people in Europe. After the fall of the Soviet Union, racist violence against Roma had increased and their fundamental civil rights were threatened.[3]

Although steps have been taken for the elimination of racism against them and the development of their rights, their situation remains a cause for concern. An incident that took place in Usti nad Labem, the Czech Republic, highlights the Roma situation: as a response to local homeowners' complaints of noise and untidiness coming from the two low-rent apartments inhabited mainly by Roma, the central administration of the town decided to build a wall to separate the Roma community from their neighbours. The wall had three gates, which were locked at 10 p.m. every night, and was patrolled by uniformed police.[4] When challenged, the Czech government noted that they did not see racial intolerance, but rather social reasons as the heart of the problem. It was only after an international outcry that the wall was eventually demolished.

The OSCE High Commissioner on National Minorities has given a short account of the main Roma problems:

> [Roma/Gypsy communities] are still faced with an unparalleled level of intolerance, mutual distrust, poor housing, exclusion, unemployment, education and systemic discrimination. In a classic downward spiral, each of these problems exacerbates the others. Sadly, the symptoms have become almost commonplace: racist attacks and segregation, Roma asylum-seekers, horrendous living conditions, extreme poverty,

and disproportionately high rates of illiteracy and ill-health including infant mortality. Images of a mother and child begging in the streets, of families reduced to living on garbage dumps, or Roma houses being burnt down by angry mobs do not tell the whole story, but they stay with us because of their poignancy. Such images seem like they should be from another time or place. But they occur – here and now ... in modern Europe, in a Europe that prides itself on being a civilized continent based on common principles, particularly respect for human rights.[5]

Owing to the gravity of the problems the Roma/Gypsies face, their situation has become the focus of several European organisations of late.

The Council of Europe has been one of the first organisations to acknowledge the problem. Since 1968, the Organisation has been involved in the understanding and dissemination of information about the Roma and their problems; since 1993 the action for their protection has become more coherent and organised. This chapter attempts to list and assess the various relevant initiatives – texts and activities – that the Council of Europe has taken over the years. To this end, the first section will review the texts adopted by the Committee of Ministers and the activities carried out by the competent bodies to implement the mandate given by the Committee of Ministers and the Parliamentary Assembly of the Council of Europe; the second section will look at the texts adopted by the other bodies of the Council of Europe; the final section will review the various relevant activities of the Council of Europe.

Texts adopted by the Committee of Ministers and the Parliamentary Assembly

1. *General instruments on tolerance and discrimination*

One of the main objectives of the Council of Europe has been to encourage member states to adopt a comprehensive approach to Roma/Gypsy issues. This has been facilitated by the recognition of Roma/Gypsies as a minority in Europe, because it explicitly links the protection provided by minority instruments with Roma/Gypsies. According to the general observations set out in the Parliamentary Assembly Recommendation 1203 (1993) on "Gypsies in Europe":

A special place among the minorities is reserved for Gypsies. Living scattered all over Europe, not having a country to call their own, they are a truly European minority, but one that does not fit in the definitions of national or linguistic minorities.[6]

For many years national histories have remained silent about Roma/ Gypsies' existence and activities. Ignoring Roma/Gypsies was eased by their exclusion from the major political, economic, cultural and social developments in Europe. Recommendation 1203 put the record straight by affirming that the Roma "greatly contribute to the cultural diversity of Europe ... in different ways, be it by language and music or by their trades and crafts".[7]

The Committee of Ministers has adopted several general texts for the protection of minorities and which may be of use to Roma. In 1968, Resolution 68 (30) "on measures to be taken against incitement to racial, national and religious hatred"[8] reaffirmed the importance of the principle of respect for human dignity and recommended the signature and ratification of the International Convention on the Elimination of All Forms of Racial Discrimination by the member states of the Council of Europe.[9] The Committee on the Elimination of Racial Discrimination (CERD), the monitoring body of the convention, has repeatedly raised the issue of Roma in its concluding observations to states' reports.[10] Resolution (72) 22 of the Committee of Ministers "on the suppression of and guaranteeing against unjustifiable discrimination"[11] focused on the national laws on prohibition of discrimination and recommended, *inter alia*, their strengthening. The consequent (1981) "Declaration regarding intolerance – a threat to democracy"[12] condemned all ideologies that deny the intrinsic equality of all human beings and expressed the Committee's aim to promote a climate of "active understanding and respect for the qualities and culture of others".[13] A decade later, Recommendation (92) 10 reaffirmed the importance of the implementation by states of international instruments protecting minority rights.[14]

The Committee of Ministers has not been the sole body to express its concern on minorities. The Parliamentary Assembly of the Council of Europe reaffirmed in Recommendation 1134 (1990) on "the rights of minorities"[15] that respect for minorities is an essential factor for peace, justice, stability and democracy, and emphasised the contribution of minorities to the pluriformity and cultural variety in Council of Europe member states. The recommendation also stressed that "the revival of minority languages and cultures is a sign of the richness and vitality of European civilisations". Two years later, Recommendation 1177 (1992)[16] reaffirmed these concepts.

Roma/Gypsy communities are also protected by several general instruments on human rights that have been adopted by the Council of Europe. The (1992) European Charter for Regional or Minority Languages[17] includes provisions specifically for non-territorial languages, such as the Romani language. According to the charter, the nature and the scope of the measures to be taken "shall be determined in a flexible manner, bearing in mind the needs and wishes, and respecting the traditions and characteristics of the groups which use the languages concerned".[18] The Charter came into force in 1998 and has now thirty signatures and seventeen ratifications.

The Convention

More complete protection is guaranteed by the 1994 Framework Convention for the Protection of National Minorities,[19] the first international treaty on ethnic minorities. States party to it undertake the obligation to promote the conditions necessary for the maintenance and development of minority cultures and cultural heritages, as well as the essential elements of their identity, namely their religion, language, traditions and cultural heritage. States party also agree to take, where possible, "special measures that take into account the specific conditions of persons concerned"[20] in order to favour equality of opportunities for persons belonging to national minorities. Other rights particularly helpful for Roma communities include intercultural dialogue and self-identification, transfrontier co-operation and conclusion of bilateral and multicultural agreements between neighbouring states on respective minorities.

A number of states, including Macedonia and Slovenia, have made declarations expressly recognising that the Framework Convention applies to members of the Roma community living within their territory.[21] More cautiously, Germany has declared that the Convention will "be applied to the Sinti and Roma of German citizenship".[22] While not specifically referring to the Roma, other states, such as Estonia and Switzerland, have also restricted the scope of the Framework Convention to members of minorities who are citizens of the respective states.[23]

As emphasised in the first chapter of this book, the existence of minorities does not depend on their recognition by the state.[24] The Advisory Committee on the Framework Convention has repeatedly commented on the situation of Roma in the various states. For instance, in September 2000, the committee noted that the situation of Roma in Slovakia, Hungary and Finland varied from unsatisfactory to worrying, and elaborated on the various problems they face within the respective states.[25] The Committee plays an important role in identifying and disseminating the existing problems of the Roma/Gypsy minorities in Europe.[26]

The Court of Human Rights

In deciding on several cases concerning Roma,[27] the European Court of Human Rights has been reluctant to acknowledge the distinctiveness of the Roma culture or to accommodate their distinct characteristics adequately.[28] The earlier decisions of the Court seem to produce little practical benefits for the improvement of Roma rights. Lately the court has been more helpful in affirming Roma rights. In *Assenov and others v.*

Bulgaria, decided in 1998,[29] the Court ruled that, although there was reasonable suspicion that the police injured the applicant during his arrest, the investigation following his claim was not thorough and effective. This amounted to a violation of the right not to be subjected to torture, inhuman or degrading treatment or punishment, and a violation of the right to an effective remedy.

The Court was particularly startled by the statement of the Bulgarian Military Prosecution Office that "even if the blows were administered on the body of the juvenile, they occurred as a result of disobedience to police orders".[30] Following Mr Assenov's arrest and detention, the Court found violations of his right to an effective remedy.[31] Bulgaria had also violated its obligation not to interfere with the right to petition the Strasbourg organs, by pressuring two of the applicants into denying having made an application at a time when Assenov was being held in detention.

In *Velikova v. Bulgaria,* decided in 2000,[32] the Court ruled that the state had violated Mr Tsonchev's right to life and that he had died "as a result of injuries inflicted while he was in the hands of the police".[33] The state was further responsible because the police failed to conduct an effective investigation into his death. Unfortunately, the Court was reluctant to find that the motive for these violations was racial prejudice based on the victim's ethnic origin; it was held that discrimination was not established "beyond reasonable doubt".

A similar reluctance to accept discrimination against Roma is obvious in *Cyprus v. Turkey* (2001), where the Commission and the Court agreed that, although Roma living conditions in Northern Cyprus had been atrocious, discrimination beyond reasonable doubt could not be established.[34] The Court reiterated this argument in 2002 in *Anguelova v. Bulgaria,* another case of un-remedied police violence that resulted in the death of a Roma.[35] Although disappointing, it is interesting to note that the language and arguments provided by the Court in all cases does not rule out completely the occurrence of discrimination.[36] It is expected that the new Protocol No. 12, which concerns a general prohibition of discrimination, will provide the Court with the machinery to deal with cases involving discrimination.[37]

Notwithstanding their possible shortcomings, the above decisions represent an important tool for Romani victims of alleged police abuse and for victims of non-violent acts of racial discrimination in general and their use may ultimately contribute to shape and transform the law.[38] The future will no doubt evidence several opportunities for such a use: the number of cases dealing with Roma issues will undoubtedly increase as a consequence of the ratifications of the European Convention on Human Rights by central and eastern European states.[39]

In June 2003, the Court found admissible the case of *Moldovan and others v. Romania* and *Rosta and others v. Romania.*[40] According to the twenty-five Roma applicants, following the death of a non-Roma in a conflict with three Romas, many villagers of Hădăren, Romania, together killed Roma persons, set fire to their houses and destroyed their property with the tolerance and even encouragement of the police. After the events, the police failed to properly investigate the case and covered for the non-Roma villagers, and the judiciary imposed light penalties on the defendants. The court found the case admissible. It will be interesting to see the final judgment of the Court, especially on issues of discrimination against the Roma. This case is especially important, because it highlights the unparalleled exclusion and brutality that Roma/Gypsies face in their everyday lives in the communities in which they live.

Other general documents

Other instruments of the Council of Europe that can be used for the protection of Roma/Gypsies include:

• the European Convention on Human Rights,

• the European Social Charter, and

• the European Convention for the Prevention of Torture and Inhuman or Degrading Treatment or Punishment.

Important also are the monitoring bodies of the above instruments, which have repeatedly commented on Roma issues.

2. Specific texts

The first text focusing on Roma/Gypsies, Recommendation 563 (1969) on "the situation of Gypsies and other travellers in Europe" was adopted in 1969 by the Parliamentary Assembly.[41] Six years later, the Committee of Ministers adopted Resolution (75) 13 "on the social situation of nomads in Europe".[42] Resolution (75) 13 urged governments to take necessary measures to prevent discrimination against nomads and to safeguard their identity and cultural heritage. Specific areas of concern were identified, such as residence within states, education, health and social welfare action.

In 1983, Recommendation R (83) 1 on "stateless nomads and nomads of undetermined nationality"[43] set out principles for the nomads related to non-discrimination; residence and movement; reunion of families; links with the state; and extended protection. The recommendation urged member states to take all the necessary measures to implement these principles. Both these documents reflect the spirit of that period: Roma are defined as nomads and the language used is soft and state-friendly. Nevertheless, their importance cannot be underestimated: apart from recognising a situation that had been overlooked for such a long time, they constitute the first seeds of setting down specific standards for the protection of Roma/Gypsies.[44]

New commitments of the 1990s

During the 1990s, Roma numbers within the province of the Council of Europe increased considerably, due to the expansion in membership to include member states of central and eastern Europe. New information about the continual violations of Roma/Gypsy rights became widely disseminated, and newly emerged Roma activism started pressing for more action. The Roma/Gypsies issue fell within all the Organisation's top priorities, namely the protection of minorities, the fight against racism and intolerance, and the fight against social exclusion. The Council of Europe responded to the challenge and intensified their efforts to improve the situation of Roma/Gypsies. The new texts indicated a firmer commitment to Roma/Gypsy issues, including a more Roma-friendly language and a stronger tone concerning the obligations of member states.

Recommendation 1203 (1993) of the Parliamentary Assembly "on Gypsies in Europe"[45] reflected the stronger commitment towards Roma protection. Using a strong tone, the recommendation affirmed that although general resolutions and recommendations on the rights of minorities "are important to Gypsies, ... as one of the very few non-territory minorities in Europe, Gypsies need special protection". The text linked the idea of a genuine cultural identity with the contribution of minority cultures to overall diversity and observed that the Roma greatly contribute to the cultural diversity of Europe.[46] It also made mention of the intolerance and hatred experienced by the Roma over the ages and proclaimed that "[r]espect for the rights of Gypsies, individual, fundamental and human rights and their rights as a minority, is essential to improve their situation".[47]

The recommendation proposed that the Committee of Ministers initiate, where appropriate, measures in the field of culture, education, information, equal rights and everyday life, and suggested that the Council of Europe "grant consultative status to representative Gypsy organisations".[48] It also suggested that "a mediator for Gypsies (...) be appointed by the Council of Europe after consultation with representative organisations of Gypsies".[49]

However, the idea of a mediator entrusted to advise governments and the Council of Europe in matters relating to Roma/Gypsies, to investigate related national policies and to review the progress in implementing related Council of Europe measures has never materialised. In 1999, the Committee of Ministers decided that "it did not see fit to appoint a specific mediator for Roma/Gypsies".[50] This approach suggests an unwillingness to accept a body that would monitor states' actions and progress concerning Roma rights. Nevertheless, Recommendation 1203 included a monitoring mechanism:

> Member states should report to the Secretary General of the Council of Europe in two years' time on the progress made in improving the situation of Gypsies and implementing Council of Europe recommendations.[51]

In the aftermath of Recommendation 1203, a report on the situation of Gypsies (Roma and Sinti) in Europe, issued by the European Committee on Migration (CDMG) was completed.[52] The report reviewed the social and economic situation of the Roma/Gypsies, their legal status, their culture, their participation in public life and the role of the local authorities in their protection. It also examined the role of Gypsy organisations as well as international organisations in the protection of Roma/Gypsies. Both Recommendation 1203 and the report constitute landmarks in the protection of the Roma/Gypsies and initiated new activities and studies on the issue.

The group of specialists on Roma/Gypsies and travellers

The complementary reply to Recommendation 1203 of the Parliamentary Assembly, adopted by the Committee of Ministers in 1995,[53] established important steps for the long-term improvement in the situation of Roma/Gypsies. The most effective measure was the establishment of a specialist group on Roma/Gypsies, appointed by the Committee of Ministers to advise member states on all Roma/Gypsy-related matters and to encourage international authorities to take action where needed.

The group consists of thirteen experts, with representatives of the OSCE, the UNHCR and the European Commission attending as observers. The specialist group has been very active and has played the role of a catalyst for other departments of the Council of Europe by encouraging and stimulating activities. It has carried out numerous visits,[54] studies on related issues – notably the 1998 report on the international mobility of the Roma/Gypsies[55] – and has organised training sessions and meetings that bring together the main actors in the protection of Roma/Gypsies at European level.

Some of the themes that the group progressively addresses include Roma/Gypsy human rights violations and discrimination; training for the police and the judicial administration; the question of the legal status of Roma/Gypsies as a minority; questions connected with citizenship; problems faced by nomadic groups and travellers; housing and caravan sites; the role of the media in the promotion of tolerance;

training for journalists; the situation of the Romani media; education, schooling, training and culture; problems connected with health care and health education; the situation of Roma/Gypsy women; and community relations.

The group has also carried out other urgent actions, each of which led to a report: in 1996, a fact-finding mission to Bosnia and Herzegovina on the situation of the Roma/Gypsies; in 1997, a study visit to Valdemingomez (Madrid); and in 1999, a joint field mission by the OSCE Office for Democratic Institutions and Human Rights (ODIHR) and the Council of Europe on the situation of the Roma in Kosovo. The group has also adopted a draft recommendation on housing and town planning that was submitted to the Committee on Migration and then to the Committee on Ministers for adoption. The group is also currently elaborating another draft recommendation on the free movement on travellers as well as a major draft recommendation on policies towards Roma/Gypsies in Europe, which will incorporate previous texts on housing, education, employment, health and culture.[56]

At the turn of the millennium

Apart from Recommendation 1203 and its complementary reply, the Parliamentary Assembly also adopted in 1998 Recommendation 1353 (1998) on "access of minorities to higher education".[57] The recommendation repeated that Roma/Gypsies are a recognised European minority and noted that their socio-economic situation constitutes an obstacle to their access to higher education. Two years later, the Committee of Ministers adopted Recommendation R (2000) 4 on "the education of Roma/Gypsy children in Europe",[58] which set down guiding principles for the implementation of relevant educational policies.

The recommendation asserted that educational policies applied on Roma/Gypsies should be flexible to accommodate their itinerant or semi-itinerant lifestyle and should take into account the particular features of the Romani culture: Romani history and culture should be introduced in the teaching materials; and opportunities to learn Romani, wherever the language is taught, should be provided for. The recommendation also set out guidelines on the communication between schools and Roma parents, which has been a very sensitive issue.

In November 2001, the Committee of Ministers adopted Recommendation (2001) 17 on "improving the economic and employment situation of Roma/Gypsies and Travellers in Europe". The Committee invited governments to take steps to improve the economic situation of Roma/Gypsies and Travellers and stressed that discrimination against Roma, coupled with social exclusion and shortcomings in the areas of training, education and information, impedes their access to the labour market. The resulting economic deprivation that Roma face has very damaging knock-on effects on areas such as housing, education or health.

The recommendation repeated the need to introduce legislation and instruments to combat racial discrimination in access to employment and in the workplace; requested that member-states foster projects that would generate income for businesses run by Roma/Gypsies; and also requested that measures be taken that would involve them in the construction, implementation and assessment of programmes geared to their needs; the latter was highlighted as a key factor in improving their economic situation.

In 2002, the Assembly adopted Recommendation 1557 (2002) on "the legal situation of Roma in Europe". The recommendation is a general instrument that paints a damning picture of widespread discrimination in every field of personal and public life, marginalisation and segregation of Roma, and it incorporates observations and suggestions from previous documents. It stresses that Roma form a special minority group, because they are an ethnic community and most of them belong to socially disadvantaged groups of society. It acknowledges that in recent years the nature and direction of Roma migration has changed and its illegal aspect has grown significantly, and even former transit countries have become final destinations; therefore, it proposes a series of confidence-building and advisory measures to help:

> Romany migrants from central and eastern Europe already living in the countries of western Europe and to prevent their further marginalisa-tion. At the same time, it is also necessary to provide effective support for the reintegration of those Romany migrants who return to their homeland.[59]

The recommendation also touches upon sensitive issues, such as the conditions of Romany women, the portrayal of Roma in the media, the need for harmonisation of the work of European organisations; Roma participation in decision-making; and the creation of special institutions for Roma. It repeats the idea of a European Ombudsman for Roma and goes further to suggest the creation of a European Roma consultative forum and an additional protocol to the European Convention on Human Rights on the rights of persons belonging to minorities.

In its reply,[60] the Council of Ministers agreed with the idea of a con-sultative forum for Roma. Concerning the suggestion of an additional protocol, the committee repeated that:

> the Ministers' Deputies considered that it was somewhat premature to reopen the debate on the proposal for an additional protocol to the European Convention on Human Rights concerning the rights of

national minorities (799th meeting, 13 June 2002, item 4.2). It stressed that "when *Protocol No. 12* to the European Convention on Human Rights comes into force, any discrimination against a member of a national minority, including discrimination based on association with such a minority, will be covered by the general prohibition on discrimination.[61] *[emphasis as in the original text]*

The Parliamentary Assembly has also issued several recommendations on the situation of Roma in specific countries. For example, Recommendation 1419 (1999) on "honouring of obligations and commitments by Slovakia" referred to positive steps taken in Slovakia for the protection of Roma. Recommendation 1459 (2000) on "an action plan for the children of Kosovo" stressed that the Roma children in Kosovo were in danger and asked for steps to protect them; whereas Recommendation 1424 (1999) on "the Evaluation of the humanitarian situation in the Federal Republic of Yugoslavia, particularly in Kosovo and Montenegro" referred to the general situation of Roma in Kosovo. Finally, in Recommendation 1338 (1997) on "the obligations and commitments of the Czech Republic as a member state", the Assembly commented on the discrimination against the Roma minority in the country.[62]

The Congress of Local and Regional Authorities of Europe (Congress)

The Congress of Local and Regional Authorities of Europe has issued several resolutions and initiated practical projects concerning the participation of Roma/Gypsies in local and regional authorities. One of its earlier texts on the issue, Resolution 125 (1981) on "the role and responsibility of local and regional authorities in regard to the cultural and social problems of populations of nomadic origin",[63] suggested, among other things, the creation of a legal instrument related to Roma/Gypsy free movement. Although the suggestion did not materialise at this level, a group of specialists is currently working on a draft recommendation on the free movement and encampment of Travellers.

In 1991, the hearing on "The Gypsy people and Europe, continuation of the tradition in a changing Europe",[64] which took place with the active participation of Roma/Gypsies, set the foundations for their active participation in those CoE activities which concern them. It was also suggested that a large organisation representing all Roma/Gypsies be established and that genuinely representative Roma/Gypsy organisations in Europe be granted consultative status.

The next year, the colloquy on "Gypsies in the locality"[65] concluded that there is a need for information about Roma, and that local and regional authorities have an essential role to play as partners in the true sense. Among other things, the colloquy suggested the launch of a network of towns chosen from those most experienced in the reception of Gypsy communities and the publication of a series of case studies. Furthermore, the Council for Cultural Co-operation (CDCC) was urged to explore the possibility of launching a European Gypsy Route.

Congress Resolution 249 (1993) on "Gypsies in Europe: the role and responsibility of local and regional authorities"[66] repeated the latter suggestion and proposed other practical measures aimed at breaking down the barriers between Roma and non-Roma, and facilitating Roma integration into the societies where they live. The resolution adopted a strong tone, beginning by "regretting that the [texts on Roma] have as yet been followed up with little concrete action"[67] and that the media "all too often project a negative image of Gypsies, encouraging rejection, expulsion and violence".[68]

In 1994, the Congress established a "Network of Cities". The network organised various activities that encouraged exchanges of information and experience among local authorities and facilitated twinning arrangements and the implementation of various community development projects.[69] The subsequently renamed "European Network of Cities on Provision for Roma in Municipalities" is independent of the Council of Europe and aims to promote better provisions for Roma in towns through developing a network of cities in each of the Council of Europe member states and by highlighting good practices and examples.[70]

In 1995, the Congress adopted Recommendation 11 (1995) and Resolution 16 (1995) "towards a tolerant Europe: the contribution of Roma/Gypsies".[71] Resolution 16 reaffirmed several of the suggestions of Resolution 249 on education, access to health care, training, employment, and the fight against racism and discrimination of Roma/Gypsies. Moreover, it suggested the establishment of national centres for mediation and dialogue between the authorities and Roma/Gypsy communities as well as a "solidarity covenant" between Roma/Gypsies and local and regional authorities with the participation of national and international bodies. It encouraged measures to ensure Roma control over their affairs, such as "the possibility of electing or appointing their representatives democratically", the setting-up of consultative committees of Roma/Gypsies or minorities as a whole, and states' support of Roma associations. The most important feature of Resolution 16, however, concerned the principle of self-identification, as it urged local and regional authorities to ensure that any reference to the Roma/Gypsies in public life uses a name for them that meets their approval and does not have connotations that they or others regard as pejorative.

Recommendation 11 (1995)[72] also repeated previous suggestions, including the need to appoint a European Roma/Gypsy mediator; the setting up a small ad hoc group of experts; the establishment of several bodies within the framework of the Council of Europe to promote Roma rights; the drawing up of an international instrument on the movement of persons; the completion of a thorough study on Roma; and the possibility of revising national legislation in order to guarantee full Roma protection. Moreover, the recommendation appealed to member states to sign the relevant international texts, notably the Framework Convention for the Protection of National Minorities and the Convention on the Participation of Foreigners in Public Life at Local Level. Most of the above suggestions have since materialised.

The Congress has also contributed to the Roma/Gypsy issue with hearings and exchange of information. The Network of Cities organised three hearings on Roma/Gypsy rights. The first one, which took place in Kosice in 1995, focused on past experiences, innovative strategies and models in education, culture, social problems and employment, and it emphasised the need to increase co-operation among European organisations on Roma/Gypsies and to allow more Roma participation in the action taken.[73] The second hearing, the 1996 Ploiesti round table on "the legal and institutional framework of the national minorities of Roma in municipalities"[74] discussed perceptions and images of Roma/Gypsies. The round table concluded that:

> popular perception of the gypsies portrays their identity as a lifestyle rather than as the cultural heritage of an ethnic group which parallels those of other nations and their problems as deriving from a conflict of social behavioural patterns, rather than one of ethnic identity and ethnic hostility towards them.[75]

Issues of definition and terminology highlight fundamental differences in views about the roots of the Roma/Gypsy situation and the ways of solving the existing problems. Participants of the round table agreed that problem-solving strategies must try to accommodate Roma rather than assimilate them, and invited Congress to launch a series of events devoted to the theme "the image of the Roma: reality of an ethnic identity versus the myth of 'social behaviour'".

Several limitations in protecting Roma using the existing European legal framework were identified, including restricted access to legal remedies, restrictions of the institutional framework, limitations of official fora and conflicts with the police. It was recommended that the Congress appealed for the co-operation of the Council of Europe and other multilateral organisations in monitoring the situation of Roma regarding human rights, providing information on appeal paths and advising lawyers representing Roma on issues concerned with human rights. The hearing also suggested that the Congress explore the possibility of a permanent monitoring of the situation of the Roma regarding human rights from a legal standpoint.

On 7 March 1997, the Congress adopted Resolution 44 (1997) on "towards a tolerant Europe: the contribution of Roma (Gypsies)" where it approved the conclusions of the Ploiesti round-table discussion and encouraged its implementation. The third hearing, which took place in Pardubice (Czech Republic) in 1997, focused on a comprehensive approach of Romani questions at the local level – housing, health and social affairs – and discussed racism, discrimination and related violence against Roma/Gypsies.[76]

Texts of other bodies of the Council of Europe

The Council for Cultural Co-operation (CDCC)

Following Congress Resolution 125 (1981),[77] the Council for Cultural Co-operation (CDCC), the body responsible for educational and cultural issues within the Council of Europe, prepared in 1984 a report on Gypsies and Travellers. A revised and expanded edition of this study was published in 1994 under the title *Roma, Tziganes et Voyageurs* ('Roma, Gypsies and Travellers'). The CDCC has also been very active in organising projects, mostly related to schooling: since 1983, it has offered a series of training courses for teachers and seminars on schooling for Gypsy and Traveller children as part of the Teacher Bursary Scheme, which led to several reports.[78] Also, the CDCC has supported the Gypsy Research Centre through producing and distributing a spelling primer in standardised Romany language[79] and a teachers' manual in Central Europe.[80]

In another project, the CDCC highlighted the importance of history teaching for the understanding of minority cultures: drawing on national history textbooks, the project aimed to use local history to give more prominence to minorities. The result of this programme led to the preparation of a methodological guide for history teachers working with Roma/Gypsy pupils. The knowledge gained by the activities, the courses and the publications are used continuously by the CDCC as the basis for future work and action.

In 1993, the CDCC initiated a four-year project entitled "Democracy, human rights and minorities: educational and cultural aspects". Within the framework of this project, three case studies on Roma were launched in 1996. The first study focused on the Secondary School of Arts and Romanthan Theatre (Kosice, Slovakia) as a "good practice" example of positive management of diversity. This secondary school provides students with an opportunity to study arts related to the Gypsy culture. It is addressed to both the Roma and the non-Roma communities, promotes recognition and professional qualifications to the Roma community and takes into account the dynamics of the community.[81]

The second case study compared the election of Gypsy self-government in Hungary with the experience of the Saamis in Norway; the report maintained that minority self-government has a positive effect on the ethnic identity of both the minority and the majority, but also enumerated the obstacles that need to be overcome for the realisation of self-government, including interethnic hostility.[82] The third study used the "LXXVII Act on the Rights of the National and Ethnic Minorities" passed by the Hungarian Assembly in 1993 to analyse Roma/Gypsy self-government and local self-governments in Hungary.[83] The project was concluded in May 1997 with a final conference held in Strasbourg.

In 1997, the CDCC launched a three-year project on "Education for democratic citizenship". The project activities were divided into three groups: concepts and definitions; citizenship sites; and training and support systems. "Citizenship sites" were a series of initiatives in Bulgaria, Spain, Ireland and Portugal rooted in the civil society, which aimed at strengthening the use of participatory and representative democracy at the local level. They included partnerships between different institutions, setting up innovative participatory structures, mediation, community development, learning strategies, intercultural dialogue and democratisation in schools.[84]

In 1994, the Council for Cultural Co-operation presented an introductory report on a Gypsy Cultural Route to the Advisory Committee on Cultural Routes. The Roma/Gypsy Route would consist of networking various existing initiatives, including museums of Roma culture, exhibitions and theatres. The Gypsy Cultural Route would be the only one of the Council of Europe's cultural routes devoted to a living culture rather than a historical one. The Advisory Committee on Cultural Routes has been positive on the matter; thus, a feasibility study was authorized in April 1994. The project requires careful examination of the ground to be covered and the partners who should be involved in the route. The second report of this study was submitted in 1997 and the Specialist Group on Roma/Gypsies is now examining the practical possibilities for its implementation.

Other Council of Europe bodies

Other bodies of the Council of Europe have also been involved in specific aspects of Roma/Gypsies. The European Commission against Racism and Intolerance (ECRI) has followed the request of the Committee of Ministers "to pay attention to discrimination, prejudice and violence against Roma/Gypsies" and has referred to Roma/Gypsies in most of its reports.[85] Also, besides general policy recommendations on racism and xenophobia, the ECRI has drawn up a recommendation specifically on Roma.

General Policy Recommendation No. 3 on "combating racism and intolerance against Roma/Gypsies" notes that Roma/Gypsies suffer throughout Europe from persisting prejudices and are victims of racism and discrimination in many fields of social and economic life as well as exclusion. The recommendation urges member states to take several measures for the improvement of Roma/Gypsies' situation. The ECRI monitors the implementation of all general policy recommendations. Also, a recent booklet of ECRI on examples of good practice focuses on the theme of combating racism and intolerance towards Roma/Gypsies. The ECRI has recently adopted a programme of action aimed at involving various sectors of society in an intercultural dialogue based on mutual respect. As part of this, the committee organised in 2002 a Round Table in Romania, focusing on the implementation of anti-discrimination legislation in Romania, Romania's strategy to improve the situation of the Roma and the role of the media in fighting racism and xenophobia.

In addition, the European Conference against Racism – "All different all equal: from principle to practice", the European contribution to the World Conference against Racism, Racial Discrimination, Xenophobia and Related Intolerance – considered the issue of Roma/Gypsies and Travellers, and the general conclusions and the Political Declaration included two paragraphs on Roma/Gypsies. Finally, the European Youth Campaign against Racism, Xenophobia, Anti-Semitism and Intolerance has also been involved in more practical activities concerning young Roma leaders.[86]

The Ad hoc Committee of Experts for Identity Documents and Movement of Persons (CAHID) has also been working in areas affecting Romas: following a 1982 request by the Conference of European Ministers of Justice, CAHID examined problems of identity documents and movement, issues of residence and movement, discrimination, links with the state and family reunion. CAHID carried out a number of activities based on Recommendation R (83) of the Committee of Ministers and in 1982 adopted the final activity report on legal problems linked with the movement of nomads.[87] Unfortunately, the conclusions of this report were not formally adopted by the Committee of Ministers.

Another committee, the Committee on Experts on Nationality (CJ-NA), has since 1989 co-operated with several countries on the issue of statelessness and nationality and has studied various questions concerning Roma/Gypsies in individual countries. Furthermore, in co-operation with the European Committee on Legal Co-operation (CDCJ), the committee drew up the European Convention on Nationality, which was opened for signature by member states in November 2000. The convention serves as a European code on nationality.

Yet another committee of the Council of Europe, the Steering Committee on Human Rights (CDDH) was asked in 1995 to give its opinion to the Committee of Ministers on the interpretation of the term "vagrants" in Article 5.1.*e* of the European Convention on Human Rights, in response to Recommendation 1203 (1993) of the Parliamentary Assembly.[88] Article 5.1.*e* of the ECHR states:

> No one shall be deprived of his liberty save in the following cases and in accordance with a procedure prescribed by law: ...
>
> e. the lawful detention of ... vagrants.

The CDDH noted that the notion "vagrant" has been interpreted restrictively by the European Court of Human Rights as well as in the legislative and administrative texts in several member states. The Committee agreed that it should be asked whether or not the term be maintained in the European Convention on Human Rights.[89]

The Steering Committee for Equality between Women and Men (CDEG) also became involved in Roma issues and in 1995 organised a hearing of Roma/Gypsy women. Several problems were identified, including widespread illiteracy, low rates of schooling, obstacles in access to education, deficiencies in health protection and family planning, gaps in the implementation of existing legislation and growing unemployment, as well as racism and violence against them. Roma women face double discrimination, because of their origin as well as their gender.

Finally, the Ad hoc Committee of Experts on Legal Aspects of Territorial Asylum, Refugees and Stateless Persons (CAHAR) adopted in 1999 an opinion on the international mobility of Roma/Gypsies and on the granting of refugee status to the victims of pogroms.[90] The committee held that, although the fact of being a victim of a pogrom does not in itself constitute a well-founded fear of persecution in the sense of the 1951 Geneva Convention, yet

> planned acts of devastation directed against the life and the property of helpless, undefended groups of people or a reasonable fear for such devastation can, in individual cases, amount to persecution, if they are encouraged or permitted by the official authorities.[91]

Other activities of the Council of Europe

In 1993, the Council of Europe initiated a programme entitled "Promoting confidence-building measures relating to minorities" in order to implement specific initiatives aimed at changing hostile attitudes in inter-ethnic communities. The projects funded are usually of a preventive nature aimed at practical, positive effects at the local level. Activities have included regional meetings on ethnic relations, educational programmes and advisory programmes for the Roma, work-shops for opinion leaders, media programmes, seminars on media, and confidence-building programmes between Roma and their governments.[92] Several projects on Roma/Gypsies were set up, including educational programmes for the Roma, workshops for opinion leaders, media and confidence-building programmes.

One such project was launched in the Czech Republic and in Slovakia, aimed at the improvement of relations between the Roma/Gypsy minor-ity and the majority in the suburbs of Prague and the Slovakian town of Krimnica. After a sociological study of the respective communities' per-ceptions of each other, a series of practical activities co-ordinated by the relevant municipal authorities was undertaken in order to improve living conditions and intercultural education. Other relevant local projects included the setting-up of kindergartens for deprived and marginalised children of Rudnany (Slovakia); a study on the situation of the Roma in Bosnia that identified possible confidence-building measures; the creation of a centre of Romany culture in the Czech Republic; and several other projects in Hungary, Bulgaria, Romania and the Czech Republic.[93]

In 1994, the Secretary General of the Council of Europe decided to appoint a Co-ordinator for Activities concerning Roma/Gypsies. The co-ordinator has taken several steps to disseminate information about the Roma/ Gypsies: an interdepartmental co-ordination group was set up within the Secretariat, an information centre has been created, and several public information documents concerning Roma/Gypsies have been widely circulated. The co-ordinator acts as a contact person with several Roma/Gypsy organisations and has established working ties with other relevant international organisations, notably the High Commissioner for National Minorities of the OSCE and the European Commission. The Secretariat has participated in several international meetings and seminars concerning the situation of the Roma/Gypsies and missions have been carried out in several states.[94]

The co-ordinator is also in charge of the implementation of the project on Roma/Gypsies in central and eastern Europe. Launched in 1996 by the Committee of Ministers, the project has assisted several activities, such as conferences, seminars, assessment missions and training sessions.[95] In 1998, the scope of the project was extended to include all member states of the Council of Europe.[96] It is now entitled "Project of Roma/Gypsies in Europe" and operates on the basis of voluntary contri-butions by member states of the Council of Europe and a programme of co-operation and assistance to the member states.

In 1999, the Development Bank and the Council of Europe signed a co-operation programme to identify projects which might be eligible for loans from the bank. The first project launched under this programme concerned Roma and was an integrated housing, employment and community development project in the city of Brno (Czech Republic). Other programmes for the research and documentation of Roma issues include the assistance programme set up in central and eastern Europe, which offers opportunities to work with governments on Roma issues,[97] and the "Confidence-building measures programme", which provides the possibility of making small grants to projects that would improve relations between minorities and society as a whole.

The Council of Europe has also developed links with other European organisations on Roma issues. In September 1994, the CSCE (now the Organisation for Security and Co-operation for Europe) and the Council of Europe organised a Human Dimension Seminar on Roma, which examined national and international policies in the legal field as well as community relations and equal opportunities. This event gave new impetus for more work on the Roma issue in the Council of Europe, the OSCE and the European Union.[98] In 1995, the Budapest Summit of the OSCE established a Contact Point for Roma and Sinti. The Council of Europe has collaborated with the Contact Point for Roma and Sinti by organising two meetings of representatives of national consultative bodies between Roma/Gypsies and governments.[99] The OSCE/ODIHR and the Council of Europe realised a joint field visit to Kosovo in order to investigate the situation of the Roma community there.[100]

Apart from the OSCE, the Council of Europe has also collaborated with the European Union on Roma issues. The Joint Programme between the European Commission (PHARE Programme) and the Council of Europe – "Minorities in central Europe" – was completed in 1998 and included a study visit to Spain to review the Roma situation and a workshop on Roma issues with the active participation of Roma/Gypsies. Since 1999, all three organisations, namely the Council of Europe, the OSCE and the European Union have united their efforts under the Stability Pact for South-Eastern Europe, signed in Cologne. The first project under the Stability Pact, launched in 1999, focused on addressing the most acute crisis situations affecting Roma and on developing policies on Roma issues with Roma participation.[101] The second project was launched in 2000 and focused on implementing national strategies on Roma at the local level, reinforcing co-operation between local authorities and Roma NGOs and developing trans-border co-operation on Roma issues. A third project launched at the beginning of 2003 is based on the work of the previous project; it examines policy implementation on Roma issues at the national and local level and attempts to strengthen regional co-operation on Roma issues.

Concluding remarks

The Council of Europe has been very active in promoting and protecting Roma/Gypsy rights, through both standard-setting documents and practical programmes. One of the most important contributions of the Organisation has been the recognition that Roma constitute a minority in Europe and should be protected as such. The work of the Council of Europe has placed protection of the Roma high on the human rights agenda and has highlighted the problems they face. Moreover, the general instruments on human rights, minority rights and racism can be very useful for the Roma. The monitoring mechanisms of these instruments repeatedly address violations of Roma rights.

Even though some states have tried to link this protection to citizenship, which would have serious implications for Roma, the monitoring committees have not accepted this diversion of the standards of current international law and repeatedly comment on the situation of Roma, irrespective of their citizenship. On the other hand, so far the judicial process of the Council of Europe has been of limited use to Roma; yet, a closer look at the case law indicates a gradual move towards the recognition that flagrant discrimination often underlies human rights violations against Roma.

The instruments specifically on Roma/Gypsy rights apply the general human rights standards to the Roma/Gypsy reality. They consist of several resolutions and recommendations issued by various bodies of the Council of Europe and refer to a wide range of rights, notably self-identification, anti-discrimination, participatory rights, education and cultural rights. Although they are not directly a source of legal obligation, they are of major importance as an expression of contemporary political thinking and are used by policy-making, semi-judicial and judicial bodies as interpretative texts, when evaluating the scope and limits of binding general legal texts. Unfortunately, the gap between the standards set in the documents and the conduct of states is often vast.

Nevertheless, the Council of Europe has addressed this and has urged member states to take measures for the implementation of the existing standards. Additional monitoring procedures and stronger language towards some states may prove helpful. In this respect, the suggestion of a Roma mediator requires further consideration: the mediator would have the authority to advise governments and the Council of Europe in matters relating to Roma/Gypsies, investigate national policies related to them and review the progress in implementing Council of Europe measures to benefit them. Unfortunately, so far the member states have been reluctant to commit to such an extent. Further, a legally binding instrument on Roma rights, or on aspects of them, would contribute to the improvement of the situation. The adoption of an international convention that would guarantee freedom of movement for Roma/Gypsies in member states would be a positive step.

Legal documents aside, the Council of Europe has also initiated several projects aimed at promoting Roma rights. Some of them work towards a long-term vision; others focus at urgent action. Particular attention has been given to encouraging interaction between Roma and non-Roma communities as the first step towards eliminating interethnic tensions. This is particularly important because of the phenomenon of ghetto-isation of Roma communities, which is often evident on the outskirts of European cities. Projects promoting dissemination of information, such as case studies and reports focusing on cultural, educational and partic-ipatory rights, are also important to familiarise people with the Romani culture and the problems faced. In all these projects, particular thought has been given to achieving the participation of the communities involved, through Roma/Gypsy representatives and associations. Several training courses have focused on Roma activists and the improvement of those abilities that will help them defend the rights of their communities at both the national and international level.

Greater impact could be achieved by follow-up activities to these pro-jects, for example, political decisions based on conclusions of relevant studies and new activities that build on previous ones. There have been a variety of Roma projects run by different bodies of the Council of Europe; but, though this has guaranteed successes at different levels, it has also meant a lack of collaboration, coherence and adherence to the long-term vision. The co-ordinator has improved the situation in the last few years; yet the cynics would view this post as a weak compromise for the post of a mediator.

Nevertheless, even the most cynical commentator would agree that both standard-setting activities and specific projects of the Council of Europe have seriously contributed to raising awareness of the Roma situation in Europe. Several improvements have been made, both at the national and the international level. Unfortunately, the existing reality for many Roma/Gypsies is a sad reminder that there is still a lot to be achieved.

Notes

1.   There is some confusion about the terminology used. The term Roma (Gypsies), which is followed in most recent Council of Europe documents, seems to correspond most with the principle of self-identification of the ethnic group in question. The term includes ethnic groups that originate from north-eastern India, started immigrating after the 11th century and have had an itinerant or semi-itinerant culture. Despite common characteristics, there are various branches of the original ethnic group, known under different names, such as Roma, Gypsies, Sinti and Tsiganes. This chapter does not deal with nomadic groups that are not ethnically related to the Roma.

2.   European Union, *EU support for Roma Communities in CEECs: Basic Information on Roma in Central and Eastern Europe*, Brussels, 14 July 1998, MEMO/98/54. The numbers differ, depending on who is counting (states give different numbers from non-governmental organisations), the definition of Roma/Gypsies and whether Travellers are included or not. Jean-Pierre Liégeois estimates that there are currently at least 7 to 8.5 million Roma, Gypsies and Travellers in Europe; see Jean-Pierre Liégeois, *Roma, Gypsies, Travellers* (Strasbourg: Council of Europe, 1994), p. 34.

3.   *Report of the central and eastern European regional seminar of experts on the protection of minorities and other vulnerable groups and strengthening human rights capacity at the national level: World Conference against Racism, Racial Discrimination, Xenophobia and Related Intolerance*, A/CONF.189/PC.2/2, 14 August 2000, paragraph 56.

4.   See "Late Night Live – 25 October 1999: Gypsies – The Roma Wall", http://www.abc.net.au/rn/talks/lnl/stories/s61928.htm

5.   Mr van der Stoel, High Commissioner on National Minorities of the OSCE, Address in September 1999 to the Supplementary Human Dimension Meeting on Roma and Sinti Issues in Vienna, quoted in "The human rights problems and protections of the Roma", *Working paper prepared by Mr Y.K.J. Yeung Sik Yuen pursuant to Sub-Commission decision 1999/109*, E/CN.4/Sub.2//2000/28, paragraph 17. Also see OSCE, *Report on the Situation of Roma and Sinti in the OSCE Area*, High Commissioner on National Minorities, March 2000.

6.   Recommendation adopted on 2 February 1993.

7.   Citations from paragraphs 2 and 3 of the *General Observations*.

8.   Resolution (68) 30 was adopted by the Committee of Ministers on 31 October 1968.

9.   Adopted and opened for signature by General Assembly Resolution 2106 A (XX), 21 December 1965.

10.   For instance, see the concluding observations of the following states: Bulgaria, CERD/C/304/Add.29, 23 April 1997, paragraph 8; Spain, CERD/C/56/Misc.37/Rev.3, 23 March 2000, paragraph 10; Austria, CERD/C/304/Add.64, paragraph 7; Finland, CERD/C/304/Add.66, 7 April 1999, paragraph 11; United Kingdom, CERD/C/304/ Add.20, 23 April 1997, paragraph 8; Italy, CERD/C/304/Add.68, 7 April 1999, paragraphs 11-12, 14-15; Slovakia, CERD/C/304/Add.110, 1 May 2001, paragraphs 9-14; Czech Republic, CERD/C/304/Add.109, 1 May 2001, paragraphs 6, 9-12; Romania, CERD/C/304/Add.85, 12 April 2001, paragraphs 4, 11, 14, 15; Slovenia, CERD/ C/62/CO/9, 21 March 2003, paras. 10-11; Poland, CERD/C/62/CO/6, 21 March 2003.

11.   Resolution (72) 22 was adopted in 29 June 1972.

12.   Adopted by the Committee of Ministers on 14 May 1981 at its 68th Session.

13. For a general review, see *Council of Europe Activities on Roma/Gypsies and Travellers*, MG-S-ROM (2000) 17, Strasbourg, 2000.

14. Recommendation No. R (92) 10 on "the implementation of the rights of persons belonging to national minorities" was adopted in 21 May 1992 during the 476th meeting of ministers' deputies.

15. Recommendation 1134 (1990) on "the rights of minorities" was adopted by the Assembly on 1 October 1990.

16. Text adopted by the Assembly on 5 February 1992.

17. See Chapter 3 of the present work.

18. Article 7.5 of Part II of the charter.

19. See Chapter 2 of the present work.

20. Section II, Article 4, paragraphs 1 and 2.

21. Committee of experts on issues relating to the protection of national minorities (DH-MIN), *Results of the exchange of information on the question to which groups the Framework Convention will be applied*, Strasbourg, 15 January 1999, DH-MIN (98) 4, Addendum I.

22 Ibid.

23. Ibid.

24. See Chapter 1 of the present work.

25. See Advisory Committee on the Framework Convention for the Protection of National Minorities, Opinions on Finland, Hungary and Slovakia, adopted on 22 September 2000; see Chapter 2 of the present work.

26. For more analysis on the Framework Convention and the work of the Advisory Committee, see ibid.

27. For a deep analysis on Roma cases and the issues raised see Chapter 1; particularly the analysis of the following decisions of the Court: *Buckley v. the United Kingdom* (1996); *Assenov and Others v. Bulgaria* (1998), *Velikova v. Bulgaria* (2000), *Cyprus v. Turkey* (2001) and *Chapman v. the UK* (2001). Also see the following decisions of the Commission: *Kalderas Gypsies v. Federal Republic of Germany and the Netherlands* (1977); *X v. Ireland* (1983); *Powell v. the United Kingdom* (1990); *Beckers v. Netherlands* (1991); and *Van De Vin v. Netherlands* (1992).

28. I. Pogany, "Accommodating an emergent national identity: the Roma of central and eastern Europe", *International Journal on Minority and Group Rights*, 6 (1999), pp. 149-67, at pp. 163-64.

29. European Court of Human Rights, case of *Assenov and others v. Bulgaria* (90/1997/874/1086), judgment, 28 October 1998.

30. See paragraph 104 of the judgment in the Assenov case.

31. The Court found that the applicant's right to an effective remedy was violated because: i. he was not brought before an "officer authorized by law to exercise judicial power"; ii. he was denied a "trial within a reasonable time"; iii. he did not have the continuing lawfulness of his detention determined by a court.

32. European Court of Human Rights, case of *Velikova v. Bulgaria* (Application No. 41488/98), judgment, 14 November 2000.

33. Assenov case, paragraph 74.

34. See Chapter 1.

35. European Court of Human Rights, case of *Anguelova v. Bulgaria* (Application No. 38361/97), judgment, 13 June 2002.

36. For more analysis on the Court's approach on discrimination against minorities, see Chapter 1 of the present work.

37.   See relevant section in Chapter 1.

38.   See James A. Goldston, "Race discrimination litigation in Europe: problems and prospects", http://errc.org/rr_aut1998/notebook-discrimination.shtml

39.   For more on the subject, see L. Clements, P.A. Thomas and R. Thomas, "The rights of minorities: a Romany perspective", *Patrin Web Journal*, 2 May 2000, http://www.geocities.com/Paris/5121/romany-perspective.htm

40.   See Final Decision as to the Admissibility of Applications nos. 41138/98 by Iulius Moldovan and others, and 64320/01 by Octavian Rostas and others against Romania, 3 June 2003.

41.   Recommendation adopted by the Parliamentary Assembly on 30 September 1969.

42.   Recommendation adopted by the Committee of Ministers on 22 May 1975.

43.   Recommendation adopted by the Committee of Ministers on 22 February 1983.

44.   In 1998, the European Committee on Migration (CDMG) suggested the possible updating of Resolution (75) 13 in order to reflect developments and newer trends in this area. See opinion on the possible updating of Resolution (75) 13 on "the social situation of the nomads" adopted by the European Committee on Migration at its 39th meeting, 14-16 October 1998. http://www.coe.fr/cm/dec/1999/656/63.htm, Appendix 1.

45.   Text adopted by the Assembly on 2 February 1993, *General Observations, 9*. See also Doc. 6733, Report of the Committee on Culture and Education (Rapporteur: Mrs Verspaget).

46.   *General Observations*, paragraph 3, see above.

47.   Ibid.

48.   Recommendation 1203, paragraph xxi.

49.   Ibid., paragraph xxii.

50.   See *Appointment of a mediator for Roma/Gypsies*, Reply of the Committee of Ministers to written question No. 372 by Mrs J. Verspaget, 656th meeting – 19 January 1999, http://www.coe.fr/cm/dec/1999/656/63.htm

51.   Recommendation 1203, paragraph xxiii.

52.   Doc. CDMG (95) 11 Final, see below.

53.   The complementary reply was adopted on 17 October 1995 at the 547th meeting of the Committee of Ministers.

54.   For example, there has been an expert mission to Kosice (Slovakia) to examine urban rehabilitation problems in a district with a substantial Roma population, 3-6 September 1996; a study visit to Bulgaria, 15-20 October 1996, Sofia and other locations; assessment of community relations affecting the Romani minority in Brno (Czech Republic), Prague and Brno, 17-19 December 1997. More recent visits include a visit to Greece in 2001 and another one to Travellers' camps in Ireland.

55.   See European Committee on Migration, *Problems arising in connection with the international mobility of the Roma in Europe*, Report by Y. Matras, and conclusions adopted by the European Committee on Migration at its 36th meeting (April 1997), Strasbourg, 20 March 1998, CDMG (98) 14.

56.   For more information, see the reports of the activities of the specialist group: for 1996, see documents MG-S-ROM (96) 6 and MG-S-ROM (97) 1. For 1997, see MG-S-ROM (97) 6; MG-S-ROM (97) 15 rev., MG-S-ROM (98) 3. For 1998, see MG-S-ROM (98) and MG-S-ROM (98) 1; for 1999, see MG-S-ROM-(99) 7 and 11; for 2000, see MG-S-ROM (2000) 8 and 20; for 2001, see MG-S-ROM (2001) 11 and 25 Rev. En; and for 2002, see MG-S-ROM (2002) 7 revised and 20.

57. Text adopted by the Parliamentary Assembly on 27 January 1998 (3rd Sitting).

58. Recommendation R (2000) 4 was adopted on 3 February 2000 by the Committee of Ministers at the 696th meeting of the Ministers' Deputies.

59. Paragraph 8 of the Recommendation.

60. Reply to the Committee of Ministers, Doc. 9828 (Reply).

61. Paragraph 21 of Doc. 9828.

62. Other similar documents are Recommendation 1521 (2001) on "Csango minority culture in Romania" and Rec. 1333 (1997) on the "Aromanian culture and language".

63. Resolution adopted on 29 October 1981.

64. 12-13 July 1991. The hearing secured the participation of representatives of Gypsy communities from twelve European countries, on the occasion of the European Gypsy festival held in Strasbourg. See Appendix 1 of the memorandum CPL/Cult (26) 6.

65. See Coll/Tsi (92) 1, *Studies and Text Series* No. 38, Strasbourg: Council of Europe Publishing, 1994.

66. Congress Resolution 249, adopted in March 1993.

67. Ibid., paragraph 5.

68. Ibid., paragraph 11.

69. See Congress of Local and Regional Authorities of Europe, *European Network of Cities on Provisions for Roma in Municipalities: Statutes of the Network*, CG/GT/TSI (3) 2 rev; also see *Activities of the Council of Europe concerning Roma/Gypsies and Travellers*, Strasbourg, 2000, MG-S-ROM (2000) 17.

70. For further details on the work of the network, see CG/GT/TSI (3) 2 rev and CG/GT/TSI (3) 7.

71. Resolution adopted on 31 May 1995 at its second session.

72. See Recommendation 11 (1995) on "Towards a tolerant Europe: the contribution of Roma (Gypsies)", debated by the Congress and adopted on 31 May 1995, second sitting, see Doc. CG 2(3), Part I.

73. See Congress of Local and Regional Authorities in Europe, *Hearing, Roma (Gypsies) in Municipalities: What provision for education and culture, social problems training and employment? Some innovative experiences and models*, Report prepared by J.P. Liégeois, Strasbourg, 25 November 1996, AUD/KOS (2), p. 18.

74. See the conclusions of the round table in Congress of Local and Regional Authorities of Europe, *Round Table, Legal and institutional framework of the national minorities: the situation of Roma/Gypsies in Municipalities*, Ploiesti (Romania), 28-29 November 1996, Strasbourg, 28 February 1997, AUD/PLO (3), p. 10.

75. Ibid., p. 3.

76. See published report in AUD/PLO (3), p. 10.

77. Resolution on "the role and responsibility of local and regional authorities in regard to the cultural and social problems of populations of nomadic origin", see above.

78. Such reports include: *The training of teachers of Gypsy children*, Donaueschingen (Germany), 2-7 May 1983 (doc. DECS/EGT (83) 63); *Schooling for Gypsies' and Travellers' children: evaluating innovation*, Donaueschingen (Germany), 18-23 May 1987 (doc. DECS/EGT (87) 36); *Gypsy children in school: training for teachers and other personnel*, Montauban (France), 4-8 July 1988 (doc. DECS/EGT (88) 31); *School provision for Gypsy and Traveller children: distance learning and pedagogical follow-up*, Aix-en-Provence (France), 10-13 December 1990 (doc. DECS/EGT (90) 47); *Education for Traveller and refugee pupils: promoting achievement*, London, 22-28 March 1995 DECS/SE/Sem (95) 9.

79. Marcel Kurtiade, *Sirpustik amare chibaqiri* (Midi-Pyrénées: CRDP, 1994).

80. Marcel Kurtiade, *Sikavipen sar te siklo, e chavorre e sirpustikaça* (Midi-Pyrénées: CRDP, 1994).

81. See the report for the study in DECS/SE/DHRM (96) 18.

82. See the report of the study in DECS/SE/DHRM (96) 17.

83. See the report for the study in DECS/SE/DHRM (96) 23.

84. For more information on the project, see DECS/EDU/CIT (99) 58.

85. For example, see the following reports: CRI (2000) 3; CRI (2000) 4; CRI (2000) 5; CRI (2000) 32 and CRI (2000) 35; CRI (2001) 5; CRI (2001) 36; CRI (2002) 2; CRI (2002) 3; CRI (2002) 4; CRI (2002) 20; CRI (2003) 5. For a full discussion of ECRI work, see Chapter 11 of the present work.

86. For example, in Strasbourg, 18-25 April 1995; and in Helsinki, 21 October-2 November 1997, see EYCS/TC Rom (97) 2.

87. CAHID (86) 3.

88. This request responds to point 11.xii of Recommendation 1203 (1993) of the Parliamentary Assembly.

89. See CCDH, *Opinion on the interpretation of the term "vagrants" in Article 5.1.e of the European Convention on Human Rights*, http://www.cm.coe.int/dec/1999/656/63.htm, Appendix 2.

90. See opinion of CAHAR, http://www.coe.fr/cm/dec/1999/656/63.htm, Appendix 3.

91. Ibid.

92. See Council of Europe, *Newsletter: Activities on Roma/Gypsies*, No. 10.

93. See http://www.coe.fr/dase/en/cohesion/action/romanews.htm

94. See *Activities of the Council of Europe concerning Roma/Gypsies and Travellers*, MG-S-ROM (2000) 17.

95. For example, see Council of Europe, *Project on the Roma/Gypsies in Europe, report of activities*, MG-S-ROM (99) 10.

96. See Committee of Ministers, ministers' deputies – decision 645/6.6 (October 1998), 645th meeting, 20 October 1998, Item 6.6.

97. Among other activities, the programme has organised a seminar on "Perspectives for Roma in Bosnia today" (Tuzla, 15-16 November 1997); a training course for teachers in Bulgaria (September-November 1997), an international seminar on the education of disadvantaged children (Prescov, Slovakia, 13-15 November 1997) and a training course on the European Convention on Human Rights, (Cordoba, Spain, 29-31 January 1998).

98. See Council of Europe, *Council of Europe Activities concerning Roma/Gypsies and Travellers*, Strasbourg 1996, CDMG (96) 5 E, 27.

99. The first meeting was held in Budapest, 21-22 November 1996 and the second in Helsinki, 30 October-1 November 1997.

100. See *Report on the Joint OSCE/ODIHR-Council of Europe Field Mission on the situation of the Roma in Kosovo, 27 July-6 August 1999*, prepared by N. Gheorghe and J. Verspaget, http://www.romnews.com/a/kosovooscerep.html.

101. See 2nd Newsletter of Council of Europe activities, *Roma under the Stability Pact*, July 2001.

Chapter 5

Council of Europe summits and decisions of the Committee of Ministers (CoM)

Introduction

In examining intergovernmental co-operation with regard to minority protection within the Council of Europe, the decisions adopted by the highest decision-making instances – the Committee of Ministers (CoM) and the Council of Europe summits – acquire particular relevance. Given the important role of the CoM in maintaining political dialogue within the Organisation, its role in providing political orientation to the intergovernmental activities and determining the institutional functioning of the Organisation, particularly in relation to its enlargement process,[1] the study of some of the decisions it has adopted is highly relevant to understanding how the Council of Europe approaches the minority question.

The holding of the two Council of Europe summits (so far) has served not only to renew the focus of the CoM on the minority question and to provide impetus to its activities with regard to minority protection, but also to emphasise that this protection should be one of the main tasks of the Organisation. This has been very important in view of the "ideological" difficulty faced by the Organisation in responding to the challenge posed by the minority question in Europe,[2] experienced in particular, by its intergovernmental structures, until the early 1990s.[3]

The convening of the first Summit of Heads of State and Government of the Council of Europe in Vienna in 1993, brought the minority question out into the open. Since then, the issue has stood out in the final declarations resulting from the two Council of Europe summits and in CoM meetings (including those held at the ministers' deputies level). This has brought the Council of Europe to the forefront of minority protection in Europe. However, it has been mainly through the follow-up provided by the CoM that these decisions have been reflected in practice, with various degrees of success.

In the following pages, specific attention is devoted to the summit declarations and decisions of the CoM directly linked to them and to minority protection, including some adopted at the deputy level.[4] Attention is also devoted to various ministerial decisions and other forms of follow-up that CoM decisions have received, including those within the context of the Stability Pact for South-Eastern Europe. There are also references to related decisions taken by subsidiary intergovernmental bodies, which the CoM has set up in accordance with Article 17 of the Statute of the Council of Europe, closely connected with the summit declarations and decisions of the CoM. Additional related aspects of the work of these subsidiary bodies, which are also relevant to understanding the work of the Council of Europe in relation to minority protection, are discussed in Chapter 7.

Background

In 1989, when the CoM was deciding on the future role of the Organisation and priority lines of intergovernmental action were being established, the emphasis placed on the reinforcement of pluralist democracy and human rights – by reference to the ECHR and the European Social Charter – was the only element that could answer expectations on minority protection. Minority protection was not yet an explicit object "of the open and practical dialogue with European non-member countries".[5]

Nevertheless, the statement that "co-operation with these East European countries should lead to the promotion of human rights, the rapprochement of individuals and groups across frontiers and the finding of solutions to the challenges of society..."[6] was an encouraging sign. Soon after, another positive sign was offered by the attention paid by the CoM to the question of transfrontier co-operation. In the "Declaration on transfrontier co-operation in Europe on the occasion of the 40th anniversary of the Council of Europe", the CoM indicated that:

> their common interests make frontier communities the major protagonist of regional development and an ideal proving ground for co-operation and, this being so, encourages the work being done to prevent these regions from ever again being drawn towards an unbalanced and marginal situation and to commit them instead to the future, thanks to transfrontier co-operation, and to a harmonious process of development with due regard to the powers prescribed by the domestic law of each state.[7]

Three years later, in Recommendation R (92) 12 of the CoM to member states "on Community Relations"[8] the CoM acknowledged that:

> as a result of migration flows during recent decades, substantial populations of different national or ethnic origins from those of the host

society, and who initially came as temporary migrants, have now settled down permanently in most of the member states of the Council of Europe.[9]

Bearing in mind, among other things, the final report of the Council of Europe's project "Community and ethnic relations in Europe",[10] the CoM recommended that governments adopt explicit policies on community relations based on principles such as security of residence, real equality of opportunity, taking effective measures to combat racism and xenophobia, fullest possible participation in the life of the society, and an attitude of openness towards the cultures and customs brought by migrants in so far as they are compatible with national law.[11]

Against the background of the conflict in the former Yugoslavia, and only after the minority situation in that country had deteriorated over a period of time, the CoM adopted several declarations endorsing the endeavours of other international organisations which aimed at ending the hostilities and reiterating its availability to provide assistance.[12] In the "Declaration on the conflict in the former Yugoslavia" adopted on 11 September 1992, the CoM was "convinced that a lasting solution to the conflict can be found only through respect for international law and principles and commitments of the Council of Europe and of the CSCE, in particular the inviolability of frontiers and respect for human rights, fundamental freedoms and the rights of persons belonging to national minorities". The CoM condemned "ethnic cleansing"; declared that it would not recognise any situation created by a policy of *faits accomplis*; and insisted that forced expulsion, deportation and attempts to change by force the ethnic composition of regions, as well as illegal detention, cease immediately. It also called for detainees to be released and displaced persons and forced migrants to be permitted and helped to return to their homes.[13]

The CoM also made two declarations in connection with specific practices of massive human rights violations, of which minorities became the target, such as that on the systematic practice of rape in Bosnia and Herzegovina (9 December 1992) and on the rape of women and children (18 February 1993).[14] These declarations did not make specific reference to minorities, although the second one referred to the women and children belonging to the Muslim community in Bosnia and Herzegovina.[15] The declarations were confined to condemning those practices, proclaiming their criminal character and subjection to international criminal jurisdictions. They also expressed the willingness of the Council of Europe to participate in efforts at co-ordination of assistance and support organised by member states and NGOs in favour of the victims.

The CoM also adopted Recommendation R (92) 10 on the implementation of rights of persons belonging to national minorities, according to
which the CoM:

> Conscious that states do not always fulfil their obligations and commit-
> ments under international instruments resulting in national minorities
> being treated badly and also that states do not make use of existing
> mechanisms which could resolve some of the disputes .... Recommends
> that the governments of member states should, as a matter of urgency,
> ensure that they implement all their obligations and commitments in
> international instruments to persons belonging to national minorities
> and make use of the existing mechanisms which could alleviate
> problems facing persons belonging to national minorities.[16]

However, at the time the Council of Europe did not have in place
either the international standards or the mechanisms that could contribute substantially to such alleviation, in spite of previous calls by the
Parliamentary Assembly for action in this regard.[17] During the same
meeting of the ministers' deputies in which Recommendation R (92) 10
was adopted, initial steps were taken by the CoM towards a more substantial approach to the minority question, by means of the ad hoc terms
of reference given to the Steering Committee for Human Rights (see
below).

This was in contrast to the progress achieved at the intergovernmental
level in the framework of other international organisations active in
Europe, such as the United Nations and the OSCE, at the level of
standard-setting and of the establishment of relevant monitoring
mechanisms.[18] While in the Council of Europe context the precarious
referent for minority protection was Article 14 of the ECHR,[19] the
General Assembly of the United Nations had adopted Resolution 47/135
containing the "Declaration on the rights of persons belonging to
national or ethnic, religious and linguistic minorities", on 18 December
1992,[20] which built on Article 27 of the International Covenant on Civil
and Political Rights.[21] Similarly, the OSCE had already adopted the majority of its long list of substantive standards relating to minority protection,
and particularly those contained in the Vienna Concluding Document of
1989 and the Document of the Copenhagen Conference on the Human
Dimension of the CSCE of 1990 (OSCE 1990 Copenhagen Document).[22]

Monitoring mechanisms relevant to minority protection in Europe which
were already in place in the framework of the UN, prior to the Vienna
Summit, included: several treaty bodies (such as the Human Rights
Committee, the Committee on the Elimination of Racial Discrimination,
the Committee on the Rights of the Child and the Committee on
Economic, Social and Cultural Rights); the Sub-Commission on
Prevention of Discrimination and Protection of Minorities (later renamed

the Sub-Commission on the Promotion and Protection of Human Rights) through its confidential 1503 procedure; and the activities of some of the country and thematic rapporteurs of the Commission on Human Rights, especially those on contemporary forms of racism, racial discrimination, xenophobia and related intolerance,[23] on freedom of religion or belief,[24] and on violence against women, its causes and consequences.[25]

They all already had the capability to address minority questions and had been actively involved in dealing with them. The World Conference on Human Rights adopted a recommendation on 25 June 1993, contained in the Vienna Declaration and Programme of Action, leading to the creation of the UN "High Commissioner for the promotion and protection of all human rights".[26] The UN High Commissioner for Human Rights was later to receive a specific request to promote the principles contained in the UN "Declaration on the rights of persons belonging to national or ethnic, religious and linguistic minorities" within its mandate.[27]

In the context of the OSCE,[28] the High Commissioner on National Minorities was established in 1992 "as an instrument of conflict prevention at the earliest possible stage".[29] Various OSCE long-term field missions had already been deployed in areas of conflict in connection with minority situations.[30] The OSCE human dimension mechanism had developed its main features and been extensively used in connection with situations involving minorities,[31] and the Berlin emergency mechanism for consultation and co-operation with regard to emergency situations had been established and activated in relation to minority questions.[32] Hence the Council of Europe organs, and especially the Parliamentary Assembly, often found invaluable references to international instruments, and mechanisms of the UN and the OSCE in particular, when addressing minority situations.[33]

Meanwhile, intergovernmental co-operation at the Council of Europe had led only to the start of the process of searching for appropriate minority protection standards and mechanisms. The decision adopted on 21 May 1992 by the Committee of Ministers to give its Steering Committee on Human Rights (CDDH) the mandate "to study the possibility ... of formulating specific legal standards relating to the protection of national minorities in the spirit of the European Convention on Human Rights..."[34] was followed by its more momentous decision of 9 March 1993, mandating the CDDH "to propose specific legal standards relating to the protection of national minorities". This gave way to the establishment of the Committee of Experts on Issues relating to the Protection of National Minorities (DH-MIN), and the corresponding working party.[35] The results of their work were approved after examination and revision at an extraordinary meeting of the CDDH, in time for the first Council of Europe summit to be held in Vienna the following month.

The Vienna Summit Declaration

The declaration resulting from the first Summit of Heads of State and Government of the Council of Europe, held in Vienna on 9 October 1993, did not contain references to specific situations concerning minority protection, with the exception of a generic reference to the "peoples of former Yugoslavia".[36] Nevertheless, the declaration placed unprecedented emphasis on the concepts of "stability" and "democratic security" within the Council of Europe. The protection of national minorities was highlighted as an essential element of these concepts.

The impetus given to the minority question at the Vienna Summit was substantial. Most of the decisions adopted at the summit were relevant to minority protection. The Heads of State and Government resolved:

> to enter into political and legal commitments relating to the protection of national minorities in Europe and to instruct the Committee of Ministers to elaborate appropriate international legal instruments ....

They also resolved to pursue a policy for combating racism, xenophobia, anti-semitism and intolerance, and to adopt for this purpose a declaration and a plan of action. These two decisions were further developed at the summit, through the corresponding appendices to the summit declaration (see below). In addition, the heads of state and government resolved "to approve the principle of creating a consultative organ genuinely representing both local and regional authorities in Europe".[37] Furthermore, they invited the Council of Europe to study the provision of instruments for stimulating the development of European cultural schemes in a partnership involving public authorities and the community at large.

Protection of national minorities

In connection with the first decision of the Vienna Summit Declaration, in Appendix II of the declaration, the heads of state and government instructed the CoM: i. to draw up confidence-building measures aimed at increasing tolerance and understanding among peoples; ii. to respond to requests for assistance for the negotiation and implementation of treaties on questions concerning national minorities as well as agreements on transfrontier co-operation; iii. to draft with minimum delay a framework convention specifying the principles that contracting states would commit themselves to respect, in order to assure the protection of national minorities (this instrument would also be open for signature by non-member states); and iv. to begin work on drafting a protocol complementing the European Convention on Human Rights in the cultural field by provisions guaranteeing individual rights, in particular for persons belonging to national minorities.[38]

i. *Confidence-building measures*

Regarding the first aspect of the instructions given to the CoM, a programme called "Confidence-building measures in the field of minorities" was already in place at the Council of Europe before the Vienna Summit. This programme was considered by the Secretariat as the culmination of Council of Europe action in the field of confidence-building measures in human relations, which included the development of intercultural teaching methods, the promotion of community relations and local self-government, as well as the formulation of fundamental principles corresponding to a democratic and pluralistic society. According to its original format, the programme was managed by the Secretariat, which was responsible for the selection, co-ordination and monitoring of the pilot projects of the programme, acting under the authority of the CoM, to which it had to report regularly.[39] Although the start of the programme was modest, involving five pilot projects (which obtained mixed results), the programme greatly expanded following its endorsement at the Vienna Summit.

The present confidence-building measures programme, which takes the Vienna Summit Declaration as a base, comprises over 200 projects in countries of central and eastern Europe. The programme is discussed in more detail in Chapter 7. However, in connection with the Vienna Declaration a couple of features of the programme should be highlighted. The first is that a substantial difference exists between the present confidence-building measures programme resulting from the Summit and that originally established. The final decision as to the selection of the projects and as to the kind of support that they will receive no longer rests in the hands of the Secretary General, but with a small steering group of the CoM. Thus, the present programme has been subjected to an increased level of governmental control.

The second feature concerns terminology. At the summit, the heads of state and government, in their instructions to the CoM, differentiated between confidence-building measures on the one hand, and responses "to requests for assistance for the negotiation and implementation of treaties on questions concerning national minorities as well as agreements on transfrontier co-operation" on the other. In contrast, the Secretariat, as indicated above, tends to subsume the latter also under "confidence-building". This illustrates a broader understanding of this concept than that emanating from the heads of state and government. The "confidence-building measures" to which reference was made during the summit, and which comprise the grass-root level projects supported by the Council of Europe discussed in Chapter 7, are further qualified by the Secretariat as "confidence-building measures in civil society".[40] They have been incorporated into the new "Council of Europe Civil Society Programmes in the promotion of inter-ethnic relations" organised by the recently established "Division of NGOs and Civil Society" of the Secretariat.

ii. *Assistance for the negotiation and implementation of treaties*

The second item, in the list of instructions addressed by the heads of state and government to the CoM, asks the latter to respond "to requests for assistance for the negotiation and implementation of treaties on questions concerning national minorities as well as agreements on trans-frontier co-operation". Thus the text of the Vienna Declaration brings together the issues of transfrontier co-operation and minority protection at the intergovernmental level. This is an important conceptual step, given the relevance of their inter-relation in practice.[41]

Previous endeavours at the Council of Europe had contributed to establishing a legal basis for the negotiation and implementation of agreements on transfrontier co-operation. On 21 May 1980, the European Outline Convention on Transfrontier Co-operation between Territorial Communities or Authorities had been adopted.[42] After the Vienna Summit, the first additional protocol to this convention was also adopted, in order to overcome various difficulties which had been encountered in the implementation of the convention.[43] In 1998, a second additional protocol was adopted, this time in order to address a new modality of transfrontier co-operation: "interterritorial co-operation" between non-neighbouring states.[44] Neither the outline convention on transfrontier co-operation nor the two additional protocols adopted after the Vienna Summit contain any express reference to minority protection.

Although these instruments refer to "communities" within their title, this reference is interpreted in a legal/administrative sense rather than in a socio-cultural one. According to Article 2 of the convention, the phrase "territorial communities or authorities" "shall mean communities, authorities or bodies exercising local and regional functions and regarded as such under the domestic law of each state". Nevertheless, possibilities are open for each contracting state to "name the communities, authorities or bodies, subjects and forms to which it intends to confine the scope of the Convention or which it intends to exclude from its scope". Thus, a wide margin of discretion exists for minority empowerment by states. A series of model and outline agreements, statutes and contracts appended to the convention aim to serve as guidance to states willing to engage in transfrontier co-operation.[45]

The assistance provided by the Council of Europe for the negotiation and implementation of treaties on questions concerning national minorities[46] requested in the Vienna Declaration seems to have developed mainly in connection with the contacts established by the Organisation in the accession negotiations of the states of central and eastern Europe, and in the framework of the planning and development of co-operation programmes with these states.[47]

The EU initiative on a Pact on Stability in Europe,[48] launched in the early 1990s to reaffirm the international authority of the EU under the shadow of the conflict in the former Yugoslavia, encouraged the requests for assistance to the Council of Europe by the states concerned with the activities of the pact, mainly central and eastern European states. Similarly, requests for assistance often originated from initiatives encouraged and channelled by the Secretariat, with the support or endorsement of the political organs of the Council of Europe, or by means of intergovernmental contacts or contacts established by members of the Assembly. In the provision of assistance, the Secretariat has often relied on outside expertise or on the support of advisory bodies, the Venice Commission in particular.

iii. *The Framework Convention and additional protocol complementing the ECHR in the cultural field*

On 4 November 1993, the Committee of Ministers (CoM) set up an Ad hoc Committee of [governmental] Experts for the Protection of National Minorities (CAHMIN). Its terms of reference were identical to the latter two instructions given by the heads of state and government at the Vienna Summit, that is, to draft with minimum delay a framework convention specifying the principles that contracting states would commit themselves to respect, in order to assure the protection of national minorities; and to begin work on drafting a protocol complementing the European Convention on Human Rights in the cultural field by provisions guaranteeing individual rights, in particular for persons belonging to national minorities. Priority was given in CAHMIN to the drafting of the Framework Convention, the final text of which was adopted at the 95th session of the CoM on 10 November 1994, and opened for signature on 1 February 1995. Chapter 2 of this book is devoted to the analysis of this text.

The work on the additional protocol, for its part, once started, was suspended by the CoM on the basis of a report prepared by CAHMIN in

January 1996. According to a public Council of Europe report, the experts of CAHMIN met six times between November 1994 and November 1995 to define and frame individual, universal and enforceable rights suitable for inclusion in an additional protocol to the ECHR.[49] According to the same report, the main difficulties encountered in the deliberations of CAHMIN to achieve this goal were three-fold: economic – "the costs engendered by the enactment of these rights might induce states to restrict the benefits"; constitutional – "certain rights being proposed might lead to a 'transfer of competence' from the executive and legislative arms to the judiciary, for example in the field of state education"; and legal – "the introduction of new rights in the additional protocol might restrict the current extensive interpretation by the Court of the European Convention on Human Rights and its protocols. Besides, one would have to identify these new individual rights such as, for example, cultural identity".[50] These arguments show the strong reluctance of states to take serious steps to adopt legal standards in this field that would fall under the scope of the ECHR.

Nevertheless, CAHMIN drew up a draft protocol granting four rights: i. the right to one's name; ii. the right to use the language of one's choice; iii. the right to learn the language of one's choice; and iv. the right to create cultural and educational institutions. These rights, as enumerated, would have implied little progress in relation to existing minority protection and human rights standards.[51]

In addition to the agreed text of the draft protocol, a document produced at the end of the six meetings lists all the proposals made by the members of the committee – drawn from various different nationalities – potentially suitable for inclusion in the text of the protocol. These draft articles related to:

- cultural identity;
- access to cultural activities;
- the right to one's name;
- the right to use the language of one's choice, particularly in dealing with public authorities;
- public signs and notices (topographical or other) also to be worded in the minority language;
- the right to learn the language of one's choice;
- the right to an education in one's language;
- the right to quality education;
- the right to lifelong education;
- the right to create institutions;

- the right to one's cultural heritage;
- the right of access to information;
- the right of reply;
- the right to intellectual property.[52]

This document suggests a very diverse and occasionally unusual approach to the nature and character of the rights to be included in the protocol. These features largely derive from the fact that the mandate of the Vienna Summit has been interpreted as indicating that the protocol is to contain cultural rights applicable to every individual, including "in particular" to persons belonging to national minorities. The opportunity of protection "of the specific" – that is, the cultural rights of persons belonging to minorities – on which good ground for agreement seems to have existed at least from a substantive perspective (on the basis, for example, of the recent texts of the Framework Convention[53] and the Languages Charter,[54] which might well have inspired several of the areas of protection mentioned above), seems to have been missed as a result of the impossibility of agreement on the protection "of the whole" – that is, the cultural rights of every individual.

CAHMIN suggested the following options to the CoM for the follow-up of its own mandate: i. to open the draft additional protocol for signature by states; ii. to complete the draft protocol, by including in it supplementary rights; iii. to suspend the work and possibly resume it in several years' time; iv. to abandon totally the idea of an additional protocol as a means of ensuring the legal protection of cultural rights.[55] In January of 1996, the CoM finally decided:

- to suspend the work of the CAHMIN on 'the drafting of an additional protocol to safeguard the rights of the individual in the cultural field', its working papers being declassified and made available to interested circles;
- to continue reflection on the feasibility of further standard-setting in the cultural field and in the field of protection of national minorities, taking into account the Declaration adopted at the Summit.[56]

Given the very minor progress in relation to cultural protection demonstrated by the four rights contained in the CAHMIN preliminary draft of the additional protocol, the CoM decision to leave the question of the additional protocol open may not have been the worst possible outcome.

It should be noted that the wording of this decision of the Committee of Ministers, and of its first paragraph in particular, differs substantially from the original mandate given by the heads of state and government at the Vienna Summit, which expressly refers to "complementing the European Convention on Human Rights in the cultural field 'by provisions guaranteeing individual rights, in particular for persons belonging to national minorities'".[57]

While in the first paragraph a reference to minorities is omitted, in the second paragraph the fields of culture and national minorities are separated. More worryingly, the decision to reflect "on the feasibility" of further standard-setting, seems to have brought into question not only whether the option of the adoption of an additional protocol in the cultural field is workable at present, but even whether the adoption of any type of instrument in this field is practicable. Later decisions of the CoM have insisted on the question of further standard-setting as pending, and still on the agenda.[58]

The Parliamentary Assembly has been a strong defender and promoter of the adoption of the additional protocol.[59] In a 1999 reply of the CoM to several Parliamentary Assembly recommendations expressing regret that the CoM had interrupted its work on a draft protocol, the CoM fully subscribed to the statement made by its Steering Committee on Human Rights (CDDH) on this issue. According to this statement:

> it seems doubtful that an attempt to prepare an additional protocol would at this stage have a chance of achieving a more successful result than the previous attempt. It therefore would not recommend that this work currently be taken up again. The CDDH does not exclude the possibility that further developments, and in particular the experience drawn from the implementation of the Framework Convention for the Protection of National Minorities, may reveal a need to consider further standard-setting. The CDDH furthermore draws attention to the fact that it is currently carrying out work on the elaboration of a possible additional protocol to the European Convention on Human Rights, widening the scope of Article 14, which expressly refers to national minorities.[60]

After the suspension of the work of CAHMIN, intergovernmental co-operation in relation to minority protection focused on the implementation mechanism under Articles 24 to 26 of the Framework Convention.[61] An ad hoc working party of the ministers' deputies on the implementation mechanism of the Framework Convention (GT-MIN) was created in 1996. As a result of its work, the CoM adopted Resolution (97) 10, on 17 September 1997 at the 601st meeting of the ministers' deputies, on the rules adopted by the CoM on the monitoring arrangements under Articles 24 to 26 of the Framework Convention for the Protection of National Minorities.[61] Also, at a later stage, an "Outline for reports to be submitted pursuant to Article 25 paragraph 1 of the Framework Convention for the Protection of National Minorities" was adopted by the CoM.[62]

Differential treatment of racism, xenophobia, anti-semitism and intolerance

With regard to the decision adopted at the Vienna Summit to pursue a policy for combating racism, xenophobia, anti-semitism and intolerance, and to adopt for this purpose a declaration and a plan of action, these are already included in Appendix III of the Vienna Summit Declaration. The declaration, emphatically worded, stresses the need for active engagement of Council of Europe member states, and "European peoples, groups and citizens, and young people in particular". It incorporates the undertaking by the heads of state and government of the Council of Europe member states "to combat all ideologies, policies and practices constituting an incitement to racial hatred, violence and discrimination, as well as any action or language likely to strengthen fears and tensions between groups from different racial, ethnic, national, religious or social backgrounds".[64] It also includes their commitment "to strengthening national laws and international instruments and taking appropriate measures at national and European level".

The plan of action, for its part, envisages: the launching of a European Youth Campaign; the revision of state legislation and the implementation of legislation aimed at combating racism and discrimination; and the reinforcement and implementation of preventive measures, giving special attention to awareness-raising and confidence-building measures. The summit largely follows the proposals made by the Parliamentary Assembly in its Recommendation 1222 (1993).[65]

Finally, the plan of action previews the establishment of a committee of governmental experts. This would result in the establishment of the European Commission against Racism and Intolerance (ECRI). The committee of experts is given the mandate: i. to review member states' legislation, policies and other measures in this area as well as their effectiveness; ii. to propose action at local, national and European level; iii. to formulate general policy recommendations to member states; and iv. to study international legal instruments applicable in the matter with a view to their reinforcement where appropriate.[66] The membership of the committee and the modalities for its functioning were to be decided by the Committee of Ministers.[67]

Although persons belonging to minorities are unmistakably the main targets of racism, xenophobia, anti-semitism and intolerance,[68] the Vienna Summit Declaration differentiated between Council of Europe action concerning the protection of national minorities, on the one hand, and action dealing with those practices on the other. Such a differentiation had a precedent in the UN context, where various international instruments specifically devoted to establishing a substantial set of standards aiming to counter discrimination against any person were adopted before the minority question was thoroughly addressed.[69] In the OSCE, the development of standards in both areas can be considered as simultaneous processes.[70]

In 1981, the Committee of Ministers of the Council of Europe had adopted a "Declaration regarding intolerance – a threat to democracy", in which the main referent on this topic was the International Convention on the Elimination of All Forms of Racial Discrimination (ICERD), and the Committee of Ministers' own Resolution (68) 30, of 31 October 1968, on measures to be taken against incitement to racial, national and religious hatred.[71] The declaration contained a decision on the implementation of "a programme of activities including, in particular, the study of legal instruments applicable in the matter with a view to their reinforcement where appropriate".[72]

However, the role of the Council of Europe in standard-setting on this matter at that time was perceived by the member states as one of closing possible loopholes existing under international instruments adopted in the framework of other international organisations (mainly the United Nations Declaration on the Elimination of All Forms of Racial Discrimination and the ICERD) rather than one of developing a thorough set of norms within the Council of Europe.[73] This resulted in the consolidation of its incomplete and indirect regulation under the European Convention on Human Rights,[74] and was reflected in the statement by the CoM that states "will make every effort so that the principles enunciated above prevail within other international organisations".[75] This was in spite of the support of the Parliamentary Assembly for the adoption of norms in this field within the Council of Europe.[76] As late as 1995, the Assembly was still placed in the position of having to recommend that the CoM call on member states of the Council of Europe to sign and ratify the International Convention on the Elimination of All Forms of Racial Discrimination, if they had not already done so.[77]

At the Vienna Summit, the different paths of Council of Europe action concerning the protection of national minorities on the one hand, and action against racism, xenophobia, anti-semitism and intolerance on the other, were taken at a time when – because consensus on standard-setting in the field of minority protection could be reached – it is likely that consensus on standard-setting in relation to the latter topic would also have been possible.

However, the Council of Europe took a reverse approach to that of other international organisations. General standards, regulating thoroughly and specifically the issues of equality and non-discrimination, tolerance and protection against violence in various areas of life, have been adopted in relation to persons belonging to minorities before they have been adopted in relation to all persons in society generally. It was necessary to wait for the convening by the Council of Europe of the European Conference "All different, all equal: from principle to practice" on 11 to 13 October 2000, for the purpose of elaborating the European contribution to the World Conference against Racism, Racial Discrimination, Xenophobia and Related Intolerance, for ministers of Council of Europe member states to adopt a "political declaration" addressing comprehensively those phenomena in relation to everyone (see below).[78]

One of the practical reasons for the divergent approach to action in both fields – protection of minorities and intolerance – at the Vienna Summit could probably be traced to the sense of "alarm" experienced by the heads of state and government in connection with the "resurgence of racism, xenophobia and anti-semitism, the development of a climate of intolerance, and increase in acts of violence, notably against migrants and people of immigrant origin, and the degrading treatment and discriminatory practices accompanying them" in the early 1990s.[79] This seems to have prompted states to take immediately applicable measures to monitor these practices, without previously engaging in a law-making process. The aforementioned tradition of relying on universal international standards could also have had an impact.

The paragraph of the declaration quoted above could create the impression that the differential treatment given to both fields responds to a wish to divorce national minority questions from those of immigrant populations, to which it particularly seems to refer. Nevertheless, the paragraph of the declaration which follows rules out this hypothesis: the heads of state and government are "equally alarmed also by the development of aggressive nationalism and ethnocentrism which constitute new expressions of xenophobia". Old, long-established minorities are equally as liable to suffer from all these types of aggression as immigrant communities, and the plan of action of the Vienna Declaration seems to relate to both. A former chairman of ECRI has stated that the need for swift action was the reason for the establishment of this monitoring mechanism without the previous drafting of a convention.[80] This also points to the sense of urgency as the explanation for the course of action adopted at the summit.

An interesting linkage in the 1993 "Declaration and Plan of Action on combating racism, xenophobia, anti-semitism and intolerance" is that established between the deterioration of the economic situation and the generation of forms of exclusion likely to foster social tensions and manifestations of xenophobia. However, the action plan envisages only the use of Council of Europe co-operation and assistance programmes,[81] with the general aim of reinforcing mutual understanding and confidence between people, and in particular the development under the programmes of "policies to combat social exclusion and extreme poverty". An intensification of work under the co-operation and assistance programmes in the fields of inter-community relations and equality of opportunities is also requested in the action plan. The encouragement of transfrontier co-operation between local authorities highlights not only the relevance of transfrontier co-operation in combating the practices contemplated under the action plan, but also, indirectly, the link between combating these practices and minority protection.[82]

The plan of action envisages the incorporation of research and education in the co-operation and assistance programmes, including: the study of "the deep-seated causes of intolerance and considering remedies"; the promotion of "education in the fields of human rights and respect for cultural diversity"; and the strengthening of "programmes aimed at eliminating prejudice in the teaching of history by emphasising positive mutual influence between different countries, religions and ideas in the historical development of Europe".[83] Finally, the heads of state and government include in the plan of action a direct request for the media to report and comment on acts of racism and intolerance factually and responsibly, calling for the development of professional codes of ethics in this regard.

Monitoring commitments

An aspect of the more general provisions of the Vienna Declaration which may have a strong impact on minority protection is the impulse given to intergovernmental co-operation in relation to the monitoring of compliance with commitments accepted by the member states. The heads of state and government of the Council of Europe, after declaring that guaranteed freedom of the media, protection of national minorities and observance of the principles of international law must remain decisive criteria for assessing any application for membership, stated their resolve to ensure full compliance with the commitments accepted by all member states within the Council of Europe.[84] They also stated their resolve "to make full use of the political forum provided by our Committee of Ministers and Parliamentary Assembly to promote, in accordance with the competencies and vocation of the Organisation, the strengthening of democratic security in Europe. The political dialogue within our Organisation will make a valuable contribution to the stability of our continent".[85]

In spite of the emphatic language used, no specific instructions were given to the CoM to facilitate the above. The follow-up provided by the CoM to these general statements included in the Vienna Summit

Declaration resulted in milder-worded compromises, and in the establishment of a specific monitoring mechanism, which has come to be known as "The Committee of Ministers' monitoring procedures".[86] The Parliamentary Assembly monitoring procedures, for their part, were to continue following their own, independent course of action.[87]

In the "Declaration on compliance with commitments accepted by member states of the Council of Europe" adopted by the CoM on 10 November 1994, the CoM, following a reference to the Vienna Summit Declaration, underlined "the need to facilitate the fulfilment of these commitments, through political follow-up, carried out constructively, on the basis of dialogue, co-operation and mutual assistance".[88] The CoM stated its statutory responsibility "for ensuring full respect of these commitments in all member states, without prejudice to other existing procedures, including the activities of the Parliamentary Assembly and conventional control bodies".[89] The commitments referred to were those to "democracy, human rights and the rule of law accepted by the member states under the Council's Statute, the European Convention on Human Rights and other legal instruments". Thus, minority rights standards could be subsumed under the scope of the monitoring mechanism.[90]

It should be emphasised that the 1994 declaration on compliance was adopted by the Council of Europe member states on the same date that the text of the Framework Convention for the Protection of National Minorities was adopted, pointing to a possible and implicit link between both instruments.[91] This is particularly relevant in view of the fact that the details of the working of the monitoring mechanism under the convention were yet to be fixed, and its effectiveness unknown. Besides the convention, several other legal instruments highly relevant to minority protection discussed in this work had already been adopted.[92]

Thus, the monitoring of commitments related to minority protection undertaken by the Council of Europe member states could and should become the object of the CoM monitoring mechanism, especially in the light of the emphasis placed on the protection of national minorities in the text of the Vienna Summit Declaration. The latter text was to serve as the basis for its establishment. Given the relevance which the CoM monitoring procedure may have for minority protection, Chapter 6 is devoted to its analysis. In reply to several Parliamentary Assembly recommendations regarding minority protection, the Committee of Ministers recently stated that this issue "may be touched upon by the Committee of Ministers, not only in exercising the functions attributed to it under the relevant conventions, but also in the context of its general monitoring procedures".[93]

Subsequent decisions of the Committee of Ministers

The results of the meetings of the CoM which followed the Vienna Summit serve to illustrate, by way of comparison, the political impetus given to minority protection at the summit. Little was added in the final communiqués resulting from these meetings to what had been decided at the summit, particularly in relation to minority protection. For example, the importance of protection of national minorities "for stability" and "in maintaining stability and strengthening democratic security in Europe" was highlighted at the 96th (11 May 1995) and 97th (9 November 1995) sessions of the CoM, respectively, as it had been highlighted in the Vienna Summit Declaration.[94] The renewal of the support for the CoM to continue its work in drawing up an additional protocol to the European Convention on Human Rights in the cultural field expressed at the 96th session of the CoM does not seem to have been successful.

At the 97th session, the less ambitious hope was expressed that the year 1996 would see the first concrete results of the work initiated in the field of national minorities. At this session, the ministers instructed their deputies to start to implement, as from the beginning of 1996, the "Declaration on compliance with commitments accepted by member states of the Council of Europe". They noted that this endeavour should be combined with effective support for all reform efforts and for consolidating democratic structures in member states.[95] In addition, the ministers made a general statement on "the readiness of the Council of Europe to contribute ... to the process of democratic reconstruction in Bosnia-Herzegovina and in other parts of former Yugoslavia".[96] This statement was made soon before the conclusion of the Dayton Agreement.[97]

The Strasbourg Summit Declaration

The second Summit of Heads of State and Government of the Council of Europe (Strasbourg Summit) was the result of an initiative launched by the President of the Parliamentary Assembly, L. Fischer, in March 1996. In September 1996, the Parliamentary Assembly adopted a recommendation proposing that a second Council of Europe summit be held in Strasbourg. In November 1996 the CoM agreed to this initiative.[98] In the final declaration of the second summit, adopted on 11 October 1997, the heads of state and government, "having reviewed the developments" since the first summit, "as well as the implementation" of the decisions concerning "the establishment of a single European Court of Human Rights; the protection of national minorities; and the fight against racism, xenophobia, anti-semitism and intolerance" do not actually take substantial steps forward in relation to minority protection. The main achievement seems to have been that this issue was mentioned among the priorities included in the action plan appended to the declaration.

The action plan "seeks to define the main tasks for the Council of Europe in the coming years, particularly in the period leading to its 50th Anniversary".[99] The intergovernmental programmes of activities and the "Activities for the development and consolidation of democratic stability" (ADACS) took account of the objectives established in the action plan.[100] Similarly, the priorities established at the Strasbourg Summit seem to have become the leitmotif of the revision of the structures and *modus operandi* of the Council of Europe subsequently undertaken. The other main achievement of the action plan, relevant to minority protection as a constituent element of human rights protection, is the high-level endorsement of the Finnish initiative to create the office of the Commissioner for Human Rights.[101]

Nevertheless, references were made, to the minority question in the text of the Declaration, in the section dealing with human rights and plural-ist democracy, both considered as factors contributing to stability in Europe. The heads of state and government asserted their determination to step up co-operation in respect of the protection of all persons belong-ing to national minorities. Further in the same section, the fundamental role of the institutions of local democracy in the preservation of stability was acknowledged.

Another interesting reference appeared in the section entitled: "Recog-nising that social cohesion is one of the foremost needs of the wider Europe and should be pursued as an essential complement to the pro-motion of human rights and dignity". Under this heading, the heads of state and government affirmed their "determination to protect the rights of lawfully residing migrant workers and to facilitate their integration in the societies in which they live." Finally, under the heading "Aware of the educational and cultural dimension of the main challenges to be faced by Europe in the future as well as of the essential role of culture and edu-cation in strengthening mutual understanding and confidence between peoples" the heads of state and government reaffirmed the importance they attach "to the protection of our European cultural and natural heritage and to the promotion of awareness of this heritage".[102]

In the action plan appended to the Strasbourg Summit Declaration the "four main areas where there is scope for immediate advances and prac-tical measures" are defined. These four main areas coincide with the main headings under which the declaration is structured. The area deal-ing with democracy and human rights includes a reference to protection of national minorities. The heads of state and government, "taking into account the imminent entry into force of the Framework Convention for the Protection of National Minorities, resolve to complement the Council of Europe's standard-setting achievements in this field through practical initiatives, such as confidence-building measures and enhanced co-operation, involving both governments and civil society".[103] Although the unequivocal inclusion of the question of the protection of national minorities in the context of democracy and human rights constitutes a positive outcome, no real innovations are introduced, in relation to minority protection. The same applies to action to combat racism, xeno-phobia, anti-semitism and intolerance:

> the heads of state and government welcome the action taken in this field by the Council of Europe since the Vienna Summit and resolve to intensify, for this purpose, the activities of the European Commission against Racism and Intolerance, while stressing the importance of close co-operation with the European Union.

No indication is given as to how the activities of ECRI are to be intensi-fied, although this statement would serve ECRI as a basis to consolidate its own initiatives.[104] No specific action is envisaged in relation to those other areas of interest for minority protection included in the declaration mentioned above. Only in relation to the enhancement of the European heritage is it decided "to launch a campaign in 1999 on the theme 'Europe, a common heritage', respecting cultural diversity, based on existing or prospective partnerships between government, education and cultural institutions, and industry". The location of the quotation marks enclosing the title to be given to the campaign however, pointed to commonalities, rather than differences, as its main focus.

In spite of the focus of the campaign on heritage protection, and although aspects of cultural diversity relevant to minority protection were present in it, hardly any emphasis was placed on minority aspects in its design, and no stable frameworks aiming at improving majority-minority relations seem to have resulted from it.[105] Thus, the main devel-opment resulting from the text of the Strasbourg Summit Declaration and Action Plan is the statement included in the latter that "the heads of state and government welcome the proposal to create an office of Commissioner for Human Rights to promote respect for human rights in the member states and instruct the Committee of Ministers to study arrangements for its implementation, while respecting the competencies of the single Court".[106] The Strasbourg Summit seems also to have created the momentum for a number of ratifications which enabled the Framework Convention for the Protection of National Minorities to enter into force.[107]

The text of the Additional Protocol to the Convention on Cybercrime concerning the Criminalisation of Acts of a Racist and Xenophobic Nature Committed through Computer Systems,[108] opened for signature on 29 January 2003, mentions the Action Plan in its preamble. In particular, the aim of the Action Plan: "to seek common responses to the developments of the new technologies based on the standards and values of the Council of Europe".[109] The relevance of the Protocol for minority protection is clear, as it envisages the criminalisation of the use of computer systems for: dissemination of racist and xenophobic material;[110] threatening persons for the reason that they belong to a group, distinguished by race, colour, descent or national or ethnic origin, as well as religion, or threatening those groups as such, with the commission of a serious criminal offence as defined under domestic law;[111] publicly insulting similar persons or groups;[112] the denial, gross minimisation, approval or justification of genocide or crimes against humanity;[113] and aiding or abetting the commission of the previous offences.[114] Particularly relevant from a minority protection perspective is the fact that the group as such becomes an explicit object of protection.

The crimes envisaged in the protocol needed to be brought outside the scope of the Convention on Cybercrime,[115] due to lack of consensus among Council of Europe states on its inclusion in the convention, on the basis of freedom of expression concerns.[116] Although the protocol has not yet entered into force, the grounds for collision between its provisions (especially Article 3) and the jurisprudence under the ECHR are broad. Especial attention should be devoted to jurisprudence established by the European Court of Human Rights under Article 10 of the ECHR in connection with hate speech and related issues.[117]

A final element of interest of the Strasbourg Summit Declaration is contained in its penultimate paragraph, instructing the CoM "to carry out the structural reforms needed to adapt the Organisation to its new tasks and its enlarged membership and to improve its decision-making process". This served as a basis for the CoM to decide at its subsequent 101st session (Strasbourg, 6 November) on the setting up of a "Committee of Wise Persons with a limited membership reflecting a geographical balance of the member states, to be chaired by an eminent political figure, responsible for drawing up proposals for structural reform, and reporting back to the 103rd session of the Committee of Ministers".[118]

The report of the Committee of Wise Persons

In accordance with the mandate received by the Committee of Wise Persons,[119] the report resulting from its activity, dated 12 October 1998, focuses on the existing and future role of the Council of Europe structures and on the ways in which they operate, rather than on establishing new priority areas of action for the Organisation. So it is mainly from the former perspective that it has relevance for minority protection. Some specific references to the minority question are contained in the report. However, none of them was included among the so-called "main recommendations" which, selected from the report, emphasise certain aspects of its content, by reiterating them at the beginning of its text.[120] These "main recommendations" would seem to have focused the attention of the CoM in the follow-up of the report.[121]

In the report, the Committee of Wise Persons pointed to the need for the Council of Europe to develop its "outreach function". One of the two tasks envisaged in this regard was "helping in a concrete manner all member states – and in particular the more recent ones – to fulfil their obligations and commitments to the Organisation, in the field of human rights and fundamental freedoms – including the protection of minorities – through the widest implementation of the principles and provisions contained in the Framework Convention for the Protection of National Minorities and the European Charter for Regional or Minority Languages."[122]

According to the Committee of Wise Persons, reports drawn up within the framework of monitoring procedures, including monitoring reports on various conventions, such as the Framework Convention for the Protection of National Minorities "should, whenever possible be made public, taking into account the delicate political nature of such information."[123] Furthermore, the Committee of Wise Persons proposed that: "in specific cases, time limits should be fixed within which recommendations made in the report should be implemented, failing which the report about the country will be published".[124] Another interesting proposal was the granting to the Secretary General of further responsibilities in the field of monitoring: "in particular, he/she should be responsible for proposing to the Committee of Ministers concrete measures in the context of co-operation programmes, stemming from the conclusions of the monitoring".[125] Initial steps in this direction seem to have recently been taken in the context of the Committee of Ministers' monitoring procedures.[126]

Furthermore, according to the Committee of Wise Persons, the Secretary General should be given the capability: i. "to commission reports from outside public figures with recognised authority, or to appoint special thematic 'rapporteurs' to look into particular areas of concern, in consultation and agreement with the Committee of Ministers"; and ii. "to carry out joint missions (with the Chairperson of the Committee of Ministers) in the member states concerned".[127] The ability of the Secretary General to appoint special rapporteurs has implicitly taken shape in the context of the CoM monitoring procedures, through the appointment of experts on specific topics who have visited some countries, although no

216

form of "rapporteurship" has been established to deal with minority questions specifically so far.

The possibility of dealing with minority situations on an individual, specific country-based approach in connection with situations of crisis would probably be more easily accepted than the establishment of a thematic rapporteur system on minority questions with a "Council of Europe wide" mandate. This would imply giving to the aforementioned term "areas" a geographical interpretation. The sensitivity of the minority issue, and the reluctance of some western European states in particular to address this issue within their own borders, would probably make the acceptance of a rapporteur system with an "all states inclusive" mandate more difficult. Thus an interpretation of the term "areas" in a "thematic" sense, although in principle more desirable, would more likely be doomed.

As to the proposal made by the Committee of Wise Persons for the Secretary General to carry out missions, qualified by the requirement that missions be "joint", the latter requirement has not been "formally" met in recent visits to states by the Secretary General, during which issues such as the political situation in the respective state, and the respect by the state of Council of Europe standards and commitments have been discussed.[128] This is despite the fact that the Secretary General may have informally received the endorsement and support of the CoM chairmanship. The CoM monitoring procedures have further allowed for the "mission activity" of the Secretary General to develop, as discussed in Chapter 6.

The proposals of the Committee of Wise Persons to reform CoM action at the deputies' level, by the reduction of automatic procedures in relation to the setting-up of the agendas to allow debates on essential matters, such as issues on the Organisation's core functions,[129] could be instrumental in bringing minority questions onto the agenda of the deputies. The same applies to the proposal that the Secretary General submits a short report to the Parliamentary Assembly and to the CoM on a yearly basis "on the state of the Council of Europe", including proposals for developing the activities of the Organisation.[130] Emphasis is placed on the Congress of Local and Regional Authorities of Europe being more widely consulted by the CoM on issues falling within the responsibilities of local and/or regional authorities.[131]

The Committee of Wise Persons further recommended that "every year, the Committee of Ministers should approve a plan for the Organisation and establish clear priorities in each field and sector in the light of the main priorities for the Organisation as a whole. This might imply freezing or postponing certain activities for a period of time and concentrating resources on a smaller number of activities in order to speed up their completion. In addition, a greater proportion of appropriations should be allocated to operational expenditure, in particular democracy-building programmes".[132]

The emphasis placed by the Committee of Wise Persons on the Council of Europe focusing on matters considered as essential, because of belonging to the Organisation's core functions, could be regarded in principle as good news for minority protection. This is not only because minority protection, as a part of human rights protection, should automatically belong to the main aims of the Council of Europe, as it flows from the Council of Europe Statute, but also because minority protection has persistently been emphasised as one of the main objects of concern for the Council of Europe at high-level intergovernmental meetings in recent years. Consequently, the Committee of Wise Persons' call for "concentration", according to which "steering committees should review existing activities in order to put an end to obsolete programmes or freeze marginal ones and, to this effect, make stricter application of the selection criteria for intergovernmental activities laid down by the Committee of Ministers"[133] should not have a negative effect on successful minority-related activities.

However, in practice, "freezing or postponing certain activities for a period of time and concentrating resources on a smaller number of activities in order to speed up their completion" has proved to be detrimental in relation to activities concerning minorities. Some of the intergovernmental activities in the field of minority protection, including those of the Committee of Experts on Issues relating to the Protection of National Minorities (DH-MIN) were suspended from March 1999 for want of funding.[134] The discontinuation of some of the minority-related activities took place following additional suggestions of the Committee of Wise Persons for strengthening the role of the Council of Europe Secretariat.

According to the Committee of Wise Persons: "greater discretion should be given to the Secretariat in the management of programmes and in budgetary management, coupled with increased accountability to the Committee of Ministers for results achieved. This could include a more flexible approach to the allocation of appropriations to prioritised activities."[135] The emphasis on "operational expenditure" and "democracy-building programmes" advocated by the Committee of Wise Persons has proved not to be good news for minority protection until now, given the little emphasis given to minority issues within these programmes so far.[136]

It remains to be seen whether recent structural changes undergone by the Secretariat along the lines of budget reforms, leading to the ending of ADACS in the year 2000, and the new inclusion of the activities of the Secretariat under so called "co-operation activities" will result in increased attention to minority questions. They will also raise the question of whether the discontinuation of activities related to minorities (such as in the case of the Joint Programme with the EU Commission open to Council of Europe states generally considered), their increase or decrease, result from a decision of the CoM or directly from the Secretariat. So far, only in connection with the monitoring of the implementation of instruments such as Languages Charter, and more in particular the Framework Convention, have new types of activities relating to minority protection susceptible of being undertaken in all Council of Europe states (albeit individually considered) started to be developed.[137]

Other proposals of the Committee of Wise Persons are relevant in particular with regard to the possibilities for the Council of Europe to speedily respond to situations of crisis where the fate of minorities can be at stake. These include the proposal for the enlargement of the responsibilities of the Chairperson of the CoM, so that he/she: i. convenes urgent meetings; ii. invites, for discussions of special importance in the Committee of Ministers, high-ranking representatives from non-member states and from international organisations; and iii. appoints, with the consent of the Bureau of the CoM, special representatives to fulfil political missions.[138] These proposals have already started to be implemented, and have contributed to bringing the Council of Europe machinery closer to that existing in the OSCE. In the latter Organisation, however, the possibilities for non-governmental consultation, including on a periodic basis, by inter-governmental structures have been more widely developed.[139] The Committee of Wise Persons did not make a call to the effect that intergovernmental bodies of the Council of Europe receive input from NGOs, particularly in connection to point ii. above.[140]

The perception by the Committee of Wise Persons of the possible contribution of non-governmental organisations to the future role of the Council of Europe has been confined to the area of "[i]mproving the visibility" of the Organisation.[141] The Committee of Wise Persons has also encouraged the involvement of NGOs in the implementation of the intergovernmental programme of activities and the elaboration of a framework for consultation with them, without providing further guidelines.[142]

The activities of the Council of Europe Secretariat in connection with NGOs enjoying consultative status seem to be on the increase, as the most recent annual report of the Organisation illustrates. L. Gogberidze, Ambassador of Georgia, was named the Committee of Ministers' Rapporteur on relations between the Council of Europe and NGOs on 30 October 2000.[143] Activities in connection with NGOs in the field of minority protection seem to have been restricted mainly to those undertaken in the framework of the confidence-building measures at the grass-roots level and the intergovernmental programmes (more recently in the framework of the so called "co-operation activities").[144] The pro-active role of relevant expert bodies in recent times, especially those responsible for monitoring the implementation of the Framework Convention and the Languages Charter (supported by their respective secretariats within the general secretariat structure) seem to provide at present the main, yet limited impulse to co-operation with the non-governmental sector on minority issues in Council of Europe member states.[145]

Another important aspect of the Committee of Wise Persons' report relates to the emphasis on the complementarity of the existing monitoring procedures of the Committee of Ministers and the Parliamentary Assembly[146] as well as "of the Congress of Local and Regional Authorities of Europe in its specific field of competence".[147] It is suggested that "in order to create more synergy between the different bodies", the reports of the European Committee for the Prevention of Torture and Inhuman or Degrading Treatment or Punishment and ECRI, as well as the findings based on the European Social Charter should, to a larger extent, be included in the monitoring work".[148] No reference is made, however, to the findings of the Advisory Committee under the Framework Convention[149] and the Committee of Experts under the Languages Charter,[150] which should also be taken into consideration in the context of the monitoring work of the various organs of the Council of Europe. Minority protection is an area which would benefit most from complementarity and mutual reinforcement among the various monitoring organs, bodies and procedures.

To conclude, the Committee of Wise Persons has stated that "the Committee of Ministers, in close co-operation with the Secretary General, should be responsible for follow-up action and should monitor implementation of the recommendations" contained in the Committee of Wise Persons' report. No role is foreseen for the Parliamentary Assembly or the Congress in connection with this follow-up. The fact that the decision to set up the Committee of Wise Persons originated from the CoM and the former had a duty to report to the latter does not seem enough reason to have side-stepped such involvement.

Nevertheless, the CoM invited the Parliamentary Assembly to give an opinion on the Committee of Wise Persons' report. It also decided to set up an ad hoc Working Party on Follow-up Action on the Final Report of the Committee of Wise Persons (GT-SAGES) within its own structures, with a duty to report to the Deputies and to the 104th session of the CoM.[151]

Other decisions of the Committee of Ministers

It was actually at the 103rd session of the CoM that the report of the Committee of Wise Persons was considered, following a presentation by former Portuguese President M. Soares, Chairman of the Committee of Wise Persons. The CoM congratulated the Wise Persons for their work and instructed their Deputies to examine the proposals contained in their report with a view to the adoption of structural reforms at the 104th session of the CoM.[152]

The 104th session, held in May 1999 in Budapest, coincided with the celebrations of the 50th anniversary of the Council of Europe. During the session a strong emphasis was placed on the achievements of the fifty years of activity of the Council of Europe. However, this session was not perceived as the culmination of a period in the Council of Europe's development initiated at the Strasbourg Summit, as initially foreseen at that summit, but rather as an interim stage.[153] The CoM, in view of the "fundamental *acquis*" of the Council of Europe decided "to move still further ahead" ... and "expressed its determination to pursue the process of renewal of the Council of Europe in particular by the adoption of a structural reform of the Organisation".[154]

One out of the ten paragraphs of the conclusions adopted by the CoM was devoted to the crisis in Kosovo, a topic on which, according to the chairman, "very strong views" had been expressed, where the Ministers endorsed the Council of Europe contribution to the Stability Pact for South Eastern Europe (see below).[155] They also took note of the declaration on the Kosovo crisis by the chairman of the CoM, appended to the conclusions of the meeting. In this declaration, the chairman condemned those responsible for the massive deportations and violations of human rights and humanitarian law against the civilian population, reiterating support for the action of the International Criminal Tribunal for the former Yugoslavia. The declaration also reiterated the willingness of the Council of Europe to contribute, in its fields of competence, to the implementation of the political settlement and to political and institutional reconstruction in the region.[156]

The "Budapest Declaration for a greater Europe without dividing lines"

The highlight of the 104th session of the CoM was the adoption of the "Budapest Declaration for a greater Europe without dividing lines" of 7 May 1999. In the declaration, the ministers of foreign affairs undertake among other things:

• to continue to consolidate the stability of the continent based on democratic institutions, and to this effect, among other things, "honour all the commitments they have given to each other, to the Council of Europe and to their citizens";

- to seek to strengthen the political, legal, social and cultural cohesion of greater Europe, and to this effect, among other things, "combat the decisive factors constituted by racism and xenophobia, intolerance – whether political, cultural or religious – and discrimination against minorities" and "build on the community of culture formed by a Europe enriched by its diversity, confident in its identity and open to the world;

- to reaffirm the primacy of the human person in their policies and for this purpose promote the rights protected under the European Convention on Human Rights and other basic Council of Europe instruments "in particular through the action of the Council of Europe Commissioner for Human Rights" established in a resolution appended to the declaration; and

- to continue to promote their shared commitment to democracy and the rule of law by developing the existing partnership between, among others "national governments and parliaments, represented in the Committee of Ministers and the Parliamentary Assembly; the statutory organs of the Council of Europe; local and regional authorities, represented in the Council of Europe by the Congress of Local and Regional Authorities of Europe; and structures making it possible to associate non-governmental organisations and civil society with intergovernmental co-operation".

Finally, the Ministers express their determination "to continue, in the 21st century, to contribute to building democratic stability and co-operation in Europe", and accordingly undertake:

   i. to complete the reform of the structures and activities of the Council of Europe and adapt them to the future challenges;

   ii. to seek political and legal solutions making it possible to transcend state frontiers and promote peaceful and harmonious co-existence of the nations, minorities, and cultural, linguistic and religious communities which together make up the continent; in this spirit, they "shall implement the Council of Europe contribution to the stability programme for South-eastern Europe and work for peace as well as full respect for human rights and the rule of law throughout Europe".[157]

Thus, the profile of minority protection as one of the main matters of concern for the Organisation seems to have had its heyday at the CoM's 50th anniversary commemoration, at the level of political declarations. However, this has been consolidated only by the unambiguous endorsement of the Council of Europe contribution to the Stability Pact for South-Eastern Europe. As to operational measures agreed on in the document resulting from the meeting itself, it is probably the adoption of the mandate of the Council of Europe Commissioner for Human Rights, through a resolution appended to the declaration, that bears the greatest significance for minority protection. Given the importance of this institution, Chapter 12 is devoted to it.

Other topics addressed by the ministers, and resulting in the corresponding declarations appended to the "Budapest Declaration for a greater Europe without dividing lines" also illustrate an unprecedented level of sensitivity towards minority questions at the intergovernmental level. These have been: the CoM "Declaration on a European policy for new information technologies" and the declaration and programme on "Education for democratic citizenship based on the rights and responsibilities of citizens" (contained in Appendixes I and III to the Budapest Declaration, respectively).

The "Declaration on a European policy for new information technologies", which includes a series of instructions to governments in this area, has made the respect for "diversity of content and language" one of its five main areas of concern. The CoM urged governments "to encourage the development of a wide range of communication and information networks, as well as the diversity of content and language, so as to foster political pluralism, cultural diversity and sustainable development". The CoM also urged the promotion of "the full use by all, including minorities, of the opportunities for exchange of opinion and self-expression offered by the new information technologies", and instructed governments to acknowledge "the usefulness of these technologies in enabling all European countries and regions to express their cultural identities".

Furthermore, the CoM urged governments "to encourage the provision of cultural, educational and other products and services in an appropriate variety of languages and to promote the greatest possible diversity of these products and services". Finally, they instructed governments "to ensure, as far as possible, that information systems, in the administrative and legal fields, offer material which takes account of regional and linguistic criteria and which meets the specific needs of concerned minorities".[158]

As to the "Declaration on education for democratic citizenship, based on the rights and responsibilities of citizens", its title could, at first sight, raise doubts as to its "inclusion" or "exclusion" from its scope of those members of minority groups who do not fully enjoy "citizenship" status in the legal sense, that is, including the rights, privileges and duties inherent to citizenship. However, the usage of the term "citizenship" in the declaration would seem to respond to its wider meaning, which includes all individuals viewed as members of society.[159] Such interpretation would seem to better fit the aims and concepts proclaimed in the declaration, in which the Council of Europe's mission to build a freer, more tolerant and just society based on solidarity, common values and cultural heritage enriched by its diversity, is stated.

Local communities are considered as one of the various contexts where education for democratic citizenship develops. Further, democratic citizenship "prepares people to live in a multicultural society and to deal with difference knowledgeably, sensibly, tolerantly and morally"; "strengthens social cohesion, mutual understanding and solidarity"; and "must be inclusive of all age groups and sectors of society".[160] Further in the declaration, member states of the Council of Europe are called upon to "promote democratic citizenship based on the maintenance and further realisation of human rights and fundamental freedoms".

Possible grounds for the aforementioned 'exclusivism' *vis-à-vis* those who do not enjoy the citizenship of the state could be perceived in the reference to "the core competencies for democratic citizenship based on citizens' rights and responsibilities", included among the key issues to receive attention under the programme which follows the declaration. However, the preceding reference made in this text to "the relationships between rights and responsibilities as well as common responsibilities in combating social exclusion, marginalisation, civic apathy, intolerance and violence", brings the aims of the programme into correspondence with those of minority protection, including of non-citizens.[161]

"Human rights, including their social dimension and each person's obligation to respect the rights of others" are considered another key issue under the programme.[162] The programme establishes a link between human rights education, civic education, intercultural education, history teaching, democratic leadership training, conflict-resolution and confidence-building. The main activities previewed under the programme fall under the purview of policy-making, research and data collection, training and awareness-raising, including support for regional and local information and training workshops and seminars.

It should be noted that the "Education for democratic citizenship" programme launched by the Council of Europe actually pre-dated the Strasbourg Summit, having already been adopted in the framework of the medium-term work programme adopted by the 19th session of the Conference of Ministers of Education of the Council of Europe, held in Kristiansand earlier during the year 1997. The main components of the medium-term work programme, including the project on "Education for democratic citizenship", were endorsed at the Strasbourg Summit as matching the Council of Europe's general lines of action and priorities.[163]

In the draft "Common guidelines for education for democratic citizenship" presented by the Ministers of Education of the Council of Europe at their 20th Session, held in Kraków on 15 to 17 October 2000 – and thus after the "Declaration on education for democratic citizenship" had been adopted – specific reference is made to the role of democratic citizenship in the fight against violence, xenophobia, racism, aggressive nationalism and intolerance.[164] A cultural dimension of education for democratic citizenship is acknowledged, comprising: "respect for all peoples, fundamental democratic values, both a shared and divergent history and heritage and contributing to peaceful intercultural relations". Emphasis is placed on human rights and intercultural education, as well as on a number of practical experiments, the so-called "sites of citizenship" which work on responses to exclusion and discrimination, as well as the fostering of communication between different ethnic groups in a multicultural setting.[165]

The contribution to the Stability Pact for South-Eastern Europe

The endorsement by the CoM of the Council of Europe contribution to the Stability Pact for South-Eastern Europe in the document "Stability programme for South-Eastern Europe, a Council of Europe contribution",[166] which was adopted in parallel with the "Budapest Declaration for a greater Europe without dividing lines", has possibly been the Committee of Ministers' decision with a more concrete impact on the policies of the Council of Europe towards minorities in recent years, and may be the decision with the most direct repercussions in the short run. The "specific action" previewed under the contribution includes the general and ambitious aim to: "redress the human rights situation and prepare for the return of refugees and displaced persons from Kosovo and assist all civilian victims of the conflict".

Under the general guideline that "human rights and social protection activities should be devised in support of the return of refugees and displaced persons from Kosovo and assistance in providing adequate protection mechanisms after their return" the Council of Europe envisages its "assistance for the establishment and functioning of existing (and possible future) protection mechanisms (in co-operation with UNHCR, UNHCHR, OSCE, ICTY)" in the area of human rights, including minority protection. It also envisages the "[d]evelopment of national human rights protection institutions (including ombudsman type institutions)". Assistance is also foreseen in the field of "human rights education and awareness-raising, aiming at combating racism and intolerance and fostering a culture of respect of the other's difference (in close co-operation with ECRI)" and in the field of "identifying and implementing activities fostering the concept of policing in a democratic and multi-ethnic society".[167]

Another aim of "specific action" is a contribution to "the establishment and stabilisation of democratic constitutional and institutional frameworks". This includes specific Council of Europe proposals for its own contribution as a partner in "the implementation of a [political] settlement within its field of competence and with its own instruments and capabilities", as well as input into the strengthening of local and regional authorities, based on the principles of the European Charter of Local Self-Government, including a proposal for involvement of the Congress in this respect.[168] Another contribution of the Council of Europe concerns "legislative frameworks, which underpin relations between individuals (civil code and civil procedure code) and which should ensure the necessary balance between public order and security concerns with respect to individual rights (penal code and code of penal procedure) ..." and assistance in the effective implementation of these legal frameworks.

Under the Council of Europe contribution to the Stability Pact for South-Eastern Europe, "specific action" also aims at developing "a culture of democratic citizenship: confidence-building, civil society and independent media", including via: i. the adoption of confidence-building measures[169] in a regional perspective; ii. the training of media professionals, especially on issues like reporting in a multi-ethnic society and their role in promoting a climate of tolerance; iii. support for partnership between local communities and the establishment of a forum in this connection; iv. initiative to facilitate the holding of a meeting of representatives of various churches and religious communities "to discuss the future in the region from an ecumenical perspective"; and v. "assistance to liaison between NGOs working in favour of mutual understanding, cultural dialogue and tolerance among peoples from different origins with special attention to the problems of Roma people".[170]

In addition, "specific action" aims "to promote culture and education in an intercultural perspective". The activities previewed in this field include:

- reinforcing projects for democracy at and through school, expanding the existing South-Eastern European schools network, assisting with history teaching, providing expert advice on legislation and policy;
- promoting education towards democratic citizenship and community development for peaceful conflict resolution using school as a focal point for the reconstruction of the social fabric;
- encouraging the re-organisation of cultural life through appropriate strategies ... defining an action plan in the field of cultural heritage, including damage assessment and plans for reconstruction;
- re-instating intercultural dialogue and communication by way of thematic encounters and exchanges among intellectuals, cultural actors and artists in the region ..."[171]

One of the first outcomes yielded by the Council of Europe contribution to the Stability Pact for South-Eastern Europe in connection with minority protection is related to this latter aspect of "specific action". It consisted in the convening of the Informal Conference of the Ministers of Education of South-Eastern Europe, held in Strasbourg on 2 and 3 December 1999, and attended by the ministers of education of: Albania; Bosnia and Herzegovina; Bulgaria; Croatia; Greece; Romania; Slovenia; "the former Yugoslav Republic of Macedonia" and Turkey, as well as Austria and Hungary.

In a declaration adopted at the conference, the ministers express their conviction "that education and educational co-operation have a fundamental role to play in the development of tolerance, mutual understanding and a common awareness both within and between the member states in the European context".[172] The ministers present a series of aspects of ongoing or planned reforms to the education systems of south-eastern Europe on which the Council of Europe activities should focus. The first among these aspects concerns "legislative and structural reforms linked to the Organisation, infrastructure, and functioning of the education system, including: the evaluation of the impact of education policies, particularly those relating to cultural diversity and the needs of minority groups". Another aspect refers to practical activities in thematic areas such as education for democratic citizenship, history teaching (including sensitive issues and periods of conflict) and the development of language teaching.

In November 2001 a Second Informal Conference of Ministers of Education for South-East Europe was convened, with the additional participation of Moldova and Serbia and Montenegro, as well as France, the Holy See, the Netherlands, Poland and the Russian Federation. Representatives of UNESCO, the Stability Pact for South-East Europe, the OHR, the OECD and UNMIK, as well as experts, also attended the conference.[173] Besides praising the role of the "Enhanced Graz Process" under the Stability Pact as a catalyst for the implementation of educational reforms in south-east Europe, with the participation of the Council of Europe, the ministers discussed the initial conclusions of the thematic reviews on educational reforms which the OECD has conducted within the framework of the Graz Process.

In their conclusions they emphasise the importance of the solutions and policies to be implemented being identified in the context of individual countries, and express their hope for increased participation by the competent authorities, decision-makers and experts from the region in defining medium- to long-term strategies. They insist on the need for a tailor-made approach by the international community. They also call for internal co-operation within the region, by emphasising the importance of multilateral and bilateral co-operation as well as co-ordination with the ministers of education in the countries concerned. The ministers further bring their own reform process in parallel "with those of all member states" and recommend that the CoM "give particular consideration, in the years ahead, to the training and status of teachers, to support for the implementation of general education reforms covering pre-school and primary education, vocational training and adult education, to diversification in higher education and to equitable access to quality education".

All these aspects would seem relevant for minority education, although no reference is made to it. A connection with minority protection can only be indirectly derived from general references to the content of the previous, first informal conference, the content of which has already been described. The ministers include an explicit reference to the Declaration adopted at the 20th Session of the ministers of education held in Kraków in October 2000, in which "the role of education in strengthening the stability of south-east Europe" was emphasised.

Finally, the "specific action" of the Council of Europe contribution to the Stability Pact for South-Eastern Europe by the CoM addresses "the protection and participation of national minorities – whilst respecting each country's territorial integrity". Reference is made in this regard to the promotion of stability and confidence "through common European values and principles based on its legally binding instruments in the human rights field ...". The Framework Convention for the Protection of National Minorities is mentioned in this connection. The convening of a high-level governmental conference with the participation of representatives of national minorities aimed at "demonstrating the relevance and operational character of the Council of Europe's principles and values for the purposes of ensuring the protection of ethnic communities and their full and equal participation in democratic processes in the region" is envisaged.[174]

At the meeting of Working Table I of the Stability Pact for South-Eastern Europe (dealing with democratisation and human rights) held in Geneva on 18-19 October 1999, a decision was taken to endorse the Council of Europe's initiative to launch, in co-operation with the OSCE High Commissioner on National Minorities, a series of consultations in south-eastern Europe on human rights and minority issues. The outcome of these consultations was intended to help in the preparation of the aforementioned conference, which the Government of Slovenia offered to organise in Portorož.[175] A Council of Europe "Special Delegation" was mandated with carrying out the consultation.

The delegation (or, alternatively, the head of the delegation) visited during November and December 1999 some of the states in the region:

Albania, Bosnia and Herzegovina, Croatia, and "the former Yugoslav Republic of Macedonia". The delegation held talks "in the capitals and other places with members of government, parliament, local authorities, the administration, representatives of ethnic groups and communities and minorities, educational and research institutions, civil society, as well as field missions of international organisations (OSCE, EU, UN, etc.)".[176] The report made by the delegation, reflecting the outcome of the consultations, was submitted to the Portorož Conference on Inter-Ethnic Relations and Minorities in South-Eastern Europe held on 16 and 17 March 2000.

A joint statement, a framework programme of action and a list of projects were adopted at the Portorož conference. Several proposals made by the "Special Delegation", by then renamed as "Special Delegation of Council of Europe Advisers on Minorities" were incorporated in the framework programme of action of the conference. These included: i. the launching of an awareness-raising campaign, through the establishment of a European organising committee and a series of national committees in each state, and ii. a commitment to the implementation of existing standards, including through the launching of a "non-discrimination review".

Other issues raised by the advisers, such as the need for specific measures to deal with Roma questions, were also taken up at the conference. The framework programme of action adopted at the Portorož conference further advocated the adoption of a comprehensive political strategy at the regional level, to ensure formal recognition of the Roma as a distinct group with specific needs, to bring discrimination against the Roma to an end, and to promote affirmative action in favour of the Roma.[177] An unequivocal connection was established between the concepts of democratic citizenship and the promotion of a multi-ethnic and multicultural society by the advisers, and later endorsed at the conference.[178]

The proposals made by the advisers, and the support they received at the Portorož conference have resulted in the three Stability Pact projects concerning minorities for which the Council of Europe is responsible: the "Non-discrimination review" (Project 1); "Acceptance and implementation of existing standards" (Project 2); and "Bilateral co-operation agreements" (Project 3). They are financed through a voluntary contribution made by Switzerland.[179] Also the awareness-raising campaign "Link diversity" has been launched, and is regarded as complementary to the projects.[180]

Project 1, the "Non-discrimination review" is to be carried out by national country groups, set up jointly by the respective national governments and the Council of Europe, following a process of consultation with non-governmental organisations, including representatives of groups which are the targets of discrimination.[181] The first objective of the project consists of an overview of discrimination in the country concerned, entailing the identification by the country groups of areas of life in which different minority groups (defined by race, colour, language, religion, nationality, national or ethnic origin, or similar grounds) are in an unequal position, and an analysis of the scope of the problem which this generates. This is followed by more detailed and focused work by the country groups on areas of life that they identify as "target areas". Each country group should thoroughly analyse the factors that contribute to the situation of inequality in each of the "target areas" and prepare detailed recommendations and measures to address the problems identified. The country groups should also be responsible for assessing the programmes and measures aimed at combating these problems.

The second objective of the project consists of a review of the existing legislative framework in the country for preventing discrimination and promoting full and effective equality (including in the civil, criminal and administrative fields) and on the assessment of existing relevant provisions and their interpretation, as well as the mechanisms responsible for their implementation. This should lead to the determination of existing loopholes, and the elaboration of proposals in order to overcome them.

The third and final objective of the project is the development of measures that could address the problems identified, particularly in the selected "target areas", including proposals for positive action, and the implementation of the measures developed. It is requested that governments should be actively involved in the development and implementation of the measures, which should be carried out at as early a stage of the project as possible (see below). To this effect, each participating state nominates a governmental contact person for the project.

The importance of this project cannot be overstated. Although at first sight it would seem just to add one more to the number of international procedures dealing with issues of discrimination that already exist (and the activities of ECRI in particular), it actually constitutes an addition of the utmost importance, given that the project relies on a "domestic effort" to adapt legislation and practices from "within" the countries concerned. The project aims to build a bridge between international standards and recommendations of existing expert bodies and the internal practice of states, by directly engaging relevant actors at the domestic level. This "hands-on approach", aimed at directly affecting state practice, constitutes a very important and long overdue step forward when it comes to minority protection in the framework of the Council of Europe.

Emphasis is placed in the outline of the project on the need to avoid overlap with the activities of already existing monitoring bodies. The

230

Council of Europe prepared a "Guide for the Non-Discrimination Review" setting out the same tasks for all the country groups, and providing them with the same model reports to fill in and questionnaires to answer, so that comparable reports and results of the review could be obtained. This has also been facilitated through meetings bringing together the experts of the country groups, governmental contact persons, and Secretariat/expert support.

Given the design of the project, the non-discrimination review is called to play a complementary role in relation to the activities of other international bodies. The non-discrimination reviews in the various countries can constitute a very useful tool in translating the recommendations given by international monitoring bodies (particularly those of ECRI; the Advisory Committee under the Framework Convention for the Protection of National Minorities;[182] the Committee of Experts under the European Charter for Regional or Minority Languages,[183] and the Commissioner for Human Rights[184]) into domestic measures, to be implemented by the states concerned.

The individual non-discrimination reviews can also provide a substantive input into the implementation of international standards and recommendations, as a result of the insight the country groups can offer of the domestic system and the country-specific conditions and procedures relevant to this implementation. This local knowledge can contribute to facilitate the effectiveness of those standards and recommendations. Even the mere establishment of the national country groups may already contribute to activate implementation at the domestic level. Their effectiveness will largely depend, however, on the independence and level of know-how that their members will portray as well as the strategies they will adopt.

As to the question of state involvement in the project, it should be noted that the green light given by "all participating and facilitating Stability Pact countries" in the framework programme of action adopted at the Portorož conference is considered as the basis for this involvement.[185] This opens participation to Western European countries as well. The conference had actually welcomed "the initiative to launch a non-discrimination review".[186]

In an initial stocktaking exercise concerning the project, it was noted that recent endeavours with regard to the drafting of anti-discrimination legislation in Hungary and the Czech Republic could be fed into the project. Eight countries in south-east Europe have agreed to engage in reviews so far: Albania, Croatia, Hungary, "the former Yugoslav Republic of Macedonia", Moldova, Romania, Serbia and Montenegro (including a separate review in the UNMIK/Kosovo), Slovenia and Ukraine. At the time of writing, country groups from Moldova, Romania and Hungary have already begun implementing projects in some of their selected target areas.

Project 2 concerning the "Acceptance and implementation of existing standards" is a continuation of some of the intergovernmental co-operation activities which used to be carried out under the aegis of the DH-MIN,[187] with a narrower focus on states of south-eastern Europe. These activities involve information meetings for the promotion of existing international instruments concerning minorities adopted in the framework of the Council of Europe,[188] with the aim of their signature and ratification by an increasing number of states, or for those states already party, to discuss in more detail domestic developments. They also involve training seminars on monitoring the implementation of the Framework Convention, especially on the submitting of state reports and the preparation of shadow reports by NGOs, as well as the provision of legislative expertise in order to ensure that international standards are duly respected in the development of new domestic legislation.

The meetings usually gather together MPs, government officials dealing with minority issues, minority representatives and non-governmental organisations. In a recent meeting in which the development of Project 2 was evaluated, it was indicated that the project, "aims at turning these activities into concrete initiatives".[189] Besides activities aimed at assisting states in the signature and ratification of the relevant international instruments, emphasis is placed in the context of Project 2 on their "full implementation". The concrete achievements of such endeavour remain to be accounted for.

Finally, Project 3 deals with the issue of bilateral co-operation agree-ments,[190] and presently focuses on reinforcing and encouraging bilateral co-operation in the field of minorities in a way that is consistent and co-ordinated with multilateral standards, those contained in the Framework Convention in particular. In the framework of Project 3, a report on the "Protection of national minorities through bilateral agreements in South Eastern Europe" has been elaborated at the European Academy of Bolzano/Bozen, and presented by Professor J. Marko at a stocktaking meeting on the Stability Pact projects.[191] Issues concerning the existing bilateral agreements and their implementation, such as: i. the possible involve-ment of the international community; ii. transparency in the financial assistance provided by kin-states; and iii. the issue of minorities without a kin-state, have been highlighted as needing further reflection in the context of the project.

The need to involve minority groups in the negotiation, drafting and monitoring of bilateral agreements, and to improve co-operation between the EU, the Council of Europe and the OSCE in this field has been emphasised. Some states participating at the meeting identified concrete problems either in the conclusion of bilateral agreements or in the functioning of the joint commissions established under some of the bilateral treaties already concluded. In the context of the process of dialogue initiated, Serbia and Montenegro concluded a bilateral co-operation agreement with Romania in the field of minorities.

Similarly, a process of dialogue at the domestic level has been facilitated through the organisation of seminars in partnership with NGOs, such as the Moldovan Centre for Minority Issues and the Moldovan Helsinki Committee in various parts of Moldova, addressing aspects such as the contribution of bilateral treaties to the protection of educational and cultural rights. In connection with this process, Moldova and Bulgaria recently concluded an agreement on the establishment of a Bulgarian University in Teraclia, and further co-operation in the fields of education and culture have been discussed between the two countries.

The question of joint commissions established under bilateral agreements has also become object of special attention under the project. A meeting of representatives of joint commissions, focusing on the implementation of bilateral agreements in the field of minorities was co-organised by the Romanian government and the Framework Convention Secretariat in Poiana Brasov on 18-19 November 2002. This led to the Secretariat sending a questionnaire to the states represented at the meeting about the work of their joint commissions. In connection with this process, Moldova and Ukraine have been negotiating the establishment of a joint commission in the field of minorities. Finally, the question of the protection of the Roma through bilateral and multilateral instruments has also been discussed in the project.

These three projects exhibit the concrete achievements of the Council of Europe contribution to the Stability Pact in the field of minority protection, and future progress in their development will further define the outcome of this contribution. A large number of Council of Europe states, including a few EU states (some of them belonging to the south-eastern area of Europe) have been involved.[192] In the framework of discussion on the Stability Pact project, "the need to maintain an inter-governmental forum for co-operation in the field of minorities" has been stressed, in reference to the joint programme between the Council of Europe and the European Commission, which was opened to participation by all member states and has been terminated.[193]

However, not only has this latter minority-specific joint programme been discontinued, but so also have the activities of DH-MIN, which used to serve a similar purpose at a high political and expert level. Confining intergovernmental co-operation in the field of minority protection to south-east Europe, or to stocktaking in relation to implementation of the Framework Convention for the Protection of National Minorities or other treaties, can be considered insufficient. A recent illustration of this has been provided at the 8th meeting of Government Offices for National Minorities, devoted to implementation of the Framework Convention.[194] Previous meetings of government offices, which had been organised in the framework of the joint programme between the European Commission and the Council of Europe, had a multifaceted role, and the joint programme as a whole played an important function in promoting inter-state Council of Europe wide co-operation on minority issues in various important, and often innovative, areas.[195]

Some notes on action concerning Kosovo

Reference has been made above to the fact that some of the aspects of "specific action" included in the Council of Europe contribution to the Stability Pact for South-Eastern Europe have been adopted in connection with the conflict in Kosovo.[196] The Council of Europe contribution had an antecedent in previous endeavours of the Organisation in connection with the conflict. According to the CoM, the crisis in Kosovo was regularly discussed by the CoM and its Rapporteur Group on Democratic Stability (GR-EDS) "since its outbreak", and on 11 March 1998 the chairman of the ministers' deputies "firmly condemned the escalation of violence in Kosovo".[197] The CoM gave its support to the decision of the Assembly to send a delegation, led by the Assembly's president, to Belgrade. The mission took place on 12 to 14 March 1998.[198]

In response to an initial application for Council of Europe membership from the Government of the Federal Republic of Yugoslavia (FRY) at that time, the ministers' deputies: "issued a communiqué in which they noted the application, while considering, *inter alia*, that several aspects of the present situation in the Federal Republic of Yugoslavia, in particular in Kosovo, were a cause of great concern".[199] In reply to an Assembly question early in September 1998, the CoM indicated in stronger terms that: "it has been made clear that the lack of seriousness and credibility of the Government of the Federal Republic of Yugoslavia's application for membership of the Organisation has led to suspension of discussion on this issue. A radical change of policy by Belgrade would be needed before the application can be considered".[200] The CoM also referred to three co-operation activities in the area of civil society undertaken or supported by the Council of Europe in that country.[201]

A month later, the CoM stated that it "favours a more active participation of the Council of Europe in the search for a solution for Kosovo. It welcomes in particular the work undertaken by the Venice Commission, in co-operation with the Congress of Local and Regional Authorities of Europe, in drafting an 'outline of main elements' for an agreement on Kosovo which is known to the international fora dealing with the issue".[202] The Committee also called on the parties to the conflict to ensure that the work of the humanitarian organisations could be carried out without obstacles and that the safety and protection of returnees were guaranteed.[203]

Following the endorsement of the Council of Europe contribution to the Stability Pact for South-Eastern Europe by the CoM at their 104th session in Budapest early in May 1999, the Council of Europe participated in the Bonn meeting of 27 May 1999 for the preparation of a Stability Pact for South-Eastern Europe proposed by the German presidency of the EU. The meeting resulted in the launching of the pact in Sarajevo on 30 July 1999. The Council of Europe also participated in the preparations for the civil implementation of UN Security Resolution 1244 on Kosovo, together with the United Nations, the OSCE and the European Commission.[204] On the basis of the UN Secretary General's report to the UN Security Council of 12 July 1999, the Council of Europe offered the deployment of several experts "to assist the United Nations Mission in Kosovo (UNMIK) in the fields of human rights, organisation of the judiciary, local government and civil society, *inter alia*".[205]

At the request of the Special Representative of the UN Secretary General for Kosovo, a group of Council of Europe experts examined the compatibility of the applicable penal laws with European norms. Legal advisers were appointed by the Council of Europe to assist the Joint Advisory Council on Legislative Matters, the UNMIK body working on the process of legal reforms, which is composed both of international and local experts. Council of Europe missions were sent to Kosovo to study the issues of women (in particular, victims of rape) and university matters. A joint UNICEF/Council of Europe project on psychosocial support to child victims of conflict that had been initiated in Albania was pursued in Kosovo. The Council of Europe became involved in the training of human rights monitors, and proposed several experts to staff the Ombudsman Support Unit set up within UNMIK. It also offered to UNMIK the posting of several advisers in the field of curriculum development and supervision of the training of judges and prosecutors.

The CoM later authorised the Secretariat to establish an office in Pristina "primarily concerned with the relations and communications with UNMIK", which became operational on 23 August 1999.[206] This office has assisted in the organisation of various Council of Europe missions to Kosovo, including those by Congress, Secretariat, Commissioner for Human Rights' office and Parliamentary delegations.[207] It has also supported and co-ordinated Council of Europe activities with those of other international institutions, in particular, the legal expertise provided by the Council of Europe to the Joint Advisory Council on Legal Matters of UNMIK in connection with the adoption of legislation on minor offences, on the execution of penal sanctions and on juvenile justice, and with the adoption of the penal and criminal procedure codes.

The Pristina office has also actively reported on developments in the region, particularly on the activities of the international community. In June 2000, the CoM Deputies authorised the Secretary General to respond positively to a request from the leadership of UNMIK and the OSCE to entrust the Council of Europe with an observation mission with regard to the civil registration and local elections in Kosovo, and to co-ordinate the action of the relevant bodies involved in the observation process.[208] This was mainly the result of an initiative of the Congress of Local and Regional Authorities of Europe.[209] The election observation mission was in operation from the end of June to the end of November 2000.[210] This was followed by an observation mission of the proper functioning of the local elections held on 26 October 2002.[211]

At the beginning of May 2001 the office completed a one-year pro-gramme to train all the local judges of Kosovo in Articles 5 and 6 of the ECHR. The project was financed by a voluntary contribution of the US State Department.[212] This was later expanded into seminars for defence counsel and lawyers on the same articles.[213] The office is represented in the boards of several non-governmental and academic institutions in Kosovo, and recent activities focused on the contribution to the adop-tion of cultural heritage legislation and policy as well as legislation and capacity building in the field of the performing arts.[214]

On 9 November 2000 President Koštunica of the former Federal Republic of Yugoslavia (now Serbia and Montenegro) was invited for an exchange of views with the CoM, and a new application for membership of the Council of Europe by this state was received on the same date. The CoM asked the Secretary General to enter into negotiations with the Yugoslav authorities, which would lead to the opening of a Council of Europe Secretariat Office in Belgrade during the first half of the year 2001.

The responsibilities of the office included: i. the promotion and support of the policies and activities of all Council of Europe bodies, with a view to the fulfilment of membership requirements by the Federal Republic of Yugoslavia, in particular the respect of the rule of law, human rights, rights of national minorities and fundamental freedoms; ii. the estab-lishment of contacts with the state authorities and civil society in order to support the process of reform; iii. reporting to the Secretary General and providing information on political developments as they may affect the membership procedure and monitoring commitments after acces-sion; iv. the conduct of an active media policy; and v. assistance in the preparation of Council of Europe visits by representatives of the various organs and institutions.

Although, in the mandate, emphasis has been placed on the monitoring of compliance with Council of Europe membership requirements by Serbia and Montenegro, the substantive aspects of the mandate closely resemble those of the mission previously established by the OSCE on 11 January 2001, in particular with regard to the human rights aspects, which in both cases include minority protection.[215] Although the OSCE mission includes also a military aspect, a question of possible duplication clearly arises. Nevertheless, both the OSCE and Council of Europe mandates refer to the duty to co-operate and co-ordinate field activities, and this contributes to complementary approaches rather than to competition.

In the Council of Europe mandate, no direct link is established between the evolution of the situation in Serbia and Montenegro, on the one hand, and the question of the future status of Kosovo on the other. The former, however, is called to have a bearing on the latter. The relation between both aspects is present, albeit indirectly, in the case of the OSCE mandate. With the decision on the establishment of the OSCE mission to Serbia and Montenegro, the original OSCE missions of long duration in Kosovo, Sandjak and Vojvodina (which were actually withdrawn from the field after June 1993, although formally maintained) were officially declared closed.[216] While the OSCE mission has its headquarters in Belgrade, it may open field offices in other areas of the country, subject to consultation with the state authorities and the approval of the OSCE Permanent Council.

Some notes on the involvement in Chechnya

The Parliamentary Assembly had been for a long time the main Council of Europe actor in connection with the Chechen conflict, devoting particular attention to the human rights violations taking place in its context. It has also exercised much pressure on the CoM for it to play an active role.[217] The work of the CoM has been facilitated by the close co-operation on this topic provided by the Commissioner for Human Rights, since the establishment of the latter institution. As the details of the latter inter-relation and some connected aspects of the activity of the CoM are discussed in detail in Chapter 12, other aspects of the activities of the CoM in connection with the conflict in Chechnya are presented here.

On 15 December 1999, the CoM decided to invite, among others, "the Secretary General and the Commissioner for Human Rights, in conjunction with the Russian authorities, to present proposals for a possible Council of Europe contribution" in relation to the situation in Chechnya.[218] Following the acceptance of a proposal for a Council of Europe presence in the region by the then acting President of the Russian Federation, V. Putin,[219] and exchanges of views with the Commissioner for Human Rights and with V. Kalamanov (the Special Representative of the President of the Russian Federation for ensuring human rights and freedom of people and citizens in the Chechen Republic),[220] the ministers' deputies decided "to provide consultative expertise to Mr Kalamanov's office in the form of Council of Europe consultative expert staff" on 20 March 2000.[221]

Consequently, and following an exchange of letters with the Russian authorities in accordance with the instructions given by the CoM,[222] the Secretary General concluded a Memorandum of Understanding with the Minister for Foreign Affairs of the Russian Federation.[223] The deployment of the team of advisers was delayed, mainly owing to security concerns, but the Council of Europe finally became "the first international political organisation to establish a presence in Chechnya"[224] after full-scale armed conflict – which re-started in September 1999 and led to the withdrawal of several international organisations present in Chechnya – had eased. The deployment of the team, initially composed of three experts, took place in mid-June 2000.[225]

The CoM, at its 106th meeting on 10 and 11 May 2000, welcomed the following statement which had been made earlier by President Putin: "all facts of violations of human rights and abuses in the course of the anti-terrorist operation in the North Caucasian region of the Russian Federation, whoever commits them, are thoroughly investigated and, if confirmed, all the rigours of the law will be applied to the guilty".[226] Similarly, the CoM noted with interest the establishment of the "National Public Commission for Investigating Crimes and Monitoring Human Rights in the North Caucasus", under the chairmanship of a former Minister of Justice, P. Krascheninnikov, with the support of President Putin. The CoM understood that the Commission, among other things, would "guarantee pluralistic participation embracing representatives of civil society, including human rights NGOs and legal experts" and "have the capacity to investigate promptly all alleged violations of human rights ... in order to establish the truth and identify those responsible, with a view to bringing them to justice ...".[227] The CoM welcomed the fact that delegations of the European Committee for the Prevention of Torture and Inhuman or Degrading Treatment or Punishment (CPT) had paid two visits to the North Caucasus and entered a number of detention places in the Chechen Republic.

This positive stand of the CoM towards the situation in the Russian Federation was expressed at the same time that the Secretary General issued a report on the use of his powers, under Article 52 of the ECHR, in connection with the implementation of the ECHR in Chechnya. The

Secretary General did not consider the replies received from the Russian authorities "as 'satisfactory explanations' for the purposes of Article 52 of the ECHR". The Secretary General indicated that in the opinion of the team of experts appointed in this connection "the replies given" by the Russian authorities "were not adequate" and the Russian Federation "has failed in its legal obligations as a Contracting State under Article 52 of the Convention".[228]

This led the Secretary General to take the unprecedented step officially to draw the attention of the CoM "by virtue of paragraph 1, second indent of the 1994 Declaration on compliance with commitments accepted by member States of the Council of Europe" to precisely this matter.[229] In spite of this, the positive stance of the CoM continued. Although in Recommendation 1444 (2000), the Parliamentary Assembly upheld Russian membership of the Organisation, it set a two-month deadline for progress towards a peace settlement to be achieved.

In a reply to Parliamentary Assembly Recommendation 1456 (2000) on 27 June 2000, adopted after the expiry of the deadline given by the Assembly, and in which the latter formally suspended the voting rights of the Russian delegation and demanded that the CoM start the procedure to expel Russia from the Organisation, the CoM stated that the Council of Europe had offered its assistance for working out a final status of the Chechen Republic, particularly through the Venice Commission.[230] It also expressed its belief:

> that in the present circumstances, there is no need for the Committee [of Ministers] to act in the context of Article 8 of the Statute. The Committee remains of the view that the Council of Europe has a major contribution to make to the restoration of human rights in the Chechen Republic. At the same time, it recognises that the contribution can only be made on the basis of Russia being a member of the Organisation and fulfilling its commitments to the Organisation.[231]

Only two days later, in Resolution 1221 (2000) the Parliamentary Assembly reiterated "its position that the CoM should denounce Russian conduct of its military campaign in the Chechen Republic and the resulting grave human rights violations as contrary to the principles of the Council of Europe" and expressed its deep regret that "none of the Council of Europe's governments ... have yet made use of Article 33 of the Convention and referred to the European Court of Human Rights alleged breaches by the Russian Federation of the provisions of the Convention and its protocols". The Assembly renewed its urgent appeal for member states to lodge an inter-state application with the Court under Article 33.[232]

Later, in Resolution 1227 (2000), the Assembly expressed its deep concern about:

> the most serious and ongoing violations of human rights in the Chechen Republic, which include, *inter alia*, arbitrary and indiscriminate attacks and bombardments, illegal arrests and abuse of those held in detention, extortion and harassment at check points, all of which lead to unnecessary and unacceptable suffering among the civilian population. The Assembly believes that any continuing unwillingness or inability of the prosecuting authorities to investigate crimes committed by federal servicemen against the civilian population and to bring those guilty to court will lead to a lack of accountability and a resulting climate of impunity, which fosters further human rights violations and impedes a political settlement of the conflict.[233]

At the following 107th session of the CoM on 7 November 2000, after the Secretary General had issued several disturbing reports "on the presence of Council of Europe experts in the Office of the Special Representative of the Russian Federation for ensuring Human Rights and Civil Rights and Freedoms in the Chechen Republic", the CoM was still using a mildly worded discourse in connection with the human rights situation surrounding the conflict. Admittedly, the reports focused on the activities carried out by the experts, rather than on human rights violations.[234] However, the dramatic situation in the field of human rights in Chechnya also emerged from the reports. The CoM "agreed that it was necessary to ensure concrete follow-up to the complaints made to the office of V. Kalamanov, including the prosecution of those allegedly responsible for human rights abuses, in accordance with Russian law".

It also welcomed the statement made by President Putin that the military campaign in Chechnya was coming to an end, and agreed that the conditions for a substantial improvement of the humanitarian and human rights situation were in place, while voicing "their expectation that the Russian government will continue to make every effort to achieve these aims".[235] On 17 January 2001, in a reply to Recommendation 1478 (2000) of the Parliamentary Assembly, the CoM recalled the exchanges of views with V. Kalamanov on the functioning of his office on 7 December 2000, noting in particular that: "his Office, with the support of the Council of Europe expert staff, is progressively developing into a useful instrument for the protection of human and civil rights and fundamental freedoms of individual citizens of the Chechen Republic".[236]

Only eight days later, the Assembly adopted Resolution 1240 (2001), in which it made clear that it did not share the optimistic views presented by the CoM. In the resolution, the Assembly underscores that "no dialogue on a political solution with elected representatives of the Chechen Republic has been entered into by the authorities of the Russian

Federation since 1999" and regrets among other things that "very few cases concerning alleged human rights violations and crimes committed by the armed forces have yet reached either the civilian or military courts, and that there have been no indictments as yet" in connection with three alleged mass killings, dating back to December 1999, and January and February 2000, respectively.

The Assembly further regrets that "convincing reports indicate the continuation of abuses and harassment at checkpoints, and unexplained disappearances, arbitrary arrests, illegal detention, ill-treatment and homicides, in particular in the course of the clean-up operations".[237] The Assembly reiterates its conviction "that the Russian Federation has not acted in accordance with the Council of Europe's principles and values in the conduct of its military campaign in the Chechen Republic".[238] In spite of this, the Assembly restores the voting rights of the Russian parliamentary delegation, and establishes a joint working group with the Russian State Duma, adopting two additional Recommendations 1498 (2001) "on the conflict in Chechnya" and 1499 (2001) "on the humanitarian situations of refugees and internally displaced persons".

On 21 September 2001, in the context of a mediation effort, during a meeting between the joint working group and representatives of the Chechen opposition, the latter criticised the activities of the joint working group, pointing to lack of progress since the previous meeting of the group in Strasbourg. Three days later, the Chechen opposition leader A. Maskhadov ordered the suspension of contacts with the Council of Europe. Nevertheless, in Resolution 1270 (2002), the Assembly supported the role of the joint working group, as one of the very few international fora where progress could be monitored, criticism expressed, pressure asserted, and where discussions on a political solution could take place.[239] The absence of a reference to any activity in this connection by the CoM points to the lack of relevant engagement by the latter organ.

Almost a year later, after the initiatives of the Assembly and the Secretary General seemed to have lost momentum,[240] and against the background of the disheartening responses of the CoM, which remained the master of the Council of Europe engagement, retaining it in a political rather than a legal framework, while largely disregarding the human rights situation,[241] the Assembly adopted Resolution 1315 (2003). In this Resolution, adopted after the announcement by the Russian authorities on the holding of a referendum on a draft constitution for the Chechen Republic, the Assembly expressed concern that the necessary conditions for holding such referendum were unlikely to be met by 23 March 2003, the date on which the referendum was scheduled, and called for the taking of essential steps for such conditions to be achieved.[242] The

Resolution did not contain, however, a recommendation to postpone the referendum, against the position asserted by Lord Judd, chairman of the joint working group and rapporteur of the Political Affairs Committee of the Assembly.[243] The referendum was not openly opposed by the CoM.

Finally, in Recommendation 1600 (2003), the Assembly, after stating the failure of all actors involved, including the Russian Federation Government, the Council of Europe and its member states "dismally to improve the human rights situation and to ensure that past human rights violations, and particularly war crimes, are adequately prosecuted",[244] decided among other things, to petition the CoM by virtue of paragraph 1 of its 1994 Declaration on Compliance with commitments, thereby formally triggering, for the first time at its own initiative, the CoM "monitoring procedures".[245] Given the meagre results delivered by these procedures with regard to minority protection, and especially with regard to the situation in Chechnya so far, the prospects for them leading to any substantial progress in the future remain bleak. While there is not a clear indication that in the future the CoM will take a firmer stand on the Chechen issue,[246] the latter continues to put the Council of Europe's statutory principles into question.

Recent decisions on cultural diversity and on the security of residence of long-term migrants

The CoM has recently adopted some texts that provide for an instrumental approximation to two important aspects of the present European reality, of particular relevance to minority protection. These texts relate to the question of cultural diversity and of the security of residence of long-term migrants in their host countries.

i. *Cultural diversity*

A "Declaration on cultural diversity" was adopted by the CoM on 7 December 2000. This declaration should be brought into the wider context of the approach to "culture" in connection with minority protection within the Council of Europe, which, as already described, remains a problematic one.[247] The declaration may well constitute an effort to provide a more direct way forward than the zigzag route by which this topic has been addressed so far. No reference to minority protection is included in the text of the declaration. However, building on the "Declaration on education for democratic citizenship based on the rights and responsibilities of citizens" already mentioned, emphasis is placed on the new challenge faced by modern democratic states to develop policies "for assuring the recognition and expression of forms of cultural diversity co-existing within their jurisdictions".[248]

The relevance of media pluralism for democracy and cultural diversity is affirmed, as well as the need to respect "the legitimate objectives of member states to develop international agreements for cultural co-operation, which promote cultural diversity.[249] The economic role that cultural diversity can play "in the development of the knowledge economy" is recognised. The role that the wide distribution of diverse cultural products and services, and the exchange of cultural practices in general, can play in stimulating creativity and in enhancing access to and widening the provision of such cultural services, is acknowledged. The important function of public service broadcasting in the safeguarding of cultural diversity is underscored, and states "are called upon to examine ways of sustaining and promoting cultural and linguistic diversity in the new global environment at all levels". Finally, "the competent organs of the Council of Europe are requested to identify those aspects of cultural policy that are in need of special consideration in the context of the new global economy, and to elaborate a catalogue of measures, which may be useful to member states in their quest to sustain and enable cultural diversity".[250]

With this declaration, the CoM expanded the scope of the steps it had already taken in the specific area of transfrontier co-operation earlier in the year. The content of Recommendation R (2000) 1 of the CoM to member states on fostering transfrontier co-operation between territorial communities or authorities in the cultural field[251] should not be dismissed, in spite of its brevity, as it places emphasis on one aspect of transfrontier co-operation that is of the utmost importance for minority protection. Nevertheless, its importance lies more in the text appended to the recommendation than on the text of the recommendation as such. The appendix contains a set of "Guidelines for fostering transfrontier co-operation between territorial communities or authorities in the cultural field".

The title of the guidelines strongly links them to the text of the European Outline Convention on Transfrontier Co-operation between Territorial Communities or Authorities and its two additional protocols, mentioned earlier in this chapter.[252] The guidelines actually follow the definition of transfrontier co-operation provided in those treaties, with minor adaptations.[253] The guidelines, however, provide for "content"-orientated guidance as to the substance of transfrontier co-operation in the field of culture, in contrast with the treaties, the purpose of the latter being rather the establishment of a legal base and procedural framework for the development of transfrontier co-operation generally.

The guidelines actually suggest "specific areas of action" and contemplate specific types of activities which could be undertaken to promote inter-territorial transfrontier co-operation in the fields of education, culture, youth and sports, cultural heritage and the media. Even the pro-cedural and institutional arrangements suggested, aimed at promoting inter-territorial cultural co-operation, are very much characterised by a content-orientated approach specific to the cultural field. The guidelines include remedies to problems that could be foreseen in the promotion of co-operation, suggesting some measures to eliminate possible legal, administrative, technical and even financial obstacles.

With this approach, the guidelines actually provide, if not a fully com-prehensive, at least a user-friendly reference framework for practical engagement in this form of transfrontier co-operation, which strongly contributes to de-dramatise it. Thus the guidelines can very much facilitate the approach of both territorial authorities and the central state authorities to transfrontier co-operation in the cultural field, which is often of much importance for minority protection, and which frequently goes a long way in satisfying minority demands.

ii. *The security of residence of long-term migrants*

On 13 September 2000, the CoM adopted Recommendation (2000) 15 of the CoM to member states, concerning the security of residence of long-term migrants. This recommendation, which deals with a very topical issue in Europe at present, constitutes the latest approach by the CoM to the issue of "new minorities".[254] Its political relevance has been such that it has become the object of an explanatory memorandum, including a number of reservations by a substantial number of Council of Europe states, mostly EU members, which have been appended to the text of the recommendation.[255]

In the recommendation, the security of residence of long-term migrants is considered "not only vital for their integration but also to social stability in the member states".[256] The recommendation refers to various international instruments on the protection of migrants and the members of their families already adopted in the European context,[257] and stresses the importance of the acquisition of nationality of the country of residence by long-term immigrants as an important factor in facilitating their integration into the society. Accordingly, the recom-mendation regulates the acquisition and withdrawal of "secure residence status" for long-term immigrants. This is a goal which the text of the recommendation aims at achieving, besides supporting the protection of immigrants during their residence in their host country in various areas of life.

Very importantly, the recommendation provides for a definition of "long-term immigrant" as a special category of alien. The concept includes also family members whose residence on the territory of a member state has been authorised. It should be noted that the "soft-legal" certainty which this definition provides is very much curtailed by an express acknowl-edgement of the fact that "each member state should have the option to add further conditions to those mentioned" as requirements in order to qualify as a "long-term migrant".[258] The definition is framed around a requirement of a minimum period of legal/authorised residence of five years. The reference to a ten-year period as a maximum seems to place this recommendation against the background of the legal framework established in the European Convention on Nationality,[259] and the work-ing assumption that acquisition of citizenship has been possible within that period. Additional reference is made in the text of the recommen-dation to long-term migrants with more than twenty years of residence in the host country, in order to exclude the possibility of their expul-sion.[260] This further indicates that the ten-year qualification included in the definition is not intended to exclude those immigrants exceeding that period of residence.

The recommendation aims at securing the entitlement to residence status "and in particular to the renewal of the relevant documents" as well as the guarantee of "no less favourable treatment" in various fields. This would seem geared to encourage, as a minimum, equal treatment and the elimination of negative discrimination, although it in no way rules out positive discrimination if appropriate. The areas of non-discrimination identified, which actually reflect areas covered by already existing international legal instruments in the field, include:

- access to employment and other economic activities, with the excep-tion of statutory professions;
- working conditions;
- right of association;
- membership of and active and passive participation in trade unions;
- access to all forms of housing;
- social security and assistance;
- all forms of healthcare;
- schooling and vocational training;
- active and passive participation in public life at local level;
- free movement on the territory of the state of residence.[261]

The recommendation establishes conditions for the withdrawal of "secure residence status". These are mainly linked to the commission of illegal or fraudulent acts or a minimum of six months' interruption in the exercise of the residence entitlement. The recommendation puts forward considerations to be taken into account in the withdrawal of the resi-dence permit and in deciding on expulsion, which relate to the applica-tion of the principle of proportionality and the case-law under the ECHR.

As regards expulsion, the relevant considerations relate, in addition, to the length of the periods of residence after which expulsion should no longer be possible. The entitlement of immigrants to legal protection on an equal footing with the citizens of the state under administrative procedures regarding the withdrawal of the residence permit is established. Similarly, the right of immigrants to present an appeal before an independent administrative authority or court competent "to review the case on its merits and on the conformity of the decision with the law" in connection with the adoption of a decision on expulsion is also established.[262]

Finally, the recommendation includes a standard clause regarding its non-infringement on more favourable applicable rules, and a recommendation to states to ratify existing international instruments adopted in the European context which relate to the protection of migrants. In particular: "the European Convention on Establishment (1955); the European Convention on the Legal Status of Migrant Workers (1977); the Convention on the Participation of Foreigners in Public Life at Local Level (1992); the Revised European Social Charter (1996); and the European Convention on Nationality (1997)".[263]

More recent developments

Aspects of minority protection have continued to be present on the agenda of the CoM since the start of the twenty-first century, although conflict-related aspects have strongly determined this presence still. The attention of the CoM has continued to focus on Council of Europe states where conflict or post-conflict situations develop. In this context, aspects which directly touch upon minority protection have occasionally been addressed.

In some instances this has been done in connection with the examination of compliance of accession requirements, such as the question of co-operation between the authorities of Serbia and Montenegro with the International Criminal Tribunal for the former Yugoslavia (ICTY),[264] or in the expression of support for political settlement processes in the context of post-conflict situations, both recent (such as the efforts to form an enlarged government coalition and the so called 'Europe Committee' in the Former Yugoslav Republic of Macedonia)[265] or long-lasting (such as the encouragement of compliance with commitments, acquired by Armenia and Azerbaijan on accession, concerning conflict settlement).[266]

In addition, the CoM has taken up general human rights questions in specific states that affect minority protection in particular (such as the question of media freedom in Ukraine)[267] or "minority-specific" questions

(such as the concern expressed by Georgia about the unilateral introduction of a simplified visa regime with separatist regions, including
Abkhazia).[268]

The terrorist attacks on the United States on 11 September 2001 have
strongly influenced the agenda of the CoM since they took place. Even
though the action of the CoM has focused on intensifying previous
co-operation to combat terrorism, especially in the legal field, the need
to safeguard the requirements of democracy, the rule of law and human
rights in this process has also been emphasised. So has been the need to
avoid negative stereotyping of particular cultures, and to promote intercultural and inter-religious dialogue, permitting societies to achieve
greater cohesion and reduce the risks of misunderstanding.[269] Thus, in
spite of possible problematic aspects of recent international regulatory
exercises, the element of diversity and identity protection has not been
totally absent from the discussion.

The resulting dialectic between restrictions on human rights on the one
hand, and minority protection on the other, is best illustrated by the
adoption of the Additional Protocol to the Convention on Cybercrime
concerning the Criminalisation of Acts of a Racist and Xenophobic
Nature Committed through Computer Systems in January 2003 discussed above. The importance of addressing the root causes of terrorism
has been emphasised by the CoM,[270] which has called "for efforts to
develop pilot schemes aimed at multicultural and inter-religious dialogue at different levels (north–south, transfrontier, regional and local)
while confirming interest in programmes geared to better control of
migratory flows and integration of migrants, whose fundamental rights
must be safeguarded".[271] Although this call has not yielded very substantial results so far, some initial, modest initiatives have been undertaken
in this direction.[272]

Concluding remarks

The Council of Europe can be considered a latecomer in the development of intergovernmental co-operation in the field of minority protection. Not even in the late 1980s, when the Organisation started its
eastward expansion, were the governmental bodies of the Organisation
ready to assume responsibility in this field. These bodies, however,
started to regulate other aspects of state co-operation, leading to the
adoption of international treaties in areas such as local self-government
and transfrontier relations, which are highly relevant for minority
protection, even if this relevance was not recognised by these governmental bodies at the time of their adoption.

The only exception in this respect have been the endeavours that led to the adoption of the European Charter for Regional or Minority Languages, following an initiative of the Standing Conference of Local and Regional Authorities of Europe, supported by the Parliamentary Assembly. The treaties adopted have contributed to place the Council of Europe in a prominent position in relation to minority protection, once their role in this connection started to be acknowledged. This only happened, however, after the intergovernmental organs began to assume responsibility in connection with minority protection.

In the early 1990s, even when situations of ethnic conflict had started to devastate a part of Europe and the process of eastern expansion of the Organisation was well under way, the intergovernmental approaches to the minority question were still limited to declaratory statements, in which express qualifications of the issues at stake as "minority" situations were normally omitted. Although in 1992 the intergovernmental structures started dialogue on minority protection, it was only in 1993 that more serious attempts to address the minority issue started to take shape, with the mandate given to the CoM Steering Committee on Human Rights to propose specific legal standards relating to the protection of national minorities.

It was with the convening of the first Summit of Heads of State and Government of the Council of Europe in 1993 (the Vienna Summit), and the reassertion of the role of the Organisation in post-communist Europe, that a breakthrough in the approach of the intergovernmental structures towards the minority question took shape. The summit served to fuel the minor pre-existing initiatives in this area, and minority protection became a major issue on the agenda of the political bodies. This affected especially the standard-setting activity. It has been in the transformation of already existing international "political" standards into "legal" obligations that the Council of Europe has found a place among existing international organisations dealing with the minority question.

The summit's impulse resulted in the speedy adoption of the Framework Convention for the Protection of National Minorities. The subsequent attempts to draft an additional protocol to the ECHR on the cultural field with provisions guaranteeing individual rights in particular for persons belonging to minorities, following the mandate in this connection given at the summit, has not yielded any significant results yet.

Another important outcome of the first summit has been the consolidation of the idea that the governmental bodies should become actively engaged in monitoring the implementation by states of the commitments undertaken. This has led to the decision on the establishment of the CoM monitoring procedures, which are analysed in detail in the next chapter. These procedures have a general scope, and various aspects of minority protection treated in this book are liable to be addressed under them. A specific monitoring mechanism in the area of minority protection, the European Commission against Racism and Intolerance, discussed in Chapter 11 also finds its origin in the Vienna Summit.

The second Summit of Heads of State and Government of the Council of Europe (1997) seems to have lacked the political energy that characterised the first one, and introduced no major breakthrough in relation to minority protection. It contributed, nevertheless, to keeping the minority question at the top of the agenda of the Council of Europe and brought onto this agenda new issues of relevance. The engagement undertaken at the summit to adapt the Organisation to the main tasks it had set upon itself, led the CoM to establish a Committee of Wise Persons to provide guidelines, some of which have already been implemented.

In relation to minority protection, the most interesting proposals by the Committee of Wise Persons relate to calls for increased levels of transparency and of monitoring of state compliance with the commitments undertaken. The proposals for improving the working methods of the intergovernmental bodies and for increasing the powers of the Secretary General could have positive repercussions for minority protection. Another important proposal has been the call for wider consultation with the Congress of Local and Regional Authorities of Europe, a body which – as discussed in Chapter 10 – is becoming a leading actor in addressing minority questions.

Although the proposal by the Committee of Wise Persons for a definition of priorities and consequent reallocation of resources would seem, at first sight, a positive one for minority protection, given the high profile acquired by this issue in the context of high-level political declarations, recent exercises undertaken have actually had a negative impact on the progress made towards involving all member states, not just those in central and eastern Europe, in addressing the minority question. In spite of the fact that the Committee of Wise Persons has called for the elaboration of a framework for NGO consultation, no substantial steps seem to have been taken by the intergovernmental co-operation bodies to establish such a framework in connection with the minority issue.[273]

The "Budapest Declaration for a greater Europe without dividing lines", adopted in 1999, and in particular the "Declaration on a European policy for new information technologies", appended to the declaration, have shown an unprecedented level of awareness of minority questions and sensitivity towards them by the intergovernmental bodies. It is to be hoped that the intergovernmental approaches to policy-making will continue to develop along these lines and be followed through at the domestic level. It is also to be hoped that the work of the mechanisms to monitor state compliance with commitments in the area of minority protection established in recent decisions such as ECRI will receive sufficient support from the CoM to lead to substantive accomplishments at the domestic level. With the Budapest Declaration, a new institution, the Commissioner for Human Rights of the Council of Europe, has been established, which has also been undertaken to facilitate the implementation of existing commitments in the field of minority protection. This could be facilitated if resources allocated to this institution are increased in order to match the size of the enormous task it has been assigned.

The special attention paid by the intergovernmental structures to efforts regarding the Stability Pact for South-Eastern Europe since the Budapest Declaration must be applauded. This should not serve, however, as an excuse to abandon those intergovernmental co-operation processes in the field of minority protection with a Europe-wide approach that have already been initiated, especially since these processes have contributed to finding solutions to minority problems, including through the establishment of political and institutional mechanisms. These intergovernmental co-operation processes have led to progress in aspects of minority protection which have not been covered under other existing international instruments (including Council of Europe sponsored treaties) and organisations.

The activities undertaken by the Committee of Experts on Issues Relating to the Protection of National Minorities (DH-MIN), a body subsidiary to the CoM, and under the joint programme between the European Commission and the Secretariat of the Council of Europe on minorities, discussed in Chapter 7, are particularly relevant in this respect. Both types of activities, open to participation by all member states, have been brought to a halt, the CoM bearing ultimate responsibility in this connection.

Minority protection has become a "mantra" for the intergovernmental structures of the Council of Europe at the level of general statements and political declarations. Their latest approaches show, in addition, substantial improvements in the manner in which they address the minority question from a conceptual perspective, and in the elaboration of policy guidelines which respond to existing and emerging minority concerns. However, relatively little is being done with regard to guaranteeing the implementation of these guidelines. The tendency of the intergovernmental structures of the Council of Europe to consider the minority question as confined to the states of central and eastern Europe still persists, as does the tendency to place political stress on considering solutions to minority questions only in connection with conflict situations.

The channelling of the minority protection discourse and co-operation initiatives to the central and eastern areas of Europe has become an excuse for the Organisation not to deal with the minority issues in the member states of the Organisation as a whole. The increased focus of the attention of the Organisation into those regions where conflict is taking place or regions undergoing post-conflict situations, fuelled by the accelerated pace of enlargement of the Organisation, has brought the Council of Europe field of activities closer to that of other international organisations, but deflected its attention away from filling the vacuum still existing in Europe with regard to general progress concerning minority protection.

A tendency to leave the latter responsibility to expert bodies, including those operating under international treaties, but which often seem to lack enough political support by the CoM, can be identified. Further, the targeting of specific regions has not often resulted in substantial achievements, given the rather timid stand of the CoM in connection with the violation of minority rights. The role of other Council of Europe organs and bodies in attracting the attention of the CoM structures to the minority issue will remain of the utmost importance.

It is to be hoped that the oft declared belief in the need to protect minority rights as a precondition to building a fair Europe by the Heads of State and Government and the CoM will increasingly be reflected in governmental policy-making and implementation, both at the international and domestic levels. It is also to be hoped that recent calls for inter-cultural and inter-religious dialogue will lead to the establishment of stable mechanisms for such dialogue between majorities and minorities in all Council of Europe member states, and increased minority participation in their societies. A final desideratum is that the minority question does not fall into oblivion, in the context of "achieved enlargement".

Notes

1.   These various aspects of the work of the Committee of Ministers are highlighted and thoroughly described in G. de Vel, *The Committee of Ministers of the Council of Europe* (Strasbourg: Council of Europe, 1995), pp. 25-56.

2.   See A. Liebich, "Janus at Strasbourg: the Council of Europe between East and West", *Helsinki Monitor*, Vol. 10, No. 1 (1999), pp. 7-24.

3.   On the more decisive approach of the Parliamentary Assembly in this connection, see Chapter 8.

4.   Minority issues have also been treated by the Committee of Ministers in reply to Parliamentary Assembly Recommendations, as illustrated in Chapters 7, 8 and 9, for example.

5.   "Declaration on the future role of the Council of Europe in European construction", adopted and signed at the 84th Session of the Committee of Ministers, 5 May 1989, Council of Europe, Committee of Ministers Internet website, paragraph 16.

6.   Ibid., paragraph 13.

7.   Declaration adopted by the Committee of Ministers on 6 October 1989, at the 429th meeting of the ministers' deputies, Council of Europe, Committee of Ministers Internet website, operative paragraph 2.

8.   Adopted by the Committee of Ministers on 21 September 1992 at the 480th meeting of the ministers' deputies, Council of Europe, Committee of Ministers Internet website.

9.   Ibid., first preambular paragraph.

10.   "Community and ethnic relations in Europe" – Final report of the Community Relations Project of the Council of Europe, Doc. MG-CR (91) final E. The content of the report and the context in which it was adopted are discussed in P. Thornberry and M.A. Martín Estébanez, *The Council of Europe and Minorities*, Doc. COEMIN, pp. 86-89. See further, Chapter 7.

11.   Operative paragraphs 1-4 of Recommendation No. R (92) 12.

12.   Declarations on Yugoslavia adopted on 5 July 1991 and 8 October 1991, at a special meeting of the ministers' deputies and at the 463rd meeting of the ministers' deputies, respectively. Council of Europe, Committee of Ministers Internet website.

13.   Declaration adopted by the Committee of Ministers at a special ministerial meeting held in Istanbul, paragraph 3. Available from the Council of Europe, Committee of Ministers Internet website.

14.   *Collection des recommandations, résolutions et déclarations du Comité des Ministres portant sur les droits de l'homme*, 1988-1995, (Strasbourg: Council of Europe, 1996), pp. 151-52.

15.   On the issue of violence against women in situations of armed conflict, see the work of Radhika Coomaraswamy, Special Rapporteur of the UN Commission on Human Rights on violence against women, its causes and consequences, in her report submitted in accordance with Commission Resolution 1997/44, contained in UN doc. E/CN.4/1998/54, 26 January 1998, Part I. This report is available through the United Nations High Commissioner for Human Rights Internet webpage http://www.unhchr.ch

16.   Recommendation adopted on 21 May 1992, paragraph 48.

17.   See Chapter 8.

18.   See Introduction.

19. See Chapter 1.

20. See further P. Thornberry, "The UN Declaration on the rights of persons belonging to national or ethnic, religious and linguistic minorities: background, analysis, observations and an update" in A. Phillips and A. Rosas (eds.), *Universal Minority Rights* (Åbo/Turku and London: Institute for Human Rights, Åbo Akademi University and Minority Rights Group International, 1995), pp. 13-76.

21. *Human Rights. A Compilation of International Instruments*, Volume I (First Part): Universal Instruments (New York and Geneva: United Nations, 1994), UN doc. ST/HR/1/Rev.5 (vol. I/Part 1), 30. Also available, free of charge, on the UN United Nations High Commissioner for Human Rights Internet website: http://www.unhchr.ch

22   M. Pentikäinen, "Human rights commitments within the CSCE process: nature, contents and application in Finland", 3, *Publications of the Advisory Board for International Human Rights Affairs* (1993), pp. 65-69.

23. G. Alfredsson, "Minority rights: a summary of existing practice", in A. Phillips and A. Rosas (eds.), *Universal Minority Rights* (Åbo/Turku and London: Institute for Human Rights, Åbo Akademi University and Minority Rights Group International,1995), pp. 78-79. For a recent report of the Special Rapporteur of the Commission on Human Rights on Contemporary Forms of Racism, Racial Discrimination, Xenophobia and Related Intolerance, see UN doc. A/56/228, 31 July 2001. This report is available on the Internet website of the United Nations High Commissioner for Human Rights http://www.unhchr.ch

24. For a recent report by the Special Rapporteur of the Commission on Human Rights on Freedom of Religion or Belief, see UN doc. A/56/253, 31 July 2001. This report is also available on http://www.unhchr.ch.

25. See the reports of R. Coomaraswamy (as cited above, note 15).

26. Vienna Declaration and Programme of Action, UN Doc. A/CONF.157/23, Part II, paragraph 18.

27. UN Doc. A/Res/49/192, operative paragraph 8.

28. See M. Bothe, N. Ronzitti and A. Rosas (eds.), *The OSCE in the Maintenance of International Peace and Security* (The Hague, London, Boston: Kluwer Law International, 1997), and V-Y. Ghebali, *L'OSCE dans l'Europe post-communiste 1990-1996: vers une identité paneuropéenne de sécurité* (Brussels: Bruylant, 1996). With a focus on the OSCE and minority protection, see M.A. Martín Estébanez, "Minority protection and the Organisation for Security and Co-operation in Europe" in P. Cumper and S. Wheatley (eds.), *Minority Rights in the "New" Europe* (The Hague, London, Boston: Martinus Nijhoff, 1999), pp. 31-52.

29. See R. Zaagman and H. Zaal, "The CSCE High Commissioner on National Minorities: prehistory and negotiations" in A. Bloed (ed.), *The Challenges of Change: The Helsinki Summit of the CSCE and its Aftermath* (Dordrecht: Kluwer Law International, 1994), pp. 95ff. For a recent account of the High Commissioner's activity, see W. Kemp (ed.), *Quiet Diplomacy in Action: The OSCE High Commissioner on National Minorities* (The Hague, London, Boston: Kluwer Law International, 2001).

30. See A. Rosas and T. Lahelma, "OSCE long-term missions" in M. Bothe, N. Ronzitti and A. Rosas (eds.), op. cit., pp. 167-91 at pp. 169-70. For a brief description of the various OSCE field presences see W. Kemp, M. Olejarnik, V-Y. Ghebali, A. Androsov and K. Jinks (eds.), *OSCE Handbook* (Vienna: Organisation for Security and Co-operation in Europe, 2000), pp. 44-84, available free of charge on the OSCE website http://www.osce.org/publications. On the same website, the *OSCE Annual Report*, including its activities and presences in the field, is also available.

31.   R. Brett, "Is more better? – An explanation of the CSCE Human Dimension mechanism and its relationship to other systems for the promotion and protection of human rights", *Papers on the Theory and Practice of Human Rights* No. 9 (1994).

32.   M. Nowak, "Lessons for the international human rights regime from the Yugoslav experience", in Academy of European Law (ed.), *VIII: Collected Courses of the Academy of European Law* – 2 (2000), pp. 170-71. See also A. Bloed, "The OSCE main political bodies and their role in conflict prevention and crisis management", in M. Bothe, N. Ronzitti and A. Rosas (eds.), op. cit., pp. 35-52.

33.   See Chapter 8.

34.   See Reply from the Committee of Ministers to written question No. 344 by Mr Worms on the rights of minorities, Parliamentary Assembly Doc. 6641, 26 June 1992, 2.

35.   On the role of working parties in intergovernmental co-operation at the Council of Europe, see G. de Vel, *The Committee of Ministers of the Council of Europe* (Strasbourg: Council of Europe, 1995), pp. 92-93. See also "Working methods, ministers' deputies, rapporteur groups, rapporteurs and working parties: vademecum", doc. CM (2002) 155, 5 December 2002, pp. 6-7. With regard to the role of the DH-MIN in particular, see Chapter 7.

36.   Fourth preambular paragraph of the Vienna Declaration.

37.   In January 1994, the Congress of Local and Regional Authorities in Europe (CLRAE) was set up by Statutory Resolution (94) 3 and the Charter of the Congress was adopted on the same date. See further, Chapter 10.

38.   Vienna Summit Declaration, Vienna, 9 October 1993, Appendix II.

39.   A set of proposals concerning "pilot projects" for 1993 was the object of a document prepared by the Council of Europe Secretariat dated May 1993. See P. Thornberry and M.A. Martín Estébanez, op. cit., doc. COEMIN, pp. 96-98.

40.   Ibid., p. 3.

41.   See P. Thornberry and M.A. Martín Estébanez, op. cit., doc. COEMIN, pp. 67-80. See further, Chapter 10.

42.   See European Treaty Series 106. At the time of writing, thirty-four states have become party to this convention, and thirty have ratified it.

43.   European Treaty Series No. 159. At the time of writing, twenty states had become parties to this protocol, out of which eleven had ratified it. See P. Thornberry and M.A. Martín Estébanez, op. cit., doc. COEMIN, pp. 71-74. See further, Chapter 10.

44.   European Treaty Series No. 169. At the time of writing, sixteen Council of Europe member states have become parties to this protocol, out of which nine have ratified it.

45.   At the time of writing, thirty-three Council of Europe member states have become parties to the convention, and twenty-five have ratified it.

46.   On the issue of bilateral treaties, see K. Gal, "The role of bilateral treaties in the protection of national minorities in central and eastern Europe", UN doc. E/CN.4/Sub.2/AC.5/1998/CRP.2.

47.   On these programmes, see Chapter 7.

48.   See F. Benoît-Rohmer and H. Hardeman, *The Pact of Stability in Europe: a Joint Action of the Twelve in the Framework of the Common Foreign and Security Policy*, and F. Benôit-Rohmer, *The Minority Question in Europe: Texts and Commentary* (Strasbourg: Council of Europe, 1996), pp. 30-36. See further, E. Greco, "Il patto di stabilità", in E. Greco (ed.), *L'Europa Senza Muri: Le Sfide della Pace Freda* (Milan: Stampa Tipomonza, 1995), pp. 94-98. See also M.A. Martín Estébanez, "The protection of national or ethnic, religious and linguistic minorities" in N. Neuwahl and A. Rosas (eds.), *The European Union and Human Rights* (London: Kluwer Law International, 1995), pp. 154-55.

The Pact of Stability in Europe should not be confused with the Stability Pact for South-East Europe, which concerns mainly the situation in the Balkan region, and which resulted from an initiative of the German presidency of the European Union in 1999. The latter was officially launched at a summit organised in Sarajevo on 31 July 1999. M. Wisse Smit, "The jury is still out on the Stability Pact for South East Europe", *Helsinki Monitor*, Vol. 11, No. 2 (2000), pp. 7-20. On the contribution of the Council of Europe to the Stability Pact for South East Europe, see below.

49. Report, "Cultural Rights at the Council of Europe (1949-1996)", CDCC, doc. DECS/SE/DHRM (97), pp. 5, 7.

50. Ibid.

51. See Chapter 1.

52. Report, "Cultural rights at the Council of Europe (1949-1996)", p. 80.

53. See Chapter 2.

54. See Chapter 3.

55. Report, "Cultural rights at the Council of Europe (1949-1996)", p. 80.

56. Recommendations of the Assembly, replies from the CoM, Parliamentary Assembly Doc. 8306, 26 January 1999, grouped reply to Recommendations: 1134 (1990); 1177 (1992); 1201 (1993); 1255 (1955); 1285 (1996); 1300 (1996) and 1345 (1997), section A. See also activities of the Council of Europe, 1995 report (Strasbourg: Council of Europe, 1996), pp. 72-73. Present authors' emphasis.

57. Appendix II to the Vienna Summit Declaration, 9 October 1993. Present authors' emphasis.

58. Committee of Ministers' Decision 656/4.1. See further, Chapter 1. On the difficulties experienced by the international community in agreeing on standards in relation to the cultural rights of minorities, see further W. Mannens, "The international status of cultural rights for national minorities", in Cumper and Wheatley, op. cit., pp. 187-91.

59. See Chapter 8.

60. Recommendations of the Assembly, replies from the CoM, Parliamentary Assembly Doc. 8306, 26 January 1999, grouped reply to Recommendations: 1134 (1990); 1177 (1992); 1201 (1993); 1255 (1955); 1285 (1996); 1300 (1996) and 1345 (1997), Appendix to the reply of the CoM to Parliamentary Assembly Recommendation 1345 (1997), Opinion of the CDDH on Parliamentary Assembly Recommendation 1345 (1997) on the protection of national minorities, paragraph 9. On the explanations given by the CoM to the Parliamentary Assembly in this connection, see further, Chapter 8. On the Additional Protocol widening the scope of Article 14 of the ECHR, see Chapter 1.

61. See Chapter 2.

62. The text of the resolution is available at the Council of Europe Internet website. It is also included in M.A. Martín Estébanez and K. Gal, *Implementing the Framework Convention for the Protection of National Minorities*, ECMI Report No. 3 (Flensburg: European Centre for Minority Issues, 1999), pp. 78-84.

63. At the 642nd meeting of the ministers' deputies, on 30 September 1998. The text, equally available on the Council of Europe website, has also been published at ibid., pp. 85-102. See further, Chapter 2.

64. The political sanctions originally adopted by EU States against the coalition government resulting from recent parliamentary elections in Austria would have seemed to fall in line with this undertaking, even if parallel initiatives were not adopted by other Council of Europe states, and this remained mainly as an EU internal (and evolving) approach.

65. Chapter 8.

66. Compare with the proposals made by the Parliamentary Assembly in Recommendation 1222 (1993).

67. Chapter 11.

68. This linkage was to be given a high profile at a later date, in "The Budapest Declaration for a greater Europe without dividing lines" adopted by the foreign ministers of the Council of Europe during the celebration of the 50th anniversary of the organisation, at the 104th Session of the CoM on 7 May 1999, operative paragraph 2. On this declaration see further below.

69. See further, N. Lerner, "The evolution of minority rights in international law" in C. Brölman, R. Lefeber and M. Zieck (eds.), *Peoples and Minorities in International Law* (Dordrecht: Martinus Nijhoff, 1993), pp. 77-101, at pp. 93-98, and also the comments on the latter contribution by M. Nowak, at ibid., pp. 103-18, at pp. 104-12. Action concerning minority protection on the one hand, and the fight against racism, xenophobia and intolerance on the other, would be brought conceptually closer together at a political level in the Durban Declaration resulting from the World Conference against Racism, Racial Discrimination, Xenophobia and Related Intolerance, organised from 31 August to 8 September 2001 in South Africa, although aspects of these phenomena other than minority protection acquired a higher profile in the text of the declaration than minority protection as such. The text of the Durban Declaration is available at the Internet website of the UN High Commissioner for Human Rights http://www.unhchr.ch. See also Chapter 11.

70. See J. Helgesen, "Protecting minorities in the Conference on Security and Co-operation in Europe (CSCE) process", pp. 162 et seq. See also M.A. Martín Estébanez, "The OSCE and human rights" in R. Hanski and M. Suksi (eds.), *An Introduction to the International Protection of Human Rights: A Textbook* (Åbo/Turku: Institute for Human Rights, Åbo Akademi University, 2nd, revised edition, 1999), pp. 334-35.

71. Preambular paragraph 6 of the declaration, adopted by the CoM at its 68th Session, on 14 May 1981.

72. Ibid., at operative paragraph I. Several conferences were convened following the declaration. A seminar was convened in Klagenfurt, Austria, 28-30 October 1991 on "Intercultural Learning for Human Rights", the principal purpose of which was to take stock of the difficulties encountered by states in view of mounting tendencies and tendencies to ethno-centrism, nationalism, xenophobia and racism "re-emerging fairly generally", and to identify solutions. A second seminar was convened in March 1993 to ensure practical follow-up to the first meeting, at which several specific projects in the fields of the media and education were proposed and considered. Although the possibility of developing new standards was highlighted, and references were made to previous attempts in that field, no serious standard-setting initiatives seem to have taken root at that time. See "Intercultural Learning for Human Rights", Seminar at Klagenfurt (Austria) 28-30 October 1991. doc. ICL-DH (91), Strasbourg, 23 September 1991, pp. 3-5.

73. This implies a continuation of the previous line of thinking in this matter, as the Committee of Ministers' Resolution (68) 30 of 31 October 1968 on measures to be taken against incitement to racial, national and religious hatred illustrates.

74. See Chapter 1.

75. "Declaration regarding intolerance – a threat to democracy", adopted by the Committee of Ministers at its 68th Session, on 14 May 1981, at operative paragraph V. Present authors' emphasis.

76. P. Thornberry and M. A. Martín Estébanez, op. cit., doc. COEMIN, 40.

77.   See Parliamentary Assembly Recommendation 1275 (1995) on the fight against racism, xenophobia, anti-semitism and intolerance, paragraph 7, iii.

78.   See Political Declaration adopted by Ministers of Council of Europe member states on Friday 13 October 2000 at the concluding session of the European Conference against Racism, doc. 'Activities of the Council of Europe, 2000 report', p. 372. See further, Chapter 11.

79.   Vienna Summit Declaration, Vienna 9 October 1993, Appendix III.

80.   M.A. Martín Estébanez and K. Gal, *Implementing the Framework Convention for the Protection of National Minorities* (Flensburg: European Centre for Minority Issues, 1998), pp. 31-32. On the subsequent drafting of a specific instrument on the issue of non-discrimination, see Chapter 1.

81.   For an overview of these programmes before the Vienna Summit, see A. Drzemczewski, "The Council of Europe co-operation and assistance programmes with central and eastern European countries in the human rights field 1990 to September 1993", *Human Rights Law Journal*, Vol. 14, No. 7-8, pp. 229-344. For a discussion on the contribution of these programmes in their present format to minority protection, see the section on the Activities for the Development and Consolidation of Democratic Stability (ADACS) in Chapter 7.

82.   See further, Chapter 10.

83.   See in particular the initiative undertaken by the Secretary General of the Council of Europe in the latter connection, Chapter 7.

84.   Vienna Summit Declaration, preambular section.

85.   Ibid. These sections of the text of the declaration are also highlighted in "Compliance with member states' commitments: background information concerning the Committee of Ministers monitoring procedure set up in November 1994", doc. Monitor/Inf (96) 1, 4 November 1996, p. 3 (see below).

86.   Chapter 6 is devoted to their analysis.

87.   See Chapter 9.

88.   "Compliance with member states' commitments: background information concerning the Committee of Ministers monitoring procedure set up in November 1994", Monitor/Inf (96) 1, 4 November 1996, p. 4.

89.   Preambular section of the declaration. The text of the declaration is included in "Compliance with member states' commitments: background information concerning the Committee of Ministers monitoring procedure set up in November 1994", doc. Monitor/Inf (96) 1, 4 November 1996, pp. 4-5.

90.   In this regard it should be recalled that, according to one author, the first reference to minority rights as a constituent part of human rights was probably made in the Council of Europe only in 1990, by the Parliamentary Assembly of the organisation. A. Spiliopoulou-Åkermark, op. cit., p. 221.

91.   This is testified to in the document "Framework Convention for the Protection of National Minorities and explanatory report", doc. H (94) 10, Strasbourg, November 1994.

92.   This had been the case, for example, of the European Charter of Local Self-Government; the European Convention on the Legal Status of Migrant Workers; the Convention on the Participation of Foreigners in Public Life at Local Level; the European Charter for Regional or Minority Languages; the European Outline Convention on Transfrontier Co-operation between Territorial Communities or Authorities; and of course the ECHR, as already mentioned in the text of the declaration.

93.   See "Recommendations of the Assembly, replies from the Committee of Ministers", Parliamentary Assembly Doc. 8306, 26 January 1999, grouped reply by the CoM to Recommendations: 1134 (1990); 1177 (1992); 1201 (1993); 1255 (1955); 1285 (1996); 1300 (1996) and 1345 (1997), section B.

94.   Final Communiqué of the 96th Session of the Committee of Ministers of the Council of Europe (Strasbourg, 11 May 1995), press release, ref. 240 (95), 11 May 1995, 2. Final Communiqué of the 97th Session of the Committee of Ministers (Strasbourg, 9 November 1995). Press release, ref. 563 (95), 9 November 1995, 2.

95.   The concrete implications of the decisions adopted by the CoM in connection with the implementation of the latter declaration are further discussed in Chapter 6.

96.   "Final Communiqué of the 97th Session of the Committee of Ministers (Strasbourg, 9 November 1995)". Press release, ref. 563 (95), 9 November 1995, 2.

97.   The Dayton Agreement was reached on 21 November 1995 and formally signed on 14 December 1995. For a review of the agreement and its antecedents, see M. Nowak in "Lessons for the international human rights regime from the Yugoslav experience" (see note 32), pp. 173-96. See further J. Mertus, "The Dayton Peace Accords: Lessons from the Past and for the Future" in P. Cumper and S. Wheatley (eds.), *Minority Rights in the 'New' Europe*, pp. 261-283.

98.   Second Summit of Heads of State and Government of the Council of Europe (Strasbourg, 10-11 October 1997), "Information Report, rapporteur: Mr Miguel Ángel Martínez, 6 November 1997", Parliamentary Assembly Doc. 7958, 6 November 1997, p. 1.

99.   Last paragraph, Final Declaration, 2nd Summit of Heads of State and Government of the Council of Europe (Strasbourg, 10-11 October 1997), contained in *Activities of the Council of Europe: 1997 report*, appendix B, Strasbourg, September 1998, p. 192.

100. On these programmes see Chapter 7.

101. See the speech given at the second summit by M. Ahtissari, President of the Republic of Finland, Council of Europe Internet website: http://www.coe.int

102. Final Declaration, 2nd Summit of Heads of State and Government of the Council of Europe (Strasbourg, 10-11 October 1997), contained in *Activities of the Council of Europe: 1997 report*, appendix B, Strasbourg, September 1998, p. 192.

103. Section I, paragraph 6, Action Plan, 2nd Summit of Heads of State and Government of the Council of Europe (Strasbourg, 10-11 October 1997), contained in *Activities of the Council of Europe: 1997 report*, appendix B, Strasbourg, September 1998, p. 193.

104. See Chapter 11.

105. See Appendix I and II of decision "'Europe, a common heritage' – a Council of Europe Campaign"; Reply by the Committee of Ministers to Parliamentary Assembly Recommendation 1465 (2000), adopted at the 748th meeting of the ministers' deputies, 3 April 2001. For a discussion of activities in the cultural field, see Chapter 7.

106. Section I, paragraph 2, Action Plan, 2nd Summit of Heads of State and Government of the Council of Europe (Strasbourg, 10-11 October 1997), contained in *Activities of the Council of Europe: 1997 report*, appendix B, Strasbourg, September 1998, p. 193.

107. 2nd Summit of Heads of State and Government of the Council of Europe (Strasbourg, 10-11 October 1997), "Information Report, rapporteur: Miguel Ángel Martínez, 6 November 1997", Parliamentary Assembly Doc. 7958, 6 November 1997, p. 1.

108. European Treaty Series No. 189.

109. See the final paragraph of the preamble.

110. Article 3.

111. Article 4.

112. Article 5.

113. Article 6.

114. Article 7.

115. Adopted in Budapest on 23 November 2001. European Treaty Series No. 185.

116. Explanatory Report on the Additional Protocol, introduction, paragraph 4.

117. This is discussed in Chapter 1.

118. The Committee of Wise Persons membership comprised former President M. Soares (chairman), Ombudsperson G. Haller, Minister T. Halonen, Minister L. Kovács and Ambassador V. Shustov. A number of authorities and Council of Europe officials were also fully involved in its activities. See "Building greater Europe without dividing lines", Report of the Committee of Wise Persons to the Committee of Ministers, Parliamentary Assembly Doc. 8261, 25 November 1998, Appendix III, p. 25 et seq.

119. The terms of reference given to the Committee of Wise Persons are also contained in Appendix III, at ibid., pp. 25-26.

120. Ibid., p. 4.

121. See further below.

122. Ibid., p. 9, paragraph 15 of the report.

123. Ibid., p. 18, paragraph 71 of the report.

124. Ibid.

125. Ibid., p. 15, paragraph 58 of the report.

126. See extract from ministers' deputies 663rd meeting, doc. CM/Del/Dec (99) 663, item 2.2, 9 March 1999, as quoted in "Compliance with member states' commitments: 'Decisions' taken within the context of the Committee of Ministers' monitoring procedure". Doc. Monitor (2000) 2, 7. On the role of the Secretary General under the monitoring procedure/s, see Chapter 6.

127. "Building greater Europe without dividing lines", Report of the Committee of Wise Persons to the Committee of Ministers, Parliamentary Assembly Doc. 8261, 25 November 1998, p. 18, paragraph 71 of the report. As to other possibilities for non-governmental input into monitoring procedures, see Chapter 6.

128. See, for example, the report "Moldova, official visit of the Secretary General, Mr Walter Schwimmer (Chişinău, 14 to 15 October 2002)". The visit was undertaken following an invitation of the President of the Republic of Moldova to the Secretary General. See doc. SG/Inf (2002) 46, 12 November 2002.

129. Ibid., p. 14, paragraph 47 of the report.

130. Ibid., p. 15, paragraph 57 of the report.

131. Ibid., p. 15, paragraph 54 of the report. See further, Chapter 10.

132. Ibid., p. 16, paragraph 63 of the report.

133. Ibid., p. 23, Appendix II of the report, section on "Reorganisation of intergovernmental co-operation".

134. *Activities of the Council of Europe: 2000 report*, p. 198.

135. "Building greater Europe without dividing lines", Report of the Committee of Wise Persons to the Committee of Ministers, Parliamentary Assembly Doc. 8261, 25 November 1998, p. 16, paragraph 64 of the report.

136. See further, Chapter 7.

137. Chapter 7.

138. Ibid., p. 14, paragraph 46 of the report.

139. M.A. Martín Estébanez, "Minority protection and the Organisation for Security and Co-operation in Europe", in P. Cumper and S. Wheatley (eds.), *Minority Rights in the "New" Europe* (The Hague, London, Boston: Kluwer Law International, 1999), pp. 31-52, at p. 38 and p. 44.

140. Possibilities for NGO consultation, including with regard to emergency situations, have been opened by the OSCE both informally, including at the ministers deputies' level, and in the formal framework of general inter-governmental review conferences, as well as at the (currently annual) general Human Dimension Implementation (review) Meetings, and (at least three times a year) in the context of (mono-thematic) Supplementary Human Dimension meetings.

141. "Building greater Europe without dividing lines", Report of the Committee of Wise Persons to the Committee of Ministers, Parliamentary Assembly Doc. 8261, 25 November 1998, p. 18, paragraph 76 of the report.

142. Ibid., p. 19, paragraph 77, point 4 of the report. On the present, highly formalised organisation of NGO involvement with the Council of Europe, still providing for a rather distant framework for NGO consultation by the governmental structures, see the "NGO and Council of Europe" section on the Council of Europe website: http://www.coe.int.

143. See *Activities of the Council of Europe: 2000 report*, pp. 145-47.

144. See further, Chapter 7.

145. The Advisory Committee of the Framework Convention Third Activity Report, covering the period from 1 November 2000 to 31 May 2002, paragraphs 36-40, serves to illustrate this. See further, Chapter 7.

146. This issue has recently raised the concern of the Assembly, as illustrated by its Recommendation 1536 (2001). See further, Chapters 6 and 9.

147. "Building greater Europe without dividing lines", Report of the Committee of Wise Persons to the Committee of Ministers, Parliamentary Assembly Doc. 8261, 25 November 1998, p. 17, paragraph 70. On the monitoring activities of these organs, see Chapters 6, 9 and 10, respectively.

148. Ibid., pp. 17-18.

149. See Chapter 2.

150. See Chapter 3.

151. 'Letter from the Chairman of the Ministers' Deputies to the President of the Assembly, dated 16 November 1998', in "Building greater Europe without dividing lines", Report of the Committee of Wise Persons to the Committee of Ministers, Parliamentary Assembly Doc. 8261, 25 November 1998, pp. 1-2.

152. 'Final Communiqué of the 103rd Session of the Committee of Ministers, Strasbourg, 3-4 November 1998', contained in *Activities of the Council of Europe: 1998 report* (Strasbourg: Council of Europe, 1999), p. 216.

153. Conclusions of the Chair, 104th Session of the Committee of Ministers, Budapest, 7 May 1999, *Report on the activities of the Council of Europe: 1999, provisional edition*, Appendix B, Strasbourg, 2000, p. 378, paragraph 6.

154. Ibid.

155. Ibid., paragraph 8. See M. Wisse Smit, "The jury is still out on the Stability Pact for South-Eastern Europe, pp. 7-20.

156. Declaration on the Kosovo Crisis by the Chairman of the Committee of Ministers of the Council of Europe", *Helsinki Monitor*, Vol. 11, No. 2 (2000), (7 May 1999), at ibid., p. 379.

157. The "Budapest Declaration for a greater Europe without dividing lines", adopted by the CoM on 7 May 1999, at its 104th Session, *Report on the activities of the Council of Europe: 1999, provisional edition*, Appendix B, Strasbourg, 2000, pp. 380-81, extracts from operative paragraphs 1-4, and closing operative paragraph.

158. "Declaration on a European policy for new information technologies", adopted by the CoM on 7 May 1999 at its 104th Session, Appendix I to the "Budapest Declaration for a greater Europe without dividing lines", adopted by the Committee of Ministers on 7 May 1999, at its 104th Session, Appendix B, Strasbourg, 2000, pp. 382-85 at p. 384. Present authors' emphasis.

159. See *Webster's Encyclopaedic Unabridged Dictionary of the English Language* (New York, Toronto, London, Sydney, Auckland: Dilithium Press, 1989), p. 270.

160. "Declaration and Programme on education for democratic citizenship based on the rights and responsibilities of citizens" adopted by the CoM on 7 May 1999 at its 104th Session, Appendix III of the "Budapest Declaration for a greater Europe without dividing lines", adopted by the CoM on 7 May 1999, at its 104th Session, *Report on the Activities of the Council of Europe: 1999, provisional edition*, Appendix B, Strasbourg, 2000, pp. 389-90.

161. Ibid., at p. 391.

162. Ibid.

163. See Resolution on results and conclusions of the completed projects in the 1997-2000 medium-term programme, adopted by the Standing Conference of the Council of Europe Ministers of Education at their 20th session, Kraków, Poland, 15-17 October 2000, preambular paragraph 2.

164. Ibid., Appendix, section on "definition and objectives".

165. Ibid. In connection with "Education for democratic citizenship" see also Parliamentary Assembly Recommendation 1401 (1999) on education in the responsibilities of the individual, adopted by the Standing Committee of the Assembly on 30 March 1999. See also references in Chapter 7 to the activities of the Council for Cultural Co-operation (CDCC) in this field, including reports on the concept of "sites of citizenship" and other related topics.

166. Henceforth, "Council of Europe contribution to the Stability Pact for South-Eastern Europe".

167. See "Stability Programme for South-Eastern Europe – A Council of Europe contribution", 104th Session of the CoM, Budapest, 6-7 May 1999, Section III, p. 1.

168. See Chapter 10.

169. See above. See also Chapter 7.

170. "Stability Programme for South-Eastern Europe – A Council of Europe contribution", Section III.

171. Ibid.

172. See "Declaration adopted at the Informal Conference of the Ministers of Education of South-Eastern Europe", Doc. CM/Inf (99) 86 (unclassified), 10 December 1999.

173. Austria seems to have been absent from this second informal conference. See doc. CM (2002) 22, 12 February 2002, p. 1.

174. See "Stability Programme for South-Eastern Europe – A Council of Europe contribution", 104th Session of the CoM, Budapest, 6-7 May 1999, Section III, p. 2.

175. See "Stability Pact for South-Eastern Europe, Working Table I on: Democratisation and human rights, promotion of multi-ethnic society, and democratic citizenship", Report of the Special Delegation of Council of Europe Advisers, Strasbourg, 6 March 2000, doc. CM/Inf(2000)2, 27 March 2000, p. 1.

176. Ibid.

177. Joint statement, framework programme of action and list of projects adopted by the Portorož Conference on Inter-Ethnic Relations and Minorities in South-Eastern Europe, Portorož, 17 March 2000, doc. without a reference, made available by the Council of Europe Secretariat (with the exception of the list of projects).

178. Ibid., "Framework Programme of Action" section II, and doc. CM/Inf(2000)2, 27 March 2000, p. 2.

179. See "Eighth meeting of government offices for national minorities and meeting on Stability Pact projects concerning minorities, 21-22 May 2001, Strasbourg", doc. G0 8 (e), 16 July 2001, p. 7, available at the Council of Europe Internet website http://www.humanrights.coe.int.

180. Ibid., p. 11.

181. See "Methodology for the 'non-discrimination review' under the Stability Pact for South-Eastern Europe", doc. GO 4 (e), p. 6, available at the Council of Europe Internet website http://www.humanrights.coe.int The main characteristics of the country groups and the criteria for the selection of the members, including independence and knowledge of the subject area, are specified in the document, among other aspects concerning the organisation of the review.

182. Chapter 2.

183. Chapter 3.

184. Chapter 12.

185. See "Eighth meeting of government offices for national minorities and meeting on Stability Pact projects concerning minorities, 21-22 May 2001, Strasbourg", op. cit., p. 8.

186. See "The Framework Programme of Action", op. cit., section II.

187. The activities of DH-MIN, which have been amongst those most relevant to minority protection undertaken in the framework of the Council of Europe are discussed in Chapter 7.

188. See "The Framework programme of action", op. cit., section II. The international instruments specifically mentioned in this context are the Framework Convention for the Protection of National Minorities, the European Charter for Regional or Minority Languages, and Protocol No. 12 to the ECHR.

189. See "The Framework programme of action", op. cit., section II, p. 9.

190. The importance of this question had been underlined in the context of the Joint Programme on "National minorities in Europe" between the EU Commission and the Council of Europe. See ibid., "Project IV: Participation of minorities in decision-making processes, Comment on Activity IV.1", p. 35. See further A. Bloed and P. van Dijk (eds.) *Protection of Minority Rights Through Bilateral Treaties: the case of Central and Eastern Europe* (The Hague: Kluwer Law International, 1999).

191. Ibid., p. 10.

192. Ibid.

193. Ibid., p. 9.

194. Ibid., pp. 2-7.

195. For a recent review of the joint programme see "Final Report to the European Commission on the Implementation of the European Commission/Council of Europe Joint Programme on 'National Minorities in Europe'", Strasbourg, June 2000. See later, Chapter 7.

196. "Stability Programme for South-Eastern Europe – a Council of Europe contribution", 104th Session of the CoM, Budapest, 6-7 May 1999, Section III, p. 1.

197. See "Crisis in Kosovo", reply to Parliamentary Recommendation 1360 (1998), paragraphs 3-4, adopted at the 628th meeting of ministers' deputies.

198. The delegation visited Belgrade and Pristina. The chairmen of the political groups and the Assembly's rapporteur on the Federal Republic of Yugoslavia were also part of the delegation. See further, *The Europeans*, Electronic newsletter of the Council of Europe Parliamentary Assembly, March 1998, Council of Europe Internet website, http://assembly.coe.int

199. See "Crisis in Kosovo", reply to Parliamentary Recommendation 1360 (1998), paragraph 6.

200. See "Federal Republic of Yugoslavia, request for accession to the Council of Europe in the light of the events in this country and in particular in Kosovo...", reply to Assembly Recommendations 1368 (1998) and 1376 (1998) adopted at the 639th meeting of ministers' deputies, 7-9 September 1998.

201. These were the support for a seminar on freedom of expression organised by the NGO "Article XIX" in Podgorica (3-4 July 1998), the civil society school programmes carried out by the Local Democracy Agency in Subotica within the framework of the Confidence-Building Measures Programme, and the support to a seminar on conscientious objection. On the Local Democracy Agencies, see Chapter 10.

202. "Current political questions. the crisis in Kosovo and the situation in the Federal Republic of Yugoslavia (including a proposal to organise an international conference on the future status of Kosovo) and the situation of the Kosovo refugees, asylum-seekers and displaced persons", reply to Assembly Recommendations 1384 and 1385 (1998) adopted at the 646th meeting of ministers' deputies, 21-22 October 1998.

203. Ibid.

204. See "Crisis in Kosovo and situation in the Federal Republic of Yugoslavia and humanitarian situation of the Kosovo refugees and displaced persons", Reply to Parliamentary Assembly Recommendation 1403 (1999), point 17.iii, adopted at the 675th meeting of ministers' deputies, 15 June 1999.

205. See "Current political questions, the crisis in Kosovo and situation in the Federal Republic of Yugoslavia", reply to Assembly Recommendation 1414 (1999), adopted at the 678th meeting of ministers' deputies, 8-9 September 1999.

206. The last detailed report on the activities of the office is contained in the document "Pristina Office report", October 2000, Doc. SG/Inf (2000) 49/5, December 2000. Presently, information on the work of the office can be found in the "News from the Council of Europe field offices" – see for example, Doc. SG/Inf (2001) 21/15 June 2001.

207. Ibid. The Chairman of the CoM and the Secretary General visited Kosovo early in January 2000.

208. See *Activities of the Council of Europe: 2000 report*, p. 14.

209. Ibid., p. 66.

210. See "Final Report of the Council of Europe election observation mission", 6 November 2000, Doc. SG/Inf (2000) 41/8 November 2000.

211. See "111th Session of the Committee of Ministers (Strasbourg, 6-7 November 2002), Conclusions of the Chair", CM (2002) 171 final, 7 November 2002, p. 2.

212. See "Situation in Kosovo and the neighbouring regions – Human rights and rule of law in Kosovo – Humanitarian situation of returnees to Kosovo", Reply to Assembly Recommendations 1508 (2001), 1509 (2001) and 1510 (2001), adopted at the 758th meeting of ministers' deputies, 21 and 25 June 2001.

213. "Activities of the Council of Europe Secretariat Office in Pristina, June and July-August 2001, News from the field offices", Secretary General Information docs., section of the CoE Website.

214. "Activities of the Council of Europe Secretariat Office in Pristina, November 2002, News from the field offices", at ibid.

215. The decision on the establishment of a field presence followed the admission of the Federal Republic of Yugoslavia as a participating state of the OSCE on 10 November 2000. See OSCE Decision No. 401, on the establishment of the OSCE Mission to the Federal Republic of Yugoslavia,. doc. PC Journal No. 315, Agenda item 5 (a).

216. *OSCE Handbook*, p. 56.

217. See Chapter 8. Besides information provided by the Assembly, a good source of information on the situation surrounding the Chechen conflict is the website of Memorial, a Russian NGO, in its English version at http://www.memo.ru/eng/hr/. See also the reports previously elaborated by Human Rights Watch, including: *Field Update on Chechnya* (Brussels: Human Rights Watch, 22 January 2001) and *Memorandum on Domestic Prosecutions for Violations of International Human Rights and Humanitarian Law in Chechnya* (Brussels: Human Rights Watch, 9 February 2001). For a summary, consult *Human Rights Watch World Reports*, such as *The Human Rights Watch World Report 2000: Events of 1999* (New York, Washington, London, Brussels: Human Rights Watch, 2000), pp. 286-87. See also the International Helsinki Federation for Human Rights and Amnesty International *Annual Reports*.

218. See Summary Report of the meeting of the Joint Committee, Strasbourg, 27 January 2000, doc. CM/AS-Mix (2000) PV1, 24 July 2000, section 2, p. 2.

219. See Parliamentary Assembly Recommendation 1444 (2000) 1, adopted on 27 January 2000, p. 14.

220. On the establishment of this post see "The contribution of the Council of Europe towards restoration of the rule of law, respect for human rights and democracy in Chechnya", Statement by the Secretary General, Appendix, "Decree of the President of the Russian Federation", unofficial translation. See further, Chapter 12.

221. See *Activities of the Council of Europe, 2000 report*, p. 15.

222. See "Conflict in Chechnya", Reply of the Committee of Ministers to Parliamentary Assembly Recommendation 1444 (2000), adopted at the 705th meeting of the Ministers' Deputies, doc. 8691, 3 April 2000.

223. See 'Letter from the Secretary General to Mr Igor Ivanov, Minister for Foreign Affairs of the Russian Federation', in *Activities of the Council of Europe, 2000 report*, Appendix B, pp. 370-71. The letter is dated 30 March 2000.

224. See *Activities of the Council of Europe, 2000 report*, p. 6.

225. On 6 October 2000 the Committee of Ministers first decided to extend the provision of consultative expertise for another six months into the year 2001, which has been periodically renewed ever since. In contrast, on 31 December 2002 the OSCE Assistance Group to Chechnya withdrew after the negotiations to renew the mandate of the group failed.

226. *Activities of the Council of Europe, 2000 report*, p. 357.

227. Ibid., p. 358.

228. See "Compliance with member states' commitments: 'Decisions' taken within the context of the Committee of Ministers' monitoring procedures", Secretariat memorandum prepared by the Monitoring Department of the Directorate of Strategic Planning, doc. Monitor/Inf (2001) 3, Strasbourg 4 May 2001, Appendix II.

229. Ibid. See further, Chapter 6.

230. See "Conflict in the Chechen Republic – implementation by the Russian Federation of Recommendation 1444", Reply from the Committee of Ministers to Recommendation 1456 (2000), adopted at the 715th meeting of ministers' deputies, doc. 8783, 27 June 2000, Part A, fourth paragraph.

231. Ibid., penultimate paragraph.

232. See Parliamentary Assembly Resolution 1221 (2000), on the conflict in the Chechen Republic – follow-up to Recommendation 1444 (2000) and 1456 (2000) of the Parliamentary Assembly, adopted by the Assembly on 29 June 2000, paragraphs 20 and 22.

233. See Parliamentary Assembly Resolution 1227 (2000) on the conflict in the Chechen Republic: recent developments (follow-up to Recommendations 1444 (2000) and 1456 (2000) of the Parliamentary Assembly), adopted on 28 September 2000, paragraph 9.

234. See Secretary General's Interim Reports (first and second, respectively) on the presence of Council of Europe experts in the Office of the Russian President's Special Representative for Human Rights in Chechnya, SG/Inf (2000) 27 Revised and Addendum, 27 September 2000, and SG/Inf (2000) 34, 10 October 2000.

235. See *Activities of the Council of Europe: 2000 report*, p. 363.

236. See Parliamentary Assembly Recommendation 1478 (2000) on conflict in the Chechen Republic: recent developments (follow-up to Recommendations 1444 (2000) and 1456 (2000) of the Parliamentary Assembly), adopted at the 737th meeting of ministers' deputies, 17 January 2001, paragraph 9. At paragraph 10, the CoM further indicates that the Chairman of the CoM "will be seeking, in the course of his forth-coming visit to Moscow, more information" concerning the achievements of the Commission chaired by P. Krasheninnikov.

237. See Parliamentary Assembly Resolution 1240 (2001) on the conflict in the Chechen Republic – recent developments, adopted by the Assembly on 25 January 2001, paragraphs 3 and 8.

238. Ibid., paragraph 3.

239. Paragraph 26 of the Resolution, adopted on 23 January 2002.

240. Following the eighth meeting of the joint working group, held in Moscow on 20 March, the head of the Assembly's delegation, Lord Judd, indicated that talks with-out A. Maskhadov were pointless. For an overview of the Secretary General's activities, see his dismayed speech on the occasion of the third part of the 2001 Ordinary Session of the Parliamentary Assembly of the Council of Europe: "One year's presence in the Chechen Republic", Strasbourg 28 June 2001.

241. Also the institution of the Commissioner for Human Rights has been treated by the Committee of Ministers as an instrument of the political process it has mastered, by not leaving it much scope of independent action coupled with insufficient resources. The fact that the Council of Europe experts appointed to V. Kalamanov's office at the initiative of the Commissioner were mandated to act under the authority of the Secretary General, to whom they must report, rather than under the authority of the Commissioner, illustrates this. See further, Chapter 12.

242. Paragraph 8 of the Resolution, adopted on 29 January 2003.

243. This led to Lord Judd presenting his resignation. See statement by Lord Judd, Rapporteur of the Political Affairs Committee of the Assembly on Thursday 30 January 2003, Council of Europe Website, Press Service, PACE Session 27-31 January 2003. See also the article "L'Europe s'apprête à fermer les yeux sul la "farce" du référendum en tchéchène", in the Swiss edition of *Le Temps*, 18 February 2003.

244. Paragraph 4 of the Recommendation, adopted on 2 April 2003.

245. See further, Chapter 6.

246. For a recent outlook, see "Evaluation of the prospects of a political solution to the conflict in the Chechen Republic. Reply to Parliamentary Assembly Recommenda-tion 1593 (2003)" adopted by the CoM on 28 May 2003.

247. See above in this chapter, and in Chapter 7 in particular.

248. Eighth preambular paragraph of the declaration, adopted at the 733rd meeting of the ministers' deputies.

249. Ibid., preambular paragraphs 9 and 12.

250. Ibid., paragraphs 3.2 and 3.3 of the declaration.

251. Recommendation adopted at the 693rd meeting of the ministers' deputies, on 12 January 2000.

252. ETS 106, 159 and 169, respectively. See further, Chapter 10. The CoM actually refers to the resolutions of the Congress calling for the drawing up of a model for transfrontier co-operation in the cultural field.

253. See section 1 of the guidelines.

254. See R. Wolfrum, "The Emergence of 'New Minorities' as a Result of Migration", in C. Brölman, R. Lefeber and M. Zieck (eds.), *Peoples and Minorities in International Law*, (Dordrecht, Boston, London: Martinus Nijhoff, 1993), pp. 153-66. On the treatment of migrants as a category of minorities in the Council of Europe context, see further, Chapter 7.

255. The recommendation was adopted at the 720th meeting of ministers' deputies. Although the high political profile acquired by this recommendation has led to its consideration in the context of the present chapter, other aspects of the protection of migrants are considered in other chapters – Chapter 7 in particular.

256. Fourth preambular paragraph of the recommendation.

257. Those instruments are enumerated below.

258. Operative paragraph 1.*a*.

259. See ETS 166, Strasbourg 6 November 1997, Article 6 in particular.

260. Paragraph 4.*b* of the recommendation.

261. The fields covered are a reflection of some of the international treaties mentioned in the preamble of the recommendation. In the area of civil and political rights, for example, these fields are actually covered under the Convention on the Participation of Foreigners in Public Life at Local Level, ETS. 144, Strasbourg, 5 November 1992. See further, P. Thornberry and M.A. Martín Estébanez, "The Council of Europe and minorities", doc. COEMIN, pp. 62-65. See also Chapter 7.

262. Paragraph 5.*c* and *d* of the recommendation.

263. Paragraph 6.*a* and *b* of the recommendation. Aspects of the content of the two former conventions are further discussed in Chapters 7 and 10.

264. See 'Communiqué of the 111th Session of the Committee of Ministers (Strasbourg, 6-7 November 2002)', doc. CM (2002) 164 final, 7 November 2002, p. 3.

265. See Final Communiqué of the 108th Session of the Committee of Ministers (Strasbourg, 10-11 May 2001), paragraph 9.

266. See 109th Session of the Committee of Ministers (Strasbourg, 7-8 November 2001), Conclusions of the Chair, third paragraph. The question of political prisoners has been specific object of Council of Europe concern. See further, Chapter 6.

267. See 108th Session of the Committee of Ministers (Strasbourg, 10-11 May 2001), Conclusions of the Chair, paragraph 7.

268. Ibid. It should be noted that no reference is made to the responsibility of the Russian Federation for the establishment of the special visa regime in this specific case.

269. See Communiqué on international action against terrorism, 109th Session of the Committee of Ministers (8 November 2001).

270. See 109th Session of the Committee of Ministers (Strasbourg, 7-8 November 2001), Conclusions of the Chair, third paragraph.

271. See 110th Session of the Committee of Ministers (Vilnius, 3 May 2002), Communiqué, doc. CM (2002) 58 final, 3 May 2002.

272. These have consisted in the encouragement by the CoM that the Secretary General pursue contacts with the Arab League and the Organisation of the Islamic Conference with a view to developing co-operation in this field, and the convening of a colloquy on "Dialogue serving intercultural and inter-religious communication", held in Strasbourg on 7-8 October 2002. The CoM has also referred to the (OSCE) Conference held in Baku on the "Role of religion and belief in a democratic society: searching for ways to combat terrorism and extremism" on 10-11 October 2002. See 111th Session of the Committee of Ministers (Strasbourg, 6-7 November 2002), Communiqué and Conclusions of the Chair, respectively.

273. Discussions are under way on the articulation and possible acceptance of the Finnish initiative to establish a "European forum for Roma" where Roma NGOs will be represented. At the time of writing, however, the position envisaged for this body in relation to the Council of Europe is still to be determined. See 111th Session of the Committee of Ministers (Strasbourg, 6-7 November 2002), Communiqué, final paragraph.

Chapter 6
The Committee of Ministers' monitoring mechanism

Introduction

The impulse which intergovernmental co-operation in the Council of Europe received in convening the first Council of Europe summit resulted, among other things, in the adoption by the Committee of Ministers (CoM) of the "Declaration on compliance with commitments accepted by member states of the Council of Europe" on 10 November 1994.[1] The declaration has resulted in the establishment of the so-called "Committee of Ministers' monitoring procedures".[2]

The main objective of the CoM monitoring mechanism is to facilitate the fulfilment of the commitments undertaken by the member states of the Council of Europe through constructive political follow-up, dialogue, co-operation and mutual assistance.[3] The commitments referred to are those "to democracy, human rights and the rule of law accepted by member states under the Council's Statute, the European Convention on Human Rights and other legal instruments".[4] Thus, there is reason to believe that Council of Europe instruments relevant to minority protection also fall under the scope of the declaration and the monitoring mechanism.[5]

The establishment of this mechanism took place once the process of enlargement of the Council of Europe had gained full speed. The need to monitor compliance by states with the basic principles of the Organisation, considered with laxity during the accession process,[6] has required an increased level of involvement of the intergovernmental structures to monitor state performance after accession. However, it would seem that compliance with the commitments contained in international instruments relevant to minority protection, which had become a major focus of attention during accession procedures,[7] has not become a priority under the CoM monitoring mechanism.

Although many aspects of the development of monitoring are secret, the information available indicates that minority protection has not become an explicit "theme" (see below) under this monitoring mechanism. On 25 October 2000, the CoM selected the topic of "Non-discrimination, with emphasis on the fight against intolerance and racism",[8] and scheduled initial debate on the theme "Freedom of conscience and religion" for 3 July 2002. Various other issues already covered under this monitoring mechanism have touched upon aspects of human rights protection and democratic practice that are relevant to minority protection. The high political profile given to this monitoring mechanism, the high-level, intergovernmental monitoring it involves, as well as its potential for addressing questions related to minority protection, call for its detailed examination.

Background

The 1994 Declaration on Compliance

In operative paragraph 1 of the "Declaration on compliance with commitments accepted by member states of the Council of Europe" – adopted by the CoM on 10 November 1994 (henceforth the 1994 Declaration on Compliance) – the CoM decided that it "will consider the questions of implementation of commitments concerning the situation of democracy, human rights and the rule of law in any member state" which will be referred to it either: i. by member states; ii. by the Secretary General; or iii. on the basis of a recommendation from the Parliamentary Assembly.

It was also decided that when considering such questions the CoM would take into account all relevant information available from different sources such as the Parliamentary Assembly and the OSCE. Information available from non-governmental sources, although not mentioned, is not excluded. In operative paragraph 2, the Secretary General of the Council of Europe is requested to forward to the CoM information deriving from contacts and co-operation with member states that are liable to call for the attention of the CoM.

The non-confrontational character of the monitoring mechanism is emphasised. Under operative paragraph 3 of the 1994 Declaration on Compliance, the CoM "will consider in a constructive manner matters brought to its attention, encouraging member states, through dialogue and co-operation, to take all appropriate steps to conform with the principles of the Statute of the Council of Europe in the cases under discussion".[9,10] Nevertheless, under operative paragraph 4, activities other than dialogue and co-operation are also envisaged. The CoM, "in cases requiring specific action, may decide to: i. request the Secretary General to make contacts, collect information or furnish advice; ii. issue an opinion or recommendation; iii. forward a communication to the Parliamentary Assembly; iv. take any other decision within its statutory powers".[11]

The 1995 procedure

The scope of the 1994 Declaration on Compliance has been further delimited by the Council of Ministers with the adoption of the "Procedure for implementing the Declaration of 10 November 1994 on compliance with commitments accepted by member states of the Council of Europe" on 20 April 1995 (henceforth: the 1995 Procedure).[12] In the light of recent documents of the Monitoring Department of the Directorate of Strategic Planning, which has taken up the Secretariat duties in connection with the monitoring mechanism originally carried by the "Monitoring Unit" of the Secretary General,[13] the use of the term "monitoring procedure" as a title to name the CoM's monitoring mechanism has given way to the use of the term "monitoring procedures". The motive for and relevance of this change in denomination is discussed in the pages which follow.

Operative paragraph 5 of the 1994 Declaration on Compliance, which refers to the process of searching for greater efficacy in CoM procedures as an open-ended one, should be kept in mind in this connection. Mr Kallas, Chairman-in-Office of the CoM, in a statement to the Parliamentary Assembly at its 1996 Ordinary Session, indicated that "the Committee of Ministers will continue to consider the questions of implementation of commitments concerning the situation of democracy, human rights and the rule of law in any member state referred to it: by member states; by the Secretary General; on the basis of a recommendation from the Parliamentary Assembly. The Assembly has an agreed role to play in the Committee of Ministers' procedure. I hope it will play it to the full".[14] The use made of these various options, especially the actual character of the Assembly's involvement, which did not address a recommendation for the triggering of the procedure until April 2003, as well as other aspects of the efficacy of the envisaged CoM monitoring mechanism and how it has actually been implemented, are discussed below.

The 1995 Procedure developed the 1994 Declaration on Compliance in a manner difficult to predict in the light of the text of the latter. The 1994 Declaration on Compliance indicated that the "Committee of Ministers will consider the questions of implementation of commitments concerning the situation of democracy, human rights and the rule of law in any member state which will be referred to it ..."[15] and that "the Committee of Ministers will consider in a constructive manner matters brought to its attention".[16] This seemed to point at cases of specific state performance being brought to the attention of the CoM in concrete situations as the main object of the monitoring mechanism. However, in the 1995 Procedure, steps were taken for the monitoring mechanism to move in a particular, yet different, direction, based on a "thematic" and "non-discriminatory" approach by the CoM. This is why reference is made here to "thematic monitoring", following the designation given by the Monitoring Unit/Department.[17]

An attempt to overcome this tendency was made by the Secretary General on 26 June 2000, with his initiative to direct the efforts of the CoM by virtue of paragraph 1 of the 1994 Declaration on Compliance, in connection with the situation in Chechnya (Russian Federation).[18] However, as described below, this attempt did not lead to successful results. Although "thematic" and "non-discriminatory" approaches were predominant for the period of almost a decade from the time the monitoring mechanism was established, their monopoly was broken in the year 2000 – six years after the establishment of the monitoring mechanism – with the incorporation of the monitoring of the situation in Armenia and Azerbaijan under the mechanism.

The monitoring of these states, initially considered as an alternative and exceptional "monitoring procedure" (so-called "ad hoc monitoring"), entailed a departure from the previous practice under the monitoring mechanism, solely conducted under the "thematic" and "non-discriminatory approaches" of the 1995 Procedure until then (see below). The ad hoc monitoring of Armenia and Azerbaijan was at that time presented in "monitoring documents" as separate from and in conjunction with the mainstream "thematic monitoring" and "monitoring undertaken by virtue of paragraph 1 of the 1994 Declaration", which, as already noted, reflected the previous, yet unsuccessful attempt to make the monitoring mechanism operational on a "country-specific" basis.[19]

The introduction of ad hoc monitoring paved the way for subsequent "country-specific" approaches under the monitoring mechanism, and reclassifications of the various forms of monitoring, which at present distinguish between: i. "Monitoring compliance with commitments by member states by virtue of the 1994 Declaration on compliance with commitments" both by virtue of paragraph 1 and paragraph 4 of the Declaration; ii. "Thematic monitoring", which takes the 1995 Procedure as its base; and iii. "Specific post-accession monitoring" under which the initial ad hoc monitoring with respect to Armenia and Azerbaijan and other "periodic", yet permanent, country-specific monitoring exercises are now being considered.

The present classification is, however, the result of a complicated evolution of the monitoring mechanism, which is still in a process of transformation and search for a balance between utility considerations on the one hand and political consensus on the other. A study of the evolution of the monitoring mechanism in practice, from its inception as a thematic monitoring mechanism alone, to its broadening to include country-specific approaches, is undertaken below. As already discussed in the previous chapter, and as discussed in more detail in the pages will follow, it will largely depend on the course of action taken by the monitoring mechanism whether its potential to become an effective minority protection instrument is realised.

Thematic monitoring and non-discrimination

The first principle put forward in the 1995 Procedure for implementing the Declaration on Compliance, is that "dialogue will be based on" the principle of non-discrimination.[20] This reference, which could seem a common reminder of a general principle of fairness, has had a strong impact on the form and character of the monitoring mechanism. As a result of the application of this principle, and even if, as already noted, since the year 2000 exceptions to the "thematic approach" started to consolidate, so that it has been possible to speak of "simultaneous" thematic and country-specific monitoring, the dominant course of the monitoring mechanism since its establishment has been thematic. A permanent feature of the mechanism since its establishment in 1994 has been the simultaneous monitoring of the situation in all member states, regarding performance in relation to a group of selected human rights or rule-of-law "themes".

Topics such as: "freedom of expression and information"; "functioning and protection of democratic institutions"; "functioning of the judicial system"; "local democracy"; "capital punishment"; "police and security forces"; "non-discrimination, with emphasis on the fight against intolerance and racism" and, most recently, "freedom of conscience and religion" have been selected by the CoM to become the object of thematic monitoring. The theme "effectiveness of judicial remedies" has also been selected, while its character as a formal sub-theme of the topic "functioning of the judicial system" has been recognised by the Secretariat, pointing to a slow, yet increasing, narrowing of thematic monitoring.[21] Since 2002, the mainstream "thematic monitoring" has also started to develop an increasingly country-specific focus in connection with one of the themes addressed, freedom of expression and information, giving rise to the country-specific cases of "specific action" currently being classified by the Secretariat under point i. above (monitoring by virtue of paragraphs 1 and 4 of the declaration), as further discussed below.

A list of "items" or "issues" within each theme has always been selected, and agreed upon by the CoM, to constitute the concrete object of monitoring. Until recently, this was done through the elaboration of the so-called "outline of basic issues" by the CoM itself.[22] At the time of writing, however, the Secretariat is responsible for the elaboration of a "questionnaire" which the CoM must agree on.

The guidelines on the organisation of the monitoring mechanism, elaborated "on the basis of decisions taken by the Ministers' Deputies in April 1998 and April 2000", indicated that, for the selection of themes, the formal "proposals" made, seemingly originating from the CoM alone (as further discussed below), should: i. "be clearly focused, with sub-themes identified if a broad theme is being proposed"; ii. include an "outline of basic issues" to be considered; iii. include suggestions as to the possible procedure for that theme's follow-up and implementation (if possible, providing an indication of which existing Council of Europe mechanisms might be utilised); and iv. establish a clear time-line for the consideration of each theme by the CoM.[23] The process of elaborating the "outline of basic issues" and later the questionnaire thus becomes the initial filter of the actual content of thematic monitoring.

The non-discriminatory or "simultaneous" approach characterising thematic monitoring has had the advantage of responding to the demand, often voiced at the Council of Europe after the start of the process of enlargement of the Organisation, that the performance of all member states of the Council of Europe be brought under surveillance, and not just that of those states that are "newcomers" to the Organisation. Thus, the "unquestionable performance" of the "old western democracies", underlying political co-operation in the Council of Europe for many years, seems to start bending, at least at the declaratory level, and a more egalitarian principle starts to be introduced.

However, although non-discriminatory approaches may have a positive impact in the search for solutions to minority questions in Europe over-all, including its Western section, they may also easily lead to the acceptance of minimum common denominators of state performance involving both Western and Eastern European states. Another question is whether the untouchable character of "western democracies" is still present in practical terms in the internal development of the CoM monitoring mechanism, in particular concerning the possible bias in the selection of themes for monitoring, or in the selection of "issues" or "questions" which thematic monitoring focuses on. This is related to the realpolitik surrounding the monitoring mechanism, which, in the case of an essentially intergovernmental one such as that of the CoM, is hardly possible to dismiss.

This is why the theme "minority protection" – which countries of central and eastern Europe have been willing to address in their process of accession to western European institutions – may encounter difficulties for its approval as a general theme for the "all states inclusive" thematic monitoring by the CoM, especially once the states that have recently acceded to the Organisation stop feeling they are "newcomers". More chances seem to exist for the introduction of aspects of minority protection into the "issues" or "questions" selected under a particular theme. As already mentioned and further discussed below, aspects of minority protection have been touched upon in the treatment of some of the themes already selected.

A drawback of the mainstream development of the 1994 Declaration on Compliance – along the lines of a thematic, non-discriminatory approach – has been the scant additional attention paid to the monitoring mechanism becoming instrumental in responding to concrete cases of human rights violations in specific situations and at specific moments in time. Under thematic monitoring, specific country situations have been dealt with by their "automatically" becoming objects of consideration under the broader theme selected, following the previous general agreement on the specific "issues" or "questions" object of monitoring.

It is doubtful whether such an approach can be useful with respect to urgent, fast-emerging situations resulting from human rights violations, especially when their main aspects have not been chosen and agreed on in advance as a particular theme. The reluctance, still predominant, to use those elements of thematic monitoring which serve to address specific aspects of states' wrong practice, particularly when this relates also to the "old democracies", may impede, as discussed below, its effective contribution to the solution of situations involving human rights violations (including emergent or urgent) especially those involving minorities.

Thematic monitoring, secrecy, the role of the Parliamentary Assembly and NGOs

Another important principle introduced in the 1995 Procedure for implementing the Declaration on Compliance is confidentiality. While the principle of non-discrimination has been eroded with the evolution and broadening of the monitoring mechanism away from strictly thematic and non-discriminatory approaches, the principle of confidentiality surrounding the content of the CoM debates has remained constant. In paragraph 7 of the 1995 Procedure, it is stated that: "in accordance with Article 21 of the Statute, the discussions should be confidential and held in camera, to encourage a constructive dialogue with the member states concerned".[24] This principle was not mentioned in the 1994 Declaration on Compliance, and its introduction in the 1995 Procedure has been strongly criticised, particularly by the Parliamentary Assembly.[25]

The fact that CoM meetings are held "in private" or "in camera" rather than in public, and that the results of such meetings are only made public in a very limited form, constitutes the rule rather than the exception when it comes to CoM proceedings, in accordance with paragraph 21 of the Statute of the Council of Europe. According to the Monitoring Unit/Department, an initial decision was taken to consider "overviews prepared by the Monitoring Unit and the information, observations and comments of member states' governments relating to the overviews" as "confidential" rather than "secret". This does not seem to have a very strong impact, however, in the publicity of the content of the procedure in practical terms, since most monitoring documents are not publicly accessible.[26]

The fact that individual decisions on the declassification of documents for the purpose of "the information of the Parliamentary Assembly" have been adopted since that decision was taken,[27] and the fact that the majority of the documents relating to the monitoring mechanism have not been published through the CoM homepage at the Council of Europe public information Internet website, testifies to their restricted availability. It should be noted, however, that the expansion of thematic monitoring into country-specific has been accompanied by increasing publicity of documentation relating to the monitoring of states undergoing country-specific monitoring, following their individual acceptance, and on a case-by-case basis. The information documents and memoranda previously prepared by the Monitoring Unit and now prepared by the Monitoring Department remain the main sources of public information on the monitoring mechanism and its work. These documents, however, contain little information on the substantive approaches to monitoring by the CoM and they deal mainly with procedural aspects.

One of the main arguments advanced by the Parliamentary Assembly against the secrecy of the CoM monitoring mechanism has been that of ensuring synergy between the Parliamentary Assembly's monitoring activities and those of the CoM.[28] The CoM's statutory right to undertake an activity without informing the Parliamentary Assembly of its content and the possibility that the CoM could hold information on serious neglect of commitments by member states without informing the Parliamentary Assembly have also been challenged.[29] The CoM has been urged "to reconsider its decision on secrecy and to envisage, for instance, transmission of relevant information to the [Assembly] co-rapporteurs concerned. It is proposed to organise further joint committee meetings devoted to monitoring at least once a year".[30]

In response, the CoM agreed to inform the Parliamentary Assembly of its decisions concerning any follow-up action decided upon and to establish formal and informal dialogue with it in this respect.[31] With regard to decisions concerning follow-up action, this would seem to have been confined to those decisions adopted during the formal follow-up which thematic monitoring has developed, that is, the measures agreed on by the CoM after it has reached its conclusions (see below). As to the establishment of formal and informal dialogue, "annual consultation in the Joint Committee will be supplemented by informal contacts between the Chairman in Office" of the CoM "and the Assembly's Monitoring Committee ... exchange of information on a confidential basis is envisaged".[32]

Statutory Resolution (51) 30 of 1951 regulates annual consultation, co-ordination and discussion of common concerns between the Parliamentary Assembly and the CoM, through the joint committee.[33] According to the progress report of the monitoring committee of the Parliamentary Assembly (1998-99):[34] "formal meetings between representatives of the CoM and of the Assembly in which monitoring issues were discussed included two Joint Committee meetings".[35] The information report of the Monitoring Committee of the Parliamentary Assembly during the subsequent yearly period (1999-2000) contains no section on relations between the Assembly and the CoM in relation to monitoring issues.[36] According to information of the year 2001, annual consultation under Statutory Resolution (51) 30 of 1951 was "supplemented by informal contacts between the Chairman of the CoM and the Parliamentary Assembly Monitoring Committee. At least one Joint Committee meeting is devoted specifically to monitoring. Exchange of information takes place on a confidential basis, with due regard to the essentially different but complementary nature of the two monitoring procedures".[37] The call contained in the information report 1998-99 of the Monitoring Committee for the Assembly to adopt a thematic approach to its own monitoring procedures, such as that followed by the CoM, may indicate attempts on the Assembly's side at bringing the monitoring procedures of both Council of Europe organs closer together.[38]

In Parliamentary Assembly Recommendation 1536 (2001), the Assembly warned: "against the real risk of diverging assessment of states' honouring of their obligations and commitments by the Assembly on the one hand and the CoM on the other hand, and against the real risk of creating confusion in the states concerned by a duplication of procedures".[39] It also supported the prevalence of "its monitoring procedure which has proven in most cases its effectiveness and efficiency" while stressing that "consideration should be given to ways of increasing the impact on the activities of the CoM of Assembly recommendations on the monitoring of obligations and commitments".[40]

This uneasiness on the Assembly's side was seemingly fuelled by the start of ad hoc monitoring of Armenia and Azerbaijan and the establishment, under the CoM monitoring mechanism, of a specific monitoring group (GT-SUIVI-AGO).[41] Thus, in spite of the existence of formal dialogue between the two organs, the Assembly has perceived the CoM monitoring mechanism as a possible source of competition and as undermining its own monitoring activity, rather than as a reinforcement.

In the CoM reply to Parliamentary Assembly Recommendation 1536 (2001), the Committee stated its will to improve dialogue with the Assembly on monitoring issues. Achievements in this regard previously mentioned above were recalled,[42] and the suggestion was made that a joint working group on monitoring between the CoM and the Parliamentary Assembly (such as that which met on 7 November 2001 following an initiative of the Liechtenstein chairmanship of the CoM) – composed of the President and Group Leaders of the Assembly on the one hand, and the chairman and vice-chairman of the CoM, as well as the chairman of the deputies' Rapporteur Group on Democratic Stability (GR-EDS) on the other – could meet regularly and offer a forum to exchange information both on the timetables and on the substance of monitoring.

While this initiative does not seem to have been consolidated, the fact that the Assembly has not actively engaged in the follow-up of the monitoring procedure when requested (see below), and only made use of its competence under paragraph 1 of the 1994 Declaration on Compliance to trigger the monitoring mechanism almost a decade after it was established and with regard to an issue on which other forms of dialogue had persistently led to no positive result,[43] further testifies to the Assembly's alienation from the CoM monitoring mechanism.

Rather, the 1995 Procedure confined the possibility of triggering thematic monitoring (the only form of monitoring under the CoM mechanism known at the time of its adoption) to an initiative originating from a state delegation or from the Secretary General, although such initiative could be taken by these bodies "with reference to a discussion in the Parliamentary Assembly".[44] The 1995 Procedure thus gave the Assembly a secondary, very limited role. According to its paragraph 8: "the Clerk of the Parliamentary Assembly may be invited to be present to provide information on any discussions in Assembly bodies on the States concerned".

Thus, under thematic monitoring in accordance with the 1995 Procedure, the Assembly seems deprived of the power of initiative regarding the monitoring mechanism allotted to it in paragraph 1 of the 1994 Declaration of compliance. Even the character of the presence of the Clerk of the Assembly (the provision of information) and the type of information that he/she can provide, if invited, is pre-defined. No further reference is made in the 1995 Procedure to external contributions, including those by non-governmental organisations or bodies, to the monitoring process. It is thus unsurprising that the recent exercise of the Assembly's competence to trigger the monitoring mechanism has been in connection with a country situation instead of a thematic issue, without a reference to the 1995 Procedure, and after the CoM monitoring mechanism has evolved from being solely thematic to also include country-specific monitoring.

Only after other forms of dialogue between the Assembly and the CoM on a specific country situation seemed exhausted, and with regard to a long-lasting human rights emergency, has the Assembly made use of its prerogative under the 1994 Declaration, even if the previous attempt to trigger the monitoring mechanism by the Secretary General, precisely to address the same situation, was unsuccessful (see below). On 2 April 2003, that is, almost a decade after the monitoring mechanism was first established, the Assembly decided, in Recommendation 1600 (2003), "to petition the Committee of Ministers by virtue of paragraph 1 of its 1994 Declaration on compliance ... and recommends that the Committee of Ministers instruct the Secretary General to make contacts, collect information and furnish advice on the human rights situation in the Chechen Republic, in accordance with paragraph 4 of the said declaration".

The results of this endeavour of the Assembly, and what the response of the CoM will be, are as yet unknown at the time of writing. It is to be hoped that this attempt to trigger the monitoring mechanism will not suffer the same fate as the previous one of the Secretary General, but finally provide an appropriate avenue to deal satisfactorily with the situation in Chechnya, although, as the evolution of the monitoring mechanism has shown so far, expectations are rather bleak.

Returning to the evolution of the monitoring mechanism, in 1998, in a document entitled "Compliance with commitments entered into by member states: development of the Committee of Ministers' monitoring procedure", the Monitoring Unit of the Council of Europe Secretariat emphasised the existence of two procedures deriving from that of 1995:

> one based on the Secretary General's factual overviews carried out every two years (paragraph 3, 1995 Procedure) and one that may be initiated by any Delegation or the Secretary General at least one month before any of the 'at least three meetings of the Ministers' Deputies at A level" which, in accordance with paragraph 2, shall be devoted each year to the issue of compliance with commitments ... The second procedure, which has so far not been used, is dealt with in paragraphs 5 and 6. This ad hoc procedure will be considered in the section entitled 'future prospects"...[45]

Thus, no reference is made to any Parliamentary Assembly initiative. The CoM decided to engage in "specific action", one of its prerogatives in

279

accordance with paragraph 4 of the 1994 Declaration on Compliance, involving the Parliamentary Assembly in the process, on one occasion.

As already indicated, one of the options expressly recognised to the CoM in paragraph 4 is deciding to "forward a communication to the Parliamentary Assembly". In the context of one of its thematic monitoring exercises, when dealing with the theme "Functioning and protection of democratic institutions, including matters relating to political parties and free elections", the CoM decided (in mid-November 1999): "to instruct the Secretariat to prepare the text of a draft communication to be forwarded to the Parliamentary Assembly in accordance with paragraph 4 of the 1994 Declaration ... inviting the Parliamentary Assembly to undertake an examination of issues surrounding the functioning (and banning) of political parties, including strategies for enhancing the democratic functioning of parliament".[46]

Accordingly, a communication was transmitted by the Chairman of the Ministers' Deputies to the President of the Parliamentary Assembly in January 2000. No information seems to be available as to any follow-up provided by the CoM in the framework of the monitoring procedure to any possible action taken by the Parliamentary Assembly in this connection, or as to any such action by the Assembly.[47]

The lack of direct channels of communication between civil society (on the one hand) and the CoM and monitoring mechanism (on the other) can negatively affect the monitoring, especially regarding complex, concrete and often urgent matters, such as those normally characterising minority situations and inter-ethnic conflict, since information highly relevant to the object of the monitoring may be missing.[48] The special restrictions applied to public access to CoM documentation in the areas of human rights and monitoring, not only entail lack of transparency, but also make any contribution by the civil society to the monitoring mechanism particularly difficult.

The possibilities for regular input from civil society into thematic monitoring seem to be limited to contacts with individual governmental delegations to the Council of Europe or with the Council of Europe Secretariat (especially its Monitoring Department), in the framework of the contribution of the Secretary General to the procedure, as described below. Only in the few instances where thematic monitoring has become country-specific have additional opportunities arisen for contact with sections of the civil society concerned, including at the domestic level, through the "information and assistance" and "expert missions" of the Secretariat described below. Besides this, in a few instances, the CoM has received direct expert advice from academia, as indicated below.

Thematic monitoring and the role of the Secretary General

An important role concerning the provision of information is that originally given under paragraph 3 of the 1995 Procedure to the Secretary General, who "at the first meeting and subsequently every second year, unless otherwise decided ... shall present a factual overview of the compliance with the commitments accepted by member states". Originally this presentation seemed to include all the commitments accepted by member states concerning the situation of democracy, human rights and the rule of law in any member state, since this constitutes the object of the monitoring procedure, in accordance with the 1994 Declaration on Compliance.

No reference is made as to any choice of specific themes.[49] Thus, the Secretary General's broad mandate, under paragraph 2 of the 1994 Declaration on Compliance, to forward information on state compliance to the CoM seemed, at first sight, to have been facilitated under the 1995 Procedure. However, the role of the Secretary General took in practice a different shape than that envisaged in the 1994 Declaration on Compliance and in the 1995 Procedure.

The confidentiality of the procedure, as already indicated, prevents public access to its exact content. Nonetheless, it seems that for the elaboration of its overviews of state compliance, the Secretariat has used both governmental and non-governmental sources of information.[50] According to a Secretariat document, the first "factual overview" was prepared within a few months by one Council of Europe official: "It offered a succinct and general statement on the situation in each member country ... under four broad headings: respect for human rights and the rule of law, the prevention of degrading treatment, freedom of the media and compliance with other commitments".[51]

However, this "overarching approach", in which the Secretariat seems to have mastered the choice of the topics addressed, was abandoned almost immediately.[52] It gave way to the monitoring process being articulated around various "themes", agreed on in advance by the states and treated in a cascading manner, which is still being applied. This second approach restricted the activities of the Secretary General in providing information to only those themes previously selected by the CoM. The scope of the Secretariat's activities was further circumscribed with the adoption by the CoM of "outlines of basic issues" on which the monitoring under the various themes started to focus,[53] until recent times, when the aforementioned questionnaire system was implemented (see below).

The Monitoring Unit was established in August 1996 to assist the Secretary General in carrying out his/her tasks within the monitoring procedure.[54] The small size of this unit may have contributed to the difficulties of implementing the initial overarching approach. However, this implementation should have been possible, given the strategic position of the unit in the Secretariat's structure.[55] Political, rather than practical considerations seem to have contributed to the initial constriction of the reporting activities of the Secretary General. The Monitoring Unit later defined its own role in a Secretariat document of 1998 as follows:

> since only the Committee of Ministers itself can undertake monitoring, the Monitoring Unit is required to confine its activities to collecting the information necessary for the Committee of Ministers' work and to present this information in a neutral fashion, in particular in the form of the aforementioned overviews. Its role in drawing the Committee of Ministers' attention to possible failures by member states to fulfil their obligations (areas of concern) has now been substituted by the need for it to provide 'comments'.[56]

Given that this description follows a reference to paragraphs 1, 2 and 4 of the 1994 Declaration on Compliance, it appears to include all the activities undertaken by the Secretary General in relation to those paragraphs of the declaration. This would indicate not only that the role originally envisaged for the Secretary General (including under the 1995 Procedure) had been substantially diminished by then, but also that this had already been admitted by the Secretary General, most probably as a result of political considerations.

Another interesting feature of the role of the Monitoring Unit was again reflected in the same Secretariat document:

> the Ministers' Deputies became aware of the difficulties faced by the Monitoring Unit in taking on, without clear instructions, the dual task of presenting the relevant facts in a neutral fashion without expressing any opinions, while at the same time drawing the Committee of Ministers' attention to possible failures by member states to fulfil their obligations. They then agreed that henceforth the documents produced by the Monitoring Unit would only constitute the first part of a larger document, the second part of which would comprise factual descriptions presented by the governments themselves. As a result, the word 'factual' was no longer added to the word 'overview' after April 1996.[57]

Then, in April 1998 it was decided "to change the method of drafting the presentation of the situation in each country: for the next overview, the national authorities would describe the situation and the Monitoring Unit would be responsible for adding "comments". Hitherto, the reverse procedure had applied."[58]

It would seem that the ability of the Secretariat "to comment" on violations of human rights to which states make no reference, in their factual descriptions regarding the specific themes, may have not been foreclosed. However, this evolution of the procedure resulted in a reduced responsibility of the Secretariat in determining the concrete object of thematic monitoring. In addition, according to the afore-mentioned document of the Secretariat:

> the notion of two-year cycles was rapidly abandoned in favour of a more flexible approach, since it soon became clear that monitoring was a continuous exercise which must not be broken up artificially. The system of cycles was abandoned, not as a result of a formal decision but because the Committee of Ministers continued to include themes already dealt with on the agenda of monitoring meetings even after the first two years elapsed...[59]

In fact, the possibility of including themes already dealt with on the agenda of monitoring meetings, even after the first two years had elapsed, seemed to have been formally opened by the 1995 Procedure, which in paragraph 4 indicates that "if during the deliberations, a need to continue the discussion on the situation in a member state is voiced, the matter will be put on the agenda of the next meeting".[60]

The abandonment of the two-year cycles previewed in paragraph 3 of the 1995 Procedure – which envisaged the presentation of comprehensive overviews where input from the Secretariat on the questions addressed was a possibility – seems to have further reduced the chances for the Secretariat to present fresh and comprehensive factual information every two years on compliance with the commitments accepted by member states. This, in turn, seems to have impaired the ability of the Secretary General to formally introduce new topics at his/her own initiative (from the perspective in which the monitoring procedure has been envisaged under the 1994 Declaration on Compliance and the 1995 Procedure), or at least new aspects of the general themes agreed upon by the CoM (from the perspective of thematic monitoring as it has evolved) other than those contained in the "outline of basic issues" agreed upon by states. As a consequence, the chances for the introduction of various aspects of human rights protection "less attractive" for states, including minority questions, under the monitoring procedure have been reduced.

The role of the Secretary General has been further delimited in accordance with the "Chairman's conclusions following the 589th meeting of the Minister's Deputies on monitoring" (17-18 April 1997).[61] At this meeting, it was agreed "that a four-stage sequence should be followed" in relation to each of the themes chosen for the monitoring exercise: "overview, debate, conclusions and follow-up".[62]

The overview – later also called "factual overview" and "first stage of the preparatory phase" of thematic monitoring – was described in 2001 as consisting in:

> the preparation and presentation of a country-by-country overview drawn up by the Secretary General, based on national contributions of no more than 10 pages of length (maximum of 7000 words) established in accordance with the outline of basic issues ... national contributions are then supplemented by 'short general and country-by-country comments' prepared by the Secretariat, in which the latter identifies issues which might merit further consideration.[63]

However, in 2002, the description of the Secretariat's role was subtly yet substantially changed. As a result of the streamlining of the procedure, the Secretariat acquired a responsibility to elaborate the questionnaire, which, subject to CoM approval, constitutes the basis for the national contributions submitted by states.

Thus, the responsibility to draw up the initial list of ("no more than three") questions subsequent to the choice of theme by the CoM, which replaces the "outline of basic issues", now rests with the Secretariat.[64] The length of the replies by states to the questionnaire has been substantially limited (at present they should not exceed 1000 words).[65] This facilitates a sharper focus. Also, an eight-week term has been fixed before the monitoring meeting for the state to make its submission, allowing for increased operability of the procedure. Although the content of the Secretary General's "comments" on state submissions is not public, their previous description in connection with the "outline of basic issues" as "short" and "general", would indicate that the role of the Secretary General consists mainly in identifying loopholes or violations of commitments, which states may have omitted or inappropriately described in their "national contributions" or replies on each "theme".[66]

While the curtailment of the Secretary General's role envisaged in the 1995 Procedure in determining the content of thematic monitoring has probably resulted in "low-profile" and "less politically acceptable" issues concerning the protection of human rights, such as most of those which relate to minority protection, becoming less likely objects of thematic monitoring overall, the recent partial, albeit restricted retrieval of his capacity to influence the content of thematic monitoring on practical grounds has possibly increased the chances that minority questions will be brought into the monitoring agenda.

A positive element in the evolution of this initial stage of monitoring has been an increasing level of publicity. The national contributions elaborated by the states are made public even though, as a rule, they have not been made available through the Council of Europe Website, a measure which would facilitate public access to their content. Thus, chances for civil society to provide input to the Monitoring Department, additional to that provided by states, may arise. The latter body, in preparing its comments: "relies on national contributions provided by the member states and on all relevant information it has been able to obtain".[67] Input from civil society may prove of practical relevance during the subsequent part of the "preparatory phase". Then:

> a provisional text of the comments made by the Monitoring Department is distributed to member states. Each state receives only general comments and the sections concerning it. Bilateral contacts then take place between Delegations of member states and the Monitoring Department. The relevant authorities in each member state are able to propose corrections and updates to the provisional texts before a specific deadline. The final version of the Monitoring Department's comments – which remain confidential – are then issued according to a schedule approved by the Committee of Ministers at the outset.[68]

The possibilities for peer review by states from the earliest stage of the proceedings thus seem to have been reduced by limiting distribution to each state only of those sections of the Secretariat's "comments" concerning it.

The possibilities for the Secretary General, and more specifically for the Monitoring Department, to uphold human rights protection, seems to acquire a more "political" character at this stage, based on its capacity to mediate and build compromises with and between states as to the content of monitoring. With the conclusion of the "first stage of the preparatory phase" and the start of the "debate" on compliance with commitments by the CoM, the role of the Secretary General in determining the content of monitoring normally dwindles (although expert input under the aegis of the Secretariat, such as those exceptions concerning the theme "freedom of expression" described below, have extended the Secretariat's contribution into the "debate" section of thematic monitoring). The CoM then becomes the master of the monitoring process, although the Secretariat is still responsible for presenting a consolidated version of the overview after the CoM "debate". This is followed by the summing-up carried out by the chairman of the CoM.[69]

The breaking of the original two-year cycles introduced increasing levels of flexibility in thematic monitoring. This has also been reflected in the activities of the Secretary General, who, by way of example, has occasionally been instructed to prepare lists of sub-items which merit priority treatment, following the debate in the framework of the CoM (see below).[70] Another interesting example has been the organisation of two seminars by the Secretariat in accordance with a special mandate to that effect given by the CoM in connection with the theme "freedom of expression and information".[71] This mandate was given following the debate on compliance by member states. While each member state was to designate up to two persons to participate in the seminars, another participant was to be selected by the Secretariat on the basis of proposals submitted by organisations representing the media sector, in consultation with the states' permanent representations.[72]

In addition, the Secretariat has increasingly been asked to become involved in the final, follow-up stage of thematic monitoring on the basis of special requests of the CoM and under its authority (see below). The Secretariat has been requested, among other things: to make proposals to the CoM or its steering committees for the purpose of readjusting intergovernmental programmes, confidence-building projects, and "Activities for the development and consolidation of democratic stability" (ADACS),[73] now "co-operation activities"; to prepare background papers and studies for stocktaking exercises; and to assess the way in which intergovernmental programmes and ADACS have been readjusted to reflect priorities highlighted as a result of thematic monitoring.[74] In the few instances that thematic monitoring has allowed for the specific targeting of country situations through expert investigation, concretely with regard to the theme "freedom of expression and information" and in connection with a limited number of states so far (see below), the Secretariat has acquired additional responsibility to feed back information for the determination of the content of subsequent monitoring under a specific theme.

In a section of the document "Compliance with commitments entered into by member states: development of the Committee of Ministers' monitoring procedure" of the Monitoring Unit, reference was made to "specific actions" (referred to in paragraph 4 of the 1994 Declaration on Compliance and paragraph 10 of the 1995 Procedure) on the one hand, and to "ad hoc procedures" (provided for in paragraph 1 of the Declaration on Compliance and paragraphs 5 and 6 of the 1995 procedure) on the other. Both were considered "procedures that would supplement the existing thematic reports system".[75] In the sentence that followed, "'specific action' was seen as a particular form of 'operational follow-up' in the current procedure". This latter statement implies that "specific action" was initially considered and treated as part and parcel of "thematic monitoring", the only form of monitoring implemented until then.

As already indicated, among the options highlighted by the CoM under paragraph 4 of the 1994 Declaration of compliance "in cases requiring 'specific action'", is the CoM decision "to request the Secretary General to make contacts, collect information or furnish advice".[76] Given that the practice of involving the Secretary General during the "follow-up" stage (of the thematic procedure previously described) became common, it seemed at first sight as if the original expectation raising "specific action" (in accordance with paragraph 4) had been identified with those current Secretary General follow-up activities, and lost, therefore, their exceptional character.

Nevertheless, in a recent document of the Monitoring Department, it was underlined that the CoM made use of paragraph 4 of the 1994 Declaration on Compliance only in the context of the follow-up to work carried out on two specific themes.[77] The first concerned the theme "the functioning and protection of democratic institutions" and consisted of the communication addressed to the Assembly, inviting the latter to examine issues surrounding the functioning (and banning) of political parties, including strategies for enhancing the democratic functioning of parliament.[78] As already discussed in the previous section, this led to no direct results.

The second concerned the theme "freedom of expression and information" and involved the Secretary General. In 1999, the CoM: "requested the Secretary General to make contacts and collect information on this theme" and invited the Secretary General "to provide the Deputies with the results by the end of the year" 1999. This deadline was later extended to 28 February 2001, and the deputies decided to resume consideration of this issue at their second meeting in camera in 2001.[79]

The aspect of the request addressed to the Secretary General which concerns "collection of information" does not seem to differ much from other requests for follow-up which have been made to the Secretariat.[80] So it has been mainly the "making contacts" that has introduced a differential element.[81] As already described, the Secretariat contacts are a normal feature of the development of the overview stage of thematic monitoring.[82] However, "making contacts" in the follow-up stage of the procedure – following debate on a theme by the CoM and a decision on "specific action" – has gained a new significance with the recent appointment by the Secretary General of experts "who are at work gathering objective information in 'all' member states. This work, currently in full swing, will be reviewed by the Ministers' Deputies in early 2003".[83]

According to a recent Secretariat document, on the basis of "specific action", experts appointed by the Secretary General visited four member states: and "at the request of the Committee of Ministers, the Secretary General will pursue his contacts to collect information on this theme in all member states, including through additional expert missions".[84] So even if "making contacts" seems to be geared towards the "collection of information", the Secretary General's activity in connection with expert missions conducted under his aegis provides the possibility of extending "making contacts" to the domestic level, so that this activity becomes more "political", and increases the possibility of influencing the domestic situation.

It can be argued that, as a result of the channelling of the implementation of the 1994 Declaration on Compliance mainly through the adoption of the 1995 Procedure and its implementation, the Secretary General has seen his role initially envisaged under the monitoring mechanism strongly eroded. The Secretary General's unhindered role in referring questions to the CoM under the formal structure originally envisaged under paragraphs 2 and 3 of the 1994 Declaration on Compliance has given way to governmental initiative as the main avenue for implementing the 1994 Declaration, in application of the 1995 Procedure.

However, the need to provide the CoM monitoring activity with substantive input and follow-up has progressively led to a renewed reinforcement of the Secretary General's position in practice. This relates not only to his function in the implementation of monitoring decisions (the current "follow-up" demands placed on him with regard to all themes) but especially since the year 2000 with regard to the more targeted role vested in him in the context of the monitoring mechanism, as a result of the need to address specific country situations. This acquisition of an increasingly relevant profile by the Secretary General in the context of the monitoring mechanism, partially due to his own proactive stance, is discussed further below. Before that, a presentation of how thematic monitoring has developed so far, follows.

Thematic monitoring and the role of intergovernmental co-operation

In the 1995 Procedure, the responsibility for monitoring is delegated from the ministers to the ministers' deputies. However, other demands contained in the 1995 Procedure aim at keeping the high political profile of the monitoring mechanism. This high profile includes the encouragement of the presence of senior officials from state capitals at meetings (paragraphs 2 and 7). A vade mecum on the procedure indicates that "[e]xperts from capitals may assist Delegations in carrying out initial consideration of themes".[85]

An important element introduced under paragraph 2 of the 1995 Procedure is the minimum number of meetings – three – of the ministers' deputies to be devoted to monitoring annually.[86] Recently, the ministers' deputies "agreed that no more than one theme be dealt with in depth at each meeting devoted to monitoring. With respect to other themes under consideration, discussion – if any – be based on short progress reports presented at each monitoring meeting".[87] It was also agreed that "procedural matters (and discussion of follow-up on monitoring issues) should, wherever possible and appropriate, be dealt with at regular meetings of the Deputies. Such discussions will be in camera, as required".[88]

According to paragraph 5 of the 1995 Procedure, any state delegation may ask to put the situation in any member state on the agenda of one of the CoM meetings devoted to monitoring, under the same conditions which apply to the Secretary General, even if the latter possibility does not seem to have been implemented, as already indicated. Further, as has also been indicated, according to paragraph 4, "if during the deliberations, a need to continue the discussion on the situation in a member state is voiced, the matter will be put on the agenda of the next meeting".[89] Although the evolution of thematic monitoring may have somehow distorted these provisions, these paragraphs would seem to indicate that, at least theoretically, the will of just one state would constitute sufficient grounds to bring a human rights situation in another state to the consideration of the CoM.

This possibility acquires special relevance in view of the fact that the permanence of a situation on the agenda of the CoM for a "reasonable" number of meetings, in accordance with paragraph 10 of the 1995 Procedure,[90] seems to provide sufficient basis for consideration of such a situation as a "case requiring specific action" under paragraph 4 of the 1994 Declaration on Compliance (see below).[91] It should be noted, however, that (as further discussed below) the undertaking of "specific action" by the CoM has not entailed the adoption of any drastic measures by this organ with regard to one or more states. It has resulted only in increased Secretariat action and intergovernmental pressure, either slight, in the form of alternative follow-up in the framework of thematic monitoring, as described above, or more incisive in allowing for the targeting of some specific country situations through expert involvement.

With regard to the internal development of thematic monitoring as it has evolved, state co-operation starts with the agreement on the theme to be addressed and on the common endorsement of the questionnaire (formerly of the "outline of basic issues", as already described) on which monitoring is focusing. According to a recent vade mecum on the procedure: "Proposals for themes to be selected should be clearly focused, with sub-themes identified if a broad theme is being proposed".[92] Individual state activity and initiatives are also present at the "first stage of the preparatory phase" of monitoring, with the elaboration and presentation of national contributions and their discussion with the Monitoring Department.[93]

However, it is during the so-called "second stage" of the preparatory phase – "which consists of debate on compliance, by member states, with commitments entered into ... the Chairman of the Ministers' Deputies then has the possibility to present his summing-up"[94] – that mutual scrutiny gains momentum. This has been the case especially since each state stopped receiving an overview concerning compliance of all other participating states at the first stage of the preparatory phase, as had been the original practice, and started to receive only "the sections concerning it".[95]

Similarly, intergovernmental co-operation is the main component of the so-called "operational phase" of thematic monitoring, in which a set of "conclusions" is agreed upon by the deputies. This leads into so-called "follow-up", in which measures such as adjustment to intergovernmental work, review of co-operation activities (formerly of ADACS), and "specific action" in accordance with paragraph 4 of the 1994 Declaration on Compliance, may be decided upon.[96]

It would seem as if a practice of stock-taking of progress made on the various themes, including an examination of the concrete results obtained, is also becoming a constituent element of follow-up.[97] This would allow for an assessment of the effectiveness of the measures taken under the monitoring mechanism and of state responses to recommendations made. It would also allow for bringing in new initiatives to promote state implementation. However, a tendency for the CoM to transfer responsibility for follow-up action to other Council of Europe bodies, including not only the Secretariat, but also the Parliamentary Assembly, as well as the Congress of Local and Regional Authorities in Europe, has been increasingly present, as further described below. The CoM has also increasingly requested the active involvement of its subsidiary bodies.[98]

"Specific actions" under paragraph 4 of the 1994 Declaration on Compliance would appear to be the area of the monitoring mechanism where the greatest powers of intergovernmental co-operation reside. No guidelines are provided as to which type of situation requires specific action, either in the 1994 Declaration on Compliance or in the 1995 Procedure. Decisions seem to emanate from CoM discretion. No indication has been given on the majorities required for decision on specific action, either in the 1994 Declaration or in the 1995 Procedure. Given that a requirement of unanimity would render monitoring worthless, it could be expected that a (probably qualified, perhaps two-thirds)[99] majority is applicable.

In the text of the 1994 Declaration on Compliance no reference is made to any requirements, or to the prerequisite of following other sections of the procedure for the CoM to decide that a case requires "specific action". However, as already noted, paragraph 10 of the 1995 Procedure seems to have introduced the requirement that a question should be on the agenda of the CoM for a reasonable number of meetings before "specific action" can be undertaken. This being the case, the possibility of dealing swiftly with human rights violations requiring a fast response is substantially reduced. According to a document of the Secretariat, "'specific action' is seen as a particular form of 'operational follow-up' in the current procedure ... these would therefore be measures to be taken when normal operational follow-up is not giving satisfactory results".[100]

This means that "specific actions" in situations involving gross violations of minority rights could not be expected under thematic monitoring, unless the series of time-consuming steps which the procedure has developed are followed. Further, as a result of the usual interpretation given to the "specific action" provision of the 1994 Declaration, consisting in practice of an alternative form of follow-up in the framework of thematic monitoring, whether "specific action" has been undertaken in connection with a specific theme often has not had any groundbreaking implications. The undertaking of "specific action" by the CoM normally has not entailed the adoption of any drastic measures by this organ with regard to one or more states.

It has only been more recently, and with regard to the theme "freedom of expression" alone, that "specific action" has started to acquire real significance. As acknowledged by the CoM, thematic monitoring received "a new impetus" when in the framework of "specific action" requested by the CoM in June 2000, experts "appointed by the Secretary General visited four member states ... and at the request of the CoM, the Secretary General will pursue his contacts to collect information on this theme in all member states, including through additional expert missions".[101] This introduction of an expert mission element into thematic monitoring has been possible against the background of the increasing emergence of country-specific forms of monitoring alternative to thematic monitoring in the context of the monitoring mechanism, often endowed with an expert input. This introduction has been largely due to the Secretary General's initiative, as discussed further, below.

The unwillingness of the CoM to engage in forms of monitoring alternative to the cumbersome "thematic monitoring" under the monitoring mechanism until late 2000, and the resulting inability of the mechanism to deal with urgent human rights situations (particularly those affecting the fate of minorities) until then, is best illustrated by the CoM's rejection of the Secretary General's initiative to trigger the monitoring mechanism in connection with the situation in Chechnya, discussed below. The transposition of this Secretary General's initiative adopted in the framework of the monitoring mechanism into the current political agenda of the CoM leads to the conclusion that the monitoring mechanism as such proved not to be instrumental, until late 2000 at least, in addressing urgent situations and massive violations of minority rights. Only the evolution of the monitoring mechanism since 2001 towards forms other than thematic monitoring has allowed for such instrumentality to loom on the horizon, although it is still far from being realised.

Before discussing this aspect, an overview of the relevance of thematic monitoring practice for minority protection follows.

Practice concerning minorities under thematic monitoring

After the selection of the theme "Functioning and protection of democratic institutions, including matters relating to political parties and free elections", and submission of the overview on this topic in February 1997, as well as subsequent debate by the CoM between February 1997 and March 1999, in the conclusions adopted by the CoM, the Secretariat was requested "to consider whether, and if so, how, a multilateral approach could relate to member states concerned, where appropriate subjects can be identified, which would merit priority treatment". It was also decided to consider proposals submitted by the Secretariat, preferably not later than at the ministers' deputies meeting of 1 and 2 June 1999.[102]

Then, at the ministers' deputies meeting of 15 and 17 November 1999, the CoM Rapporteur Group on Human Rights and two other rapporteurs were given mandates to consider the advisability of the preparation of texts (proposals) relevant to the topic. The ministers' deputies urged member states to sign and ratify the European Convention on the Recognition of the Legal Personality of International Non-Governmental Organisations.[103] Finally, in the exercise of "specific action" the deputies decided "to instruct the Secretariat to prepare the text of a draft communication to be forwarded to the Parliamentary Assembly in accordance with paragraph 4 of the 1994 Declaration on Compliance ....", as already described.[104] This communication was transmitted by the Chairman of the Ministers' Deputies to the President of the Parliamentary Assembly in January 2000.[105] However, no information is available on the direct results of this specific action, as already noted.

"Specific action" in this case seems to have become just an additional means of follow-up under thematic monitoring leading to no extraordinary outcome, and to have taken a rather circuitous path. While the number of organs acting as front-runners on the theme has been increased, the call for the Assembly's involvement in the monitoring mechanism does not seem to have resulted in its active intervention. Admittedly, the focus of attention on the particular theme seems to have become more narrow in the process.

The focusing on a topic as relevant for minorities as the functioning and banning of political parties, including the enhancement of the democratic functioning of the parliament, especially in those states where minorities have – or aspire to have – parliamentary representation, may possibly lead to progress in this field, including the issue of restrictive domestic legislation and practices which directly concern minorities.

However, as already indicated, no evidence exists of minority issues or minority protection as such being specifically considered under this theme. Finally no urgent, overriding, or even incisive measures by the CoM vis-à-vis any particular state or group of states with negative practices in this connection seems to have resulted from the monitoring, even if "specific action" was undertaken.

"Local democracy" – also of great significance for minorities – has been another theme addressed. Among the conclusions of the ministers' deputies debate on the basis of seven "basic issues" approved on 7 July 1997, following an initial overview, were: i. the existence of "shortcomings in legislation (constitutions/national legislation) that made no reference to the general principles of local democracy and/or did not provide legal guarantees for local and regional self-government; ii. the lack of specific legislation and/or laws on the status of local and regional authorities; ... and iii. problems regarding the operation of the institutions of local and regional democracy."[106]

The deputies agreed to assist governments in resolving these problems through intergovernmental co-operation activities and through "local authorities activities" under the ADACS programme.[107] They invited the CoM Steering Committee on Local and Regional Democracy (CDLR), in the context of the implementation of the local and regional democracy section of the intergovernmental programme of activities, to further develop those activities aimed at:

- achieving the right balance in the relationship between central government, sub-national levels of government (regional and local authorities) and local population, so that, firstly, all tiers of government have proper regard for the needs and wishes of the local population, and that, secondly, each tier of government discharges its powers and responsibilities in a co-ordinated and co-operative manner;
- promoting sound and stable financial arrangements for regional and local authorities, which not only support the efficient and effective operation of those authorities, but also contribute to the effective working of the economy as a whole;
- improving the structures and operation of regional and local authorities in order to increase the transparency and value for money of their actions and to help them respond to the needs and wishes of the local population...;
- promoting active involvement in public life at local and regional level through appropriate machinery for representative and direct democracy.[108]

The deputies invited member states which had not signed/ratified the Council of Europe instruments in the field of local democracy, and in particular the European Charter of Local Self-Government, to do so, and invited governments to reconsider reservations/declarations they had made upon accession to these instruments and to withdraw them "whenever possible".[109]

The deputies endorsed the monitoring work carried out by the Congress of Local and Regional Authorities of Europe (Congress) in various ways,[110] including the need for the ADACS programmes to take account of the results of this work. They also supported the reinforcement or inclusion of a local and regional democracy dimension in the joint programmes between the Council of Europe and the European Union.[111] They further decided to continue keeping local democracy on the agenda of the monitoring procedure. At a subsequent meeting, on February 2000, the deputies requested the Secretariat to assess the way in which intergovernmental and ADACS programmes had been readjusted, and invited the Congress to provide information on progress made in connection with previous decisions by November 2000. They finally decided to carry out stocktaking on the theme at one of its monitoring meetings in the year 2001, instructing the Secretariat to prepare a background paper in this regard.[112]

The corresponding monitoring meeting took place on 1 March 2001. Its results are particularly relevant, not only because it marked the closing of the monitoring cycle on this theme (the suspension of its consideration "for two or three years"),[113] but also because it took place in the midst of the transition from ADACS to "co-operation activities".[114] At this meeting, among other things, the ministers' deputies instructed the Secretariat: i. to draw up "specific proposals for action to be implemented in 2002 and 2003 within the framework of the intergovernmental work programme in order to help the member states where problems have been identified to resolve the difficulties encountered"; ii. "to give thought to multilateral initiatives on specific matters of mutual interest to several states, which could be included in the annual programme"; and iii. "to prepare a detailed comparative study on the extent and nature of local authorities' responsibilities in Council of Europe member states".

At the same time, the deputies also instructed the CDLR: "to verify whether it would be helpful, in respect of certain specific problems and in the light of precise decentralisation targets to be achieved" to elaborate a menu of good practices in accordance with the European Charter of Local Self-Government and recommendations from the CoM and "to undertake other activities which might help to solve the problems encountered, and particularly a targeted updating of its previous work in fields such as the status of local elected representatives and local authority staff recruitment and service conditions".[115]

The deputies encouraged the Congress to proceed with its monitoring work and to inform the CoM of the results regularly, and welcomed the Latvian chairmanship's initiative of holding an international conference on the topic of "Local and regional democracy at the dawn of the 21st century", inviting the chairmanship to promote debate on the subject and "to put forward proposals for action which the CoM could examine at a forthcoming meeting before the end of the year 2001".

Thus the closing of the monitoring cycle on the theme "local democracy" has resulted in a set of instructions by the CoM for its subsidiary bodies or other Council of Europe organs to act, rather than in the adoption of concrete measures with regard to state action or a set of instructions for state performance. Whether important steps forward in state performance have resulted from the monitoring process as such, and in particular from the political debate and negotiations taking place under its framework, remains an open question, in view of the lack of reporting on any such achievements. The aforementioned transfer of responsibility for progress on the object of monitoring to other bodies and organs, and even to a single conference, point to stagnation rather than progress within the framework of the monitoring mechanism as such.

An important breakthrough for minority protection seemed to result from the acceptance of the theme "Non-discrimination, with emphasis on the fight against intolerance and racism" and the corresponding outline of basic issues by the ministers' deputies on 25 October 2000.[116] Debate on this theme followed in July 2002.[117] According to the initial agenda of the deputies, the outline of basic issues and thus the object of debate on this theme comprised:

i. Legislation and governmental programmes (existence of comprehensive non-discrimination legislation);

ii. Measures to combat discrimination, in particular incitement to hatred as well as racist and xenophobic acts in the light of the Political Declaration adopted at the European Conference against Racism, Racial Discrimination, Xenophobia and Related Intolerance on 13 October 2000.[118]

However, in October 2002, the CoM decided: "to suspend consideration of this theme for 'at least' two years".[119] It also decided to transmit relevant documents to ECRI, to the Advisory Committee on the Framework Convention and to the Commissioner for Human Rights. Thus, the first instance in which the monitoring mechanism has engaged in monitoring most likely to address minority questions in a direct manner has seemingly resulted in a deadlock, and no deadline for continuation, but rather a minimum period of postponement of the treatment of this theme by the CoM has been fixed.

It is to be hoped that the theme "freedom of conscience and religion" accepted by the ministers' deputies on 30 October 2002 will not suffer a similar fate. The question addressed to states under this theme so far is as follows: "How is freedom of conscience and religion ensured in your country? – please provide one or two recent examples of progress made in this respect (e.g. recognition of religions, respect for their autonomy, legal status, including property questions, issues relating to co-existence of various beliefs and creeds, non-discrimination)".[120]

The content of this inquiry, regardless of its generality and open-endedness, does not exclude the question of minority protection, but rather seems to indirectly pave the way for its treatment. The problem, however, is that its broadness and untargeted character leaves to state discretion the choice of specific questions addressed, and thus an effective monitoring function with regard to minority protection is absent in practical terms. Although the possibility for the monitoring mechanism to keep away from minority questions remains, it is to be hoped that, if not otherwise, minority protection aspects will be addressed through the Secretariat "comments".

A final theme which deserves particular consideration is "Freedom of expression and information". Although the minority question has not become a specific target of this thematic monitoring, specific issues related to minority protection have been touched upon in addressing it. It also has special interest on procedural grounds. The initial overview on the theme in March 1996 contained "an outline of the way incitement to racial, national and religious hatred (hate speech) and its dissemination in the media were dealt with. This was followed by country-by-country descriptions of the situation in all the member states".[121]

Nevertheless, the specific issue "freedom of expression and restrictions included in penal codes and other legal texts" seems to have taken precedence over other aspects of this theme.[122] Aspects of the theme which particularly affect minorities, such as restrictions on the use of minority languages in the public sphere, including in the media, do not seem to have been addressed. The persistence of problems in this area has been evidenced recently by the adoption, under the sponsorship of the OSCE High Commissioner on National Minorities, of a set of "Guidelines on the use of Minority Languages in the Broadcast Media".[123]

With regard to "freedom of expression and restrictions included in penal codes and other legal texts", two seminars were held in 1997 in Budapest (1-2 September) and Strasbourg (13-14 October), as mentioned above.[124] Following these meetings, a team of independent experts elaborated an interim report, later presented by the chairman of the team of experts to the CoM. Particular regard has been paid to the "opportunity for frank discussion on a number of issues" provided by the presentation of the interim report. This seems to be the only instance in which non-governmental experts have been given direct input, through dialogue, into thematic monitoring. The final version of the experts' report and written comments provided by delegations were later forwarded by the ministers' deputies to two of its steering committees (the CDMM and the CDDH) so that they would be taken into account in intergovernmental work.[125]

From that moment on, thematic monitoring on this theme followed a rather normal, albeit prolonged course, until June 2000, when the CoM decided to undertake specific action by requesting the "Secretary General to make contacts and collect information".[126] More precisely, it was later stated by the CoM that "the Secretary General, in accordance with the Deputies' previous decisions ... will further pursue his contacts and collect information on the theme freedom of expression and information in 'all' member states and will provide the Deputies with the results by the end of 2002".[127]

A subsequent CoM decision indicated that experts appointed by the Secretary General had visited Albania, Russia, Turkey and Ukraine, and (as already noted) it was also restated that "at the request of the CoM, the Secretary General will pursue his contacts to collect information on this theme in 'all' member states, including through additional expert missions".[128] Since then the mission activity of the experts has seemingly extended to Azerbaijan, Georgia, Moldova and the Former Yugoslav Republic of Macedonia, while Bosnia and Herzegovina has also been targeted.[129]

However, there is no evidence of missions in Western European states so far, even if the question of freedom of expression is an object of concern also in those states.[130] So it remains to be seen whether expert missions in the context of thematic monitoring will follow the non-discriminatory approach characterising this procedure. The relevance of this development for minority protection, although seemingly remote, can still be glimpsed both in the long-run and in the shorter term. While the success of expert involvement with the theme "freedom of expression and information" may lead to this being repeated with other themes, possibly including the theme of minority protection if it is ever addressed by the CoM, expert involvement can also act as a facilitator in bringing minority concerns into the CoM thematic monitoring agenda when themes other than minority protection are addressed.

Information on expert involvement with regard to the theme "freedom of expression and information" in Moldova and Georgia has been made public and available through the Council of Europe Website. The expert report on the situation in Moldova touches upon questions of freedom of expression relevant to minority protection, even if such relevance is not mentioned. The experts address the issue of the closing of a newspaper that expressed views seemingly reflecting the position of the Transnistrian secessionist authorities, on the basis of allegations of their threat to territorial integrity, national security, public safety, public order and the prevention of crime, but in what would seem *prima facie* a clear breach of the ECHR.[131] More generally, the experts address the allegations that the Audio-Visual Co-ordinating Council of Moldova "has not monitored the equality of access of political parties and social groups to public radio and television".[132]

The expert report on the situation in Georgia makes specific reference to the situation regarding "freedom of expression and information" in the three autonomous regions of the state: Abkhazia, Ossetia and Ajaria, mainly inhabited by ethnic minorities and characterised by a fettered level of state control. The report, however, only touches on minority questions tangentially, through a short reference to issues of law enforcement and "unpunished religious violence".[133] The issue of freedom of expression as it relates to persons belonging to minorities in the country is not addressed. Nevertheless, it would seem as if, at least with regard to countries where the minority situation clearly affects in practical terms the organisation and even the viability of the state as such, minority questions have started to be introduced, even if through the side door of expert involvement, into the CoM thematic monitoring agenda.

The Secretary General, paragraph 1 of the 1994 Declaration on Compliance, and other alternatives to thematic monitoring

On the only occasion when the Secretary General took the initiative to trigger the monitoring mechanism, he used operative paragraph 1 of the 1994 Declaration on Compliance as a basis. This was done on 26 June 2000, in connection with the situation in the Russian Federation, and with regard to the conflict in Chechnya.[134] In giving a breath of life to the mandate given to him under operative paragraph 1 of the 1994 Declaration, the Secretary General attempted to start a parallel, alternative procedure to that of thematic monitoring and open new avenues for the development of the – up to then – linear and cumbersome thematic monitoring mechanism. This attempt was unsuccessful, as further discussed below.

The Secretary General did not include any reference to the 1995 Procedure. Paragraph 5 of the 1995 Procedure allows the Secretary General "on the basis of its own concerns or with reference to a discussion in the Parliamentary Assembly" to "ask to put the situation in any member state on the agenda" of one of the CoM meetings devoted to monitoring, "by request made a month before each of these meetings". By not including any reference to the 1995 Procedure, the Secretary General may have missed the opportunity to incorporate his own capacity of initiative into the mainstream thematic monitoring, developed in accordance with the procedure.

A reference to paragraph 5 of the 1995 Procedure could have possibly permitted the Secretary General to make an independent entry into thematic monitoring, to become a militant actor in its triggering and possibly one of the masters in its development, including that of its most political stages and aspects. Similarly, given the reference in paragraph 5 of the 1995 Procedure to the Parliamentary Assembly, such a step of the Secretary General might have opened the door for the Assembly's indirect involvement in thematic monitoring. Admittedly, the willingness on the CoM side to allow any of the above remains questionable, as may be seen from the discussion below.

The exercise by the Secretary General of his prerogative under paragraph 1 of the 1994 Declaration on Compliance is presented in a letter dated 26 June 2000, sent by the Secretary General to the chairman of the ministers' deputies. In this letter the Secretary General states that he "did not consider the replies ... received from the Russian authorities as satisfactory 'explanations' for the purposes of Article 52 of the European Convention on Human Rights". According to Article 52 of the ECHR,[135] "On receipt of a request from the Secretary General of the Council of Europe any High Contracting Party shall furnish an explanation of the manner in which its internal law ensures the effective implementation of any of the provisions of this Convention".

The Secretary General further refers to the findings made by a team of independent experts who have confirmed his views, by indicating that "the replies given" by the Russian Federation "were not adequate and ... the Russian Federation has failed in its legal obligations as a Contracting State under Article 52" of the ECHR.[136] By making use of the prerogatives under paragraph 1 of the 1994 Declaration in connection with a situation of lack of compliance of Article 52, the Secretary General took an important step in trying to give some teeth to the latter provision, and opening a new possibility for pro-active engagement by the CoM in the framework of the monitoring mechanism. He possibly aimed at establishing a stable link between Article 52 and the monitoring mechanism.

Nevertheless, the initiative of the Secretary General did not meet with a positive response from the CoM. The CoM seems to have waited for several months (until October 2000) to provide an official response to the initiative by the Secretary General.[137] According to the response given:

> the Ministers' Deputies, 'without prejudice to the continued validity of the 1994 Declaration on Compliance with commitments accepted by member states', recalled their decision at their previous meeting (5-6 October 2000) 'to resume consideration of the contribution of the Council of Europe towards restoration of the rule of law, respect for human rights and democracy in Chechnya on the basis of a periodic report by the Secretary General' and noted that, in the context of such discussions, the Secretary General would provide them with additional relevant information.[138]

Thus, the CoM does not seem to have engaged in urgent action, not even the convening of an urgent meeting, in connection with the exercise by the Secretary General of his competence under paragraph 1 of the 1994 Declaration on Compliance.

The initiative of the Secretary General seems to have been re-conducted into the current agenda of the CoM, outside the framework of the 1994 Declaration and the monitoring mechanism generally. In spite of the reference to the "continued validity" of the 1994 Declaration by the CoM, the aforementioned initiative of the Secretary General to trigger the monitoring mechanism by making use of his powers under paragraph 1 was effaced, and the possibility for the latter organ to become a real interlocutor of the CoM in the context of the monitoring procedure, in accordance with the text of the 1994 Declaration on Compliance, obliterated.

For the time being, the Secretary General's ability to get involved in stages of monitoring other than overview have depended on CoM discretion, in the form of decisions taken at random, even if in the case of normal follow-up within thematic monitoring they have become constant, as already described. Nevertheless, the Secretary General has continued to adopt a pro-active role in connection with the monitoring mechanism, and it has been largely due to this that the monitoring mechanism has diversified and become more operative.

The Committee of Ministers, at its 107th session on 8 November 2000, adopted Resolutions (2000) 13 and (2000) 14, inviting Armenia and Azerbaijan respectively to become members of the Council of Europe, while deciding that the date for accession would be fixed at the deputies' 737th meeting, on 17 January 2001. At the same session, the CoM took "account, with some concern, of the situation in respect to the meeting of the standards of the Council of Europe, as required from both countries, including the elections held in Azerbaijan on 5 November 2000".[139]

The CoM "took note with satisfaction of statements made by the two Ministers for Foreign Affairs of these countries". It emphasised that Armenia and Azerbaijan "should continue to strengthen their democratic institutions, respect for human rights and the rule of law" reiterating the readiness of the Council of Europe to co-operate to this end. It urged both states "to reach tangible results without delay in the solution of the Nagorno-Karabakh conflict". The Committee decided "to monitor on a regular basis the democratic development" of the countries and to "create in this context a monitoring group which will report before the 737th meeting of the deputies (17 January 2001)".[140] The name given to the monitoring group created was "GT-SUIVI-AGO".

On 22 November 2000, the ministers' deputies took note of the Secretary General's initiative to send an information mission of the Secretariat to Armenia and Azerbaijan with a view to reporting back to the Rapporteur Group for Democratic Stability of the CoM (GR-EDS) on 1 December. In addition, the deputies:

> taking into account the decision of the Ministers to monitor on a regular basis the democratic development of Armenia and Azerbaijan, in the light of the exchange of letters of October 2000 between the Chairman of the Committee of Ministers and the Ministers for Foreign Affairs of the two countries, if necessary with the help of working groups to be set up for that purpose, invited their Rapporteur Group GR-EDS to place an item 'Monitoring of the democratic development of Armenia and Azerbaijan' on the agenda of all its meetings until the next part-session of the Parliamentary Assembly in January 2001, and to report back to them on a regular basis.[141]

Thus, CoM monitoring under the mechanism in connection with Armenia and Azerbaijan started before these two states became members of the Council of Europe. It should be recalled that as the full title of the 1994 Declaration emphasises, the "Declaration on Compliance with commitments accepted by member states of the Council of Europe" concerns "the situation of democracy, human rights and the rule of law in any 'member State'".[142] Thus, it could be questioned whether this ad hoc monitoring actually fell under the scope of the 1994 Declaration on Compliance, and therefore, under the CoM monitoring mechanism as such. It has been nevertheless brought under its framework. Initially, ad hoc monitoring has been presented in Secretariat documents in parallel with other forms of monitoring described earlier in this chapter, namely thematic monitoring and the monitoring as envisaged by the 1994 Declaration on Compliance attempted by the Secretary General.[143]

At the time of writing, the term "ad hoc" has been phased out from the continued monitoring of Armenia and Azerbaijan, which now, curiously heads the "Specific post-accession monitoring" section of the current classification of the monitoring mechanism.[144] The monitoring of these two countries has provided the basis for a transition in denomination of the monitoring mechanism, from the term CoM monitoring "procedure" to "procedures". Formal aspects aside, the importance of ad hoc monitoring resides in the substantial change it has introduced into the monitoring mechanism, allowing its until then rather monolithic and cumbersome working to develop and diversify, becoming more useful.

Its relevance further resides in the fact that ad hoc monitoring did not simply become a unique monitoring exercise established in connection with the accession of two particular new states with a very poor human rights and rule-of-law record, undergoing a post-conflict situation. The monitoring with regard to these two countries has served to open the door for the monitoring mechanism to be applied to other specific country situations, and to expand more broadly along paths alternative to thematic monitoring, all of which involve stronger participation of the Secretariat, including through various forms of expert contribution.

It is interesting to note how the initial ad hoc monitoring of Armenia and Azerbaijan, which acceded to the Council of Europe on 25 January 2001, developed. Following the initiative of the Secretary General to send an information mission to both countries at the end of the year 2000,[145] the CoM adopted a decision on a "proposal by the Secretary General on a possible expert study of cases of alleged political prisoners in Armenia and Azerbaijan". The ministers' deputies decided that "in the context of the specific monitoring procedure for Armenia and Azerbaijan, cases of alleged political prisoners in these countries be transmitted to the Secretary General by Delegations to the Committee of Ministers before 28 February 2001".

The emphasis on the specificity of this particular monitoring exercise testifies to the perception by the deputies at that time that it was applicable only to the current situation in these two particular countries. The deputies also approved the initiative of the Secretary General to refer these cases to a group of independent experts, and requested the Secretary General to submit on a confidential basis the experts' opinion on the referred cases of alleged political prisoners, as soon as available, to their monitoring group GT-SUIVI-AGO.[146]

Finally, the deputies also decided on the "terms of reference given to a group of independent experts to inquire into cases of alleged political prisoners in Armenia and Azerbaijan". According to these terms of reference:

1. The Secretary General, in the context of the specific monitoring procedure for Armenia and Azerbaijan, instructs three independent experts to inquire into the cases of alleged political prisoners in Armenia and Azerbaijan referred to them.

2. The experts shall prepare a confidential opinion on the said cases indicating whether the persons in question may be defined as political prisoners on the basis of objective criteria in the light of the case-law of the European Court of Human Rights and the Council of Europe standards.

3. The experts shall transmit their opinion to the Secretary General by the 30 June 2001.[147]

The endorsement by the CoM of the initiatives of the Secretary General in connection with ad hoc monitoring, and in particular with regard to the "expert study of cases of alleged political prisoners" should be highlighted. The substance of operative paragraphs 1 and 2 of the 1994 Declaration on Compliance on the competencies of the Secretary General seem to have been put into effect, albeit informally and indirectly, as a result. The fact that the "terms of reference given to a group of independent experts" was actually adopted by the CoM points, however, to the high level of control exercised by the CoM over the Secretary General's activities. At the same time, the duty for the experts to report to the Secretary General has given the latter some scope for independent action.

It should be noted that the monitoring group GT-SUIVI-AGO has not only paid attention to the question of political prisoners on the basis of the Secretary General's reports, but also addressed issues such as freedom of the media, of NGOs and religion. The questions of freedom of religion and alternatives to military service were raised by the monitoring group in visiting Armenia, and the question of registration of religious associations has been raised in visiting Azerbaijan.[148]

References to the minority question as such have been rather absent from the work of the group, even if the minority situation permeates the situation in those states.[149] The results achieved, however, especially in the liberation and fair trial of a large number of political prisoners, can also be viewed from this perspective.[150] The mutual reinforcement of particular efforts regarding the political prisoners under the CoM monitoring mechanism and the Parliamentary Assembly's own monitoring procedures deserves to be highlighted.[151]

The experience gained with Secretariat involvement in monitoring Armenia and Azerbaijan in connection with accession, and further developed in the subsequent monitoring of other Council of Europe states in connection with thematic monitoring, further discussed below, seems to have facilitated the progressive "institutionalisation" of periodical monitoring under the CoM monitoring procedure of countries of central and eastern Europe upon their accession to the Organisation. This started with Bosnia and Herzegovina, which acceded on 22 April 2002. Again in this case, the ministers' deputies agreed "with the procedure proposed by the Secretary General concerning the monitoring of commitments by BIH".

This procedure, agreed on 29 May 2002, that is, after the accession of Bosnia and Herzegovina to the Council of Europe, provides for quarterly Secretariat progress reports on the honouring of commitments, "as well as developments in the co-operation programmes (and their possible updating). These regular reports are discussed at the Committee of Ministers' Rapporteur Group for Democratic Stability (GR-EDS) meetings".[152] The ministers' deputies also agreed that the first quarterly report should be drawn up following a Secretariat "Information and Assistance Mission" to take place within the first three months after accession.[153]

A similar pattern has been followed in connection with the accession of Serbia and Montenegro, which took place on 3 April 2003. In the latter case, the invitation that Serbia and Montenegro become a member of the Council of Europe; the post-accession co-operation programme with regard to this state; and the decision on the setting-up of the specific monitoring procedure regarding the country were adopted by the CoM simultaneously, on 26 March 2003.[154] Therefore, a tendency to include the intervention of the CoM's monitoring mechanism in an accession deal can be increasingly identified.

Unsurprisingly, the reporting on Bosnia and Herzegovina is impregnated with minority issues. A separate sub-section on these issues is included in the initial and subsequent Secretariat reports, which explicitly introduce this aspect of human rights protection on the agenda of the monitoring mechanism for the first time,[155] following agreement by the CoM in this respect.[156] Although the "minority protection" sub-section is confined to examination of the status of ratification of the Framework Convention and the Languages Charter, as well as to the Roma issue, other minority questions are addressed throughout the text of the initial report without being qualified as such.

Under the heading "priority issues of a political nature" the questions of: i. the implementation of the Dayton Peace Agreement; ii. the timely preparation of the 5 October 2002 general elections; iii. constitutional and legislative amendments necessary to comply with the Constitutional Court decision on the "constituent peoples of Bosnia and Herzegovina"; iv. co-operation with the ICTY [International Criminal Tribunal for the former Yugoslavia]; and v. safe return of refugees and displaced persons, and creation of sustainable conditions for return, are addressed.[157]

It should be highlighted that under iii. the report notes that whilst measures taken to ensure the implementation of the decision of the Constitutional Court constitute a positive development as compared with the prior situation, "this leaves open a number of questions, in particular for those who do not wish to declare their ethnicity or are not part of any of the three Constituent Peoples".[158] Therefore, the report hints at the weakness of the Constitutional Court decision, from an international human rights perspective, and particularly for minority protection standards.

A less veiled criticism is contained under the "'minority'" sub-section by reference to a report requested "in co-operation with UNICEF and OSCE missions to Bosnia and Herzegovina on "Access of Roma to Education and Health Care Services in Tuzla Canton" which highlights wide-ranging discrimination against the Roma.[159] This sub-section also refers to the initiative to establish an Advisory Council "on" Roma, although no reference is made to the need to include Roma representatives in the membership of the Council. In the analysis of the status of the Frame-work Convention and the Languages Charter in Bosnia and Herzegovina, delays on compliance with reporting duties and on accession are pointed at, respectively.

Finally, under the sub-section on "promotion of social cohesion, in particular the return of refugees and displaced persons through reinte-gration policies" of the human rights section, reference is made to the fact that "minority returns are generally located in self-contained and sharply delimited areas, within a majority municipality" and to the seg-regation deriving from this.[160] The problem of "possible disinterest [i.e., 'lack of interest'] of majority municipalities for the effective integration of returnees" is pinpointed.[161]

In the list of different types of action recommended in the report for the Council of Europe to undertake, the promotion of "the development of good community relations policy and practice" and "capacity within local authorities to promote local economic development" as well as the facil-itation and encouragement of "donor investment, particularly through integrated investment projects that combine housing, infrastructure, employment and health" (and education) are included. Educational issues relevant to minority protection, such as training for human rights and civic education teachers, the elimination of "objectionable" material from textbooks as well as differences in levels of education – and acces-sibility of public education in one Canton for the residents of another – of new residents are also addressed.[162]

Although in the second periodic report the minority sub-section is not further developed, other aspects of the situation in the country highly relevant to minority protection are analysed, including aspects relating to the selective implementation of property laws,[163] the adoption of legislation in the field of local self-government,[164] and education reform.[165] Subsequent reports have followed a similar pattern, although the reporting outline has been changed to fall under four main headings: i. democratic institutions; ii. human rights; iii. rule of law; and iv. educa-tion. Particularly relevant has been the reference in the most recent report to the issue of lack of implementation by the authorities in the

Republika Srpska of the BiH Human Rights Chamber ruling regarding the failure by these authorities to disclose information on the fate of missing persons, in connection with the Srebrenica massacre.[166]

As to Serbia and Montenegro, a "National minorities" sub-section has been introduced in the first periodic report.[167] The current situation with regard to legislation is discussed in detail, including concerns relating to the introduction of preferential treatment of the "Albanian community" in the draft law on national minorities in Montenegro.[168] Council of Europe involvement with regard to the implementation of existing legislation, and the drafting of new, is advocated in relation to each constituent state.

Periodic monitoring, based on a series of reports elaborated at regular intervals, has also been established with regard to Georgia since January 2003. It should be noted that the periodic monitoring of the latter state is presently classified under the heading "Specific post-accession monitoring" together with that regarding Armenia, Azerbaijan and Bosnia and Herzegovina[169] (in the future probably also Serbia and Montenegro), even though Georgia acceded to the Organisation in April 1999, long before this form of monitoring took shape.

It should also be noted that country-specific monitoring had previously been undertaken regarding Georgia, on the basis of "specific action", as described in the paragraphs which follow. However, according to the initial, six-monthly,[170] periodic report prepared by the Directorate of Strategic Planning, it was on the basis of a visit by a delegation from this directorate to Tbilisi in December 2002, and the examination of the resulting report by the CoM, that the latter organ "noted that there was agreement on ensuring regular monitoring of Georgia's respect of its obligations and commitments on the basis of proposals by the Secretary General".[171]

The report resulting from the visit by the Secretariat actually included a request for the CoM to review "at six-monthly intervals, progress achieved until such time as Georgia has complied with commitments accepted in 1999",[172] that is, at the time of its accession to the Organisation. Under a "Human rights" section, the fact that no progress has been registered as regards the ratification of the Framework Convention is emphasised, although the fact that Georgia was the first state to ratify Protocol 12 to the ECHR is also noted.[173] Reference is made to the problem of violence against religious movements and to the issue of the repatriation of the persons deported during the period 1940-44 (the Meskhetian population). These issues had already been raised in the previous monitoring of Georgia under the monitoring mechanism (see below).

It is interesting to note that among the concrete concerns and proposals raised by the Secretariat was the information provided by Human Rights Watch, Amnesty International and the OSCE concerning the decision of the Georgian Supreme Court to de-register Jehovah's Witnesses as a legal entity in Georgia. The Secretariat proposed that the draft Law on Religious Organisations be submitted to the Council of Europe for legal expertise prior to its transmission to Parliament.[174]

The six-monthly periodic monitoring on Georgia[175] is to concentrate on three priority areas: preparations for the parliamentary elections, with associated legislation and institutional arrangements; the functioning of the judiciary and law enforcement agencies; and combating corruption.[176] Nevertheless, the issues of "freedom of conscience and religion", "national minorities" and "repatriation of deported persons during the period 1940-44" are still treated as "other important matters".

With regard to freedom of expression, reference is made to the increasing manifestations of intolerance and attacks against various churches, with the alleged involvement of members of the Georgian Orthodox clergy in acts of intolerance. The fact that the Draft Law on Freedom of Conscience and Religious Entities was submitted to the Council of Europe for expert appraisal in June 2003 is mentioned, and so is the fact that the progress achieved in all member states, including Georgia, on freedom of conscience and religion is to be discussed by the CoM under its thematic monitoring procedure on 3 July 2003.[177] With regard to national minorities, the existence of no major breakthrough in the process of ratification of the Framework Convention is reported, and ratification is demanded. Finally, with regard to the repatriation of the Meskhetian population, a new version of the draft Law on Repatriation of Formerly Deported People is also demanded.[178]

As mentioned above, the experience gained through Secretariat involvement in monitoring Armenia and Azerbaijan, in connection with their accession to the Organisation, may have contributed to facilitating its involvement in successive monitoring exercises and in diversifying the monitoring mechanism. In the chairman's summing-up of the deputies' 754th meeting on 7-8 June 2001, the chairman concluded "that the decisions on the Secretary General's proposals concerning Ukraine, following the ministers' informal meeting on 10 May 2001, had been taken within the framework of the 1994 Declaration on compliance with commitments accepted by member states of the Council of Europe".[179] Thus again a country-specific monitoring, officially brought under the 1994 Declaration on Compliance, was started, following an initiative and political decision apparently taken outside the framework of the monitoring mechanism and even outside the official agenda of the CoM, in the context of an informal meeting of the latter dealing with a specific country.

Taking as a basis, firstly, the Secretary General's proposals concerning Ukraine, following the ministers' informal meeting on 10 May 2001, secondly, Parliamentary Assembly Recommendation 1513 (2001), and thirdly, a letter from the foreign minister of Ukraine, the deputies "decided to ask the Secretary General to send, at the earliest opportunity, a Secretariat mission with a view to assisting the Ukrainian authorities to fulfil their remaining commitments and to providing relevant information to the CoM" on 8 June 2001.[180]

It should be noted that although an Assembly Recommendation was mentioned, its text does not make any reference to the monitoring mechanism of the CoM, the 1994 Declaration on Compliance or the 1995 Procedure. Therefore, the possibility that this reference may have related to the exercise by the Assembly of its competencies, under the 1994 Declaration on Compliance in particular, can be dismissed. It rather seems as if the CoM decided to refer to the Assembly's independent monitoring endeavours in justifying the new steps taken under its own monitoring mechanism. This practice has started to develop into a pattern in the context of country-specific monitoring. It undeniably contributes to the CoM response to the Assembly's demands regarding follow-up by the CoM of the Assembly's monitoring (post-accession in particular),[181] although reference has been made above to the reservations expressed by the Parliamentary Assembly in this connection.[182]

The report resulting from the "Secretariat Assistance and Information to Ukraine, 26-29 August 2001" addresses issues of "pluralist democracy" (including the item "local self-government"); "rule of law"; "human rights" (including the item "minorities") and "others" (including the item: "Church's independence and restitution of church property").[183] The item "minorities" is confined to a description of the current procedural stage of monitoring of Ukraine under the Framework Convention. It is also stated that no request for expertise on the new draft law on national minorities has been submitted by the Ukrainian government to the Council of Europe Secretariat, while such expertise was demanded from the OSCE.

References are also made to the difficulties encountered in the ratification of the Languages Charter, and a proposal for follow-up action by the Council of Europe is put forward, which consists in co-operation with the OSCE High Commissioner on National Minorities in the provision of legislative expertise concerning the draft law on the State Language, as well as the possible organisation of an information seminar on this issue.[184]

A similar procedural course was taken by the monitoring mechanism when on 17 October 2001, again by reference to an Assembly "monitoring" Recommendation – No. 1533 (2001) – the deputies decided "to send, at the earliest opportunity, a Secretariat mission" to Georgia, "by virtue of paragraph 4 of the 1994 Declaration on compliance ... with a view to assisting the Georgian authorities to fulfil their remaining commitments and to providing relevant information to the Committee of Ministers".[185] Thus 'specific action' was formally activated in connection with this country.

The "Information and Assistance Mission to Georgia (3-5 December 2001)" dealt with issues relating to the "political context", "democratic institutions", "the rule of law" and "human rights". No separate reference is made to the minority question in the resulting report, although the fact that Georgia neither ratified the Framework Convention within the set deadline of one year following accession, nor signed the Languages Charter, is discussed under the "Council of Europe Conventions" sub-section in the "human rights" section.[186]

The issue of the repatriation of the Meskhetian population, a question on the political agenda of the Council of Europe during previous years, is discussed under a specific sub-section on the "Repatriation of deported persons during the period 1940-44 (Meskhetian Turks)" also within the "human rights" section.[187] The principle that "their living conditions in the regions of temporary residence should be improved, especially as regards their residence status to avoid statelessness situations" is supported.[188] The idea that "bilateral discussions and negotiations between Georgia and the countries of temporary residence should be encouraged" is endorsed, as is the involvement of the Council of Europe in the elaboration of a census of the population concerned, in order to ascertain how many people wish to return to Georgia.

The need to legally prosecute those responsible for "incidents of violence in Georgia against non-traditional religious groups" and to change the law on legal organisations in order to end with the practice of unfair detention of "cult" members, possibly with Council of Europe assistance, is discussed under the item "freedom of conscience and religion".[189] Finally, by reference to previous Council of Europe Secretariat activities outside the framework of the monitoring mechanism in the field of local self-government, it is stated that previous proposals made by the Secretariat in relation to the local electoral system were not taken into consideration by the Georgian authorities.[190] Thus, the opportunity is used to take up previous recommendations made outside the framework of the monitoring mechanism, aiming to provide them with additional political weight within it.

As already described, the monitoring of Georgia has gone a step further than in the case of Ukraine. In addition to requests to the groups GT-SUIVI-AGO and GR-EDS, and especially to the Secretary General, to provide follow-up, in February 2003 the deputies "noted that there was agreement on ensuring regular monitoring of Georgia's respect of its obligations and commitments on the basis of proposals from the Secretary General, and instructed the GR-EDS to finalise the arrangements for implementing this procedure". Consequently, the six-monthly "regular monitoring with respect to Georgia" has been implemented since early 2003, as already described.

Finally, reference should be made to the decision of the CoM in March 2002 "to invite the Secretary General to send, at the earliest opportunity, a Secretariat Information and Assistance mission ... to Moldova, by virtue of paragraph 4 of the 1994 Declaration on Compliance". This resulted in a mission headed by the Council of Europe Deputy Secretary General to Chisinau, on 16-18 April 2002. The main aspect of relevance for minorities, in the Secretariat report of the visit, is the reflection of the claims by the head of a territorial authority (and minority representative) regarding the inadequacy of existing laws in the field of territorial self-government – specifically, the law on the special legal status of Gagauzia, elaborated with Council of Europe assistance. The report also reflects his allegations of violations of existing legislation by the central authorities of the state.[191]

Although in a subsequent reply by the CoM to Assembly Recommendation 1554 (2002), the CoM acknowledged that the implementation of Moldova's obligations and commitments vis-à-vis the Council of Europe "still gives cause for concern and should continue to be followed closely" no decision on periodic monitoring (such as that adopted with regard to Georgia) was taken with regard to Moldova. It should be highlighted, however, that in adopting this reply, the CoM expressly referred to the case of Church of Bessarabia,[192] brought against Moldova before the European Court of Human Rights, as a matter raising particular concern.[193]

Concluding remarks

The Committee of Ministers has become the master of the monitoring mechanism established in the "Declaration on Compliance with commitments accepted by member states of the Council of Europe". Although according to the 1994 Declaration on Compliance, the Parliamentary Assembly and the Secretary General were also to have a leading role, this has been eroded, mainly as a result of successive steps taken by the CoM to this effect. This applies to the main course taken by the monitoring mechanism, thematic monitoring, in particular, and its implementation through the 1995 Procedure (this has been the case in particular for the Parliamentary Assembly) or just through subsequent practice (especially with regard to the Secretary General).

This development has not been good news for the activation of the monitoring mechanism, and for its potential to address minority questions, given the general reluctance by states, especially those in western Europe, to address this aspect of human rights protection. The lack of transparency and restricted access to information on CoM monitoring makes it difficult for civil society to contribute to its activation and development. The successive calls of the Parliamentary Assembly for increased transparency are highly relevant in this context.

It should be noted, however, that the later evolution in the implementation of thematic monitoring has resulted in a growing devolution of responsibility on Council of Europe actors other than the CoM, which are entering the procedure by the hand of the latter organ. Thus, although the role of these actors as independent initiators of the procedure and in determining the content of the agenda for thematic monitoring as originally envisaged has dwindled, their role in the implementation of the procedure and its follow-up has been progressively increased. This has possibly been the result of the CoM's search for ways to fulfil its monitoring aims, seemingly impossible to achieve through internal debate alone. This applies, in particular, to the growing involvement of the Secretary General.

The existence of a will to involve directly the Parliamentary Assembly in the procedure is far less evident. The Congress of Local and Regional Authorities of Europe, for which no role had been envisaged in the 1994 Declaration, has also been brought into the "operational phase" of thematic monitoring by the CoM. Some analytical input from the academic community and expert involvement has also been made possible under the aegis of the Secretary General's involvement. The latter has been particularly instrumental in bringing issues relating to minority protection into the monitoring agenda.

The very existence of the 1994 Declaration on Compliance has been linked to the on-going enlargement process of the Organisation, a process in which the minority issue has slowly moved to the top of the political agenda. However, the very nature of the course mainly taken by the CoM's monitoring mechanism along thematic lines, characterised by "non-discriminatory" approaches to monitoring, has acted as an impediment to minority questions being addressed, given the difficulty of "minority protection" being accepted as a "theme" object of "egalitarian" monitoring of all member states, particularly those of Western Europe. The non-discriminatory character of thematic monitoring also greatly weakens its ability to respond to human rights crisis situations involving minorities in specific states. Other aspects of the procedure, such as the high level of formality and secrecy that it has developed in practice, contribute to this shortcoming.

An important element introduced in the monitoring mechanism, and started under thematic monitoring, has been that of the reassessment of the "Activities for the development and consolidation of democratic stability", and the succeeding co-operation activities, from the perspective of monitoring concern. Given the low level of attention paid to the minority question that had traditionally characterised these programmes, their revision in the future could lead to their stronger focus on the minority question. This is especially important since the Council of Europe-wide Joint Programme between the European Commission and the Secretariat of the Council of Europe on minorities (which almost exhausted the activities concerning minority protection considered under the ADACS heading) was discontinued. A window of opportunity is currently provided through the Co-operation Activities, especially in connection with the implementation of relevant international instruments (such as the Framework Convention) and procedures.

An encouraging element resulting from existing monitoring practice has been the endorsement of the activities of the Congress of Local and Regional Authorities of Europe under the theme "local democracy", and in particular of the Congress's monitoring activity, which has implemented in practice a non-discriminatory approach to monitoring, under which questions of minority protection have been considered.[194] It remains to be seen whether particular aspects of local democracy related to minority protection – and addressed by the Council of Europe in specific conventions (such as that on transfrontier co-operation or the participation of foreigners in public life at local level) – will become objects of the monitoring mechanism in the future.

In addition to addressing the theme of local democracy – while monitoring freedom of conscience and religion is yet to yield specific results – it has been mainly in the framework of country-specific approaches to monitoring involving expert participation, both under the scope of thematic monitoring with regard to the theme freedom of expression and with regard to other types of country-specific monitoring developed since 2001, that questions relating to minority protection have been brought to the attention of the CoM under the monitoring mechanism. It should be noted, however, that specific treatment of minority questions as such under these forms of monitoring has been scant. Similarly, there is no evidence of such expert missions being conducted in countries of western Europe so far. The concrete results that expert involvement under the monitoring mechanism may achieve, and their effects on the development of monitoring and on the addressing of the minority question, remain to be seen.

The question should be put forward as to whether the monitoring mechanism has fulfilled the expectations generated by its establishment.

The CoM has not addressed numerous pending human rights questions under it, including those ranking high on its own political agenda. Various aspects of minority protection constitute the most vivid example of this. While the approach which has dominated the procedure has been "non-discriminatory" and "thematic", no set of instructions for the swift implementation of measures by the member states as a whole seems to have resulted from the procedure.

When it comes to concrete situations of massive violations of minority rights, the monitoring mechanism has so far been rejected as an instrument, the CoM preferring to address the topic under its current political agenda. The encouragement of more active involvement by other Council of Europe organs in the procedure, accompanied by appropriate follow-up of their initiatives, could act as an activator of the mechanism, and prevent the neglect of important human rights questions as a result of realpolitik, which strongly influence the capacity of initiative and action of the CoM. While the principle of egalitarian treatment of states in the framework of the monitoring mechanism should be upheld, alternative avenues to time-consuming, deadlock-prone "thematic monitoring" in its present form should be developed, allowing for the operationalisation of the monitoring mechanism not only to deal with exceptionally urgent and grave violations of human rights, particularly of minorities, but also to address minority questions within all member states in a systematic manner.

Notes

1.   For the text of the declaration see the appendix of this publication. The text is also included in "Compliance with member states' commitments: background information concerning the Committee of Ministers monitoring procedure set up in November 1994", Monitor/Inf (96) 1, 4 November 1996, pp. 4-5.

2.   On monitoring mechanisms at the Council of Europe generally, see A. Drzemczewski, "The prevention of human rights violations: monitoring mechanisms in the Council of Europe", in L.-A. Sicilianos (ed.) and C.B. Bouloyannis-Vrailas (assoc. ed.), *The Prevention of Human Rights Violations* (The Hague, New York, London: Kluwer Law International; and Athens: Ant. N. Sakkoulas, 2001), pp. 139-77. Also available in French: "La Prévention des violations des droits de l'homme: les mécanismes de suivi du Conseil de L'Europe", 11 *Revue Trimestrielle des Droits de L'Homme*, No. 43, 1 Juillet 2000, pp. 385-428. For an analysis of the CoM monitoring mechanism in particular see, by the same author: "Monitoring by the Committee of Ministers of the Council of Europe: a useful 'human rights' mechanism?", 2 *Baltic Yearbook of International Law*, pp. 83-103. For an early description and critical remarks on the original monitoring procedure, see B. Petranov, "Council of Europe launch confidential monitoring procedure", *10 Interights Bulletin*, 1996, p. 85. Finally, for a collection of essays providing relevant background information see A. Bloed, L. Leicht, M. Nowak and A. Rosas (eds.), *Monitoring Human Rights in Europe* (Dordrecht, Boston, London: Martinus Nijhoff, 1993).

3.   Doc. Monitor/Inf (96) 1, p. 4.

4.   Second preambular paragraph of the declaration. See also paragraph 1 of the operative section of the declaration, quoted below.

5.   As already noted in Chapter 5, the fact that both the text of the Framework Convention for the Protection of National Minorities and the declaration were adopted on the same date would seemingly point to an implicit link between both instruments. However, this link has not materialised in practice, as described below.

6.   See K. Drzewicki, "The future relations between eastern Europe and the Council of Europe", in A. Bloed and W. de Jonge (eds.), *Legal Aspects of a New European Infrastructure* (Utrecht: Europa Institute and Netherlands Helsinki Committee, 1992), pp. 41-60. See also Chapter 9 of this book.

7.   See Chapter 9.

8.   According to the initial agenda of the CoM, this theme was to be considered until March 2002. (See "Compliance with member states' commitments: 'Decisions' taken within the context of the Committee of Ministers' monitoring procedures", Doc. Monitor/Inf (2001) 3, Strasbourg, 4 May 2001, p. 24.) However, this topic was also discussed at the CoM's 801st meeting of 1 July 2002.

9.   See "Monitoring procedure – background information", Doc. Monitor/Inf (96) 1, 4 November 1996, p. 4. Present authors' emphasis.

10.   This aspect is emphasised again in operative paragraph 5. Ibid., p. 5.

11.   Ibid.. Present authors' emphasis. The non-confrontational character of the procedure will be re-emphasised in each of the subsequent stages of its development, including in the "Procedure for implementing the Declaration of 10 November 1994 on compliance with commitments accepted by member states of the Council of Europe" (see below).

12.   The text is included in "Monitoring procedure – background information", Monitor/Inf (96) 1, 4 November 1996, p. 6, and subsequent vade mecum documents on the development of the monitoring mechanism. For a more recent one, see "Compliance with commitments entered into by member states: vade mecum of the Committee of Ministers' Thematic Monitoring Procedure", doc. Monitor/Inf (2003) 2, 6 February 2003.

13. The change in denomination took place in September 2000.

14. 1996 Ordinary Session, Third part, Official Report, 21st sitting, contained in Parliamentary Assembly Document AS (1996) CR 21 of 26 June 1996, included in ibid., p. 11.

15. Operative paragraph 1 of the 1994 Declaration on Compliance, contained in ibid., p. 4. Present authors' emphasis.

16. Operative paragraph 3 of the 1994 Declaration on Compliance, at ibid. Present authors' emphasis.

17. Ibid., Appendix II.

17. Ibid., Appendix XII.

18. See "Monitoring procedure – decisions", doc. Monitor/Inf (2001) 3, Strasbourg, 4 May 2001, Appendix II.

19. Ibid., p. 2. See below.

20. See operative paragraph 1 of the 1995 Procedure in "Monitoring procedure – background information", doc. Monitor/Inf (96) 1, 4 November 1996, p. 6.

21. See "Monitoring procedure – decisions", doc. Monitor/Inf (2001) 3, Strasbourg, 4 May 2001, p. 3.

22. See statement by Mr Kallas, Chairman-in-Office of the CoM, to the Parliamentary Assembly at its 1996 Ordinary Session, fourth part, Official Report, 27th sitting, contained in Parliamentary Assembly Document AS (1996) CR 27, 24 September 1996, extracts of which are included in "Monitoring procedure – background information", doc. Monitor/Inf (96) 1, 4 November 1996, p. 15.

23. See "Compliance with commitments entered into by member states: vade mecum on the Committee of Ministers' thematic monitoring procedure", ["Monitoring procedure – vade mecum"] Doc. Monitor/Inf (2001) 1, Strasbourg, 4 January 2001, 2.

24. Ibid., p. 6.

25. Ibid., pp. 7-17.

26. See "Monitoring procedure – development", doc. Monitor/Inf (98)2, 23 November 1998, endnotes 49 and 50. On the specific rules applicable to publication of documents of the CoM, consult the CoM home page on the Council of Europe website. For a recent example of the Assembly's demands for the declassification of documents relating to the monitoring mechanism, see the Question asked by Mrs Tytti Isohookana-Asunmaa, General Rapporteur of the Parliamentary Assembly on the Media to the Chairman of the Committee of Ministers, and the corresponding reply, quoted in "Compliance with member states' commitments: the Committee of Ministers' monitoring procedures", doc. Monitor/Inf (2003) 1 Addendum, 6 February 2003, p. 14.

27. See decision of the ministers' deputies 699th meeting, doc. CM/Del/Dec (2000) 699, item 2.4.*e*, as quoted in "Monitoring procedure – decisions", doc. Monitor (2000) 2, Strasbourg, 7 March 2000, p. 13. It should be noted in this context that the general rule according to which documents are made public one year after a decision on their declassification has been taken does not apply to "human rights" and "monitoring" documents, which are subjected to more stringent rules.

28. See questions by Mr Severin, Mr Gross and Mr Antretter (parliamentarians) to Mr Kallas, Chairman-in-Office of the Committee of Ministers, in "Monitoring procedure – background information", doc. Monitor/Inf (96) 1, 4 November 1996, pp. 9-12.

29. "Monitoring procedure – development", Doc. Monitor/Inf (98) 2, 23 November 1998, p. 12.

30. Text within brackets added by the present authors. See "Progress of the Assembly monitoring procedures (April 1997-April 1998)", Report of the committee on the honouring of obligations and commitments by member states (monitoring committee), rapporteur: Mr Guido de Marco. Parliamentary Assembly Doc. 8057, 2 April 1998. It should be noted that the plenary session of the Assembly took a milder stand in this connection. In Resolution 1155 (1988), which followed the presentation of the report by Mr de Marco, the Assembly stated that "monitoring of obligations and commitments of member states should be regularly on the agenda of the Joint Committee" without any reference to specific meetings of the Joint Committee which should be devoted to this topic. See Parliamentary Assembly Resolution 1155 (1988) on progress of the Assembly monitoring procedures (April 1997-April 1998), paragraph 6.

31. Ibid., footnote 47. See also Doc. CM Del/Dec (98) 630 item 2.1 as quoted in "Monitoring procedure – development", Doc. Monitor/Inf (98)2, 23 November 1998.

32. See "Monitoring procedure – development", Doc. Monitor/Inf (98)2, 23 November 1998, endnote 47. See also Doc. CM Del/Dec (98) 630 item 2.1 as quoted at ibid.

33. See "Monitoring procedure – vade mecum", Doc. Monitor/Inf (2001) 1, Strasbourg, 4 January 2001, endnote 3.

34. "Progress report of the Monitoring Committee (1998-99)", Information report, Committee on the honouring of obligations and commitments by member states of the Council of Europe (monitoring committee), rapporteur: Mr Jordi Solé Tura, Parliamentary Assembly Doc. 8359, 19 March 1999, pp. 2, 3, 11.

35. The first, held on 23 April 1998, was devoted to monitoring issues generally, and the second, held on 28 January 1999, was devoted to an exchange of views on co-operation between the Ukraine and the Council of Europe in the light of the previous discussion in the Parliamentary Assembly. As regards informal meetings, according to the same source, the monitoring of Ukraine gave rise to the first informal meeting, held on 11 January 1999 between the Bureau of the Monitoring Committee of the Parliamentary Assembly and the Assembly rapporteurs on Ukraine and on the death penalty, on the one hand, and the Chairman of the Ministers' Deputies as well as the permanent representative of Ukraine on the other. The second informal meeting, held on 26 January 1999 between the Acting Chairman of the CoM and the Chairman of the Monitoring Committee of the Assembly, "marked the interest of the Hungarian Presidency in reinforced co-operation between the Committee of Ministers and the Monitoring Committee". See "Progress report of the monitoring committee (1998-99)", Information report, Committee on the honouring of obligations and commitments by member states of the Council of Europe (monitoring committee), rapporteur: Mr Jordi Solé Tura, Parliamentary Assembly Doc. 8359, 19 March 1999, p. 3.

36. See "Progress report of the Monitoring Committee (1999-2000)", Information report, Committee on the honouring of obligations and commitments by member states of the Council of Europe (monitoring committee), rapporteur: Mr Juris Sinka, Parliamentary Assembly Doc. 8734, 4 May 2000.

37. See ibid.

38. "Progress report of the monitoring committee (1998-99)", p. 3.

391. See paragraph 4 of the recommendation.

40. Paragraphs 5 and 6 of the recommendation.

41. See Parliamentary Assembly Recommendation 1536 (2001), "Progress of the Assembly's monitoring procedure (2000-2001)", para. 3. See further, A. Drzemczewski, "Monitoring by the Committee of Ministers of the Council of Europe: a useful 'human rights' mechanism?", op. cit., p. 100. On the activities of GT-SUIVI-AGO, see below. This *Groupe de Travail – Suivi* ('follow-up working group') is named after its chairman, Mr P.E. Ago, Permanent Representative of Italy.

42.   Annual joint committee meetings devoted to monitoring, and informal meetings previously held by the chair of the ministers' deputies and the chair of the Assembly's monitoring committee. See "Relations with the Parliamentary Assembly, Parliamentary Assembly Recommendation 1536 (2001) on progress of the Assembly's monitoring procedure (2000/2001)", doc. CM/Del/Dec (2001) 767/2.3 and 778/2.8, 8 January 2002.

43.   See further, Chapters 5 and 9 in particular.

44.   Paragraph 5 of the 1995 Procedure, "Monitoring procedure – background information", Monitor/Inf (96) 1, 4 November 1996, p. 6.

45.   Doc. Monitor/Inf (98)2, 23 November 1998, p. 5.

46.   See "Monitoring procedure – decisions", Doc. Monitor/Inf (2001) 3, Appendix VI, Strasbourg, 4 May 2001, p. 13.

47.   In Resolution 1308 (2002) "Restrictions on political parties in the Council of Europe member states" adopted by the Assembly on 18 November 2002, two years after the invitation was made no reference is made to the CoM monitoring mechanism and no direct connection seems to exist between the two. Reference is made instead to the fact that the question of the banning of democratically elected political parties in Council of Europe member states was raised in the Assembly two years before the European Court's judgment of 31 July 2001 in the Case *Refah Partisi and Others v. Turkey*. That means that this issue was raised in the Assembly before the CoM requested its involvement on this topic in connection with the monitoring mechanism, and independently from it. Before Resolution 1308 (2002), the Assembly seems to have addressed only one more topic related to the functioning of political parties: their financing, in Recommendation 1516 (2001), also without any clear connection with the CoM monitoring mechanism.

48.   The convening of two expert seminars – in connection with the sub-theme "freedom of expression and restrictions included in the Penal Code and other texts" organised in the framework of monitoring the theme "freedom of expression and information" – seems to constitute the only exception in this connection as it comes to thematic monitoring (see further, below). In the context of the OSCE, for example, meetings with non-governmental actors are articulated not only through institutionalised, periodical means of dialogue, but also via more informal means, and often in connection with situations involving human rights crises or interethnic conflict. See further, M.A. Martín Estébanez, "Minority protection and the Organisation for Security and Co-operation in Europe", in P. Cumper and S. Wheatley, *Minority Rights in the New Europe* (The Hague/London/Boston: Martinus Nijhoff, 1999), p. 38 and pp. 43-45.

49.   See "Monitoring procedure – development", Doc. Monitor/Inf (98)2, 23 November 1998, p. 6.

50.   See below.

51.   "Monitoring procedure – development", Doc. Monitor/Inf (98)2, 23 November 1998, p. 9.

52.   See statement by Mr Kallas, Chairman-in-Office of the CoM, to the Parliamentary Assembly at its 1996 Ordinary Session, Third part, Official Report, 21st sitting, contained in Parliamentary Assembly Document AS (1996) CR 21 of 26 June 1996, and also question by Mr Davis and reply by Mr Kallas, Fourth part, Official Report, 27th sitting contained in Parliamentary Assembly Document AS (1996) CR 27 of 24 September 1996, at ibid., pp. 7 and 17.

53.   See above.

54.   Three permanent Council of Europe officials, two administrators and their assistant have constituted the permanent staff of the Monitoring Unit, which was deemed to "liaise with different directorates, depending on the theme it has been instructed to work on". See "Monitoring procedure – development", Doc. Monitor/Inf (98)2, 23 November 1998, p. 7.

55.   In a recent vade mecum, the role of the Monitoring Department of the Secretariat, which has replaced the Monitoring Unit, is still defined as one of co-ordinator of the Secretariat Directorates General activities. Thus the large resources provided by most of the Council of Europe Secretariat can be drawn upon by the Monitoring Department for the development of its activity. See doc. Monitor/Inf (2002) 2.

56.   Ibid.

57.   Ibid., pp. 6-7.

58.   Ibid., p. 8.

59.   Ibid., p. 7.

60.   See "Monitoring procedure – vade mecum", Doc. Monitor/Inf (98) 1, Strasbourg, 13 July 1998, p. 7.

61.   Adopted at the 591st Meeting of ministers' deputies on 30 April. See "Compliance with commitments entered into by member states: information concerning the Committee of Ministers' monitoring procedure", Doc. Monitor/Inf (97) 2 rev., p. 6.

62.   Ibid.

63.   See "Monitoring procedure – vade mecum", Doc. Monitor/Inf (2001) 1, Strasbourg, 4 January 2001, p. 3. Present authors' emphasis.

64.   See "Compliance with commitments entered into by member states: vade mecum on the Committee of Ministers' thematic monitoring procedure", Doc. Monitor/ Inf (2003) 2, p. 2.

65.   Ibid., p. 3.

66.   This is also supported by an earlier description provided by the Monitoring Unit according to which the "first stage of the preparatory phase" consists "of the preparation and presentation of a country-by-country overview drawn up by the Secretary General's Monitoring Unit, based on national contributions of between five and ten pages in length, established in accordance with the "outline of basic issues". These are to be supplemented by "short" comments prepared by the Secretariat, in which the latter is to identify issues "which might merit further consideration". See "Monitoring procedure – vade mecum", Doc. Monitor/Inf (98) 1, Strasbourg, 13 July 1998, p. 2. (Present authors' emphasis).

67.   See "Monitoring procedure – vade mecum", Doc. Monitor/Inf (2001) 1, Strasbourg, 4 January 2001, p. 3.

68.   Ibid.

69.   The "debate" section of the procedure has remained rather constant since its inception, in accordance with the vade mecum documents. For a recent update see doc. Monitor/Inf (2003) 2, 6 February 2003, p. 3.

70.   See "Monitoring procedure – decisions", Doc. Monitor (2000) 2, Strasbourg, 7 March 2000, p. 9.

71.   In connection with the monitoring procedure on this theme, "the Committee of Ministers instructed the Secretary General's Monitoring Unit to produce proposals for the organisation of seminars on 'freedom of expression and restrictions included in penal codes and other legal texts', a sub-theme of the general report on freedom of expression which the report had picked out as being of particular importance". See "Compliance with commitments entered into by member states: development of the Committee of Ministers' monitoring procedure", ["Monitoring procedure – development"] Doc. Monitor/Inf (98)2, 23 November 1998, p. 9. See further, "Compliance with commitments entered into by member states: information concerning the Committee of Ministers' monitoring procedure, freedom of expression and restrictions included in the penal code and other legal texts: Seminars held in Budapest and Strasbourg in 1997", Doc. Monitor/Inf (97) 3, 14 November 1997. These seminars were held in September and October 1997, respectively, at a time when "defamation laws" in some states of central and eastern Europe were receiving widespread criticism.

72.   See "Compliance with commitments entered into by member states: information concerning the Committee of Ministers' monitoring procedure, freedom of expression and restrictions included in the penal code and other legal texts: Seminars held in Budapest and Strasbourg in 1997", Doc. Monitor/Inf (97) 3, 14 November 1997, p. 3.

73.   The ADACS programme now comes under the heading of co-operation programmes.

74.   See "Monitoring procedure – decisions", Doc. Monitor (2000) 2, Strasbourg, 7 March 2000, pp. 6, 9, 13. On the programmes and activities mentioned see the annual reports on both topics published by the Council of Europe. For a focus on minority protection aspects, see Chapter 7.

75.   See "Monitoring procedure – development", Doc. Monitor/Inf (98) 2, 23 November 1998, pp. 8,13. On the thematic character which the monitoring procedure has developed, see further, below. The fact that: i. the thematic report system is qualified as the only existing one; ii. "specific actions" and "ad hoc procedures" are referred to as possible avenues of action; and iii. that they have been addressed under the heading "future prospects" in the Secretariat document, underlines the lack of use of alternative avenues for the development of the monitoring procedure to the (general and) thematic, from its establishment until 23 November 1998, when the document is dated.

76.   Present authors' emphasis.

77.   See "Monitoring procedure – decisions", Doc. Monitor/Inf (2001) 3, Strasbourg, 4 May 2001, p. 2. See also "Compliance with member states' commitments: the Committee of Ministers' monitoring procedures", doc. Monitor/Inf 2002 1 rev., paragraph 6.

78.   Ibid., paragraph 11.

79.   Ibid., p. 2.

80.   By way of example, in the context of monitoring of the theme "local democracy", in which the monitoring cycle has been already been stopped, the Secretariat has been instructed "to prepare a detailed comparative study on the extent and nature of local authorities' responsibilities in Council of Europe member states". See at ibid., Appendix VIII, p. 19.

81.   Ibid., Appendix V, p. 10.

82.   From this it would seem to derive that, for the Secretariat to engage in "contacts" with states in the "follow-up" stage of thematic monitoring, once the Committee of Ministers has engaged in debate on a particular theme, a special mandate of "specific action" would be required from the Committee of Ministers. Seemingly, the role of the Secretariat would not just entail "contacts" of an "administrative type", in connection with the collection of information on the particular theme, but possibly also its engagement in more "political" consultations.

83.   See "Extract from statement by Mrs Lydie Polfer, Deputy Prime Minister, Minister for Foreign Affairs and Foreign Trade of Luxembourg, Chairman of the Committee of Ministers (May-November 2002) at the closing sitting of the Conference" in "Compliance with member states' commitments: the Committee of Ministers' monitoring procedures", doc. Monitor/Inf (2003) 1, Addendum, p. 12.

84.   Ibid., p. 9.

85.   See "Monitoring procedure – vade mecum", Doc. Monitor/Inf (2001) 1, Strasbourg, 4 January 2001, 4, paragraph 8.

86.   The meetings of the ministers' deputies have recently been lasting for two days. See "Monitoring procedure – development", Doc. Monitor/Inf (98)2, 23 November 1998, p. 8.

87.   See "Monitoring procedure – decisions", Doc. Monitor/Inf (2001) 3, Strasbourg, 4 May 2001, p. 4.

88. See "Monitoring procedure – vade mecum", Doc. Monitor/Inf (2001) 1, Strasbourg, 4 January 2001, 4, paragraph 10.

89. See "Monitoring procedure – background information", Doc. Monitor/Inf (96) 1, 4 November 1996, p. 6.

90. Ibid. Emphasis added. No further definition exists of what may be considered "reasonable".

91. Ibid., p. 5.

92. See "Monitoring procedure – vade mecum", Doc. Monitor/Inf (2001) 1, Strasbourg, 4 January 2001, p. 2.

93. See above.

94. "Monitoring procedure – vade mecum", Doc. Monitor/Inf (98) 1, Strasbourg, 13 July 1998, p. 3.

95. Ibid.

96. The types of follow-up action have been enumerated in more detail above.

97. In support of this see "Decisions" paragraph 1 of Doc. CM/Del/Dec (99) 674, item 2.5.b; "Decisions" paragraph 6 of Doc. CM/Del/Dec (98) 639, item 2.3; and "Decisions" paragraph 10 of Doc. CM/Del/Dec (98) 644, item 2.4.b, as quoted in document "Monitoring procedure – decisions", Doc. Monitor (2000) 2, Strasbourg, 7 March 2000, at pp. 6, 9, and 12 respectively.

98. By way of example, see the decisions undertaken in the context of thematic monitoring of the theme "functioning of the judicial system" in "Monitoring procedure – decisions", Doc. Monitor/Inf (2001) 3, Appendix VII, Strasbourg, 4 May 2001, p. 14.

99. On the majorities required for decisions to be adopted by the CoM and the ministers' deputies generally, see G. de Vel, *The Committee of Ministers of the Council of Europe* (Strasbourg: Council of Europe Publishing, 1995), pp. 58-61, especially at p. 60. See also the decision that no delegation should request the application of the rule of unanimity to block the adoption of recommendations, adopted at the 519th bis meeting of ministers' deputies quoted at ibid., p. 140.

100. See "Monitoring procedure – development", Doc. Monitor/Inf (98) 2, 23 November 1998, p. 13.

101. See "Relations with the Parliamentary Assembly, Parliamentary Assembly Recommendation 1536 (2001) on progress of the Assembly's monitoring procedure (2000-2001)", doc. CM/Del/Dec (2001) 767/2.3 and 778/2.8, paragraph 4.

102. See "Monitoring procedure – decisions", Doc. Monitor (2000) 2, Strasbourg, 7 March 2000, p. 7.

103. ETS 124.

104. See "Monitoring procedure – decisions", Doc. Monitor/Inf (2001) 3, Appendix VI, Strasbourg, 4 May 2001, p. 13.

105. See "Monitoring procedure – decisions", Doc. Monitor (2000) 2, Strasbourg, 7 March 2000, 7, endnote 4.

106. "Decisions" of the ministers' deputies 650th meeting, doc. CM/Del/Dec (98) 644, item 2.4.b, as quoted in "Monitoring procedure – decisions", Doc. Monitor (2000) 2, Strasbourg, 7 March 2000, p. 11.

107. See Chapter 7.

108. "Decisions" (as cited in note 106), pp. 11-12.

109. Ibid., p. 11.

110. See further, Chapter 10.

111. On the Congress of Local and Regional Authorities of Europe and the joint programme between the Council of Europe and the European Union, see Chapters 10 and 7 of this book respectively.

112. See "Monitoring procedure – decisions", Doc. Monitor/Inf (2001) 3, Appendix VIII, Strasbourg, 4 May 2001, p. 17.

113. Ibid., p. 19.

114. See Chapter 7.

115. See "Monitoring procedure – decisions", Doc. Monitor/Inf (2001) 3, Appendix VIII, Strasbourg, 4 May 2001, p. 19.

116. See "Monitoring procedure – decisions", Doc. Monitor/Inf (2001) 3, Appendix XI, Strasbourg, 4 May 2001, p. 24.

117. See "Compliance with member states' commitments: the Committee of Ministers' monitoring procedures", doc. Monitor/Inf (2003) 1 Addendum, p. 38.

118. "Monitoring procedure – decisions", Doc. Monitor/Inf (2001) 3, Appendix XI, Strasbourg, 4 May 2001, p. 24.

119. See "Compliance with Member States' Commitments: The Committee of Ministers' Monitoring Procedures", doc. Monitor/Inf (2003) 1 Addendum, p. 38. Present authors' emphasis.

120. Ibid.

121. See "Monitoring procedure – development", Doc. Monitor/Inf (98)2, 23 November 1998, p. 9. A second overview took place in September 1996. See "Compliance with Member States' Commitments: The Committee of Ministers' Monitoring Procedures", doc. Monitor/Inf (2003) 1 Addendum, p. 21.

122. See "Monitoring procedure – development", Doc. Monitor/Inf (98)2, 23 November 1998, p. 9.

123. Soon available at the OSCE HCNM Website: http://www.hcnm.org. See also T. McGonagle, B. D. Noll, M. Price (eds.) *Minority-Language Related Broadcasting and Legislation in the OSCE* (Oxford/Amsterdam: PCMLP Centre for Socio-Legal Studies Institute for Information Law, 2003).

124. The organisation of these seminars followed an exceptional mandate given to this effect by the Committee of Ministers to the Secretariat (see below).

125. See "Monitoring procedure – decisions", Doc. Monitor/Inf (2000) 2, 4. See also "Monitoring procedure – decisions", Doc. Monitor/Inf (2001) 3, Appendix V, Strasbourg, 4 May 2001, p. 11.

126. Extract from the ministers' deputies 712th meeting, doc. CM/Del/Dec (2000) 712, item 2.1, 5-6 June 2000. See doc. Monitor/Inf (2003) 1 Addendum, p. 8.

127. Extract from the ministers' deputies 761st meeting, doc. CM/Del/Dec (2000) 712, item 2.1, 5-6 June 2000. See at ibid. Present authors' emphasis.

128. See "Relations with the Parliamentary Assembly, Parliamentary Assembly Recommendation 1536 (2001) on progress of the Assembly's monitoring procedure (2000-2001)", doc. CM/Del/Dec (2001) 767/2.3 and 778/2.8, paragraph 4. Present authors' emphasis.

129. See "Council of Europe standards with respect to freedom of expression and information", doc. Monitor/Inf (2003) 3, p. 9.

130. In this regard, Maud De Boer-Buquicchio, Deputy Secretary General of the Council of Europe referred generally to the problems encountered in media legislation of long-standing members of the Council of Europe, which is in contradiction to the ECHR, at a conference organised by the Luxembourg Chairmanship of the Committee of Ministers on 30 September-1 October 2002. See ibid.

131. A breach of the ECHR jurisprudence is signalled by the experts in their report. See "Freedom of expression and information: experts' report on the situation in Moldova, following their visit to the country from 22 to 24 January 2002", doc. CM/Monitor (2002) 7, 25 March 2002, p. 3.

132. Ibid., p. 11.

133. See "Freedom of expression and information, experts' report on the situation in Georgia, following their visit to the country from 22 to 25 July 2002", doc. CM/Monitor (2002) 17, 30 September 2002, p. 3.

134. Ibid., p. 2.

135. Ibid., Appendix II, p. 6.

136. Ibid. On the approach by the CoM to the conflict in Chechnya, see further, Chapter 5.

137. Ibid., p. 7.

138. Ibid. On the approach of the CoM, within its own general agenda, to the conflict in Chechnya, see Chapter 5.

139. See *Activities of the Council of Europe: Report 2000*, p. 362.

140. See "Monitoring procedure – decisions", Doc. Monitor/Inf (2001) 3, Appendix XIII, Strasbourg, 4 May 2001, p. 25.

141. It was decided that this group would be composed of the permanent representatives of the following member states: Austria, France, Georgia, Greece, Italy, Latvia, the Netherlands, Romania, the Russian Federation, Sweden, Switzerland, Turkey and Germany (the latter as holder of the chairmanship of the GR-EDS), under the chairmanship of Italy. See *Activities of the Council of Europe: Report 2000*, p. 14.

142. Title and operative paragraph 1 of the 1994 Declaration. Present authors' emphasis.

143. See "Monitoring procedure – decisions", Doc. Monitor/Inf (2001) 3, Strasbourg, 4 May 2001, p. 2.

144. See "Compliance with member states' commitments: the Committee of Ministers' monitoring procedures", doc. Monitor/Inf (2003) 1 Addendum, p. 3.

145. See docs. SG/Inf (2000) 46 revised and SG/Inf (2000) 47 revised.

146. See "Monitoring procedure – decisions", Doc. Monitor/Inf (2001) 3, Appendix XIII, Strasbourg, 4 May 2001, pp. 25-26. The expert reports have been published in documents SG/Inf (2001) 34 and Addenda 1 and 2.

147. Ibid, p. 26, endnote.

148. See "Monitoring group (GT-SUIVI-AGO) – progress report", doc. CM (2002) 79 revised, 4 June 2002, paragraphs 30 and 41 respectively.

149. The report of the work of GT-SUIVI-AGO serves as an illustration. The word "minorities" is used only in one instance, and in rather general terms (see at ibid., paragraph 53).

150. See documents SG/Inf (2001) 34, and its Addenda 1, and 2, of 24 October 2001. See also doc. SG/Inf (2003) 15 of 2 April 2003.

151. See doc. CM/Del/Dec (2001) 765bis, 21 September 2001, para. 2 as quoted in "Compliance with member states' commitments: the Committee of Ministers' monitoring procedures", doc. Monitor/Inf (2003) 1 Addendum, p. 44.

152. See "Bosnia and Herzegovina, Follow-up to Committee of Ministers decisions regarding the monitoring of commitments and implementation of the post-accession co-operation programme, Document presented by the Secretary General, second quarterly report", doc. SG/Inf (2002) 40, 16 October 2002, paragraph 2.

153. See "Bosnia and Herzegovina, Follow-up to Committee of Ministers decisions regarding the monitoring of commitments and implementation of the post-accession co-operation programme, first quarterly report following the first Secretariat assistance mission to Bosnia and Herzegovina (2-6 July 2002)", doc. SG/Inf (2002) 27, 15 July 2002, paragraph 2.

154. See "Serbia and Montenegro: Compliance with obligations and commitments and implementation of the post-accession co-operation programme, Document presented by the Secretary General, first quarterly report (April-June 2003), doc. SG/Inf (2003) 28, 7 July 2003, p. 3.

155. This is done under the under the "Full respect for European Human Rights standards, including through an effective protection system, and promotion of tolerance, social cohesion and social rights" heading, paragraphs 62-67.

156. The structure of the first and second reports followed the outline agreed by the ministers' deputies on 29 May 2002. See "Bosnia and Herzegovina, Follow-up to Committee of Ministers decisions regarding the monitoring of commitments and implementation of the post-accession co-operation programme, Document presented by the Secretary General, second quarterly report (July-October 2002)", doc. SG/Inf (2002) 40, 16 October 2002, paragraph 7.

157. See "Bosnia and Herzegovina, Follow-up to Committee of Ministers decisions regarding the monitoring of commitments and implementation of the post-accession co-operation programme, first quarterly report following the first Secretariat assistance mission to Bosnia and Herzegovina (2-6 July 2002)", doc. SG/Inf (2002) 27, 15 July 2002, paragraphs 9-34.

158. Ibid., paragraph 20.

159. Ibid., paragraph 64.

160. Ibid., paragraph 74.

161. Ibid., paragraphs 72-75.

162. Ibid., paragraphs 92-93.

163. See "Bosnia and Herzegovina, Follow-up to Committee of Ministers decisions regarding the monitoring of commitments and implementation of the post-accession co-operation programme, Document presented by the Secretary General, second quarterly report (July-October 2002)", doc. SG/Inf (2002) 40, 16 October 2002, paragraph 28.

164. Ibid., paragraph 41.

165. Ibid., paragraphs 50-62.

166. See "Bosnia and Herzegovina, Compliance with obligations and commitments and implementation of the post-accession co-operation programme, Document presented by the Secretary General, fourth quarterly report (March 2003-June 2003)", doc. SG/Inf (2003) 21, 23 June 2003, paragraph 21.

167. See "Serbia and Montenegro, Compliance with obligations and commitments and implementation of the post-accession co-operation programme, Document presented by the Secretary General, first quarterly report (April-June 2003)", doc. SG/Inf (2003) 28, 7 July 2003, paragraphs 28-30.

168. Ibid., paragraph 30.

169. See "Compliance with member states' commitments: the Committee of Ministers' monitoring procedures", doc. Monitor/Inf (2003) 1 Addendum, p. 3.

170. Instead of quarterly, as is the case of the other "specific post-accession monitoring" exercises mentioned above.

171. See "Compliance with commitments and obligations: the situation in Georgia, six-monthly report prepared by the Directorate of Strategic Planning (DSP), (January-June 2003)", doc. SG/Inf (2003) 25, 24 June 2003, paragraph 1.

172. See "Compliance with commitments and obligations: the situation in Georgia, report prepared by the Directorate of Strategic Planning (DSP), (subsequent to Secretariat Delegation visit to Tbilisi on 8-11 December 2002)", doc. SG/Inf (2003) 1, 17 January 2003, p. 1.

173. Ibid., p. 5.

174. Ibid., p. 23.

175. Instead of quarterly, as it is the case of the other "specific post-accession monitoring" exercises mentioned above.

176. See "Compliance with commitments and obligations: the situation in Georgia, six-monthly report prepared by the Directorate of Strategic Planning (DSP), (January-June 2003)", doc. SG/Inf (2003) 25, 24 June 2003, paragraph 2.

177. Ibid., paragraphs 38-41.

178. Ibid., paragraphs 42-43.

179. See "Compliance with member states' commitments: the Committee of Ministers' monitoring procedures", doc. Monitor/Inf (2003) 1, Addendum, p. 15.

180. Ibid.

181. See further, Chapter 9.

182. For further discussion on this question, see A. Drzemczewski, "Monitoring by the Committee of Ministers of the Council of Europe: a useful 'human rights' mechanism?", 2 *Baltic Yearbook of International Law*, pp. 87-89.

183. See doc. SG/Inf (2001) 27, 6 September 2001, p. 1.

184. Ibid., p. 20.

185. See "Compliance with member states' commitments: the Committee of Ministers' monitoring procedures", doc. Monitor/Inf (2003) 1, Addendum, p. 16.

186. See Report of the Secretariat's information and assistance mission to Georgia (3-5 December 2001), doc. SG/Inf (2001) 45, 19 December 2001, p. 12.

187. See ibid., paragraphs 44-45.

188. Ibid., p. 14.

189. Ibid., p. 16.

190. Ibid., p. 9.

191. See "Moldova, Secretariat information and assistance mission, headed by the Deputy Secretary General, Mr H. C. Krüger (Chisinau, 16-18 April 2002)", paragraphs 16-17.

192. See further, Chapter 1.

193. See "Relevant extract from the ministers' deputies' reply to Parliamentary Assembly Recommendation 1554 (2002) on the functioning of democratic institutions in Moldova (doc. CM/Del/Dec (2002) 808, item 2.4, 18 September 2002)", quoted in doc. "Compliance with member states' commitments: the Committee of Ministers' monitoring procedures", doc. Monitor/Inf (2003) 1, Addendum, p. 18.

194. See Chapter 10.

Chapter 7

Other intergovernmental co-operation and activities of the Secretariat

Introduction

Although the high-level political declarations and decisions adopted by the intergovernmental structures of the Council of Europe are important in understanding the approaches of the Organisation to the minority question, it is through the activities of the various intergovernmental committees and the Secretariat that these decisions are articulated and implemented.

An important aspect in the setting of guidelines is the adoption by the ministers' deputies of the intergovernmental programme of activities linked to the annual budget of the Organisation.[1] This programme is prepared by the Secretariat on the basis of information provided by the main intergovernmental "committees of experts" appointed by member states. These specialised committees are also responsible for the implementation of the annual programme of activities.[2] Each committee receives specific terms of reference and the ministers' deputies are responsible for decisions on their functioning, including the approval of the terms of reference of subordinate committees.[3]

Some of these committees and subordinate committees have developed activities that touch upon minority protection. Attention here focuses on the activities of those which have contributed substantially to promoting minority protection since this issue became an important item on the intergovernmental agenda – and especially on the Committee of Experts on Issues Relating to the Protection of National Minorities (DH-MIN), even though its activities have been suspended; the European Committee on Migration (CDMG); the European Population Committee (CAHP, formerly CDPO); the Council for Cultural Co-operation (CDCC) and more recently the Rapporteur Group on Education, Culture, Sport, Youth and the Environment (GR-C).

A short reference will be made to the work of the Steering Committee on Local and Regional Democracy (CDLR), given the overall relevance of inter-governmental work on the development of local democracy and territorial structures for minority protection. These questions, however, are mainly addressed in Chapter 10. Finally, reference should be made to the fact that an "ad hoc Working Party with the task of examining proposals of the Secretary General on multicultural and inter-religious dialogue" has been established in the context of the post-September 11th approaches. However, as already mentioned in Chapter 5, the level of intergovernmental activity in this connection seems to have been rather limited so far.[4]

In "serving" the organs of the Council of Europe in accordance with Article 10 of the statute of the Organisation, the Secretariat has become the main executor of the activities included in the intergovernmental programme of activities, including those relating to minority protection. A major aspect of the work of the Secretariat has been the Activities for the development and consolidation of democratic stability (ADACS) formerly known as "Co-operation and assistance programmes with central and eastern European countries" but with the broader aim to include all Council of Europe states. It was under this heading that most Council of Europe activities related to minority protection within the member states of the Organisation or candidates for accession used to be framed. This included the two joint programmes between the European Commission and the Secretariat of the Council of Europe, which have been the most comprehensive activities involving practical interstate co-operation in the field of minority protection undertaken by the Organisation so far.

In 2001, the ADACS-specific budget was brought to an end and the various Council of Europe departments responsible for implementing activities were given individual budgetary allocations to finance their own projects. The funding and those activities relevant to minorities that were previously organised under the ADACS budgetary scheme were decentralised. This resulted in the present organisation of the Secretariat activities under the so-called Co-operation activities, which are mainly confined to countries of central and eastern Europe once more. The so-called new initiative of the Secretary General and the follow-up given to it are also briefly presented below. Finally, the programme of confidence-building measures in civil society, which involves direct co-operation with NGOs, is discussed.

Activities of intergovernmental committees[5]

DH-MIN

Following a decision of the Committee of Ministers (CoM) of December 1997, the Committee of Experts on Issues Relating to the Protection of National Minorities (DH-MIN), a sub-committee of the CoM Steering

Committee for Human Rights (CDDH), was established as an intergovernmental forum for the exchange of information, views and experience on policies and good practice for the protection of national minorities at the domestic level and in the context of international instruments.[6] Although in the Intergovernmental Programme of Activities for the year 2000 the activities of DH-MIN still ranked high on the agenda,[7] these were suspended at the end of 1999 for budgetary reasons. The deputies' ministers, however, invited in July 2003 their Rapporteur Group on Human Rights (GR-H) to consider the proposal to re-establish DH-MIN.

The terms of reference of DH-MIN are:

- to act as a forum for the exchange of information, views and experience on policies and good practice for the protection of national minorities at the domestic level and in the context of international instruments.

- to identify and assess ways and means of further enhancing European co-operation on issues relating to the protection of national minorities and, where appropriate, to make proposals to this effect for consideration by the CDDH;

- in so doing it shall, where appropriate:

  - carry out or commission relevant policy research;

  - involve in its work representatives of national minorities and non-governmental organisations with recognised competence in this field.[8]

Already at the first meeting of DH-MIN, held from 17 to 20 March 1998, this committee prepared the draft opinions of the CDDH on recommendations of the Parliamentary Assembly pending from the two previous years.[9] During its second meeting, held from 20 to 23 October 1998, DH-MIN also prepared a draft opinion of the CDDH on Recommendation 43 of the Congress, on territorial autonomy and national minorities.[10] The CDDH adopted an opinion on this recommendation for the attention of the CoM in 1999.[11]

DH-MIN has been the main Council of Europe forum for intergovernmental co-operation in relation to minority protection. It used to be presented as an important actor in the activity on "Legal and political aspects of the protection of national minorities" included in the intergovernmental programme of activities.[12] The objectives pursued under this activity, which provided a more detailed description of the issues in relation to which the work of DH-MIN developed, included:

i. to improve, through practical initiatives, the protection of persons belonging to national minorities as an integral part of the international protection of human rights and democratic stability in Europe, in accordance with the action plan of the Strasbourg Summit;

ii. to facilitate further signatures and ratifications of the Framework Convention for the Protection of National Minorities;

iii. to increase knowledge and awareness of the Framework Convention in member states;

iv. to promote the pooling of experience and practices through inter-governmental exchanges of views on policies and good practices for the protection of persons belonging to national minorities at the domestic level in the context of international instruments; and

v. to identify and assess, in intergovernmental exchanges of views, ways and means of further enhancing European co-operation on issues relating to the protection of national minorities.[13]

The majority of the results expected from this activity remained rather constant. They were: i. continuation of the work of DH-MIN to exchange views on policy issues and further European co-operation; ii. elaboration of possible guidelines and collection of good practices; iii. information meetings, conferences, seminars at national and local level on the Framework Convention for government officials, parliamentarians, local authorities and NGOs; iv. preparation of materials on the Framework Convention for NGOs; and v. legislative and policy counselling on request.[14] Two new elements were introduced among the results expected for the year 2000: vi. involvement of DH-MIN in the follow-up to a high-level meeting on minorities foreseen in the Council of Europe Stability Programme for South-Eastern Europe and the contribution of DH-MIN to furthering the aims of the stability programme[15] and vii. the elaboration of studies. The results of the initiatives undertaken by DH-MIN were still on the agenda of the CDDH during the years 2000 and 2001.

DH-MIN held consultations with non-governmental organisations with expertise in the field of protection of national minorities. It also considered the question of the participation of minorities in decision-making processes.[16] The latter topic was addressed during the second and third meetings of DH-MIN, and led to the elaboration of a questionnaire on this issue. On the basis of a compilation of the responses, a study was prepared at the Max Planck Institute in Heidelberg, Germany.[17]

The study, carried out by Professor J. Frowein and Dr R. Bank, aims "to develop a typology of different forms of participation of minorities in decision-making processes and identify parameters relevant to the choice of a specific form for a given situation".[18] It addresses measures adopted in the fields of:

i. parliamentary representation of minorities and exercise of parliamentary control;

ii. representation of minority interests in governmental agencies;

iii. informal channels of participation, such as round tables or councils;

iv. different forms of autonomy; and

v. the approaches taken in federal systems.[19]

In spite of the suspension of the activities of DH-MIN this study seems to have been an object for consideration within the CDDH, although no information on follow-up action is available.

At its 650th meeting, held on 24 and 25 November 1998, the CoM gave the following ad hoc terms of reference to DH-MIN:

• to undertake a study on "dispersed ethnic minorities" as well as prospects for co-operation between the Council of Europe on the one hand and the European Institute for Dispersed Ethnic Minorities and other bodies pursuing similar objectives on the other hand;

• to submit its findings to the Committee of Ministers through the CDDH.[20]

The first aspect of these terms of reference resulted in a very important exercise. In order to carry out its study on dispersed ethnic minorities, DH-MIN addressed a questionnaire to member states requesting information about which groups could be considered as dispersed ethnic minorities within their territory. DH-MIN thus engaged member states in an exercise of "identification" of these groups. However, the report contains replies from only fifteen member states: Austria, Cyprus, Finland, Germany, Hungary, Lithuania, Poland, Portugal, Romania, Russia, Slovakia, Slovenia, Sweden, Switzerland and "the former Yugoslav Republic of Macedonia". Most member states seem to have shown no willingness to become involved. On the basis of the information collected, "DH-MIN firstly discussed, completed and collated the information received from member states", and then it went on to consider "whether it would be desirable and/or possible to propose a definition of 'dispersed ethnic minorities' that would be capable of mustering general acceptance".[21]

DH-MIN concluded that there was no need to propose the adoption of a definition in view of: i. the differing approaches of the member states to the term and the perception that this should not preclude establishing forms of practical co-operation where possible; and ii. the fact that no normative, standard-setting work was envisaged.[22] Nevertheless, DH-MIN identified "a number of elements which in the majority of cases would all or mostly apply to groups of persons which could be considered 'dispersed ethnic minorities'", while emphasising "that these elements are to be regarded as beacons for practical orientation and do not constitute a definition".[23] These elements "which appear to apply to the great majority of groups"[24] are the following:

• they have no kin-state;

- they live in more than one state;

- persons belonging to these groups share common ethnic, religious, linguistic or cultural characteristics;

- they do not form a majority in any Council of Europe member state.

The emphasis placed by DH-MIN on the lack of a "kin-state", further highlighted in the report, is illustrated by its direct and indirect introduction in the first and fourth elements that have been identified respectively. The second element – "they live in more than one state" – has been interpreted in the report as "dispersed".

The origin of this approach could again be rooted in the weight that the idea of kin-state bears when states consider the minority question. The need for a "dispersed group" to live in the territory of several states in order to qualify as such seems limiting, and works against the principle of providing protection for those groups which are particularly vulnerable as a result of their scattered demography, not necessarily across borders. This is especially the case for small minorities, which may be in most urgent need of protection, and for which existence in more than one state may prove too demanding a requirement.[25]

Finally, the third element identified could be considered as informing the concept of "minority" that DH-MIN has developed. It is important to note in this respect the statement in the report that:

> DH-MIN underlines that the term 'dispersed ethnic minorities' should not be understood as excluding groups of persons whose principal ties are religious, linguistic or cultural, rather than ethnic. In this context it is suggested that the terminology may be adapted, either by introducing the term 'dispersed ethnic, religious, linguistic or cultural minorities', or by introducing the shorter term 'dispersed minorities', it being understood that it has the same material scope as the longer term.[26]

Another important issue raised in the report is that of group self-identification: "DH-MIN emphasised the sensitivity of the issue of self-identification and stressed that this terminology should not be used in reference to groups against their will".[27] It should be noted that the aspect of self-identification being addressed here is collective, that of the group as such, rather than the more classic aspect of self-identification, which relates to the will of individual members to belong to the group. The latter has become a common feature of the international minority rights instruments and discourse,[28] but the former introduces an innovative element in the context of discussions at the intergovernmental level in the Council of Europe.[29]

Again in connection with the question of identification, the report indicated:

> DH-MIN also considered whether qualifying a group as a 'dispersed ethnic minority' excludes such a group from being qualified at the same time as a 'national minority'. It noted that the approach to this question differs from state to state.[30]

This seems to suggest that there was no agreement on the establishment of strict, restrictive categorisations and that states are bound to adopt flexible approaches to the issue. It should be noted in this context that the issue of defining which groups constitute a specific category of minority is no longer considered an exclusive prerogative to be exercised by states individually, and the idea of taking internationally accepted, objective criteria as a basis has gained ground, as the exercise in which DH-MIN engaged as regards dispersed minorities illustrates.

While the divergent approaches by states to the issue of whether a group deserves to be considered under more than one specific category of protection illustrate that no government has the monopoly of reason, the adoption of common approaches to guarantee human rights protection is called for. In this light, states should willingly adapt their particular categorisation of a determined minority, or adopt elements of protection included in a different category than that originally envisaged for a particular group.[31] Conversely, the use of categories and compartmentalisation as a means of adopting restrictive approaches to minority rights recognition and protection does not seem to be an approach commonly accepted by the international community.[32]

In implementing the second aspect of the terms of reference given to DH-MIN by the CoM – to study the prospects for co-operation between the Council of Europe on the one hand and the European Institute for Dispersed Ethnic Minorities and other bodies pursuing similar objectives on the other hand – DH-MIN also put forward relevant views concerning minority protection.

DH-MIN expressed the view that:

> such groups [dispersed ethnic minorities] might need, *inter alia*, additional support ... DH-MIN considers that, in light of the difficulties facing 'dispersed ethnic minorities' and the limited resources available, the establishment of a network, allowing for the exchange of relevant information, the pooling of resources and co-operation on projects between institutes, NGOs and individuals at a European level, would be a welcome development.[33]

DH-MIN further discussed the appropriateness of the CoM taking the initiative in creating such a network, concluding that it was preferable to leave the initiative to the parties that would form part of it. DH-MIN indicated, however, that the CoM could support the establishment of the network, by means, for example, of dissemination of information contained in the report, leaving open the possibility that the CoM grants its auspices to the network once it is established, "if such a request is made".[34]

DH-MIN considered that such a network, once established, could potentially be a relevant interlocutor for the Council of Europe, for example, but by no means exclusively, in the framework of the work of DH-MIN.[35] Thus, DH-MIN brought to the attention of the CoM the possibility of opening a forum for dialogue with civil society on the issue of dispersed minorities, and indirectly with the groups concerned. The consolidation of this initiative involving civil society as well as academic institutions would have meant a step forward for minority consultation and co-operation with Council of Europe structures.[36]

The final activity report by DH-MIN on dispersed ethnic minorities was forwarded by the CDDH to the CoM for its attention in 1999,[37] and, after its consideration by the ministers' deputies, was made public. The publication of this document has in itself been a very positive achievement, not only because of its specific content, and the light it has shed on the position of states on this issue, but also because it has provided detailed information on the substance of the work of DH-MIN, and on intergovernmental co-operation in minority protection within the Council of Europe generally. Finally, the third meeting of DH-MIN took place in conjunction with the sixth meeting of government offices for national minorities under the joint programme between the European Commission and the Council of Europe: "National minorities in Europe". A section of this chapter is devoted to this important programme, where the content of the exercise in which DH-MIN was involved is discussed.

To conclude the review of DH-MIN activities, the information meetings – part of the intergovernmental programme of activities – consisted mainly of information meetings on the Framework Convention for the Protection of National Minorities organised and/or participated in by the Secretariat in Sofia (Bulgaria), Opava (Czech Republic) and Vilnius (Lithuania) during 1998. In 1999, similar meetings took place in Chisinau (Moldova), Skopje ("former Yugoslav Republic of Macedonia") and Baku (Azerbaijan).[38] Legislative counselling missions were carried out at the request of the national authorities in Latvia and Slovakia.[39] The latter were continued during 1999.[40] At present, information meetings regarding the Framework Convention for the Protection of National Minorities and the Languages Charter are conducted mainly under the framework of the co-operation activities of the Secretariat (see below).

The CDMG

The European Committee on Migration (CDMG), which has been the intergovernmental committee responsible for co-operation in relation to migration at the Council of Europe since 1984, has engaged in efforts to promote the European Convention on the Legal Status of Migrant Workers,[41] adopted in 1977. This convention, which grants certain minimum levels of legal protection to migrants and their families in the economic and social spheres, has been ratified by only eight Council of Europe member states at the time of writing: France, Italy, the Netherlands, Norway, Portugal, Spain, Sweden and Turkey. Another five states, Germany, Greece, and Luxembourg, which signed the convention as far back as November 1977, Belgium, which signed it in February 1978, and Moldova, which signed it in July 2002, have not ratified it yet.[42]

This is despite the fact that the convention largely considers migration as a temporary phenomenon, "assuming the early return to the country of origin" by migrants and their families, an approach which many states of the Council of Europe are still willing to embrace.[43] This assumption, however, seems to be giving way to more realistic approaches to the actual situation in European states, as reflected in the growing attention paid to integration policies, including legal aspects, such as the consolidation of long-term residence status.[44] Nevertheless, even shorter-term approaches to the phenomenon of migration than those underlying the European Convention on the Legal Status of Migrant Workers seem to be taking the lead at present, increasing emphasis being placed on so-called "short-term migration", involving short-term or seasonal working contracts and a limited, non-extendable stay in the host country.

In this context, "migration management" has recently been studied at the Council of Europe. At the same time, increasing attention has been paid to the integration of those immigrants with a permanent presence in the host states, and the members of their families leading to the continuation of previously existing programmes[45] and the start of new ones focusing on these issues. An interesting development is the closer link established between the issues of these so-called "new minorities"[46] resulting from migration and the "old" or "historical" minorities, normally qualified as "national" in Council of Europe approaches. States had shown reluctance concerning the establishment of such a link in the past. In practice, the characterisation of the "new" minorities as "religious", "linguistic" or "ethnic" is even harder to question.

The CDMG has pursued its work regarding the situation and social integration of populations of migrant origin and refugees, as well as community relations, since 1987. Increasingly also, old minorities, and particularly those which are the most disadvantaged from a socio-economic perspective, have become the focus of attention in the work of the CDMG. This has been especially the case in relation to the Roma/Gypsies. In 1994 the CoM requested that the CDMG prepare an in-depth study on the situation of Roma/Gypsies in Europe. Furthermore, the CoM decided to set up a group of specialists on Roma/Gypsies (MG-S-ROM) which would advise the CoM through the CDMG on issues concerning the Roma. The activities of this group of specialists are discussed in Chapter 4. A number of aspects of the work of the CDMG are discussed below.

At the time of writing, the following committees of experts are working under the aegis of the CDMG: the Committee of Experts on Integration and Community Relations (MG-IN); the Committee of Experts on the Legal Status and other Rights of Immigrants (MG-ST); and the Committee of Experts on the Implementation of the Migration Management Strategy (MG-FL).

i. *Migratory movements*

Using a constructive approach which studies the root causes of migration, the CDMG collected factual information on various aspects of repatriation movements of involuntary migrants or members of ethnic groups and minorities in several European countries, following the political upheavals in central and eastern Europe in the late 1980s and early 1990s. This included an examination of their size, "push and pull factors", technical organisation, and the role of specialised agencies. Also the normative aspects involved were investigated.[47] However, this project does not seem to have been followed-up, probably as a result of the easing of migratory tensions in central and eastern Europe.

ii. *Migration management*

Following the emphasis placed by the conference of ministers on the Movement of Persons from Central and Eastern European Countries, held in Vienna on 24 and 25 January 1991, on short-term migration,[48] and the subsequent activities carried out by the so-called Vienna group, in 1994 the mandate and mission of the group were entrusted to the Council of Europe. It was agreed that the Council of Europe might concentrate on the broader aspects of migration flows and policies such as: i. the need to take a comprehensive view of migration phenomena affecting Europe, including consideration of root causes and integration policy; and ii. the definition of principles for orderly migration movements into and within Europe.[49]

A reflection group on "Managing migration in the wider Europe" was set-up by the CDMG in the late 1990s following the call at the sixth Conference of European Ministers responsible for Migration Affairs, for the Council of Europe to play a role in developing a comprehensive approach to migration questions affecting the European continent as a whole.[50] According to the proposals of the reflection group the aim is not to stop immigration but to control it: "this does not rule out rather strict control measures where appropriate, and indeed a more robust approach to returning people without the right to stay, but the starting point should be freedom to travel and the positive impact of controlled migration on European countries."[51]

The reflection group refers to mobility as a human right,[52] and stresses the importance that "the control element in immigration policies is placed in an overall strategy that values international migration and the presence of immigrants". The reflection group puts forward policy suggestions and standards in connection with integration, including in the field of: i. residence rights; ii. naturalisation and citizenship; iii. measures to promote equality of opportunities; iv. action to combat racism, xenophobia and intolerance; and v. the building of a coherent national strategy including co-ordination between the various ministries concerned.[53] Some of the areas of concern pinpointed by the experts have subsequently been addressed in CoM Recommendations, particularly in the field of security of residence and family reunification.[54]

The report of the reflection group was forwarded to the CDMG for examination. In 1999, a restricted group of experts was entrusted with its revision in the light of the comments submitted during a seminar organised in Strasbourg in October 1998, in order to test reactions to the proposals contained in the report. The aim is "to move towards consensus on the principles which should underlie a realistic and modern approach to migration in Europe".[55] The result of the work of the restricted group of experts was adopted by the CDMG in May 2000 as the Council of Europe policy for a coherent and orderly migration management.[56] This was published in November 2002, under the title: "Towards a migration management strategy".[57]

In addition, from the year 2000, particular attention started to be devoted to south-eastern Europe.[58] On the basis of a request from the CoM, the CDMG extended its activities concerning "clandestine migration" and a questionnaire on the prevention of irregular immigration was sent to member states. The aim was to draw up, on the basis of the replies, a report on the prevention of irregular migration in Europe. The results of this inquiry have not yet been published. In the meanwhile, a conference on "irregular migration and migrants' dignity" was held in Athens in October 2001.[59]

iii. *Building better integrated communities*

After the conclusions of the final report of the "Community relations" project in which the CDMG had been engaged were presented,[60] leading

335

to the adoption of Recommendation R (92) 12 of the same title by the CoM, the project "The integration of migrants, towards equal opportunities", was started in 1991, in order to examine the practical application of the principles laid down in the final report on community relations. While the initial aim of the project was to promote exchanges of experience and the elaboration of practical guidelines for integration,[61] work was soon to focus on the less action-orientated theme of "investigating practical measures taken in various countries, often in partnership between government, local and regional authorities and non-governmental bodies, to overcome the obstacles to equality for immigrants".[62]

The project, which came to an end in 1996, was articulated through the convening of various meetings and the elaboration of expert reports on specific topics, in the following areas: i. immigrants' opportunities in the labour market; ii. access by immigrants to housing and social welfare; iii. prevention of racism and xenophobia and promotion of active tolerance; iv. full recognition of the cultural rights of immigrants; and v. participation by immigrants in the decision-making processes of society.

Then, at the sixth conference of European Ministers responsible for Migration Affairs, held in Warsaw in 1996, the project "Tensions and tolerance: building better integrated communities across Europe" was launched. The Specialist Group on Integration and Community Relations (MG-S-INT), responsible for implementing the programme, was given the following mandate: i. to prepare, with a view to publication, good-practice guidelines and studies on new issues for integration policy; ii. to provide practical assistance to countries seeking to develop or review their integration policies; and iii. to promote networking and exchange of experience between practitioners in the various fields of integration policy. This was articulated through the organisation of expert meetings; the promotion of activities within the member states; the encouragement of networking among persons and organisations involved in the practical implementation of integration and community relations; and reflection on new issues arising in this area.[63]

During 1997, the following activities were implemented: two round tables on identity and integration, a seminar on the political and social participation of immigrants through consultative bodies, and a comparative study on administrative arrangements for dealing with the integration process, including specialist bodies and units responsible for co-ordination.[64] The latter activity was continued during 1998. Other activities implemented during this year included a seminar on religion and the integration of immigrants, round tables on initiatives taken by governments on a national, regional or local level, with a view to promoting recruitment and employment of immigrants/ethnic minorities in the public service, and a comparative study on administrative arrangements for dealing with the integration process, including specialist bodies and units responsible for co-ordination.[65] The latter activity was finalised in 1999.

As a result, a so-called draft matrix of integration measures was worked out in 1997-99. It outlined the political action required at specific stages or in particular areas, offering guidance to new-immigration countries and to newer member states. It was also intended to serve as a checklist for older countries of immigration. Similarly, a series of national round tables on community relations in the "newer immigration countries" were organised over those same years.[66] The MG-S-INT concluded its work with the presentation of a final activity report to the CDMG in the autumn of 1999.

Subsequently, a conference held in Namur on 7 and 8 September 2000 brought together national policy makers "to enable them to share Council of Europe member states' positive experience and good practice concerning the devising or revising of integration and community relation policies".[67] At this conference, the new report on community relations – "Diversity and cohesion: new challenges for the integration of immigrants and minorities" – and a report on the "'Framework of integration policies" were presented.

The former report, elaborated by J. Niessen, Director of the Migration Policy Group, in co-operation with the European Cultural Foundation, discusses commonalities between immigrants and minorities.[68] It studies, among other things, strategic goals and comprehensive approaches to integration, including examples of governmental and non-governmental policies. Similarly, the latter report, elaborated by M. Coussey, Chair of MG-S-INT, adopts a comprehensive approach to "old" and "new" minorities, dealing with policies and measures to be adopted in connection with "multi-ethnic populations" in the fields of: i. legal measures; ii. employment; iii. housing; iv. health and other services; v. religion, culture and language; vi. education; vii. the media; viii. government functions; and ix. monitoring and evaluation. In some sections of this study a "division into policies for new arrivals and more established populations" has explicitly been found as inappropriate, and "has not been applied".[69] The promotion and dissemination of the two reports became a priority for the CDMG in the year 2001. A small seminar on intercultural mediation practice relating to migrant groups in Europe was also organised on 3 May 2000.[70]

iv. *Security of residence, family reunification, access to employment*

Building on the work of the Committee of Experts on the Legal Situation of Long-Stay Migrants in Host Countries (MG-JU),[71] and on the basis of a report analysing national legislation and policies on the security of residence of long-term migrants, the CDMG set up a Select Committee of Experts on Security of Residence for Long-term Immigrants (MG-R-ES). The select committee finished its work on a draft recommendation of the CoM in 1998, which was then submitted to the CDMG.[72] The CDMG then adopted a revised text of the recommendation, taking into account national positions of member states as well as developments within the European Union in the year 2000.[73]

This resulted in the adoption of Recommendation (2000) 15 of the CoM to member states concerning the security of residence of long-term migrants, which exceptionally includes an explanatory memorandum, pointing to the political sensitiveness of the issues addressed.[74] As the content of the recommendation has been thoroughly discussed in Chapter 5, it is sufficient to note here that the importance of security of residence as a facilitator of integration has been underscored not only by the CoM but also by the Parliamentary Assembly.[75]

Although aspects of family unity were touched upon in the recommendation, the question of family reunification later became the object of specific treatment by the CDMG. On the basis of a report on "The legal status of persons admitted for family reunification" published in the year 2000, the MG-ST "decided to draw up draft guidelines and principles relating to legislation and practice on the residence status and other rights of persons admitted to national territory for the purpose of family reunification". The relevant draft recommendation was transmitted to the CDMG[76] and the CoM finally adopted (on 26 March 2002) Recommendation Rec (2002) 4 "to member states on the legal status of persons admitted for family reunification". The recommendation contains a series of principles that states are advised to apply in their legislation and administrative practice.

The concepts of residence status recognition as well as best interests and wellbeing of children, in line with the (UN) Convention on the Rights of the Child and other international legal instruments,[77] inform the recommendation. The principle of autonomy of the family member's residence status in relation to that of the principal right-holder is supported, on the basis of legal residence time frames. The availability of appeal procedures to competent independent administrative authorities or courts is also supported.[78] Political participation of persons admitted for family reunification is upheld, in accordance with the provisions of the Convention on the Participation of Foreigners in Public Life at Local Level,[79] and so is equal access to the labour market, to education and to social rights of family members. Although no specific reference is made to the European Convention on the Legal Status of Migrant Workers in the latter connection,[80] the latter principle is based on its text.

The recommendation thus plays an important role in putting forward standards recognised in European instruments that a large number of Council of Europe member states have not yet adhered to. It should be noted, however, that with regard to the principle of equal enjoyment of social rights, as with regard to other principles addressed in the recommendation, such as free movement and facilitation of access to citizenship, the recommendation incorporates an "in accordance with internal law" clause, adding to the precariousness of its obligational character.

In connection with the question of equal enjoyment of social rights, a draft report on access to employment of foreigners, immigrants and national minorities was discussed by MG-IN during the year 2000. This draft report was based on a study elaborated by a consultant and on national reports elaborated in reply to a questionnaire drawn up by MG-IN. On the basis of the report, MG-IN is to prepare guidelines for access to employment by immigrants and minorities, resulting in the drawing-up of recommendations,[81] which will focus on access of foreigners to the public sector.

The CAHP

The European Population Committee (CAHP, formerly CDPO) is responsible for studying population developments for the Council of Europe. A group of specialists formed by government representatives examined the situation of national minorities in a number of European countries. Although originally intending to undertake an analysis of the minority situation across Europe, the rejection of the concept of "national minorities" altogether by some Council of Europe states soon led to the studies becoming country-based and initiated on a voluntary basis.

The series of minority studies started with a comparative study on the methods used in census elaboration in Europe to enumerate groups belonging to national minorities.[82] This was followed by specific studies on the demographic characteristics of the two communities in Northern Ireland, and of national minorities in Hungary, Romania and Slovakia. The latter studies were published in December 1998.[83] They include a description of the demographic situation in the countries studied, although no special censuses were made for this specific purpose. They also include references to the level of fertility of minority groups as compared to that of the majority population, the effects on minority groups of external migration to other countries, patterns of marriage, and related matters.

Subsequent studies were devoted to ethnic groups in Bulgaria, national minorities in Estonia, the Swedish-speaking population in Finland, the linguistic/religious groups in Switzerland and the Roma/Gypsies in a number of European countries. They were finalised in 1999 and, with the exception of the study on Bulgaria, were published as a second volume in January 2000.[84] A study was also completed on internal migration and regional population dynamics in ten member states – the Czech Republic, Estonia, Germany, Italy, the Netherlands, Norway, Poland, Romania and the United Kingdom – and was published in 1999. It is accompanied by a CD-ROM containing case studies on the aforementioned countries.[85] A study on the demographic implications of social exclusion covered the following topics: i. identification of vulnerable groups and areas of vulnerability; ii. welfare regimes and trends in social exclusion policies; and iii. an analysis of demographic characteristics and behaviour of main vulnerable groups. It was published in 2002.[86]

Furthermore, between 1998 and 2001, the European Population Committee conducted a series of studies on the demographic and social impact of migration, analysing the convergence or divergence in the demographic behaviour of migrants with respect to the rest of the population. Each study begins with an overview of today's migrant groups in Europe and the main findings are summarised in a comparative synthesis report. They describe the origin of migrants, the demographic dynamics of immigrant populations (inflows and outflows), fertility, family formation, intermarriage, mortality and the spatial distribution in the countries of settlement. The results of this work were published in 2002.[87]

It is to be hoped that the investigation on the situation of minorities will be continued, in spite of the sensitivity of the question for many Council of Europe member states. The information provided by the CAHP may prove invaluable in the adoption of policies concerning minority protection in the future, as it provides an international source of data and analysis, possibly less vulnerable to distortions resulting from political considerations than those provided at the domestic level.

The CDCC/GR-C

The Council of Europe work in the fields of education, culture, youth and sport has traditionally developed in the framework of the European Cultural Convention of 1954, an instrument open to accession by non-member European states, but which, as a product of its time, did not pay particular consideration to minority concerns. Four specialised committees – on culture, cultural heritage, general education, and higher education and research – which soon became steering committees, as well as the standing conference on university problems, helped the CDCC to carry out its tasks under the European Cultural Convention, as well as in relation to the regular conferences of specialised European ministers responsible for education, culture and cultural heritage.[88] The Rapporteur Group on Education, Culture, Sport, Youth and Environment

(GR-C) has recently taken over activities of the Council for Cultural Co-operation (CDCC), the inter-governmental body traditionally responsible for work on education and culture at the Council of Europe, with an additional expansion of competencies to the environment, youth and sport.

In 1993 the CDCC and its four specialised committees launched a multi-disciplinary project under the title "Democracy, human rights, minorities: educational and cultural aspects" with three objectives: i. "to develop civics, intercultural education and cultural democracy through practical field activities"; ii. "to examine the educational and cultural aspects of the management of diversity in a democratic society"; and iii. "to produce, at the end of the activity, guidelines for governments on educational and cultural rights".[89]

The project leadership, composed of about twenty people nominated by the ministries of education of states parties to the European Cultural Convention, aimed to gather previous experience of the CDCC in the field of intercultural co-operation and to examine its application in relation to minority issues. Seminars dealt with questions such as the role of the media in constructing the public image of minorities, the cultural heritage of the Balkans, the dialectic of specificities and universality, intercultural education, cultural and educational rights and identities, minorities in the new democracies, minorities in the Balkans, the media and minorities, and cultural communities and social cohesion.[90]

Five pilot activities were organised to set up an innovative network of training officers ready to intervene in a variety of situations. The first pilot activity involved forty primary and secondary school teachers from sixteen different European countries in a training seminar; the rest of the pilot activities concerned projects in particular member states at their own request. The second pilot activity "An analysis of the issue of minorities and the potential role of history teaching",[91] launched at the initiative of the Slovak authorities, dealt with how history textbooks can support the cultural identity of minorities, and was primarily concerned with the Roma/Gypsy population of Slovakia. The third pilot project "Education in democratic citizenship in Russia" aimed at encouraging the emergence of "ethnic schools" promoting interaction between cultures and communities. The fourth pilot project, "Identity and history", was launched at the initiative of the Austrian authorities and comprised comparative research into national identities in central Europe. Finally, the pilot project "The right to heritage and education" was jointly suggested by Italy and Greece and aimed at the use of cultural heritage for transmitting values of human rights, democracy and intercultural understanding.

In addition, case studies were undertaken, geared at analysing examples of good practice and to lay down markers for governments to develop their policy towards minorities. Given the goals of this activity, more west European states volunteered to participate: Luxembourg, France, Italy, Denmark, Albania, Slovenia, Belgium, Slovakia, Hungary, the Netherlands and the United Kingdom.[92] Education professionals of various levels were brought together in seminars at Klingenthal (Germany), Sofia (Bulgaria); Lohusalu (Estonia); Strasbourg (France) and Graz (Austria) "to analyse the conceptual grid informing the actions that have been undertaken".[93] Finally, studies on rights in the field of education; information; the management of diversity; and on the evolution from the notion of "minorities" to that of "cultural communities" were carried out,[94] supported by documentary research, dissemination and publication activities.

The third objective of the project, "to produce, at the end of the activity, guidelines for governments on educational and cultural rights", included a final conference held from 21 to 23 May 1997 in Strasbourg. The conference "assessed the many advances made, laid down guidelines for the policies to be implemented and served as a springboard for disseminating the theoretical and practical results of the project".[95] In the final declaration, the participants noted the importance of multiculturalism at all levels of social, cultural, economic and political life. They also noted that:

> the expectations of populations – and in particular of groups constituting cultural minorities – are not adequately addressed by the mere implementation of optional educational and cultural policies. Awareness of this situation leads to realisation of the need to set the issues in an ethical framework of cultural rights. Even though the specific legal substance of such rights remains extremely difficult to determine, especially when their individual and collective elements have to be reconciled, the importance to be attached to them as essential conditions for the protection and promotion of human dignity should be highlighted.[96]

Thus, the participants emphasised the importance of establishing a legal framework for cultural protection, even if they recognised the difficulties involved. This acquires especial relevance when placed against the background of the failure of the Council of Europe member states to reach an agreement in adopting an additional protocol on cultural rights to the ECHR.[97]

The participants at this 1997 conference also considered the principles on which action in various policy areas should be based. They proclaimed that cultural identity: i. should be considered as a key element of human dignity and as an essentially dynamic and evolving concept, and ii. understood as a body of cultural elements through which persons or groups define themselves, manifest themselves and wish to be recognised. They advocated the recognition of cultural communities, which are perceived as actors within the territorial community. They dealt with the situation of minorities more specifically, supporting the adoption of specific measures in relation to situations of discrimination, poverty and exclusion, measures which aim to re-establish equal opportunities for the weakest.

Although the position of the participants still remains to be accepted by most Council of Europe member states, especially when it comes to actual policy-making and implementation, it still falls short of more demanding views, which advocate the maintenance of special measures "as long as the groups concerned wish".[98] Finally, the participants encouraged the recognition of the notion of plural citizenship, that is, "that each individual may wish to see his or her problems and aspirations addressed in distinct political arenas, which in some instances may be essentially territorial and in others more clearly cultural, without membership of or participation in one arena being deemed subordinate or alternative to the others".[99]

An important contribution of the project has been its integration of minority questions into the wider context of the cultural diversity of society at large, particularly relevant in the light of the failing attempts at standard-setting mentioned above. From the recommendations of the project it can be deduced that, even if no express reference to cultural autonomy has been introduced,[100] the latter has been perceived by the project group as a possible solution to the question of minorities' cultural identity and sense of belonging to a differentiated cultural community. In addition, the participants proposed various measures to promote the accommodation of cultural diversity in several policy areas: i. the media; ii. languages and literature; iii. heritage and especially history; iv. the religious dimension of cultural identity; v. communities' cultural life and development; vi. education for citizenship and vii. human rights.

The progressive character and corresponding political sensitivity of the recommendations resulting from the project has possibly been at the origin of the negative stand of the CDCC towards its conclusions. This is reflected in the fact that they did not lead to the adoption of a recommendation by the CDCC to the CoM endorsing the results of the project. Instead, the CDCC "carried out an internal evaluation of the project ... inviting the specialised committees to take this internal evaluation into account when implementing new projects with the same transversal and multidisciplinary character, in particular concerning the implementation of the follow-up to the Action Plan of the Second Summit".[101] The emphasis placed on "education for democratic citizenship" in the Final Declaration of the 1997 Strasbourg Summit and the "Budapest Declaration for a greater Europe without dividing lines" adopted by the CoM on 7 May

1999,[102] and the ongoing Council of Europe programme on this topic, may open the way for the consideration of the results of the project in the context of the adoption of future political texts.

As already indicated in Chapter 5, the education for democratic citizenship "concept" actually pre-dated the Strasbourg Summit, and it was defined as a priority objective for the CDCC and its Education Committee already at the 19th session of the Standing Conference of European Ministers of Education held in Kristiansand (Norway) in June 1997.[103] The Education Committee launched its project on this topic in February 1997, and the final conference of the project was held in Strasbourg, from 14 to 16 September 2000. Four reports present the results of the project, which have touched upon questions of intercultural education,[104] identity and multiculturalism,[105] and questions of "inclusiveness", participation and culture in the work of so-called "sites for citizenship" at the grass-roots level.[106] The findings of the project resulted in the "draft common guidelines on education for democratic citizenship" adopted by the European Ministers of Education at the 20th session of the Standing Conference held in Kraków in October 2000. These "draft common guidelines" led to the adoption in 2002 of a policy instrument – the CoM Recommendation on Education for Democratic Citizenship.[107]

The CDCC was involved in the implementation of the CoM's "Declaration on a European policy for new information technologies" appended to the "Budapest Declaration for a greater Europe without dividing lines".[108] Some of the CDCC specialised committees have participated in the drafting work for a text which offers a framework for Council of Europe action in this field.[109] One of the aims of the work plan was to prepare guidelines for European cultural policies for the new information society, including the field of cultural diversity and sustainable development.[110] Nevertheless, the outlook for minority protection concerns to be addressed does not seem very positive, at least in the shortrun. Following a preliminary feasibility study, the Culture Committee intends to develop an analysis which focuses on the possible sources of conflict between international trade and cultural policies.[111]

In 1985, the Culture Committee of the CDCC started developing its European programme of "Cultural policy reviews", now continued under the aegis of the GR-C. In the framework of this programme, the way in which the key principles of cultural policy – more concretely the promotion of cultural identity and diversity, support for artistic creativity, and enhancement of participation – have been put into practice by member states has been analysed. The programme has comprised individual state "national cultural policy reviews" and "transversal (comparative) cultural policy reviews".

The "national" reviews are carried out at the initiative of individual states volunteering to be subjected to the review, and on the basis of a national report describing the cultural policy of the state, elaborated by its Ministry of Culture. Then a group of experts appointed by the Council of Europe elaborates a report on the basis of the national report and visits to the state under review, which contains an assessment and recommendations. This is followed by a discussion in the Council of Europe and a national debate in the state concerned.

The states reviewed so far are: Albania, Armenia, Austria, Azerbaijan, Bosnia and Herzegovina, Bulgaria, Croatia, Estonia, Finland, France, Georgia, Italy, Latvia, Lithuania, Malta, Moldova, the Netherlands, Portugal, Romania, the Russian Federation, Slovenia, the Slovak Republic and Sweden. Reviews on Andorra, Cyprus, Serbia and Montenegro, and "the former Yugoslav Republic of Macedonia" are currently under way.

The level of thoroughness of the expert assessments has substantially increased over time, and so has the consideration of cultural identity in multicultural rather than mono-cultural terms, in spite of the predominant use of the concept national cultural "identity" over "identities" in the reports.[112] However, although cultural diversity aspects, and issues of minority protection in particular, have received an increasing level of attention in the reviews, not much attention has been devoted to finding solutions as to their specific articulation in domestic policy and practice so far.

The "transversal (comparative) cultural policy reviews", consist on thematic analyses on specific topics across countries, illustrating policy alternatives in responding to similar problems occurring in different cultural contexts. The topic of the first so-called "transversal analysis" dealt with "National cultural institutions in transition: decentralisation and privatisation" and analysed different policy models and options available to enable national cultural institutions to operate in the prevailing context of decentralisation and privatisation. Only six countries became involved in this review: the Netherlands, Finland, Hungary, Poland, Cyprus and Germany.[113]

The theme of the second "transversal analysis" currently under way is "Cultural policy and cultural diversity".[114] The overall objective of the project "is to understand and support the development of democratic cultural policy in the context of culturally diverse societies".[115] It analyses aspects of diversity resulting from the process of migration into and across different states, in particular those patterns that characterise post-war periods and also so-called *in situ* forms of diversity "that have resisted assimilation into dominant national communities over long periods of time".[116] It involves Austria, Belgium, Bulgaria, Canada (a non-member state), Luxembourg, Switzerland and the United Kingdom.

National reports from each participating country and seven research position papers on key issues for cultural diversity have resulted from the project so far.

The research position papers have dealt with aspects of high relevance for minority protection, such as European media policies, practices and organisational structures regarding cultural diversity; assessing cultural diversity policies; cultural planning and cultural diversity; international copyright law and cultural diversity; media and cultural practices of diaspora; and cultural diversity and biological diversity. In addition the final report of the first year of the project explores the challenges associated with adapting existing cultural policies to accommodate diversity rather than homogeneity as a normative policy, while identifying broad policy contexts that shape cultural policy approaches to diversity.[117]

Finally, the Steering Committee for Education deals with the issue of language policy formulation and development, creating the framework for the work of the Language Policy Division of the Secretariat. Policy issues relating to the promotion of multilingualism in society, and the development of multilingualism among individuals, have been examined at a conference on "Languages, diversity, citizenship: policies for plurilingualism in Europe" organised by this division and attended by policy makers in November 2002. This took as a basis the previous discussions in the context of a conference co-organised by the modern languages division of the Austrian Ministry of Education and Cultural Affairs and held in Innsbruck on 10 to 12 May 1999,[118] attended by policy makers, experts and social partners. That conference had dealt with the challenges and obstacles regarding effective diversification of language learning and teaching with a view to developing multilingualism among individuals, and maintaining it in society. A survey on language policies was subsequently undertaken, followed by the elaboration of a synthesis of factors encouraging or hindering linguistic diversity.[119]

The 2002 conference launched the so called "Guide for Language Education Policy in Europe" intended to promote greater diversification in the range of languages offered in the curriculum and a more coherent approach to all languages in education: mother tongue, second language, and 'foreign' languages. A new activity consisting in offering assistance to member states with a self-evaluation of their national language policy has been initiated, the so called "Language Education Policy Profile". This activity focuses on aspects of language education of minorities and immigrant populations, and it has involved a pilot scheme implemented in Hungary, being currently underway in Norway, Slovenia, and Cyprus, with other states to follow in subsequent years. This is complemented by targeted assistance activities in South-East Europe and CIS countries. Finally, the dissemination of an "European Language Portfolio scheme" which aims to evaluate the linguistic competence of individuals and to assist them in diversifying their language learning throughout life, is in progress since its presentation during the European Year of Languages (2001).

The CDLR

The activities of the CoM's Steering Committee dealing with issues of Local and Regional Democracy, the CDLR, have been on the increase over recent years, fuelled by the growing role of the Congress of Local and Regional Authorities of Europe (Congress/CLRAE) in promoting this field of Council of Europe activity (see Chapter 10). The work of the CDLR has focused on three themes: i. democratic citizenship, public services at local level, and urban problems; ii. institutional framework, structure and operation of local and regional democracy; and iii. local finance, financial management and the economic role of local and regional authorities.

Besides the responsibility of preparing the periodical conferences of European Ministers responsible for local (and more recently also "regional") government,[120] the CDLR has been the main interlocutor for the Congress and the Parliamentary Assembly in preparing CoM replies to recommendations by the latter organs, and a substantive contributor to CoM policy-making in its specific field of competence.[121] This has extended, for example, to its contribution on the drafting process of the CoM Recommendation Rec (2002) 4 on the question of the legal status of persons admitted for family reunification, described above.[122] In addition the CDLR has been the main body responsible for the CoM's groundwork on the elaboration of a legal instrument on regional self-government following the Congress's initiative in this connection.[123]

The CDLR has been particularly active in analysing aspects of the finance and delivery of services of territorial authorities, as well as aspects of transfrontier co-operation. Especially relevant has been its role in assessing the implementation by states of the European Outline Convention on Transfrontier Co-operation between Territorial Communities or Authorities, on the basis of the specific mandate given by the CoM in this regard on 6 September 2000.[124] This mandate was given in response to Congress Recommendation 85 (2000).[125]

On the basis of this mandate, a questionnaire was sent to all states members of the CDLR, irrespectively of whether they were signatories of the convention or not, for the purpose of collecting information on the actual situation regarding transfrontier co-operation by local and regional authorities. An innovative feature and important step forward was the fact that the questionnaire was not aimed at the states' central governmental authorities, but especially addressed "to one or preferably more territorial authorities in border areas (municipalities, provinces and regions)" although some of the questions "could also be answered by the Ministries concerned".[126] Through this questionnaire, the CDLR aimed to complement its previous report on the "current state of the administrative and legal framework of transfrontier co-operation in Europe", which had been based on a questionnaire "sent only to the central or federal authorities of States concerned by these transfrontier issues".[127]

The second report adopted by the CDLR is especially important, as it highlights the main problems encountered by territorial authorities in making transfrontier co-operation effective in practice.[128] In this report it is stated that the majority of local authorities expect the central or federal authorities: i. to improve cross-border infrastructure (roads and frontier crossing points); ii. to facilitate transfrontier co-operation in the legal field (especially by overcoming current customs problems relating to time-consuming procedures for the granting of visas and for border-crossings); and iii. to give them greater responsibilities, especially financial.[129]

Another aspect of particular relevance for minority protection is the reference to the fact that local and regional authorities in some countries lack the necessary legal powers to implement their own decisions directly, or for example, to recruit directly.[130] Stock is taken of the little knowledge that exists about the model agreements appended to the European Outline Convention on Transfrontier Co-operation between Territorial Communities or Authorities, which aim at facilitating the implementation of the convention.[131] Additional note should be taken in this regard of the First Additional Protocol to the convention, which has a similar aim.[132] Further, the CDLR recently adopted a separate report on transfrontier co-operation in civil protection and mutual assistance in natural/technological disasters occurring in frontier areas, forwarding to the CoM a draft recommendation in this connection.[133]

The activities of the secretariat

ADACS

In 1998, the so-called "Co-operation and assistance programmes with central and eastern European countries"[134] of the Council of Europe were renamed "Activities for the development and consolidation of democratic stability" (ADACS). This change of denomination opened the programmes not only to applicant states but also to member states of the Council of Europe. The co-operation and assistance programmes with central and eastern European countries were established to assist non-member states in the building of democratic institutions, and in particular to help applicant member states to meet the requirements for membership.[135] The stated aim of ADACS was to "gradually become a means of helping any state in difficulties – as revealed in particular by the various procedures for monitoring compliance with obligations or special undertakings given as members of the Council of Europe".[136] As already indicated above, in 2001, ADACS gave way to so-called co-operation activities, which so far have been confined to countries of central and eastern Europe.[137]

ADACS were funded under a specific vote (IX) of the Council of Europe budget, although increasing importance was given to the development of a closer partnership with the European Commission in particular, and several programmes were co-financed under so-called joint programmes between both institutions, as well as on the basis of voluntary con-tributions. Although not very substantial overall, the minority-related activities under ADACS increased significantly from the time the co-operation and assistance programmes were established in 1990, when such activities were almost non-existent. Actually, what increased more substantially with the introduction of the ADACS was their profile. At the time of the Vienna Summit, only minor activities in relation to minority protection were the subject of sporadic references among the also meagre activities in relation to human rights carried out in the various countries.[138] By the time of the Strasbourg Summit, minorities had become one of the identified fields of activity specifically envisaged under ADACS.[139]

The number of ADACS activities on minorities was not large. Even after the Strasbourg Summit, most were developed under the joint programme on minorities between the European Commission and the Council of Europe, and subsequently under joint programmes of a more general scope but focusing on certain countries, such as the joint programme on Ukraine or the joint programme on South Caucasus. A special section of this chapter is devoted to the joint programme on minorities.

In 1997, the year of the Strasbourg Summit, for example, those activities not included in the joint programme on minorities were confined to: i. legal assistance in relation to an appraisal of the bill on education of minority communities in Croatia, ii. the contribution to a course for senior police management in Romania, iii. a study visit for three Azeri experts to Budapest, and iv. the contribution to a seminar on the legal status and socio-economic situation of Roma in Bosnia organised by the International Romani Union.[140] A similar pattern applies to subse-quent years.[141] Progressively, projects undertaken under the confidence-building measures programme (see below) were also included under the ADACS heading. For example, for the year 1999, the projects on minorities in relation to Croatia under ADACS consisted only of those undertaken in the framework of the confidence-building measures programme.[142]

Country-specific joint programmes of a general scope between the European Commission and the Council of Europe Secretariat were also developed *inter alia* in relation to Albania, Estonia, Latvia, Lithuania, Romania, the Russian Federation and Ukraine, as well as South Caucasus, and some of them are still under way. Even when minority protection was not a specific item on their agenda, several of the activities undertaken with regard to those states, particularly those in relation to local authorities and national human rights institutions, can be considered of relevance for minority protection.[143]

Questions of local government co-operation were the subject of seminars under the joint programmes with regard to Estonia and Latvia.[144] Although the joint programme for the "Assistance for the integration of the populations of foreign origin in Estonia and Latvia" (between the European Commission and the Council of Europe) expired in 1998, a seminar on bilingual education was organised in 1999 in Estonia, launching the project to elaborate "a handbook compendium for teachers and administrators of immersion programmes".[145] Similarly, a seminar on co-operation with the Ministry of Education on new models for bilingual education for minority education programmes was organised in Latvia.[146]

During 1999, the Council of Europe Secretariat took part in several missions to Riga, together with the OSCE High Commissioner on National Minorities, with a view to providing assistance and advice on the amendments to the State Language Law (adopted on 9 December 1999) and its implementing regulations.[147] A conference was held on "Integration in society through education and language" attended by representatives from Latvia, Lithuania, Moldova and the Russian Federation, and to which several states sent observers. Similarly, the conference "Cultural autonomy of minorities: in search of a new model in Latvia" was organised by the Council of Europe Information and Documentation Centre, the Institute of Philosophy and Sociology and the Ministry of Culture of Latvia on 28 September 1999.[148]

The activities of the Council of Europe relevant to the protection of minorities, and in particular to the large non-citizen Russian minority population living in the country seem to have prioritised the implementation of social and cultural rights over civil and political: a seminar to discuss the consequences for Latvia of a possible ratification of the European Convention on Nationality, with the participation of experts from the Council of Europe, led to the conclusion that "the citizenship law of Latvia is in conformity with the general principles of the European Convention on Nationality",[149] instead of concentrating on its drawbacks for the large non-citizen population.

Nevertheless, even before this seminar, and quite apart from the country-specific joint programmes, a thematic joint programme between the European Commission and the Council of Europe had been developed to give assistance with the integration of populations of foreign origin in Estonia and Latvia, as an accompanying measure to the EU Pact of Stability in Europe.[150] The aim of the programme was "to create the necessary conditions in the naturalisation process for the integration of populations of foreign origin, thereby contributing to stability in the region".[151]

The activities under the programme focused on: i. assistance in legislative, administrative and procedural matters with respect to the granting of citizenship and residents permits in Estonia and Latvia; ii. assistance in introducing, developing and maintaining an efficient, objective and consistent system of standardised testing for assessing and certifying the language competence of applicants for citizenship in Estonia and Latvia; and iii. the development of bilingual education policies. Assistance to Latvia also dealt with the question of the "history and other knowledge" test required by the Latvian authorities for naturalisation purposes. Assistance both to Estonia and to Latvia dealt with the improvement of language testing for professional purposes.[152] These activities, which were aimed mainly at the Russian minority living in the states, were concluded by the end of 1998.[153]

The programme for the Russian Federation in 1997-98 focused on "strengthening the federal structures, introducing human rights protection mechanisms and reforming the legal system".[154] In 1997, co-operation activities for the strengthening of the federal structures

> were marked by a series of seminars held on key areas in the improvement of federal structures such as the division of powers and hierarchy of legal standards in a federal state, budget and taxes in a federal state and international relations, including external economic links of the Subjects of the Federation ... The development and promotion of local democracy ... took as its reference point in 1997 the principles of the 'European Charter of Local Self-Government' ... As far as legislative assistance was concerned, ongoing co-operation with the Committee on Local Government of the State Duma led to the adoption by the Federal Parliament of the Local Authorities' Financial Basis Act and the first reading of the Status of Municipal Management Act. Special emphasis was laid on supporting the process of ratifying the European Charter of Local Self-Government.[155]

In 1998, co-operation activities for the development of federalism "concentrated on four main themes: the strengthening of fiscal federalism and of regional aspects of taxation policy; legislative initiatives on improving co-operation between the federal authorities and the public authorities of the entities of the Federation; improving the forms of mechanisms of inter-regional co-operation; and finally, on the international and external economic links of the regions".[156] The item specifically devoted to minorities under the programme was limited to the organisation of two seminars in relation to the implementation of the Framework Convention for the Protection of National Minorities.[157]

Activities, either of a multilateral character or with regard to specific countries carried out under the Council of Europe LODE (LOcal DEmocracy) development programme, which included the training of elected representatives and officials, have also been relevant for minorities. These activities have comprised the provision of legal assistance, such as the drafting of laws on local self-government and administrative territorial organisation,[158] and technical assistance. Questions of power-sharing between central government authorities on the one hand, and local and regional authorities on the other,[159] as well as decentralisation,[160] including fiscal matters, have been on the agenda. A special sub-programme, the "fiscal decentralisation programme for central and eastern Europe", has been devoted to the latter aspect.[161] Questions of local policy and municipal management have also been addressed in various seminars.[162]

With the increasingly active role played by the Congress of Local and Regional Authorities in Europe (Congress/CLRAE), some of the activities under the LODE programme after the Strasbourg Summit were devoted to the provision of assistance to the establishment and activities of "local democracy embassies" in the Balkan area.[163] This assistance, however, does not seem to have put an end to the financial problems that the local democracy embassies/agencies faced. LODE activities also supported the monitoring of local elections by the Congress.[164]

Finally, mention should be made of the so called "New initiative of the Secretary General" (1996-98), under which the Council of Europe carried out a series of national seminars concentrating on curricula and standards for history teaching;[165] the preparation and publication of new history textbooks; and initial and in-service training in history teaching in Albania, Belarus, Georgia, Moldova, Romania, the Russian Federation and Ukraine. Multilateral seminars on "the preparation of new history textbooks in European countries in democratic transition" and "initial and in-service training of history teachers in European countries in democratic transition" were organised respectively in Poland and Ukraine, bringing together participants from all the Council of Europe's new partner states.[166]

On the basis of a regional seminar, "The reform of history teaching in secondary schools" held in Tbilisi in September 1997 and which constituted the first activity of the Council of Europe on history teaching in the Caucasian region, a recommendation was made for the preparation and publication of a textbook. The aim of this textbook was to create a balance in teaching local, national, regional and world history, to establish democratic approaches in teaching the histories of the majority and the national minorities of each country, to help strengthen confidence, mutual understanding and democratic stability in the region, and to promote democratic values and tolerance. In the framework of the initiative, the elaboration of a handbook for teachers on how to teach sensitive and controversial issues was also envisaged.[167]

Besides the so-called "Tbilisi initiative", a similar project was started in relation to Bulgaria, Georgia, Moldova, Romania, the Russian Federation, Turkey and Ukraine under the title "The Black Sea initiative on history". Under this project, a seminar on "The preparation of new history textbooks and teaching resources" was held in Odessa on May 2000.[168] Also a working group on "History and history teaching in south-eastern Europe" was established under the Stability Pact for South-Eastern Europe.[169] Since then, other projects have been organised in the framework of co-operation activities by DG IV (Education, Culture and Heritage, Youth and Sport), including an expert meeting devoted to evaluation held in Kyiv, under the title: "Educational policy and minorities – working group on the assessment and evaluation of the pilot project".

Co-operation activities

The disappearance of ADACS led to new articulation through the decentralised Council of Europe "Co-operation activities" funded under Vote II, the Programme of activities section of the Council of Europe budget. The co-operation activities fall under one or more of five objectives: i. to protect and promote respect for human rights in all member states without discrimination; ii. to foster the setting up and development of democratic institutions and procedures at national, regional and local level; iii. to ensure the observance of the rule of law; iv. to promote a European cultural identity, while taking into account Europe's cultural diversity and heritage, with special emphasis on the role of education; and v. to promote tolerance, social cohesion and social rights.[170]

It should be noted that in spite of the non-discrimination reference under objective i., activities under this as well as under the remaining objectives focus on countries from central and eastern Europe.[171] The only exception in this connection seems to arise in the context of the follow-up activities relating to the implementation of the Advisory Committee opinions and corresponding CoM Resolutions, in which the Advisory Committee and the corresponding section of the Secretariat have recently engaged (see below).

Since their re-organisation into co-operation activities, Secretariat activities relevant to minorities seem to have focused on awareness-raising and implementation of the Framework Convention for the Protection of National Minorities and the European Charter of Regional and Minority Languages. Information meetings organised by the Secretariat responsible for the latter instrument in co-operation with the national authorities of various states and attended by government officials (especially local authorities), parliamentarians, and NGOs or minority representatives, have been organised to encourage its signature and ratification. In December 2002, an NGO seminar was organised by the Languages Charter Secretariat, in which NGO representatives from all the states party to the Charter participated.

Similarly, legislative expertise and technical working meetings with those states preparing ratification of these two treaties have been organised by the Secretariat upon request of the states concerned. With regard to the Languages Charter, seminars have been organised in Azerbaijan, the Czech Republic, Moldova, Poland, Romania and the Russian Federation (Moscow, Khakass Republic and Bashkortostan), in which the role of the different partners concerned with the functioning of the monitoring mechanism, in particular: the central authorities of the state, local authorities and NGOs, has been explained.

As to the Framework Convention for the Protection of National Minorities, co-operation activities have comprised bilateral meetings of Council of Europe officials with local experts, including those responsible for the drafting of laws on minorities (such as in the Federal Republic of Yugoslavia); assistance with the preparatory work related to the drafting of state reports on the application of the Framework Convention (such as in Bosnia and Herzegovina); or the training on minority protection standards of Roma advisers (this was the case in the Czech Republic).[172]

Multilateral meetings have also been held, including the "Regional Ministerial Conference on National and Ethnic Communities and Minorities in South-Eastern Europe – Domestic and Regional Confidence-Building", funded by the Stability Pact. Other Stability Pact projects – "Acceptance and implementation of existing standards", organised in most Stability Pact countries,[173] the non-discrimination review, and the bilateral co-operation agreements, thoroughly discussed in Chapter 5 – are implemented as co-operation activities by the Framework Convention Secretariat.

The eighth meeting of government offices for national minorities – intended as a continuation of the previous meetings of government offices, which were organised under the joint programmes between the Council of Europe and the European Commission "on minorities" (see below) – was also included in the co-operation activities for 2001 on the

Framework Convention for the Protection of National Minorities. This eighth meeting actually dealt with the implementation of the Framework Convention alone.[174]

The ninth meeting of government offices, held in Vilnius in April 2002, attended by Azerbaijan, Belgium, Bulgaria, Croatia, Cyprus, the Czech Republic, Denmark, Estonia, Finland, Georgia, Germany, Hungary, Ireland, Latvia, Lithuania, Moldova, Poland, Romania, the Russian Federation, the Slovak Republic, Slovenia, "the former Yugoslav Republic of Macedonia", the United Kingdom and Serbia and Montenegro (not then a member state), as well as a handful of international non-governmental organisations, dealt with the same topic. In addition, it addressed the issue "towards effective participation of national minorities in public life" taking up a topic partially addressed during the sixth meeting (see below).

It remains to be seen whether the topic of effective participation in public life, as well as other aspects of minority protection, besides progress on the implementation of the Framework Convention will be addressed in subsequent meetings of government offices, or in any other intergovernmental structure (such as DH-MIN), in pursuance of the aforementioned joint programmes between the Council of Europe and the European Commission "on minorities" open to all Council of Europe member states, and which in spite of their usefulness, as described below, have been discontinued.[175]

In the country-specific joint programmes between the Council of Europe and the European Commission concerning Ukraine on the one hand, and the three states of the South Caucasus (Georgia, Armenia and Azerbaijan) on the other, which deal with various areas of Council of Europe activity and are under way at the time of writing, a minority protection aspect has been introduced.[176] This aspect falls under the responsibility of the Framework Convention Secretariat. It aims at the ratification of the Framework Convention by Georgia and the implementation of this treaty by the three states, as well as awareness-raising about its standards, including among the NGO community.

Involvement in co-operation activities of countries not covered by the geographical scope of the joint programmes seems presently confined to the possibilities opened under a final area of activity of the Framework Convention Secretariat to which special reference should be made: the support of the monitoring activities of the Advisory Committee under the Framework Convention, and in particular the recent Advisory Committee's initiatives to follow up its implementation. This is done through the organisation of meetings (follow-up seminars) at the domestic level, which bring together authorities, representatives of minorities and NGOs to discuss the implementation of the initial results of monitoring under the Framework Convention.[177] Discussion focuses on the implementation of the respective Advisory Committee Opinion and corresponding CoM Resolution by the state concerned. The first such meeting was held in Finland on 1 February 2002,[178] and similar follow-up seminars have since been organised in Croatia, Romania, Hungary, Estonia, Armenia, Germany, Slovakia, Ukraine and Moldova.

These meetings have been characterised by the Advisory Committee as inclusive in their approach, providing an opportunity for governmental and non-governmental views to be "expressed in an open and constructive manner". They have also been characterised as transparent and flexible, opening the door to additional international external involvement in follow-up. Such outsiders included members of the Committee of Experts on the Languages Charter, in the case of the Finnish or the German seminars, where the implementation of the Languages Charter also became an object of discussion, as well as officials of the OSCE permanent mission in Croatia and members of ECRI, in the case of the Croatian seminar.[179]

The characteristics of these seminars have been contrasted by the Advisory Committee with those of the meetings taking place in the context of regular country visits before the Advisory Committee issues its Opinion (the formal monitoring under the Framework Convention), which are held in close session.[180] The Advisory Committee has advocated publication of the results of the seminars on the Internet.[181] This would contribute to the broadening of the dialogue on the implementation of the Framework Convention at the domestic level. The fact that follow-up seminars have been held also in Western countries points to this type of co-operation activity adopting a non-discriminatory approach among all Contracting Parties. This constitutes a welcome exception and an encouraging element of current minority protection practice within Council of Europe, which deserves to be pursued.

Finally, also in connection with co-operation activities, reference should be made to three projects recently launched by the Cultural Policy and Action Department of the Council of Europe. Two of these projects aim at assisting countries in south-east Europe on the one hand, and countries in the South Caucasus on the other, in the transition of their cultural policies, as well as to create a framework for exchange and co-operation amongst them. The first is the Managing an Open and Strategic Approach to Culture (MOSAIC) project launched in 1998, financed through voluntary contributions,[182] and the second is the Support for Transition in the Arts and Culture in Greater Europe (STAGE) project launched in 2000, falling under objective iv. of the co-operation activities. Albania; Bosnia and Herzegovina; Bulgaria; Croatia; Moldova; Romania; Slovenia; the Former Yugoslav Republic of Macedonia; Serbia and Montenegro and UNMIK/Kosovo have participated in MOSAIC, which has targeted cultural policy makers and administrators at national, regional and local level, as well as representatives of the cultural sector (practitioners, managers, researchers and so on).

The project has been implemented through national debates, sectorial reviews and advisory activities (to accompany legislative or regulatory reforms, carried out by panels of experts), as well as seminars, workshops and training-related activities. Various publications have resulted from the project, which has been developed in two phases: MOSAIC I (1998-2001) and II (2002-03).[183] Cultural diversity has been included among the "crucial issues" to be tackled through multilateral activities under the project. As to the activities organised at national level, these have responded "to the specific requirements formulated by each of the participating countries". Consequently, some important aspects of cultural diversity at the domestic level have not been addressed.

The 2002 programme for the project relied on specific requests made by individual states involved, so the treatment of cultural diversity aspects relating to minority protection seems to have rested on their discretion. In spite of the large number of activities carried out, specific references to minority protection aspects have been very limited.[184] However, many activities of the project have been of indirect relevance for minorities, in particular those relating to national policy reform and decentralisation, and to the establishment of local cultural institutions of various kinds (such as cultural centres, libraries or museums).

The general objectives of STAGE have aimed at tackling some of the basic problems generally subjacent in the South Caucasus states, especially aspects of transparency in policy-making and management, as well as stability, with regard to the cultural sector. The first year of the project, 2001, was devoted to the drawing of guidelines for technical assistance and co-operation activities on the basis of a colloquy of the ministers of culture of the states participating in the project, Armenia, Azerbaijan and Georgia, held in December 2000. Reviews of the cultural policies of these states, organisation of workshops and seminars to provide assistance to "the various sectors" involved in cultural activity, and support for the training of cultural managers, were provided. A group of experts visited the three states and took note of the areas in which assistance was needed, and of the concrete proposals of the representatives of the respective ministries of culture and of civil society.[185]

On this basis, the strategy of the project for the period 2002-03 was prepared, including the continuation of the review of national policies in Azerbaijan and Georgia; national debates on the national reports and experts' reports resulting from the review process; the organisation of a workshop on "cultural policies in transition: dilemmas and strategies", the setting-up of regional cultural strategies in areas such as cultural tourism, and the organisation of national or multilateral seminars, one of them in relation to the question of the development of partnerships with civil society. Aspects of protection of the cultural rights of minorities have not become, however, an express object of the project, although questions such as decentralisation are among the key issues addressed, especial emphasis being also placed on cultural exchanges.

A third relevant project launched by the Cultural Policy and Action Department is entitled Intercultural Dialogue and Conflict Prevention. This has seemingly become the main channel for confidence-building as opposed to terrorism-combating approaches in the aftermath of the 11 September 2001 attacks on the United States of America, to which reference has been made in Chapter 5.

The project involves research activities, an analysis of good practices, and support for cultural action. It has the overall aim to promote inter-cultural and inter-religious dialogue, and mutual respect and under-standing between the different communities and to prevent conflicts through cultural policies and cultural action.[186] In the framework of the project, an informal meeting of the European ministers responsible for cultural affairs on "the new role and new responsibilities of ministers of culture in initiating intercultural dialogue, with due regard to cultural diversity" was held in Strasbourg on February 2003. However, no partic-ular action plan seems to have derived from that meeting.[187]

Field presences

The work of relevance to minorities done by the Council of Europe's offices established in several member states at the Secretariat's initiative is illustrated by the work of the offices in Pristina and Belgrade, already described in Chapter 5. While this mainly consists in the support of general Council of Europe and Secretariat activities in the states where they are based,[188] a separate reference should be made to the presence of Council of Europe experts in the Office of the Russian president's Special Representative for Human Rights in Chechnya, given its special charac-ter and the specific nature of its activities. As described in Chapter 12, this field presence was established at the initiative of the Council of Europe Commissioner for Human Rights.

Since the arrival of the experts at the Special Representative's office in Znamenskoye on 21 June 2000, theirs has been the only permanent presence of an international, intergovernmental organisation in Chechnya, especially since 31 December 2002, when the mandate of the OSCE Assistance Group to Chechnya, previously in and out of the region, finally expired as a result of the failure of the Russian authorities and the OSCE to reach an agreement on the conditions for its extension.

The only exception to the Council of Europe's permanent presence has been the withdrawal of the experts during the period from 19 to 28 March 2003, immediately preceding the referendum in which the draft Chechen constitution, as well as the draft acts on presidential and parliamentary elections in Chechnya, were approved. This withdrawal, resulting from a reversal of mainstream policy, took place when the Council of Europe decided not to observe the said referendum as the appropriate conditions established by the Parliamentary Assembly had not been met, while the OSCE sent a technical, fact-finding mission, under the aegis of its Dutch chairmanship.[189]

While the work of the Council of Europe experts initially focused in assisting the Special Representative's office, at first headed by V. Kalamanov, in putting together a system for receiving complaints, registering applications and forwarding them to the competent authorities of the Russian Federation, as well as following up their further processing, it soon started to involve visits to detention centres.[190] The periodic reporting of the Secretary General on the activity of the experts has since become an important source of information, not only on the activities of the (currently twelve) branch offices of the Special Representative (position presently held by A-K. Sultygov following the resignation of V. Kalamanov), but also on the lack of progress with regard to human rights in Chechnya.[191] However, as described in Chapter 5, this direct access to information on the situation by the CoM has not resulted in pro-active steps on its side.

Although much emphasis has been placed on the recent renewal of the "Agreement on the establishment of the joint working group between the Office of the Special Representative and the Prokuratura", originally supported by the Council of Europe and concluded on March 2003, no substantial improvement in the human rights situation has resulted so far. The most problematic issues remain, as identified by the joint working group itself: i. human rights violations committed by members of the federal forces during special operations and when "targeted measures" are implemented; ii. disappearances of persons, especially at night; iii. prevailing climate of impunity resulting from the fact that responsible persons are not brought to justice; iv. lack of adequate detention facilities; and v. lack of adequate means to carry out efficiently forensic examination.[192]

The permanence of this state of affairs is aggravated by the massive scale at which this human rights emergency situation is allowed to continue. As to the current situation, recent Secretary General reports point to the danger that recent initiatives concerning an amnesty "may be used to 'wipe-out' serious violations committed by members of the federal forces, thus leaving the population with a feeling that, in the name of reconciliation, these crimes will be left unpunished".[193]

The joint programmes between the Council of Europe (Secretariat) and the European Union (Commission) on minorities

The joint programmes between the European Commission and the Secretariat of the Council of Europe on minorities have generated a range of co-operation and assistance activities in relation to minority protection in a number of countries. The joint programmes had their origin in a proposal for structured co-operation between the various governmental offices for national minorities, in the framework of the measures accompanying the EU-sponsored Pact of Stability in Europe, addressed to the countries of central and eastern Europe in the mid-1990s.[194] The proposal was made by the Hungarian authorities following the first meeting of government offices for national minorities, organised by the Hungarian Office for National Minorities in November 1994.[195]

An initial joint programme entitled "Minorities in central European countries" ran from 1 July 1996 to 31 March 1998. The seventeen states participating in that programme were Albania, Belarus, Bulgaria, Croatia, the Czech Republic, Estonia, Hungary, Latvia, Lithuania, "the former Yugoslav Republic of Macedonia", Moldova, Poland, Romania, the Russian Federation, Slovakia, Slovenia and Ukraine. It was structured into four main projects:

- MIN I: consisting of regular meetings of the governmental offices for national minorities;

- MIN II: comprising study visits for representatives of offices for national minorities to similar institutions in other countries;

- MIN III: consisting in the organisation of seminars/workshops on topical subjects common to all (or several) offices for national minorities; and

- MIN IV: under which specific follow-up action was to be considered.[196]

Following two preparatory meetings held in Budapest, the third meeting of government offices for national minorities, held in Romania already under MIN I, coincided with the launching of the joint programme. While this meeting dealt with quite general topics – the implementation of the Framework Convention, and programmes for organisations of national minorities – subsequent meetings became increasingly targeted, particularly in relation to the question of the integration of national minorities in civic society.

360

The issues addressed included: i. modalities of participation of national minorities in decision-making processes at state level; ii. the role of language in the integration process; and iii. the role of culture in the integration process. Whereas topic i. was referred to a seminar under MIN III for discussion, the latter two topics were addressed at the "higher-profile" fifth meeting of governmental offices for national minorities, under MIN I in two separate working groups. The issue of tolerance was also addressed at the same meeting in two working groups, dealing, respectively, with iv. the role of education and v. the role of civil society, including political parties.[197]

The meetings organised under MIN I seem to have achieved satisfactory results since, according to the Secretariat, initial diplomatic reserve gave way to open discussions and exchange of information, including a professional approach to problem-solving. This had a positive impact on the development of informal, bilateral relations between the government offices, which in some cases were formally structured in the framework of existing bilateral treaties between the states participating in the programme. This exercise, in turn, seems to have had a positive impact on the overall climate regarding the protection of minorities at the domestic level.[198] At the third meeting, representatives from national minorities were invited to attend as observers.[199]

The study visits organised under MIN II and made by members of the government offices participating in the joint programme to their counterparts in various Council of Europe states also received, with some minor exceptions,[200] a positive overall evaluation, mainly because of their contribution to increasing "awareness of the way in which minority questions are dealt with, both at the legal level and in practice, in other European countries", and to developing contacts that are "valuable, if difficult to quantify, assets when it comes to developing and implementing policies in the home country".[201]

Under MIN III, seminars on the themes "Minorities and media", "Minorities and education", and "Participation of national minorities in decision-making processes" were organised for all seventeen states participating in the programme.[202] The topics for the seminars were chosen on the basis of their relevance to minority protection by reference to the text of the Framework Convention for the Protection of National Minorities. The seminars aimed at the identification of other relevant international standards that give guidance for the understanding and implementation of the legal standards established in the Framework Convention. They also examined existing related experience, at the national and European levels. As an innovative feature, minority representatives were allowed to participate, the selection of participants being left to the discretion of the states. The involvement of minority representatives received a very positive assessment.[203]

Under MIN IV, a few proposals for follow-up activities were tentatively put forward, which included a number of pilot projects for the training of professionals (government officials, journalists, cultural administrations, teachers and so on), developing their professional activities in relation to national minorities.[204] In spite of the fact that these proposals did not prosper – and it was later concluded that the introduction of such proposals (under the item on "future co-operation") from the very start of the co-operation initiated by the joint programme had been premature[205] – the item as such became a permanent feature on the agenda of subsequent meetings organised under MIN I. This allowed, if not for specific follow-up action at the domestic level, at least for the articulation of the follow-up action in connection with the development and enhancement of the joint programme as such.

The first joint programme received a very positive evaluation by the participating states, which led to the agreement that a concrete proposal for a new joint programme should be put forward. A proposal entitled "National Minorities in Europe" was subsequently submitted to the European Commission and approved for the period January 1999 to June 2000. Very importantly, following suggestions put forward by the states participating in the first programme, expressing their wish for states from western Europe to become involved in the activities under MIN I and III, the second joint programme was opened to all Council of Europe member states as well as applicant states.

The structure of the second programme was more thematic, rather than built exclusively around working methods,[206] although the description here follows the original structure, for the sake of consistency. The main topics addressed were: education, the media, integration and participation.[207] Preference was given to sub-regional or bilateral projects. A greater involvement of minority representatives was also envisaged and put into practice.[208] Of the numerous activities undertaken, which involved thirty-six member states in one way or another, a handful are described below.[209]

With regard to MIN I, at the sixth meeting of government offices for national minorities, held in Strasbourg, state participation had substantially increased. Twenty-six countries were represented: Albania, Armenia, Austria, Bulgaria, Croatia, the Czech Republic, Estonia, Finland, Georgia, Germany, Greece, Hungary, Latvia, Lithuania, Moldova, Poland, Portugal, Romania, the Russian Federation, Slovakia, Slovenia, Switzerland, "the former Yugoslav Republic of Macedonia", Turkey, Ukraine and the United Kingdom. In addition, Italy, Norway, Spain and

Sweden expressed their interest in the programme, although they argued they could not be represented at the meeting.[210] Not only the Framework Convention, but also the European Charter for Regional or Minority Languages and activities of the Council of Europe in relation to minorities were on the agenda.

An important feature of the meeting, devoted to an exchange of views on the subject of participation of minorities in decision-making processes, was that the members of DH-MIN joined the meeting.[211] On the basis of the state replies to a questionnaire on the subject of the participation of minorities in decision-making processes, different models of minority participation were presented. Several international NGOs – the Federal Union of European Nationalities (FUEN), the European Bureau for Lesser Used Languages (EBLUL) and the European Centre for Minority Issues (ECMI) – were invited by DH-MIN to attend the meeting. The seventh meeting of government offices for national minorities, held in Latvia in June 2000, when the second joint programme was coming to a close, was devoted to taking stock of the development of the joint programmes.[212]

In relation to MIN II, the programme of study visits proceeded along the same lines as during the first joint programme,[213] consisting mainly in visits of officials from countries of central and eastern Europe to institutions and bodies in western European states. According to the final report on the programme, greater emphasis was placed on quality over quantity than in the previous programme.[214] With regard to MIN III, many other activities (described in detail in the final report of the second joint programme) were undertaken in a large number of states, under the themes: "Minorities and the media", "Education and minorities", "Participation of minorities in decision-making processes" and "Integration and tolerance".[215] Only a few are described below, to illustrate the type of activities undertaken.

A seminar on the role of non-governmental minority associations in the exercise of minority rights was held in Croatia in June 1999. In spite of the sensitivity of the topic for many Council of Europe states, the seminar was attended by representatives of ten states: Austria, Croatia, the Czech Republic, Hungary, Italy, the Netherlands, Romania, Slovakia, Slovenia and the United Kingdom. Other Council of Europe states showed interest yet declined the invitation to attend for internal reasons: Denmark, France, Germany and Spain.[216] One participant per country was requested "to make a general presentation of the legal system in use in his/her respective country in terms of foundation of minority associations and their role in civil society" in plenary session.[217] Then, separate workshops were organised on the role that minority associations play in the exercise of minority rights and the implementation of European legal instruments aimed at the protection of national minorities.

Discussions on the relations between different minority associations, and between minority associations and the majority population were encouraged. Members of minority associations in Croatia participated and took the floor during the discussions, and contributed to a review of the situation in relation to minority protection in Croatia. The conference resulted in further initiatives for bilateral interstate co-operation as well as co-operation between local and international NGOs.[218] The support which the first joint programme had received by the states which had participated in it was renewed, and this support also extended to the newcomers to the joint programme. At the end of the seminar, representatives of the United Kingdom and the Netherlands for example "indicated that this seminar did away with a number of stereotypes, as well as enlarged the reflection on national minority issues".[219]

A conference on the representation of minority interests and participation of minorities in political decision-making processes was organised in Budapest at the initiative of the Hungarian Office of the Parliamentary Commissioner for the Rights of National and Ethnic Minorities in consultation with Minority Rights Group International. The aim of the conference was to address the issue of the promotion of the parliamentary representation of minorities in Hungary through an analysis of relevant good practices in Europe. Representatives of minority parties or organisations, members of minorities represented in the parliament of their countries and representatives of various minorities in national political parties from Austria, Finland, Germany, Italy, Poland, Romania, Slovakia, Slovenia, Spain, and the United Kingdom were invited, besides governmental and international organisation representatives.[220]

Similarly, a multilateral round table on national minority policies in central and eastern Europe was also organised in Bratislava at the initiative of the cabinet of the Deputy Prime Minister and the Ministry for Foreign Affairs of Slovakia, the Centre for European Policy and the city of Košice. The attendance of participants from Ukraine, the Czech Republic, Poland, Hungary and Romania, as well as of minority NGOs and representatives of minorities in Slovakia, was envisaged. The round table aimed at the exchange of information on national policies, especially on the political, social and economic conditions of life of persons belonging to national minorities, with emphasis on cultural, religious and educational aspects.

A good climate for dialogue and co-operation at the political level, as well as a substance-orientated approach, seems to have prevailed throughout the development of the joint programmes. The professionals from the governments involved seemingly found in their counterparts from other states valuable sources of information on how to approach domestic questions. The increasing involvement of NGOs and the positive assessment of their role, in what started as an intergovernmental exercise alone, broke new ground, and opened new perspectives for future co-operation between governments and civil society in relation to minority protection. The joint programmes became the object of unprecedentedly detailed and open reporting and evaluation, reflected not only in the final reports on the programmes addressed to the EU Commission, partner in the projects, but also in their newsletters, which have provided current information on their development. Assessments of state participation in the programmes were carried out, and means to improve it discussed. This has broken new ground when it comes to transparency of activities undertaken in the framework of the Council of Europe.

In the conclusions of the stocktaking exercise undertaken during the seventh meeting of government offices, the second joint programme received a very positive assessment, due among other things, to its "undisputed value ... from the standpoint of harmonisation of European legislation, greater co-operation between governments and the effective involvement of civil society in the decision-making process".[221] The need to continue the meetings of government offices for national minorities was underlined. So was the need to maintain the pan-European character of the programme, especially for the meetings of government offices, although most thematic activities should focus on particular geographical areas. The possibility was envisaged of developing websites for all government offices, in order to facilitate communication and networking among them, if need be through the provision of technical assistance. Similarly, a higher level of NGO involvement, including the possibility of developing a parallel series of trans-European meetings for NGOs representing minorities, was recommended, in order to encourage national organisations to open up to Europe and work at the pan-European level.[222]

The term of the second joint programme on minorities expired and the joint programmes on minorities came to an end. In spite of the wave of activity in relation to intergovernmental and non-governmental co-operation that the joint programmes generated, and the constant endorsement and support for their continuation by the states participating, at the time of writing no formal proposals have been put forward by the Council of Europe as to their continuation. The fact that the eighth and ninth meetings of government offices for national minorities[223] were organised outside the framework of the joint programmes points to the fact that the broader activities initiated under their framework have been brought to an end. This raises a question of commitment to practical co-operation which extends to the governments and public administrations in all member states in the field of minority protection.

365

Council of Europe Civil Society programmes in the promotion of inter-ethnic relations

The Civil Society programmes of the Council of Europe are currently made up of four main elements: Civil Society initiatives, the Democratic Leadership Programme (DLP), the schools of political studies, and Confidence-Building Measures in civil society (CBM). Their common strategy aims at encouraging various sectors of civil society to play an active role in strengthening pluralist democracy in their respective countries and to contribute to mutual understanding and reconciliation in those parts of Europe that have been affected by conflicts. The "Civil Society initiatives" focus *inter alia* on the role of civil society in inter-community and inter-religious dialogue and include, for example, a series of seminars implemented in different parts of Bosnia and Herzegovina with a view to facilitating concrete co-operation among the different communities, on issues such as human rights protection, reconstruction and sustainable return. Current geographic priorities include south-east Europe, Moldova, Belarus, Cyprus and the south Caucasus.

While the Democratic Leadership Programme (DLP)[224] and the Schools of Political Studies[225] are of indirect relevance for minority protection, the Confidence-Building Measures (CBM) programme addresses exclusively the question of minority–majority relations. The full name of the programme, in accordance with the denomination given by the Secretariat is "Confidence-building measures in civil society", in order to differentiate it from other related activities of the Council of Europe.[226] According to a recent description of the origin of the confidence-building measures programme of the Council of Europe "the increasing prominence of minority problems, especially in central and eastern Europe, revealed" the need for Council of Europe work in promoting a climate of mutual understanding, tolerance and respect for different cultures "to be supplemented by specific initiatives on the ground undertaken in close collaboration with the communities concerned".[227] This is the first major initiative of the Council of Europe involving civil society and the NGO community at the domestic level in a wide operational programme related to minority protection. It is open to groups and organisations active in Europe, including those originating from non-member states.

Although the programme is mainly geared towards civil society,[228] activities which involve public authorities have also been included. This has been the case for example in the organisation of round tables bringing together relevant authorities, local or others, and minority representatives; as well as activities concerning the interaction between the police and the Roma population. Similarly, support for Local Democracy Embassies/ Agencies[229] has also been brought under the programme. According to a Secretariat document, the initiatives for a project could originate from member states or European non-member states, regions or local authorities, schools, universities, media, NGOs and so on, as well as from the Council of Europe Secretariat.[230] More recent descriptions of the programme place increasing emphasis on civil society as the source of initiatives, referring to "local or international NGOs, media, educational establishments or local or regional authorities" as examples.[231]

By December 2002, over 331 projects in twenty-seven countries of central and eastern Europe had been undertaken in the framework of the programme, including projects in states which are not actively considered under the accession procedures, such as, as the time of writing, Belarus.[232] Within the EU, some projects have been developed in Austria and Germany.[233] While some projects are financed by the Council of Europe through a special account for confidence-building measures,[234] other projects received only the general endorsement of the programme by the organisation and are opened for voluntary contributions within its framework.

The ambitious goal of the programme as stated in 1993, "the elimination of tension liable to develop into serious conflicts through managing the multicultural nature of European societies and changing people's mentalities and their approaches to 'others' on the basis of respect for pluralism and respect for minority protection", has progressively been replaced by more modest aims. Firstly, it was defusing tensions that could otherwise lead to serious conflicts, helping "to break down barriers between different communities at the grass roots through dialogue and opportunities to learn or work together on specific projects".[235]

The stated intention was "to promote mutual knowledge and understanding and a rejection of violence as a means of solving problems" through the shared experience resulting from the projects organised under the aegis of the programme.[236] According to the most recent description of the programme, its aim is: "to provide moral and financial support for civil society projects, of which the main objective is to promote relations between persons belonging to different ethnic groups within a specific country or between two or more neighbouring countries".[237]

While responding to this overall objective, the nature of the projects varies widely. Main areas identified by the Secretariat include the media, education, culture, human rights, democracy, transfrontier co-operation, youth, local and regional democracy and also, more recently, social cohesion;[238] projects on economic or entrepreneurial development have been explicitly excluded.[239] Some projects have a primarily political character, such as those concerning the establishment of forums for dialogue between leading representatives of the authorities and the minorities in a given state, or the support of international conferences on minority protection. The projects have been considered to be pilot projects that, if successful, will have a multiplier effect "and stimulate others to follow the example given".[240]

Many of the projects in the programme concern the media, including the elaboration of television and radio programmes aimed at the majority population, the minorities, or both. Educational programmes for journalists, including on the provision of multicultural information, or programmes especially geared towards journalists originating from minority communities, as well as workshops for opinion leaders, are also included.

Projects in the field of education, including taught courses, the elaboration of history books, as well as "training of trainers" programmes on intercultural approaches, have received support. Also educational projects for youth and children have received support, as well as video courses, including those in the majority language aimed at the integration of minority groups. Intercultural institutes, such as the European Institute for Dispersed Ethnic Minorities recently established in Vilnius and already mentioned above, when discussing the activities of DH-MIN, have been included under the programme. So have been summer camps, youth meetings and children's activities, many of them involving the Roma.

A team based in the Directorate of Political Affairs of the Secretariat is in charge of the management of the programme. It receives applications for projects to be considered under the programme, and carries out a preliminary selection. "It then consults the different Directorates concerned and, if need be, arranges interdepartmental meetings". Projects are then submitted to the Steering Group on the Confidence-Building Measures programme of the CoM, "to examine the projects which have already been vetted and filtered by the Secretariat and for which the necessary information has been provided, and to take the final decisions as to whether to approve the projects and what form the Council of Europe's support should take".[241]

According to the Secretariat, the expected impact of the projects is to be mainly local, and their results should be felt in the medium and long term.[242] However, the period for implementation of the projects should not exceed twelve months,[243] although an extension of up to 24 months is envisaged in exceptional and motivated cases.[244] The Secretariat has provided information on the criteria for the selection of projects, as well as guidelines for the submission of applications and the financial and administrative procedures to be followed.[245] To ensure that projects continue to achieve their objectives, on-the-spot ex-post evaluations of a selection of projects are carried out either by the Secretariat or by an external consultant.

Concluding remarks

During the last decade and especially in the period 1998 to 2003, the issue of minority protection has progressively trickled down to the day-to-day activities of the intergovernmental structures of the Council of Europe, not only with regard to the setting of standards but also in the area of policy making. DH-MIN started to tackle issues (some of which could be considered as theoretical at first sight), which carry important implications for the establishment of appropriate and accepted practices concerning minority protection by states throughout Europe. DH-MIN directly engaged member states in considering issues of minority protection in a concrete and targeted manner. The increasing interaction of DH-MIN with non-governmental actors similarly became an important step forward in the area of minority protection.

The proposals put forward and initiatives undertaken by DH-MIN regarding closer interaction with civil society, including the establishment of mechanisms of dialogue on minority questions, have been ground-breaking. The publication of the final activity report of the "Study on dispersed ethnic minorities", in particular, can be considered an exercise in transparency (an aspect recently recognised as urgently requiring attention in the overall work of the Organisation)[246] which contributes to the credibility of the bodies and organs responsible for it, as well as the states mentioned in the report. This type of activity benefits not only minority protection, but also the relations between the Council of Europe institutions and the member states involved on the one hand, and the civil society at large on the other.

Similarly, the activities of the CDMG (the European Committee on Migration) have also implied important progress at the conceptual level, especially regarding the integration of so-called new minorities in their host countries. The CDMG has carried out very thorough analyses identifying the general problems present in this area, and is increasingly looking for appropriate solutions to specific, well-defined concerns identified throughout the member states. The activities of the CDMG have resulted in highly relevant proposals for policy-making in topical areas, such as those relating to the security of residence of long-term migrants.

However, the outlook does not seem as positive when it comes to the intergovernmental decision-making bodies following up the results of work carried out by the CDMG. The reluctance of member states to recognise the social rights of migrants largely remains, as illustrated by the low level of accessions to the European Convention on the Legal Status of Migrant Workers. In spite of the increasing recognition of the permanent character of residence of most immigrants and their families in their host countries, at the level of intergovernmental discussion and declarations, and the initial, timid steps taken to safeguard their permanence in the host countries, there is still a high level of reluctance to recognise the civil and political rights of the new minorities and their access to social services on an equal footing with the majority population. This has already been discussed in Chapter 5 and is further discussed in Chapter 10. The attention of states is currently mainly focused on finding formulas for "migration management", although the facilitation of integration is gaining ground as a crucial element also in this context.

The activities of the CAHP (the European Population Committee) in the analysis of various aspects concerning the situation of minorities in member states, is of paramount importance, especially in identifying minority questions and finding appropriate solutions to problems that already exist or that may emerge in the future. These activities have proved particularly beneficial with regard to international co-operation, as they provide the basic information necessary to take reasoned and adequate decisions on action. Its work, as well as that of its predecessor, the CDPO, has thus become a useful basis for international policy-making, although the level of support for international action in areas identified in the course of its work (and which may raise international concern) seems to largely depend still on the particular interests of states and their domestic situation at any given moment, rather than serving for the adoption of "objective" and long-term approaches to the problems perceived.

In keeping minority issues high on its agenda and on that of the inter-governmental structures, the role of the GR-C (the Rapporteur Group on Education, Culture etc.) has been – like that of the CDCC – particularly important for minority protection. The lack of political follow-up to the findings resulting from the major project in which the CDCC was involved in relation to minority protection – "Democracy, human rights, minorities: educational and cultural aspects" – has shown the reluctance, which still persists at the level of the intergovernmental structures of the Organisation, to adopt minority-sensitive approaches in the cultural field, especially when this touches upon granting legal recognition to specific aspects of minority protection or upon aspects of the political organisation of the state. It is to be hoped that this reluctance will be overcome in favour of human rights considerations, especially in view of the existing difficulties in achieving results in cultural protection, including at the standard-setting level, as discussed in Chapter 5. The work started in this field by the CDCC should not be abandoned, but built on.

Similarly, opportunities which should not be missed include those provided by the follow-up to be given to the "Budapest Declaration on a European policy for new information technologies", which, as indicated in Chapter 5, has paved the way for minority protection to be included as a priority concern in the development of future policies in that field. Another opportunity is in connection with the development of policies in Europe concerning multilingualism. It is to be hoped that Secretariat programmes in the cultural field would emphasise the importance of intergovernmental co-operation acting on previous achievements. The work started by the CDLR (the Steering Committee on Local and Regional Democracy) should be similarly further built upon. This should include its endeavours with regard to the development of local territorial structures and the promotion of regional ones, an issue discussed in detail in Chapter 10.

This raises a more general question about the overall activity of the intergovernmental committees and other CoM subsidiary bodies in their various forms. In the context of their work, a common feature has been the establishment of wider frameworks of expert consultation, research and analysis in order to identify solutions to existing problems, frequently involving actors from civil society. However, often the results obtained have not found appropriate follow-up at the higher political levels of intergovernmental co-operation. As a result of a lack of positive responses, findings have not been pursued or given further practical application. Often, the main outcome that could be expected from these processes has been the progressive creation of states of opinion as to what may constitute appropriate state responses to existing monitoring problems, without medium-term or even foreseeable impact on state behaviour.

A second general concern results from the frequent interruption of the processes started and the progress achieved within the context of the work of the intergovernmental committees or subsidiary bodies, in order to respond to new priorities as they arise. If the interruption of these processes is treated as a temporary measure, taken in response to current budgetary constraints, and intergovernmental co-operation is resumed at the point where it had been left in the short run, substantial progress can still be expected in the medium term. This may not be the case, however, if – as a consequence of periodical shifting of priorities – ongoing processes are frequently suspended for long periods, or simply terminated. The momentum of political co-operation reached may simply be lost.

This concern about lost momentum arises especially in connection with the suspension of the work of certain committees (such as DH-MIN) or the re-structuring or re-naming of existing committees or subsidiary bodies (as has been the case with regard to the discontinuation of certain areas of activity initiated by the CDCC in the framework of GR-C). It equally applies to those intergovernmental co-operation frameworks created in the context of Secretariat-sponsored programmes, such as the joint programmes between the European Commission and the Council of Europe on minorities which, following a process of internal evolution, aimed at involving the totality of Council of Europe member states in a common endeavour of practical co-operation with substantial domestic impact. In both cases, interstate co-operation on minority protection at the level of all member states of the Council of Europe is what is at stake.

The increasing importance given to the minority question in the highest and lowest echelons of intergovernmental co-operation at the Council of Europe was not adequately reflected in ADACS. While minority issues became a major policy concern in most states involved in the ADACS programmes, work in this field mainly concentrated on promotional activities related to accession to the Framework Convention. Greater attention for minority protection is needed, especially in view of the fact that the minorities activities under ADACS in most Council of Europe states had been those included in the joint programmes with the European Commission on minorities, which have been halted.

In spite of the fact that the co-operation activities that started in the year 2000 have tended to concentrate on the states of central and eastern Europe, a window of opportunity has been opened in the context of the follow-up to the conclusions of the monitoring of the Framework Convention. It is to be hoped that this responsibility given to the co-operation activities will be given adequate attention and support. Similarly, it is to be hoped that field presences will acquire a more active role in improving the actual situation of minorities on the ground, whenever the security situation allows.

A very positive assessment must be given to the two joint programmes between the European Commission and the Council of Europe "on minorities". These proved to be one of the most useful multilateral enterprises in relation to minority protection undertaken at the Council of Europe. They had the benefit of involving in an unprecedented partnership the governmental agencies directly concerned with minority questions at the domestic level in a large number of member states of the Council of Europe, and of making them the protagonists in the co-operation process. The flexibility with which the organisation of the programmes was approached, to take into account the concerns and interests of the various governmental offices involved, seems to have facilitated the abandonment of rigid and formalistic positions which often characterise intergovernmental co-operation. Further, NGO involvement was progressively considered as a valuable element in the process, proving that dialogue between governmental structures and domestic civic groups can make a positive contribution to finding concerted solutions to minority problems.

The detailed description and open assessment by the Secretariat of the Council of Europe of each of the activities undertaken under the programmes (including study visits), and its open advice to states on questions such as the selection of participants, point to the success of the programme from the perspective of organisation and follow-up. The programmes also presented ground-breaking approaches as to transparency and openness. Probably the fact that reporting was not just for internal purposes, but that the Council of Europe was responsible to an external partner, in this case the European Commission, contributed to this. At all these levels, the programmes established a very good model, which deserves to be continued, and followed in similar programmes. Under the aegis of these programmes, practices have been developed as to transparency and flexibility, as well as direct minority involvement, which should be extended to other areas of activity of the Organisation.

In spite of these achievements, the joint programmes on minorities have been discontinued. The comments previously made in relation to the interruption of ongoing intergovernmental co-operation processes concerning minority protection by the Council of Europe, and the resulting lost opportunities for achieving progress in this field, especially apply to the substance of the joint programmes. For the Council of Europe to take up the leadership in minority protection in Europe that it has often proclaimed, the political momentum and positive climate created under the joint programmes still provides an opportunity of co-operation in relation to minority protection throughout the Council of Europe member states, which should not to be lost. Their relaunching would constitute an expression of the truthfulness of the Council of Europe states' commitment to make minority protection a reality throughout the Council of Europe region.

The programme of confidence-building measures in civil society seems to present a more positive outlook as to its continuation in the short run. The high level of growth experienced by the programme in recent years does not seem to be threatened, at least for as long as the minority issue continues to rank highly on the Council of Europe agenda, and states – including some on an individual, voluntary basis – are willing to make financial contributions to the programme. Improvements to the programme could be introduced, however, at the level of transparency and follow-up. Especially regarding public information on the criteria applied in the selection or rejection of project applications and the results achieved in their implementation.

The importance of an open and detailed assessment of Secretariat projects in the field of confidence-building measures as well as in other fields, is of the utmost importance. Even if the likelihood of obtaining mixed results in this type of project is high, increased transparency and non-partisan, external, assessment as well as publicity, would contribute to the credibility of the programme, facilitate its non-politicisation and benefit its future development. It would also encourage good practice within the states where the projects are carried out, including by the authorities and civic groups involved in its implementation. The joint programme between the European Commission and the Council of Europe on minorities has provided a model in this domain, which could be followed by other programmes.

Notes

1. See G. de Vel, *The Committee of Ministers of the Council of Europe*, pp. 42-43.

2. Ibid.

3. Ibid., p. 44. On the current organisation of the presently called "Deputies' subsidiary groups" see the Committee of Ministers' Webpage in the Council of Europe Website.

4. Activities carried out by the Secretariat in connected fields are discussed in the present chapter.

5. On these committees of experts, formed in pursuance to Article 17 of the Statute of the Council of Europe, as well as on rapporteur groups, working parties and other bodies, see generally, G. de Vel, op. cit., pp. 42-44 and pp. 88-93.

6. See recommendations of the Assembly, replies from the Committee of Ministers, Parliamentary Assembly Doc. 8306, 26 January 1999, grouped reply to Recommendations 1134 (1990); 1177 (1992); 1201 (1993); 1255 (1955); 1285 (1996); 1300 (1996) and 1345 (1997), section C.

7. See first activity in the Human Rights section (Activity I.8) of the "Intergovernmental programme of activities for 2000", p. 21.

8. Recommendations of the Assembly, replies from the Committee of Ministers, Parliamentary Assembly Doc. 8306, 26 January 1999, grouped reply to Recommendations 1134 (1990); 1177 (1992); 1201 (1993); 1255 (1955); 1285 (1996); 1300 (1996) and 1345 (1997); Appendix to the reply of the Committee of Ministers to Parliamentary Assembly Recommendation 1345 (1997); Opinion of the CDDH on Parliamentary Assembly Recommendation 1345 (1997) on the protection of national minorities. See Council of Europe Internet website, human rights/minorities homepage.

9. Recommendations: 1291 (1996) on Yiddish culture; 1333 (1997) on the Aromanian culture and language; and 1345 (1997) on the protection of national minorities. *Activities of the Council of Europe: 1998 Report* (Strasbourg: Council of Europe, October 1999), p. 107.

10. See further, Chapter 10.

11. *Report on the activities of the Council of Europe 1999, provisional edition* (Strasbourg: Council of Europe Publishing, 2000), p. 191.

12. This has been the case over recent years. On 2000, see *Intergovernmental Programme of Activities for 2000*, p. 21.

13. See *Intergovernmental Programme of Activities for 1999*, Doc. MEP (99) 3, p. 21 and *Intergovernmental Programme of Activities for 2000*, p. 21.

14. Ibid.

15. On the Portorož conference and the Stability Programme for South-Eastern Europe, see Chapter 5.

16. *Activities of the Council of Europe: 1998 Report* (Strasbourg: Council of Europe, October 1999), p. 107. On the issue of the "Effective participation of national minorities in public life" see the Lund Recommendations elaborated under the aegis of the OSCE HCNM (The Hague: Foundation on Inter-Ethnic Relations, 1999). This and other sets of general recommendations of the OSCE HCNM are also available at the Internet website: http://www.osce.org/hcnm/documents/recommendations

17. See "The participation of minorities in decision-making processes – expert study submitted on request of the DH-MIN of the Council of Europe by the Max-Planck-Institute for Comparative Public Law and International Law, Heidelberg, Authors: Professor Dr. Dres. h.c. J.A. Frowein and Dr. R. Bank, November 2000", Doc. DH-MIN (2000) 1.

18. Ibid., p. 1.

19. Ibid.

20. See Final activity report on "Dispersed ethnic minorities", Steering Committee for Human Rights (CDDH), Committee of Experts on issues relating to the Protection of National Minorities (DH-MIN), CM (99) 173, Addendum, 22 December 1999, 694th Meeting of the Ministers' Deputies, 19 January 2000.

21. Ibid., paragraphs 4-5.

22. Ibid., paragraph 5.

23. Ibid., paragraph 6.

24. Ibid., emphasis added.

25. See, for example, the case of the Csango minority in Romania highlighted by the Assembly as discussed in Chapter 8.

26. Ibid., paragraph 7.

27. Ibid.

28. This is an important feature of the international instruments relevant to minority protection discussed in other Chapters, especially Chapter 1 and 2.

29. Aspects of this issue are currently under discussion by the Grand Chamber of the European Court of Human Rights in the Case *Gorzelik and Others v. Poland.* See further, Chapter 1.

30. See also the conclusions on this question reached in the framework of the project "Democracy, human rights and minorities: educational and cultural aspects" undertaken in the framework of the CDCC, discussed below.

31. Various aspects of the overlap of aspects of indigenous peoples and minority rights protection, and the attitudes upheld by states in this connection are discussed elsewhere in this work, especially in Chapter 2.

32. This issue is also discussed in Chapter 2.

33. Final Activity Report on "Dispersed ethnic minorities", paragraph 10.

34. Ibid., paragraphs 11-12.

35. Ibid., paragraph 13.

36. See further, Chapter 5. Reference is made in that Chapter to the recent initiative for the establishment a "Roma forum", launched by the Finnish government. In this connection it should be mentioned that a specific "Working Party with the task of examining the question of a possible forum for Roma and Travellers" (GT-ROMS) was established by the ministers' deputies in January 2003. However, the currently Franco-Finnish proposal, as it stands at the time of writing, consists in the establishment of an "international association" outside Council of Europe structures, and relations between the forum and the Council of Europe would be formalised by an agreement of association whereby the Council of Europe would undertake to use the Forum as a consultative body while providing it with the practical means enabling it to perform this role.

37. *Report on the activities of the Council of Europe: 1999, provisional edition* (Strasbourg: Council of Europe, 2000), p. 191.

38. Ibid., p. 193.

39. *Activities of the Council of Europe: 1998 Report,* op. cit., p. 107.

40. *Report on the activities of the Council of Europe: 1999, provisional edition,* op. cit, p. 193.

41. European Treaty Series No. 93, Strasbourg, 24 November 1977. On the content of the convention see P. Thornberry and M.A. Martín Estébanez, op. cit, pp. 82-85.

42. Source: Council of Europe chart of signatures and ratifications, European Treaties, Council of Europe Internet website.

43. P. Thornberry and M.A. Martín Estébanez, op. cit., p. 84. See further, Chapter 10 in this book.

44. See below. See also Chapter 5.

45. For example, the project "Community and ethnic relations in Europe" – Final report of the community relations project of the Council of Europe, Doc. MG-CR (91) final E. The project is also described at ibid., pp. 87-89.

46. The term "new minorities" has started to be used by the Parliamentary Assembly (Chapter 8). On this term see R. Wolfrum, "The emergence of 'new minorities' as a result of migration", in C. Brölmann, R. Lefeber and M. Zieck (eds.), *Peoples and Minorities in International Law* (Dordrecht; Boston, London: Martinus Nijhoff, 1993), pp. 153-66.

47. *Activities of the Council of Europe: 1995 Report*, p. 89.

48. See P. Thornberry and M.A. Martín Estébanez, op. cit., pp. 90-91.

49. *Activities of the Council of Europe: 1995 Report*, p. 89.

50. *Activities of the Council of Europe: 1998 Report*, p. 127.

51. Ibid.

52. "Towards a migration management strategy", Final report, Reflection Group on Managing Migration in the Wider Europe (MG-MAN), Strasbourg 8 July 1998, p. 14.

53. Ibid., pp. 22-24.

54. These are presented in an upcoming section of this chapter and in Chapter 5.

55. *Activities of the Council of Europe: 1997 Report*, p. 90.

56. "Towards a migration management strategy", doc. CDMG (2000) 11.

57. The document is available on the Council of Europe Website.

58. *Activities of the Council of Europe: 2000 Report*, p. 229.

59. Ibid.

60. P. Thornberry and M.A. Martín Estébanez, op. cit., pp. 86-90, at p. 89.

61. Ibid., p. 90.

62. *Activities of the Council of Europe: 1995 Report*, p. 88.

63. See *Activities of the Council of Europe: 1997 Report*, pp. 89-90.

64. Ibid.

65. *Activities of the Council of Europe: 1998 Report*, pp. 126-27.

66. *Report on the Activities of the Council of Europe: 1999, provisional edition,* (Strasbourg: Council of Europe Publishing, 2000), pp. 219-20.

67. *Activities of the Council of Europe: 2000 Report*, p. 227.

68. J. Niessen and the European Cultural Foundation, *Diversity and Cohesion: New Challenges for the Integration of Immigrants and Minorities* (Strasbourg: Council of Europe Publishing, July 2000), pp. 27-28.

69. See M. Coussey, *Framework for Integration Policies* (Strasbourg: Council of Europe Publishing, July 2000), p. 5.

70. Ibid.

71. P. Thornberry and M.A. Martín Estébanez, op. cit., p. 85.

72. *Activities of the Council of Europe: 1998 Report*, p. 127.

73. *Report on the Activities of the Council of Europe: 1999, provisional edition* (Strasbourg: Council of Europe Publishing, 2000), p. 221.

74. See further, Chapter 5.

75. On the approaches of the Parliamentary Assembly to this and other related issues, see Chapter 8.

76. *Activities of the Council of Europe, 2000 Report*, p. 227.

77. See the preambular section of the recommendation.

78. See sections III and IV of the recommendation.

79. European Treaty Series 144, P. Thornberry and M.A. Martín Estébanez, op. cit., pp. 62-64.

80. European Treaty Series 93, P. Thornberry and M.A. Martín Estébanez, op. cit., pp. 82-85.

81. *Activities of the Council of Europe, 2000 Report*, p. 228.

82. For a discussion on political aspects connected with census elaboration see D. Kertzer and D. Arec (eds.) *Census and Identity. The Politics of Race, Ethnicity and Language in National Censuses* (New York: Cambridge University Press, 2002).

83. W. Haug, Y. Courbage, and P. Compton (eds.), "The demographic characteristics of national minorities in certain European states – Vol. 1", *Population Studies No. 30* (Strasbourg: Council of Europe, 1998).

84. W. Haug, Y. Courbage and P. Compton (eds.), "The demographic characteristics of national minorities in certain European states – Vol. 2", *Population Studies No. 31* (Strasbourg: Council of Europe, 2000).

85. P. Rees and M. Kupiszewski, "International migration and regional population dynamics in Europe: a synthesis", *Population Studies No. 32* (Strasbourg: Council of Europe, 1999).

86. D. Avramov, "People, demography and social exclusion", Population Studies No. 37 (Strasbourg: Council of Europe, 2002).

87. See W. Haug, P. Compton and Y. Courbage (eds.), "The demographic characteristics of immigrant populations", *Population Studies No. 38* (Strasbourg: Council of Europe, 2002). The 2002 issue of the yearbook *Recent demographic developments in Europe* comprises a 120-page volume accompanied by a CD-ROM presenting the main demographic characteristics of the population of forty-six European states as of January 2002. It includes developments on fertility, mortality, life expectancy, marriage and divorce, migration and the like. See *Recent demographic developments in Europe* (Strasbourg: Council of Europe, 2002).

88. Report on "Cultural rights at the Council of Europe (1949-1996)", Project "Democracy, human rights, minorities: educational and cultural aspects", CDCC, Doc. DECS/SE/DHRM (97) 5, introductory section.

89. Ibid., p. 92.

90. César Bîrzéa, *Methodology and Results of the Project "Democracy, Human Rights, Minorities: Educational and Cultural Aspects"*, Final Conference, CDCC, Doc. DECS/SE/DHRM (97) 2, p. 7.

91. On the issue of history teaching, see also the so-called "New initiative of the Secretary General" presented below.

92. Ibid., C. Bîrzéa, *Methodology and Results of the Project "Democracy, Human Rights, Minorities: Educational and Cultural Aspects"*, Final Conference, CDCC, Doc. DECS/SE/DHRM (97) 2, pp. 12-15.

93. Report on "Cultural rights at the Council of Europe (1949-1996)", CDCC, Doc. DECS/SE/DHRM (97) 5, introductory section.

94. Ibid., pp. 93-94.

95. Ibid., p. 94.

96. Final declaration, Final conference of the project "Democracy, human rights, minorities: educational and cultural aspects", CDCC, Doc. DECS/SE/DHRM (97) 8, 2.

97. See Chapter 5.

98. W. McKean, op. cit., p. 288, quoted and supported by A. Spiliopoulou-Åkermark, op. cit., pp. 27-28. See further, Chapter 1, as well as the Introduction.

99. Final declaration, Final conference of the project "Democracy, human rights, minorities: educational and cultural aspects", CDCC, Doc. DECS/SE/DHRM (97) 8, 4.

100. See A. Eide, "Cultural autonomy: concept, content, history and role in the world order", in M. Suksi (ed.), op. cit., pp. 251-76.

101. *Activities of the Council of Europe: 1998 report,* p. 139.

102. Final declaration, Strasbourg Summit, and Action Plan, section IV: "Democratic values and cultural diversity". The "Budapest Declaration for a greater Europe without dividing lines", adopted at the 104th Session of the Committee of Ministers, 7 May 1999, Appendix III: "Declaration on education for democratic citizenship, based on rights and responsibilities of citizens" (paragraph 11) and "Programme on education for democratic citizenship, based on rights and responsibilities of citizens", section 3: "Key issues", especially at 3.8. See further, Chapter 5.

103. See "Education for democratic citizenship activities", EDC project, 1997-2000, EDC activities 2001-2004, Information Document, Council for Cultural Co-operation (CDCC), DGIV/EDU/CIT (2001) 12, Strasbourg 22 March 2001, p. 2.

104. See K. Duerr, V. Spajic-Vrkaš and I. Ferreira Martins, *Strategies for Learning Democratic Citizenship,* CDCC, DECS/EDU/CIT (2000) 16, pp. 39-40.

105. Professor F. Audigier, *Basic Concepts and Core Competencies for Education for Democratic Citizenship,* CDCC, DGIV/EDU/CIT (2000) 23, Strasbourg 26 June 2000, 19-20.

106. L. Carey and Dr K. Forrester, *Sites of Citizenship: empowerment, participation and partnerships,* CDCC, DECS/EDU/CIT (99) 62 def. 2, Strasbourg 17 July 2000. Another report of the project has been elaborated by C. Bîrzéa, *Education for Democratic Citizenship: a Lifelong Learning Perspective,* DGIV/EDU/CIT (2000) 21, Strasbourg, 20 June 2000, A report on the final conference of the project has also been published: K. Forrester, *Project on "Education for Citizenship" Final Conference, Strasbourg 14-16 September 2000,* CDCC, DGIV/EDU/CIT (2000) 41, Strasbourg 28 November 2000.

107. Recommendation 2002 (12) of the Committee of Ministers to member states on education for democratic citizenship, adopted by the CoM on 16 October 2002 at the 812th meeting of the ministers' deputies, DGIV/EDU/CIT (2002) 38.

108. On this declaration, from the perspective of minority protection, see Chapter 5.

109. *Report on the Activities of the Council of Europe: 1999, provisional edition,* Strasbourg 2000, p. 287.

110. *Activities of the Council of Europe: 1998 Report,* p. 160.

111. *Report on the Activities of the Council of Europe: 1999, provisional edition,* Strasbourg 2000, p. 288.

112. Compare the content and level of criticism in the reports on France, dating from 1988; Slovenia, 1996; and Albania, 2000. These three reports, together with those on Finland, Italy, Malta, the Netherlands, the Russian Federation and Sweden are available on the Council of Europe Website, section on Cultural co-operation.

113. Ibid.

114. The original title of the transversal study was "Management of cultural diversity". See Report on the *Activities of the Council of Europe: 1999, provisional edition,* Strasbourg 2000, p. 289.

115. *Activities of the Council of Europe: 2000 Report,* pp. 270-71.

116. See "Cultural policy and action", Cultural Co-operation section on the Council of Europe Website, Description of transversal studies.

117. Ibid.

118. *Report on the Activities of the Council of Europe: 1999, provisional edition,* Strasbourg 2000, p. 251.

119. Ibid.

120. "Steering Committee on Local and Regional Democracy (CDLR), abridged report of the 28th meeting (Strasbourg 10-12 December 2001)", doc. CM (2002) 10, 27 February 2002.

121. See further, Chapter 10.

122. "Steering Committee on Local and Regional Democracy (CDLR), abridged report of the 28th meeting (Strasbourg 10-12 December 2001)", doc. CM (2002) 10, 27 February 2002, Appendix II.

123. "Final activity report of the Steering Committee on Local and Regional Democracy (CDLR) to the Committee of Ministers on the completion of the groundwork for the elaboration of a legal instrument on regional self-government", doc. CM (2002) 10 Addendum I – Part A, 1 February 2002. See further, Chapter 10.

124. The ad hoc terms of reference in this connection were given through decision No. CM/719/06092000.

125. "Steering Committee on Local and Regional Democracy (CDLR), abridged report of the 28th meeting (Strasbourg 10-12 December 2001)", doc. CM (2002), p. 5.

126. "Report on the progress in implementation of the European Outline Convention on transfrontier co-operation between territorial communities or authorities", doc. CM (2002) 10 Addendum, p. 52.

127. Ibid., p. 3.

128. Ibid., p. 5.

129. Ibid., p. 7.

130. Ibid.

131. See P. Thornberry and M.A. Martin Estebanez, op. cit, pp. 68-72. See further, Chapter 10.

132. European Treaty Series No. 159.

133. See "Steering Committee on Local and Regional Democracy (CDLR), abridged report of the 28th meeting (Strasbourg 10-12 December 2001)", doc. CM (2002), p. 4.

134. See A. Drzemczewski, "The Council of Europe's co-operation and assistance programmes with central and eastern European countries in the human rights field, 1990 to September 1993", *Human Rights Law Journal,* Vol. 14, No. 7-8, 30 September 1993, pp. 229-344. With a focus on minority protection, see P. Thornberry and M.A. Martín Estébanez, op. cit., pp. 93-96.

135. Ibid., p. 93.

136. "Activities for the development and consolidation of democratic stability (ADACS) programme 1998", Doc. SG/INF (98) 2, p. 7.

137. "Draft programme of activities for 2002: Co-operation activities – synoptic tables by country", doc. RAP-PROG (2001) 5, 12 November 2001.

138. "Council of Europe co-operation and assistance programmes with central and eastern European countries, Bi-annual report, prepared by the Directorate of Political Affairs", Doc. SG/INF (93) 4, Strasbourg, 1 September 1993. In the course of 1993 two activities were undertaken with reference to minorities, in Albania and Lithuania. See ibid., at pp. 7 and 16.

139. "Activities for the development and consolidation of democratic stability (ADACS), Annual report 1997", [ADACS annual report 1997], Doc. SG/INF (98) 1, 5.

140. See ibid., at 19, 54, 92 and 102, respectively.

141. "ADACS annual report 1998", Strasbourg, 26 February 1999, and ADACS annual report 1999, Doc. SG/INF (2000) 5, Strasbourg, February 2000. At the time of writing the annual report of ADACS for the year 2000 has not been made public.

142. See ADACS annual report 1999, Doc. SG/INF (2000) 5, Strasbourg, February 2000, p. 21.

143. See, for example, ADACS under the joint programme in relation to Ukraine, in ADACS annual report 1997, Doc. SG/INF (98) 1, p. 80.

144. Ibid., pp. 27 and 36.

145. ADACS annual report 1999, Doc. SG/INF (2000) 5, Strasbourg, February 2000, pp. 27-28.

146. Ibid., p. 35.

147. On the work of the OSCE High Commissioner in this connection see the "Country recommendations" regarding Latvia, which can be downloaded from the OSCE HCNM website: http://www.osce.org/hcnm/documents/recommendations.

148. "ADACS annual report 1999, Doc. SG/INF (2000) 5, Strasbourg, February 2000, p. 35.

149. Ibid.

150. As already indicated this "original" pact of the mid-1990s, focusing on countries of central and eastern Europe, should not be confused with the Stability Pact for South-Eastern Europe, focused mainly on the Balkan region and adopted in the late 1990s (see further, Chapter 5). On the Pact of Stability in Europe, see F. Benoît-Rohmer and H. Hardeman, "The Pact of Stability in Europe: a joint action of the Twelve in the framework of their common foreign and security policy" in *Helsinki Monitor*, Vol. 5, No. 5 (1994), pp. 39-53. See also E. Greco, *L'Europa Senza Muri: Le Sfide della Pace Fredda* (Milano: Stampa Tipomonza, 1995), pp. 94-98. For additional comments, see M.A. Martín Estébanez, "The protection of national or ethnic, religious and linguistic minorities" in *The European Union and Human Rights*, op. cit., pp. 154-56.

151. ADACS Programme 1998, op. cit., p. 199.

152. Ibid. See also ADACS annual report 1998, op. cit., pp. 29 and 37.

153. Ibid.

154. ADACS annual report 1997, Doc. SG/INF (98) 1, p. 55.

155. Ibid., p. 56.

156. ADACS annual report 1998, op. cit., p. 55.

157. ADACS annual report 1997, op. cit., p. 66.

158. See, for example, ADACS activities in relation to Moldova, and Bosnia and Herzegovina, with specific regard to the Republika Srpska, in the ADACS annual report 1997, op. cit., pp. 44 and 99.

159. For example, the conference organised in November 1997 in Plovdiv, Bulgaria, under the title "The sharing of rights and responsibilities between municipal councils and district councils", in co-operation with the Foundation for the Reform of Local Authorities. See ibid., p. 17.

160. For example, the multilateral conference on regionalisation held in Warsaw in December 1997, at ibid., p. 48.

161. Activities under the "Fiscal decentralisation programme" have included exploratory missions and the organisation of seminars. For example, the conference: "Municipal creditworthiness and financial risks of local authorities" organised in June-July 1997 in Budapest. See ibid., pp. 12 and 30, respectively.

162. For example, the hearing organised in Pardubice (Czech Republic): "Provisions for Roma in the municipality: housing/sites, health, social affairs". Ibid., p. 24.

163. This included support for the local democracy embassy of Subotica, in the Federal Republic of Yugoslavia. ADACS annual report 1998, op. cit., p. 106. See further, Chapter 10.

164. See ADACS annual report 1997, op. cit., pp. 21 and 77. See also ADACS annual report 1998, op. cit., at pp. 24 and 102.

165. See also the initiatives in this field undertaken by the CDCC mentioned above.

166. Ibid., p. 261.

167. ADACS Programme 1999, Doc. SG/INF (99) 2, Appendix I, p. 309.

168. See *Activities of the Council of Europe, 2000 Report*, p. 252.

169. Ibid.

170. "Draft programme of activities for 2002: co-operation activities – synoptic tables by country", doc. RAP-PROG (2001) 5, 12 November 2001.

171. Ibid.

172. This information is based on a non-paper made available by the Publications Department. These activities were treated under the heading "Co-operation activities 2001 on the Framework Convention for the Protection of National Minorities – DG II".

173. Albania; Bosnia and Herzegovina; Bulgaria; Croatia; Hungary; "the former Yugoslav Republic of Macedonia"; Moldova; Romania; Serbia and Montenegro; UNMIK/Kosovo; and Ukraine.

174. See "Eighth meeting of government offices for national minorities and meeting on Stability Pact projects concerning minorities, 21-22 May 2001, Strasbourg", Doc. GO 8 (e), Strasbourg 16 July 2001.

175. See further, Chapter 5.

176. Visit, on the Council of Europe Council of Europe Website, "Activities in the field of protection of national minorities", Section on "co-operation activities concerning the protection of persons belonging to national minorities (including the stability pact)".

177. See "Advisory Committee of the Framework Convention, Third Activity Report, covering the period from 1 November 2000 to 31 May 2002", doc. ACFC/INF (2002) 001, paragraph 36.

178. The leading role of the Finnish government in facilitating effective monitoring by the Advisory Committee under the Framework Convention should be highlighted in this connection. The fact that also the first country visit undertaken by the Advisory Committee in the context of formal monitoring under the Framework Convention was to Finland points to the pro-active role of this state in encouraging procedural means aimed at improving the implementation of this instrument, as well as the Languages Charter, as discussed below.

179. See "Advisory Committee of the Framework Convention, Third activity report, covering the period from 1 November 2000 to 31 May 2002)", paragraph 39.

180. See further, Chapter 2.

181. See "Advisory Committee of the Framework Convention, Third activity report, covering the period from 1 November 2000 to 31 May 2002)", paragraph 38.

182. By Andorra, Austria, Finland, Germany, Hungary, the Netherlands, the United Kingdom and Belgium (its Flemish community in particular).

183. See "Cultural policy and action", Cultural co-operation section of the Council of Europe Website, description of the MOSAIC project.

184. One of the few instances in which minority aspects were addressed directly was a multilateral seminar on cultural diversity held on 29-30 September 2000 in Slovenia, which dealt with "Public authority instruments for the protection of cultural rights of minorities". See at ibid., "Evaluation of the MOSAIC project (1998-2001)" in the section on national debates and multilateral sectorial seminars.

185. See "Cultural policy and action", Cultural co-operation section of the Council of Europe Website, "STAGE project: 2002-2003 strategy".

186. See "Cultural policy and action", Cultural co-operation section of the Council of Europe Website, project: "Intercultural Dialogue and conflict prevention".

187. As to the general Intercultural Dialogue and Conflict Prevention project, exploratory work in the framework of the latter has also resulted so far on studies entitled: "The role of culture in conflict prevention – culture plays an important role in Nordic co-operation by building bridges between differences"; "Culture and conflict in Northern Ireland"; "Sirens and muses: culture in conflict and peace processes in the Former Yugoslavia" and "Experiences about intercultural co-operation in the Barents Euro-arctic Region".

188. Other offices, often headed by special representatives of the Secretary General, have been established in Tirana, Podgorica, Sarajevo, Mostar, Yarevan, Baku, Chişinău and Skopje.

189. See "Addendum to the twenty-seventh interim report by the Secretary General on the presence of Council of Europe's experts in the Office of the Special Representative of the president of the Russian Federation for ensuring human rights and civil rights and freedoms in the Chechen Republic", doc. SG/Inf (2003) 23 Addendum, 19 May 2003, paragraph 29.

190. "Secretary General's Interim Report on the presence of Council of Europe's experts in the Office of the Russia's president Special Representative for Human Rights in Chechnya", doc. SG/Inf (2000) 27 Revised, 5 September 2000, paras. 10 and 12.

191. For an eloquent description of this lack of progress, see "One year's presence in the Chechen Republic", speech by the Secretary General on the occasion of the third part of the 2001 ordinary session of the Parliamentary Assembly of the Council of Europe (Strasbourg, 25/29 June 2001).

192. "Twenty-seventh interim report by the Secretary General on the presence of Council of Europe's experts in the Office of the Special Representative of the president of the Russian Federation for ensuring human rights and civil rights and freedoms in the Chechen Republic. Period from 19 February to 13 May 2003", doc. SG/Inf (2003) 23, 14 May 2003, paragraph 21.

193. Ibid., paragraph 28.

194. See above. See further, Chapter 5.

195. "Final report to the European Commission (Phare programme) on the implementation of the joint programme with the Council of Europe entitled "Minorities in central European countries", Council of Europe Doc. with no reference, Strasbourg, April 1998, p. 4.

196. Ibid., p. 5.

197. Ibid, appendices 2.*a*, at 21 and 3.*c*, at p. 29.

198. Ibid., p. 8. For a detailed account of the meetings, see ibid., appendices 1-3, pp. 14-32.

199. Ibid., appendix 1.*a*, p. 14.

200. For a detailed account of the study visits, see ibid., appendices 4 to 18, pp. 33-67.

201. Ibid.

202. On these issues see the Hague Recommendations regarding minority education rights (October 1996); the Lund Recommendations on the effective participation of national minorities in public life (June 1999); and the Guidelines on the use of minority languages in the broadcast media (forthcoming) adopted under the aegis of the OSCE High Commissioner on National Minorities. (The Hague: Foundation on Inter-Ethnic Relations/OSCE High Commissioner on National Minorities, http://www.hcnm.org)

203. Ibid., p. 11.

204. Ibid., appendix 1.*a*. at p. 14.

205. Ibid.

206. ADACS programme 1999, Doc SG/INF (99)2, p. 299.

207. "Final report to the European Commission on the implementation of the European Commission/Council of Europe joint programme on 'national minorities in Europe'", Strasbourg, June 2000, p. 28.

208. See ADACS programme 1999, Doc SG/INF (99)2, 301. During the 7th meeting of government offices, the question of appointment of NGO representatives was thoroughly discussed. See final report to the European Commission on the implementation of the European Commission/Council of Europe joint programme on "national minorities in Europe", Strasbourg, June 2000, p. 14. On the participation of NGOs generally, see at ibid., pp. 18-28.

209. For a full account of the activities undertaken, see ibid. (final report).

210. Joint programme between the European Commission and the Council of Europe, "National minorities in Europe", Council of Europe and European Commission, Newsletter, No. 1 revised, September 1999, p. 2.

211. On DH-MIN, see above.

212. "Final report to the European Commission on the implementation of the European Commission/Council of Europe joint programme on 'national minorities in Europe'", Strasbourg, June 2000, p. 30.

213. Joint programme between the European Commission and the Council of Europe, "National minorities in Europe", Council of Europe and European Commission, Newsletter, No. 1 revised, September 1999, pp. 3, 5, 8, 10, 12.

214. "Final report to the European Commission on the implementation of the European Commission/Council of Europe joint programme on 'national minorities in Europe", Strasbourg, June 2000, p. 29.

215. See ibid., p. 30.

216. Ibid., p. 6.

217. Ibid., p. 7.

218. Ibid.

219. Ibid.

220. Ibid., p. 11.

221. Ibid., p. 43.

222. Ibid., p. 44.

223. On the organisation of these meeting of government offices for national minorities in the context of the newly established "Co-operation activities", see above.

224. This programme provides young people interested in pursuing a politically active life (within their respective liberal profession and management functions, with national, regional or local administrators, as well as in active politics) with practical training in the necessary skills that will enable them to take responsibilities in political and civil society structures (for example on leadership, confidence-building and conflict resolution techniques). The programme promotes democratic stability by networking, including between majority and minority communities in south-east Europe, and in a wider European context.

225. The schools of political studies are local initiatives operating with the support of the Council of Europe. They provide training and development in democratic practice, including human and minority rights, for young political leaders and decision makers. At present, the Council of Europe is preparing, together with local civil society partners, the launch of a Network of Schools of Political Studies in south-east Europe, in which the question of minority–majority relations will be on the curriculum. The school in Sofia is already operational. During 2003 initial seminars will be held in Sarajevo, Chisinau, Belgrade and Pristina.

226. On the differing terminological approach between the Secretariat and the intergovernmental structures, regarding the programme as illustrated by the Vienna Summit Declaration, see Chapter 5.

227. "Confidence-building measures, – description of the programme and list of projects approved", Doc. CBM-_INF (99) 1, Strasbourg, May 1999, p. 4.

228. Ibid.

229. On the Local Democracy agencies, see Chapter 10.

230. "Confidence-building measures – description of the programme and list of projects approved", Doc. CBM_INF (97) 6, Strasbourg, July 1997, p. 4.

231. Doc. CBM-_INF (99) 1, p. 5. See also Doc. CBM-_INF (2001) 02, Strasbourg, November 2001, p. 4.

232. Ibid., p. 9.

233. Ibid., p. 9 and CBM-_INF (97) 6, p. 13, respectively. For the list of projects approved in 2003, see "The Confidence-building measures programme: presentation of the programme, guidelines for applicants for grants and application form", Directorate General of Political Affairs, Confidence-building measures programme, CBM-_INF (2003) 01A, Strasbourg, September 2003.

234. See at ibid., section on eligibility requirements, p. 4. According to the current requirements, the amounts requested under each project should not exceed 27 000 Euros, although this limit may be exceptionally raised.

235. CBM_INF (97) 6, at p. 9 and p. 14 respectively.

236. "Confidence-building measures – description of the programme and list of projects approved", Doc. CBM_INF (97) 6, Strasbourg, July 1997.

237. See "The Confidence-building measures programme: presentation of the programme, guidelines for applicants for grants and application form", p. 3.

238. "Description of the programme", Directorate General of Political Affairs, CBM_INF (2000) 02, Strasbourg, May 2000, p. 4.

239. See "The Confidence-building measures programme: presentation of the programme, guidelines for applicants for grants and application form", section on eligibility requirements, p. 4.

240. "Confidence-building measures, description of the programme and list of projects approved", Doc. CBM_INF (99) 1, Strasbourg, May 1999, p. 5.

241. Ibid., p. 6.

242. Doc. CBM_INF (99) 1, p. 5.

243. "Description of the programme" Directorate General of Political Affairs, CBM-INF (2000) 02, Strasbourg, May 2000, p. 5.

244. See "The Confidence-building measures programme: presentation of the programme, guidelines for applicants for grants and application form", section on eligibility requirements, p. 4.

245. Ibid., p. 11.

246. See Chapter 5.

Chapter 8

The evolution of the work of the Parliamentary Assembly in relation to minority protection

Introduction

The Parliamentary Assembly has been the engine of minority protection in the Council of Europe since the Organisation was established. Parliamentarians have been responsible for continually bringing the minority question onto the political agenda of the Organisation, even at times when states were most willing to ignore it. In addition, the Parliamentary Assembly has acted as the watchdog of minority protection at the Council of Europe, by devoting particular attention to specific minority situations, and by encouraging and following up the process leading to the establishment of legal standards. When appropriate, the Assembly has brought to the attention of the Council of Europe the fact that it was lagging behind other international organisations in this area of human rights protection, and made an effort to bring the Organisation to the forefront of minority protection in the international arena.

Although the general attitude of the Assembly towards minority protection has always been more positive than that of the intergovernmental structures of the Council of Europe, political considerations have also played a role in the attitudes of the Assembly on this issue. Political factors have determined the approach of the Assembly at different times to questions such as standard-setting, in the aspects of minority protection with which the Assembly has been concerned. Accordingly, the discussion of the work of the Parliamentary Assembly follows here mainly a chronological, evolutionary perspective. It treats separately the responses of the Assembly to the minority question before and after the processes of transformation in central and eastern Europe, taking the start of the 1990s as a referential breaking-point.

However, while the political climate of east–west confrontation before the 1990s, for example, strongly determined approaches to minority protection, "political determinism" has only been one among many factors influencing the Assembly. Social, economic and cultural evolution, even the evolving perceptions towards the new information technologies, to cite an example, have influenced the content of the various approaches of the Assembly to the minority question, as illustrated below.

The work of the Assembly before the 1990s

The setting of standards regarding minority protection

The work of the Parliamentary Assembly in relation to minority protection dates back to its first meeting in 1949 (the Parliamentary Assembly was then known as the Consultative Assembly), and the endeavours of its Committee on Legal and Administrative Questions in relation to the introduction of an article concerning minority protection in the European Convention on Human Rights (ECHR).[1] Although these efforts did not get sufficient support, the Parliamentary Assembly insisted on maintaining the minority question on the agenda of the Council of Europe, through the establishment of a special sub-committee of its Committee on Legal and Administrative Questions dealing with issues of minority protection. This sub-committee started to examine the possibility of adopting an additional protocol to the ECHR and prepared a draft article in this connection, which was presented to the Assembly in 1961.[2] Although the Committee of Ministers (CoM) instructed its Committee of Experts on Human Rights to study the draft, the latter deferred the issue, in view of the progress of the Belgian Linguistics case brought before the European Commission of Human Rights.[3]

In 1973 the committee of experts finally took a negative view on the need for an additional protocol, asserting, among other things, that from the strictly legal point of view there was no need for one in the context of the European Convention.[4] In spite of the fact that the activity of the Assembly was to adopt a lower profile in the following years, the Assembly did not abandon the issue totally. The expert report "The status of minorities and ethnic groups in the member states of the Council of Europe", elaborated by E. Grisel at the initiative of the Legal Affairs Committee of the Assembly and presented in 1988, is an illustration of this. The approach adopted in the study aimed, for example, at identifying existing rules and "possible future guarantees which would be desirable in the future".[5]

Other minority protection concerns

Minority questions were, however, not going to drop off the Parliamentary Assembly's agenda. The Parliamentary Assembly committees – on culture and education, on relations with European non-member countries, on migration, refugees and demography, and on regional planning and local authorities – would, in particular, be responsible for the adoption of various reports and subsequent Assembly resolutions and recommendations to the CoM, in relation both to general issues concerning minority protection and specific situations where the fate of minorities was at stake. An account of some of these, which give an idea of the wide spectrum covered by the Assembly, is presented below.

i. *General minority issues*

A first example at hand is the issue of minority languages. In Recommendation 928 (1981)[6] on the educational and cultural problems of minority languages and dialects in Europe, the Assembly made suggestions to the CoM with regard to state action in relation to: i. the adoption of correct toponymical names based on the original language of each territory, however small;[7] ii. the gradual adoption of children's mother tongues for their education;[8] iii. respect and official use of standardised minority languages, and for their current use in higher education and by the local mass media, in so far as this approach is favoured by the communities which speak them; and iv. in all areas which have a language of their own and some degree of administrative structure within the state of which they are a part, the possibility of adoption of that language by those areas' authorities as the official or joint official language.[9] Further, the Assembly recommended that "the Committee of Ministers consider the feasibility of undertaking action for the purpose of gathering and disseminating information on developments in this field".[10]

However, it was necessary to wait for the adoption of the European Charter for Regional or Minority Languages on 5 November 1992 for such a proposal to materialise, with the establishment of the periodical reporting mechanism under the charter.[11] In the Assembly's Opinion No. 142 (1988) on Resolution 192 (1988) on regional or minority languages in Europe, adopted by the Standing Conference of Local and Regional Authorities of Europe, the Parliamentary Assembly strongly endorsed the initiative of the Standing Conference of Local and Regional Authorities of Europe (Congress/CLRAE) in preparing the Charter.[12]

In Recommendation 1043 (1986), on Europe's linguistic and literary heritage, the Assembly showed its concern in relation to other aspects of linguistic diversity, and in particular "the new challenges and possible threats posed for many European languages by the rapid industrialisation of natural languages and the increased commercialisation of language products, as a consequence of the growing interface between these natural languages on the one hand and informatics and electronics on the other".

The Assembly recommended that the CoM "defend and encourage multilingualism in Europe, both in written material (whether in book or other form) and the audiovisual media" and "take active steps to safeguard

Europe's linguistic and literary heritage, and encourage its continued creative development". It also recommended that the CoM "urge the governments of member states to support through appropriate measures the development of the language industries with due respect for Europe's linguistic diversity".[13] This wary approach to the impact of new technologies and commercialisation on cultural and linguistic diversity was to be slightly revised one year later.

In Recommendation 1067 (1987) on the cultural dimension of broadcasting in Europe, the Parliamentary Assembly adopted a more positive approach. The Assembly expounded on the possible usefulness of these developments for promoting diversity, including by "increasing the opportunities and opening up new fields of cultural creation and expression" and "assisting awareness of other European languages and cultures". This change in approach followed the proposal made at the Conference of Ministers responsible for Cultural Affairs held in Sintra in September 1987 for developing practical measures to promote European cultural diversity, taking into account the development of communication technologies.[14]

The Assembly kept pointing, however, to the visible risks, including: "the undermining of the cultural identity of smaller countries and minor language groups, and of the cultural diversity of Europe as a whole".[15] The Assembly recommended, among other things, that the CoM "draw up proposals for maintaining and encouraging the linguistic diversity of the mass media, for example by: i. joint production funds on which minor language nations may also draw; ii. the inclusion of minor language interviews in news bulletins; iii. ensuring the right for national languages, and where appropriate minor local and regional languages, to be carried on national, regional and local networks".[16]

The Assembly made use of the momentum created after the adoption of the European Outline Convention on Transfrontier Co-operation between Territorial Communities or Authorities, by Council of Europe member states in May 1980,[17] to address the cultural aspect of this co-operation in particular. In Recommendation 1013 (1985), on transfrontier co-operation in Europe,[18] the Parliamentary Assembly recommended that the CoM foster "transfrontier cultural co-operation intended in particular to promote teaching of the languages of neighbouring regions" and remove "all obstacles to transfrontier cultural exchanges catering for national minorities and their identity".[19]

In this recommendation, the Assembly built on pre-existing OSCE commitments in the area of co-operation and exchanges in the field of culture.[20] It adopted an advanced approach, as it specifically addressed the question of minority protection in relation to countries of central and eastern Europe, at a time when east–west dialogue in this field was characterised by a climate of confrontation. However, it also adopted a discriminatory approach, as it aimed specifically at the development of transfrontier co-operation in peripheral Council of Europe member countries bordering states from the Eastern bloc.

The Assembly addressed the issue of long-term migration in Recommendation 1034 (1986), on the improvement in Europe of mutual understanding between ethnic communities "daring to live together". Taking a realistic approach, at the time yet to be reflected in legal standards, the Assembly noted "that a very large majority of foreigners who have lived in Europe for a number of years have not chosen to return to their countries of origin, notwithstanding policies to encourage this adopted in certain host countries" and recommended that the CoM urgently invite the governments of the member states "to give existing or expressly created national committees responsibility for" among other things, "launching initiatives – and where appropriate, enhancing those already in existence – aimed at improving understanding between ethnic communities".[21]

One year later, in Recommendation 1089 (1988),[22] on improving community relations the Assembly recommended that the CoM "take into consideration the existence in member states of large minorities from non-member countries when considering the legal and political rights of foreigners"; "prepare a comparative study of the media policies pursued by the different member states with regard to migrant communities and ethnic minorities"; and "devote adequate resources to the project on community relations."[23]

The approach of the Parliamentary Assembly reflected an increasing awareness of the need for new attitudes to the phenomenon of long-term migration in Europe, based on recognition of the identity of the communities concerned. These new attitudes implied not only the recognition of basic economic and social rights to the members of these communities, an approach guiding intergovernmental action at the Council of Europe during the 1970s, as reflected in the text of the European Convention on the Legal Status of Migrant Workers,[24] but also the granting of basic legal status and at least a certain level of political participation to migrants. It was necessary to wait until the early 1990s for the CoM to take up this new approach, starting with the adoption of the Convention on the Participation of Foreigners in Public Life at Local Level on 5 February 1992.[25]

The recommendations of the Assembly started to focus increasingly on various aspects relevant to the legal status of migrants and to the interaction between the members of these communities and society at large. This is the case with Recommendation 1081 (1988) on problems of nationality in mixed marriages; Recommendation 1082 (1988) on the right of permanent residence for migrant workers and members of their families; Recommendation 1093 (1989) on the education of migrants' children; Recommendation 1148 (1991) on the Europe of 1992 and migration policies; Recommendation 1154 (1991) on North African migrants in Europe; Recommendation 1187 (1992) on relations between migrants and trade unions; and Recommendation 1206 (1993) on the integration of migrants and community relations.

In addressing a different issue also relevant to minority protection – freedom of conscience and religion – the Assembly adopted Resolution 908 (1988). In this text the Assembly recommended that the CoM invite the governments of the Council of Europe member states to ensure that the concluding document of the forthcoming OSCE conference to be held in Vienna, or any other forthcoming conference within the CSCE process that took place in any COMECON country, would include the content of an extensive list of rights in the area of freedom of conscience and religion.[26] Actually the comprehensive list proposed by the Assembly was quite adequately reflected in the OSCE Vienna concluding document adopted in January 1999, with the proviso that the OSCE document was formulated in terms of state duties rather than subjective rights for those concerned.[27] This proposal of the Assembly is still the most thorough document adopted by a Council of Europe organ in relation to freedom of religion. The Framework Convention for the Protection of National Minorities contains only a two-and-a-half line article on this issue (Article 8).[28]

ii. *Specific minority situations*

As already indicated, in addition to questions of general interest for minority protection, the Parliamentary Assembly also became increasingly concerned with addressing specific situations where the fate of minorities was at stake. It should be noted, however, that the minority situations directly addressed corresponded only to countries that were not members of the Council of Europe. Although the situation in member states with important minority concerns, such as Turkey and Cyprus, was the object of various Parliamentary Assembly recommendations during that time,[29] these recommendations did not make particular reference to the situation of minorities in those countries, and in the case of Cyprus referred only to the fate of the majority communities resulting from the actual division of the island. The new minorities thereby created would be liable to become only indirect beneficiaries of some of the measures proposed.[30]

Parliamentary Assembly recommendations focused their attention instead on minority situations in non-member countries of central and eastern Europe. The Assembly often took OSCE commitments and negotiations as its reference point on its proposals for standards and instruments aiming at the facilitation of the implementation of minority rights in those countries.[31] A common feature of the recommendations adopted by the Parliamentary Assembly during this period was its direct appeal for the states concerned to take concrete measures to remedy their minority situations, as well as its call upon the governments of the Council of Europe member states to exercise political pressure in their relations with the states concerned.

By way of example, in 1983 the Parliamentary Assembly addressed, in its Recommendations 795 (1983) and 972 (1983), the situation of the Jewish community and the German ethnic minority in the Soviet Union. In the first of these recommendations, which followed a series of recommendations on the same topic adopted by the Assembly during the late 1960s and the 1970s, among other things the Assembly qualified the Jewish community as "an oppressed cultural minority" and recognised its cause to be an issue of international concern.[32] In the latter recommendation the Assembly pointed to the violations of the rights of the German minority in the areas of freedom of religious worship; rights to education and non-discrimination; free exchange of information; freedom of speech and freedom to travel abroad. In both resolutions the Assembly urged the speeding-up of procedures for obtaining exit visas by members of these communities.

In 1984 it was again the situation of these particular minorities, but in Romania, that became the focus of the Assembly's attention. The argument was that, among the different minorities in Romania, these were the communities with a stronger incentive to emigrate.[33] Thus, not only human rights concerns but also the political interests present in some western European states could be identified as a driving force behind these decisions.

The situation of the Jews in the Soviet Union became an object of renewed concern for the Assembly, and in particular the continual attitude of anti-semitism prevailing in many areas of Soviet life and the restricted possibilities for Jews to emigrate to Israel or to other countries.[34] The Assembly made an appeal for the Soviet government to adopt various measures to remedy the situation and for the governments of the Council of Europe member states to exercise pressure in this regard. Also "the situation of the German ethnic minority in the Soviet Union" was to become an object of renewed concern for the Assembly two years later.[35]

In the first paragraph of Resolution 846 (1985) on the situation of ethnic and Muslim minorities in Bulgaria, the Assembly referred generally to the "right of members of ethnic minorities to enjoy their own culture, to profess and exercise their religion, to speak their own language, to keep their traditions and customs and to preserve their national and cultural identity" by reference to the OSCE Helsinki Final Act and the International Covenant on Civil and Political Rights. The Assembly expressed concern about the "alarming reports that members of the ethnic and Muslim minorities in Bulgaria are being deprived of the right to enjoy their own culture, to profess and exercise their religion and to speak their own language". Also, parliamentarians were concerned about the "information that the Bulgarian authorities, in their attempt at complete assimilation of the Turkish minority, have undertaken a systematic campaign in order to force the members of this minority to adopt Bulgarian names" and other acts of violence against the minorities.

Once more, the Assembly requested the government of the country among other things, to adopt various measures to put an end to the repressive policies against the Turkish minority and to the violation of the rights of members of the ethnic and Muslim minorities, and invited the governments of the Council of Europe member states to report the requests made in their contacts with the Bulgarian government and within the framework of the Helsinki Process. The Assembly even authorised its Committee on Relations with European Non-Member Countries and its rapporteur to visit the areas concerned and to report back to the committee on the results of their findings. A visit by a sub-commission of the Assembly was carried out in 1989.[36]

Another interesting example, in relation to the question of freedom of conscience and religion in particular, is Resolution 908 (1988) on the situation of the Church and freedom of religion in eastern Europe. In this resolution, the Assembly addressed the specific situations of several religious minorities in various central and eastern European states simultaneously, and as part of a larger package of concerns in relation to religious freedom in those countries. The requests of the Assembly included: the recognition of the Ukrainian (Uniate) Catholic Church in the Soviet Union and the end of the persecution of the Lithuanian Catholic Church; an end to the persecution of ethnic Turks and to the elimination of the Muslim identity in Bulgaria; an end to Romania's resistance to any improvement in its treatment of churches and religious believers, and to its plans to eliminate villages with their churches and Christian heritage; as well as an end to the ban on religious belief and practice in Albania.[37]

In this resolution, the Assembly recalled its previous Recommendation 1086 (1988) of the same title, in which a reference had been included to previous resolutions on the situation of the Jews in the Soviet Union, on the situation of minorities in Romania and on the situation of the ethnic and Muslim minorities in Bulgaria,[38] and focused its attention on the current situation in the Soviet Union.

394

Finally, the Assembly was also to take a minority-conscious approach to the changes starting to take place in Europe due to the fall of the Berlin Wall and, in particular, the population movements, especially of persons of German origin, taking place at that time. In Recommendation 1106 (1989) on the reception and settlement in the Federal Republic of Germany of refugees and settlers of German origin coming from countries in central and eastern Europe, after recalling the OSCE commitments in relation to free movement of persons, the Assembly considered that "any interference with minorities' right to their own cultural identity constitutes a violation of human rights".[39]

The Assembly welcomed the efforts made by the governments of member states, and particularly the government of the Federal Republic of Germany, to assist refugees and settlers while "paying tribute to the policy pursued by the Hungarian authorities, in co-operation with those of the Federal Republic of Germany, with a view to preserving the cultural identity of the German minority resident in Hungary".[40] At the same time, the Assembly praised the adoption of a liberal policy on the granting of visas to Polish nationals of German origin, while expressing its rejection of the approaches and measures taken by the authorities of Romania and the German Democratic Republic in connection with minorities and the visa applications submitted in these countries.

The work of the Assembly during the 1990s

During the 1990s, the Parliamentary Assembly again showed a higher degree of awareness of minority questions than the CoM.[41] At the beginning of the decade the Assembly continued to address the minority issue as a general phenomenon rather than concentrating on specific country situations alone. As to this latter aspect, it showed a clear inclination to focus on the problems concerning minorities in countries of central and eastern Europe. The series of changes taking place in Europe, and the ensuing conflicts, encouraged the Assembly to address the issue of international standard-setting with renewed impetus, and this issue was to occupy a prominent place on its agenda.

Standard-setting regarding minority protection

On the basis of a report of the Committee on Legal Affairs and Human Rights' rapporteur Mr Brincat,[42] the Assembly adopted Recommendation 1134 (1990) on the rights of minorities. In this recommendation the Assembly stated that:

> with the change towards democracy in central and eastern European states, grave minority problems also had come to light in these countries. These problems had been ignored and neglected for many

years by authoritarian rule. It is obvious that the Council of Europe must have the interests of minorities at heart – one of the main assignments given to this Organisation being the maintenance and further realisation of human rights and fundamental freedoms. Minorities was one of the major subjects for co-operation and consultation with the countries of central and eastern Europe.[43]

The Assembly also stated that "adequate legal protection of minorities requires certain minimum standards" and proceeded to indicate what it considered to be "basic principles on the rights of minorities". This included equal access to the courts for all citizens, and their protection under the ECHR and its supervisory machinery, including the right of individual petition.

The Assembly advocated the introduction of a "general" non-discrimination clause in the ECHR, possibly without the constraints affecting the clause in Article 14 of the Convention,[44] an initiative which would consolidate only in the early 2000s, with the adoption of Protocol 12 to the ECHR. In addition, the Assembly endorsed the adoption of "special measures" in favour of minorities by reason of their "special situation". Further, the Assembly advocated that minorities "shall be allowed to have free and unimpeded peaceful contacts with citizens of other states with which they share a common origin or heritage, without however, infringing the principle of the territorial integrity of states".

The call for an unconstrained application to minorities of the principle of non-discrimination and their possibility for maintaining contacts across frontiers was already present in the Vienna Document adopted by the OSCE almost two years earlier. Similarly, the favourable view of the Assembly towards the adoption of specific measures towards minorities drew upon the provision contained in the OSCE Copenhagen Document adopted the same year as the resolution. However, certain innovative features of these "basic principles" in relation to OSCE documents were also present. One was the highlighting of the ECHR as an instrument of minority protection and the other was the fact that the favourable stance in relation to positive measures was not subject to conditions. In the OSCE Copenhagen Document the adoption of special measures was geared towards "ensuring to persons belonging to minorities full equality with the other citizens in the exercise and enjoyment of human rights and fundamental freedoms".[45]

In defining minority rights the Assembly mainly drew upon standards already adopted within the framework of other international organisations, and in particular the OSCE, taking actually a reductionist approach as to the level and scope of the standards accepted by the European states in the OSCE framework. Some aspects of the content and the approach adopted in the recommendation deserve to be highlighted. An innovative feature, in addressing "basic principles", is the reference to the term "minorities" without any further qualifications. This would imply that, in the opinion of the Assembly at that time, a minimum set of principles should have been applicable to any type of minority.

Another interesting feature is that the Assembly mostly makes use of a language of "subjective rights", which refer both to minorities as such and to their members. These approaches diverged from mainstream Council of Europe thinking, particularly at the intergovernmental level. As the Framework Convention for the Protection of National Minorities illustrates, member states of the Council of Europe have been, and are still reluctant to deal with minority issues in terms of subjective rights. Similarly, in Council of Europe documents, references to minority protection have been mostly worded in the following terms "persons belonging to national minorities".

The categorisation which the Assembly established also deserves attention from a formal perspective. Following its statement on "basic principles on the rights of minorities" generally, the Assembly first adopted principles in relation to "national minorities" and then additional ones in relation to "linguistic minorities". The Assembly included under the category of national minorities "religious, linguistic, cultural, or other characteristics", an example later to be followed in the Framework Convention.

However, the Assembly simultaneously devoted a parallel section to one additional category of minority (that is, linguistic), for which specific rights are recognised. Thus, this is done on the basis of the selection of one among the various sets of characteristics already considered under the concept "national minorities". The question arises as to whether the Assembly was just adopting a cascading approach, by which additional rights are granted to one particular sub-category of national minority, or whether linguistic minorities were considered as a category independent from that of national minorities, entitled to a different set of rights. The work undertaken at the initiative of the Congress of Local and Regional Authorities of Europe (henceforth: "Congress") for the elaboration of a specific instrument devoted to linguistic matters and the recommendation adopted by the Assembly in this context, may have been at the origin of this separate treatment at this early stage of conceptual elaboration.[46]

An important provision introduced in the recommendation is the statement of the right of national minorities "to participate fully in decision-making about matters which affect the preservation and development of their identity and in the implementation of those decisions", which will only find a denaturalised, reductionist reflection in Article 15 of the Framework Convention.[47] The provision on the right of national minorities "to be recognised as such by the states in which they live" remains unparalleled by any international instrument relevant to minority protection in Europe. It addresses a question which has not only become one of the major issues in relation to the implementation and effectiveness of the Framework Convention,[48] but has also affected the implementation of almost every other international legal instrument relevant to minority protection.

Nevertheless, it has not found further reflection in the Council of Europe's thinking. Thus, the provisions of the recommendation with more practical significance have been those concerning the Assembly's insistence that "the Council of Europe is the appropriate organisation for the elaboration of a legal instrument in this field" and its recommendation "that the Committee of Ministers draw up a Protocol to the European Convention on Human Rights or a special Council of Europe convention to protect the rights of minorities".[49]

In Order No. 456 (1990), adopted by the Parliamentary Assembly on the same day as Recommendation 1134, the Assembly instructed its Committee on Legal Affairs and Human Rights to organise a parliamentary conference or symposium "to further elaborate and define the principles on the stated rights of minorities which may be included in an additional protocol to the European Convention on Human Rights or in a special Council of Europe convention".[50] It also decided to play a role of mediation and conciliation in minority conflicts whenever such a role was requested and accepted by its enlarged Bureau. It invited its enlarged Bureau to set up a special group of rapporteurs in this connection.

Following the Order of the Assembly, a colloquy on "The rights of minorities" was organised in Paris on 13 and 14 November 1991 "to suggest to Council of Europe member governments constructive action which would take effect rapidly".[51] In the final declaration of the colloquy, the two rapporteurs (two parliamentarians, Mr Brincat and Mr Worms) indirectly pointed to the opportunities which enlargement of the Council of Europe could open in relation to the role of the Organisation with regard to minority protection.[52] The rapporteurs put forward a series of proposals by the participants for both urgent and long-term action by the Council of Europe. With regard to urgent action, they advocated the adoption of a declaratory text, which would be adopted rapidly by the Council of Europe, bringing together the points (concerning minority protection) on which there was already agreement and which could be used as a reference base for decisions or action in specific cases.

They also advocated that the Council of Europe rapidly create a suitable mediation instrument for urgent, on-the-spot action. As to the composition of the body to be created in this connection, they pointed to representatives from the highest courts in the Council of Europe member states, as well as the European Commission of Human Rights and European Court of Human Rights. As to the functions to be given to this body, they referred to powers: i. to observe and record, including the "constant monitoring of changes in the situation of minorities in all states in Europe"; ii. to advise and prevent, "taking immediate action to help states and minorities to define the rules governing their relations before open conflict developed"; and iii. to discuss and mediate, "in cases of open conflict, it would be expected to draw on its international backing and own achievements in making on-the-spot efforts to find ways of reconciling the parties in dispute and lasting and peaceful solutions to the problems which opposed them".[53] Although discussions on the establishment of a mediation instrument of the kind were engaged upon at various levels of the Organisation, these were to diminish with the consolidation of the negotiations leading to the establishment of the unipersonal institution of the OSCE High Commissioner on National Minorities in 1992.[54]

With regard to long-term action, "the participants think it essential to give the rights of minorities ... a solid basis in international law". The rapporteurs further indicated that the Parliamentary Assembly:

> and its relevant committees now have everything they need to move ahead in making their recommendations to the Committee of Ministers more specific and in defining a realistic and gradual implementation strategy. One crucial point remains: the political ability and determination of the Committee of Ministers, in other words of the Council of Europe's member governments, to make the decisive move into action.[55]

The rapporteurs further pointed to the fact that:

> some west European States which have traditionally defined 'nation' and 'citizenship' in terms which make it hard to recognise minorities, in practice and above all in law, have succeeded in delaying the introduction of these new rights. This hanging back has now become dangerous. Unless minorities are given the right to preserve certain aspects of their own identity within broader state structures, they may well try to win that right by violent means and to guarantee it by setting up a new and supposedly homogeneous state (this is both impossible and dangerous, particularly since it results in a new flood of refugees). The actual effect of this would be long-term disruption of Europe's essential balance at the very time when Europe is trying to recreate its unity by rediscovering the common basis of its civilisation and using its diversity in the service of a shared endeavour. Promoting the rights of minorities today is an essential part of building the Europe of tomorrow.[56]

The far-sighted conclusions of the colloquy, which were incorporated in the Parliamentary Assembly report on the rights of minorities of 29 January 1992, prepared by Mr Brincat and Mr Worms (the same rapporteurs of the colloquy), were taken up by Recommendation 1177 (1992) of the Parliamentary Assembly. In this recommendation, the Assembly took note of the terms of reference given by the CoM to its Steering Committee for Human Rights (CDDH), according to which "consideration is to be given to the proposal for a European convention for the protection of minorities".[57] Nevertheless, the Assembly still insisted on the need to elaborate an additional protocol to the European Convention on Human Rights.

The Assembly also indicated its preference for the supplementary drawing up and rapid adoption by the CoM of a declaration, setting the basic principles relating to the rights of minorities "although this can in no way substitute for a legal instrument" (that is, the additional protocol to the ECHR). According to the Assembly, this declaration "should serve as a basic reference against which applications for membership of the Council of Europe can be judged".[58] The additional proposal for urgent action made at the colloquy, regarding the creation of a suitable mediation instrument, was also included in the recommendation. On a different front, the Assembly, although expressing awareness of certain weaknesses in the draft European Charter for Regional or Minority Languages, recommended that the CoM conclude its work on the charter as quickly as possible and that it do its utmost to ensure its rapid implementation.[59]

The Assembly requested that this recommendation be implemented by the CoM in the same year as its adoption, before 1 October 1992. In Order No. 474 (1992) on the rights of minorities adopted on the same day as Recommendation 1177, the Parliamentary Assembly stated that "should the Committee of Ministers be unable to implement this Recommendation by 1 October 1992, the Assembly instructs its Committee on Legal Affairs and Human Rights, its Political Affairs Committee and its Committee on Culture and Education to prepare as soon as possible a draft protocol on minorities to the European Convention on Human Rights and a draft mediation instrument".[60]

The perception by the Parliamentary Assembly that no swift progress was being made by the CoM along the lines of its recommendations is evidenced by the content of the Assembly's Written Question No. 344, addressed to the CoM on 7 May 1992. The Assembly asked, among other things, "why the protection of the rights of minorities was not included in the agenda for the 90th session (7 May 1992) of the Committee of Ministers, as was apparently planned ..." and "when it is planning to adopt the European Charter on Regional or Minority Languages".[61] In reply, the CoM indicated that it never intended to include the situation of minorities as a separate item at the 90th session of the CoM. It also referred the Assembly to CoM Recommendation R (92) 10 on the implementation of the rights of minorities,[62] adopted by the CoM on 21 May 1992, and stated the new, ad hoc terms of reference given to the CDDH:

> to study the possibility, having in mind the principle of complementarity of the work of the Council of Europe and that of the CSCE, of formulating specific legal standards relating to the protection of national minorities in the spirit of the European Convention on Human Rights. Work carried out within the United Nations will also be taken into account. The Committee will carry out its work in the light of the draft European convention for the protection of minorities drawn up by the European Commission for Democracy through Law[63] as well as the Austrian proposal for an additional protocol to the European Convention on Human Rights[64] and other proposals for legal solutions.[65]

With regard to the adoption of the European Charter for Regional or Minority Languages, the CoM announced its decision to open this convention for signature.[66]

In spite of this reply, the persistent perception by the Assembly that intergovernmental activity was not developing along its own line of thinking, in relation to the urgent provision of an effective guarantee of minority protection, led the Assembly to elaborate its own proposal for an additional protocol to the European convention on the rights of minorities. The proposal was based on the "Report on an additional protocol on the rights of minorities to the European Convention on Human Rights" prepared by the Committee on Legal Affairs and Human Rights, rapporteur Mr Worms.[67]

In the well-known Recommendation 1201 (1993) on an additional protocol on the rights of national minorities to the European Convention on Human Rights, adopted by the Parliamentary Assembly on 1 February 1993, the Assembly referred to its previous requests to the CoM made in Recommendations 1134 (1990) and 1177 (1992), as well as to its Orders Nos. 456 (1990) and 474 (1992) on the rights of minorities. Although the Assembly welcomed the adoption of the European Charter for Regional or Minority Languages on 22 June 1992, which had met one of its requests, it pointed to the fact that the question of the rapid implementation of the charter still remained.

The Assembly fully supported the terms of reference given by the CoM to the CDDH and subsequently to its Committee of Experts on Issues relating to the Protection of National Minorities (DH-MIN).[68] It insisted, however, that the CoM adopt an additional protocol on the rights of minorities to the European Convention on Human Rights. It ought to do so by drawing on the "proposal for an additional protocol to the Convention for the Protection of Human Rights and Fundamental Freedoms, concerning persons belonging to national minorities", which the Assembly itself had elaborated. The text of this proposal was appended to the text of the recommendation.

The content of the proposal for an additional protocol has already been described in detail elsewhere.[69] However, some aspects of its text deserve to be highlighted here. The proposal illustrates the efforts of the Assembly to provide a more developed text than that which the Assembly itself had provided in Recommendation 1134 (1990). It no longer attempts to present a sketchy picture of the rights of "national" and "linguistic" minorities, but rather to take a thorough, developed approach, dealing with most of the main conceptual questions relating to minority protection.

Additional elements in the definition of the concept "national minority" by the Assembly are introduced in Article 1 of the proposal, including the idea of "sufficient representation" and what has come to be known as the "subjective element" that is, the will of the members of a minority to preserve together a common identity. The principle that the exercise of minority rights should be a matter of free, personal choice and the fact that no disadvantage must result from such choice is introduced by the Assembly in Article 2, while in Article 3 the issue of the individual and collective exercise of minority rights is touched upon.

Besides the introduction of a general non-discrimination clause in Article 4 of its proposal, the Assembly significantly develops its list of minority-specific rights, especially in the linguistic and educational spheres. Article 11, which refers to the right of persons belonging to a national minority, in the regions where they are in a majority, "to have at their disposal appropriate local or autonomous authorities or to have a special status, matching the specific historical and territorial situation and in accordance with the domestic legislation of the state" has generated strong reactions, especially on the part of a significant number of states. Given that the wording of this article closely relates to Provision 35 of the 1990 Copenhagen Document, adopted almost three years earlier by OSCE participating states, it was probably its introduction as a subjective right rather than as an example of good practice that gave rise to such polemic.

The reference to collective rights included in draft Article 12 has also been polemical, in spite of the fact that the proposed protocol adheres to the wording "persons" belonging to national minorities throughout its text. The express extension of the protection provided under the proposal, to "the persons belonging to the majority in the whole of the state but who constitute a minority in one or several of its regions" under Article 13,[70] seems to anticipate the diverging views of the Human Rights Committee. The Human Rights Committee, in its consideration of the merits of the case *Ballantyne et al. v. Canada*, concerning the applicability of Article 27 of the International Covenant on Civil and Political Rights to members of the majority in the state as a whole which constitute a minority within any of the territorial subdivisions of the state, observed that: "the minorities referred to in Article 27 are minorities within such a State, and not minorities within any province. A group may constitute a majority in a province but still be a minority in a State and thus be entitled to the benefits of Article 27. English-speaking citizens of Canada cannot be considered a linguistic minority".[71]

The views of the Human Rights Committee on this point have raised much controversy, and even a substantial share of the members of the Committee expressed their disagreement with the fact that persons are necessarily excluded from the protection of Article 27:

> where their group is an ethnic, linguistic or cultural minority in an autonomous province of a State, but is not clearly a numerical minority in the State itself, taken as a whole entity. The criteria for determining what is a minority in a State (in the sense of Article 27) has not yet been considered by the Committee and does not need to be foreclosed by a decision in the present matter, which can in any event be determined on other grounds.[72]

To conclude, although Parliamentary Assembly Recommendation 1201 (1993) has broken new ground in relation both to the approaches of the Assembly to minority protection and to international standards in the matter, the apprehension with which the recommendation was received by states could have been at least partly dissipated with a comprehensive look at its content and wording.

Actually, the protocol proposal can be criticised for being too restrictive in certain aspects, such as the introduction of a citizenship requirement in the definition of "national minority" introduced in its Article 1. Other international standards, including universal ones, such as the UN Declaration on the Rights of Persons Belonging to National or Ethnic, Religious and Linguistic Minorities, do not introduce such a restriction, and the same applies to existing practice under international instruments such as the Framework Convention (see Chapter 2) and OSCE commitments.[73] Besides the structuring of the proposed protocol around the exercise of individual rights already mentioned, Article 14 allows for restrictions in the exercise of the rights envisaged, based on considerations such as national security, territorial integrity or public safety, the prevention of disorder or crime, the protection of health and morals, and the protection of the rights and freedoms of others.

As the Assembly itself has pointed out (see below) several bilateral treaties – including those between Hungary and Slovakia, Hungary and Romania, and Romania and the Ukraine – have incorporated this recommendation,[74] illustrating that its text was considered as an appropriate legal option by a substantial number of Council of Europe states. Actually, this treaty incorporation may have been encouraged by the fact that Recommendation 1201 has become one of the key instruments to which state candidates to Council of Europe membership must adhere in order to fulfil the requirements for acceding to the Organisation. Also, in the post-accession monitoring procedures it has become a key reference.[75] This has progressively made Recommendation 1201 a commonly accepted Council of Europe instrument in the context of the process of enlargement of the Organisation.[76]

In spite of the Assembly's insistence that the CoM adopt an additional protocol on the rights of minorities to the ECHR along the lines of its proposal, the decisions of the Vienna Summit Declaration were evidence that Council of Europe states were not ready to follow this path.[77] In Recommendation 1231 (1994) on the follow-up to the Vienna Summit, the Assembly deeply regretted that the summit did not follow its recommendation on an additional protocol and recommended that the CoM revise its decision in this connection. The Assembly adopted, however, a pragmatic approach and further recommended that if the CoM maintained its position, "at least the principles formulated in the framework of the CSCE and laid down in the Copenhagen Document be enshrined in the framework convention and in the additional protocol on cultural rights" and that the Assembly be consulted at an early stage of the development of these texts.

Following the adoption of the Framework Convention, and during the week of its opening for signature, the Assembly adopted Recommendation 1255 (1995) under its urgent procedure.[78] In this recommendation the Assembly expressed reservations as to both the content of the Framework Convention and its legal nature, as well as the fact that the convention was weakly worded and that it formulated a number of vaguely defined objectives and principles, "the observation of which will be an obligation of the contracting states but not a right which individuals may invoke".[79]

The Assembly also expressed criticism that "its implementation machinery is feeble and there is a danger that, in fact, the monitoring procedures may be left entirely to the governments". The Assembly recommended that the CoM: i. "make sure that the Advisory Committee to be set up ... is as independent, effective and transparent as possible" (making two specific proposals in relation to the composition of the committee to facilitate this);[80] ii. allows the Advisory Committee to draw its information from a wide range of sources and to act on its own initiative; and iii. allows the Advisory Committee to enter into a dialogue with the government of the contracting state concerned and to publish its reports and recommendations with the authorisation of that government.[81]

Further, the Assembly recommended that the CoM bring to a satisfactory and rapid conclusion its work on a draft protocol to the ECHR "in the cultural field by provisions guaranteeing individual rights, in particular for persons belonging to national minorities", quoting directly from the Vienna Summit Declaration. The Assembly also recommended that the CoM submit this draft protocol, once concluded, to the Assembly for its opinion. As already discussed in Chapter 5, in spite of this groundwork laid by the Assembly, these recommendations have not been followed so far.

In addition, the Assembly introduced a list of provisions of Recommendation 1201 (1993) on national minorities that could be included in an additional protocol on cultural rights. This list included provisions dealing with the following matters:

- the right to express, preserve and develop one's cultural identity;
- the individual and collective exercise of rights and freedoms by persons belonging to national minorities;
- equality before the law and non-discrimination;
- the right to use the minority language in private and in public, including in the audiovisual sector;
- the right to use first names and surnames in the minority language;
- the right to use the minority language in relations with the administration;
- the right to display local names, street names, and the like, in the minority language;
- the right to learn and receive education in the minority language, including in state educational and training establishments, located in accordance with the geographical distribution of the minority;
- the right to set up and manage schools, educational and training establishments;
- the right to an effective remedy;
- the right to free and unimpeded contacts with the citizens of another country;
- the relation between the text of the protocol and domestic legislation and other international instruments.

Following the initial steps of intergovernmental work on an additional protocol to the ECHR "in the cultural field by provisions guaranteeing individual rights, in particular for persons belonging to national minorities", resulting from the mandate of the Vienna Summit Declaration, and the subsequent decision of the CoM to suspend work and continue reflection on this topic,[82] the Assembly adopted Recommendation 1285 (1996). In this recommendation, elaborated on the basis of a report of the

Committee on Legal Affairs and Human Rights on the rights of national minorities by rapporteur Mr Bindig,[83] the Assembly reiterated the regrets expressed in Recommendation 1255 (1995) concerning the fact that the Vienna Summit did not follow the Assembly's proposal for an additional protocol on the rights of national minorities to the ECHR, as contained in Recommendation 1201.

Nevertheless, in an indirect reference to the Vienna Summit decision to begin work on drafting a protocol to the ECHR in the cultural field, the Assembly indicated that "yet, if a 'maximalist' approach were to be made for the new protocol the Assembly might be satisfied as many of the rights of minorities are either already covered by the Convention itself or may be considered as 'cultural' rights".[84] The Assembly expressed its disappointment with "the recent decision of the Committee of Ministers to suspend its work on a draft protocol"[85] and recommended that the CoM immediately resume this work and bring it to a satisfactory and rapid conclusion. The Assembly demanded that the protocol should be made as comprehensive as possible and should formulate the obligations incumbent on states as precisely as possible, so as to make the rights to be conferred upon individuals by states clear and justiciable.[86] Furthermore, the Assembly insisted that the CoM submit the draft protocol, once concluded, to the Assembly for its opinion.[87]

Furthermore, the Assembly reiterated its recommendation that the CoM ensure the independence, effectiveness and transparency of the Advisory Committee to be established under the Framework Convention, repeating its previous suggestions, included in Recommendation 1255, to facilitate this, and making new ones.[88] The Assembly also fine-tuned its previous recommendations concerning operational aspects of the work of the Advisory Committee. First, the Assembly added to its previous proposal for the Advisory Committee to enter into a dialogue with the governments of the contracting states, contained in Recommendation 1255, the possibility that the Advisory Committee enter into dialogue with national minority groups as well.[89] No restrictions as to the character of the dialogue were envisaged by the Assembly.

With regard to the need to seek permission for the Advisory Committee to publish its reports, the Assembly further proposed that publication could take place, in special cases, without the authorisation of the government concerned.[90] The Assembly also recommended that the CoM consult the Assembly before taking its final decisions on the Advisory Committee. In Parliamentary Assembly Order No. 513 adopted subsequently, the Assembly instructed its own Committee on Legal Affairs and Human Rights "to ensure that the Advisory Committee to be set up by the Committee of Ministers, in accordance with Article 26 of the

Framework Convention may be as independent, effective and transparent as possible".[91]

The Assembly returned to the issue of the regulation of the Advisory Committee under the Framework Convention in Recommendation 1300 (1996) on the protection of the rights of minorities, adopted on the basis of a report by the Committee on Legal Affairs and Human Rights, rapporteur Mr Bindig.[92] In this recommendation, the Assembly revised and developed its proposals in relation to the composition and working methods of the Advisory Committee.

These recommendations of the Assembly were roughly taken up the following year by the CoM in Resolution (97) 10 on rules adopted by the CoM on the monitoring arrangements under Articles 24 to 26 of the Framework Convention for the Protection of National Minorities.[93] However, for key areas of the work of the Advisory Committee, such as its power of initiative to obtain information and its role in assessing the adequacy of state compliance with the Framework Convention provisions, the Assembly proposals for wide powers and a strong position of the Advisory Committee were curtailed in the resolution of the CoM.[94] The CoM would not follow either the Assembly proposal regarding a system of election of the members of the Advisory Committee along the lines of that of members of the European Commission of Human Rights or election along the lines of the European Committee for the Prevention of Torture and Inhuman or Degrading Treatment or Punishment.

This would lead the Assembly, in Recommendation 1345 (1997) on the protection of national minorities, elaborated on the basis of a report by its Political Affairs Committee (rapporteur Mr Gjellerod),[95] to greatly regret "that the Committee of Ministers did not follow the proposals of the Assembly ... when laying down the rules for the election of the Advisory Committee of the Framework Convention for the Protection of National Minorities and on the ways it may seek and obtain information".

The Assembly called upon the CoM to reconsider its decision. One of the main concerns of the Assembly resided in the method of election of the members of the Advisory Committee. The Assembly regretted the fact that the election procedure would be entirely controlled by the CoM, and thus there would be no opportunity for Assembly input. Another matter of concern for the Assembly was the procedure for the Advisory Committee to seek and obtain information, and "the potential danger to the freedom of action of the Advisory Committee".[96] The Assembly restated its regrets about the fact that the CoM was unable to continue the work on a draft protocol to the ECHR in the cultural field.

The Assembly proposals for the second Council of Europe summit, held in Strasbourg on 10 and 11 October 1997, insisted once more on the elaboration of a protocol to the ECHR protecting the cultural rights of minorities.[97] However, no reference to the protocol was included in the Final Declaration of the Strasbourg Summit.[98]

The CoM, following the adoption of "interim replies" to the recommendations adopted by the Parliamentary Assembly during the 1990s in connection with the elaboration of standards relating to minority protection and their implementation, finally gave a "grouped reply" to Recommendations: 1134 (1990); 1177 (1992); 1201 (1993); 1255 (1955); 1285 (1996); 1300 (1996) and 1345 (1997), the latter being the only recommendation which had not received an interim reply previously. This "grouped reply", adopted at the 656th meeting of the ministers' deputies on 19 January 1999 took "stock of the achievements of the Council of Europe in this field".[99] The CoM justified its previous adoption of interim replies on the basis of the rapid evolution in questions pertaining to the protection of national minorities, while indicating that developments in this field would most certainly continue.[100]

The CoM noted the disappointment of the Assembly at its decision to suspend the work on the drafting of an additional protocol "to safeguard the rights of the individual in the cultural field".[101] However, the Committee also noted that:

> an approach to an additional protocol as recommended by the Parliamentary Assembly, notably in Recommendation 1201, has proved not to be feasible for several reasons, *inter alia* because it contains certain elements (the definition of a national minority, the nature and scope of certain rights, etc.) which do not muster the general support of all member States. It further notes that its decision to suspend the work does not imply a final decision on an additional protocol, but indeed leaves open the possibility of re-examining the question in the light of subsequent experience with the implementation of existing standards.[102]

In relation to the rejection by the CoM of the Assembly's proposals concerning the election procedure of the members of the Advisory Committee, the CoM indicated that it "was not considered appropriate in the light of the role of the Advisory Committee as a body established to advise it [the CoM] on the adequacy of measures taken to implement the Convention".[103]

On this issue the CoM adopted the approach followed by its Steering Committee on Human Rights (CDDH), which had further expounded on this, by pointing out "that this Advisory Committee, unlike for example the European Commission of Human Rights, is a subsidiary body of the Committee of Ministers and was established accordingly".[104] The CoM stressed, however that: "in electing and appointing experts to the Advisory Committee, it gives full attention to the requirements of independence, impartiality and availability as laid down in Resolution (97) 10".[105]

Another issue of concern for the Assembly was the procedure for the Advisory Committee to seek and obtain information. The CoM "emphasises the fact that the Advisory Committee is free to receive information and that procedural requirements apply only to ensure that the Committee of Ministers is aware of requests for information being made. The Committee of Ministers will ensure that this procedure does not hinder the effective and efficient functioning of the Advisory Committee".[106] In addition, the CoM fully subscribed to the statement by the CDDH on this issue "that it would not be appropriate to change the agreed rules at this stage. The rules should be now put into practice and experience will show whether these working arrangements prove satisfactory".[107]

Finally, the CoM followed the suggestion of the CDDH for the CoM to express "its recognition of the importance and the need for maintaining or initiating dialogue with representatives of national minorities and civil society"[108] by actually doing so.[109] Thus, although the CoM did not foreclose the possibility to review its approaches, it maintained its previous position vis-à-vis the questions raised by the Assembly.

Other minority questions addressed by the Parliamentary Assembly during the 1990s

Besides devoting continual attention to establishing appropriate Council of Europe standards concerning minority protection, the Parliamentary Assembly has devoted its attention to other aspects of this protection. It has dealt with special concerns of specific types of minorities, religious minorities in particular. It has also dealt with general phenomena of society which especially affect minorities (such as the question of racism and intolerance), and with general minority questions (such as the access of minorities to higher education). The Assembly has addressed the problems of certain minorities dispersed throughout the territory of several states, and which are facing extinction (such as the Yiddish, Uralic or Aromanian) and the situation of minorities in specific countries, including in situations of conflict.

i. *Special concerns of specific minority groups: religion*

The rights of religious minorities were hardly touched upon in the text of the proposal for an additional protocol contained in Recommendation 1201, with the exception of a short reference in Article 3 of the proposal. This reference was to the right of every person belonging to a national minority "to express, preserve and develop in complete freedom his/her religious ... identity, without being subjected to any attempt at assimilation against his/her will".

One day after the adoption of Recommendation 1201, the Assembly adopted Recommendation 1202 (1993) on religious tolerance in a democratic society. In spite of pointing to some of the questions in relation to religious tolerance relevant to minority protection, this recommendation did not address the most burning issues relevant to the protection of religious minorities. These include the questions of recognition, the non-discriminatory treatment of minority religions, or their ability in practice to establish and manage their own institutions. Following a general statement indicating that "[w]estern Europe has developed the model of secular democracy within which a variety of religious beliefs are in theory tolerated",[110] the Assembly focused its attention instead on the three main monotheistic religions and the values of tolerance that these religions portray.

Nevertheless, the Assembly stated among other things that "the secular state should not impose any religious obligations on its citizens. It should also encourage respect for all recognised religious communities and ease their relations with society as a whole".[111] It also recommended that the CoM call upon the governments of the member states, the European Community as well as the responsible authorities and organisations, among others, "to ensure that studies of religions and ethics are part of the general school curriculum, and to work towards a differentiated and careful depiction of religions in school books (including history books) and in classroom teaching with a view to achieving a better and deeper understanding of the various religions".[112]

The Assembly has made an important conceptual contribution to the determination of adequate state policies concerning the right to freedom of conscience and religion, touching on aspects particularly relevant to minority protection. Besides the contributions of the Assembly before the 1990s, mentioned above, the adoption of Recommendation 1178 (1992) on sects and new religious movements, pre-dating Recommendation 1202, implied an important step forward, particularly against the background of the restrictive legislation and policies in this field that had been implemented by European states, including in Western Europe – and which in some states still persist and continue to be implemented. In Recommendation 1178, the Assembly acknowledged its need to make further inquiries into this topic, but made a straightforward statement that "it considers that the freedom of conscience and religion guaranteed by Article 9 of the European Convention on Human Rights makes major legislation on sects undesirable since such legislation might well interfere with this fundamental right and harm traditional religions. It considers, however, that educational as well as legislative and other measures should be taken in response to the problems raised by some of the activities of sects and new religious movements".[113]

The Assembly recommended that the CoM call on the member states to adopt a series of measures, such as that "the basic educational curriculum ... include objective factual information concerning established religions and their major variants, concerning the principles of comparative religion and concerning ethics and personal and social rights".[114] The Assembly also advocated the dissemination of this type of information among the general public. Furthermore, the Assembly stated that "consideration should be given to introducing legislation, if it does not already exist, which grants corporate status to all sects and new religious movements which have been registered, together with all offshoots of the mother sect".[115]

The Assembly paid particular attention to the question of the protection of minors, indicating among other things that "existing legislation concerning the protection of children should be more rigorously applied".[116] In addition, the Assembly indicated that "those belonging to a sect must be informed that they have the right to leave" and that "persons working for sects should be registered with social welfare bodies and guaranteed social welfare coverage, and such social welfare provision should also be available to those deciding to leave the sects".[117]

Illustrating that concerns post-September 11th 2001 in connection with the issue of religious extremism are not new, in Recommendation 1396 (1999) on religion and democracy the Assembly dealt mainly with that issue, and the possibility that religion might become an instrument which generated tension within society. The Assembly underscored the need to ensure that manifestations of religion comply with the limitations set out in Article 9 of the ECHR, while stating that "democratic states, whether secular or linked to a religion, must allow all religions that abide by the conditions set out in the European Convention on Human Rights to develop under the same conditions and enable them to find an appropriate place in society".[118]

The Assembly re-emphasised the role of education in eliminating religious stereotypes, and the need to safeguard freedom of conscience and religious expression. It recommended that the CoM invite the governments of the member states to:

> safeguard religious pluralism, by allowing all religions to develop in identical conditions; facilitate ... the observation of religious rites and customs ...; denounce any attempt to foment conflict within and between religions for partisan ends; ensure freedom and equal rights of education to all citizens regardless of their religious belief, customs and rites; and ensure fair and equal access to the public media for all religions.[119]

The Assembly also recommended, among other things, that the CoM invite the governments of the member states to ensure equal conditions for the maintenance and conservation of religious buildings and of the assets of all religions, as an integral part of the national and European heritage, as well as safeguarding cultural traditions and different religious festivals.[120]

Finally, in Recommendation 1412 (1999) on illegal activities of sects, the Assembly further refines its standing on these issues. It reiterates its position regarding the adoption of major legislation on sects as undesirable, while insisting that "it recognises religious pluralism as a natural consequence of freedom of religion. It regards state neutrality and equal protection before the law as fundamental safeguards against any form of discrimination and therefore calls upon state authorities to refrain from taking measures based on value judgement concerning beliefs".[121] The Assembly states that it "has come to the conclusion that it is unnecessary to define what constitutes a sect or to decide whether it is a religion or not". In addition, the Assembly

> takes the view that it is essential to ensure that the activities of these groups, be they of religious, esoteric or spiritual nature, are in keeping with the principles of our democratic societies and, in particular, with the provisions of Article 9 of the European Convention on Human Rights, as well as being legal. It is of prime importance to have reliable information on these groups that emanates neither exclusively from the sects themselves nor from associations set up to defend the victims of sects, and to circulate it widely among the general public, once those concerned have had the chance to comment on the objectivity of such information.[122]

It is understood that by using the concept "being legal" the Assembly is simply referring to the need for these groups not to commit illegal acts. Special attention should be given in this connection to the current tendency of some states to use formal legal requirements, including registration, as a means of placing various religious denominations in a position of illegality, which opens the door to unfair restrictions and encroaches on the right to religious freedom.

Further, the Assembly expresses once more its concern, in particular, with the fate of minors, "and particularly the children of members of religious, esoteric or spiritual groups, in case of ill-treatment, rape, neglect, indoctrination through brainwashing and non-enrolment at school, which makes it impossible for welfare services to exercise supervision".[123] Consequently, the Assembly calls on the governments of the member states, in addition to other recommendations previously made, and among other things:

> a. to use the normal procedures of criminal and civil law against illegal practices carried out in the name of these groups;

b. to ensure that legislation on the obligation to enrol children at school is rigorously applied, and that appropriate authorities intervene in the event of non-compliance;

c. to encourage an approach to religious groups which will bring about understanding, tolerance, dialogue and resolution of conflicts;

d. to take firm steps against any action which is discriminatory or which marginalises religious or spiritual minority groups.[124]

Furthermore, the Assembly recommends that the CoM should "where necessary provide for specific action to set up information centres on groups of a religious, esoteric or spiritual nature in the countries of central and eastern Europe in its aid programmes for those countries" and set up a European observatory on these groups to make it easier for national centres to exchange information.[125]

ii. *General phenomena which affect minorities in particular*

Another kind of approach by the Assembly to minority protection has resulted from its addressing general phenomena that affect minority groups in particular. This approach is best illustrated by the adoption by the Assembly of Recommendation 1222 (1993), on the fight against racism, xenophobia, anti-semitism and intolerance. This voluminous recommendation results from the Assembly's alarm at the resurgence of these phenomena, and it was adopted against the background of acts of violence committed in several Council of Europe member states.[126]

The Assembly "stresses the importance of addressing the root causes of racism, xenophobia and intolerance", and "of applying existing national and international legal instruments to combat these phenomena".[127] With regard to the former, the Assembly states that "action by national, regional and local authorities, as well as by non-governmental organisations, should further include prevention through education, support for the victims and protection and promotion of cultural diversity", while recalling its previous statement in this connection included in Recommendation 1206 (1993) on the integration of migrants and community relations.[128]

The Assembly underlines the role of young people, the media and the advertising industry, and calls on the member states "to introduce or reinforce, as a matter of the utmost urgency, an active education and youth policy stressing the combat of intolerant, racist and xenophobic attitudes; special attention should be given to human rights education and language teaching".[129] It also calls on member states: i. "to support and fund activities by non-governmental organisations aimed at promoting tolerance and, where appropriate, initiate such action as the establishment of multicultural centres and the organisation of language courses for immigrants, training courses for youth leaders, multi-ethnic travel and other forms of cultural exchange" and ii. "to set up at national level organisations for the promotion of tolerance, with responsibility for encouraging dialogue between young people from immigrant and indigenous communities and for advising governments on the direction to be taken by their policies to promote tolerance".[130] Thus, on the positive measures side, the Assembly supports integration policies originating not only from the state authorities, but also from the grass-roots level.

From a negative measures side, and with regard to domestic legislation, the Assembly recommends that states "adopt legislation in line with the principles and guidelines to be drawn up by the Council of Europe for the punishment of persons initiating racist, xenophobia, or anti-Semitic remarks or acts, as well as any act of discrimination of this kind perpetrated by the public authorities".[131] The Assembly also recommends that the CoM include in the draft plan of action to be discussed in the forthcoming first Council of Europe summit: "a decision to re-examine urgently the question of possible obstacles to acquisition of citizenship, in order to facilitate the integration of migrants". However, this is followed by the somehow contradictory proviso, which illustrates the political tensions embedded in the Assembly's work: "if under the national legislation of the host country the requirements of such acquisition are met".[132]

With regard to the application of international legal instruments, the Assembly addresses a practical and burning aspect, stating that "in certain member states, public opinion seems to be that the burden resulting from the application of the Geneva Convention of 1951 relating to the status of refugees is not fairly shared by all European countries. This belief contributes to the rise of xenophobic and racist sentiments".[133] The Assembly recommends "the creation, in close co-operation with UNHCR, of a European refugee commission or forum to promote policies and measures which would be aimed at improving solidarity between member states as regards the consequences of receiving refugees and asylum seekers".[134] The Assembly calls on member states to ratify the International Convention on the Elimination of All Forms of Racial Discrimination and the International Covenant on Civil and Political Rights, to accept in full their corresponding complaints procedures and to ensure that "interested lawyers and immigrant support organisations" are aware of their provisions as well as those of the ECHR.[135]

Finally, the Assembly recommends that the CoM include in the draft plan of action, to be discussed in the forthcoming summit, the following:

    a. a European youth campaign enabling the young people of Europe to unite in a common struggle for European values;

414

    b. an interdisciplinary comparative study in all member states on the root causes of racism, xenophobia and other manifestations of intolerance and exclusion as well as on other measures taken at the national level, in order to lay down guidelines and common principles of a Europe-wide strategy;

    c. the setting up of an independent group of experts which should: i. monitor member states' compliance with international legal obligations; ii. exchange information and stimulate action at national, regional and local level; iii. consider communications addressed to it by non-governmental organisations; iv. report regularly to the Committee of Ministers, which should transmit these reports to the Assembly.[136]

As already described in Chapter 5, these proposals were partly reflected in the Vienna Declaration resulting from the first Council of Europe summit. It is worth noting the much weaker wording finally used in the Vienna Declaration, [137] especially in relation to the mandate of the committee of experts to be established, and which would later result in the creation of the European Commission Against Racism and Intolerance (ECRI).[138] Substantial differences can also be easily identified between the approach of the Parliamentary Assembly and that of the heads of state and government towards the nature and content of the mandate of the committee of experts, unnecessary to spell out here. The title of the committee as an "independent group of experts" proposed by the Assembly, and that of a "committee of governmental experts" finally included in the Vienna Declaration suffices to illustrate the divergent approaches of these two Council of Europe organs.

In 1995, the Assembly adopted Recommendation 1275 (1995), with the same title as Recommendation 1222 (1993), in which it re-emphasised certain policy concerns, filled in gaps with regard to its policy suggestions, and developed ideas already expressed in the latter recommendation. The Assembly recommended, for example, that the CoM strengthen the mandate of the ECRI to include the right to monitor the compliance of member states with their international legal obligations, as already supported in Assembly Recommendation 1222 (1993), and to lay down guidelines and common principles for a Europe-wide strategy in this area.[139] It also recommended that the CoM promote the work on an additional protocol to the ECHR strengthening the non-discrimination clause of Article 14,[140] and that the CoM appoint a mediator for "Gypsies" (Roma and Sinti) along the lines proposed in Recommendation 1203, on Gypsies in Europe.[141]

The Assembly requested state action in areas already identified in Recommendation 1222, but on which no specific action had been taken, such as media regulation. In addition, it recommended that the CoM call on the Council of Europe member states among other things:

a. to conduct their policy according to the principles laid down in Assembly Recommendation 1201, on an additional protocol on the rights of minorities to the ECHR, and to incorporate in their domestic law, and implement in practice, minority rights in line with this recommendation;

b. to incorporate in their domestic law, and implement in practice, provisions aiming at preventing or reducing statelessness, in order to attack the roots of current problems;[142]

c. to examine their national legislation and practice, and to abolish those still existent which have a direct or indirect discriminating effect and to introduce new legislation on a national level against racism, xenophobia, anti-semitism and all religious and other forms of intolerance;

d. to adopt measures for the release of persons imprisoned on the sole ground of having conducted non-violent information campaigns in order to secure recognition for ethnic and linguistic minorities;

e. to set up supervisory and consultative bodies of the ombudsman or commission type on the problems of racism, xenophobia, anti-semitism, and all religious and other forms of intolerance, authorised to examine individual complaints, and to enhance the mandate of such bodies in the cases where they already exist;

f. to conduct national and local awareness-raising campaigns against those problems and guarantee accessible judicial and social assistance to their victims;

g. to grant voting rights in local elections to resident aliens;[143]

h. to encourage the drawing up of self-regulatory codes of conduct, as previously proposed in Recommendation 1215 (1993) on the ethics of journalism, setting professional and ethical standards for journalists and broadcasters, prohibiting the instigation to racial discrimination, violence, hatred and intolerance in the media while respecting freedom of speech;

i. to promote the setting up and the activity of self-regulatory bodies supervising the implementation of codes of conduct for the media;

j. to support electronic media projects for programmes on national minorities and migrant groups and their history and religion.

Finally, the Assembly recommended that the CoM call on the Council of Europe member states to sign and ratify the Framework Convention for the Protection of National Minorities, the European Charter for Regional or Minority Languages and the International Convention on the Elimination of All Forms of Racial Discrimination, if they had not already done so.

iii. *General minority questions*

Yet another approach of the Parliamentary Assembly to minority protection – that of addressing general minority questions which the Assembly has come to identify – is illustrated by the attention devoted to the issue of the access of minorities to higher education. In Recommendation 1352 (1998) on this topic, the Assembly pointed to the fact that "members of national minorities are often under-represented in higher education. The cost of provision, problems of recognition of qualifications, the lack of suitable primary and secondary education and, in some cases, political opposition contribute to this situation".[144] Thus, attention is raised to the precarious situation of minorities not only in the enjoyment of civil but also economic and social rights. The text contains an enumeration of a series of principles which the Assembly recommends the CoM ask states to consider.

The adoption of this recommendation was preceded by the drafting of "The Hague recommendations regarding minority education rights", under the auspices of the office of the OSCE High Commissioner on National Minorities, published in October 1996. The Assembly recommendations follow a similar line of thinking as those delineated by the High Commissioner's expert group, which they occasionally complement, as some Assembly proposals focus on very specific aspects, while others establish broad policy guidelines.

For example, the Assembly points to the need for governments to "recognise the fundamental liberty to engage in higher education activities and to establish institutions for that purpose", in line with paragraph 8 of The Hague recommendations. The Assembly makes specific suggestions on how to facilitate access by members of minorities to higher education, for example indicating that "higher education institutions should develop out-reach programmes designed to facilitate the access of minorities, for example by collaborating more closely with secondary education institutions".[145] The Assembly also indicates that "students from minority groups should have the possibility to sit entrance examinations to higher education in their mother tongue".[146]

It further indicates that "new information and communications technologies should be used more widely as these are well suited for the education of minority groups and of students in geographically remote areas".[147] The Assembly recommends that the CoM "provide expert assistance ... to universities and governments in countries where minorities experience difficulties in acceding to higher education".[148] This has been an issue to which the OSCE High Commissioner on National Minorities has devoted much attention.[149]

iv. *The situation of specific minorities in various states*

Finally, as already indicated, the Assembly has devoted special attention to the situation of specific minority groups, expressing its special concerns towards them. This is illustrated by the adoption of Recommendation 1291 (1996) on Yiddish culture; Recommendation 1333 (1997) on the Aromanian culture and language; and Resolution 1171 (1998) on endangered Uralic minority cultures.[150] These "cultures"[151] have as a common characteristic the fact that the minority groups from which they originate constitute dispersed ethnic minorities, living in more than one state.[152]

A common concern expressed in these texts relates to the fact that the very existence of these groups is in jeopardy, as their number of members is dwindling dramatically, mainly as a result of assimilation into the larger societies surrounding them. In these recommendations the Assembly also raises particular concerns in relation to each of the respective cultures. Some of those concerns have been subsequently studied by the Assembly in more detail.[153]

In the three recommendations, the Assembly calls for state support, especially from states where these groups live and from neighbouring states where at least a part of the population has greater affinities with the respective cultures. The Assembly does not advocate "kin-state" interference, but assistance, particularly for members of these groups to receive education in their mother tongue, and for the provision of appropriate teacher training. The Assembly requests support also for the promotion of research, publications and cultural activities aiming at a better knowledge and preservation of the respective identities. It refers to the need to include information on the culture of these groups in history books, and to support publications in their languages as well as their access to the media.

Another common feature of these texts is support for the establishment of a "laboratory for dispersed ethnic minorities" with the responsibility to do research and collect information about these groups, to monitor their situation and to promote legislation to protect their cultures against discrimination or "annihilation".[154] In the reply from the CoM to Recommendation 1333, adopted at the 674th meeting of the ministers' deputies held on 8 and 9 June 1999, and with regard to this interesting initiative of the Assembly, the CoM:

> draws attention to the fact that it decided, on 25 November 1998, to grant Council of Europe auspices to the 'European Institute for

Dispersed Ethnic Minorities' (EIDEM) which was set up in July 1998 in Vilnius, on a private initiative, with the support of the Lithuanian Government. While this institute is not under Council of Europe authority, the Committee of Ministers recalls that it has given terms of reference to the Committee of Experts on Issues Relating to the Protection of National Minorities (DH-MIN) to undertake a study on 'dispersed ethnic minorities' as well as on prospects for co-operation between the Council of Europe on the one hand and the European Institute for Dispersed Ethnic Minorities and other bodies pursuing similar objectives on the other hand.[155]

While the results of the DH-MIN study have not resulted in further follow-up, as discussed in Chapter 7, Council of Europe support for EIDEM seems to have been finally confined to that provided under the Confidence-Building Measures Programme, as stated in the same chapter.

Also dealing with the situation of a group dispersed in several countries, in Parliamentary Assembly Recommendation 1377 (1998) on the humanitarian situation of the Kurdish refugees and displaced persons in south-eastern Turkey and northern Iraq, the Assembly recalls and reaffirms previous adopted texts, including those related to the conflict in the region and on the conditions faced by the Kurds as a result. Then, taking a western "Eurocentric" approach, the Assembly addresses the humanitarian situation of these groups in connection with the issue of clandestine migration into the European industrialised countries, which raises the Assembly's anxiety.

Besides stating its position in relation to the conflicts in the region, and expressing its concern about their impact on the humanitarian situation, the Assembly states its worry "that the number of asylum-seekers and illegal migrants of Kurdish origin has increased in certain European countries".[156] It also stresses "that although this phenomenon is of great concern for receiving countries, it is also disturbing for the countries on the transit route" and "the fact that any criticism addressed to a member state such as Turkey is made in a constructive spirit, emphasising the importance of the Turkish participation alongside other European states and the need to reconcile absolute respect for its territorial integrity and respect for minority rights".[157]

The Assembly addresses several recommendations to the CoM. Among others, it invites Turkey: "to sign and ratify the Framework Convention for the Protection of National Minorities and the European Charter for Regional or Minority Languages and apply its provisions to the Kurds; to bring to light the fate of the missing persons" and "to adopt policies and take adequate measures to enable Turkish citizens of Kurdish origin to exercise their cultural and political rights".[158] In addition to this, the Assembly recommends that the CoM invite Turkey

> to implement, in co-operation with international humanitarian organi-
> sations, a major programme with a view to encouraging those members
> of the Kurdish population who so desire to return to their homes; to
> ensure particular protection for returning women, children and elderly
> people; to present reconstruction projects to be financed by the Council
> of Europe's Social Development Fund, in the framework of return pro-
> grammes; to adopt measures to integrate those displaced persons of
> Kurdish origin who wish to settle in other parts of Turkey, and provide
> them, as well as returnees, with compensation for damaged property.[159]

The Assembly suggests that the CoM "set up, together with the European Union, a joint programme of co-operation with Turkey aimed at
providing assistance for the promotion of cultural rights of the Kurdish
population and other groups of the local population in south-eastern
Turkey".[160]

In Recommendation 1455 (2000) on repatriation and integration of the
Tatars of Crimea, the Assembly, among other things, recommends that
the CoM invite the states concerned, notably the Russian Federation,
Kazakhstan, Kyrgyzstan and Tajikistan (with the exception of the
Russian Federation, these are not members of the Council of Europe so
far) "to enter into bilateral negotiations with Ukraine with a view to
agreeing on a simplified procedure for the acquisition of Ukrainian
citizenship, accessible to Crimean Tatars residing in those states".[161]

The Assembly takes the not very felicitous step of making the experience
of other member states of the Council of Europe, concerning the representation of minorities and indigenous peoples, "generally" a model,
without giving any concrete examples. It also recommends that the CoM
invite the government of Ukraine to take into account the Framework
Convention for the Protection of National Minorities and the "Lund recommendations on the effective participation of national minorities in
public life", elaborated at the request of the OSCE High Commissioner on
National Minorities, with a view to securing effective representation of
the Crimean Tatars at central, regional and local levels of government.[162]

The Assembly asks for "the study of the experience of other multi-ethnic
states", with a view to restoring and securing the rights of the Crimean
Tatars to education in the Crimean Tatar language, and the use of their
language in all private and public affairs. For this purpose, the Assembly
asks the Ukrainian authorities to take into account the European Charter
for Regional or Minority Languages, the Framework Convention for the
Protection of National Minorities, "as well as the October 1996 Hague
recommendations regarding the education rights of national minorities

and the February Oslo recommendations regarding the linguistic rights of national minorities, elaborated at the request of the OSCE's High Commissioner".[163] As to the aforementioned suggestion to study the experience "of other multi-ethnic states", the question remains of how many states are not multi-ethnic, particularly in Europe, notwithstanding that state policies may tend to ignore this fact.

v. *The situation of specific minorities in individual states*

The Assembly has also occasionally dealt with specific minorities when addressing the general situation in countries independently considered. An example at hand is that of Resolution 1113 (1997) on the situation in Cyprus. In contrast with the initial approach of the Assembly to this matter before the 1990s, earlier referred to, the Assembly specifically addressed in this resolution the situation of one of the minority groups living in the country, expressing concern about the "treatment of the Greek Cypriots living in the northern part of Cyprus. The Assembly calls upon the Turkish Cypriot administration to change its policies that, at present, amount to violations of human rights".[164]

This points to an evolution in the Assembly's standing, by which the minority issue has become an important element to consider when addressing the situation of specific Council of Europe member states. As discussed below, this evolution will continue into the 2000s, as the adoption in 2003 of a resolution on the "rights and fundamental freedoms of Greek Cypriots and Maronites living in the Northern Cyprus" illustrates. Therefore, the evolution of approaches of the Assembly in the treatment of the minority question in Northern Cyprus serves well to illustrate the evolution of the standing of the Assembly vis-à-vis questions of minority protection generally.

Again dealing with a concrete minority, in Resolution 1172 (1998) on the situation of the French-speaking population living in the Brussels periphery, the Assembly thoroughly addressed the special situation of this particular group, against the background of recent tensions arising between the Flemish authorities and the French-speaking communities of Belgium, to which the Assembly addresses itself directly. The Assembly calls on the Flemish Government to "seek to integrate, but not assimilate, speakers of other languages (especially French-speaking Belgian citizens) in Flanders", while recognising their right to keep their own identity and language, and to develop their own culture.

At the same time, the Assembly "recommends that the French-speaking inhabitants of the Brussels periphery and in particular their political representatives": i. "seek to integrate into the region they live in, ... by, for example, trying to learn Dutch or improving Dutch language skills, and taking part in the cultural life of Flanders"; ii. cease trying to enlarge the linguistic facilities into actual bilingualism. Finally, the Assembly also addresses two recommendations to the Belgian government: that it "encourage cultural communication and co-operation across the language borders within the Belgian state" and "consider signing and ratifying the European Framework Convention for the Protection of National Minorities.[165] As discussed below, this aspect of minority protection will also be taken up by the Assembly in the 2000s.

vi. *The situation of specific minorities in armed conflict situations*

Kosovo

Further, the Parliamentary Assembly has dealt with the situation of minorities in some states by addressing armed conflict situations. Although an analysis of the approaches of the Assembly to conflict cannot be undertaken here, some notes on the Assembly's recent responses to conflict related to minority protection follow. The development of those conflicts – almost all with an interethnic component – which have affected European states since the 1990s, has been closely followed by the Assembly, whose responses have included:

- support for mediation and peaceful settlement initiatives, including those provided by the international community: the Assembly has occasionally offered or exercised its direct involvement in mediation efforts;

- support for international permanent presences in post-conflict areas, and occasionally for "international military intervention to end conflict";

- demands for the protection of refugees and displaced persons and creation of the adequate conditions for their voluntary return; and

- request for inquiries into and investigation of human rights violations committed in connection with the situations of conflict.

Only some of the decisions adopted by the Assembly in this connection are recorded below, particularly those concerning the recent conflict in Kosovo.

The Assembly has carried out a continuous follow-up of the conflict in Kosovo, paying special consideration to minority concerns. Already in its Recommendation 1360 (1998) on the crisis in Kosovo, adopted on 18 March 1998, the Assembly expresses its concern about the escalation of violence, and states its expectation that the Yugoslav authorities will implement "the agreement on education concluded in September 1996 between Mr Milošević, then President of Serbia, and Mr Rugova, leader of the Albanian community in Kosovo". The Assembly "calls for the establishment of an international monitoring presence in Kosovo, and for an independent inquiry into the recent events in the Drenica region". It states its belief that "a long-term solution to the crisis can only be found on the basis of a greater autonomy for Kosovo within the Federal Republic of Yugoslavia, and calls for an immediate start to genuine negotiations on this issue between the Yugoslav authorities and representatives of the Albanian community in Kosovo", reiterating its offer to assist in those contacts.[166]

In Recommendation 1368 (1998), adopted on 22 April 1998, on the latest developments in the Federal Republic of Yugoslavia and situation in Kosovo the Assembly welcomes the beginning of the implementation of the 1996 education agreement, while indicating that the request of the Yugoslav government for Council of Europe membership of 18 March 1998 can only be considered if the Federal Republic of Yugoslavia, among other things, complies with the requests of the international community, notably with regard to Kosovo.[167]

In Recommendation 1376 adopted on 24 June 1998, on the crisis in Kosovo and situation in the Federal Republic of Yugoslavia, by which the Assembly initiates a series of decisions of the same title, the Assembly requests that the Yugoslav authorities immediately end those operations harmful to the civilian population and create conditions for the resumption of negotiations with representatives of the Kosovo Albanians, stating that "security throughout Kosovo, for the Albanian population as well as others living in Kosovo, is vital for the resumption of negotiations with representatives of Kosovo Albanians". The Assembly also asks the Kosovo Albanian community to do its utmost to prevent a further escalation of violence.[168] The Assembly calls on the authorities of the Federal Republic of Yugoslavia, among other things, to agree to the deployment of international observers "to monitor the activities of the police and the Yugoslav army, as well as armed groups of ethnic Albanians".[169] It also points to the possible use of "all options at the disposal of the international community, including military ones ... to prevent further bloodshed".[170]

Under the shadow of the further escalation of the conflict, in Recommendation 1384, adopted on 24 September 1998, the Assembly puts forward some elements considered as essential in reaching a lasting peaceful solution, including: the guarantee of the security of people living in Kosovo, achieved through the withdrawal of the Serbian security forces; the disarmament of armed groups of ethnic Albanians and the deployment of an international peace force; and a new political status for Kosovo, based on a high level of autonomy within the Yugoslav federation and comprising, among other things, the respect for the rights of Serbs and other minorities.[171] In Recommendation 1385 (1998) adopted on the same date, the Assembly deals with the situation of the Kosovo refugees, asylum seekers and displaced persons.[172]

In Recommendation 1397 adopted on 28 January 1999, the Assembly expresses its strongest condemnation of the killings of forty-five ethnic Albanians in the village of Racak on 15 January 1999 by the Serbian security forces, while taking note of reports by the OSCE Kosovo Verification Mission (KVM)[173] stating that some of the victims, including women, elderly persons and at least one child, had been shot at close range. It strongly condemns all acts of terrorism by the Kosovo Liberation Army (KLA/UCK) and other armed groups, and calls for the deployment of substantial international military forces on the frontier between the Federal Republic of Yugoslavia and Albania with a view to preventing the smuggling of arms to fighting groups in Kosovo. The Assembly recommends to the CoM, among other things, that it "increase its support to civil society in the Federal Republic of Yugoslavia and use all possible means to make this support known to non-governmental organisations, to the authorities of the Federal Republic of Yugoslavia and to the Yugoslav population at large, for example by organising meetings on the spot and fact-finding missions".[174]

In Resolution 1182 adopted on 30 March 1999, the Assembly "highly appreciates the efforts of the Contact Group, which led to the holding of the Rambouillet meeting, and considers that the Interim Agreement for Peace and Self-Government in Kosovo resulting from this meeting represents a fair and equitable proposal for the solution of the Kosovo conflict".[175] In addition, "the Assembly regrets that, due to the intransigent policy of the leadership of the Federal Republic of Yugoslavia and the inability of the United Nations Security Council to reach a unanimous decision, military action had to be taken by NATO to prevent a human tragedy in Kosovo".[176] In Recommendation 1400, adopted on the same date as Resolution 1182, and making direct reference to it, the Assembly invites member states to pursue: "the strengthening of the United Nations in their responsibility to protect threatened ethnic minorities, in the full respect of the territorial integrity of all states".[177]

In Recommendation 1403 (1999) the Assembly further adds that the Nato decision "to take limited military action ... was aimed at preventing the already existing human tragedy in Kosovo from worsening and bringing the authorities of the Federal Republic of Yugoslavia to sign the proposed Rambouillet Interim Agreement". The Assembly acknowledges that "so far the military action taken by NATO has not succeeded in stopping the humanitarian tragedy in the region. Since the beginning of the air strikes, the Serb authorities have accelerated ethnic cleansing in Kosovo and increased the risk of spill-over of the crisis into neighbouring countries", and:

> strongly condemns the policy of systematic ethnic cleansing carried out by the Yugoslav military and Serb paramilitary forces in Kosovo which

has led to the destruction of entire villages, the killing of innocent civilians, the perpetration of war crimes, particularly the abduction and rape of women as a systematic tool of war, and the expulsion of hundreds of thousands of persons into neighbouring countries.[178]

The Assembly holds President Milošević, the Yugoslav and the Serb leadership responsible for these crimes against humanity, and demands those responsible for these criminal acts to be brought before the International Criminal Tribunal for the Former Yugoslavia. It also demands that all governments which are in possession of evidence of criminal acts immediately hand it over to the tribunal.[179] The Assembly recommends among other things that the CoM "open a Council of Europe Secretariat office in 'the former Yugoslav Republic of Macedonia' in order to help that country overcome the difficulties it is facing due to the conflict in Kosovo" and "prepare the opening of a Council of Europe Secretariat office in Pristina with the task of building democratic institutions in Kosovo".[180]

In Recommendation 1414 (1999) the Assembly "deeply regrets that the Yugoslav authorities only accepted a political solution following the intensive use of military force by NATO, and demands an appropriate representation of the Council of Europe in the UN Mission in Kosovo (UNMIK).[181] It welcomes the adoption of the Stability Pact for South-Eastern Europe and the full participation of the Council of Europe in it.[182] After the establishment of UNMIK and later, the presidential elections leading to the ousting of President Milošević, the Assembly redirected its attention to analysing developments in the Federal Republic of Yugoslavia on the one hand, paying particular attention to developments in connection with the renewed application for membership of the Council of Europe by this state,[183] and to specific aspects of the situation in Kosovo and its neighbouring regions, on the other.

Chechnya

As regards the conflict in Chechnya, the Parliamentary Assembly has been particularly active in connection with the second outbreak of the Chechen conflict, which started in September 1999, over three years after the Russian Federation had become a member of the Council of Europe, although the Assembly had already been active with regard to the first stage of the conflict.[184]

In November 1999 the Assembly adopted Resolution 1201 on the conflict in Chechnya, in which among other things, the Assembly deplored the fact that the 1996 cease-fire had not led to a peaceful settlement of the crisis in Chechnya. The Assembly requested that persons guilty of terrorist acts, human rights violations and abductions be prosecuted, and made an appeal for the Russian authorities to avoid military raids against the civilian population and to introduce a cease-fire. The Assembly also supported "all efforts aiming at peaceful dialogue between the Russian authorities and democratically elected President Maskhadov".[185] However, most of the Assembly's decisions have been taken since the year 2000, as discussed further below.

The Assembly in the early 2000s

The activities of the Assembly in connection with minority protection in the early 2000s have been strongly marked by the Assembly's involvement with the situation in Chechnya, as further discussed below. However, other important aspects of minority protection have also called for the attention of the Assembly. Most of them had already been present on the agenda of the Assembly since the 1990s, although in some cases they have taken interesting turns, as also described below. Further, in addressing minority situations in specific countries, the Assembly has contributed to the delimitation of concepts which are central to the definition of international minority protection standards generally, consolidating a Council of Europe contribution in this field.

A very important aspect addressed by the Assembly has been that of the applicability of minority protection standards to persons who belong to the majority population of the state generally considered, but who can be considered as belonging to a minority within a specific section of its territory, as a result of state decentralisation. In Resolution 1301 on Protection of minorities in Belgium, the main concern of the Assembly is the introduction by Belgium of a reservation that "risks undermining most" of the Framework Convention provisions.[186]

This results from the restriction of protection under the convention to those groups which constitute a numerical minority in the state generally considered but are excluded from the power-sharing arrangements resulting from the system of territorial subdivisions existing in the state, which take linguistic differentiation as a base. In the opinion of the Assembly, this restriction does not take into account the de facto minority situation of the groups concerned within the specific territorial subdivisions of the state to which power has been devolved. By reference to an analysis of the situation in Belgium by the Venice Commission carried out at the request of the Committee on Legal Affairs and Human Rights of the Committee of Ministers,[187] the Assembly states that "the following groups are to be considered as minorities in Belgium within the context of the Framework Convention: at state level, the German-speaking community; at regional level, the French-speakers in the Dutch-language region and in the German-language region, and the Dutch speakers and German-speakers in the French-language region".[188]

With this approach, the Council of Europe organs seem to deviate from the views of the Human Rights Committee in *Ballantyne et al. v. Canada* (see above),[189] and taking into consideration the factual situation of specific groups, and the specific distribution of powers between the central and territorial authorities of the state, consider persons belonging to a minority within a specific territorial subdivision (or possibly other type of entity) as subject to protection under an international minority protection instrument. With this active standing of the Assembly in regard to the interpretation by an individual state of the framework convention provisions, the idea is reinforced that the interpretation of international treaties is not just a discretionary act of the state authorities (or a monopoly of the government in power at the time when a particular international instrument is ratified), but a concern for the international community at large, including its civil society.

Such a clear message has not been so present in other texts recently adopted by the Assembly.[190] However, the Assembly has taken up the issue of the interpretation of the framework convention with regard to a particular country, and following the steps already taken under the aegis of the CoM in this connection. Therefore, the contribution of the Assembly to the broadening of the discussion on the interpretation of the obligations under the framework convention, an issue which has become object of concern for the Advisory Committee with regard to a large number of states,[191] has been very narrow, and strongly affected by political considerations.

Another very important aspect examined by the Assembly has been that of the role of the state in supporting kin minorities in other states. This issue has been addressed in Resolution 1335 (2003) on Preferential treatment of national minorities by the kin-state: the case of the Hungarian Law on Hungarians Living in Neighbouring Countries ("Magyars") of 19 June 2001. While the Assembly evaluates positively the emergence of new and original forms of minority protection, particularly by their kin-states,[192] it stresses that kin-states must take care that the form and substance of the assistance given are also accepted "by the states of which the members of the kin-minorities are citizens and to which the basic rules contained in the Framework Convention on National Minorities ... are applicable".[193]

Two technical drawbacks can be identified in the text between quotation marks. The first is the introduction of the citizenship limitation, since the rule could also be suitable to apply to persons belonging to minorities which are residing in the state, and not just to those who hold the state's citizenship. The exclusion of the citizenship limitation could possibly contribute to a better protection of the interests of the state where the persons actually live. The second technical drawback is the apparent restriction of the principle drawn by the Assembly only to states signatory to the Framework Convention.

In the resolution, the Assembly discusses the situation of political tension created by the adoption in the Hungarian Parliament of the Law on Hungarians Living in Neighbouring Countries on 19 June 2001, and by reference to the report of the Venice Commission on the preferential treatment of national minorities by the kin-state presented in December of the same year, reminds states of the principles to be respected in adopting unilateral measures on the protection of kin-minorities abroad. These include: territorial sovereignty; *pacta sunt servanda*; friendly relations among states and respect for human rights and fundamental freedoms, in particular the prohibition of discrimination.[194] The Assembly reflects on issues such as: i. the definition of "nation" under that law being interpreted by neighbouring states as a non-acceptance of existing frontiers,[195] ii. the expressed concern of those neighbouring states about the unilateral character of the measures adopted, and iii. the general concerns which these measures have raised concerning the discrimination of the majority population in the neighbouring states.[196]

The latter concerns, in particular, would seem however mitigated from the perspective of the legitimacy and acknowledged non-discriminatory character of special measures in favour of persons belonging to national minorities under international law.[197] Criticism about the "unilateral" and "unnegotiated" character of the measures and its collision with the principle of friendly relations and co-operation among states would remain inescapable. In the latter connection, the Assembly has noted that amendments on the law introduced by the Hungarian Parliament on 23 June 2003 were not based on bilateral agreements. The Assembly has urged the government and parliament of Hungary that the law be amended, so that it meets all the concerns expressed.[198]

The adoption of legal standards

With regard to the ever-present question of the adoption and implementation of legal standards regarding minority protection, in Recommendation 1492 (2001), on the rights of national minorities, the Assembly has taken up its long-standing request for states to begin drafting an additional protocol to the ECHR, "drawing on the principles contained in Recommendation 1201 (1993)".[199] It has also re-affirmed the value of the principles contained in its proposal as an appropriate regulatory framework, by pointing to their acquisition of international legal status in several friendship treaties (see above).

The Assembly has emphasised the need to include in the protocol envisaged the definition of national minority contained in Recommendation 1201, although, as already discussed, the convenience of the introduction of a citizenship limitation remains questionable. The Assembly has, among other things, asked those states which have not signed and/or ratified the Framework Convention for the Protection of National Minorities to do so as soon as possible. It has called upon member states generally to sign and ratify as soon as possible Protocol No. 12 to the ECHR and to adopt a generous attitude in applying specific minority policies and implementing relevant Council of Europe instruments.[200]

Furthermore, the Assembly has made the unprecedented recommendation that the CoM "begin drafting an additional protocol to the Framework Convention for the Protection of National Minorities giving to the European Court of Human Rights or to a general judicial authority of the Council of Europe the power to give advisory opinions concerning the interpretation of the Framework Convention".[201]

The purpose of this proposal is somewhat unclear. On the one hand, the Assembly seems to be driven by the intention to provide a judicial guarantee to the implementation of the provisions of the Framework Convention. On the other hand, the choice of the provision of "advisory opinions" as the means of involvement envisaged for a possible judicial involvement seems to distort this attempt to a certain extent. The Assembly seems to adopt this "middle way" in order not to over-ride the validity of the existing monitoring mechanism under the Framework Convention, while searching for additional guarantees of compliance with its provisions.

The call for the involvement of the European Court may aim at providing further guarantees of a non-political, non-partisan interpretation of the framework convention as well as its straightforward implementation. It may also aim at ensuring that decisions on the implementation of the Framework Convention do not depart from the legal doctrine developed by the Court.[202] It should be borne in mind, however, that reliance on the Court alone does not necessarily imply a "developmental" approach to minority protection, at least in some of its aspects, as the jurisprudence existing so far illustrates and as is discussed in Chapter 1.

The Assembly also takes a "conceptual" step. It recognises that "immigrant populations whose members are citizens of the state in which they reside constitute special categories of minorities, and recommends that a specific Council of Europe instrument should be applied to them".[203] This statement of the Assembly probably responds to the tendency of states to establish differences between so called "historical" minorities and those minorities resulting from recent migratory trends, as illustrated in the process of ratification of the Framework Convention and the Languages Charter now under way. The Assembly requests the adoption of an additional instrument to deal with the situation of these minorities[204] – a request which if ever successful, would involve a time-consuming exercise – rather than requesting that the states party to existing international instruments abandon their current approaches and adopt a more generous interpretation of the existing provisions.[205]

Soon before the adoption of the Convention on Cybercrime on 23 November 2001, the Assembly adopted Recommendation 1543 (2001) on Racism and xenophobia in cyberspace. In this recommendation besides deploring the fact that several member states have not yet ratified the International Convention on the Elimination of All Forms of Racial Discrimination, the Assembly calls attention to the fact that the Convention on Cybercrime does not address the dissemination of racist propaganda using computer technology.[206] It demands that the Committee of Experts on the criminalisation of racist or xenophobic acts using computer networks, mandated by the CoM to prepare a draft additional protocol to the Convention on Cybercrime, gets sufficient means to complete its tasks before its terms of reference expire. It also asks for the inclusion of the concept of "unlawful hosting" in the drafting process, and for the specification of means for the effective prosecution of those responsible for the existence of racist sites. The Assembly encourages dialogue between Internet users, technical operators and prosecuting authorities, as well as the establishment of a consultation or joint regulation body within the Council of Europe to help prepare codes of conduct, serve as a mediator in specific disputes and function as a permanent observatory of racism and xenophobia in the Internet.[207]

The Assembly takes a narrow view of the concept of racism as such, in emphasising that "not only racism, but also the dissemination of hate speech against certain nationalities, religions and social groups must be opposed".[208] It should be recalled in this regard that Article 1 of the Convention on the Elimination of All Forms of Racial Discrimination, includes the concept of national or ethnic origin, although no reference is made to religion and social status, so the Assembly references to the latter constitutes a broadening of the scope of the groups considered.

In Opinion No. 240, on a Draft additional protocol to the Convention on Cybercrime concerning the criminalisation of acts of a racist and xenophobic nature committed through computer systems, adopted almost a year later, the Assembly expresses its opposition to the refusal to include the concept of "unlawful hosting" as a result of the opposition of a single non-member state,[209] and against the defence of what the Assembly identifies as the "European continent's common values".[210] As already noted in Chapter 5, however, the need to adopt the protocol seems to have resulted from the lack of a European consensus on the introduction in the Convention of Cybercrime of a section on the criminalisation of certain forms of expression, as this might facilitate state interference with the right to freedom of expression.

It should be recalled in this connection that access to specific types of information on the Internet is most often the result of an individual and conscious attempt, so state control of content becomes harder to legitimise than in the case of other types of media. In this regard, the avoidance of undue interference with the right to freedom of expression as a result of the implementation of the protocol should become the object of specific attention in the future. Importantly, in this opinion the Assembly advocates the introduction of "language" as a ground of discrimination to be considered in the qualification of communication material as racist or xenophobic in nature.[211] Against the Assembly's advice, however, discrimination on the basis of language was not included in the definition of racist and xenophobic communication of the final text of the protocol.[212] In contrast, the aforementioned recommendation on the inclusion of religion as a consideration was followed.

"Immigrants"

Three days after the adoption of Recommendation 1492 (2001), the Assembly voted Recommendation 1500 (2001) on the participation of immigrants and foreign residents in political life in the Council of Europe member states. Very importantly, in this decision the Assembly "underlines that respect for human rights in Europe is independent of citizenship and country of origin".[213] This statement would point at the Assembly overcoming its restrictive conceptual approach to the definition of minorities expressed in Recommendation 1201, where the minority definition contained in its proposal for an additional protocol to the ECHR, limits its scope to non-citizens.

The whole text of Recommendation 1500 comes in support of the recognition of minority rights to non-citizens. Following a line of thinking already present in the Council of Europe since the 1960s and 1970s,[214] although not sufficiently reflected in the European Convention on the Legal Status of Migrant Workers,[215] the Assembly acknowledges that "lawful residence of non-citizens ... is now a permanent feature of European societies and that the number of long-term immigrants and foreigners legally settled in Council of Europe member states is rising".[216] The Assembly further indicates that "although the integration of immigrants and foreign residents has considerably increased in economic, social, cultural and educational terms, political participation has always given rise to controversy". The Assembly favours the latter type of participation as a promoter of integration and harmonious co-existence between citizens and non-citizens, pointing to lack of integration as a source of tension and conflict.[217]

The Assembly recommends that the CoM, among other things,

> reappraise the desirable minimum standards for the treatment of non-citizens residing in a country, in particular concerning their political participation at all levels, with a view to granting the right to vote and stand in local elections to all legally established migrants irrespective of their origin, and invite member governments to take all appropriate action to ensure their implementation.[218]

The Assembly recommends the initiation of a political dialogue on this issue, with the participation of representatives of immigrant communities, and the prioritisation of integration programmes involving foreign communities – showing a somewhat patronising approach – "with a view to preparing them for political participation".[219] The Assembly urges states to grant the right to vote and stand in local elections within a three-year period to all legal migrants. This is a shorter term than the five-year period envisaged in Chapter C of the European Convention on the Participation of Foreigners in Public Life at Local Level, although the possibility of applying reductions to this period is expressly foreseen in the convention.[220]

The Assembly also urges states to review their national legislation to better respond to the needs of immigrants and foreign residents, and especially the criteria for granting citizenship and the organisation of political participation at all levels. It asks for the development of programmes aiming at the promotion of political participation, the promotion of migrants' organisations and their activities. Finally, the Assembly urges states to ratify the Convention on the Participation of Foreigners in Public Life at Local Level and the European Convention on Nationality.[221]

On 14 March 2001, the Assembly adopted Recommendation 1504 (2001) on the non-expulsion of long-term immigrants. This recommendation builds on the CoM Recommendation (2000) 15, of which detailed account has been given in Chapter 5. In response to the "spirit" of the latter recommendation, which upholds expulsion as a valid practice although subjecting it to limitations, the Assembly invites states to recognise that the expulsion of long-term immigrants "is a disproportionate and discriminatory sanction" and "an obstacle to integration".[222] The Assembly urges states to take steps to ensure that the sanction of expulsion of immigrants "is applied only to particularly serious offences affecting state security of which they have been found guilty".[223]

Adopting an innovative approach to this question, the Assembly proposes that the CoM formulate a protocol to the ECHR concerning the protection of long-term migrants against expulsion.[224] The Assembly advocates the application of the principle of equality before the law to non-citizens, including equal access and subjection to existing ordinary procedures, as well as the principle of presumption of innocence until guilt has been legally established. In the latter connection, and in contrast with the CoM recommendation, which refers to administrative procedures and authorities as competent to deal with expulsion cases, the Assembly advocates "the right to a judge" and "the right to a trial in the presence of all parties", as well as to legal assistance by counsel and "an appeal with suspensive effect, because of the irreversible consequences of enforcing expulsion".[225] The Assembly also seems to advocate the exclusion of expulsion after the serving of a prison sentence, on the basis of the principle *non bis in idem.*[226] The Assembly reinforces the principle of non-expulsion of "long-term immigrants born on the territory" of the state already present in the CoM recommendation, as well as the principle of guaranteeing appropriate consideration of the consequences of expulsion for the immigrant and his/her family, which is also present in the CoM Recommendation.[227]

Finally, in Order No. 570 (2001) on non-expulsion of long-term immigrants, the Assembly takes the unprecedented step of addressing the situation of foreign illegal residents, considering that "the penalty of expulsion, which may be combined with a prison sentence" imposed for violations of legislation on foreigners are "at least as disproportionate as those imposed on lawfully resident immigrants who have committed an ordinary-law offence".[228] Further, the Assembly regrets "the dearth of information on expulsion practice in the countries of central and eastern Europe, particularly in connection with residents who became foreigners in the wake of the dismantling of certain states".[229] Even if it instructs one of its committees to further study these issues,[230] the Assembly does not refer to any specific states.

The situation of minorities in specific countries

As in the 1990s, the Assembly has continued to focus its attention on the situation of minorities in specific countries, increasingly engaging, in addition, in addressing particular aspects. In Recommendation 1521 (2001) on the Csango minority culture in Romania,[231] the Assembly follows the line of the decisions adopted during the 1990s for the protection of various minority "cultures" (see above) which, like the Csango, are facing the danger of extinction. A difference with the previous decisions is that this particular minority culture is seemingly present only in one state. References to the role of "kin-states" are absent from the Recommendation.

The Assembly insists once more, however, in the "non-political" character of the claims by this minority group, pointing at existing demands as focusing instead on education in the mother tongue and the use of the Csango language in the Roman Catholic religious services attended by

433

this group. The Assembly recommends that the CoM encourage Romania to meet these demands, as well as to ensure information and research on the Csango culture. Innovative features of this recommendation are the Assembly's requests that Romania should provide information to Csango parents so that they are able to exercise their rights under existing legislation in the field of education, and that it provides recognition and support for Csango associations, including access to modern mass media facilities. Another innovative aspect in the Assembly's approach (already present in that of the Congress)[232] is the encouragement of the establishment of small- and medium-sized enterprises in Csango villages, to promote their welfare and contribute to their survival.

The Assembly has continued to address the minority situation in Cyprus during the early 2000s. As already noted, the treatment by the Assembly of the situation in Cyprus serves as an illustration of the evolution of the Assembly's approaches to the minority situation in specific states over the last decades. In Resolution 1333 (2003) and Recommendation 1608 (2003), the Assembly has not only addressed the minority situation when dealing with the situation in the country generally as it occurred during the 1990s, but has been directly concerned with the "Rights and fundamental freedoms of Greek Cypriots and Maronites living in the northern part of Cyprus" and the "Colonisation by Turkish settlers of the occupied part of Cyprus" as indicated on the title of the respective adopted texts.

In the resolution, adopted on 24 June 2003, the Assembly considers that a general settlement of the Cypriot conflict should never be achieved at the expense of the communities that have chosen to stay where they have always resided,[233] and by reference to the judgment of the European Court of Human Rights in the case of *Cyprus v. Turkey*, asserts Turkey's obligation to secure respect for the rights recognised under the ECHR in areas controlled by the Turkish Cypriot administration.[234]

The Assembly demands from the latter i. the cessation of the humiliation of the Greek and Maronite communities and of their intimidation; ii. the return of property to members of these communities which have been arbitrarily dispossessed, individually or collectively, or the offering of just compensation to them; iii. the guarantee of the freedom of education and worship for Orthodox Christians and Maronites; iv. the end of the movement restrictions across the demarcation line and the recognition to Greek Cypriots at least of the same rights as those already granted to Maronites; v. the granting to all inhabitants of the right to an effective remedy; vi. equal access to medical care; vii. that communities are allowed to choose their own representatives.[235] These requests are not exempt from escape clauses, such as the undefined character of the concept "arbitrarily" or the presentation of just compensation (under ii.) as an "alternative" rather than as a remedial, secondary option. However, the Assembly's dealing with the collective aspect of minority protection deserves to be highlighted.

In Recommendation 1608 adopted on the same date as the previous resolution, the Assembly addresses the other side of the coin in the situation of northern Cyprus, stating that the presence of settlers originating from mainland Turkey "constitutes a process of hidden colonisation and an additional and important obstacle to a peaceful negotiated solution to the Cyprus problem.[236] The Assembly recommends to the CoM a series of actions to counteract the colonisation process, including that Turkey and its Turkish Cypriot subordinate local administration in northern Cyprus, be called upon to stop such process,[237] and that the European Population Committee (CAHP) be instructed to conduct a population census throughout the island in order to replace estimates with reliable data.[238]

In Resolution 1309 (2002) on Freedom of religion and religious minorities in France, and by reference to the law adopted on 12 June 2001 on the reinforcement of the prevention and suppression of sects which infringe on human rights and fundamental freedoms, the Assembly questions the compatibility of this law with the ECHR, pointing in particular to the lack of clarity of the concept of "offence" and "offender" under the law.[239]

Finally, and also in addressing a specific country situation, in Recommendation 1454 (2000) on education in Bosnia and Herzegovina, the Assembly actually addresses some of the problems concerning minority education in a post-conflict environment generally. The Assembly takes note of the existing "problems relating to the ethnic segregation of children, language issues, ethnic stereotyping in school textbooks". More specifically to the country situation, it also notes "the authorities' refusal to develop a common curriculum or to co-ordinate the different curricula". According to the Assembly, "these problems are incompatible with the principles of the Council of Europe and unworthy of a state signatory to the European Cultural Convention".[240]

The Assembly recommends that the CoM works in conjunction with other international organisations in applying the principle of conditionality in the granting of financial aid to overcome the existing problems. It also recommends that the CoM supports local educational initiatives to counteract the negative phenomena mentioned and give consideration to the setting-up of multi-ethnic schools in areas where they will have the broadest impact. It also suggests that the CoM consider "using distance learning to overcome ethnic segregation at university level",[241] possibly because it foresees the difficulty of solving existing practical problems at this level. As indicated below, the Assembly has also addressed this same aspect of minority protection in connection with the post-conflict situation in Kosovo.

Armed conflict situations

Chechnya

The conflict in Chechnya has very much focused the attention of the Assembly since the start of the 2000s. On 27 January 2000, the Assembly adopted Recommendation 1444 (2000) in which the Assembly "recalls the declaration of the Parliamentary Assembly's Bureau on the situation in Chechnya of 13 December 1999, according to which 'persistence in violations could lead the Parliamentary Assembly to put under question Russian participation in the Assembly's work and in the Council of Europe in general' and takes note of the findings of its delegation during its recent visit to Moscow, Chechnya and Ingushetia (16-20 January 2000)".[242] The Assembly condemns the conduct of military operations in Chechnya and stresses the need to exclude indiscriminate and disproportionate use of force affecting the civilian population.[243]

The Russian Federation is found by the Assembly "to be violating some of her most important obligations" under both the ECHR and international humanitarian law.[244] It notes with some satisfaction the fact that the acting President of the Russian Federation, V. Putin, has accepted the proposal for a Council of Europe presence in the region.[245] The Assembly resolves to monitor closely respect for some of the requests made in the recommendation, while emphasising "that failure to meet them will inevitably necessitate, at the Assembly's April 2000 part-session, a review of Russian continued membership of, and participation in, the Assembly's work and in the Council of Europe in general".

The Assembly also instructs several of its committees to make arrangements for their respective rapporteurs to pay a visit to the region before the April part-session, "in order to review whether such a review is necessary".[246] Thus, the Assembly starts to make use of the most powerful political leverages available to it, in order to try to influence the state's approach, placing additional pressure by indicating the timeframes for the Assembly's re-evaluation of existing conditions.

In Recommendation 1456 (2000) on the conflict in the Chechen Republic – implementation by the Russian Federation of Recommendation 1444 (2000) adopted on 6 April 2000 – after taking note of "certain positive measures which the Russian Federation has taken in keeping with Recommendation 1444 ...", the Assembly affirms that the Russian Federation "has not yet, however, responded to the two key political demands made by the Assembly, namely the introduction of an immediate and complete cease-fire and the initiation of political dia-logue without preconditions with the elected Chechen authorities".[247]

The Assembly regrets the unsatisfactory replies to the explanations requested by the Secretary General under Article 52 of the ECHR.[248] It recalls that "assurances were made that the accession of the Russian Federation would not result in the lowering of the high standards of the Organisation" and considers that substantial grounds for concern exist, as noted in some of the paragraphs of the recommendation, that the ECHR: "is being violated by the Russian authorities in the Chechen Republic both gravely and in a systematic manner".[249] The Assembly appeals to the member states of the Council of Europe: "to make use of Article 33 as a matter of urgency and to refer to the European Court of Human Rights alleged breaches by the Russian Federation of the provi-sions of the Convention and its Protocols".[250]

It also recommends that the CoM, "should substantial, accelerating and demonstrable progress not be made immediately ... initiate without delay, in accordance with Article 8 of the Statute, the procedure for the suspension of the Russian Federation from its rights of representation in the Council of Europe", and report to the parliamentary Assembly in this connection.[251] Reference has already been made in Chapter 5 to the fact that the CoM, in its reply to Recommendation 1456 (2000) stated that there was no need for the Committee to act in the context of Article 8 of the Council of Europe Statute. Council of Europe states have not made use either of their prerogatives under Article 33 of the ECHR with regard to the situation in Chechnya.

In Resolution 1221 (2000) adopted on 29 June 2000, the Assembly con-siders it unacceptable that the CoM has neither denounced the conduct by the Russian Federation of its military campaign in the Chechen Republic and the resulting grave human rights violations, nor seriously considered the implications of this for Russian membership of the Council of Europe. It also regrets that the Council of Europe's govern-ments have not made use of Article 33 of the ECHR, and renews its appeal in this connection.[252] Nevertheless, it also refers to the earlier withdrawal of the voting rights of the Russian parliamentary delegation by the Assembly, expressing "its wish that the Russian Federal Assembly will actively and substantially use its influence to improve the human rights situation in the Chechen Republic, and as a consequence, the voting rights of the Russian Parliamentary delegation could be restored".[253]

In Resolution 1227 (2000) adopted on 28 September 2000, the Assembly urges the Russian Federation to take action, in line with its previous decisions, in areas relevant to human rights protection in the Chechen Republic. The Assembly addresses concrete aspects of the human rights situation, and asks for the facilitation of the work of the various bodies established by the Russian authorities to investigate crimes committed by federal service personnel against the civilian population.[254] However, in view of all previous unsuccessful attempts to lead the CoM to take more drastic action, the Assembly's recommendations lose additional steam, although the Assembly still calls on the CoM to monitor the action taken by the Russian Federation "in response to the Assembly's recommendations and resolutions".

The Assembly starts to focus its attention instead on approaches by the Council of Europe to specific aspects of the human rights situation on the ground, in order to better follow up those initiatives already accepted and undertaken. The Assembly calls on the CoM "to closely monitor progress on investigations and prosecutions of those responsible for abuses and urges member states, 'in the absence of meaningful progress', to pursue other avenues of accountability including an interstate complaint before the European Court of Human Rights",[255] in accordance with its previous recommendations. The Assembly "resolves to make the necessary practical arrangements to assess progress at its January 2001 part-session" and "expresses the hope that by then progress will have proved sufficiently convincing for the Russian delegation to enjoy its full rights".[256]

On 25 January 2001, the Assembly decided to ratify the credentials of the Russian delegation, restoring its voting rights, even if these were challenged on substantial grounds in relation to the conflict in the Chechen Republic. The Assembly believed: "that the Russian parliamentary delegation deserves to be given another chance to prove that it is willing – and able – to influence the situation in the Chechen Republic for the better".[257] In Resolution 1240 (2001), on the conflict in the Chechen Republic – recent developments, the Assembly reiterates its determination to join forces with Russian parliamentarians in their efforts to implement a series of recommendations regarding the conflict, adopted by the State Duma in September 2000. A joint working group of the Assembly and the Russian Duma is established for this purpose, due to report both to the relevant committees of the Assembly and to the Duma "with regard both to the human rights situation and to the overall reconstruction effort".[258] The Assembly also decides to co-operate closely with Mr Kalamanov's office.[259]

While the development of the Assembly's approaches thereafter have already been discussed in detail in Chapter 5, additional reference should be made here to the more recent ones, especially the adoption of Resolution 1315 (2003) on the Evaluation of the prospects of a political solution to the conflict in the Chechen Republic, adopted on 29 January 2003. In this resolution the Assembly states that the Russian prosecuting bodies are either unwilling or unable to find and bring to justice the guilty parties, despite the fact that some investigations of the most high-profile cases of mass killings and disappearances have now been proceeding for more than three years without tangible results. The Assembly deplores the climate of impunity which consequently reigns in the Chechen Republic and which makes normal life in the republic impossible.[260]

The Assembly calls upon the competent authorities to ensure, among other things, that military Orders Nos. 80 and 46 concerning the conduct of military operations and especially operations to check citizen's registration are enforced, and that more police units of mixed ethnicity are formed for law enforcement activities, as well as that police units follow training on human rights. The Assembly demands that legal action against suspects be brought to a less delayed and more convincing conclusion and that the proliferation of weapons to Chechen fighters be curbed, armed fighters being encouraged to surrender their weapons voluntarily. It is interesting to note that in connection with the current amnesty proposals discussed in Chapter 7, the Assembly supports the granting of pardons in accordance with the previous Decree of the Head of Administration of the Chechen Republic of 24 October 2002, without suggesting the need for additional amnesty initiatives.[261]

The Assembly requests that the reports by the Committee for the Prevention of Torture are published and its recommendations implemented, and that the Russian authorities provide it with an updated and detailed list of all criminal investigations by military and civilian law enforcement agencies into crimes against the civilian population by service personnel and members of all police and special forces, and also into crimes committed by Chechen fighters.[262]

The Assembly sets a series of conditions necessary for the holding of the constitutional referendum on 23 March 2003,[263] which, as already noted in Chapter 5, were later considered by the Assembly as not having been met. It also supports the right for Chechen IDPs (internally displaced persons) to stay in Ingushetia and to take up residence in that republic, calling on the Russian authorities not to exercise pressure on or coerce displaced people to return to the Chechen Republic.[264] The Assembly calls for the drawing of a collaborative plan for reconstruction and humanitarian aid between the Chechen authorities and the international community, which ensures the proper and transparent use of such aid.[265] Finally, it also calls upon the Chechen fighters to lay down their arms and commit themselves to a serious political process, as well as to distance themselves from terrorist acts and to immediately release all kidnapped people.[266]

In Recommendation 1593 (2003), adopted on the same date as Resolution 1315 (2003), the Assembly deals with some additional, practical aspects, including a call for the implementation of the recommendations made by the Commissioner on Human Rights "on certain rights that must be guaranteed during the arrest and detention of persons following 'cleansing' operations in the Chechen Republic of the Russian Federation"[267] and for the consideration of ways in which the work of the Council of Europe experts "could still be more effective".[268]

Whatever the CoM responses to the Assembly's requests,[269] the Assembly goes on to reiterate the aforementioned recommendations in Resolution 1323 on the Human rights situation in the Chechen Republic, adopted on 2 April 2003. Renewing its pro-active stand, the Assembly in this resolution criticises the climate of constant fear, destruction and massive human rights violations in which the Chechen Republic had lived for nearly a decade, and points at the lack of effectiveness of judicial and non-judicial redress mechanisms set up by the Russian authorities, including the Office of the Special Representative of the President of the Russian Federation for Human Rights in the Chechen Republic.[270] It refers to lack of co-operation of the Russian government with the European Committee for the Prevention of Torture and its non-renewal of the mandate of the OSCE Assistance Group to Chechnya.

It points out that the European Court of Human Rights cannot cope effectively with systematic human rights abuses on the scale of those committed in Chechnya via individual complaints, and laments that no member state or group of states has yet found the courage to lodge an interstate complaint with the Court.[271] The Assembly calls on member states to pursue all avenues of accountability with regard to the Russian Federation, including of the latter type, without delay. It also calls on the international community to consider the setting up of an ad hoc tribunal to try war crimes and crimes against humanity committed in the Chechen Republic.[272] It urges the Russian Federation to implement the recommendations of the Commissioner for Human Rights and the European Committee for the Prevention of Torture and to ratify the Statute of the International Criminal Court without delay.[273]

As already discussed in Chapter 6, on the same date that Resolution 1323 was adopted, the Assembly adopted Recommendation 1600 (2003), in which it decided to trigger the CoM monitoring mechanism, exercising for the first time its prerogative under paragraph 1 of the 1994 Declaration on Compliance with Commitments Accepted by Member States of the Council of Europe. On 28 May 2003, the CoM adopted its reply (Doc 9821) to Recommendation 1600, which did not explicitly take position on the Assembly's proposal concerning paragraph 1 of the 1994 Declaration. However, the CoM pointed out that

> since June 2000, a monthly discussion takes place in the [meeting of] Deputies on interim reports by the Secretary General on the work of the

Council of Europe experts present in Chechnya under the item "Contribution of the Council of Europe towards restoration of the rule of law, respect of human rights and democracy in Chechnya". Relevant Parliamentary Assembly Recommendations are being taken into account during these discussions. They also take into account additional information regarding the situation in the Chechen Republic of the Russian Federation provided by the Secretary General. Both the monthly interim reports and the addenda thereto are transmitted to the Assembly.

This points to the Assembly's initiative suffering a similar fate to that suffered by the Secretary General's initiative.

Kosovo

During the early 2000s, the Assembly also devoted much attention to monitoring the post-conflict situation in Kosovo. The Assembly has started to adopt separate recommendations on specific aspects of the situation concerning human rights. For example, Recommendation 1509 (2001) on human rights and the rule of law in Kosovo deals, among other things, with the situation of prisoners and conditions of arrest and detention, pointing to the slowness of the process of national participation in the provisional administration set up by the United Nations, and welcoming the creation of a domestic, multi-ethnic local police force. The Assembly has encouraged the adoption of an electoral law enabling elections to be contested "by parties of citizens", instead of "parties based on ethnic affiliation".[274]

It has adopted Recommendation 1510 (2001), on the humanitarian situation of returnees to Kosovo[275] and Recommendation 1511 (2001) on the cultural situation in Kososvo (as well as in the field of education). With regard to the latter, the Assembly addresses questions of segregation, nationalist stereotyping and hate speech similar to those addressed with regard to Bosnia (see above). On the geo-political aspects, the Assembly has addressed the "situation in Kosovo and its neighbouring regions" in Recommendation 1508 (2001), pursuing its efforts to analyse the situation already started during the 1990s and continuing to suggest concrete measures to prevent further conflict. In this context, the Assembly has also analysed the situation in southern Serbia, Montenegro and "the former Yugoslav Republic of Macedonia", addressing recommendations to the respective authorities, as well as to those of Albania.

Finally, with regard to the conflict which violently erupted in 2001 after a long period of mounting tension in "the former Yugoslav Republic of Macedonia", the situation was initially addressed by the Assembly in Resolution 1255 (2001).[276] In this, while condemning the action by Albanian extremist groups, the Assembly "resolutely condemns acts of retaliation against the ethnic Albanian population".[277] The Assembly regrets that little progress has been achieved by the authorities in implementing the recommendations of the Assembly contained in Recommendation 1213 (2000) on the honouring of obligations and commitments by this state (see further, Chapter 9), mentioning in particular "measures regarding the use of the Albanian language in public life and education and to increase the proportion of ethnic Albanians in state institutions, the police and the army". The Assembly adds however, that "at the same time, the Albanian minority should not make excessive demands".[278]

The Assembly "asks the Government of Macedonia ... to adopt urgent measures, including constitutional ones, aimed at improving the legal and practical position of the ethnic Albanian population and other minorities", in particular with regard to the use of the Albanian language in dealings with the state administration and the courts, and the improvement of education in the Albanian language.[279] It also asks the government "to ensure efficient protection of all citizens irrespective of their ethnic origins against possible acts of retaliation and harassment and to bring to justice the perpetrators of those acts".[280] Further, it asks the government "to engage in a political dialogue with those leaders whose movements are not represented in the parliament, and who renounce violent action and have surrendered their arms".[281]

The Assembly invites the Venice Commission to offer its co-operation to the Macedonian authorities in amending their constitution, and decides on the establishment of an ad hoc committee of its Political Affairs Committee to visit the region and report to the Assembly at its next ordinary session two months later.[282] In Recommendation 1528 (2001) of the same title as the previous resolution, the Assembly advises the CoM to intensify its co-operation programmes with Macedonia with a view to assisting in the implementation of the necessary reforms, including in the fields of interethnic dialogue, education, the media and local government.[283] It also advises that the CoM provide financial and logistic help in organising a reliable population census. Furthermore, the Assembly recommends that "the Committee of Ministers call upon all governments of the member states to freeze the bank accounts and forbid the financing of the extremist groups who support from abroad the illegal activities of the extremists, in 'the former Yugoslav Republic of Macedonia'".[284]

Concluding remarks

The Parliamentary Assembly has been concerned with minority protection almost constantly since the Council of Europe was created, while the intergovernmental structures have considered it as a non-issue for most of that time. Even if the endeavours of the Assembly in legal standard-setting on minority protection were brought to a halt with the decisions adopted by the intergovernmental bodies in the early 1970s, the Assembly did not abandon the question. Especially during the early 1980s, the Assembly started to address minority questions directly. The issue of minority languages is an example.

In areas of relevance for minority protection which the intergovernmental bodies did address, such as the issue of the provision of minimum protection for migrant workers in the social and economic spheres, resulting in the adoption of a convention in this area, the Assembly was to demonstrate much more forward-looking approaches than those adopted by the intergovernmental bodies. The Assembly pointed out questions, particularly related to the long-term stay of migrants in host countries, which are highly relevant to interethnic relations in Europe today, and which most European states are still unwilling to address. The Assembly has also made substantive proposals to deal with these questions.

It should be noted, however, that during the 1980s, and even until the mid-1990s, Assembly approaches to minority protection were strongly determined by geo-strategic, political considerations. The Assembly showed readiness to address specific minority situations in countries that were not members of the Council of Europe, countries in central and eastern Europe in particular. In spite of the cold-war context, the Assembly often placed specific demands on states, aiming to address specific issues of specific groups living on the other side of the iron curtain. However, questions of freedom of religion and the situation of religious minorities became a priority for the Assembly, as this became a main tool for ideological confrontation. Other aspects of minority protection, however, were largely disregarded.

The situation of some ethnic minorities in central and eastern Europe – those which had a kin-state in the west – also became object of particular concern, especially in connection with the restrictions imposed on the freedom of movement of these groups which prevented them from leaving the country where they lived, denying them the possibility to move to their kin-state. As soon as changes in central and eastern Europe started, the Assembly became an even stronger supporter of the lifting of those restrictions, particularly in the context of the significant population movements which took place at that time.

The start of the changes in central and eastern Europe also encouraged the Assembly to take up with renewed vigour the question of the adoption of legal minority protection standards by the Council of Europe. The search for standards to assess state performance in the field of minority protection by the Assembly, linked to the acceleration of the process of accession of central and eastern European states to the Organisation, as discussed in the next chapter, seems to have been a triggering factor. The perception of the need for the adoption of appropriate guarantees and justiciable rights of minority protection has never decayed since then. The Assembly's perception of a lack of adequate efforts by applicant states led it to elaborate a draft protocol to the ECHR, contained in Recommendation 1201 (1993). The protocol has been used by the Assembly as a key instrument of assessment of compliance with accession requirements till present time. This is further discussed in the following chapter.

The Assembly has not spared efforts in guaranteeing the effectiveness of the monitoring system established under the Framework Convention for the Protection of National Minorities, a text which reflects the highest level of achievement in the field of minority protection by the inter-governmental structures of the Council of Europe so far. Nevertheless, the consideration by the Assembly that the guarantees, especially as to justiciability, provided under the Framework Convention are not sufficient, have led to its insisting on the adoption of an additional protocol to the ECHR dealing with minority protection generally. The Assembly has adopted flexible approaches, as shown by its positive attitude regarding the substitutive value of the possible adoption of an additional protocol to the ECHR in the cultural field, in accordance with the text of the Vienna Summit Declaration. The Assembly has aimed at contributing to the process of elaboration of the cultural protocol, so that it could meet its own concerns. However, little progress has been achieved by the intergovernmental structures regarding the elaboration of the cultural protocol so far, as discussed in Chapter 5.

The Assembly has continued to deal with other general questions which affected minorities during the 1990s, such as religious and other types of intolerance, giving special importance to education and the role of the media. The establishment of the European Commission Against Racism and Intolerance has been, perhaps, the initiative of the Assembly with most important practical repercussions in addressing these questions. With regard to specific minority situations, an important development has been the increasing attention paid by the Assembly to minorities when dealing with the overall situation in particular member states.

Another important trend has been the growing attention devoted to addressing specific minority situations from the perspective of human rights concerns, rather than mainly as a result of geo-political considerations. This is illustrated by the increasing attention paid by the Assembly to those minorities which do not have a kin-state and which are in the greatest danger of extinction unless prompt protective measures are adopted. Furthermore, the Assembly has started to focus on concrete aspects of human rights protection of the specific minority groups it has been dealing with, providing for in-depth analysis of their problems, and facilitating conceptual progress regarding minority protection generally. This has been facilitated, especially since the 2000s, by the Assembly's reliance on the expert analysis provided by the Venice Commission.

At the political level, and in its interaction with the Council of Europe structures, the Assembly has exercised pressure for the triggering of the most compelling mechanisms available under the Statute of the Council of Europe and the ECHR with regard to a powerful member state, the Russian Federation, in connection with the on-going conflict in Chechnya, resulting in grave and massive violations of human rights, those of the Chechen population especially. Neither the CoM nor individual member states have followed the Assembly along this path. In relation to this as well as to other conflict situations, the Assembly has constantly followed up political and human rights developments, suggesting solutions to problems identified, especially those concerning minority protection. The Assembly has often undertaken a mediating role, organising on-the-spot visits to the states where tensions and conflicts have occurred, to better study the situation and engage in direct contacts with the parties to existing tensions.

In conclusion, the Assembly has been the Council of Europe structure showing the greatest awareness of minority concerns and need of protection. Although the Assembly may have occasionally incurred "scientific" errors in approaching minority questions, or been guided by political considerations rather than human rights concerns, it has shown increasing willingness to identify and study existing problems, investigate solutions to them, and propose appropriate action both to the CoM and other Council of Europe structures on the one hand, and to the states concerned on the other. The Assembly has not given up on its efforts even when not obtaining appropriate responses or feed-back, showing flexibility and capacity to adapt its own agenda in order to pursue its work in the field of minority protection. It regularly takes stock of the situation of minorities in Europe (for example, during the autumn session 2003, report by Mr Cilevics, Doc. 9862).

The Assembly is called upon to continue playing an essential role in keeping the minority question on the agenda of the Council of Europe. Especially in the medium term, when the minority question may lose support in a broadly enlarged Organisation, where states are supposed to be treated on an equal footing, and the division between central and eastern European states on the one hand, and western European states on the other, as it comes to the tackling of the minority issue, becomes increasingly blurred. It is to be hoped, and it can be expected, that the

Assembly will continue in its efforts to make minority protection a reality, so that Council of Europe enlargement does not result in the generalisation of the minimum common denominator as it comes to minority protection standards upheld by some of the western European democracies.

Notes

1. See Chapter 1. For a detailed account of these early endeavours of the Assembly, see A. Spiliopoulou-Åkermark, op. cit., pp. 200-209. See also F. Benoît-Rohmer, *The Minority Question in Europe: Towards a Coherent System of Protection for National Minorities* (Strasbourg: Council of Europe, 1996), p. 36.

2. For the text of this article, see Chapter 1.

3. See further, Chapter 1.

4. Report of the Committee of experts to the Committee of Ministers, 9 November 1973, Doc. DH/Exo (73) as noted in P. Thornberry and M.A. Martín Estébanez, op. cit., p. 25.

5. See E. Grisel, *The Status of Minorities and Ethnic Groups in the Member States of the Council of Europe,* Assembly Doc. 6294, AS/Jur (40) 7, Strasbourg 28 July 1988, Appendix I, paragraph 5.

6. Adopted at the 33rd ordinary session of the Parliamentary Assembly.

7. Paragraph 4.*a* of the recommendation.

8. The Assembly proposes the use of dialects as the spoken language in pre-school education, and use of standardised mother-tongue language forms in primary education, the prevailing language of the country being then progressively introduced alongside the mother tongue. On this topic, see further *The Hague Recommendations regarding Minority Education Rights and Explanatory Note,* elaborated at the request of the OSCE High Commissioner on National Minorities (The Hague: Foundation of Inter-Ethnic Relations, 1999).

9. On this and other aspects of linguistic rights, see *Oslo Recommendations regarding the Linguistic Rights of National Minorities and Explanatory Note,* elaborated at the request of the OSCE High Commissioner on National Minorities (The Hague: Foundation of Inter-Ethnic Relations, 1998).

10. Final paragraph (5) of the recommendation.

11. On the European Charter for Regional or Minority Languages, see Chapter 3.

12. Opinion adopted at the 40th ordinary session of the Assembly. On the Congress, see Chapter 10

13. Adopted by the Parliamentary Assembly at its 38th session, paragraphs 3, 5, and 7.

14. Ibid., at paragraph 16.

15. Recommendation adopted by the Assembly at its 39th session, paragraphs 5 and 6.

16. Ibid., at paragraph 20, *d.*

17. European Treaty Series No. 106.

18. On the treatment of this topic at the Council of Europe, see Chapter 10.

19. Adopted by the Parliamentary Assembly at its 37th session, paragraph 10, iv. and v.

20. See in particular the CSCE Madrid Concluding Document of 1983, Chapter on co-operation in humanitarian and other fields. The OSCE Meeting on Human Rights and Fundamental Freedoms and Cultural Forum were held in Ottawa and Budapest respectively, the same year the resolution was adopted. The text of these documents is available in A. Bloed (ed.), *The Conference on Security and Co-operation in Europe; Analysis and Basic Documents, 1972-1993* (Dordrecht, Boston, London: Kluwer Law International, 1993), pp. 274-78. The text is also available on CD-ROM from the OSCE Secretariat and can also be obtained via the OSCE Internet website: http://www.osce.org

21. Adopted at the 38th session of the Assembly, paragraphs 5 and 9.*a.*

22.   Adopted at the 40th session of the Assembly, in 1988.

23.   For information on the community relations project, consult its final report under the title "Community and ethnic relations in Europe", MG-CR 1 final E. See also P. Thornberry and M.A. Martín Estébanez, op. cit., pp. 81-82 and 87-90. References to the project can also be found in Chapters 5 and 7.

24.   European Treaty Series No. 93, Strasbourg, 24 November 1977. For a commentary on the convention see P. Thornberry and M.A. Martín Estébanez, op. cit., pp. 82-85. See also Chapter 10.

25.   European Treaty Series No. 144, Strasbourg, 5 February 1992. For a commentary on the convention see ibid., at pp. 62-64. See also Chapters 5 and 10.

26.   The list refers to: i. the right of religious associations to unhindered existence and recognition under the law; ii. the right to practise religion and associate in churches, private homes and dwellings and in public, without the need for official approval; iii. the right to free election of church officers and bodies without interference; iv. the rights of religious associations to combine anywhere within the territory of the State; v. the right to erect, purchase or hire churches and prayer centres without the need for official approval; vi. the right of ownership of churches, liturgical objects and donations; vii. the right to public freedom of religious opinion on an equal footing with anti-religious propaganda; viii. the right to print and distribute religious literature without the need for official approval: in particular, the right to print religious works in the necessary quantities, or to import them; ix. the right to operate pastoral work without restriction anywhere in the territory, particularly in hospitals, old people's homes and prisons; x. the right to run religious education for children and young people, and to organise youth groups; xi. the right to operate charitable aid schemes, particularly through collection, relief funds, etc.; xii. the right to erect and run educational centres for ministers without official interference, and for free selection of candidates for the ministry; xiii. the right to run religious courses and congresses without official permission being required; xiv. the right of parents to bring up their children in a religious manner; xv. the right to contact with sister churches and religious associations abroad by correspondence, exchange of literature and participation in congresses etc; xvi. the right to freedom from discrimination on religious grounds, particularly in housing, social security, employment, education and academic life, as well as in the exercise of civil, civic and political rights; xvii. the right of churches and religious associations to uncensored access to the mass media (press, radio, television), and to broadcast religious services on Fridays, Saturdays or Sundays and at major religious festivals.

27.   See the Vienna Concluding Document of 1989, questions relation to security in Europe, section on principles, paragraphs 16 and 17. The text of this document is available in A. Bloed (ed.), *The Conference on Security and Co-operation in Europe; Analysis and Basic Documents, 1972-1993* (Dordrecht, Boston, London: Kluwer Law International, 1993), pp. 335-37. The text is also available on CD-ROM from the OSCE Secretariat and can also be obtained via the OSCE Internet website: http://www.osce.org

28.   See Chapter 2.

29.   On the situation in Turkey, see Resolutions 822 (1984), 840 (1985) and 860 (1986). See also Recommendation 974 (1983) and Resolution 816 (1984) on the situation in Cyprus.

30.   This is the case, for example, with the requests for an increase in the number of crossing points between the two parts of the island, and the requests to leaders of both the Greek and Turkish communities not to alter the demographic structure of the island. See Recommendation 1056 (1987) on national refugees and missing persons in Cyprus, paragraph 18 *c* and *g*.

31. On the human dimension of the OSCE during this period, see J. Helgesen, "Between Helsinkis – and beyond? Human rights in the CSCE process" in A. Rosas and J. Helgesen (eds.), *Human Rights in a Changing East/West Perspective* (London: Printer Publishers Ltd, 1990). See also A. Heraclides, *Security and Co-operation in Europe: The Human Dimension, 1972-1992* (London: Frank Cass, 1993) and M.A. Martín Estébanez, "The OSCE and human rights" in R. Hanski and M. Suksi (eds.), *An Introduction to the International Protection of Human Rights: A Textbook* (Turku/Åbo: Institute for Human Rights, Åbo Akademi University, 1999), pp. 329-47, at pp. 329-35.

32. This can be considered as an important precedent, since it was necessary to wait until the OSCE Geneva meeting of experts on national minorities for a general recognition of this at the intergovernmental level. The text is available on CD-ROM from the OSCE Secretariat and can also be obtained via the OSCE Internet website: http://www.osce.org

33. See opinion on the situation of minorities in Romania, presented by the Committee on Migration, Refugees and Demography, Rapporteur Mr Böhm, 12 September 1984, Parliamentary Assembly Doc. 5264.

34. Resolution 845 (1985), adopted at the 37th session of the Assembly.

35. Recommendation 1040 (1986), adopted at the 38th ordinary session of the Assembly.

36. See report on the situation of ethnic and Muslim minorities in Bulgaria (Rapporteur: M. Probst), 5 September 1989. Parliamentary Assembly Doc. 6106.

37. Adopted at the 40th ordinary session of the Assembly.

38. Resolutions 845 (1985); 830 (1984); and 846 (1985) respectively.

39. Paragraph 2 of the recommendation, adopted on 9 May 1998.

40. Ibid., paragraph 6.

41. See Chapter 5.

42. See report on the rights of minorities, Parliamentary Assembly Doc. 6294, 24 September 1990.

43. Paragraphs 6-7 of the recommendation, adopted at the 42nd session of the Assembly. See Chapter 9.

44. See further, Chapter 1.

45. See section IV, paragraph 31 of the Document of the Copenhagen meeting of the Conference on the human dimension of the CSCE (OSCE Copenhagen Document), adopted in June 1990. The text of this document is available in A. Bloed (ed.), op. cit., pp. 438-65 at p. 456. The text is also available on CD-ROM from the OSCE Secretariat and can also be obtained via the OSCE Internet website: http://www.osce.org

46. See Chapter 3.

47. On this topic, see further *Lund Recommendations on the Effective Participation of National Minorities in Public Life and Explanatory Note* (The Hague: The Foundation on Inter-Ethnic Relations, 1999).

48. See Chapter 2.

49. Paragraphs 16 and 17 of the recommendation. See further, Chapters 1 and 5.

50. Paragraph 3 of the order.

51. Fourth paragraph of Appendix II (Colloquy on the rights of minorities) to the report on the rights of minorities (rapporteurs: Mr Brincat and Mr Worms), 29 January 1992, Parliamentary Assembly Doc. 6556, p. 16.

52. Fifth paragraph of the report, at ibid.

53. Ibid, p. 17.

54. See further references in the Introduction.

55. Ibid., p. 18.

56. Ibid.

57. See P. Thornberry and M.A. Martín Estébanez, op. cit., pp. 37-38. See further, Chapter 5.

58. Paragraph 14 of the recommendation, adopted on 5 February 1992, at the 43rd ordinary session of the Assembly. On the assessment of the applications for membership of the organisation by the Assembly, see Chapter 9.

59. Paragraph 10 of the recommendation.

60. Paragraph 4 of the order adopted by the Assembly at its 43rd ordinary session.

61. On the Charter's pre-history, see Chapters 3 and 10.

62. For the content of this recommendation, see Chapter 5.

63. For comments on this proposal see P. Thornberry and M.A. Martín Estébanez, op. cit., Chapter five, pp. 36-39.

64. For comments on the Austrian proposal for a draft protocol, see P. Thornberry and M.A. Martín Estébanez, op. cit., pp. 26-27.

65. Reply from the Committee of Ministers to Written Question No. 344 by Mr Worms on the rights of minorities, 26 June 1992. Parliamentary Assembly Doc. 6641, 2, paragraph 3. Notes within the quotation added by the present authors.

66. Ibid., paragraph 5.

67. Parliamentary Assembly Doc. 6742, 19 January 1993. See also opinion of the Political Affairs Committee, Rapporteur Mr de Puig, Parliamentary Assembly Doc. 6749, 1 February 1993.

68. On DH-MIN and its work, see further, Chapter 7.

69. See P. Thornberry and M.A. Martín Estébanez, op. cit., pp. 27-30. See also the comments on the Austrian proposal for a draft protocol in which similarities with the Assembly proposal can be found, at ibid., pp. 26-27.

70. This position has been recently sustained by the Assembly in Resolution 1301 (2002). See below.

71. See *J. Ballantyne et al. v. Canada*, UN Doc. A/48/40 (1 November 1993), paragraph 11.2.

72. Ibid., individual opinion by Mrs E. Evatt, co-signed by Mr N. Ando, Mr M.T. Bruni Celli and Mr V. Dimitrijevic.

73. The OSCE High Commissioner on National Minorities, for example, has addressed the situation of the non-citizen population in the implementation of its mandate. See M.A. Martin Estebanez, "The High Commissioner on National Minorities: development of the mandate", pp. 152-53. This has been particularly the case when addressing situations of tension in Latvia and Estonia. See W. Kemp (ed.), *Quiet Diplomacy in Action*, pp. 141-65.

74. See the reference included in the Parliamentary Assembly opinion on the protection of national minorities by the Committee on Legal Affairs and Human Rights, Rapporteur Mr R. Bindig, Doc. 7922, 23 September 1997, 5, paragraph 16.

75. See Chapter 9.

76. On this process and its relevance for minority protection, see further below.

77. See Chapter 5.

78. Report on the "Rights of national minorities", rapporteur Mr Bindig, 20 December 1995, Parliamentary Assembly Doc. 7442, section III (explanatory memorandum), p. 7, paragraph 5.

79.   Paragraph 7 of the recommendation, adopted on 31 January 1995.

80.   Neither of these specific proposals was taken up literally by the CoM. With regard to the first proposal, concerning the presence at the advisory committee of one representative for each of the contracting states, it was to be revised by the Assembly one year later, as illustrated by Recommendation 1300 (1996). The large number of contracting parties to the framework convention seems to have made the option for a fixed number of members of the advisory committee, finally adopted, a preferable one. This latter approach serves better the principle of effectiveness. See further, Chapter 2. On the issue of a fixed number of members of the committee as a preferable choice, see the comments, on the experience of the European Committee for the Prevention of Torture and Inhuman or Degrading Treatment or Punishment, included in M.A. Martín Estébanez and K. Gál, op. cit., p. 40.

81.   Paragraph 12 of the recommendation.

82.   See Chapter 5.

83.   See report on the "Rights of national minorities", rapporteur Mr Bindig, 20 December 1995, Parliamentary Assembly Doc. 7442.

84.   Paragraph 13 of the recommendation, adopted on 23 January 1996.

85.   Paragraph 14 of the recommendation.

86.   Paragraph 16.vii-viii of the recommendation.

87.   Paragraph 16.ix at ibid.

88.   Paragraph 16.vi.*a-d* at ibid.

89.   Present author's emphasis. The argument underlying this proposal is clearly described in Mr Bindig's report: "The Convention can only serve its purpose usefully if it has the trust of those it seeks to protect. A system that remains exclusively in the hands of states would leave little to identify with to persons belonging to national minorities". See report on the "Rights of national minorities", rapporteur Mr Bindig, 20 December 1995, Parliamentary Assembly Doc. 7442, p. 8, paragraph 10.

90.   Paragraph 16.v.*e* of the recommendation. See the similar views held by the Committee of Wise Persons in this regard, presented in Chapter 5.

91.   Paragraph 2.iii of the order adopted by the Assembly on 23 January 1993.

92.   Report on the "Protection of the rights of minorities", Parliamentary Assembly Doc. 7572, p. 5 (June 1996).

93.   Adopted by the Committee of Ministers on 17 September 1997 at the 601st meeting of the ministers' deputies. See further, Chapter 2.

94.   See in particular, paragraph 15.vi. and ix of the Assembly's Recommendation 1300 as compared with paragraphs 31-32 and 24 of the CoM Resolution (97) 10, respectively.

95.   Report on the "Protection of national minorities", Parliamentary Assembly Doc. 7899, 8 September 1997. See also opinion on the "Protection of national minorities" by the Committee on Legal Affairs and Human Rights, rapporteur Mr Bindig, Doc. 7922, 23 September 1997.

96.   See opinion on the "Protection of national minorities", at ibid., p. 4, paragraphs 9 and 11.

97.   Press release Ref. 237 (97), Strasbourg, 22 April 1997, Council of Europe Press Service.

98.   On the Strasbourg summit declaration, see Chapter 5.

99.   See recommendations of the Assembly, replies from the Committee of Ministers, Parliamentary Assembly Doc. 8306, 26 January 1999, grouped reply to Recommendations 1134 (1990); 1177 (1992); 1201 (1993); 1255 (1955); 1285 (1996); 1300 (1996) and 1345 (1997), introductory section.

100. Ibid.

101. Section A, paragraph 2 of the reply. See further, Chapter 5.

102. Ibid.

103. Recommendations of the Assembly, replies from the Committee of Ministers, Parliamentary Assembly Doc. 8306, 26 January 1999, grouped reply to Recommendations 1134 (1990); 1177 (1992); 1201 (1993); 1255 (1955); 1285 (1996); 1300 (1996) and 1345 (1997), section B. Text within brackets added by the present authors.

104. See recommendations of the Assembly, replies from the Committee of Ministers, Parliamentary Assembly Doc. 8306, 26 January 1999, grouped reply to Recommendations 1134 (1990); 1177 (1992); 1201 (1993); 1255 (1955); 1285 (1996); 1300 (1996) and 1345 (1997), Appendix to the reply of the Committee of Ministers to Parliamentary Assembly Recommendation 1345 (1997), Opinion of the CDDH on Parliamentary Assembly Recommendation 1345 (1997) on the protection of national minorities, paragraph 6.

105. Ibid., section B.

106. Ibid.

107. Ibid., Appendix to the reply of the Committee of Ministers to Parliamentary Assembly Recommendation 1345 (1997): Opinion of the CDDH on Parliamentary Assembly Recommendation 1345 (1997) on the protection of national minorities, paragraph 6.

108. Ibid., paragraph 13.

109. Ibid., section C.

110. Paragraph 6 of Recommendation 1202 (1993), adopted by the Assembly on 2 February 1993.

111. Ibid., paragraph 15.

112. Ibid., paragraph 16.iii.

113. Paragraphs 5-6 of Recommendation 1178 (1992), adopted on 5 February 1992. Present authors' emphasis.

114. Ibid., paragraph 7.i.

115. Ibid., paragraph 7.iii.

116. Ibid., paragraph 7.v.

117. Ibid., paragraph 7.v-vi.

118. Paragraph 6 of Recommendation 1396 (1999), adopted on 27 January 1999.

119. Ibid., paragraph 13.i.*a-e*.

120. Ibid., paragraph 13.iv.*a* and *c*.

121. Paragraph 2 of Recommendation 1412 (1999), adopted on 22 June 1999.

122. Ibid., paragraphs 6-7.

123. Ibid., paragraph 9.

124. Ibid., paragraph 10.iii-iv and vi-vii.

125. Ibid., paragraph 11.

126. The reaction of the Council of Europe intergovernmental structures to these phenomena will be reflected in the text of the Vienna Summit Declaration. See Chapter 5.

127. Paragraph 3 of the recommendation, adopted on 29 September 1993.

128. Ibid., paragraph 5.

129. Ibid., paragraph 12.i

130. Ibid., paragraph 12.ii-iii.

131. Ibid., paragraph 12.vii. No follow-up seems to have been given to this somehow awkward initiative of the Assembly. In the Political Declaration adopted by the ministers of Council of Europe member states on 13 October 2000 at the concluding session of the European Conference Against Racism, the governments of the member states of the Council of Europe described the role of the Council of Europe in combating racism, xenophobia, anti-semitism and intolerance as involving: i. the ECHR and its additional protocols, as well as the European Court of Human Rights and its case-law; ii. the adoption by the Committee of Ministers of Protocol No. 12 to the ECHR, which introduces a general prohibition of discrimination; iii. the organisation's other human rights and legal instruments providing for equality and non-discrimination, including the Framework Convention for the Protection of National Minorities; iv. the action of the European Commission against Racism and Intolerance (ECRI); and v. the contribution of the Commissioner for Human Rights. See *Activities of the Council of Europe: Report 2000*, p. 373. On the approach to this issue at the Council of Europe as compared with other international organisations, see Chapter 5.

132. Ibid., paragraph 11.v.

133. Ibid., paragraph 9.

134. Ibid., paragraph 11.iv.

135. Ibid., paragraph 12.iv-v and vi.

136. Ibid., paragraph 11.i-iii.

137. On the way this recommendation was reflected in the Vienna Summit Declaration, see Chapter 5.

138. On the ECRI, see Chapter 12.

139. On the way these recommendations of the Assembly have come to be implemented, see Chapter 12.

140. See Chapter 1.

141. This recommendation contained some interesting proposals in relation to the Roma, such as that the provisions of any additional protocol or convention relating to minorities should apply to non-territorial minorities, and the appointment of a mediator for Gypsies by the Council of Europe with various specific tasks. See further, Chapter 4, devoted to the Roma/Gypsies.

142. On this issue, see Committee of Ministers Recommendation R (99) 18 of the CoM to member states on the avoidance and reduction of statelessness, adopted by the CoM on 15 September 1999, at the 679th meeting of the ministers' deputies. See also the European Convention on Nationality (European Treaty Series No. 166) as well as the international 1954 Convention relating to the status of stateless persons and 1961 Convention on the Reduction of Statelessness.

143. On this question see the Convention on the Participation of Foreigners in Public Life at Local Level, adopted on 5 November.1992, European Treaty Series No. 144.

144. Paragraph 3 of the recommendation, adopted on 27 January 1998.

145. Ibid., paragraph 6.v of the recommendation.

146. Ibid., paragraph 6.vi.

147. Ibid., paragraph 6.x.

148. Ibid., paragraph 7.i.

149. See W. Kemp (ed.), *Quiet Diplomacy in Action: the OSCE High Commissioner on National Minorities*, pp. 186-96.

150. As already indicated in the Introduction, an attempt to address the approaches of the Assembly to situations involving the fate of minorities in relation to situations of armed conflict falls beyond the scope of this study. Thus the comments that follow refer to minority situations not linked to situations of armed conflict.

151. On the justification of minority protection by reference to protection of culture or cultural identity under international law, see A. Spiliopoulou-Åkermark, op. cit., pp. 78-83.

152. Intergovernment bodies have been recently concerned precisely with the issue of "dispersed ethnic minorities". See final activity report on "Dispersed ethnic minorities" of the CDDH, prepared by the Committee of Experts on Issues Relation to the Protection of National Minorities (DH-MIN) Doc. CM (99) 173 Addendum. Available at the Council of Europe Internet website, Committee of Ministers home page.

It should be noted, however, that according to the definition of "ethnic minorities" provided by DH-MIN, in addition to the condition of living in more than one state, another of the requisites for a group to qualify as a "dispersed ethnic minority" is that of having no "kin-state". In this regard it is questionable whether the cultures mentioned, and the Yiddish culture in particular, qualify under the definition provided by DH-MIN. See further, Chapter 7.

153. This is the case, in particular, with the issue of the return of cultural property to Yiddish academic institutions, which was taken up again by the Assembly in Resolution 1205 (1999) on looted Jewish cultural property.

154. This proposal was mainly outlined by the Assembly in Recommendation 1291 (1996), paragraph 9.vii.

155. For the specific opinions of the Committee of Ministers' Steering Committee on Human Rights and Council for Cultural Co-operation in this connection, see appendices to Recommendation 1333, Parliamentary Assembly Doc. 8438, 15 June 1999.

156. Paragraph 6 of the recommendation, adopted on 25 June 1998.

157. Ibid., paragraphs 10 and 11. Present authors' emphasis.

158. Ibid., paragraph 13.i v.

159. Ibid., paragraph 13.iv.*k-n.*

160. Ibid., paragraph 13.vii.

161. Paragraph 7.vii of Recommendation 1455 (2000), adopted on 5 April 2000.

162. Ibid., paragraph 7.viii. The recommendations concerning various areas of minority protection adopted under the aegis of the OSCE High Commissioner on National Minorities are published by the Foundation on Inter-Ethnic Relations based in The Hague. They are also available at the OSCE HCNM's website.

163. Ibid., paragraph 7.ix. See previous footnote for further sources of information.

164. Paragraph 7 of Resolution 1113 (1997), adopted by the Assembly on 29 January 1997.

165. For the full text of these recommendations, see in particular paragraphs 8, 9 and 10 of Resolution 1172 (1998), adopted by the Assembly on 25 September 1998.

166. Paragraphs 6-8 of Recommendation 1360 (1998).

167. Paragraphs 7 and 13 of Recommendation 1368 (1998).

168. Paragraphs 4-6 of Recommendation 1376 (1998).

169. Ibid., paragraph 12.iii.

170. Ibid., paragraph 11.

171. Ibid., paragraph 3.i and ii.

172. This issue will be taken up again later by the Assembly, in Recommendation 1404 (1999) on the humanitarian situation of the Kosovo refugees and displaced persons.

173. This OSCE operation was deployed to verify Federal Republic of Yugoslavia compliance with UN Security Council Resolutions 1160 and 1199, to verify the cease-fire, monitor movement of forces, and promote human rights and democracy-building. Following a deterioration of the security situation, the KVM was withdrawn from Kosovo in March 1999. See further, *OSCE Handbook*, 3rd ed, (Vienna: OSCE, June 2000), p. 47.

174. Recommendation 1397 (1999) paragraphs 1, 6-7 and 15.vi.

175. Resolution 1182 (1999), paragraph 1.

176. Ibid., paragraph 4.

177. Recommendation 1400 (1999), paragraph 2.ii.

178. Paragraph 6 of the recommendation, adopted on 28 April 1999.

179. Ibid., paragraphs 4-8.

180. Ibid., paragraph 17.ix and xi.

181. Paragraphs 4 and 16.B.i.a of Recommendation 1414 (1999), adopted on 23 June 1999.

182. See further, Chapter 5.

183. Paragraphs 4 and 16.B.i.*a* of the recommendation.

184. See, for example, Resolution 1086 (1996) on developments in the Russian Federation in relation to the situation in Chechnya, adopted on 24 April 1996. The Russian Federation became a member of the Council of Europe on 22 February 1996. On the decisions of the Assembly on accession, see further, Chapter 9.

185. Resolution 1202 (1999), adopted on 4 November 1999 by the Standing Committee of the Assembly, paragraphs 2, 3 and 9.

186. Paragraph 4 of the resolution, adopted on 26 September 2002.

187. Ibid., paragraph 12.

188. Ibid., paragraph 18.

189. This also amounts to building upon the individual opinion of various members of the Human Rights Committee (E. Evatt, N. Ando, M.T. Bruni Celli and V. Dimitrijevic) with regard to this particular communication considered by the Human Rights Committee (see above).

190. See, in particular, paragraph 5 of Resolution 1309 (2002), discussed below.

191. See further, Chapter 2.

192. Paragraph 2 of the resolution, adopted on 25 June 2003.

193. Ibid., paragraph 1.

194. Ibid., paragraph 8.

195. Ibid., paragraph 10.

196. Ibid., paragraphs 10-12. Especial reference is made to the concerned expressed by the OSCE High Commissioner on National Minorities in the latter connection.

197. This includes article 4 of the Framework Convention and, more broadly, provision 31 of the OSCE Copenhagen document.

198. Paragraph 14 of the resolution.

199. Recommendation 1492 (2001), adopted on 23 January 2001, paragraph 12.xi.

200. Ibid., paragraph 12.i, iii, iv and vii.

201. Ibid., paragraph x.

202. In this regard it should be recalled that Article 19 of the FCNM establishes the precedence of the ECHR in applying the FCNM provisions.

203. Recommendation 1492 (2001), paragraph 11.

204. In Order No. 568 (2001), adopted on the same day as the recommendation, the Assembly instructs two of its own committees "to study the situation and the rights of new minorities originating from migration".

205. The latter approach would be more in accordance with the approaches adopted by the Advisory Committee under the Framework Convention and the Committee of Experts under the Languages Charter. Another "conceptual" step is taken by the Assembly in demanding that the CoM give the various sign languages utilised in Europe a protection similar to that afforded by the European Charter for Regional or Minority Languages. In spite of this demand for "equalisation", the Assembly only suggests the adoption of a recommendation to member states as a means to achieve this.

206. Paragraphs 1 and 3 of the recommendation, adopted on 8 November 2001.

207. Ibid., paragraph 6.

208. Ibid., paragraph 7.

209. This probably refers to the United States of America, which normally takes up the position of a strong defender of the right to freedom of expression in international fora.

210. Paragraph 5 of the opinion, adopted on 27 September 2002.

211. See paragraph 6 ii. of the opinion.

212. See Article 2 of the Additional Protocol to the Convention on Cybercrime concerning the Criminalisation of Acts of a Racist and Xenophobic Nature Committee through Computer Systems. (European Treaty Series No. 189).

213. Paragraph 2 of Recommendation 1500 (2001).

214. See P. Thornberry and M.A. Martín Estébanez, op. cit., pp. 81-82.

215. See Chapters 5 and 7.

216. Recommendation 1500 (2001), paragraph 1. In spite of the reference to this as a general phenomenon, the Assembly seems to aim in particular at "the situation in some member countries of the Council of Europe, where the percentage of non-citizens in the population is high, and where no adequate structures or opportunities exist for their political participation" (paragraph 8).

217. Ibid., paragraph 7.

218. Ibid., paragraph 11.i.

219. Ibid., paragraph 11.iii.

220. ETS No. 144, Strasbourg, 5 February 1992. See also, P. Thornberry and M.A. Martín Estébanez, op. cit., pp. 62-64.

221. Recommendation 1500 (2001), paragraph 11.iv.

222. Recommendation 1504 (2001), paragraph 11.ii.*a* and *b*.

223. Ibid., paragraph 11.ii.*g*.

224. Ibid., paragraph 11.i.

225. Ibid., paragraph 11.ii.*j*.

226. Ibid., paragraph 11.ii.*c-f.*

227. Ibid., paragraph 11.ii.*h* and *i.* See also Committee of Ministers' Recommendation (2000) 15, operative paragraph 4.*a.*

228. Paragraph 1 of the Parliamentary Assembly's Order No. 570, adopted on 14 March 2001.

229. Ibid., paragraph 2.

230. Ibid., paragraph 3.

231. Adopted by the Assembly on 23 May 2001.

232. See further, Chapter 10.

233. Paragraph 6 of the resolution.

234. Ibid., paragraph 3. See further, Chapter 1.

235. Paragraph 9 of the resolution.

236. Para. 6 of the recommendation.

237. Ibid., paragraph 7, iv.

238. Ibid., paragraph 7, i. On the work of the CAHP, see further, Chapter 7.

239. Paragraph 6 of the resolution, adopted on 18 November 2002.

240. Recommendation 1454 (2000), adopted on 5 April 2000, paragraphs 2 and 3.

241. Ibid., paragraph 7.ix.

242. Recommendation 1444 (2000), paragraph 2.

243. Ibid., paragraphs 6 and 7.

244. Ibid., paragraph 8.

245. Ibid., paragraph 14.

246. Ibid., paragraph 18.

247. Recommendation 1456 (2000), paragraph 6.

248. Ibid., paragraph 7. See further, Chapter 6.

249. Ibid., paragraphs 14 and 18.

250. Ibid., paragraph 18.

251. Ibid., paragraph 24.ii and iii.

252. Resolution 1221 (2000), paragraphs 20 and 21.

253. Ibid., paragraph 17.

254. See further, Chapter 5.

255. Resolution 1227 (2000), paragraph 16. Present authors' emphasis.

256. Ibid., paragraph 18.

257. See Resolution 1241 (2001) on the credentials of the delegation of the Russian Federation.

258. Ibid., paragraph 22. of the resolution, adopted on 25 January 2001.

259. Ibid., paragraph 24. See further, Chapters 5 and 12.

260. Paragraph 5 of the resolution.

261. Ibid., paragraph 6.

262. Ibid., paragraphs 6-7.

263. Ibid., paragraph 8.

264. Ibid., paragraph 9. Compare with the Commissioner's approaches on this issue, described in Chapter 12.

265. Ibid., paragraph 10.

266. Ibid., paragraph 11.

267. See further, Chapter 12.

268. Paragraphs 2 and 3 of the recommendation. See further, Chapter 7.

269. See "Evaluation of the prospects of a political solution to the conflict in the Chechen Republic", reply by the Committee of Ministers on 28 May 2003 to Parliamentary Assembly Recommendation 1593 (2003), doc. CM/AS (2003) Rec 1593 final, 2 June 2003.

270. Paragraphs 3-6 of the resolution. See further, Chapters 12 and 7.

271. Ibid., paragraph 7.

272. Ibid., paragraph 10.

273. Ibid., paragraphs 9-10.

274. Recommendation 1509 (2001), adopted on 25 April 2001, paragraph 12.v. See also, Order No. 572 (2001) of the same title.

275. See also, Order No. 573 (2001) of the same title.

276. Resolution 1255 (2001), adopted on 28 June 2001.

277. Paragraphs 2-4 of the resolution.

278. Ibid., paragraph 11.

279. Ibid., paragraph.12.1.a-b.

280. Ibid., paragraph12.v.

281. Ibid., paragraph12.iii.

282. Ibid., paragraph 13.

283. Recommendation 1528 (2001), adopted on 28 June 2001, paragraph 2.

284. Ibid., paragraph 3.

Chapter 9

The monitoring procedures of the Parliamentary Assembly in connection with Council of Europe enlargement

Introduction

The Parliamentary Assembly has acquired a pivotal role in relation to the process of accession of states to the Council of Europe, in particular in determining whether the states that are candidates for membership comply with the necessary requirements, in accordance with Articles 3 and 4 of the Council of Europe Statute.[1] The "opinions" of the Assembly in this connection, since the changes in central and eastern Europe, have resulted from a process of evaluation developed mainly by several committees of the Assembly (namely the Political Affairs Committee, the Committee on Legal Affairs and Human Rights and, until 1997, the Committee on Relations with European Non-Member Countries), which nominate rapporteurs for this purpose.

Since 1993 this has been done following an assessment provided by a team of "eminent jurists", usually members of the European Commission of Human Rights or the European Court of Human Rights.[2] Although the Committee of Ministers (CoM) is the organ responsible for inviting European states to become members of the Council of Europe,[3] through its involvement in the evaluation of compliance with membership requirements the Assembly has progressively brought the question of minority protection to the top of the Council of Europe's political agenda.

The Council of Europe's *relaxation* in requiring compliance by states before accession[4] has resulted in a growing need for establishing procedures to monitor compliance following accession. As discussed below, this has affected requirements relating to minority protection in particular. The emphasis on increased interstate co-operation and compliance with commitments, emphasised in the context of the Council of Europe summits, has served as a basis for the development of post-accession monitoring not only by the CoM,[5] but also by the Assembly.[6]

In contrast with the approach adopted by the CoM, minority protection as such has already become a very important component of the post-accession monitoring procedures of the Assembly. In the pages which follow, attention is devoted both to the monitoring activity of the Assembly in connection with its role as evaluator of compliance with accession requirements (that is, in connection with the pre-accession procedure) and to its monitoring activity concerning member states of the Organisation. This monitoring activity is increasingly resulting in the establishment of "monitoring cycles", which follow fixed patterns.

The pre-accession procedures of the Assembly

Background

Reference has been made in the previous chapter to the fact that already, in Recommendation 1177 (1992), the Assembly had asked for "the drawing up and rapid adoption by the Committee of Ministers of a declaration, setting the basic principles relating to the rights of minorities on which there is already international consensus". In the same recommendation, the Assembly considered that "such a declaration should serve as a basic reference against which applications for membership of the Council of Europe can be judged".[7]

As already discussed, the Assembly's perception of insufficient action by the CoM led to its decision to proceed with the drafting of its own proposal for a legal text, and the subsequent adoption of Recommendation 1201 (1993), on an additional protocol on the rights of national minorities to the European Convention on Human Rights.

The question of minority protection had occasionally been raised in Parliamentary Assembly reports evaluating whether candidate states fulfilled the conditions of membership, even before the adoption of Recommendation 1201.[8] However, before this adoption, specific references to minority protection were not included in the final "opinions" of the Parliamentary Assembly concerning states' applications for membership.

A constitutive element of these "opinions" is the reference to compliance with Articles 3 and 4 of the Statute of the Council of Europe. Article 4 of the Statute contains a reference to the state's ability and willingness to fulfil the provisions of Article 3, as a condition of being invited to become a member of the Council of Europe by the CoM. Article 3 indicates that "every Member of the Council of Europe must accept the principles of the rule of law and of the enjoyment by all persons within its jurisdiction of human rights and fundamental freedoms".[9] The text of the statute does not contain any separate reference to minority protection.[10]

Minority protection in the Assembly's opinions on accession[11]

Following the adoption of Recommendation 1201 by the Parliamentary Assembly on 1 February 1993, references to the protection of minorities progressively started to be included in the Assembly opinions concerning states' applications for membership, hand in hand with references to this recommendation. This took place in parallel with an increase in the length and level of detail of the opinions, as the sampling presented below illustrates. The first opinion on accession given by the Assembly following the adoption of Recommendation 1201, Opinion No. 169 (1993) on the application of the Republic of Slovenia for membership of the Council of Europe, does not contain a specific reference either to Recommendation 1201 or to minority protection generally.

Other opinions adopted during the same year – on the accession of Estonia (Opinion No. 170), the Czech Republic (Opinion No. 174), the Slovak Republic (Opinion No. 175) and Romania (Opinion No. 176) – do contain such references. In the opinions on Estonia, the Czech Republic and the Slovak Republic, the authorities of the respective state are specifically asked "to base their policy regarding the protection of minorities on the principles laid down in Recommendation 1201 (1993) in an additional protocol on the rights of national minorities to the European Convention on Human Rights".[12]

Estonia

In Opinion No. 170 (1993), the Assembly refers expressly to minority protection only in connection with Recommendation 1201. However, it also deals with questions of minority protection indirectly, when referring to the situation of the non-citizen population in Estonia. The Assembly observes "that the first electoral period covers only three years in the course of which non-citizens, now residing in the country and wishing to apply for Estonian citizenship, will have the possibility of acquiring it. They, like all non-Estonians residing permanently in Estonia, already now enjoy political rights at the local level".[13]

It should be noted that in the context of the more recent "monitoring procedure" the Assembly has not hesitated to qualify the situation of the ethnic Russian population living in this country as a minority situation. As discussed below, the lenient approach of the Assembly with regard to the treatment by this state of the non-citizen Russian minority, in particular, is in contrast with that adopted with regard to Andorra concerning the treatment of its non-citizen population one year later.

461

The Slovak Republic

In Opinion No. 175 (1993), the Assembly expounds on its reference to minority protection in a detailed manner instead, stating that

> it takes note of the Slovak authorities' commitments to adopt legislation granting to every person belonging to a minority the right to use his/her mother tongue and, in the regions in which substantial numbers of a national minority are settled, the right for the persons belonging to this minority to display in their language local names, signs, inscriptions and other similar information, in accordance with the principles contained in Recommendation 1201.

> It encourages the authorities of the Slovak Republic to continue the efforts they have begun to eliminate from its legislation all the laws or decrees adopted by previous governments which are likely to contain elements discriminating against a group of persons or an ethnic, national community living on its territory, particularly those concerning 'collective guilt'.

> It also takes note, whatever administrative divisions may be introduced in the Slovak Republic, of the declaration made by the Slovak authorities that they will respect the rights of national minorities.[14]

An important element introduced by the Assembly in this opinion is that the mere expression of the will of the state to conduct a policy along the principles set forth in Recommendation 1201 is considered a constituent element and grounding factor of the Assembly's decision to provide a positive assessment of the application for membership by the state, rather than actual compliance.

Romania

Similarly, in the case of Romania, the Assembly "appreciates the written declaration of the Romanian authorities, in which they commit themselves to basing their policy regarding the protection of minorities on the principles laid down in Recommendation 1201 (1993) ... It wishes the honouring of these commitments to be monitored in accordance with Assembly Order No. 488 (1993)".[15] In addition:

> The Assembly recommends that the Romanian authorities sign the European Charter on Local Self-Government as soon as possible ... .

> The Assembly calls upon the Romanian Government to return property to the churches and to permit the establishment and operation of church schools with a particular view to teaching children of minority groups their mother tongue.

> ... .

The Assembly proposes that the Romanian authorities and the Romanian Parliament:

i. adopt and implement as soon as possible, in keeping with the commitments they have made and with Assembly Recommendation 1201, legislation on national minorities and education;

ii. make use of the means available to a constitutional state in order to combat racism and anti-semitism, as well as all forms of nationalist and religious discrimination and incitement thereto.

The Assembly recommends that Romania sign the European Charter for Regional or Minority Languages as soon as possible.

... .

The Assembly also recommends that the Committee of Ministers encourage the Romanian authorities to continue efforts they have started to make in order to implement the principles of ... the respect for minorities.[16]

Andorra

Although the Assembly omits a reference to Recommendation 1201 in its Opinion No. 182 (1994) on the application by the Principality of Andorra for membership of the Council of Europe, it adopts a much stricter stand on the approach of this state towards its non-citizen population than it had adopted towards Estonia. Even if the Assembly acknowledged that in Andorra "the native population is numerically smaller than the immigrant population",[17] in contrast with the situation in Estonia and Latvia, the Assembly "expects the Andorran legislators to produce, taking into account the particularly sensitive background to this situation, a new version of the articles of the qualified law on nationality, annulled by the Andorran Constitutional Court, facilitating access to Andorran nationality, notably to people considered to be integrated by a long period of residence in Andorra. Adequate legislation on nationality should be in line with the established standards of the Council of Europe".[18]

Latvia

As in the case of Estonia, the Assembly adopts a milder discourse when addressing the situation of the non-citizen population in Latvia than it adopted with regard to Andorra. The Assembly, however, deals with the situation in Latvia in a much more detailed manner than with regard to Estonia. Opinion No. 183 (1995), on the application by Latvia for membership of the Council of Europe, includes an express reference to Recommendation 1201, similar, although with a stronger grip, to the reference introduced in the Estonian case. The Assembly is ready to recommend Latvia's accession on the understanding that Latvia intends "to conduct a policy along the principles set forth" in Assembly Recommendation 1201 (1993).[19]

The Assembly omits a specific reference to the Russian minority living in the country, but in a clear reference to it, addresses the situation of "non-citizens":

> Following visits by the rapporteurs of the three committees concerned ... and observation of the parliamentary elections on 5 and 6 June 1993, it was agreed that there remained outstanding the question of a law on citizenship and the definition by law of the rights and status of 'non-citizens'.

> Through the law on citizenship adopted by the Seima (Latvian Parliament) on 22 July 1994, a major pre-condition for accession to the Council of Europe was fulfilled. Such was the conclusion of the rapporteurs following meetings in Riga ... The law was approved by the President of the Republic of Latvia on 8 August 1994.

> A commitment has now been made by the Latvian Government ... 'to continue its consultations and co-operation with the Council of Europe' in implementing the law on citizenship and in drawing up a law on the rights and status of 'non-citizens': all laws and regulations, including notably those on the use of languages, must be applied without unacceptable pressures on individuals or unduly prolonged procedures.

> The Assembly 'considers that this commitment also means' that the relevant laws and regulations should very soon enter into force and will be in line with generally accepted principles of the Council of Europe .... In particular, it means that there must be no arbitrary and unjustified discrimination between citizens and 'non-citizens'. Decisions of an allegedly discriminatory character – whether taken under national, regional or municipal authority – must be subject to procedures of appeal and review.[20]

With this opinion the Assembly starts a new trend of evaluation of compliance by states with accession requirements, consisting on the provision by the Assembly of its own interpretation of the content of the commitments undertaken by the state.

Moldova

Opinion No. 188 (1995) on Moldova's application for membership, adopted by the Assembly on 27 June 1995, contains a detailed assessment of the minority situation. The Assembly refers to the intensive consultations of Moldova with the Council of Europe on the preparation of a new constitution, an organic law granting special legal status to Gagauzia as well as legislation on minorities. It examines the prospects for the peaceful settlement of the Transnistrian question in the light of the most recent electoral results,[21] and takes note of the commitments undertaken by the Moldovan Parliament. This includes minimising the potential consequences of inadequate knowledge of the official language and granting a significant time extension for learning this language.[22] It also includes the reform of laws and practice in the sphere of local self-government to bring them into line with the European Charter of Local Self-Government.[23]

The Assembly again includes in this opinion an express reference to Recommendation 1201, and to the intention of Moldova "to incorporate it into the legal and administrative system and practice of the country". Taking this issue a step further, the Assembly refers to the intention of Moldova "to sign and ratify within a year from the time of accession the Framework Convention for the Protection of National Minorities".[24]

The Framework Convention had been opened for signature only a few months earlier, on 1 February 1995, and, in the Assembly opinions on accession subsequently adopted, its text becomes a landmark in relation to minority protection along with Recommendation 1201. The difference in the Assembly's treatment of both texts is clear from the start of the simultaneous references to them: as the Framework Convention is an international treaty, it is not treated by the Assembly as a point of reference in legal or administrative practice, or occasionally as a text to be incorporated into the domestic legal system, as was the case with Recommendation 1201.[25] The Assembly adopts a forthright position, requesting the signature and ratification of the Framework Convention, usually within one year from the time of accession to the Organisation.

In the case of Moldova, the Assembly refers in addition to the intention of the state to sign and ratify within one year of accession the European Charter of Local Self-Government, and "to study, with a view to ratification ... the European Charter for Regional or Minority Languages".[26] Once more, these statements of the will of the state are formulated as constituent elements and grounding factors of the Assembly's decision to provide a positive assessment of the application for membership. Furthermore, the Assembly relies on an assumption concerning minority protection: the intention of Moldova "to confirm complete freedom of worship for all citizens without discrimination, and to ensure a peaceful solution to the dispute between the Moldovan Orthodox Church and the Bessarabian Orthodox Church",[27] as a constituent element of its positive assessment of the state's application for membership.

Albania

In the account of political developments in Albania by the Assembly preceding its positive assessment on the application for membership of this state, the Assembly refers, in its Opinion No. 189 (1995), to the election observers' conclusions that the elections held in this country on 22 and 29 March 1992: "opened the way for closer relations between Albania and the Council of Europe, with a view to subsequent membership – subject to review of the position of the ethnic Greek minority (notably in the South)".[28] The Assembly adds:

> a welcome relaxation of tension on Albania's southern border has been matched by a re-affirmation of the legal and constitutional bases of Albania's policy towards minorities – notably to the effect that no religious community will be deprived in practice of an opportunity to flourish ... The fact that this commitment will be monitored by the Council of Europe should provide continuing reassurance to ethnic minorities and communities in Albania.

Furthermore, the Assembly positively acknowledges the restraint of the Albanian foreign policy in the face of rising tensions concerning minorities and communities of Albanian ethnic origin in Kosovo.[29]

The acknowledgment by the Assembly of the state's intention: to conduct a policy towards minorities in accordance with the principles set forth in Recommendation 1201; to sign and ratify within one year from the time of accession the Framework Convention; as well as to study with a view to ratification "the European Charters for Local Self-Government and for Regional or Minority Languages, and meanwhile to conduct its policy in accordance with their principles" serve as a basis for the positive assessment of the Assembly on accession.[30]

Ukraine

In the case of Ukraine, the assessment of the situation of the Russian minority in particular forms part of the wider geo-strategic and economic evaluation of the factual situation in the country carried out by the Assembly. In Opinion No. 190 (1995),[31] among the considerations for the positive assessment by the Assembly on the suitability of Ukraine for membership, the fact that Ukraine had signed the Framework Convention and the European Outline Convention on Transfrontier Co-operation between Territorial Communities or Authorities is highlighted.

The Assembly notes that "the Constitutional Court of Ukraine will be competent to decide on the compatibility of the acts of the legislative and executive authorities of the Autonomous Republic of Crimea with the Constitution and Laws of Ukraine". It also notes that "a peaceful solution to the dispute existing among the orthodox churches will be facilitated while respecting the Church's independence vis-à-vis the state; a new non-discriminatory system of church registration and a legal solution for the restitution of church property will be introduced".[32]

With regard to the international commitments which Ukraine intends to undertake, and in contrast with the approach taken with regard to Albania, the Assembly refers to Recommendation 1201. As in the case of Moldova, the Assembly indicates the intention of the state to incorporate Recommendation 1201 into the legal and administrative system and practice of the country.[33]

"The former Yugoslav Republic of Macedonia"

A similar formula is used in Opinion No. 191 (1995) on the application by the former Yugoslav Republic of Macedonia, which includes, in addition, a reference not just to the intention of the state to study ratification, but to ratify within one year of accession, the European Charter for Regional or Minority Languages.

Russian Federation

Also in 1995, the Assembly adopted Resolution 1055, on Russia's request for membership in the light of the situation in Chechnya.[34] In this resolution the Assembly decides to suspend the procedure concerning its statutory opinion on the request for membership by this state for actions which "constitute a grave violation of the Council of Europe's most elementary human rights principles, which Russia, by requesting membership of the Organisation, pledged to uphold".[35] In a subsequent order, the Assembly instructs its Sub-Committee on Human Rights "to visit Chechnya, once the hostilities have ceased, to verify that human rights are observed".[36] The accession procedure was resumed following the 30 July 1995 peace agreement[37] and the adoption of Resolution 1065 (1995) "on the grounds that Russia was henceforth committed to finding a political solution and that alleged and documented human rights violations were being investigated".[38]

In Opinion No. 193 (1996) on Russia's request for membership of the Council of Europe and in contrast with previous opinions of the Assembly on accession, the Assembly grounds its positive assessment not in the present, but in the future[39] ability of the state to fulfil the requirements for membership "in the sense" of Articles 3 and 4 of the Statute of the Council of Europe.

Among the considerations for the Assembly's belief in the future ability of the Russian Federation to fulfil the membership requirements are plans to introduce new laws "in line with Council of Europe standards", in areas such as the role, functioning and administration of the Procurator's Office and of the Office of the Commissioner for Human

Rights, the protection of national minorities and freedom of assembly and religion.[40] The Assembly, using the current formula, also notes the intention of the Russian Federation

> to sign and ratify within a year from the time of accession the Framework Convention; to conduct its policy towards minorities on the principles set forth in Recommendation 1201, and to incorporate these principles into the legal and administrative system and practice of the country, as well as its intention to sign and ratify within a year of accession the European Charter of Local Self-Government and the European Charter for Regional or Minority Languages, and to study the European Social Charter with a view to ratification.

The Assembly refers to the intention of the state to conduct its policy in accordance with the principles of these conventions.[41] It also refers to the intentions of the Russian Federation concerning several areas of practical state action which relate to minority protection in the state. This includes the withdrawal of the 14th Army and its equipment from the territory of Moldova; the denunciation of the concept of the "near abroad" to qualify certain foreign countries treated as a zone of special influence; the negotiation of claims for the return of cultural property; and the return of property of religious institutions without delay.[42]

Three months after the adoption of the positive opinion on the accession of the Russian Federation, the Assembly adopts Resolution 1086 (1996) on developments in the Russian Federation in relation to the situation in Chechnya. In this resolution, the Assembly recalls its opinion on accession and, using a mildly worded discourse, highlights several commitments reflected in that opinion "which are currently not all being honoured by the Russian Federation".[43] The Assembly notes that the President of the Russian Federation presented a plan to solve the crisis in the Chechen Republic on 31 March 1996, proposing talks on the future status of Chechnya; the conclusion of agreements on the demarcation of authority between federal and local institutions; and a resolution by the State Duma on an amnesty for separatist fighters who have not committed the most serious crimes.[44] The Assembly:

> urges that concrete measures, beginning with a cease-fire, be taken without further delay to implement elements of this or other peace plans, and considers that these efforts will be successful only if they involve all the parties to the conflict acting in good faith, and if the Russian authorities will stop describing as bandits the Chechen combatants in action on the territory of Chechnya, who do not make use of terrorist means.

... .

The Assembly reminds the Russian authorities of their commitment, included in Opinion No. 193 (1996), to ensure that 'those found responsible for human rights violations will be brought to justice ...' and demands that documented human rights abuses, for example in the filtration camps, be investigated, and those guilty, punished.[45]

Croatia

Also in connection with a situation of conflict and illustrating an approach similar to that adopted in connection with the accession of the Russian Federation, in Opinion No. 195 (1996) on Croatia's request for membership of the Council of Europe, the Assembly states that "the procedure for an opinion on Croatia's request for membership was delayed as a result of Croatian involvement in the war in Bosnia-Herzegovina. Events in western Slavonia and the former United Nations Protection Sectors North and South further delayed the procedure".[46]

However, in contrast with the assessment of compliance by the Russian Federation, the Assembly refers to the express commitments formally undertaken by the presidents of the Republic of Croatia and of the Croatian Parliament:

- to implement the recommendations resulting from the opinion of the European Commission for Democracy through Law (the 'Venice Commission') on the constitutional law on human rights and the freedoms and rights of national and ethnic communities and minorities and human rights protection mechanisms;

- to take all necessary measures, including adequate police protection, to guarantee the safety and human rights of the Serb population in Croatia, in particular in the former UN Protected Areas, to facilitate the return of people who left these areas and to allow them, through a specific procedure established by law, effectively to exercise their rights to recover their property or to receive compensation;

    ...

- to co-operate fully and effectively in the implementation of the Dayton/Paris Agreements for Peace in Bosnia-Herzegovina;

- to co-operate with, and actively assist, the Prosecutor of the International Criminal Tribunal for the former Yugoslavia in bringing before the tribunal without delay persons indicted for war crimes, crimes against humanity and genocide;

    ...

- to comply, well before the next elections, with the recommendation made by the election observers of the Council of Europe and other international organisations, in particular with regard to the special voting block for the diaspora, minority representation, voter registration lists ... and to undertake a census of the population as soon as possible.[47]

The Assembly also refers to the commitment undertaken by the aforementioned presidents for Croatia:

> to sign and ratify within a year from the time of accession the Framework Convention for the Protection of National Minorities, the European Charter on Local Self-Government, and the European Charter for Regional and Minority Languages; to conduct its policy towards minorities on the principles set forth in Assembly Recommendation 1201 (1993), and to incorporate these principles into the legal and administrative system and practice of the country.[48]

This opinion brings the number of commitments to adopt Council of Europe standards relevant to minority protection in connection with accession to the highest level. The Assembly expects Croatia "to guarantee effectively the rights and freedoms of national and ethnic minorities ..." and "to consult the Council of Europe experts on the revision bill of the draft local administration and autonomy act sufficiently in advance of its second reading in parliament".[49]

Georgia

In Opinion No. 209 (1999) on Georgia's application for membership of the Council of Europe, the Assembly no longer refers even to an express declaration of the state's intentions to undertake a series of commitments for accession to the Council of Europe, but expresses its own detailed expectations regarding state action. The Assembly expectations include a long list of items under the headings: i. "conventions"; ii. "domestic legislation"; iii. "implementation of reforms"; iv. "human rights"; v. "the conflict in Abkhazia"; and vi. "the monitoring of commitments".[50]

The Assembly's expectations under i. concern the signature and ratification within a year of accession of the Framework Convention and the European Charter for Regional or Minority Languages, and within three years of accession, the European Charter of Local Self-Government, as well as the European Outline Convention on Transfrontier Co-operation between Territorial Communities or Authorities and its additional protocols.

Expectations under ii. include: *a.* the enactment, within two years of accession, of a legal framework determining the status of the autonomous territories and guaranteeing them broad autonomy, the exact terms to be negotiated with the representatives of the territories concerned; *b.* the adoption, within two years of accession, of a legal framework permitting repatriation and integration, including the right to Georgian nationality for the Meskhetian population deported by the

Soviet regime, as well as the starting and conclusion of the process of repatriation and integration within fixed terms; *c.* the amendment, within three years of accession, of the law on autonomy and local government to enable all the heads of councils to be elected instead of being appointed; *d.* the adoption, within two years of accession, of a law on minorities based on the principles of Assembly Recommendation 1201.

Expectations under iv. include the resolute and impartial prosecution of the perpetrators of war crimes committed during the conflicts in Abkhazia and South Ossetia, also within their own armed forces. Finally, expectations under v. include efforts to settle the conflict by peaceful means and to put a stop to the activities of all irregular armed groups in the conflict zone.[51] The Assembly decides to start its "monitoring procedure" (see below) with regard to the state "as from the country's accession".[52] The same approach will be adopted with regard to other states acceding to the Organisation subsequently. The seeds of this approach can already be traced in previous demands for acceding states to co-operate with the Assembly's own post-accession monitoring procedure as well as the CoM's monitoring procedures, already present in the opinion on Moldova's accession.[53]

Armenia and Azerbaijan

Opinions No. 221 (2000) and No. 222 (2000), on the applications by Armenia and Azerbaijan respectively, were adopted by the Assembly on the same day, and contain several common provisions, particularly those related to the settlement of the conflict in Nagorno-Karabakh. In contrast with the Opinion on Georgia's accession, where the Assembly qualified the latter state as a "pluralist democratic society", in these opinions the Assembly considers that the respective state "is moving towards a democratic, pluralist society in which human rights and the rule of law are respected". It also points at each state's "ability and willingness" to continue/pursue democratic reforms initiated "in order to bring its entire legislation and practice into conformity" with Council of Europe standards.[54]

The Assembly takes note of the promise to honour a series of commitments, expressed in writing by the president, the prime minister, the speaker of parliament, and the chairmen of the political parties in each state. These include, in the case of international instruments: i. the signature and ratification, within one year of accession, of the European Charter for Regional or Minority Languages and the European Charter for Local Self-Government; and ii. the signature and ratification, within two years of accession, of the European Outline Convention on Transfrontier Co-operation between Territorial Communities or Authorities and its additional protocols.[55] The Assembly also takes note of the promise to sign and ratify the Framework Convention within one year of accession by Azerbaijan, since Armenia is already party to it.

In relation to Nagorno-Karabakh, the Assembly takes note of the commitments by the respective authorities regarding the peaceful settlement of the conflict, and asks Armenia, in particular, "to use its considerable influence over the Armenians in Nagorno-Karabakh to foster a solution" to it.[56] In both opinions the Assembly acknowledges the promise "to amend, before the next local elections, the current legislation governing the powers of local authorities so as to give them greater responsibilities and independence, taking into account the recommendations made in this respect by the Congress for Local and Regional Authorities in Europe (CLRAE)".[57]

Finally, with regard to the promises made by the state authorities in the area of human rights and fundamental freedoms, the Assembly highlights, in the case of Armenia, the promise "to ensure that all churches or religious communities, in particular those referred to as 'non-traditional', may practise their religion without discrimination".[58] In the case of Azerbaijan, the Assembly refers instead to the promise "to adopt, within three years of its accession, a law on minorities which completes the provisions on non-discrimination contained in the constitution and the penal code and replaces the presidential decree on national minorities".[59]

Bosnia and Herzegovina

Two years later, in Assembly Opinion No. 234 (2002) on the application by Bosnia and Herzegovina, the reference to "pluralistic and democratic society" is omitted altogether, while the relaxation of accession requirements reaches a peak.[60] Reference is made, however, to the recognition by the state of the principle of the rule of law and its guarantee of respect for human rights. As in the previous opinions, the Assembly points to the ability and willingness of the state "in the sense of Article 4 of the Council of Europe statute", to continue the democratic reforms embarked upon "in order that its legislation and practice globally conform" with Council of Europe principles and standards.[61]

The Assembly takes note of the letters from the presidency of Bosnia and Herzegovina, the Speakers of the Parliament and the Prime Minister to honour a list of commitments. These include the ratification of ECHR and its Protocol 12 within one year of accession, and within two years, the signature and ratification of the European Charter for Regional or Minority Languages; the European Charter of Local Self-Government and the European Outline Convention on Transfrontier Co-operation between Territorial Communities and Authorities (the Framework Convention had already been ratified in February 2000).

Curiously, at the level of domestic legislation, the Assembly recalls the commitment for the state to adopt and implement, within one year after accession, constitutional and legislative amendments necessary to comply with the decision taken by the Constitutional Court on the "constituent peoples of Bosnia and Herzegovina of June-July 2000" without further considerations. The reservations raised by this decision, from the perspective of the principle of non-discrimination, have been discussed in Chapter 7. The Assembly also recalls the commitments to the adoption and implementation within two years of laws on schools (at the level of the state and its constituent entities) and on citizenship (by the Federation of Bosnia and Herzegovina).

The Assembly refers to the commitments to comply fully with the decisions and recommendations of the Human Rights Chamber and Human Rights Ombudsman and to ensure their adequate funding, as well as adequate funding of the Commission for Real Property Claims. It also refers to the commitment to work towards the establishment of multi-ethnic ombudsmen and a unified human rights ombudsman office at the state level, which would include the present ombudsmen institutions at the entity level.[62] The Assembly equally refers to the commitment to the elimination of segregation and ethnic discrimination in the field of education and the continuation of reforms aimed at establishing multi-ethnic police forces.

Serbia and Montenegro

Finally, in Opinion No. 239 (2002), in which the Assembly supports the accession of the Federal Republic of Yugoslavia (later known as Serbia and Montenegro), the Assembly refers to this state having become a party to the Framework Convention for the Protection of National Minorities. It also refers to the adoption by the state of a federal act on the protection of national minorities as well as legislation on procedures governing the transfer of indicted persons to the International Criminal Tribunal for the former Yugoslavia (ICTY), although the need for a more clear political will as to the implementation of the latter is understated.[63] The Assembly, again on the basis of letters received from the president of the Federal Republic, the presidents of the two chambers of the Parliament and the Prime Minister, notes that the state is determined to honour a series of commitments.

These commitments include the ratification of the Dayton Peace Agreements and effective co-operation in their implementation, as well as accession to and ratification of Council of Europe treaties relevant to minority protection, under similar conditions to those requested from Bosnia and Herzegovina (see above). They also include continued co-operation with the ICTY, co-operation in establishing the facts concerning the fate of missing people and handing over information concerning mass graves. Information of the people of Serbia "about the crimes committed by the regime of Slovodan Milošević, not only against the other peoples of the region but also against the Serbs" seems to have been another of the commitments accepted by the authorities according to the Assembly's statement.[64]

Another commitment mentioned is the improvement of constitutional and legislative provisions concerning decentralisation and the organisation of local authorities and autonomous regions. With regard to Kosovo in particular, among the commitments listed is a rather undefined contribution "to the efforts aimed at building a democratic, multi-ethnic entity in Kosovo with a view to creating a political climate conducive to reflection and dialogue on its future status".[65] In addition, the Assembly expresses its own wish that the responsibility for the protection of the rights of national minorities remain at the federal level; that the existing level of protection of these rights is maintained; and that the aforementioned federal act is duly implemented.

The Assembly also anticipates the treatment of combating discrimination against the Roma under the post-accession monitoring procedure.[66] Finally, the Assembly recommends that the Secretary General is invited by the CoM to explore "with the authorities in Belgrade and with UNMIK ways to guarantee the applicability of the substantive norms contained in Council of Europe conventions and of their supervisory mechanisms in Kosovo, including access to the European Court of Human Rights, bearing in mind the special legal situation resulting from UN Security Council Resolution 1244".[67]

Assessment

In the light of the above, it is possible to observe a substantial evolution in the approach of the Parliamentary Assembly to the evaluation of state compliance with accession requirements. The confirmation of the willingness and ability of the state to fulfil the requirements established in Articles 3 and 4 of the Statute of the Council of Europe by the Assembly no longer focuses on the determination of the existence on an appropriate level of state performance. As the opinion on the accession of the Russian Federation best illustrates, the recommendation of the Assembly for the CoM to invite a state to become a member of the Council of Europe now centres on the recognition by the Assembly of the state's intention to take a series of measures in the normative field and in the fields of policy and administrative practice concerning those areas envisaged in Articles 3 and 4 of the statute.

Thus, in the monitoring of the implementation of these articles there has been a switch in emphasis between "willingness" and "ability", weight being increasingly placed on "willingness" rather than on "ability". Lack of state compliance with the Council of Europe standards in relation to minority protection, including the most basic rights, has not prevented the Assembly from giving a positive evaluation regarding state accession.

As the accession procedure has recently evolved, the recognition by the Assembly of the state's intention to take a series of measures, in the normative field and in that of policy and administrative practice concerning the areas envisaged in Articles 3 and 4, does not necessarily take as a basis a formal declaration of intent by the highest authorities of the state. As the opinion on the accession of Georgia illustrates, just the expectations of the Assembly in relation to state behaviour may suffice for the Assembly to give a positive evaluation.

Thus, the approach of the Assembly in giving a positive evaluation of state compliance with accession requirements has been substantially relaxed, including at a formal level. This is notwithstanding the fact that from a historical perspective, and in the field of minority protection in particular, the level of demand placed on states has reached its highest level, as already described, and further discussed below. According to the prevailing approach, recognition by the Assembly of the intention by the state candidate for membership to take a series of measures (even if this intention has not been formally declared by the state) is now being considered a defining element of the state's willingness and ability to comply with Articles 3 and 4 of the Statute which the Assembly certifies.

As a result, the statement of the Assembly on compliance with these articles is no longer a closed matter. Even if the statement on compliance with Articles 3 and 4 which opens the door to membership is definite, its full realisation requires particular state action in the future to respond to the concrete measures signalled by the Assembly. As a result, the statements on state compliance of the Assembly have become "conditioned". This has fuelled the need for further scrutiny by the Assembly.

With the introduction of references to concrete measures of prospective state action, which now constitute part and parcel of compliance with requirements for accession contained in Articles 3 and 4, the Assembly has included increasing demands for state action in the field of minority protection. Actual compliance with minority protection standards, however, has not been a requisite for positive evaluation on accession by the Assembly. Failure to implement basic minority rights has not been considered as an impediment for accession. At the same time, minority protection has reaffirmed its position as an essential component of the requirements for the state to comply with Articles 3 and 4 of the Council of Europe Statute at a declaratory level.

Initially, this was mainly done through the introduction of requests for compliance with Recommendation 1201 (1993) into the Assembly's favourable opinions on accession. References to the European Charter of Local Self-Government were soon introduced. Since then, as the number of international legal instruments relevant to minority protection adopted in the framework of the Council of Europe has grown, the Assembly has increased the number of international conventions dealing with minority protection to which it is willing to refer and for which it requests compliance. This started with the European Charter for Regional or Minority Languages; references to the Framework Convention were soon to follow suit. Consequently, various international instruments relevant to minority protection adopted within the framework of the Council of Europe are now a prominent part of the prospective undertakings by the states in connection with accession.

Assembly opinions on accession have become increasingly detailed, both in analysing the current situation of the state regarding compliance with accession requirements, and in pointing to areas where action is expected. References to minority protection have also increased. Since a detailed account of specific minority issues raised by the Assembly has been given above, it suffices to note that questions of religious tolerance and the discriminatory treatment of various religious denominations or beliefs have been among those which have received a great deal of attention.

Citizenship and linguistic issues, especially in connection with education, have also received attention, as have questions of territorial organisation and local self-government, and to a lesser extent property return and compensation. The opinions of the Assembly have addressed the factual situation of minorities mainly in cases where a kin-state exists, and mainly in relation to situations of conflict or tension, although exceptions to both of these have been provided with reference to the Roma/Gypsies. Normally, express references to the need to address concrete aspects of the protection of other minorities living in the countries have been missing. In considering the role of kin-states, the Assembly has adopted positive and negative stands. A positive stand has been adopted in the consideration of the role of the kin-state as a possible contributor to conflict settlement. A negative stand was adopted in considering the kin-state as a promoter of tensions.

Often, specific measures in relation to minority protection have become one of the main areas where prompt action by the state is expected. The type of action requested has varied, but it has concerned mainly the legislative field. This has ranged from requests for the signature and ratification of international instruments to the adoption of general pieces of legislation on minority protection. It has also included the adoption of concrete norms in relation to specific minority problems. Increasingly, the Assembly refers to the need to comply with the content of international instruments before formal ratification is achieved. The request for the incorporation of minority protection principles into the administrative system and practice of the state has also become a common feature.

The (post-accession) monitoring procedure

Background

As already discussed, the increasing weight given to the recognition by the Assembly of the states' intention to undertake a series of concrete measures, as reflected in the favourable opinions on membership, resulted in the need for the Assembly to develop a system to monitor state performance after accession. The Assembly initially proceeded to develop the so-called monitoring procedure. The aim of this post-accession monitoring activity has been defined by the Assembly as follows: "the monitoring is the expression of the Assembly's political will to ensure that: no unnecessary strains are placed on the European Court of Human Rights; commitments entered into upon accession to the Council of Europe be met; the principles of pluralist democracy are respected; a crisis of state authority does not put basic human rights at risk".[68]

The Assembly's monitoring procedure has been developed progressively to improve monitoring capacity and to better meet monitoring needs as perceived by the Assembly at a given time. The Parliamentary Assembly first adopted Order No. 488 (1993) on the honouring of commitments entered into by new member states in June 1993.[69] In Resolution 1031 (1994) on the honouring of commitments entered into by member states when joining the Council of Europe, the Assembly decided to extend its monitoring capacity to all Council of Europe member states.[70]

In this resolution the Assembly observed that in addition to the obligations which all member states of the Council of Europe are required to respect (the Council of Europe Statute; the European Convention on Human Rights and all other conventions to which they are parties):

> the authorities of certain states, which have become members since the adoption in May 1989 of Resolution 917 (1989) on a special guest status with the Parliamentary Assembly, freely entered into specific commitments on issues related to the basic principles of the Council of Europe during the examination of their request for membership by the Assembly. The main commitments concerned are explicitly referred to in the relevant opinions adopted by the Assembly. In Order No. 488

(1993), adopted on 29 June 1993, the Assembly instructed its Political Affairs Committee and its Committee on Legal Affairs and Human Rights to monitor closely the honouring of these commitments ... . The Assembly considers that this monitoring process should be regarded as a stimulus and guidance for the consolidation of democracy in the states which have become members since the adoption in May 1989 of Resolution 917 (1989). Persistent failure to honour commitments freely entered into will have consequences however. For this purpose the Assembly could use the relevant provisions of the Council of Europe's Statute and of its own Rules of Procedure, as well as paragraph 2 of Order No. 488 (1993).[71]

The following year, in Order No. 508 (1995), which supersedes Order No. 488 (1993) and Resolution 1031 (1994), the Assembly:

instructs its Committee on Legal Affairs and Human Rights (for report) and its Political Affairs Committee (for opinion) to continue monitoring closely the honouring of obligations and commitments in all member states concerned. The Committee on Relations with European Non-Member Countries will also be asked for an opinion with regard to the member states which previously enjoyed special guest status. To start the procedure, the Committee on Legal Affairs and Human Rights must take such a decision, in accordance with normal committee procedure. Countries which are members should honour Recommendation 1201 (1993); candidates for full membership should, on their accession, commit themselves to do likewise. The honouring of this recommendation will also be followed as part of the monitoring process.[72]

As this order illustrates, the Assembly progressively delimits and stream-lines the role of its own committees involved in the post-accession "monitoring procedure". At the same time, the issue of minority protection is recognised and given a prominent position in the monitoring process, although the Assembly does not establish clear criteria for the monitoring of the "older states" (especially the western European democracies). In turn, the idea that members of the Organisation should comply with minority protection standards opens the door at least for the extension of this requirement not only to "new" member states, but also to "old" ones.

In Order 513 (1996), adopted on 23 January 1996, the Assembly instructed its competent committees (on political affairs; on legal affairs and human rights and on relations with European non-member countries) and their rapporteurs "to continue taking into account" the European Charter for Regional or Minority Languages; the Framework Convention for the Protection of National Minorities and the European Charter for Local Self-Government; "as well as the Assembly's draft for an additional protocol to the European Convention on Human Rights on the rights of national minorities, included in Recommendation 1201 (1993), in the procedures on the admission of new member states and the 'monitoring' process of the commitments accepted upon accession to the Council of Europe".[73] Thus, in the same way that the Assembly shows readiness to increase the number of Council of Europe instruments relevant to minority protection considered in connection with accession, it also shows readiness to consider this "increased number" of instruments in connection with post-accession monitoring.

In Resolution 1115 (1997), the Assembly established a Monitoring Committee devoted specifically to post-accession monitoring. The mandate of this committee covers all specific commitments and general obligations undertaken by the member states.[74] The Assembly instructs the committee to resume work on existing monitoring procedures from the point at which they stood. Thus the Monitoring Committee "took over from the Committee on Legal Affairs and Human Rights eleven procedures opened under the previous system of Order No. 508 (1995). They concerned Albania, Bulgaria, the Czech Republic, Croatia, Lithuania, Moldova, Russia, Slovakia, 'the former Yugoslav Republic of Macedonia', Turkey and Ukraine".[75] The Assembly later indicated in Resolution 1155 (1998) that committees other than the Monitoring Committee: "shall continue to deal with specific issues within their traditional areas of competence which arise in member states, but shall seek to co-ordinate their work on monitored countries with the Monitoring Committee".[76]

Given the fact that the mandate of the Monitoring Committee covers all specific commitments and general obligations undertaken by member states, an indicative list of twenty-one areas covered under the previous monitoring procedures was elaborated to facilitate its work.[77] This list includes specific references not only to

- minorities (non-discrimination; citizenship legislation; status of and education in minority languages),

but also to other issues interlinked with minority protection:

- policies to combat racism, anti-semitism, xenophobia;
- political parties (status; conditions for setting up/registration; fiscal rules/party finances);
- parliament (pluralist composition; minority representation ...);
- local and regional self-government;
- freedom of conscience and of worship.

The Monitoring Committee, in view of experience acquired under previous monitoring procedures, decided, however:

> to focus, in the first phase of its work, on well-defined specific issues, in respect of which progress should be made as a matter of priority. Co-rapporteurs have thus prepared issue papers for each state being monitored, as a basis both for initial exchanges of views with national parliamentary delegations and – in the light of these exchanges – for focusing discussions during their visits.[78]

According to the second annual progress report of the Monitoring Committee, commitments concerning the rights of minorities are among those being monitored in almost all states subject to monitoring. An exchange of views on the situation of national minorities in Croatia, Estonia, Latvia, Slovakia, "the former Yugoslav Republic of Macedonia" and Ukraine, was held between the representatives of the Monitoring Committee and the OSCE High Commissioner on National Minorities in The Hague in November 1998.

An issue of paramount importance in post-accession monitoring by the Assembly is the system followed to open the monitoring procedure in a specific state. Although all member states of the Council of Europe may be subject to the Assembly's monitoring, Resolution 1115 introduced a specific system for starting the monitoring procedure and gives the Bureau of the Assembly the authority to open the procedure. The bureau's decision can be taken on the basis of an application:

* from the Monitoring Committee or other Assembly committees, through a 'reasoned written application' to the Bureau;
* from not less than ten members of the Assembly (representing at least two national delegations and two political groups) through the tabling of a Motion for a Resolution or Recommendation;
* from the Bureau of the Assembly;

> Applications (other than those made by the Monitoring Committee itself) are referred for consultation to the Monitoring Committee. When consulted by the Bureau on a proposal for the opening of a procedure, the Committee appoints two co-rapporteurs to prepare a draft written opinion on whether a procedure should be opened, having carried out any 'necessary investigations'. The Committee seeks to determine whether there are sufficient grounds to justify the opening of a procedure for the State concerned.[79]

The Monitoring Committee presents its views in the form of a "written opinion".[80] Although the bureau takes the decision on the opening of a monitoring procedure, the Assembly as a whole has the opportunity to ratify or query this decision when adopting the report of the bureau and the Standing Committee of the Assembly.[81]

Review of existing practice concerning post-accession monitoring

Early instances

It is worth noting the fact that the first consultation on the opening of a monitoring procedure was initiated by the Bureau of the Assembly in relation to a long-standing member of the Council of Europe, Greece, and in connection with a minority situation. This was done through the presentation of:

> a Motion for an Order on the situation of the Muslim minority in western Thrace (Greece). The Motion did not itself contain a 'reasoned written application' for the opening of monitoring, as required by Resolution 1115, but only a request for authorisation of a fact-finding visit by the Committee on Legal Affairs and Human Rights. Given the nature of the allegations contained in the Motion – of discrimination against the Muslim minority – the Bureau decided to consult the Monitoring Committee.[82]

The Bureau referred the matter to the Monitoring Committee, which appointed two co-rapporteurs "for inquiry" and authorised them "to visit the region in order to verify matters on the spot and to finalise a draft 'written opinion'".[83] Following a first reading of the draft written opinion, and the decision of the Monitoring Committee to revert to the question, the Greek government agreed to repeal Article 19 of the Greek Nationality Code, and to present draft legislation to Parliament to this effect.[84]

This article had been one of the main issues giving rise to the motion for an order. The article "was criticised as discriminatory vis-à-vis persons of non-Greek ethnic origin".[85] This actually entailed discrimination against ethnic Turks. The decisions of the Greek government to repeal Article 19 were taken just six days before the meeting of the Monitoring Committee was due to be held, in which the draft opinion of the rapporteurs was to be reverted to.[86] This outcome, obtained in the context of the consultation process previous to the opening of the monitoring procedure, seems to have sufficiently satisfied the concerns of the Assembly concerning state performance. Post-accession monitoring was thus never formally opened with regard to Greece.

The Monitoring Committee proceeded to close some of the pre-existing post-accession monitoring procedures soon after taking over its functions from the Committee on Legal Affairs and Human Rights. Monitoring on Estonia, Romania, the Czech Republic, and Lithuania, in particular, was closed during the same year in which the Monitoring Committee was established. This resulted in a series of resolutions and recommendations by the Assembly, which illustrate the role of post-accession monitoring in contributing to the implementation of minority protection standards. These and subsequent decisions also illustrate the threshold of compliance required by the Assembly for states to see their post-accession monitoring closed.

Estonia[87]

In Resolution 1117 (1997) on the honouring of obligations and commitments by Estonia, the Assembly considers that the most important obligations and commitments have been honoured by this state, and decides to close the monitoring procedure (opened on 29 May 1995 under Order No. 508). The Parliamentary Assembly welcomes the ratification of the Framework Convention by Estonia.[88]

Nevertheless, among the "three problematic areas [identified] concerning Estonia's obligations under the Council of Europe's Statute and the European Convention on Human Rights",[89] the Assembly expressly refers to "the treatment of the 'non-historic' Russian-speaking minority, which has given rise to some concern over the last three years, especially as far as the granting of residence permits and citizenship (and the language test that has to be passed in order to obtain the latter) are concerned".[90] As already noted, this recognition of the Russian-speaking non-citizen population as a minority is in contrast with the previous Assembly's opinion on accession and thus constitutes a step forward.

The Assembly considers the granting of residence permits and citizenship as issues falling under the scope of the Council of Europe Statute and the European Convention on Human Rights. It urges the Estonian authorities "to seek to integrate those members of the 'non-historic' Russian-speaking minority, who so wish, by improving the teaching of Estonian as a foreign language in public schools and universities, and in adult education by offering language courses free of charge or at a reduced rate to applicants for Estonian citizenship (especially in Russian-speaking areas)". The Assembly requests the Estonian authorities "to amend the 1993 Law on Education so as to allow the continued functioning of the Russian language state-funded secondary schools as long as there is a sufficient demand by parents".[91]

In Recommendation 1313 (1997), adopted on the same day as the resolution, the Assembly "in view of Estonia's remaining obligations and commitments, which Estonia is bound to fulfil within one year", recommends that the CoM aid Estonia's efforts in the field of language education, including through a co-operation programme with Estonia.[92]

Romania[93]

In closing its monitoring procedure on Romania less than three months later through Resolution 1123 (1997), the Assembly takes note of the fact that this state was the first to ratify the Framework Convention. It also notes the state's intention to ratify as soon as possible other conventions which it has already signed, including the European Charter of Local Self-Government and the European Charter for Regional or Minority Languages.[94] Further, it notes the resolve of the Romanian authorities to further the rights of national minorities and especially to amend the 1995 Education Act so as to allow mother-tongue instruction for members of national minorities.

Among the "few problems" pending, the Assembly "wishes Romania to be firmly committed to fighting racism, xenophobia and intolerance, particularly in respect of the Rom population, while committing itself to basing its policy regarding the protection of minorities upon the principles laid down in Recommendation 1201 (1993)".[95] The Assembly requests that the Romanian authorities "promote a campaign against racism, xenophobia and intolerance and take all appropriate measures for the social integration of the Rom population".[96] In Recommendation 1326 (1997) of the same title as Resolution 1123 (1997), the Assembly recommends that the CoM aid Romania's efforts, particularly through actions under the Council of Europe-EU joint co-operation programme including by: "carrying out a campaign against racism, xenophobia and intolerance".[97]

The Czech Republic[98]

In Recommendation 1338 (1997) on the obligations and commitments of the Czech Republic as a member state,[99] by which the Assembly closes its monitoring procedure with regard to this state, the Assembly notes among the principal issues to be addressed in its dialogue with the Czech authorities the following: i. conformity with the Council of Europe principles of citizenship law (notably in regard to acquisition of citizenship) and provisions for the expulsion of non-citizens – including the implementation of both these regulations – further to the dissolution of the Czech and Slovak Federal Republic (CSFR); ii. minorities, notably measures to reduce discrimination against the Roma community; and iii. legal status of religious groups (more concretely: the membership threshold required for registration with the Ministry of Culture).[100] Thus the idea of "post-monitoring" dialogue after the closing of the monitoring procedure (see below) starts to take root.

With regard to i., the Assembly notes that:

> the citizenship law has now been amended to make easier the acquisition of Czech citizenship by those who became automatically Slovak citizens at the time of the CSFR's dissolution but were registered as permanent residents in the territory of the Czech Republic and have not cancelled this registration since, and to reduce cases of statelessness ...[101]

However, the Assembly also notes that "some problems still remain which call for a more flexible approach in applying the law and for stricter central government supervision of attitudes and actions of local officials".[102] With regard to the latter issue, raised under i., the Assembly notes that "amendments to the criminal code in regard to expulsion are now before parliament, and that new legislation in regard to aliens is being prepared".[103]

In relation to ii., the Assembly indicates that "policies and programmes are being developed against racism, xenophobia, and anti-semitism – intended to counter in particular discrimination against the Roma minority", notably in the light of the report of the ECRI on the situation in the Czech Republic, and "also in anticipation of the Czech Republic's ratification of the Framework Convention for the Protection of National Minorities (with its control mechanism)".[104] Finally, in relation to iii., the Assembly notes that "a new law has been prepared to reduce the membership threshold for registration of religious groups".[105] In closing the monitoring procedure, the Assembly recommends that the CoM address the question of the implementation of the citizenship law under its own monitoring procedure,[106] and ensure the necessary allocation of resources to the ECRI, so that its proposals concerning the situation in the Czech Republic can be effectively implemented.[107]

Lithuania[108]

In closing the monitoring procedure on Lithuania, by adopting Recommendation 1339 (1997), the Assembly notes that among the principal issues of dialogue with this state under the monitoring procedure have been: i. the implementation of local government reform, with a view to establishing units of local self-government having their own financial resources; ii. the position of the ethnic Russian and ethnic Polish minorities; and iii. the adequacy of measures to restore property or give compensation to religious communities.[109]

The Assembly does not identify outstanding problems in relation to minority protection, and simply notes that: i. the European Charter of Local Self-Government is expected to be ratified before the end of 1997; ii. the right to use national languages is legally secured, in accordance with the principles of the European Charter for Regional or Minority Languages; and iii. other minority issues and relations with religious communities are approached in a spirit of mutual accommodation. The Assembly recommends that the CoM maintain the priority areas determined for Lithuania within the frame of the Council of Europe's ADACS programmes, including the joint programme with the EU,[110] and sustain the present level of resources allocated to these programmes. In contrast with the decision on the Czech Republic adopted on the same day, the

Assembly does not find it necessary to make a reference to continuing dialogue, or to follow-up regarding minority protection under the CoM's monitoring procedure.

The Slovak Republic[111]

Two years after the initial wave of closures of the monitoring procedure on Estonia, Romania, the Czech Republic and Lithuania by the Monitoring Committee, in Resolution 1196 (1999) – on the honouring of obligations and commitments by Slovakia – the Assembly proceeds to close the monitoring procedure started in relation to this state. The Assembly refers to the ratification by the Slovak Republic of the Framework Convention and presents the principal objects of the dialogue undertaken with the Slovak authorities: i. local and regional self-government; ii. the protection of minorities, and notably the consequences of the law on the state language and the need for a law on the use of minority languages; and iii. measures to address the problems of the Roma population.[112]

In connection with i., the Assembly indicates that legislation on the restructuring of the administration in this state is in preparation to increase the powers of local self-government authorities and to introduce regional self-government. With regard to ii., the Assembly states that

> the post of a Deputy Prime Minister responsible for human rights, minorities and regional development and a parliamentary committee for human rights and minorities have been created; bilingual certificates are used in schools with instruction in a minority language; a law was adopted on 10 July 1999 to regulate, in conjunction with other specific laws, the use of minority languages in official communications.

The Assembly indicates, however, that other problems "resulting from the state language law with regard to freedom of expression, as well as the use of minority languages in other settings, notably education", still needed to be regulated in conformity with recommendations made by international organisations. The ratification of the European Charter for Regional or Minority Languages is "strongly recommended".[113] Finally, regarding iii., the Assembly notes that

> programmes have been put into place to promote the education of Roma pupils (for example, school text books in the Roma language) and motivate school attendance and further integration, through co-operation with non-governmental organisations...; measures have been taken to better monitor and prevent racially motivated attacks; the post of a government commissioner and an advisory parliamentary committee to deal with the problems of the Roma population have been

created; the situation of the Roma minority is closely followed, *inter alia*, by [the ECRI] which will assess existing measures and make further proposals in its second stage report on Slovakia, to be prepared by the end of 1999.[114]

In Recommendation 1419 (1999), adopted in parallel to Resolution 1196, the Assembly recommends that the CoM should "address the minority issues" mentioned above "when monitoring the implementation" of the Framework Convention.[115]

Bulgaria[116]

In Resolution 1211 (2000) on the honouring of obligations and commitments by Bulgaria, the Assembly qualified the following as major steps forward on this country's "road to democracy": i. the ratification of the Framework Convention; ii. "the agreements on languages concluded with 'the former Yugoslav Republic of Macedonia'"; iii. progress in the area of freedom of conscience and religion "despite widening rifts within the Orthodox Church and the Muslim religious community"; as well as iv. the contribution to a peaceful settlement of the Kosovo conflict.[117] No reference is made to the status of Bulgaria in connection with the European Charter for Regional or Minority Languages.

The Assembly notes "a number of outstanding concerns and worrying trends",[118] some of which are related to minority protection, including: "the insufficient implementation of minorities' constitutional rights as regards education and information in their mother tongue through electronic media"; "continuing cases of police brutality, particularly towards the Roma"; and "the increasing divide within society, mirroring the lack of dialogue between the governing majority and the opposition, and the rifts within the Bulgarian Orthodox Church and the Muslim religious community".

The latter allegations do not, however, prevent the Assembly from bringing the monitoring procedure concerning Bulgaria to a close, although it "launches an appeal to the Bulgarian authorities" to take a series of steps "in the near future, the implementation of which it will closely follow" and which include:

- the rights of the persons belonging to minorities, especially as regards education and broadcasting in their mother tongue, should be improved and respected;

- minorities should be better represented in the police and the public services;

- the institution of an ombudsman for human rights should be created;

- the twenty-eight newly established districts should be given directly elected councils in accordance with the European Charter of Local Self-Government;

- freedom of thought, conscience and religion should be maintained, in accordance with Article 9 of the European Convention on Human Rights, and the process of returning property to churches and the Muslim community should be continued.[119]

In Recommendation 1442 (2000), adopted in parallel to Resolution 1211, the Assembly recommends that the CoM step up its assistance to the Bulgarian authorities in the framework of the ADACS Programme, in particular in the field of minority rights and in the implementation of the European Charter of Local Self-government.[120]

"The former Yugoslav Republic of Macedonia"

In paragraph 2 of Resolution 1213 (2000) on the honouring of obligations and commitments by "the former Yugoslav Republic of Macedonia",[121] the Assembly commends Macedonia "on having preserved the fragile equilibrium between the Macedonian majority and the ethnic Albanian minority and encourages both sides to continue striving for full integration of this and the other minorities, within one state that is respectful of all citizens' rights and freedoms". The Assembly indicates that this state has signed and ratified the Framework Convention, and signed, with a view to ratification, the European Charter for Regional or Minority Languages.[122]

It encourages "the Macedonian authorities to bring to a successful conclusion the initiatives they have taken" so that "the primary focus of any government action should be the integration of the ethnic minorities, in particular the Albanian minority, in accordance with the provisions" of the Framework Convention and "the principles set forth" in Recommendation 1201. The Assembly requests that:

a. facilities for the education and training of the Albanian and other minorities in their own language should be improved and provision for such improvements should be made in the new laws on further education;

b. the use of the Albanian language in the courts, in social and welfare institutions and elsewhere in public life should be facilitated in accordance with the European Charter for Regional or Minority Languages – which Macedonia should ratify;

c. incidents involving ethnic groups, such as the killing of three Macedonian police officers in Arachinovo in January 2000, should be settled in an objective, efficient and transparent way, so as to avoid these incidents being used to disturb the ethnic equilibrium.[123]

487

The Assembly also makes a series of requests for the acceleration of the reform of the education system which, according to the Assembly, should be undertaken in co-operation with the Council of Europe, in order to:

a. encourage the training of Albanian language teachers in secondary education and give careful consideration to the proposal by the OSCE High Commissioner on National Minorities to create an Albanian State University College for teacher training;

b. increase the opportunities for official higher education conducted in the Albanian language, and start a dialogue with the governors of the so-called 'University of Tetovo' with a view to establishing formal relations in accordance with the relevant provisions in the constitution;

c. provide adequate training facilities to enable Macedonians of Albanian origin, or other minorities, to find employment in the public sector, for example by considering the proposal of the OSCE High Commissioner on National Minorities to create a privately funded higher education centre for public administration.[124]

The Assembly also indicates that the Macedonian authorities should, "in close co-operation with the Congress of Local and Regional Authorities of Europe, work towards implementation of the European Charter of Local Self-Government, which Macedonia has ratified" and "in the meantime, the central Macedonian authorities should improve implementation of the 1995 Law on Local Government in order to increase local autonomy".[125]

In the Assembly resolution, as well as in Recommendation 1453 (2000), the Assembly declares the procedure closed.[126] Conversely, the active and continuous involvement and monitoring by the Congress, including in connection with the confrontations which had arisen in the country at the local level, as further discussed in Chapter 10, openly raise the question of whether the closing of the monitoring procedure by the Assembly was not premature. In closing its monitoring, the Assembly recommends that the CoM step up the assistance of the Council of Europe with the revision of Macedonian legislation in respect of higher education, citizenship, the media and police training within the framework of ADACS.[127]

Croatia

In Resolution 1223 (2000) on the honouring of obligations and commitments by Croatia, the Assembly decides to close the monitoring procedure in relation to this country. The Assembly refers to the ratification by this state of all the Council of Europe conventions it had committed itself to upon accession, including the Framework Convention, the European Charter of Local Self-Government and the European Charter for Regional or Minority Languages. It also refers to the adoption on 11 May 2000 of two laws on minority rights: the law on education in the language and script of national minorities and the law on official use of the language and script of national minorities.[128]

The Assembly expounds on the adaptation of the electoral law, including the revision of the special rights of the Croatian diaspora, and the amendments to the law on local self-government and administration, to take into account most of the suggestions made by the Congress.[129] Similarly, the Assembly expounds on the honouring of commitments related to the consequences of the war, in relation to the implementation of the Dayton and Erdut Agreements, in areas such as: co-operation with the International Criminal Tribunal for the former Yugoslavia; agreements with Bosnia and Herzegovina on return and exercise of property rights and other aspects related to the return of refugees (including a simplification of the procedures for confirming citizenship status); and the establishment of genuine dialogue with representatives of the Serb community.[130]

In addition, the Assembly addresses a series of recommendations to the Croatian authorities, which it relates to the implementation of the Dayton and Erdut Agreements and to the process of European integration. These include the adoption by Parliament of:

a. a new, integral constitutional law on the rights of national minorities in compliance with recommendations made by the Venice Commission;

b. further amendments to the constitution in order to extend to all persons within the jurisdiction of Croatia certain rights currently reserved to citizens, in compliance with recommendations made by Council of Europe experts;

c. further amendments to the electoral law to implement remaining recommendations contained in Assembly Resolution 1185 (1999) regarding minority voting and impartiality of the HRT during electoral campaigns;

...

e. a thorough reform of the legislation governing property issues throughout the country ... including the issue of occupancy/tenancy rights, in consultation with international experts.[131]

The recommendations also concern measures to be taken by the Croatian authorities, including the non-discriminatory implementation of laws regarding access to reconstruction assistance, repossession of property and the provision of alternative or temporary accommodation, as well as a prompt and flexible implementation of the citizenship law.[132]

Both in this resolution and in Recommendation 1473 (2000) of the same title, the Assembly asks the international community to keep its

promises of prompt financial assistance to Croatia. In the recommendation the Assembly advises the CoM to help the Croatian authorities in
the framework of its co-operation and assistance programmes, in order
to assist the state in the implementation of its recommendations.[133]
Furthermore, the Assembly advises the CoM to verify progress made in
the implementation of paragraph 3 of the resolution (the relevant provisions have been quoted above) in the framework of its own monitoring
procedure "when dealing with the relevant themes".[134] In so doing, the
Assembly seems to adopt a wishful, long-term approach to the matter.[135]

As in previous decisions, the Assembly indicates that it will carry out
post-monitoring dialogue through its Monitoring Committee on the
issues referred to in paragraph 3 of the resolution, or on "any other issue
arising from the obligations of Croatia as a member state of the Council
of Europe, with a view to re-opening the procedure ... if further clarification or enhanced co-operation should seem desirable".[136] The decision to
formalise post-monitoring dialogue adopted by the Monitoring
Committee on 12 January 2000, and according to which a review of compliance with the Assembly's advice and other aspects of the obligations
derived from membership should start one year after the closing of the
post-accession monitoring (see below), should be borne in mind in this
connection. According to this, a new review of Croatia's compliance was
due to start after September 2001.

Latvia[137]

In closing the monitoring procedure on Latvia, by adopting Resolution
1236 (2001), the Assembly welcomes progress made by this state with
the adoption of amendments to the law on citizenship, which abolished
the "age-window system" for the granting of citizenship, opened its
granting to stateless children born in Latvia since 21 August 1991, simplified the language tests for persons aged over 65 years, and reduced
the number of questions in history and other knowledge tests.

The Assembly also welcomes amendments to the State Language Law
and implementing legislation, "thus completing the implementation
mechanism of the State Language Law, which is now essentially in
conformity with Latvia's international obligations".[138] It should be noted,
however, that at the same time, the Assembly calls on the Latvian
authorities to ratify as a matter of priority the Framework Convention,
"and to amend and implement legislation, in particular the amended
State Language Law in conformity with the provisions and the spirit of
the Framework Convention".[139]

The absence of any reference to the need for the adoption and ratification of the European Charter for Regional or Minority Languages by the
state should also be noted. The Assembly calls instead on the state

authorities "to devise and adopt a law on the protection of national and language minorities and establish a state body in charge of minority affairs".[140] With regard to the law on education, dating from 29 October 1998, the Assembly points to the need for the state authorities to "maintain an open dialogue with the non-Latvian speaking community on the further implementation of the law, in particular on issues concerning the introduction of Latvian as the sole language of instruction in secondary schools by 2004, and the implementation of minority education programmes in primary schools".[141] The Assembly calls for the amendment of the law, in accordance with the provisions and spirit of the Framework Convention.[142]

Regarding the "National Programme for the Integration of Society in Latvia which was adopted by the Cabinet of Ministers in December 1999", the Assembly considers its implementation "to be outstandingly important for Latvia's future development and expects the speedy establishment of the institutions foreseen in the programme".[143] The Assembly calls for the ratification "as a matter of priority" of the European Social Charter by the state.[144]

The Assembly calls "on the Russian and other neighbouring states' authorities to encourage non-citizens in Latvia to apply for Latvian citizenship".[145] It also calls on member states of the Council of Europe generally to grant technical and financial assistance as well as to fund Council of Europe confidence-building projects with a view to strengthening social integration.[146] Finally, the Assembly uses the standard formula equivalent to that employed in connection with Croatia, in order to close the procedure.

At the time of writing, ten states are subjected to the monitoring procedure of the Assembly: Albania, Armenia, Azerbaijan, Bosnia and Herzegovina, Georgia, Moldova, Russia, Serbia and Montenegro, Turkey and Ukraine. From the year 2000, the Assembly started to adopt decisions not only in connection with the closing of the monitoring procedure regarding specific states, but also regarding its continuation. This has allowed for public stock-taking of state performance, and the outlining of priority areas for future state action. It has also allowed others to identify the concrete meaning that compliance with Council of Europe standards and commitments in the field of minority protection signifies in actual country situations from the Assembly's perspective.

Albania

The first exception to the "honouring of obligations and commitments" decisions of the Assembly during the year 2000 was that provided in the Albanian case. In Resolution 1219 (2000), the Monitoring Committee did not decide on the closing of the monitoring procedure on this state, as it had with preceding states on which a resolution on the "honouring of obligations and commitments" had been passed (or as would be subsequently the case with Croatia), but decided on the postponement of this decision instead.

The Assembly makes the adoption of a decision on Albania's honouring its obligations and commitments conditional on the manner in which "the forthcoming local and general elections in Albania", foreseen for October 2000 and June 2001 respectively, are conducted. It also makes it conditional on the adoption of further legislative and administrative measures in the framework of the monitoring procedure.[147] This is done in spite of the fact that Albania has "fully co-operated in the monitoring procedure" and "made substantial peaceful contributions to the settlement of the Kosovo conflict".[148] This is also in spite of the fact that Albania had signed and ratified the Framework Convention for the Protection of National Minorities and the European Charter of Local Self-government, among other international instruments, and started the "examination with a view to ratification of the European Charter for Regional or Minority Languages".[149] No remarks are made on the treatment given to minorities in the state. This points to the Assembly's not perceiving causes of particular concern in the latter connection.

Albanian performance with regard to minority protection, according to the results of the monitoring procedure – and as compared with that of neighbouring states monitored: Bulgaria, Croatia, and "the former Yugoslav Republic of Macedonia" – presumably seemed satisfactory, especially with regard to the existence of outstanding problems concerning the treatment of minorities. In spite of the fact that Albania's performance seems comparable to, if not even more advanced than, that of the other states where the monitoring procedure has been closed, the Assembly decides on its continuation. This points to the relatively low weight of minority considerations as compared with others in the decisions of the Assembly on the closing of the monitoring procedure.

The Assembly, in encouraging the Albanian authorities to accelerate the procedures initiated by the state in various areas of concern, includes a reference to the ratification of the European Charter for Regional or Minority Languages.[150] This has not been a demand in the case of other member states which have seen their respective monitoring procedures closed. No parallel decision is made as to the provision of additional assistance by the Council of Europe to the Albanian authorities to achieve this and other requests made by the Assembly, except for the fact that the Assembly decides generally "to follow closely further developments in Albania, including the status of minorities and the implementation of the Stability Pact for South-Eastern Europe ... in order to provide further assistance and advice in this process of consolidation of democratic stability and development of civil society, and to help Albania complete the honouring of its obligations and commitments".[151]

Ukraine

As in the case of Albania the year before, in Recommendation 1513 (2001) on the honouring of obligations and commitments by Ukraine the Assembly does not proceed to close the monitoring procedure on that country. Quite to the contrary, the Assembly decides that if no progress is made by Ukraine in honouring its obligations and commitments as a member state before the forthcoming (June 2001) session, the Assembly will consider imposing sanctions against the Ukrainian parliamentary delegation in accordance with Rules 6 to 9 to the Assembly's Rules of Procedure.[152] Furthermore, the Assembly recommends that the CoM consider suspending Ukraine from its right of representation in accordance with Article 8 of the Statute of the Council of Europe, should no substantial progress be made by that date.[153]

The fact that no reference is made to the ratification of the Framework Convention by Ukraine, which had already signed this instrument before acceding to the Council of Europe, supports the idea that other considerations prevail in the decision to continue the monitoring procedure with regard to this state. In spite of a reference to the fact that Ukraine should finalise the interrupted ratification process of the European Charter for Regional or Minority Languages and ensure adequate protection for all minority groups in Ukraine,[154] the decision of the Assembly seems to rely on other considerations – in particular, the abuses of power by the state authorities in respect of freedom of expression and assembly, especially concerning the freedom of the media, and the pattern of abuses against journalists and opposition politicians, affecting, among others, the right to life and physical integrity.

Turkey

In Resolution 1256 (2001) on the honouring of obligations and commitments by Turkey, the Assembly addresses the situation in a long-standing member of the Council of Europe under the monitoring procedure.[155] In this resolution, the Assembly does not proceed to close the monitoring procedure with regard to this state, but to pursue it "in close co-operation with the Turkish delegation".[156] The Assembly evaluates positively the progress recently achieved by Turkey in honouring its obligations as a member state of the Council of Europe, including the amendment of laws in the field of criminal law and procedure.

It refers in particular to the extension of freedom of expression as a result of the adoption of the "Law on the Postponement of Sentences and Trials

in respect of Crimes Committed through the Press and Broadcasting"
and to the ongoing debate on the modification of Article 312 of the Penal
Code, "which provides for sentences of up to three years and exclusion
for life from public functions for incitement to hatred on grounds of race
or religion".[157] It also makes reference to the draft laws on the establishment of the ombudsman and on local authorities.[158] The Assembly
welcomes the reduction of hostilities in south-eastern Turkey, and the
relief programme for displaced people and returnees.[159]

The Assembly identifies a number of obligations "where progress made
cannot yet be considered to be substantial and the honouring of which
requires further action by the Turkish authorities".[160] It recommends that
the state authorities should:

> ensure that the relevant constitutional provisions and other legal rules
> cannot be interpreted in a way which prevents political parties from
> carrying out their normal functions and elected representatives from
> expressing freely their political opinions, with due respect to the princi-
> ple of refraining from engaging in any activity or performing any act
> aimed at inciting violence or discrimination, at undermining parliamen-
> tary democracy or at destroying any of the rights and freedoms set forth
> in the European Convention on Human Rights.[161]

The Assembly indicates that the decision of the Turkish Constitutional
Court to ban the main opposition Virtue Party "for activities contrary to
the principle of a secular republic", to expel two of its members from
parliament, and to impose political bans on five other members, is in
contradiction with the principles of pluralist democracy. The Assembly
further points to the potential for this decision to create political instability.[162]

The Assembly urges the authorities to accelerate the modification of
Article 312 of the Turkish Penal Code and to revise Article 8 of the
Prevention of Terrorism Act, "which in its present unclear wording opens
the door to arbitrary action by the state against individuals for 'crimes of
expression of thought', in particular journalists and politicians for having
expressed opinions which, under the existing rules, could be interpreted
as incitement to separatism", and thus avoid further contravention of the
ECHR.[163]

The Assembly states that "pending a judgment of the European Court of
Human Rights in the case of Mrs Leyla Zana and others, the legal possibility should be examined or, if necessary, be created, to revise prosecution procedures and subsequent sentences in respect of former DEP
parliamentarians imprisoned since that time".[164] Also in connection with
the ECHR, the Assembly encourages an acceleration of the procedures
for adequate follow-up to those judgments which have not yet been

completely implemented, referring specifically to the Loizidou case,[165] and the third interim resolution adopted by the CoM declaring its resolve to ensure compliance with the judgment.[166]

The Assembly also recommends that the Turkish authorities:

> take the necessary legislative and administrative measures to guarantee full respect of the human rights of the Kurdish people in Turkey and enable them to live their Kurdish cultural identity (including teaching of the Kurdish language in schools in the Kurdish regions and author-isation of Kurdish language audiovisual media).[167]

These requests do not seem demanding in the light of existing international standards; however, their implementation would imply important progress at the domestic level. The Assembly, in recommending the signature and ratification of the Framework Convention and the European Charter for Regional or Minority Languages, as well as the application of their principles in respect of the different ethnic groups living in Turkey points, indirectly, to the low level of international and domestic commitment towards minority protection in this country. The Assembly invites the Turkish authorities to consider the organisation, in conjunction with the Assembly, of a seminar on multi-ethnic societies in Turkey,[168] in an attempt to start dialogue on this issue at the domestic level.

Georgia

In Recommendation 1533 (2001) on the honouring of obligations and commitments by Georgia, the Assembly calls on this state to accelerate reforms under way. While it welcomes progress made in granting autonomous status to Adjaria in April 2000, it regrets that no substantial progress has been made on a political settlement of the South Ossetian and Abkhaz conflicts and on the return of displaced persons who wish to do so to Abkhazia. It recommends that the CoM continue co-operation with the Georgian authorities in connection with the drafting of the law "on repatriation of persons deported from Georgia in the 1940s by the Soviet regime" (an issue which mainly concerns the Meskhetian Turks, as already discussed) and the amending of the Law on Local Self-Government, as well as the implementation of the recommendations made by the Congress to enhance local and regional self-government.[169]

Russian Federation

In Resolution 1277 and Recommendation 1553, on the honouring of obligations and commitments by the Russian Federation, both adopted on 23 April 2002, the Assembly refers to various areas in which progress has been achieved by the state in the field of minority protection – in particular, the ratification of the European Charter of Local Self-Government and the Framework Convention for the Protection of

National Minorities.[170] The Assembly reminds the Russian Federation of its commitment to ratify the European Charter for Regional or Minority Languages while expressing its own concern "about a number of obligations and major commitments with which progress remains insufficient" and pointing to the conflict in Chechnya as the greatest problem.[171]

The Assembly regrets that restrictive residential registration requirements continue to be enforced, often in a discriminatory manner, against ethnic minorities,[172] and expresses its consternation regarding the measures taken by the Krasnodar authorities "with a view to the expulsion of the Meskhetian population from Russian territories", expecting the authorities of the Russian Federation to seek a permanent solution by means of dialogue with the Meskhetians concerned and the Georgian authorities.[173] Finally, the Assembly regrets the problems faced by the Salvation Army and Jehovah's Witnesses in Moscow, welcoming the decision of the Russian authorities to ensure that the problem of local discrimination and harassment of these religious communities be brought to an end.[174]

In Recommendation 1553 the Assembly takes up again the issue of Chechnya, but, as in the resolution, merely calls for a proper investigation of abuses committed while addressing the question of the peaceful settlement of the conflict. When comparing the latter texts with other decisions of the Assembly in connection with the Russian Federation and the conflict in Chechnya in particular,[175] a different approach *vis-à-vis* human rights, and minority rights considerations, can be perceived between the results of the "monitoring function" on the one hand, for which the Monitoring Committee of the Assembly is responsible, and the work for which other committees of the Assembly (such as the Political Affairs Committee and the Committee on Legal Affairs and Human Rights) are responsible.

While this could point at complementary approaches by the various committees, the concerns expressed by the Monitoring Committee in connection with its lack of sufficient involvement in the discussions of the Assembly's reports on the conflict in Chechnya in particular,[176] point to differing approaches.[177] This multiplicity of approaches would seem to have been positive in relation to the assessment of the human rights situation in Chechnya.

Moldova

In spite of the lack of any reference to the "honouring of obligations and commitments" in the title of Resolutions 1280 and 1303 (2002), as well as Recommendation 1554 (2002) on "the functioning of democratic institutions in Moldova", as in the preceding "monitoring" decisions the latter texts were adopted on the basis of a report by the Monitoring Committee of the Assembly, and have performed a similar function.[178] They were adopted, however, in a context of accentuated political upheaval.

In Resolution 1280 the Assembly expresses its expectation that Moldovan political forces agree on a compromise which should include: "an extension of the existing moratorium on the reforms concerning the teaching and status of the Russian language, and changes to the history curriculum".[179] The Assembly also expects to see execution of the judgment of the European Court of Human Rights in the *Metropolitan Church of Bessarabia case,*[180] through the immediate registration of the Church by the adoption of a government decision to this effect, and the definition of implementation arrangements under Council of Europe supervision, within a three-month deadline.[181]

The Assembly insists on the application of the Congress recommendations for improving local self-government.[182] In the parallel Recommendation 1554, the Assembly further develops the latter aspect, recommending that the CoM pursue co-operation with the Moldovan authorities, among other things, "on the clarification of the legal status of Gagauzia by thorough expert appraisal of the various applicable legislation and framing of proposals for removing existing contradictions; this appraisal could be entrusted to the Venice Commission".[183]

In Resolution 1303, the Assembly welcomes the issuing of a certificate of entry in the register of religious denominations for the Metropolitan Church of Bessarabia and the maintenance of the aforementioned linguistic moratorium. The Assembly expresses its expectation that the authorities do not breach their commitments at a later date, including those regarding freedom of religion and the autonomy of local authorities.[184] It insists on the need to implement the recommendations made by the Congress.[185] It finally issues a general warning for the Moldovan authorities to refrain from taking any new measures or adopting new legislation in contradiction with Council of Europe standards, and more specifically, with Resolution 1280.

Armenia

Although Resolution 1304 (2002) on the honouring of obligations and commitments by Armenia very much focuses on this state not honouring its commitment to ratify Protocol 6 to the ECHR on the abolition of the death penalty, aspects of minority protection also occupy a prominent place. The Assembly urges registration of the Jehovah's Witnesses as a religious organisation,[186] and draws attention to the consequences of land and property privatisation operations in urban or rural areas for persons belonging to the Yezidi community.[187] The Assembly asserts its consideration of the peaceful settlement of pending conflicts – the conflict in Nagorno-Karabakh in this particular case – as a precondition for the closing of the monitoring procedure with regard to a particular country involved.[188]

Azerbaijan

In Resolution 1305 (2002) on honouring of obligations and commitments by Azerbaijan, the Assembly points out that this state has neither signed the European Outline Convention on Transfrontier Co-operation between Territorial Communities or Authorities and its additional protocols, nor ratified the European Charter for Regional or Minority Languages. The Assembly regrets the lack of progress in the development of local self-government and calls for the adaptation of legislation to the principles of the European Charter of Local Self-Government as well as the implementation of a genuine decentralisation strategy, taking into consideration the Congress and Secretariat recommendations.[189]

Minority issues are not addressed specifically, although aspects of minority protection are contained in concerns relating to human rights and the functioning of democratic institutions generally, such as parliamentary representation,[190] or the question of registration procedures of local non-governmental organisations.[191] The Assembly re-emphasises that agreement on the peaceful settlement of the Nagorno-Karabakh is a precondition for the closing of the monitoring procedure, while referring to the inclusion in a peaceful settlement of "the occupied territories",[192] and thus taking on board Azerbaijan's concerns.

Assessment and follow-up through post-monitoring dialogue

The Assembly's decisions on closing the monitoring procedure show that minority protection has constituted a permanent point of reference. All such decisions taken so far have alluded to this question. The Assembly has devoted particular attention to the issue of whether the state concerned has signed and ratified standards relating to minority protection, or whether the state has shown its intention to do so in the near future, even if the approaches of the Assembly in this connection have not been fully consistent. However, the consideration of minority protection has been rather nominal. Even if the Assembly has identified situations of violations of minority rights, or worrying patterns in this connection, it has been ready to close the monitoring procedure. Signature and ratification of the Framework Convention, or steps undertaken by the state aiming to achieve this, have often been considered sufficient for the Assembly to close the procedure.

The level of compliance with minority protection standards that the Assembly has been ready to accept as sufficient in closing the monitoring procedure has varied widely. Sometimes the Assembly has been willing to close even when it has identified and recognised systematic practices of violations of minority rights. Thus, from the practice of the Assembly, it can be deduced that compliance with Council of Europe standards for minority protection has not been a prerequisite for closing the monitoring procedure. References by the Assembly to the fact that the state has honoured "its most important obligations" when proceeding to close the procedure, while recognising at the same time the fact that minority protection questions still require satisfactory solution, further reinforce this perception.[193]

The Assembly seems to have given priority to other mainly political considerations over minority protection when proceeding to close the monitoring procedure. However, these "political" approaches have not resulted in improving the profile of its monitoring role, but rather the contrary. The disengagement of the Assembly from monitoring in a state facing important minority questions – and inter-ethnic tensions identified by the Assembly and left unresolved in closing the procedure, such as has been the case of "the former Yugoslav Republic of Macedonia", where armed inter-ethnic conflict exploded one year after the monitoring procedure had been closed – testifies to this.

While in most cases it has been sufficient for the Assembly to observe that standards for minority protection are "in the process of being fulfilled",[194] in cases where it has identified worrying trends in this regard it has also been ready to close its post-accession monitoring procedure.[195] In such situations, the Assembly has considered it sufficient to convey to the state a series of requests concerning state practice, and to simultaneously make further references to the fact that it will follow up their fulfilment. Occasionally the Assembly has set a deadline (usually one year) within which the country concerned has an obligation to fulfil its pending commitments.[196] An interesting political bent in the approaches of the Assembly has been that of emphasising the importance of economic and social rights, relevant to the protection of minorities in particular, in those states where the granting of civil and political rights to minorities is not guaranteed.

Given the low threshold of compliance with minority protection standards required by the Assembly, a relevant issue is what kind of follow-up the Assembly foresees after the closing of the monitoring procedure. In some cases the Assembly has decided "to follow developments" with regard to concrete minority situations.[197] References to the Assembly's intention to continue dialogue with the state concerned in relation to the obligations and commitments derived from membership, including those of minority protection, have been a common feature. Occasionally, the Assembly has expressly stated its readiness to reopen the procedure, "if further clarification or enhanced co-operation" should seem desirable in the future,[198] or in more negative terms, if it considers that the state concerned is not honouring those obligations and commitments.[199]

The Assembly has warned that it could decide to reopen the procedure, should the recommendations made, including those concerning minority protection, not be fulfilled within a year after the adoption of the Assembly's decision to close the procedure.[200] As a milder alternative, the Monitoring Committee decided in 2000 to develop so called "post-monitoring dialogue", in those areas where deficient compliance with Council of Europe standards had been identified in the resolution which closed the monitoring procedure, and also more broadly. This is further discussed below.

Besides the Assembly's decisions concerning its own follow-up, this organ has often addressed recommendations to the CoM suggesting further action. A recurrent suggestion has been that the CoM address pending issues, including those in connection with minority protection, under its own monitoring procedure.[201] However, as discussed in Chapter 6, the CoM has not addressed the question of minority protection as such under its monitoring procedure so far, even if it has decided to devote attention to issues touching on minority protection aspects, such as non-discrimination, with emphasis on the fight against intolerance and racism.

The Assembly has also recommended that the CoM address the minority issues highlighted in regard to a specific state when monitoring the implementation of the Framework Convention.[202] Sometimes, the Assembly has recommended some form of technical or material support by the CoM for action in the state concerned, to be channelled through the co-operation activities organised by the Secretariat, However, as described in Chapter 7, the provision of this type of support has been meagre. Finally, the Assembly has recommended that the CoM ensure the necessary allocation of resources to the ECRI, so that the proposals made by the latter can be effectively implemented.[203]

As already noted, in the year 2000 the Assembly took decisions regarding the manner in which its post-monitoring dialogue with states should be conducted. According to a proposal made by the Monitoring Committee on 12 January 2000, this dialogue should be conducted as follows. One year after the closure of the monitoring procedure, the Monitoring Committee will proceed:

> to a discussion on the follow-up given by the authorities of the country concerned to the steps recommended by the Assembly in its resolution or recommendation closing that procedure or on any other issues arising from that state's obligations. Such discussion could be based on the assessment of the situation made by the Chairman of the Monitoring

Committee, in co-operation with the national parliamentary delegation concerned and in consultation with the former co-rapporteurs. The Monitoring Committee would address the conclusions of its discussion in a memorandum to the Bureau. The Bureau would then decide whether further clarification or enhanced co-operation would seem desirable and, where necessary, a new procedure should be opened.[204]

This proposal by the Monitoring Committee was agreed upon by the Bureau of the Assembly and later ratified by the Assembly on 3 April 2000.[205]

This "formalised" post-monitoring dialogue has been initiated with Estonia, Romania, Lithuania, the Czech Republic, the Slovak Republic, the "former Yugoslav Republic of Macedonia", Latvia, Bulgaria and Croatia.[206] The Monitoring Committee has already declared itself satisfied with its post-monitoring dialogue with Estonia, Lithuania, Romania and more recently with Croatia, and recommended that the Bureau of the Assembly conclude this dialogue.[207] In parallel to the process of post-monitoring dialogue with Latvia, the Monitoring Committee discussed the issue of re-opening the monitoring procedure in respect of that state, mainly in respect to the situation of the Russian-speaking minority and the fact that Latvia has still not ratified the Framework Convention on National Minorities.[208]

Concluding remarks

Minority protection has become an important component of the requirements placed on member states of the Council of Europe in connection with membership after the changes in central and eastern Europe, both in acceding to, and following accession to, the Organisation. Thus, minority protection has become an essential element in a state monitoring cycle, which starts with the pre-accession procedure and extends into the post-accession monitoring procedure and, after this has been closed, "follow-up" dialogue with the Assembly *vis-à-vis* countries of central and eastern Europe.

In spite of the fact that the post-accession monitoring procedure, in particular, relates to member states of the Organisation without distinction, only one long-standing member of the Council of Europe, Turkey, has formally been subjected to this procedure so far. An attempt by the Monitoring Committee pursuant to Resolution 1115 (1997) to open a monitoring procedure concerning Austria in 2000 was refused by the Assembly's Bureau.[209] The preliminaries of the monitoring procedure as such, however, have proved to be instrumental in addressing minority issues in another long-standing member, Greece.

Although various aspects of minority protection have been a constant feature of the Assembly's monitoring activity, this has not implied that actual compliance with Council of Europe standards concerning minority protection has been required by the Assembly for states to accede to the Organisation or to cease being subjected to the monitoring procedure following their accession. Preference has been given to adherence to international instruments concerning minority protection over actual respect for minority rights. Considerations other than this respect have prevailed in the opinions on accession and in the decisions on closing the post-monitoring procedure.

With regard to the latter, a growing tendency has been for the Assembly to forward monitoring responsibilities on pending questions to the CoM, under its own monitoring procedure,[210] or as the organ ultimately responsible for monitoring the implementation of the Framework Convention for the Protection of National Minorities. Similarly, the Assembly has also forwarded responsibility on the follow-up of state implementation to the Secretariat programmes or co-operation activities, which in practice have not devoted much attention to minority protection.[211]

It is to be hoped that, on the basis of demands made by the Assembly in closing the post-accession monitoring procedures, increasing attention will be paid in the future to the minority question both in the political activity of the CoM and under the recently established Co-operation activities of the Secretariat which have replaced ADACS. Of course, the responsibility of the CoM in monitoring implementation, of the Framework Convention in particular, remains unabated. Nevertheless, probably much effort will be required in bringing attention to the need to contribute to the implementation of minority protection standards by those frameworks. The post-monitoring, follow-up dialogue recently started by the Assembly, to make up for monitoring procedures closing against a background of deficient state compliance with Council of Europe standards, can constitute a useful tool in this connection. Further, the monitoring activity of the Assembly as such has proved to have a positive impact in connection with specific aspects of state performance and can continue doing so in the future.

An important aspect of the monitoring procedure has been the principle of non-discrimination which it has timidly introduced: all member states can be subjected to it. This principle has been reasserted by the Monitoring Committee in a recent progress report on its activity, where the need has been affirmed that "monitoring should concern not only commitments expressly accepted by the newer members of the Organisation – as it does – but all of the obligations that are to be honoured by all 45 member states – something that is not done". Reference is also made in the report to the current practice of excluding western European democracies from monitoring as a source of criticism for its lack of fairness.[212] This attitude of the Monitoring Committee opens new possibilities for dialogue between the Assembly and "old" member states on long-standing issues, such as minority protection. It remains to be seen whether the monitoring procedure will be applied vis-à-vis increasing thresholds of state performance, to extend to all member states, since all of them can improve their performance in the implementation of Council of Europe standards.

The proposal for the establishment of a "sub-committee on conflict settlement in monitored states" of the Monitoring Committee, even if seemingly unsuccessful so far,[213] could imply a step in the right direction. It would help to prevent the activity of the Monitoring Committee and its monitoring procedure being perceived as limited to states undergoing conflict situations only. The pro-active, non-discriminatory approaches to monitoring taken by the Congress offer a good example to follow.[214]

Otherwise, a growing perception among member states of differential treatment by the Assembly will lead to the failure of its monitoring activity. At the same time, and against the background of repeated calls by the Monitoring Committee for other parliamentary committees not to infringe upon its competencies, it should be borne in mind that a multiplicity of monitoring approaches and multifaceted perspectives in assessing state performance has proved so far beneficial for human rights, and minority protection in particular, and therefore should not be curtailed, even if mere duplication should be avoided.

In the new context created by the changes in Europe and Council of Europe enlargement, renewed possibilities exist for the treatment of the minority question by the Assembly as a matter of human rights, rather than as a matter of geo-politics. Although the Assembly should not, and cannot by its very nature, abandon its political approaches in dealing with minority questions, human rights protection is also a "political" matter, and a matter for "politics" and "politicians". The importance of the concerns of the Assembly and its endeavours in ensuring justiciable rights for minorities, facilitated through the activities of its various committees besides the Monitoring Committee, and its Legal Affairs Committee in particular, described in Chapter 8, are an illustration of this.

Although the Assembly's endeavours in this connection should be pursued, member states of the Council of Europe have already undertaken specific compromises, contained in the various conventions mentioned in this book, and especially in the Framework Convention, which are particularly relevant to minority protection. Given this substantive *acquis* of the Organisation in this field, the Assembly is now in a position to consider minority questions from the perspective of existing legal standards and the need for their realisation, given them appropriate weight vis-à-vis short-sighted geo-political considerations. It is not only the responsibility of states, but also of society at large, including parliamentarians, to make these standards work in practice, especially if further situations of conflict within societies are to be avoided.

Notes

1. See H. Winkler, "Democracy and human rights in Europe: a survey of the admission practice of the Council of Europe", *Austrian J. Publ. Intl Law*, Vol. 47 (1995), pp. 147-72.

2. On this and other important aspects of the accession procedure, see H. Klebes and D. Chatzivassiliou, "Problèmes d'ordre constitutionnel dans le processus d'adhésion d'états de l'Europe centrale et orientale au Conseil de l'Europe", 8 *Revue Universelle des Droits de l'Homme*, No. 8-9, 27 December 1996, pp. 269-86. For a more recent study on the question of accession, see M. Nowak, "Is Bosnia and Herzegovina ready for membership in the Council of Europe? The responsibility of the Committee of Ministers and of the Parliamentary Assembly", *Human Rights Law Journal*, Vol. 20, No. 7-11 (1999), pp. 285-89. For a detailed analysis of the initial development of the Assembly's accession procedure with a special focus on the minority question, see A. Spiliopoulou-Åkermark, op. cit., pp. 238-45. On the specific aspect discussed here see, in particular, p. 238.

3. This is stated in Article 4 of the Statute of the Council of Europe.

4. See K. Drzewicki, "The future relations between eastern Europe and the Council of Europe", in A. Bloed and W. de Jonge (eds.), *Legal Aspects of a New European Infrastructure* (Utrecht: Netherlands Helsinki Commité and Europa Instituut, 1992), pp. 41-60.

5. See Chapter 6.

6. See, for example, Parliamentary Assembly Resolution 1155 (1998) on the progress of the Assembly's monitoring procedures (April 1997-April 1998), first paragraph. It should be noted, however, that the first step taken by the Assembly in this connection actually precedes the convening of the first Council of Europe summit. M. Nowak indicates that the adoption by the Assembly of Order No. 488 (1993), which was adopted before the first Council of Europe summit and to which reference is made further below, was due to the need to satisfy demands by Hungary for the protection of the Hungarian minority living in Slovakia, in the context of the negotiations on accession by the latter state. See M. Nowak, "Is Bosnia and Herzegovina ready for membership in the Council of Europe? The responsibility of the Committee of Ministers and of the Parliamentary Assembly", op. cit., p. 285, footnote No. 2.

7. Paragraph 14 of Recommendation 1177 (1992), adopted on 5 February 1992, at the 43rd ordinary session of the Assembly.

8. See, as an example, the report of the Political Affairs Committee on the application for membership by Finland (1), rapporteur Mr Lied, Parliamentary Assembly Doc. 5985, 22 December 1988, explanatory memorandum, paragraph 26.

9. Statute of the Council of Europe, European Treaty Series No. 1.

10. A. Spiliopoulou-Åkermark supports the introduction of minority protection in the Statute as a separate condition of membership in the Council of Europe in *Justifications of Minority Protection in International Law*, pp. 244-45. However, in considering this, the question can be raised as to why minority protection should be receiving a different treatment in this regard vis-à-vis other aspects of human rights protection. Separate treatment could be manipulated in order to question once again the definition of minority protection as a human right.

11. On related aspects of the Assembly's opinions, see H. Klebes and D. Chatzivassiliou, "Problèmes d'ordre constitutionnel dans le processus d'adhésion d'états de l'Europe centrale et orientale au Conseil de l'Europe", 8 *Revue Universelle des Droits de l'Homme*, No. 8-9, 27 December 1996, pp. 269-86.

12. See paragraph 8 of Assembly Opinions Nos. 174 and 175 (1993) on the applications by the Czech and Slovak Republics for membership of the Council of Europe, 29 June 1993, respectively.

13. Opinion No. 170 (1993), paragraph 3.

14. Paragraphs 9-11 of Opinion No. 175 (1993).

15. Paragraph 5 of Opinion No. 176 (1993).

16. Ibid., paragraphs 6, 8, 10 and 11.

17. Opinion No. 182 (1994), paragraph 7.

18. Ibid.

19. Rather than just "expecting" the state authorities "'to base their policy' regarding the protection of minorities on the principles laid down in Recommendation 1201 (1993)" as in the case of Estonia. See paragraph 10.e of Opinion No. 183. Present authors' emphasis.

20. Opinion 183 (1995), paragraphs 4-7. Present authors' emphasis.

21. Opinion 188 (1995), paragraphs 5-6.

22. Ibid., paragraph 8.*c.*

23. Ibid., paragraph 8.*g.*

24. Ibid.

25. The Assembly has occasionally been criticised for referring to Recommendation 1201 as if it were a legally binding document. See A. Spiliopoulou-Åkermark, op. cit., p. 244.

26. Opinion 188 (1995), paragraph 8.*h.*

27. Ibid., paragraph 8.*l.*

28. Opinion No. 189 (1995), paragraph 3.

29. Ibid., paragraphs 13-14.

30. Ibid., paragraph 17.iv and xi.

31. Opinion No. 190 (1995), paragraph 8.

32. Ibid., paragraph 11.iv, x and xi.

33. Ibid., paragraph 12.v. and vii.

34. Resolution 1055 was adopted on 2 February 1995.

35. Paragraph 3 of the resolution.

36. Order No. 506 (1995), adopted on the same day as Resolution 1055 (1955).

37. Resolution 1065 (1995) on procedure for an opinion on Russia's request for membership of the Council of Europe, adopted on 26 September 1995.

38. Opinion No. 193 (1996), paragraph 3.

39. Specifically, the Assembly uses the expression "in the near future". See paragraph 7 of the opinion.

40. Paragraph 7.v. of the opinion.

41. Paragraph 10.iv of the opinion.

42. Paragraph 10.ix, and xi-xiii.

43. Paragraph 4 of Resolution 1086 1996).

44. Ibid., paragraph 5.

45. Ibid., paragraphs 6 and 10.

46. Paragraph 3 of Opinion No. 195 (1996), adopted by the Assembly on 24 April 1996. The accession procedure concerning Croatia is described in detail in H. Klebes and D. Chatzivassiliou, "Problèmes d'ordre constitutionnel dans le processus d'adhésion d'états de l'Europe centrale et orientale au Conseil de l'Europe", 8 *Revue Universelle des Droits de l'Homme*, No. 8-9, 27 December 1996, pp. 284-86.

47.   Ibid., paragraph 9.vii-viii, xiii-xiv and xix. On the issue of the effective exercise of the electoral rights by national minorities in Croatia at that time, see in H. Klebes and D. Chatzivassiliou, op. cit., p. 273.

48.   Ibid., paragraph 9.vi.

49.   Ibid., paragraph 10.iv and viii.

50.   Paragraph 10 of Opinion No. 209, adopted on 27 January 1999.

51.   Ibid., paragraph 10.i.*d* and *e*; ii.*b*, *e*, *h* and *i*; iv.*f* and v.*a*.

52.   Ibid., paragraph 11.

53.   The Opinion on the accession by Latvia, adopted in the same year as that on the accession by Moldova, contains a reference to the Assembly's own "monitoring procedure" only.

54.   Paragraph 6 of the respective opinions, adopted by the Assembly on 28 June 2000.

55.   Opinion No. 221, paragraph 13.i.*d*, *e* and *f*. Opinion No. 222, paragraph 14.i.*e*, *f* and *g*. adopted by the Assembly on 28 June 2000.

56.   Paragraph 13.ii.*b*. of Opinion 221.

57.   Paragraphs 13.iii.*h* and 14.iii.b of Opinions Nos. 221 and 222, respectively.

58.   Paragraph 13.iv.*b* of Opinion No. 221.

59.   Paragraph14.iv.*g* of Opinion No. 222.

60.   For a critical examination of the background against which this opinion was adopted, which extends to other positive opinions on accession by the Assembly, see M. Nowak, "Is Bosnia and Herzegovina ready for membership in the Council of Europe? The responsibility of the Committee of Ministers and of the Parliamentary Assembly", *Human Rights Law Journal*, Vol. 20, No. 7-11 (1999), pp. 285-89.

61.   Paragraph 13 of the opinion, adopted on 22 January 2002.

62.   Paragraph 15.v.*c*.

63.   Paragraph 6 of the opinion, adopted on 24 September 2002.

64.   Paragraph 12.iv.*c*.

65.   Pargraph 12.vi.*c*.

66.   Paragraph 16.

67.   Paragraph 18.

68.   Resolution 1155 (1998) on progress of the Assembly's monitoring procedures (April 1997-April 1998), Parliamentary Assembly Doc., 21 April 1998, paragraph 8.iii.

69.   This adoption took place on 20 June 1993.

70.   As discussed below, this decision still remains to be implemented. See "Progress of the Assembly's monitoring procedure", Progress report: Committee on the honouring of obligations and commitments by member states of the Council of Europe (Monitoring Committee), rapporteur: Ms Josette Durrieu, doc. 9651, 13 January 2003, paragraph 9.

71.   Parliamentary Assembly Resolution 1031 (1994), adopted by the Assembly on 14 April 1994, paragraphs 1-4 and 6-7.

72.   Parliamentary Assembly Order No. 508 (1995) on the honouring of obligations and commitments by member states of the Council of Europe.

73.   Parliamentary Assembly Order No. 513 (1996), adopted on 23 January 1996, paragraph 5.

74. See "Progress of the Assembly's monitoring procedures (April 1997-April 1998)", report of the Committee on the honouring of obligations and commitments by member states (Monitoring Committee), rapporteur Mr Guido de Marco, Parliamentary Assembly Doc. 8057, 2 April 1998, p. 10, paragraph 20.

75. Ibid., at p. 14, paragraph 38.

76. Resolution 1155 (1998) on progress of the Assembly's monitoring procedures (April 1997-April 1998), Parliamentary Assembly Doc., provisional edition, 28 April 1998, paragraph 4.ii.

77. See "Areas which have been covered under the monitoring procedure", indicative list, memorandum prepared by the Office of the Clerk on the instructions of the Chairman, doc. As/Mon (1997) 13, contained in Annex 3 of "Progress of the Assembly's monitoring procedures (April 1997-April 1998)", report of the Committee on the honouring of obligations and commitments by member states (Monitoring Committee), rapporteur Mr Guido de Marco.

78. Ibid., at p. 10, paragraph 20.

79. "Progress of the Assembly's monitoring procedures (April 1997-April 1998)", Report of the Committee on the honouring of obligations and commitments by member states (Monitoring Committee), rapporteur Mr Guido de Marco, p. 8, paragraphs 10-11.

80. Ibid., p. 15, paragraph 46.

81. Ibid., p. 8, paragraph 12.

82. Ibid., p. 15, paragraph 47.

83. Ibid, at pp. 15-16, paragraph 48.

84. Ibid., p. 16, paragraph 50.

85. Ibid., paragraph 49.

86. Ibid., paragraph 50.

87. On the domestic situation concerning minority protection in Estonia, see EU Accession Monitoring Programme, *Monitoring the EU Accession Process: Minority Protection* (Budapest, New York: Central European University Press, 2001), pp. 175-212.

88. Resolution 1117, adopted by the Assembly on 30 January 1997, paragraph 3.

89. Ibid., paragraph 5.

90. Ibid., paragraph 6. Present authors' emphasis.

91. Ibid., paragraph 8.i and ii.

92. Paragraph 2 of Recommendation 1313 (1997). On the co-operation programmes, see Chapter 7.

93. On the domestic situation concerning minority protection in Romania, see EU Accession Monitoring Programme, *Monitoring the EU Accession Process: Minority Protection* (Budapest, New York: Central European University Press, 2001), pp. 385-428.

94. Resolution 1123, adopted on 24 April 1997, paragraphs 3 and 4.

95. Ibid., paragraph 13.

96. Ibid., paragraph 14.

97. Recommendation 1326, adopted on 24 April 1997, paragraph 2.iii. See further, Chapter 7.

98. On the domestic situation concerning minority protection in the Czech Republic, see EU Accession Monitoring Programme, *Monitoring the EU Accession Process: Minority Protection* (Budapest, New York: Central European University Press, 2001), pp. 121-74.

99. Adopted by the Assembly on 22 September 1997.

100. Recommendation 1338, adopted on 22 September 1997, paragraph 6.

101. Ibid., paragraph 7.i.

102. Ibid., paragraph 7.ii.

103. Ibid., paragraph 7.iii.

104. Ibid., paragraph 7.v.

105. Ibid., paragraph 7.vi.

106. See further, Chapter 6.

107. Recommendation 1338, paragraph 11.i and ii.

108. On the domestic situation concerning minority protection in Lithuania, see EU Accession Monitoring Programme, *Monitoring the EU Accession Process: Minority Protection* (Budapest, New York: Central European University Press, 2001), pp. 313-42.

109. Recommendation 1339, adopted on 22 September 1997, paragraph 6.i, vii, and viii.

110. On these programmes, see Chapter 7.

111. On the domestic situation concerning minority protection in the Slovak Republic, see EU Accession Monitoring Programme, *Monitoring the EU Accession Process: Minority Protection* (Budapest, New York: Central European University Press, 2001), pp. 429-92.

112. Resolution 1196, adopted on 21 September 1999, paragraph 4.iii, v and vi.

113. Ibid., paragraph 5.iii and v.

114. Ibid., at vi.

115. Recommendation 1419 (1999), paragraph 2.

116. On the domestic situation concerning minority protection in Bulgaria, see EU Accession Monitoring Programme, *Monitoring the EU Accession Process: Minority Protection* (Budapest, New York: Central European University Press, 2001), pp. 75-120.

117. Resolution 1211 (2000), adopted on 26 January 2000, paragraph 1.

118. Present authors' emphasis.

119. Paragraph 4.iv, v, vii and viii of the resolution.

120. Paragraph 2 of Recommendation 1442 (2000). On ADACS and the charter, see further, Chapters 7 and 10, respectively.

121. Resolution 1213 was adopted on 5 April 2000.

122. Ibid., paragraphs 5 and 6.

123. Ibid., paragraph 13.i.

124. Ibid., paragraph 13.iv.

125. Ibid., paragraph 13.viii-ix.

126. Ibid., paragraph 14 and Recommendation 1453 (2000), adopted also on 5 April 2000, paragraph 2.

127. Paragraph 4 of the recommendation.

128. Resolution 1223 (2000), paragraph1.ix.

129. Paragraph 1.i and iii and iv of Recommendation 1473, adopted on 26 September 2000.

130. Ibid. paragraph 2.

131. Paragraph 3.i.of the resolution.

132. Ibid., paragraph 3.ii.*d*.

133. Ibid., paragraph 4 and paragraphs 1.v and 2.i of Recommendation 1473 (2000), adopted on 26 September 2000. On the co-operation and assistance programmes, see Chapter 7.

134. Ibid., paragraph 2.ii.

135. See Chapter 6.

136. Paragraphs 5 and 1.iii of the resolution and the recommendation, respectively.

137. On the domestic situation concerning minority protection in Latvia, see EU Accession Monitoring Programme, *Monitoring the EU Accession Process: Minority Protection* (Budapest, New York: Central European University Press, 2001), pp. 265-312.

138. Paragraph 2 of Resolution 1236, adopted on 23 January 2001.

139. Paragraph 5.i of the resolution.

140. Ibid., paragraph 5.v.

141. Ibid., paragraph 3.

142. Ibid., paragraph 5.iv.

143. Ibid., paragraph 4.

144. Ibid., paragraph 5.vi.

145. Ibid., paragraph 7.

146. Ibid, paragraph 8. See also Recommendation 1490 (2001) adopted on the same date as the Resolution, paragraph 1.iv. On the confidence-building measures programme, see Chapter 7.

147. Resolution 1219, adopted on 28 June 2000, paragraphs 9-10.

148. Ibid., paragraph 2.*i-j*.

149. Ibid., paragraph 5.*e*.

150. Actually, at the time of writing, the charter has not been signed by Albania either.

151. Paragraph 7 of the resolution.

152. See paragraph 9 of Recommendation 1513 (2001) and also paragraph 10 of Resolution 1244 (2001), adopted on the same date as the recommendation.

153. Ibid., paragraph 10 in both texts.

154. Paragraph 3 of the recommendation.

155. See "Progress of the Assembly's monitoring procedure", Progress report Committee on the honouring of obligations and commitments by member states of the Council of Europe (Monitoring Committee), rapporteur: Ms. Josette Durrieu, doc. 9651, 13 January 2003, paragraph 9.

156. See paragraph 20 of Resolution 1256, adopted on 28 June 2001.

157. Ibid., paragraph 15.

158. Ibid., paragraph 10.

159. Ibid. paragraph 13.

160. Ibid., paragraph 16.

161. Ibid., paragraph 16.*c*.

162. Ibid., paragraph 18.

163. Ibid., paragraph 16.*i*. See further, Chapter 1.

164. Ibid., paragraph 16.*d*.

165. See further, Chapter 1.

166. Ibid., paragraph 16.*j.*

167. Ibid., paragraph 16.*k.* See further, Chapters 1, 2 and 3. See also the recommendations and guidelines adopted under the aegis of the OSCE High Commissioner on National Minorities, in particular: the Oslo Recommendations regarding the Linguistic Rights of National Minorities and Explanatory Note (February 1998) and the Guidelines on the use of minority languages in the broadcast media (October 2003). Available free of charge from the OSCE HCNM office or on the OSCE HCNM Website: www.hcnm.org.

168. Ibid., paragraph 16.

169. Paragraphs 1 v, 2.v and 3 ii of the recommendation, adopted on 25 September 2001.

170. Paragraphs 2. i and iii of the resolution.

171. Ibid., paragraph 8.iii and i.

172. Ibid., paragraph 8.xii.

173. Ibid., paragraph 8.xiii.

174. Ibid., paragraph 8.xiv.

175. These approaches have been discussed in Chapters 5, 6 and 8.

176. See "Progress of the Assembly's monitoring procedure (2000-2001)", Progress report Committee on the honouring of obligations and commitments by member states of the Council of Europe (Monitoring Committee), rapporteur: Mr Mota Amaral, doc. 9198, 11 September 2001, paragraph 28.

177. Concerns about careful division of the work programme among the various Assembly committees and increasing complementarity have been expressed by the Monitoring Committee. See at ibid., paragraphs 24-33.

178. Resolution 1280 and Recommendation 1554 were adopted on 24 April 2002, while Resolution 1303 was adopted on 26 September 2002.

179. Paragraph 10.ii. of the resolution.

180. Judgment of 5 December 2001. See further, Chapter 1.

181. Paragraph 10.v. of the resolution.

182. Ibid., paragraph 14.i.

183. Paragraph 5.vi, of the recommendation.

184. Ibid., paragraph 6.

185. Ibid., paragraph 9.

186. Paragraph 15 of the resolution, adopted on 26 September 2002.

187. Ibid., paragraph 22.

188. Ibid., paragraph 24.iii.

189. Paragraph 3.v of the resolution, adopted on 26 September 2002.

190. Ibid., paragraph 6.ii.

191. Ibid., paragraph 6.iii.

192. Ibid., paragraph 9.

193. See, for example, Resolution 1117 (1997) on the honouring of obligations and commitments by Estonia, as indicated above.

194. This has been the case for "the former Yugoslav Republic of Macedonia", for example. See paragraph 14 of Resolution 1213 (2000).

195. See, for example, Resolution 1211 (2000) on the honouring of obligations and commitments by Bulgaria, as indicated above.

196. See, for example, Recommendation 1313 (1997) on the honouring of obligations and commitments by Estonia, as quoted above.

197. This is the case with Resolution 1117 (1997) and Recommendation 1313 (1997).

198. For example, this has been the case in relation to the Czech Republic, Lithuania, Bulgaria and "the former Yugoslav Republic of Macedonia".

199. For example, this has been the case in relation to Romania. See Resolution 1123 (1997) paragraph 15.

200. Ibid.

201. See, for example, Recommendation 1338 (1997) concerning the Czech Republic, and Recommendation 1419 (1997) concerning the Slovak Republic. On the monitoring procedure of the Committee of Ministers, see Chapter 6.

202. See Recommendation 1419, paragraph 2, in relation to the Slovak Republic. On the role of the Committee of Ministers in monitoring the Framework Convention, see further, Chapter 2.

203. See Recommendation 1338 (1997) concerning the Czech Republic, paragraph 11.ii. On the ECRI, see Chapter 11 in this book.

204. See "Progress report of the Monitoring Committee (1999-2000)", Information report, Committee on the honouring of obligations and commitments by member states of the Council of Europe (Monitoring Committee), rapporteur: Mr Juris Sinka, Parliamentary Assembly Doc. 8734, 4 May 2000, p. 3, paragraph 10. See further "Progress of the Assembly's monitoring procedure (2000-2001)", paragraph 10.

205. Ibid., paragraph 11.

206. Ibid., paragraph 13.

207. See further, "Progress of the Assembly's monitoring procedure", Progress report by Ms Josette Durrieu, 13 January 2003, p. 13.

208. Ibid.

209. See "Progress of the Assembly's monitoring procedure (2000-2001)", paragraph 10.

210. See Chapter 6.

211. Occasionally the Assembly has referred to the confidence-building measures programme, which has dealt with minority issues at the level of the civil society. See further, Chapter 7.

212. See "Progress of the Assembly's monitoring procedure", Progress report by Ms Josette Durrieu, 13 January 2003, p. 4.

213. See "Progress of the Assembly's monitoring procedure (2000-2001)", paragraphs 17-19.

214. See Chapter 10.

Chapter 10

The Congress of Local and Regional Authorities of Europe (CLRAE) and its monitoring procedures

Introduction

The Congress of Local and Regional Authorities of Europe (Congress) is an organ of the Council of Europe that has prominently developed its functions and status since its initial establishment in 1957 as a "Conference on Local Authorities" on the basis of Article 17 of the Statute of the Council of Europe. This article authorised the Committee of Ministers (CoM) to "set up advisory and technical committees or commissions for such specific purposes as it may deem desirable".

Thus, the initial status of the Congress was precarious, and always in a subordinate position in relation to the CoM.[1] In the most recent revision of the status of the Congress, under Statutory Resolution (2000) 1, its role as a fully-fledged, independent organ of the Council of Europe representing local and regional authorities, a role which had been established under Statutory Resolution (94) 1, has been reaffirmed.[2] Similarly, the organisation of the Congress in two chambers, one representative of local authorities (Chamber of Local Authorities) and one of regional authorities (Chamber of Regions), has been consolidated.[3]

The activities of some of the working groups through which the Congress has developed its work have been of special relevance for minority concerns, including those on: the European Charter of Local Self-Government; the situation of local democracy in member states (both groups belonging to the Chamber of Local Authorities); regionalisation and democratic stability in Europe; social cohesion and the economic development of regions (both under the authority of the Chamber of Regions); as well as federalism, regionalism, local autonomy and minorities (composed of members of both chambers). Further to the reform adopted by the CoM on the basis of Statutory Resolution (2000) 1, the Congress established statutory committees on institutional affairs, social cohesion, sustainable development and cultural matters.

The Congress's mandate is to represent local and regional authorities. Given that local and regional (also called "territorial") institutions are those where minorities have, in principle, the greatest opportunity to see their concerns reflected,[4] the Congress is, by its very nature, the organ of the Council of Europe most relevant for the overall advancement of minority interests and concerns. This has been particularly the case since the Congress has taken up the promotion of local democracy as one of its main functions.[5] This is in spite of the newly-fledged character of the Congress, which is still asserting its political role and pursuing the expansion and increase of the overall relevance of its specific competencies within the Council of Europe.

Most of the initiatives from within the Council of Europe for the elaboration of international instruments relevant to minority protection have actually originated in the Congress.[6] Some of these initiatives, presented in this chapter, have not yet received the endorsement of Council of Europe member states, although they could entail substantial progress in relation to minority protection. The Congress has also devoted several of its resolutions and recommendations to dealing specifically with the minority question.

Similarly, the Congress is gradually becoming the main organ responsible for monitoring the implementation of some international treaties relevant to minority protection, which have been adopted in the framework of the Council of Europe and for which a specific monitoring mechanism had not been previewed. This is mainly as a result of the role which the Congress has acquired in relation to the European Charter of Local Self-Government and the "monitoring of local and regional democracy", further discussed below.

Decisions on minorities

Given the aforementioned mandate of the Congress, most of its decisions have been relevant to minorities in an indirect manner. The decisions dealing specifically with minority protection, although few, have been useful especially from a conceptual perspective, as they have served to highlight the close inter-relations between various aspects of local and regional self-government on the one hand, and minority concerns on the other. By establishing this conceptual link, they have shown, indirectly, the relevance of the work of the Congress generally to minority protection.

The link between local democracy and the rights of minorities has been established in Congress decisions since the early 1990s, particularly via the adoption of Resolution 232 (1992) on autonomy, minorities, nationalism and the European Union.[7] In this resolution, the Congress calls for the preservation of the identity of minorities, the recognition of their

514

right to cultural and economic survival and the prohibition of their assimilation. It also calls upon states to ensure non-discrimination and the establishment of appropriate appeal systems in this connection, while advocating the adoption of measures of affirmative action. In addition, the Congress calls for the application of the principle of subsidiarity and the recognition of the right of minorities to play a part in public administration.[8]

The conceptual link established by the Congress has been further elaborated in recent years. In Resolution 52 (1997) on federalism, regionalism, local autonomy and minorities and in Recommendation 43 (1998) on territorial autonomy and national minorities, the Congress has underscored the connections between the principle of subsidiarity and autonomy. It has also underscored the instrumentality of the principle of subsidiarity to the solution of minority problems and the benefits, in terms of safeguarding state integrity, that can be derived from its application. The Congress has used Recommendation 43 to encourage the Committee of Ministers to endorse its own views, vis-à-vis member states, on the positive contribution of territorial autonomy to assist in solving the national minority question.[9] Moreover, the Congress has established a conceptual link between territorial autonomy, which it considers as one of the concrete forms in which the principle of subsidiarity takes shape, and local or regional self-government, which is the Congress's main area of concern.

With regard to territorial autonomy, in Resolution 52 (1997) the Congress declares that, under certain circumstances, for example when there are high concentrations (within a municipality, province or region) of persons belonging to a cultural or linguistic minority, territorial autonomy is a very effective means of helping to solve the problem of minorities while avoiding separatist tendencies.[10]

In addition, the Congress refers to the principle of cultural autonomy,[11] which it construes in relation to territorial autonomy. The Congress:

- believes that, under certain circumstances, cultural autonomy – which is an essential part of any territorial autonomy enjoyed by minorities – may complement self-government;
- believes that, in the light of the specific situation in certain regions which are directly affected by the problem of minorities, some territorial authorities may be granted more wide-ranging powers, particularly in the cultural and linguistic field and in education.[12]

The Congress instructs its Working Group on federalism, regionalism, local autonomy and minorities to prepare a draft recommendation for submission to the CoM for adoption, addressing some clear-cut questions concerning the definition of the role of local self-government in relation to minority protection. The working group is instructed to indicate, among other things,

a. under which circumstances an appropriate form of self-government should be granted to minorities ...;

b. the powers which the autonomous authorities for minorities should in principle be granted and the right of such authorities to co-operate and form consortia ...;

c. the competencies which should be given to the regional authorities on the subject of minorities, including the possibility of nominating the mediators at local and regional level to defend the rights of minorities, in co-operation, if necessary with the representative organisations of minorities.[13]

The resulting Congress Recommendation 43 (1998) does not provide clear-cut responses to the questions put forward, but rather contains general advice and principles. The Congress encourages the CoM to adopt two separate sets of recommendations to states. The first set of recommendations is to be addressed to those states "whose administrative subdivisions of state are already established" and where the minorities within them "constitute a substantial proportion of the population, justifying specific protective measures",[14] introducing, thereby, broad escape clauses.

The first set of recommendations insists, in a principle already established in Article 17 of the Framework Convention,[15] that states should abstain from engaging in gerrymandering regarding their administrative or territorial subdivisions to the detriment of minorities. This principle had already found a basis in Article 5 of the European Charter of Local Self-Government,[16] according to which "changes in local authority boundaries shall not be made without prior consultation of the local communities concerned, possibly by means of a referendum where this is permitted by statute". As opposed to gerrymandering, the Congress encourages the development of partnerships between communities bringing separated groups together, in order to facilitate their benefiting from protective measures.

The Congress advocates a legally endorsed devolution of power to communities in matters which are of the greatest significance for the preservation of the minorities' identity, such as language, education and culture, and the promotion of co-operation and partnerships aiming at the promotion of the minorities' identity in those fields. It also advocates the preservation of existing favourable legal arrangements which come in support of that differential identity, and the restoration of competencies to the local authorities with regard to the regulation of the use of the minority languages in public administration.

The approach of the Congress in this area underscores the content of the stipulations with regard to administrative authorities and public services already included in Article 10 of the European Charter for Regional or Minority Languages. The Congress touches upon the issue of the endowment of local authorities with sufficient financial means so that they are able to carry out their specific responsibilities in relation to minorities.[17] It also touches upon the issue of adequate minority representation in territorial elected bodies, including in the relations of the latter with the central organs of the state.

The Congress encourages the CoM to make a second, additional set of recommendations to those "member states planning to change their systems of administrative subdivisions", and mainly those states in central and eastern Europe undergoing administrative and territorial reforms. In this second set of recommendations, the Congress insists on the need to avoid gerrymandering with regard to minorities, requesting the establishment of administrative subdivisions which prevent the dispersal of the minority members so that they can be afforded effective protection, "unless other economic, social or geographical considerations duly motivated make this impossible".[18] Thus, although the exceptions envisaged are broad, they must be restrictively considered. The Congress asks for the consultation of the populations concerned in the marking of the territorial boundaries.

Finally, the Congress asks for the granting of sufficient powers to the administrative units being created, including in the field of territorial development, so that they can make full use of the potential provided by their history, tradition and multiculturalism. In Resolution 65 (1998) adopted on the same day that Recommendation 43 (1998) was adopted, the Congress asks its Working Group on "federalism, regionalism, local autonomy and minorities", among other things, to monitor the implementation of the recommendation.

Similarly moving on a conceptual but enlightening level the Congress refers in Recommendation 70 (1999) to the provision by states of "special status" or legislation applying to specific sections of their territories, as an appropriate response to the existence of specific cultural, historical or geographical situations. Such provision is considered a means of ensuring "on the one hand that cultural diversity within a state is not considered a threat to the state and, on the other hand, that the state is not perceived as a threat by every minority living on its territory".[19] Importantly, and in connection with the reference to "every minority" in particular, the Congress insists that this is not in contradiction with the principle of equality "provided it is designed to take due account of a particular situation and differences which need to be respected".[20] The Congress further qualifies special status as a form of special territorial "autonomy" compatible with and instrumental for the unity and territorial integrity of the state.[21]

Further, the Congress seems to indirectly refer to areas fit for the development of "cultural" autonomy, by mentioning certain fields (educational, cultural and linguistic; protection of the natural environment or historic heritage; regional planning; social and community activities; organisation of local life and democracy) as particularly suited for differential legislative systems "provided they remain consistent with a number of general principles".[22] Finally, the Congress calls upon the CoM and the governments of the member states to have recourse to the Congress (possibly in co-operation with the Venice Commission) for assistance on the "introduction or preservation of local law or forms of special status, with the aim of seeking solutions to current conflicts in Europe".[23]

Finally, although this has not been an area particularly exploited by the Congress, this organ has adopted some decisions addressing specific minority situations. This was the case with Recommendation 44 (1998) on the crisis in Kosovo, adopted at the time of the conflict in that region, when the international community was initiating measures of various kinds to respond to the conflict. The Congress proposed to contribute mainly through the establishment of Local Democracy Embassies (see below) in Kosovo and through its intention to examine, as appropriate, the situation of local and regional democracy throughout the former Republic of Yugoslavia (FRY).[24]

In addition, in Resolution 44 (1997) "Towards a tolerant Europe: the contribution of Roma", the Congress acknowledges the responsibility of local authorities in the precarious situation of Roma communities by referring to the "too passive, or even in some cases accommodating, attitude on the part of local authorities or the police". It resolves to examine, in conjunction with other Council of Europe bodies concerned, the possibilities of implementing the Conclusions of the Round Table held in Ploiesti on 28-29 November 1996, which are appended to the recommendation.

These conclusions, which contain recommendations for action and networking, actually call on the Congress to continue to address the situation and problems of the Roma, acknowledging their ethnic/national identity, and to initiate, in co-operation with other Council of Europe bodies, activities dedicated to the exchange of information and experiences among i. legal specialists and experts representing Roma in human rights related cases; ii. media representatives who take interest in continuous coverage of the legal situation of Roma.

The Congress is also called upon to approach other Council of Europe institutions to explore the possibilities of making a continuous contribution to monitoring the legal and human rights situation of the Roma by: i. establishing a mechanism which would allow continuous examination of reported cases of human rights violations of which Roma have been victims; ii. supporting media projects with the task of promoting public awareness of the legal and human rights situation of the Roma.

More recently, finding a role in the "war on terror" in Resolution 159 (2003), on tackling terrorism – the role and responsibilities of local authorities – the Congress touches upon minority aspects, by pointing to the absence of cultural dialogue and solidarity between different communities and creeds as a source of violence and conflict.[25] The Congress asks local authorities in Europe to devise strong and clear policies among other things to: i. foster social cohesion and eradicate social exclusion; ii. promote tolerance through educational and cultural programmes; iii. ensure respect for cultural diversity and the peaceful coexistence of different cultures, minorities and communities; iv. prevent residential or educational segregation; v. seek to address in an equitable manner social, political and economic problems in their populations and ensure fair and equal access to public utilities and educational and employment opportunities; and vi. encourage and promote regular dialogue among different religious faiths, between their leaders, institutions and communities, ensuring that equal conditions exist for the practice of each faith.[26]

In spite of this growing awareness of the Congress of minority protection aspects however, minority considerations have not yet fully become part of the mainstream of the work of the Congress. For example, Recommendation 119 (2002) on the state of regional print media in Europe – pluralism, independence and freedom in regional press, does not address aspects of minority language expression or identity, in spite of addressing aspects of bilingualism or negative stereotyping across state frontiers.[27] Other fields of the Congress's work where minority protection aspects have been taken into consideration are discussed below.

The monitoring of local and regional democracy

An important element of the most recent statutory reform of the Congress has been that it has explicitly received from the CoM a statutory mandate to "prepare on a regular basis country-by-country reports on the situation of local and regional democracy in all member states and in states which have applied to join the Council of Europe" and "to ensure, in particular, that the principles of the European Charter of Local Self-Government are implemented".[28]

Although those monitoring functions had been taken up by the Congress already before the statutory resolution was adopted, the statutory mandate has endorsed and strengthened the position of the Congress in this connection, and in particular its capacity to formulate recommendations to the CoM and/or to the member states. This has also contributed to increasing the weight of the Congress within the Council of Europe institutional structures and as a fully-fledged monitoring body of the Council of Europe.

Monitoring and the European Charter of Local Self-Government

As the Congress has often emphasised,[29] the European Charter of Local Self-Government,[30] which opened for signature in 1985 and entered into force in 1988, constituted the first express endorsement at the treaty level of basic principles of local democracy, such as that of subsidiarity, which the charter established in a genuine fashion.[31] In Resolution 71 (1998) on monitoring of the application of the European Charter of Local Self-Government, the Congress considers:

a. that local self-government is one of the cornerstones of pluralist democracy as understood by the Council of Europe, since, in accordance with the principle of subsidiarity, it is at local level that a citizen's right to participate in the conduct of public affairs can be most directly exercised;

b. that consequently,

i. local elected representatives must have the right and capability to manage a substantial proportion of public affairs on their own responsibility and in the best interests of the populations they represent.[32]

These and other principles enshrined in the European Charter of Local Self-Government constitute an important tool for minority protection. The Congress was not only the initiator of this international instrument, as already indicated, but has also been a promoter of its implementation.[33] The monitoring activities of the Congress actually started in connection with this convention. The question of the implementation of the charter has been at the very heart of the activities of the Congress since the Barcelona Conference on the European Charter on Local Self-Government of January 1992.[34] Several subsequent decisions of the Congress testify to this.[35]

In Recommendation 2 (1994) on monitoring the implementation of the European Charter of Local Self-Government, the Congress notes the difficulties in implementing the charter. It indicates, among other things, that in certain countries the charter has not been incorporated into domestic law, and "consequently recourse to domestic courts in cases of non-conformity of national legislation with the Charter is not always possible".[36] In Resolution 3 (1994) adopted on the same day, the Congress refers to the fact that:

> with the agreement of the Committee of Ministers it has introduced a system of monitoring the Charter in the states which have ratified it, a system which consists in the selection each year of certain articles of the Charter and, by various means, including recourse to independent experts, obtaining information on their application, the evaluation of which would enable the Congress to make proposals to governments.[37]

In addition, in the same resolution, the Congress "recalls that local authorities have the possibility, through the intermediary of their associations or national delegations to the Congress, to refer to the Congress problems relating to the implementation of the Charter in their country".[38]

These two different approaches to the monitoring of the charter, which started as a result of the Congress's initiative, have come to be known as "ex-officio monitoring" and "monitoring on request". The first approach consists of a review of the manner in which the articles of the charter are applied in all contracting states, based on the findings of a committee of independent experts, and resulting in the preparation of general reports on the implementation of various articles of the charter, which include comments and proposals to governments. The second approach consists of an examination of the situation of local democracy in a specific state, at the request of local or regional authorities in that state, acting through their representative associations or their delegations to the Congress, and this also results in a corresponding report.

The Congress has further refined the second procedure in particular. In Resolution 34 (1996) "on monitoring the implementation of the European Charter of Local Self-Government", the Congress:

- confirms the value of special country-by-country reports;
- proposes that, when such requests are likely to justify a rapid response, if necessary on the spot, the Bureau [of the Congress] contact the national authorities of the country concerned through the most appropriate channels;
- acknowledges furthermore that the reports ... can also be prepared at the request of the Bureau after consulting the Working Group or following the request of the Working Group to the Bureau, based on the conclusions of its committee of independent experts.[39]

Thus, the Congress started to take steps to adapt its procedure for "monitoring on request", in order to broaden its own capacity of initiative. Such power of initiative will further crystallise under the so-called "monitoring of local and regional democracy" procedure, which is broader in scope and has been introduced and progressively developed by the Congress, within the limits established by CoM Resolution (2000) 1 quoted above.

As a result of the Congress's monitoring of the charter, it gained increasing awareness of the problems in the implementation of this instrument. In Recommendation 39 (1998) on the incorporation of the European Charter of Local Self-Government into the legal systems of ratifying countries and on the legal protection of local self-government, the Congress reflects on the tendency of states to approach the charter as a set of recommendations rather than as an international treaty, and indicates that the provisions "which are not directly applicable because they simply require the states to achieve certain aims must be interpreted in the light of the monitoring of the implementation of the Charter carried out" by the Congress itself, "and be implemented under domestic legislation by means of positive measures taken a reasonable time after ratification".[40]

The Congress notes, among other things, that, in some states which have ratified the charter, its provisions have not been incorporated into domestic law. Thus, situations arise where it is not possible for local authorities to apply to the domestic courts in cases where national legislation or regulations are in breach of the charter. It recommends that the CoM instruct the Steering Committee on Local and Regional Authorities (CDLR) to study these questions.[41]

In Resolution 71 (1998), adopted around three months later, the Congress re-emphasises that the European Charter of Local Self-Government is the "only international treaty dealing with the defence and development of local self-government and the principle of subsidiarity in Europe"[42] and "that with the agreement of the Committee of Ministers and on the basis of the explanatory report" of the charter,[43] the Congress "is responsible for the political monitoring of its application in the member States, through an ad hoc working group assisted by a committee of independent experts from the signatory states".[44] The Congress describes the character of the procedure, while reminding those concerned that locally elected representatives are also responsible for monitoring the implementation of the charter.[45]

The main basis of the Congress's monitoring activities concerning the charter, particularly ex-officio monitoring, has been the presentation of general reports on the implementation of various articles of the charter, which include comments and proposals to governments.[46] In these reports the Congress has drawn general conclusions, highlighting principles of the charter which call for especial attention. The Congress has outlined the specific problems that are affecting its implementation more negatively in a majority of states.

This has resulted in the bringing to the attention of states particular problems in the domains of local authorities' powers and responsibilities; their financial resources; the conditions under which responsibilities at local level are exercised; the legal protection of local authorities, their right to recourse to a judicial remedy in order to secure free exercise of their powers and respect of the principles of local self-government; the rules and practice concerning dialogue within local councils, and respect of the right of the opposition to exercise fully its political role.[47] Further to the reform adopted by the CoM on the basis of Statutory Resolution (2000) 1, the Institutional Committee of the Chamber of Local Authorities was entrusted with the responsibility of monitoring the implementation of the charter.

Country-by-country monitoring

After the monitoring of the European Charter of Local Self-Government had begun, the Congress started to prepare reports on local and regional democracy generally, in member states and candidate states for membership of the Council of Europe. This was done on the basis of Article 2, paragraph 1.c of the CoM's Statutory Resolution 94 (3),[48] and taking into account a favourable opinion expressed by the CoM and forwarded to the Congress by a letter dated 26 January 1996.

In Resolution 31 (1996) "on guiding principles for the action of the Congress when preparing reports on local and regional democracy in member states and applicant states", the Congress streamlines its power of initiative in relation to this new monitoring procedure:

the Bureau [of the Congress] shall on its own initiative or on the basis of:

- either a request from local or regional authorities in member states through their representative associations or the delegations to the Congress,

- or a request from the Working Group responsible for monitoring the implementation of the European Charter of Local Self-Government, in the light of the findings of the Committee of Independent Experts working under its aegis,

- or at the request of the Committee of Ministers and/or the Parliamentary Assembly in connection with their procedures relating to compliance with the commitments accepted by member states of the Council of Europe.[49]

The Congress continues by describing the steps it will follow in monitoring local and regional democracy:

i. establish the facts through an initial fact-finding mission performed by at least two members of the Congress, making it possible to begin a frank and constructive dialogue with both the national authorities and the territorial authorities of the member state concerned;

ii. in so far as the fact-finding mission shows that the facts justify more in-depth action, having obtained the opinion of the Working Group responsible for monitoring the implementation of the Charter, set up an ad hoc Working Group instructed to draw up a detailed report, where appropriate based on new contacts in the field, among other things with the relevant national authorities, and to submit it to a plenary session of the Congress or to the Standing Committee;

iii. before the report mentioned above is finally adopted, give the relevant national authorities an opportunity to make their views known.[50]

The Congress expressly adopts a fully non-discriminatory approach as it comes to the new monitoring, asking its Bureau "to ensure that over a reasonable period of time all member States be the subject of a detailed report on local and regional democracy, even where no express request is made by a party recognised ... above".[51] The monitoring activity of the Congress has actually developed along these non-discriminatory lines, and new member states have been approached on an equal footing to the so-called western democracies.

Nevertheless, the Congress has shown a preference for monitoring those states undergoing a process of reform of their territorial and administrative structures and/or having applied for membership to the European Union. The Congress has not hesitated to refer to the standards of local self-government applied in western Europe when evaluating precarious structures in states of central and eastern Europe. Although in the course of this monitoring activity the Congress has taken the European Charter of Local Self-Government as a main reference document, increasingly other international instruments, which are also highly relevant for minority protection, have been taken as a reference point, as discussed below.

In general terms, in 1997 the Congress pointed out some states where major problems of local democracy existed: Croatia, Bulgaria, Latvia, Moldova, Ukraine and the United Kingdom.[52] All these states have become the subject of the "monitoring of local and regional democracy" procedure described below, which has emerged as a development of the monitoring of the charter.

In this framework, various visits by members of the Congress and its Secretariat as well as external consultants have been undertaken, and country-by-country reports prepared, leading to the adoption by the Congress of subsequent corresponding recommendations and resolutions on the states monitored. An important element is that the monitoring has been considered as an open-ended process, and the Congress has often expressly referred to its intention to follow up the evolution of the reform process, while expressing its willingness to contribute to its successful completion.

By December 2002 the states involved in this monitoring procedure included Albania, Bulgaria, Croatia, Cyprus, the Czech Republic, Estonia, Finland, France, Germany, Greece, Hungary, Ireland, Italy, Latvia, Lithuania, Malta, Moldova, the Netherlands, Poland, Romania, the Russian Federation, Turkey, San Marino, Slovenia, Slovakia, Spain, "the former Yugoslav Republic of Macedonia", Ukraine and the United Kingdom. In addition, Azerbaijan, Armenia, Bosnia-Herzegovina and the Federal Republic of Yugoslavia were involved as candidate states for membership of the Council of Europe. For some of these, the Congress has already issued specific recommendations for state action.

Moldova

An interesting example of the monitoring exercised by the Congress has been that undertaken in relation to Moldova.[53] In Recommendation 38 (1998) on the situation of local and regional self-government in the Republic of Moldova, the Congress refers to its initiative of involvement in that state at the time of the reform of its overall system of local self-government. The Congress addresses a series of recommendations to the parliamentary and governmental authorities due to take office as a result of the forthcoming elections, including in the areas of regionalisation and transfrontier co-operation.

It refers to the positive contribution made by the definition of a new status for the autonomous region of Gagauzia to the settlement of the political conflict in that region. It further refers to the need for certain provisions of the statute of the region to be revised, "particularly those relating to the definition of the powers and responsibilities of the autonomous region".[54] Regarding the situation in Transnistria, the Congress joins other international bodies in regretting "the fact that the 1995 agreement between the Moldovan government and the Prime Minister of the Russian Federation providing for the gradual withdrawal of the Russian 14th Army from Transnistrian territory has not been ratified and implemented so as to enable a fair statute on the autonomy of the region to be drawn up".[55] The Congress states its willingness to provide assistance in the drafting of a statute on autonomy for the region, once a political settlement is reached. Finally, the Congress gives a detailed opinion on the most recent versions of the bills on the organisation of local and regional authorities and on local government submitted for consideration by the Moldovan parliament.[56]

Two years later, the Congress issued a new Recommendation 84 (2000) on regional democracy in Moldova, in connection with the process of regionalisation undertaken by that state. This recommendation refers once more to the situation in Gagauzia, indicating that "its special autonomy should be reflected not only in laws and regulations but also in practice", while putting forward a series of comments and suggestions aiming to facilitate this.[57]

The Congress makes explicit mention of the change in the status of the "former district of Taraklyia" which has now become a new region, interpreting this as "a clear sign of the Moldovan authorities' determination to respect the rights of national minorities and testifies to their efforts to develop pluralist democracy at regional level".[58] In Resolution 103 (2000) of the same title as the previous recommendation and adopted on the same date, the Congress decides to keep the situation in Moldova under consideration and expresses its willingness to participate, together with the Venice Commission, in the activities of the working group on Gagauzia set up by the Moldovan authorities.[59]

More recently, the Congress adopted a much harder tone with regard to the internal developments in the state. Recommendation 110 (2002) on local and regional democracy in Moldova, addresses the issue of the recent legislative reform in the field of territorial organisation and local public administration adopted by the Moldovan Parliament. The Congress notes that associations representing Moldovan local and regional authorities were not consulted on such reforms,[60] and deplores the announcement of a decision to anticipate local elections, aiming to end the terms of the local and regional representatives in office. It heavily criticises various aspects of the reform, leading to increased centralisation and hierarchy between central and local authorities, while resulting in a substantial diminution of the autonomy of the latter.

The Congress also refers to the decision to hold a referendum in Gagauzia with the aim of removing the governor of the region (Bashkan) from office, and the violent arrest of a member of the regional government.[61] Besides addressing a series of recommendations to remedy the situation created, the Congress invites the Moldovan authorities to be present at the next Congress mini-session on 14-15 November to provide explanations on the measures adopted or envisaged in order to implement its recommendations.[62] While this is a practice recently adopted also in connection with other member states of the Council of Europe as well (see below), the Congress takes – in Resolution 132 (2002) – a further step, which brings its modus operandi closer to that of the Parliamentary Assembly.

The Congress invites the rapporteurs in charge of examining the credentials of national delegations to the Congress to pay particular attention to the renewal of the credentials of the Moldovan delegation. This is done while underscoring the importance of ensuring that the delegation systematically comprises local and regional representatives elected at proper elections, and that associations representing the country's local and regional authorities are officially consulted by the competent government authorities as required by the Congress's Charter and Rules of Procedure.[63] Giving a mandate which will also become normal practice in recent monitoring recommendations, the Congress further instructs its Bureau and Institutional Committee to monitor the implementation of Recommendation 110 (2002).[64]

Bulgaria

In the case of Bulgaria, the Congress, in its Recommendation 45 (1998) on the situation of local and regional self-government in the Republic of Bulgaria, adopts a less demanding approach than in the case of the initial decisions on Moldova, requesting the revision of existing wrongful practices in relation to local self-government, pointing to some specific areas where action is needed in the short term. The Congress indicates that it is "awaiting the results of a major legislative reform setting up a second level of self-government with democratically constituted decision-making bodies".[65] However, it does not make concrete proposals as to what should be the content of such a reform.

Croatia

In Recommendation 46 (1998) on the state of local and regional democracy in Croatia, the Congress recalls its own assessment of Croatia as one of the countries "in which major problems of local democracy exist" and points to the fact that when signing and ratifying the European Charter of Local Self-Government "the Croatian Government made considerable use of the options in Article 12 of the Charter and consequently did not accept certain important provisions". The Congress makes specific references to those commitments of the charter that it considers important and which have not been undertaken by the state.

This recommendation does not attempt to make a contribution to a developing process of local government reform, but rather points to the lack of willingness of the state to undertake practical steps to this effect. The Congress:

> regrets that, despite renewed promises to amend Croatian legislation on local self-government with the assistance of Council of Europe experts in accordance with the commitments entered upon its accession, no progress has been made in this respect and reiterates its support and its readiness as and when required to implement the Croatian Government's proposal that a joint committee, composed of experts from the Croatian Parliament and from the Council of Europe, be set up, in consultation with representatives of the Croatian Government

authorities, and local and regional authorities, to make a detailed examination of the various parts of the law which need to be amended.[66]

The Congress also expresses its concern about the situation in Eastern Slavonia and other areas previously falling under the United Nations Transitional Authority in Eastern Slavonia, Baranja and Sirmium (UNTAES) administration, an area particularly affected by the war and where the Serb population lives. In these areas the local authorities are undergoing "major operating difficulties" which, in the opinion of the Congress, may have a negative repercussion on their credibility and on the principle of local self-government in general, particularly in relation to the local population.[67] Resolution 67 (1998) envisages, among other things, a follow-up visit to the country by Congress rapporteurs.[68]

Latvia

Another interesting example of the Congress's monitoring in connection with a process of reform of the territorial system has been that undertaken in relation to Latvia. In Recommendation 47 (1998) on local and regional democracy in Latvia,[69] the Congress criticises the restrictive approach of this state in its adoption of the European Charter of Local Self-Government. Latvia, like Croatia, by making use of the options offered under the charter, has chosen not to undertake several of the commitments contained within its text which the Congress considers as important. The need for Latvia to comply with some of the charter commitments it has undertaken is emphasised. The Congress recommends that the Latvian parliamentary and governmental authorities base the current reforms of local and regional authorities:

a. on prior consultation with the local and regional authorities and with their representative bodies in accordance with Article 4 paragraph 6 and with Article 5 of the European Charter of Local Self-Government;

b. on the need to strengthen local and regional authorities' political, administrative and financial autonomy and to apply the subsidiarity principle as it is expressed in Article 4 paragraph 3 of the European Charter of Local Self-Government.[70]

Without making express reference to the Russian minority living in the country, but addressing its situation, the Congress:

> Considering the large number of Latvian residents who have no political or civic rights, reaching nearly 50% of the population in some cities, such as the capital, and having regard to the Preamble of the European Charter of Local Self-Government:
>
> *a.* Believes that it is important to integrate these residents into the country's democratic system and that local democracy offers a significant opportunity to achieve this;

b. Recommends that the Latvian parliamentary and governmental authorities recognise these people's right to vote on issues within the competence of local authorities by acceding to the European Convention on the Participation of Foreigners in Public Life at Local Level.[71]

Ukraine

Moving to the situation in Ukraine in Recommendation 48 (1998), the Congress recalls among other things its previous recommendations to the Ukrainian governmental authorities and parliamentary delegates concerning the need to achieve "a better balance between the requirements of central and local government in the management of Kyiv and Sebastopol and, particularly, to give their elected heads and councils their own administration, subordinate and answerable to them in line with Article 3 of the European Charter of Local Self-Government".[72] The Congress deplores the climate of confrontation between the president and the parliament, which has developed particularly in connection with issues of local self-government.

It recommends among other things that the newly elected parliament adopts legislation on local and regional self-government, in accordance with the European Charter, including a new statute for Kyiv and Sebastopol that clarifies the respective roles of central and local government.[73] Resolution 68 (1998) of the same title as the previous recommendation, the Congress previews the follow-up of its recommendation, instructing the Congress's Bureau to "take whatever steps may be considered necessary to encourage the implementation of the above Recommendation, e.g. organisation of a Seminar (s) in Ukraine with the host authorities; organisation of further fact-finding missions; preparation of a progress report".[74]

The United Kingdom

Recommendation 49 on the situation of local and regional democracy in the United Kingdom was also adopted in 1998.[75] In this recommendation, the Congress welcomes the serious steps in the area of local democracy recently undertaken by the British government. It mentions in particular the establishment of the Scottish Parliament and the Welsh Assembly, as well as the regional assembly and councils for transfrontier co-operation between Northern Ireland and the Republic of Ireland. The creation of the latter bodies in particular is believed by the Congress to endorse its own opinion, "according to which stability and peace in Europe might be fostered by granting a certain degree of regional self-government in particular areas and creating bodies in charge of regional transfrontier co-operation".[76]

Without making an express reference to minorities, the Congress recommends to the British government, among other things, that it should
establish "a legal framework giving local government a clear basis and a
general competence for the benefit of its citizens and other inhabitants,
including the issue of community leadership".[77] It "expresses the hope
that the British government will agree, in the near future, to sign and
ratify other Council of Europe conventions in the field of local and
regional government",[78] referring in particular to the European Outline
Convention on Transfrontier Co-operation between Territorial
Communities or Authorities and its additional protocols; the Convention
on the Participation of Foreigners in Public Life at Local Level; and the
European Charter for Regional or Minority Languages.

The Congress offers to the authorities of the United Kingdom its assistance with more detailed discussion on local and regional government
reforms. It also makes a series of specific proposals with a view to developing those reforms, which are included in an appendix to the recommendation. Among those proposals, the Congress makes an assessment
of the exclusion of several local and regional authorities in the United
Kingdom from the scope of application of the European Charter of Local
Self-Government. It agrees with the exclusion of the local authorities in
Northern Ireland from this scope of application "in the present situation",
although expressing its hope that the charter "could be applied there at
a later stage".[79] The Congress is more hesitant in supporting the fact that
the Scottish Parliament and the Welsh Assembly would be excluded
from the scope of the charter. It hopes that "at a later stage, the European
Charter of Regional Self-Government, when adopted by the Committee
of Ministers, would apply to these regions, and hopefully to regions in
England itself".[80]

France

Particularly interesting, given its ground-breaking character, has been
the monitoring of France, since the performance of this state, traditionally reluctant to engage in any international legal commitment to minority protection, has received a thorough international review in various
fields highly relevant to this protection as a result. The monitoring of this
country led to the adoption of the voluminous Recommendation 78
(2000) on local and regional democracy in France. In this recommendation the Congress carries out an exhaustive analysis of the situation of
local and regional self-government. The Congress makes reference to the
progress made, while voicing its pending concerns in a detailed manner.

When dealing with the issue of regional democracy, the Congress makes:

> particular reference to the Corsican regional authority, encourages the
> government and parliamentary authorities to introduce a new status

that will enable Corsica to adapt public decisions taken at central government level to the specific conditions of the island. With this in mind, and taking into consideration the solutions adopted for other European islands, it would be appropriate to:

a. strengthen the recognition of the specific nature of the territorial community concerned;

b. transfer substantial blocs of powers, particularly in the fields of regional planning, identity, culture, language and education;

c. study the possibility of endowing the Corsican territorial assembly with more important rule-making powers in the fields mentioned in paragraph b, in line with its insular and cultural identity, and strengthen its powers with regard to finance, without this engendering debate on the basic prerogatives of the central authorities.[81]

The Congress regrets the fact that France has not ratified the European Charter of Local Self-Government, despite having signed this text immediately after its adoption in 1985, and that it has also not ratified the European Charter on the Participation of Foreigners in Public Life at Local Level. Furthermore, it regrets that France has not ratified either the European Charter for Regional or Minority Languages, following the decision issued by the *Conseil Constitutionnel* in this connection.[82]

In Resolution 94 (2000) of the same title as the previous recommendation and adopted on the same day, the Congress – without engaging in criticism of the decision of the *Conseil Constitutionnel* – encourages the French elected local representatives to submit practical proposals which should focus, among other things, on the ratification of both the European Charter of Local Self-Government and the Convention on the Participation of Foreigners in Public Life at Local Level.[83]

The Czech Republic

Another interesting example of Congress's monitoring undertaken in connection with the early stages of thorough reform of the territorial system has been that of the Czech Republic. In Recommendation 77 (2000), the Congress "considers it necessary to recommend that the parliamentary and governmental authorities of the Czech Republic", among other things, continue the dialogue with the Congress "during the reform process currently under way, through consultations and exchanges of views with its members and experts, in order to benefit from their expertise and the experience of other European countries in the sphere of local and regional democracy".[84] The Congress makes a series of recommendations aiming to facilitate the transition from the old to the new territorial system and to consolidate appropriate local and regional territorial structures. It recommends that the Czech Republic increases the level of its international commitments by limiting the scope of the reservations formulated when ratifying the European Charter of Local Self-Government and signing the additional protocols to the European Outline Convention on Transfrontier Co-operation between Territorial Communities or Authorities.[85]

Once again, the Congress previews its own follow-up of the reform process. In Resolution 93 (2000), it invites its own Bureau and Institutional Committee to "follow closely the progress of the reform under way in the Czech Republic, and in particular implementation by the Czech authorities of the proposals set out in the recommendation",[86] and to submit a final report to the Congress as soon as the reform process is complete. It also previews its assistance to the Czech authorities in this process, and invites the territorial authorities of the Czech Republic to set up associations to protect and promote their common interests once the territorial reform process has been completed.

Estonia

In the case of Estonia, the Congress has again seized the opportunity provided by the process of administrative reform in the country to make a series of recommendations to influence this process. Some of the provisions contained in Recommendation 81 (2000) on the situation of local democracy in Estonia are particularly relevant for minorities.[87] The issue of gerrymandering in relation to minorities, to which the Congress had recently devoted specific attention in the resolutions on minorities mentioned above, is taken up in relation to this particular state. The Congress insists that in the restructuring of administrative subdivisions in Estonia "local authorities, local government associations concerned must be consulted prior to the final decision-making in accordance with Article 4, paragraph 6 of the European Charter of Local Self-Government. The inhabitants concerned should also be involved in the process of the change in local authority boundaries, possibly by means of a local referendum or plebiscite".[88]

A specific section of the recommendation is devoted to transfrontier co-operation and the situation of the Russian minority. In this section the Congress advocates that Estonia sign and ratify the European Outline Convention on Transfrontier Co-operation between Territorial Communities or Authorities. It also advocates the development of the "necessary legal basis of transfrontier co-operation with Russia",[89] taking into consideration existing agreements, including in relation to mutual visits of the population of the border regions. In addition, the Congress prompts Estonia to revise the content of the provision of the Local Government Council Election Act requiring proficiency in the Estonian language from candidates in local elections, before the next elections take place. The Congress recommends that legislative and government authorities "examine the ways and possibilities to protect languages of local minorities including the right to use a mother language at local government council sessions as well where it is possible", quoting the case of those areas where the Russian speakers are in a majority as an example.[90]

"The former Yugoslav Republic of Macedonia"

In Recommendation 82 (2000) on the situation of local democracy in "the former Yugoslav Republic of Macedonia", the Congress expresses awareness of the complex multi-ethnic composition of the population of this state and the negative repercussions that the Kosovo conflict has had on it, in particular the refugee crisis resulting from the conflict.[91] It notes with satisfaction the significant improvement in relations between this state and the majority of its neighbouring countries. The Congress congratulates "the Macedonian government for its efforts to develop transfrontier co-operation with Albania, Bulgaria and Greece, with the participation of local authorities ... " and

- invites the Macedonian government to sign and ratify the European Outline Convention on Transfrontier Co-operation between Territorial Communities or Authorities and its protocols;

- recommends that the Macedonian authorities, in consultation with the authorities in its neighbouring countries, take all appropriate steps to facilitate border crossings and visa acquisition, particularly for the inhabitants of border regions, for example by issuing a border resident's card or multiple-entry visas.[92]

While noting the fact that this state has ratified without reservations the European Charter for Local Self-Government, the Congress identifies numerous shortcomings in its implementation. It regrets that local authorities have only minor competencies,[93] and recommends that the Macedonian authorities transfer powers to local authorities in a number of areas, including cultural activities; primary and pre-school education; and "in general, initiative and local development".[94] The Congress notes with interest:

> the existence of neighbourhood communities ... which, within the local authority, have a council of elected representatives and promote participatory democracy and citizen participation in the management of local affairs and recommends that the Macedonian authorities encourage their work, as well as the development of participatory democracy at sub-municipal level.[95]

Making an indirect reference to the situation of the Albanian minority, and the often tense inter-ethnic relations in the country, the Congress regrets "the numerous impasses in Macedonian society deriving in part from its extreme bi-polarisation".[96]

The Congress points to the importance of promoting co-operation between local authorities, while preserving interethnic dialogue in this context:

> Sharing the desire of the Macedonian authorities to maintain the unity and integrity of the country and not to encourage the process of disintegration, which would not be the case for intermunicipal co-operation projects, and recalling that it would be advisable to make it possible for new associations of local authorities to be set up – in the spirit of Article 10 of the European Charter of Local Self-Government – on bases other than ethnic, if necessary by amending the law.[97]

The Congress points to its follow-up of the case involving the imprisonment of the mayors of Tetovo and Gostivar,[98] while recalling the "difficulties encountered in the administration" of these municipalities "following the application of Section 75 of the Local Self-Government Act concerning the dissolution, under certain circumstances, of municipal councils".[99]

In a section of the recommendation devoted to civil society, the Congress welcomes the initiatives taken by the Ohrid Local Democracy Agency to promote and develop local democracy and intercommunity dialogue,[100] expressing its belief "that the Association of Local Self-Government Units should become a genuine speaking-partner of the government, submit working proposals and defend the interests of local authorities, irrespective of the political beliefs or ethnic origin of the local elected representatives".[101] In Resolution 100 (2000), the Congress decides to monitor closely the implementation of the recommendation, including through the preparation of a report within two years.[102] Thus, the Congress seems to have been the Council of Europe organ most sensitive to the difficult interethnic situation in the country, as proved by its active engagement in following up developments, including by establishing direct contacts with the parties to the tensions.

Lithuania

In Recommendation 87 (2001) on local and regional democracy in Lithuania, the Congress welcomes the ratification by Lithuania of the European Charter of Local Self-Government without any reservations, as well as the European Outline Convention on Transfrontier Co-operation between Territorial Communities or Authorities. The Congress expresses the hope that the state will also ratify the two additional protocols to the convention, and sign and ratify the European Charter for Regional or Minority Languages and the Convention on the Participation of Foreigners in Public Life at Local Level.[103]

These recommendations are made in the context of the programme of reform of the public administration of the state, including the creation of enlarged regions. In this regard, the Congress advocates an express mention of the principle of subsidiarity within a legal text alongside the principle of local self-government, already recognised in the constitution and derived legislation.[104] Regarding this derived legislation, the Congress identifies a series of shortcomings concerning the effectiveness of the principle of local self-government, including the need to specify the full and exclusive character of the responsibilities transferred to the local administration to avoid their being undermined by reasons other than those specified in the law.[105]

The issue of the provision of sufficient financial resources for the local authorities to carry out their responsibilities is elaborated upon,[106] and so is the question of the guarantee of independent decision-making, including in the financial sphere, and through judicial guarantees.[107] The Congress addresses the question of the need for the direct election of mayors by the population,[108] and concludes underlining the necessity for the process of regional reform not to be realised artificially, but to be based on concrete socio-economic and ethnocultural needs, and to be pursued gradually, by means of regular consultation of the population.[109]

The Slovak Republic

In dealing with the situation of local and regional democracy in the Slovak Republic in Recommendation 88 (2001), the Congress regrets the large number of reservations that this state has made when ratifying the European Charter of Local Self-Government, while welcoming the adoption by the state of the European Outline Convention on Transfrontier Co-operation between Territorial Communities or Authorities and its two additional protocols.[110] The Congress highlights the determination of the Slovak government to reform the territorial system of the state and welcomes the enabling amendments recently made to the constitution to pursue a policy of regionalisation and decentralisation.[111] It notes the difficulties experienced in reaching political consensus with regard to the names of the capital towns of the future regions and the number of such regions, and recommends that the decisions on the number of regions respect the large minorities living in the state.[112]

As in previous recommendations, the Congress elaborates on various aspects relevant to the preservation of the independence of the territorial authorities, including in the financial sphere, emphasising the need to provide for appropriate financial equalisation mechanisms.[113] A specific need highlighted is that to "systematically consult local authorities and future regions and their representative associations when drawing up and discussing draft legislation concerning them".[114] The need to implement the interstate agreements concluded with neighbouring countries, thereby applying the European outline convention and its additional protocols is also highlighted. In Resolution 109 (2001), the Congress instructs its Chamber of Regions to monitor the progress in territorial reform by the Slovak Republic.[115]

Slovenia

In Recommendation 89 (2001) on local and regional democracy in Slovenia, besides addressing concerns repeatedly expressed regarding other states, including those related to the financial independence of local authorities and the need for mayors and regional councillors to be directly elected by the population, the Congress also addresses several interesting nuances of aspects of minority protection which fall under its competencies. Some relate in particular to the question of gerrymandering.

The Congress is in favour of a stricter enforcement of the Slovenian Local Self-Government Act, which sets a desirable minimum of 5000 inhabitants for the creation of a municipality, in order to prevent fragmentation coupled with inadequate funding.[116] The Congress refers to the case of a specific city, Koper, and the plans to divide it against the will of the people expressed in referenda,[117] inviting the Slovenian authorities to respect the right of the local authorities to freely associate, in accordance with Article 10 of the European Charter of Local Self-Government.[118]

Furthermore, the Congress takes a comprehensive approach to subsidiarity, by indicating the need for the powers of municipalities to be transferred to the regions only to the extent that the size of the former prevents them from carrying out responsibilities themselves, while pointing to the need for numerous central government powers to be transferred to the regions, accompanied by an adequate transfer of funding.[119]

Finally, another innovative aspect is that the Congress invites the CoM to take the Congress's recommendations into account when assessing the compliance of Slovenia with its undertakings. The achievements of the state in the field of transfrontier co-operation and the ratification of the Framework Convention and the European Charter for Regional or Minority Languages are highlighted by the Congress, which invites the government "to keep up its good work in order to protect the rights of the other minorities associated with much more recent immigration".[120]

Cyprus and Malta

In Recommendation 96 (2001) on local democracy in Cyprus, the Congress deals with the situation of local democracy in the territory under the control of the internationally recognised government of

Cyprus.[121] It is probably the de facto division of the island that prompts the Congress to take the decision to reduce the title and scope of this recommendation to the local level, in contrast with previous recommendations. This decision could have also been prompted by considerations regarding the small size of the state, notwithstanding the similar approach towards Ireland (described below).

In the subsequent Recommendation on Malta, also confined to "local democracy", the Congress expressly refers to the fact that Malta is a unitary state and no federal or regional government structures exist, while pointing out that Malta is "one of the smallest and most densely populated states of Europe" and its system of local self-government had then been in existence for less than ten years.[122] Therefore the Congress shows increasing adaptability to domestic administrative traditions and levels of territorial self-government.[123]

More striking in the Cypriot case is the fact that the Congress refers only to the European Charter of Local Self-Government, ratified by Cyprus in 1988, from among all the international instruments relevant to minority protection to which the Congress normally makes reference when addressing the situation in a particular state. The absence of a reference to the European Outline Convention on Transfrontier Co-operation between Territorial Communities or Authorities or its protocols, or to the implementation of the principles contained in them, deserves to be especially highlighted, against the background of the actual situation of division of the island. The Congress pays tribute to the Cypriot authorities for having substantially improved the legislative basis for local self-government recently, by amending the law on municipalities and adopting a new law on communities (that is, on local entities that have a rural character and do not enjoy municipal status).[124]

The Congress notes, however, the existence of provisions which may rise concern about their compatibility with the European Charter of Local Self-Government. With regard to municipalities, the Congress indicates, among other things, that the authorities should consider further devolution of responsibilities in areas such as school administration. With regard to communities, the Congress expresses concern about a number of controls to which they are subjected, including: the fact that most communities have no administration of their own; the procedure to be followed in the filling of vacant posts; or the need of the District Officer's approval for the naming or renaming of streets.[125]

The Congress advocates that the existing capital grants system to finance major development and infrastructure projects be replaced by a system of general grants, distributed between communities according to equalisation criteria, and that the state develop mandatory schemes of co-operation between local authorities, in order to develop the capacity of local authorities to fulfil their expanding responsibilities. Finally, the Congress also advocates the merging of the existing two laws into a common legal framework of local self-government, in which each category may also be the object of specific regulation.[126]

Ireland

The Congress has addressed another insular situation of division, with the adoption of Recommendation 97 (2001) on local democracy in Ireland. As in the preceding recommendation regarding Cyprus, the Congress restricts the title of the recommendation to the local level. Since the Congress actually addresses the situation of regional authorities in Ireland, the omission of the latter aspect from the title of the recommendation is somehow more striking than in the Cypriot case.

In contrast with the recommendation on Cyprus, the Congress not only takes the European Charter of Local Self-Government as a reference point as regards international standards, but refers to the need for this state to ratify also the two additional protocols to the European Outline Convention on Transfrontier Co-operation between Territorial Communities or Authorities, and the Convention on the Participation of Foreigners in Public Life at Local Level.[127] The Congress refers to the commitment within the government to ratify the charter, and welcomes the recent amendment of the constitution to include a provision on local government.[128] It calls on the Irish Parliament to explicitly accept the principle of subsidiarity when discussing the Local Government Bill 2000.[129]

The Congress points to the minor involvement of local authorities in education, health and public transport, as well as to their lack of competencies concerning policing matters. It also deals with aspects of local finance, the system of election of local councils, the lack of an executive role for the Cathaoirleach (mayor/chairperson) and other issues. With regard to regional authorities, the Congress considers that although the existing regions, unlike in other countries, "do not seem to have any historical basis or public sentiment in the Irish context", their potential could be used in finding solutions to problems arising at the central and local levels of government.[130] The Congress regrets that the legislative foundation and functions of regional authorities remain rather weak as compared with regions in other European countries.[131]

Greece

Recommendation 109 (2002), on local and regional democracy in Greece, is adopted against the background of the request from the Greek Union of Prefectures (ENAE) that the Institutional Committee of the Chamber of Regions prepare a report on the situation of local democracy in Greece. This followed a series of measures taken by the Greek government which, according to the ENAE, remove fundamental powers and responsibilities from the prefectures (regional level authorities) to transfer them to the central authorities of the state.[132]

The Congress, besides recommending that administrative reorganisation be conducted in conformity with the principles enshrined in the European Charter of Local Self-Government, advises that local authorities and their associations be consulted before any final decision in reform is taken.[133] Further, it calls for the establishment of a regional "intermediate" level of government, elected by direct universal suffrage.[134]

The Congress recommends that the CoM instruct the CDLR to provide "any legislative and technical assistance the Greek authorities may request". It also recommends that the Greek territorial authorities, their associations and the Greek delegation to the Congress monitor the reform process and regularly inform the Congress of progress. In Resolution 131 (2002) a formal request is made for the Greek government to present the new legislative reforms to the Congress, possibly "prior to the preparation of the second report on the situation of local and regional democracy in Greece".[135]

Hungary, Poland and Spain

Finally, in the recommendations on local and regional democracy in Hungary 116 (2002); Poland 120 (2002) and Spain 121 (2002), the Congress addresses various outstanding points of the current administrative organisation in those states. Only with regard to Poland does the Congress call upon the national authorities (concretely the Polish minister responsible for local and regional self-government) to present the measures taken, or envisaged, to implement the respective recommendation to the Congress's next plenary session.[136] With regard to Spain and Hungary, the Congress just instructs its subsidiary bodies (its institutional committee, in the Spanish case, and also its bureau, in the Hungarian case) to monitor developments.[137]

In the case of Hungary, emphasis is placed on the need to revise the current complex territorial structures and to clarify the distribution of responsibilities among them, in particular to create a single regional level, if necessary by carrying out regroupings, which would allow for a higher level of efficiency and rationality of management while taking into account among other considerations "the traditions and developments relating to regional identities".[138]

With regard to Poland, and even if the Polish model of territorial reform is still praised by the Congress (see above), this organ notes that over the last two years the decentralisation process in which the state engaged has slowed down, pointing at the excessive politicisation of local and regional authorities' administrations and the existence of corruption, as well as to the need for the direct election of mayors as a means to improve citizens' interest in public life. The Congress includes among its demands a clearer distribution of competencies between the various levels of territorial authorities, their financial independence (including through direct taxation) and the development of transfrontier co-operation.[139]

When it comes to Spain, the Congress again praises the territorial reform undertaken over the last twenty years, and the transformation of this state in one of the most decentralised countries in Europe through the *Comunidades Autónomas* (autonomous communities) system of regional government. In the identification of persisting problems, the Congress mainly focuses on the strengthening of the local level of self-government, and the need to devolve to local authorities a number of administrative powers and responsibilities concentrated at the level of the *Comunidades Autónomas*, accompanied by a corresponding adequate allocation of resources. The Congress highlights in particular the problem of the current practice of reliance on delegation of competencies rather than allocation of exclusive powers to the local authorities, and the transferring of responsibilities to them without introducing changes to their existing budgetary base.[140]

The Congress addresses the issue of the need for the local authorities to respond to emerging responsibilities not assigned to them by law, such as the reception and care for asylum seekers and immigrants, without a corresponding budget allocation. Finally, the Congress raises the question of the lack of appropriate links and actual frameworks for consultation between the various levels of government, referring to the absence of negotiations by particular *Comunidades Autónomas* with local authorities, and calling upon the national authorities to hold discussions with the regions on a far-reaching reform of the Senate to enable fairer representation of the interests of the *Comunidades Autónomas* at national level.[141]

Conclusions on monitoring

To conclude, the Congress has shown a high degree of timeliness and flexibility in approaching its monitoring activity. This activity has been characterised, in addition, by an unprecedented level of non-discrimination between Council of Europe member states, unknown in the monitoring practice of other Council of Europe organs. These characteristics have been intertwined to facilitate the provision of monitoring in response to current problems, in adequate political contexts allowing for targeted territorial authority reform.

They also enable monitoring to be carried out in connection with varying levels of state performance, in response to the particular needs of each state, aiming at the improvement of its specific situation in a progressive course of achievement of appropriate levels of territorial self-government. In this context, the Congress has not opted for recommending instant, optimal, yet possibly impracticable solutions, but has often opted instead for adapting to the domestic and historic context in each state, in response to its particular problem base.

In the absence of an enforcement procedure, the Congress's recommendations can generally be implemented only if the political will for change can be developed at national level. This can be facilitated by some pressure from Council of Europe bodies, in the appropriate cases. The Congress's monitoring performance has been very positive and ground-breaking overall, including from a procedural perspective. The Congress, as already mentioned, has not surrendered to complacency with state performance only to then be forced to re-start monitoring as a result of poor results (as has been the case with the Assembly), but instead has kept up monitoring exercises until acceptable levels of implementation are achieved. Continued monitoring has been matched by increasing demands for state responsiveness, including through procedural modelling, so that states have been subjected to ever increasing levels of compulsion to improve their performance.

Demands for state authorities, at an increasingly high level of public profile and political weight, to provide explanations of improvement of performance serve as an illustration. Governmental authorities of the countries concerned are regularly invited to present to the Congress the measures envisaged or adopted to fulfil its recommendations. Finally, while the development and growth of the monitoring activity of the Congress has been facilitated by the assertion of its standing as a fully-fledged Council of Europe organ, playing an important role in the Council of Europe's political activity, Congress approaches to monitoring have reciprocally contributed to the affirmation and consolidation of its position within the Organisation.

Transfrontier and inter-territorial co-operation

As described above, in monitoring the situation of local and regional democracy, the Congress has increasingly introduced references not only to state compliance with the provisions of the European Charter of Local Self-Government, but also to specific aspects of local and regional self-government, and in particular to the question of transfrontier co-operation.[142] The issue of transfrontier co-operation has received increasing attention since the adoption of the European Outline Convention on

Transfrontier Co-operation between Territorial Communities or Authorities in the framework of the Council of Europe.[143] A new impulse was given to this issue during the first Council of Europe summit, precisely in connection with the question of minority protection, when the CoM was asked to respond to requests for assistance for the negotiation and implementation of agreements on transfrontier co-operation.[144]

Two years later, in 1995, the first additional protocol to the European Outline Convention on Transfrontier Co-operation between Territorial Communities or Authorities was adopted,[145] in order to overcome the shortcomings of the convention, which had made its effective application difficult in practice. These shortcomings referred mainly to the legal status of the transfrontier co-operation bodies and of those acts resulting from the implementation of the convention.[146] At present, a select committee of experts has been established by the CoM to facilitate co-operation in this field, and, with a narrower focus, a committee of advisers for the Development of Transfrontier Co-operation in Central and Eastern Europe has also been established.

In 1998, another issue for which the Congress had shown a particular concern since the early 1990s, that of interterritorial co-operation (that is, the relations of territorial communities or authorities with other community authorities in distant states sharing common interests) was addressed through the adoption by Council of Europe states of Protocol No. 2 to the European Outline Convention on Transfrontier Co-operation between Territorial Communities or Authorities concerning interterritorial co-operation.[147] Initiatives of the Congress in this connection had included the preparation in 1993 of a preliminary draft convention on interterritorial co-operation between territorial communities or authorities.[148] Although the option favoured by the Congress, that of the adoption of a separate convention on this topic did not prevail, Protocol No. 2 is still a substantial step in view of the fact that some states have postulated a "softer law" approach, and to deal with this issue just by adopting a recommendation of the CoM rather than a treaty.[149]

A firm, normative framework for the development of interterritorial co-operation has thus been established, along the lines provided in the convention and additional protocols. It should be noted, nonetheless, that important elements of the Congress proposals on the subject of interterritorial co-operation have not been addressed in this second additional protocol. One is the issue of the involvement of local and regional authorities in decision-making processes of international organisations when the latter deal with matters which concern their field of competency. Similarly, the issue of the involvement of local and regional authorities (through consultation mechanisms or other forms of participation) in the preparation of international treaties concerning their field of competencies has not been addressed. In the explanatory report of Protocol No. 2, the unsubstantiated argument given for this exclusion has been that this so-called "external relations" aspect "has no real bearing on interterritorial co-operation".[150]

No reference is made, either in the European Outline Convention on Transfrontier Co-operation between Territorial Communities or Authorities or in its protocols to the establishment of any mechanism to monitor their implementation. The mandate given to the CoM by the Vienna Summit was confined "to respond to requests for assistance" in the implementation of agreements on transfrontier co-operation. Therein lies the importance of the references to this instrument included in the monitoring activities of the Congress in relation to local and regional democracy.

In this connection should be noted the adoption of Resolution 119 (2001) on international co-operation at regional level, in which the Congress, among other things, invites the regions to step up partnerships with the Council of Europe's new member states in central and eastern Europe, particularly in south-eastern Europe. It also invites them:

> to follow closely the activities and organs of the European institutions with a view to contributing to their democratic transparency and to the application of the principle of subsidiarity, and helping to ensure that they take into account the opinions and suggestions formulated by the elected representatives of the regions of Europe in the course of their work.[151]

The Congress also invites the Euro-regions to co-operate with others, especially in central and eastern Europe, with a view to the transfer of experience on transfrontier co-operation and technical know-how, especially in the economic, environmental and cultural fields.[152] It also invites the Association of European Border Regions to give priority to its work in central and eastern Europe, in order to contribute to democratic stability in the region and to foster good neighbourly cross-border relations, "paying particular attention to the problems of minorities".[153] In addition, the Congress instructs its Chamber of the Regions, among other things: "to prepare a study with a view to promoting regionalisation as a political tool for preventing and settling sociocultural and political conflicts at the national and European level".[154]

The Congress has looked into the matter of transfrontier co-operation with a minority-specific perspective already in previous decisions. In Recommendation 85 (2000) on democratic stability through transfrontier co-operation in Europe, the Congress stresses "the fundamental importance of transfrontier co-operation for the European construction process and for establishing a climate of confidence through tolerance, mutual understanding, solidarity and good-neighbourly relations between the inhabitants of different countries, particularly in border regions which are home to minorities".[155] It endorses the conclusions and recommendations contained in the final declaration resulting from the 7th European Conference of Border Regions,[156] and addresses a series of recommendations for action to the CoM, including in relation to the Stability Pact for South-Eastern Europe,[157] largely based on the conclusions of the conference.

The Congress recommends that state authorities, among other things, "sign and/or ratify the European Outline Convention on Transfrontier Co-operation between Territorial Communities or Authorities and its protocols, and the European Charter for Regional or Minority Languages".[158] It also recommends to state authorities:

- to set up new border crossing points in greater Europe, in view of the increase in socio-economic transfrontier activities ...;

- to pay special attention in their regional development plans to the problems of border regions and give them priority in the distribution of funds and investments concerning infrastructure and sociocultural and commercial amenities;

- to encourage devolution and provide local and regional authorities with effective powers that they can exercise at transfrontier level, in accordance with the principle of subsidiarity and the provisions contained in the additional protocols to the outline convention;

- to promote the teaching of the languages of neighbouring countries/ regions, using appropriate financial resources.[159]

The latter aspect, in particular, is developed in Resolution 104 (2000) of the same title as the previous recommendation. This time, the Congress urges local and regional authorities "to foster and encourage, in their areas of responsibility, the teaching of the languages and cultures of neighbouring countries and regions and the implementation of cultural activities designed to bring populations on either side of individual borders closer together".[160]

The Congress also urges these authorities "to continue setting up permanent transfrontier co-operation networks and implementing joint projects based on initiatives taken by senior officials at local and regional level".[161] It resolves to submit the text of the resolution and the previous recommendation "to the representatives of all border regions and municipalities in Europe and the bodies representing them".[162] It also resolves to ask its bureau to submit "a report on the implementation of the recommendations arising from the 7th European Conference of Border

Regions, in particular regarding the Stability Pact" and "in this respect, to ask its Bureau to support the colloquy on transfrontier co-operation between Bulgaria and Romania, foreseen for October 2000 in the town of Svishtov, Bulgaria".[163]

It should be noted, however, that the subsequent Recommendation 74 (2000) – on the Stability Pact for South-Eastern Europe: specific projects on local democracy and transfrontier co-operation – is mainly geared towards support for the development of local self-government generally in this region. No express reference is made to minority protection. Among the seven priority objectives of the action plan to strengthen local democracy and stability in south-eastern Europe highlighted by the Congress, relevant references are limited to the development of "democratic citizenship and intercultural dialogue at local level (with emphasis on the role of Local Democracy Agencies (LDAs))",[164] and to the fostering of transfrontier co-operation, with a general reference to the conclusions of the 7th European Conference of Border Regions.[165]

Similarly, Recommendation 117 (2002) – on Promoting transfrontier co-operation: an important factor of democratic stability in Europe – generally calls upon member states to pay particular attention to transfrontier co-operation in drawing up any projects for intercultural dialogue and conflict prevention, and to give political backing to negotiation of a multilateral regional agreement on transfrontier co-operation in south-eastern Europe. It also calls upon the CoM's Committee of Advisers for the Development of Transfrontier Co-operation in Central and Eastern Europe to contribute to the preparation and negotiation of such an agreement.[166]

More specifically, in Resolution 143 (2002) of the same title as the previous Recommendation, the Congress mandates its own bureau to give to the Congress's statutory committees the task of promoting transfrontier co-operation in their areas of competence, drawing on an informal network of members of the Congress from frontier regions and local authorities who could contribute their know-how and experience, co-ordinated by a general rapporteur.[167] In addition the Congress invites member states, among other things, to remove existing legal and administrative obstacles as well as to provide local and regional authorities with the financial and human resources allowing the implementation of transfrontier activities, providing these authorities with the necessary tools for transfrontier governance. The Congress reiterates previous requests for the states to sign and ratify the European Outline Convention and its two protocols, and calls for the making of voluntary contributions for the financing of Council of Europe programmes to promote transfrontier co-operation in south-eastern Europe.[168]

The participation of foreigners in public life at local level

Another important international instrument to which the Congress has increasingly referred when monitoring the situation of local and regional democracy, as indicated above, has been the Convention on the Participation of Foreigners in Public Life at Local Level, initially drawn up by the Congress and proposed to the CoM.[169] The convention, opened for signature in 1992, remains a landmark when it comes to the international legal protection of the civil and political rights of non-citizens, lawfully resident in the territory of the states party to it. Although the convention has already entered into force, only six states have so far ratified this treaty, and another three have signed it.[170]

Member states of the Council of Europe having a large proportion of long-term resident population that does not enjoy the citizenship of the state, and for which the convention represents a particularly useful tool to address their present situation until more adequate long-term solutions are found, have not acceded to the convention. A similar fate has affected the European Convention on the Legal Status of Migrant Workers, which deals with some aspects of the economic and social protection of those foreigners of a state party to the convention, who have been authorised "by another contracting party to reside in its territory to take up paid employment" and their closest family members.[171] This latter convention has also entered into force, but only eight member states have ratified it and another four have signed it.[172]

Although the text of the Convention on the Participation of Foreigners in Public Life at Local Level does not deal with economic and social aspects of the protection of non-citizens in the way the European Convention on the Legal Status of Migrant Workers does, an advantage of the former over the latter instrument is that it no longer considers the residence of foreigners as a short-term phenomenon, but rather as "a permanent feature of European societies".[173] The Convention on the Participation of Foreigners in Public Life at Local Level includes a section which states cannot withdraw from, and which refers to the protection of the right to freedom of expression and association of non-citizens, reiterating principles already enshrined under the ECHR. Articles 3 and 9.2, in particular, dealing with the right to freedom of expression and information, are just a mirror image of Article 10 of the ECHR.

In the explanatory report of the Convention on the Participation of Foreigners in Public Life at Local Level, the CoM Steering Committee on Local and Regional Authorities (CDLR) – responsible for the final draft of the convention – emphasises that the interpretation given to the relevant ECHR provisions is to prevail over that given to the convention, on the basis of the possibility of challenging the implementation of legislation which is in contradiction with the ECHR.[174] Another important provision of the Convention on the Participation of Foreigners in Public Life at Local Level from which states cannot withdraw is Article 4, under which each state party "shall endeavour to ensure that reasonable efforts are made to involve foreign residents in public inquiries, planning procedures and other processes of consultation on local matters".[175]

Obligations contained in other sections of the convention, and which states may decide not to undertake, deal with the establishment of consultative bodies to represent foreign residents at local level and the right of non-citizens to vote and stand as candidates in local authority elections, following a certain period of legal and habitual residence, for which the convention assumes a normal period of five years.[176] It should be noted that, although in accordance with Article 10 each state party "shall inform the Secretary General of the Council of Europe of any legislative provisions or other measure adopted by the competent authorities on its territory which relates to its undertakings under the terms of this convention", no specific mechanism seems to be presently functioning to monitor its implementation.

Nevertheless, initial steps seem to have been undertaken by the Congress to improve implementation. In Recommendation 115 (2002) – on the participation of foreign residents in local public life: consultative bodies – the Congress "invites the Committee of Ministers to ask the Secretary General to initiate an in-depth inquiry into the fulfilment of the principles" of the convention.[177] The Congress calls upon the CoM to ensure that specific Directorates General of the Secretariat are involved in this inquiry, and similarly invites the Parliamentary Assembly and various of its specialised committees to become associated with it.

In Resolution 141 (2002) of the same title as the aforementioned recommendation, the Congress focuses on the issue of consultative bodies more specifically, instructing its own Culture and Education Committee to: i. gather information on existing experience in various Council of Europe states; ii. promote the creation of a network for the exchange of experience among towns that have established this type of consultative body; iii. analyse the broad trends in their development; iv. draw up a compendium of guiding principles for their creation and smooth functioning so that it can be used by the towns where these bodies exist and "as a source of inspiration for others across Europe"; and v. convene a major conference in Stuttgart in 2003 to present the conclusions of this work.[178]

Although the Congress seems to have started laying the foundations on which to build implementation of the convention in the medium term at a general and conceptual level, it remains to be seen whether the

Congress will pursue its endeavours to consider the monitoring of the implementation of the Convention on the Protection of Foreigners in Public Life at Local Level as part and parcel of its monitoring of the situation of local and regional democracy in member states consistently. A steady practice in that connection has not developed yet.

A continuous and individualised follow-up of the implementation by states of the principles enshrined in the convention would prove that the concern of the Congress to ensure genuine democratic practices in the relations between central government on the one hand, and territorial authorities and communities on the other, also extends to ensuring democratic practices in the relations within the territorial authorities and communities themselves. This would imply a commitment by the Congress to ensure that genuine democratic principles and minority rights prevail not only in the relations among territorial structures but also in the organisation of territorial authorities and in the manner they conduct their own activities.

Cultural diversity

Although cultural diversity has frequently become an object of concern for the Congress, it has been mainly on the basis of a conference held in Innsbruck in December 2000, and a study prepared by an expert of the Congress on "Competencies and practices in European local and regional cultural policy"[179] that the Congress has articulated its approach to this theme.

More recently, the Congress adopted Resolution 112 (2001) on follow-up action to be taken on the conference "Cities and Regions: Cultural Diversity – a Precondition for a United Europe" (Innsbruck, 11-12 December 2000).[180] In this resolution, the Congress invites the cities and regions of Europe among other things to:

- contribute to understanding and recognition of, and interaction between, the diverse cultures which are Europe's great asset;

- develop interregional and transfrontier co-operation in the cultural sphere by continuing to promote initiatives such as the European cultural routes and Euro-Regions;

- take action to ensure that culture remains, or once again becomes, a driving force for the development of our local and regional communities;

- promote intercultural dialogue to help people learn to live together.[181]

Furthermore, the Congress invites the cities and regions of Europe to "take greater advantage of the new technologies to improve the supply of information to the public and find new ways for people to participate in community life",[182] and "adapt their cultural policies to the various audiences and social groups", in particular to:

- preserve regional and minority languages and cultures, as an essential frame of reference for identity purposes;

- promote immigrants' cultures and languages to enable them to keep their roots and share their culture while becoming integrated into our societies.[183]

The Congress invites cities and regions to provide support for non-governmental organisations active in the cultural, social and educational sectors, which, among other things, foster intercultural understanding and co-operation, and to assign greater importance to culture in projects submitted to EU funding under the structural funds.[184] In addition, it instructs its Committee on Culture and Education to undertake a series of activities, including the promotion of existing networks for cultural co-operation between cities and regions, and investigating the possibility of establishing a means of pooling the experiences of European cities and regions in the areas of: i. cultural responsibilities and ii. the management of cultural diversity.[185]

Recent treaty initiatives

Regional self-government

During the first session of the Congress, following its re-establishment in accordance with Statutory Resolution (94) 3, it adopted Resolution 8 (1994), in which it "invites the Chamber of Regions and the Chamber of Local Authorities: to draw up a European Charter of Regional Autonomy along the lines of the European Charter of Local Self-Government, in co-operation with the Parliamentary Assembly".[186] As a result of the activity of a working group established for that purpose, the text of a draft European Charter of regional self-government was first presented and adopted by the Chamber of Regions and then presented to the Chamber of Local Authorities.

Congress Resolution 37 (1996) followed, inviting the working group to consult all the European regions on the draft charter so as to present the Congress with a final text. Later, the working group adopted a revised version of the draft charter together with an explanatory report.[187] In Recommendation 34 (1997) "on the draft European Charter of regional self-government"[188] the Congress invites the Parliamentary Assembly to support the draft appended to the recommendation, and the CoM to examine it, with a view to its adoption as a convention. The Congress also seeks the support for this initiative at the forthcoming second Summit of Heads of State and Government of the Council of Europe.[189]

The text of the draft European Charter of regional self-government, appended to the recommendation, refers in its preamble to the awareness "that the region is an appropriate level of authority for effective implementation of subsidiarity" and affirms that "recognition of regional self-government entails loyalty towards the State to which the regions belong, with due regard to its sovereignty and territorial integrity".[190] It also states that the region, "as an essential component of the State, bears witness to Europe's diversity, contributes to the enrichment of its culture with due regard to its traditions and in keeping with its history, and furthers its economic prosperity with a view to sustainable development" and importantly affirms that "recognition of regional self-government should be accompanied by measures to implement solidarity between regions so as to foster balanced development".[191]

In Part I, Article 3 of the draft, a basic definition of regional self-government is included, which delineates the scope and aims of the text. According to this article:

> Regional self-government denotes the right and the ability of the largest territorial authorities within each State, having elected bodies, being administratively placed between central government and local authorities and enjoying prerogatives either of self-organisation or of a type normally associated with the central authority, to manage, on their own responsibility and in the interests of their populations, a substantial share of public affairs, in accordance with the principle of subsidiarity.

Thus the draft does not predetermine the type of authority that regional self-government implies, or the character of its relationship with the central authority of the state. Throughout its operative section, the draft charter does not enter into the regulation of the actual content of the competencies which should be given to regional authorities. It establishes only a series of principles which should prevail in the establishment of regional authorities and in their relations both with central and local authorities, in order to guarantee the effective exercise of their functions and independence, as well as to avoid their encroachment on the competencies of local authorities.

The draft specifies that the financial resources of the regions "shall consist mainly of own resources, which they may use freely" and addresses other questions concerning the financial independence of the regions. It points to the need for the introduction within each state "of a financial equalisation mechanism taking account of both the potential resources and the tasks of regions, with the aim of harmonising the living standards of inhabitants of different regions".[192]

550

As to the form that regional organisations should adopt, the draft refers only generally to "a representative assembly and an executive body".[193] An important breakthrough is that the draft envisages the participation of the regional authorities in decision-making processes which affect their interests both at the state level and at the level of European and international institutions.[194] It also envisages measures for the protection of regional boundaries and access by regions to judicial remedies, including in cases related to conflicts of competencies.[195]

The draft previews the establishment of a mechanism for monitoring the application of the charter, based on a state reporting system. This mechanism envisages the intervention of the Congress, which should make "observations" on state reports to the CoM, under a procedure to be determined by the CoM. The draft contemplates the possibility that states may specify the categories of regions to which they intend to confine the scope of the charter or which they intend to exclude from its scope,[196] although it includes a restriction within its text as to the articles which can be subjected to reservations.[197]

In Resolution 1118 (1997) and Recommendation 1349 (1997), the Parliamentary Assembly fully endorses the initiative of the Congress and the text of the draft.[198] However, according to the Congress's account, and to its regret, after a year of deliberation on the draft charter by the CDLR following the instructions of the CoM to this effect, "the CDLR did not make clear in its opinion its support for a conventional text preferring to leave open the question as to whether a future text should be a Council of Europe convention or a 'flexible' recommendation".[199] In response, the Congress recommended, among other things, that the CoM should

> examine as soon as possible the CDLR's Opinion on the draft European Charter of regional self-government and give the CDLR terms of reference in which priority is given to the preparation of a conventional text rather than a flexible Committee of Ministers recommendation, to be drawn up speedily, preferably by 1 July 2000, on the basis of the Congress Recommendation.[200]

In view of the not very welcoming reaction by governmental structures to the draft European Charter of regional self-government, the Congress has subsequently centred its attention on bringing to the attention of governments the advantages that can be derived from regionalisation. It has also seemed to re-focus its attention on the countries in transition, possibly pointing to a negative reaction by the Western democracies in particular. In Recommendation 83 (2000) on evaluation of regionalisation in central Europe, especially in Poland, the Congress refers to the regionalisation process in central Europe.[201] It recommends that the

CoM: "invite the CDLR to study the experiences made in member countries and especially those in central Europe with administrative and territorial reforms creating territorial communities or authorities at different levels".[202]

The Congress, however, also addresses a series of recommendations to governments of member states generally, and points first to the need that they "recognise the political, economic, social and cultural advantages of decentralised democratic structures for the development of the whole country" and "consider regionalisation as a measure to prevent conflicts and to encourage the expression of minorities' values and their integration into the structures of the civil society".[203]

In Resolution 102 (2000) of the same title as the previous recommendation, and adopted on the same date, the Congress invites its own bureau to charge its competent committee, among other things, "to continue systematically its assistance and the exchange of experience between territorial communities and national administrations of countries which have to solve during the administrative reforms problems resulting from the creation and the functioning of regional communities or authorities".[204]

Thus, it would seem that – in view of the rather negative reaction of intergovernmental co-operation structures to the proposal for adoption of a conventional text on regionalisation, regardless of the flexibility of the proposal made – the Congress has shown readiness to undertake the groundwork necessary to advance the concept of regionalisation among the member states of the Council of Europe, in an attempt to keep the adoption of an international treaty on this topic on the agenda of the political bodies.

Against this background, the CoM asked the CDLR to complete the groundwork for the elaboration of a legal instrument on regional self-government on the basis of the principles, areas and elements on which the CDLR has reached preliminary agreement and, in particular:

- to draw up model forms of regional self-government which may be included in a legal instrument as guidelines or a basis of more precise standards;

- to identify those principles which are common to all such models and which may constitute the core principles of a legal instrument designed to apply to all states wishing to establish or reform a democratic regional tier of government;

- to draft a text, which could be the core of a legal instrument, presenting principles and models and to report back to the Committee of Ministers.

On this basis, the CoM adopted the ad hoc terms of reference of a drafting committee responsible for implementing the above decisions,[205] even if the emphasis placed on "principles" and "models" illustrates the persistent political reluctance to adopt strictly binding provisions on regionalisation. In this connection, in Resolution 146 (2002) on the draft European Charter of regional self-government, the Congress follows up the CDLR's work up to December 2001. Commenting on the CDLR's proposals, the Congress emphasises in particular the need that a convention rather than a Recommendation be adopted on the subject,[206] asking for the Parliamentary Assembly's support and endorsement of this position.

In Resolution 161 (2003) – on the draft European Charter of regional self-government: progress of work for its adoption as an international convention – the Congress refers to the results of the final declaration of the thirteenth Conference of European Ministers responsible for Local and Regional Government, held in Helsinki on 27-28 June 2002,[207] which recommends that the CoM instruct the CDLR "to prepare draft legal instruments of different types, taking account of proposals and the developing experience of member states, and addressing the need for an appropriate relationship with the European Charter of Local Self-government".[208] It also refers to the corresponding mandate given subsequently to the CDLR, and its subsidiary Committee of Experts on the Framework and Structure of Local and Regional Government, taking note of the first draft legal instruments prepared and examined by the CDLR at its thirty-first meeting, held on 12-15 May 2003.

The Congress voices once again its opposition to the adoption of a Recommendation instead of a convention, while accepting that the insertion in a convention of a provision allowing states "to limit themselves, in the case of regional institutions, to the legal guarantees contained in the European Charter of Local Self-Government, meets criticism voiced by some states".[209] The Congress expounds on this point, indicating that some states had expressed concern regarding the harmonisation of a convention with Article 13 of the European Charter of Local Self-Government. This article previews the incorporation of regional authorities under the scope of the charter. The argument to exclude the adoption of a separate convention would seem to be rather lightweight.

Mountain regions

Another area of relevance for minority protection in which the Congress has promoted the adoption of a convention has been that of "mountain regions". Following the drafting of a "European Charter of Mountain Regions" endorsed by the Congress in Recommendation 14 (1995), a subsequent favourable opinion from the Committee of European Ministers

Responsible for Regional Planning,[210] and an opinion of the Directorate of Legal Affairs of the Secretariat, rapporteurs from the Parliamentary Assembly and the Congress proceeded to revise the draft and to give it the form of an outline convention.[211] In Recommendation 75 (2000), the Congress called on the CoM to examine the new draft outline convention, with a view to adopting it and opening it for signature as soon as possible.[212]

The preambular part of the draft refers to the awareness "that mountain regions of Europe, in spite of their diversity, which should be preserved and promoted, experience common economic, social and environmental problems ... [and] call for a specific, integrated policy framed according to the principles of sustainable development".[213] It also refers to the conviction that "the peculiarities of mountain regions make it more difficult for their inhabitants to provide for their basic needs and that the populations should be able to maintain living and working conditions equivalent to those of other regions".[214]

Part II of the draft, "Principles and instruments", indicates in its Article 3 that:

1. The specific nature of mountain regions must be legally established by the Contracting Parties; a policy must therefore be developed for the benefit of these regions, mainly favouring traditional activities and framed according to the principles of sustainable development.

2. The local authorities should be involved in the definition, formulation and application of measures required for the implementation of this policy, according to their respective powers and to the principle of subsidiarity. The Contracting Parties undertake to develop the role of local and regional authorities when preparing and implementing their mountain policies, by strengthening their powers and their financial resources and by facilitating, wherever necessary, transfrontier co-operation.

The appendix to the convention contains a series of "pointers with a view to the application of Article 4.1.*b* of the convention". Under this article "each Contracting Party undertakes to adapt and increase the effectiveness of the various sectorial policies already in force and ensure their co-ordination and their integration into a comprehensive approach". Many of these pointers in relation to policy development refer to issues particularly relevant for the protection of minorities' identity and the preservation of the particular identity of the areas in which they live. The aim to harmonise the economic and technological development of the regions with the preservation of the traditional activities characteristic of this identity is a continuum throughout the text.

Relevant examples are those pointers referring to: "economic diversity and multiple job-holding"; "agriculture and forestry", including both the guaranteeing of "the conditions of continuity of agricultural, forestry and pasture lands, farms and mountain crops" and the "fostering of complementary economic activities"; "industry, crafts, trade and private services", their development, including the "strengthening of co-operation, especially among small enterprises and also among the different sectors of the economy, including agriculture, forestry and tourism". "Tourism" in this context refers particularly to the "fostering and supporting of initiatives contributing to the development of quality tourism which is respectful of the natural, economic, social, heritage and cultural environments of mountain regions, especially those taken by local and regional authorities exercising their powers".

"Housing, living environment and infrastructure" includes the "consolidation and promotion of existing housing and control of the establishment of second homes" and "no practice of discrimination against mountain regions as compared with the rest of the territory with regard to housing and basic amenities and public services". "Education and training" comprises the "promotion of access to education and, taking into account the necessity of adult education, maintenance of schools in mountain areas and organisation of them so as to avoid long journeys for pupils, in particular by fostering distance learning and the development of education technologies". "Culture" includes "respect for, and reinforcement of, the identity of mountain populations and their regions" and "maintenance and promotion of the diversity and richness of their cultural heritage and of the activities of voluntary associations".

An important innovation is the participatory element introduced in the monitoring mechanism foreseen in the draft convention. This is to be carried out by a Standing Committee created for this purpose, composed of delegations comprising representatives of mountain regions, who represent the states party to the convention.[215] Among the functions expressly assigned to this standing committee are: making recommendations to the states party concerning measures to be taken under the convention and making proposals to improve its effectiveness generally, as well as recommending measures to keep the public informed about the activities undertaken in its framework.[216]

The normative framework which the draft convention establishes is rather flexible, as it mainly refers to a series of principles and approaches to be followed by states, providing suggestions as to the type of policies which should be implemented by them. Similarly, the involvement of the groups especially concerned (in monitoring) centres on making recommendations as to how the convention should be implemented, rather than taking binding decisions.

The draft European outline convention on mountain regions breaks new ground both as to its content, showing a high level of sensitivity to questions of identity, and as to the level of direct involvement of the populations concerned in the implementation of monitoring which it previews. The willingness of states to accept this type of approach, and level of direct involvement of the groups concerned, remains to be proved.

So far, the chances for success of this Congress proposal seem rather bleak. In Recommendation 130 (2003) on the European Charter for Mountains, the Congress steps back from its previous position and recommends that the CoM adopt a recommendation to member states including a new European Charter of Mountains text, appended to the recommendation. In this latest text, both the tone and the content of the original proposal are drastically watered down. The new "Charter" contains a list of actions that member states of the Council of Europe "will endeavour" to put into practice, and no monitoring mechanism, while references to the empowerment of local and regional authorities have been dissipated.

This is in spite of the political momentum provided by the celebration the previous year of the International Year of Mountains and the pompous title of Resolution 136 (2002) on the International Year of Mountains – A new political project for Europe's mountains: turning disinherited mountain areas into a resource – where again the Congress points to the situation of relegation from the new economy and the global market which Europe's mountain regions face. Adopting a somewhat patronising discourse, the Congress considers, among other things, that these regions "must build the framework for an environment-friendly development that meshes with the human capacity to create methods for utilising natural resources which involve adapting them to productive purposes, and learning to live with them and to preserve them" while pointing at the development of "the entrepreneurial capacity to create production systems that evolve in innovative technological directions" as a key factor. The Congress calls for legal, social and economic recognition of these areas, as well as for clear criteria for their classification, so that the conditions for improving the quality of life and the provision of services in mountain regions can be fostered.[217] These compromises would seem insufficient.

Local Democracy Agencies

Since their creation under the name of "Local Democracy Embassies" on the basis of an initiative of the Swiss and Belgian NGOs *Causes Communes* and their introduction by the Congress in Resolution 251 (1993) on the report on humanitarian action and aid to local democracy in former Yugoslavia,[218] these bodies – established by the Congress in the territory of the former Yugoslavia – have constituted the first and longest-lasting Council of Europe presence in the field. They also constitute the most important exercise of interterritorial co-operation sponsored by the Congress. In 2003, more than 180 cities, regions and NGOs from seventeen European countries are actively involved in a multilateral, decentralised, co-operation process.[219]

In 1998, the Local Democracy Embassies (LDEs) were renamed Local Democracy Agencies (LDAs) by the Congress, as a result of the Congress's awareness that the word "embassy" "could lead to confusion and erroneous expectations".[220] At the same time, the Congress further clarified this concept, presented the main objectives and activities of these bodies, and outlined the structure and organisation of the local democracy agencies "network". The LDAs are:

> established by an agreement between, on the one hand, a host local or regional authority in selected European countries, approved by the Congress Bureau and, on the other, a number of European local and regional authorities which are prepared to keep a permanent staff on the spot for the purpose of encouraging or preserving the democratic process via intramunicipal and intermunicipal confidence-building measures.[221]

The stated aims of the LDAs are, among other things,

- to foster peaceful co-existence and the development of civil society through mutual acquaintance and understanding, developed by means of exchanges and intermunicipal co-operation;

- to strengthen the democratic process where it exists and to put in hand confidence-building measures (in accordance with the scheme devised by the Council of Europe) through intercultural activities, human rights and peace education;

- to combat racism, intolerance and xenophobia by implementing non-violent solutions;

- to commit itself to a pluralistic society and to protect multicultural and multireligious society.[222]

Among the main duties of the LDA delegates is to ensure that the LDA "is present and visible at all times"[223] in the field, pointing to a conflict-prevention role. A Committee on Local Democracy Agencies has been established by the Congress and is responsible, among other things, for making decisions on the designation of an LDA. Also an "Assembly" of LDAs has been established, bringing together "the members of the Committee on LDAs, representatives of the towns, regions or NGOs which are project leaders, LDA delegates and the host local and regional authorities".[224]

In defining the LDAs' role, the promotion of human rights and minority rights is presented as a primary object of attention. The facilitation of mutual communication between the participating towns and their neighbouring regions is considered one of the main duties of the LDAs, together with the establishment of "constructive contacts – in a spirit consistent with the aims of the Local Democracy Agency – with local political parties, local NGOs, religious communities, youth organisations and the independent media".[225]

The creation of the Association of Local Democracy Agencies in December 1999, under the auspices of the Congress, gave a new impetus to the programme and enhanced the regional co-operation process among LDAs, which are today, according to Rapporteur Yvauz Mildon:

> a fundamental stakeholder in the stabilisation and long-term strengthening of democratic institutions in the countries of the region. The participative and multilevel inclusive approach in the planning and implementation of the action is a guarantee that the activities are corresponding to the needs and the available resources of those involved.

As for the international relevance of the programme, it was recognised as a main tool for promoting democracy and respect for human rights in southern and eastern Europe by the Council of Europe, in particular with the support and the activity of the Congress of Local and Regional Authorities. The convention signed in 2002 by the Secretary General of the Council of Europe, Mr Walter Schwimmer, and the President of the ALDA, Mr Gianfranco Martini, confirmed the importance attributed to the LDAs' activities. With the support of the Congress of Local and Regional Authorities, the agencies are working closely with the network of national associations of local authorities (NALAs) and with the working group of the elected representatives from south-eastern Europe.

The LDAs are members, together with the Congress of Local and Regional Authorities, of the Steering Committee on Local Democracy and Transborder Co-operation in the Stability Pact for South-Eastern Europe. The association of LDAs adopted in July 2003 a Position paper on ALDA's role in the Stabilisation and Association Process for South-Eastern Europe. Since 2001, several Council of Europe member states, among them Switzerland, Ireland, Liechtenstein, Luxembourg, Finland, France and Italy as well as the Cantons of Basel-City and Geneva (Switzerland), have contributed substantially to the consolidation of LDA activities in south-east Europe in the framework of the Stability Pact, notably in the fields of transborder co-operation, interethnic dialogue, youth programmes, training of LDA staff and environmental issues.

In 2003, LDAs were operative in Subotica, Nis, Niksic and Gjilane (Serbia and Montenegro) Osijek/Slavonia, Brtonigla-Verteneglio and Sisak (Croatia); Zavidovici and Prijedor (Bosnia and Herzegovina) and Ohrid ("the former Yugoslav Republic of Macedonia").[226] The opening of an agency in Mostar (Bosnia and Herzegovina) is ongoing. The LDAs have proved to be an example of co-operation with localities in the territory of Yugoslavia and support for local self-government in that country even at the time of greatest international isolation of that state. Following the escalation of the conflict in Kosovo, and the presentation by the CoM at its Budapest Meeting of the Council of Europe's contribution to the Stability Programme for South-Eastern Europe, the Congress soon responded with proposals to develop partnerships with the local and regional authorities in Kosovo.[227]

A wide range of initiatives has been implemented thanks to, and in co-operation with, other international organisations such as the OSCE, UNHCR, and the EU. The LDA programme is supported by the Congress and the Council of Europe through various resources: the "Urgent measures programme" in January 1996, "Confidence-building measures" and LODE programmes.[228] LDAs have also received support from the EU B7-7001 budgetary line, within the framework of the Phare programme and other programmes of action and assistance in Europe.[229] However, in recent years the Congress has been appealing for more consolidated means of finance.[230] Taking into account the expertise acquired in the field of intercultural dialogue and promotion of democratic practices at local level, the association is considering extending to new geographical areas. At its 2002 General Assembly, ALDA decided to launch a first pilot activity in Georgia to assess the possible extension of the programme in the Caucasus.

Concluding comments

The Congress has become an essential driving force in the progress of the Council of Europe in the area of minority protection. In recent decisions, the Congress has specifically referred to minority protection as one of its main goals. Already, before these were adopted, the most innovative initiatives of the organisation in the standard-setting field concerning minority protection in recent years originated from the Congress. Given the concern of the Congress for the implementation of the principle of subsidiarity and other important aspects of local self-government which this organ has actually contributed to defining, the Congress has established the political and ideological bedrock on the basis of which minority protection can be made effective. Furthermore, the Congress has contributed to identifying state practices which contravene these principles. The Congress has often taken the initiative to do so, even when these principles were not expressly enshrined in the international treaties which directly concern it.

The efforts of the Congress have been geared towards the establishment of strong, financially sound territorial structures, at both regional and local level, even if this has been to the detriment of the number of their units. The Congress has paid particular attention to territorial structures being endowed with a stable legal basis and their responsibilities being fenced off from undue interference from other levels of government. Concern for recognition at the highest possible level of the principle of subsidiarity as an essential element of the territorial organisation of the state has also been a constant feature, and so has been the need to provide territorial authorities with an adequate financial base, to match the powers and responsibilities they are called upon to exercise.

In the Congress's monitoring of state performance, it has increasingly sought new responsibilities in connection with the monitoring of those international instruments particularly relevant to achieving its aims, and to which member states were not devoting sufficient attention. This started with the monitoring of the European Charter of Local Self-Government. At the same time, the Congress kept its own monitoring methods under review, to make its monitoring increasingly effective. The Congress has progressively expanded the scope of its monitoring activity to increase both the number of states covered and the international instruments considered. This has crystallised in the "monitoring of local and regional democracy" in member states, a concept which seems to be constantly evolving, expanding and consolidating.

A very important aspect of the development of the Congress's monitoring activity, is that the expansion in the number of states being monitored has not taken place just eastwards but also towards western Europe, facilitated by the non-discriminatory approach which the Congress has upheld in a remarkably consistent manner, unprecedented in the practice of Council of Europe organs. This has resulted in an unmatched application of the principle of sovereign equality of states when it comes to "political" monitoring within the Organisation. It constitutes a landmark and provides a model which should followed by the two other organs, the Parliamentary Assembly and the Committee of Ministers. The Congress has demonstrated that a non-discriminatory approach to monitoring is not only feasible, but also highly recommendable, since the development of the Congress's monitoring activity has been accompanied by the strengthening of its political position and the consolidation of its institutional status.

States taking the initiative to reform their territorial structures have usually provided the basis for the Congress's intervention, attempting to influence state initiatives so that they meet the principles of local democracy which the Congress advocates. This intervention has been particularly pro-active in relation to initiatives for the reform of territorial structures that affect minorities especially, or even concern specific minority groups. The monitoring of local and regional democracy by the Congress, in spite of being conducted by a "political" body, has been characterised not only by a non-discriminatory, but also by an open-ended character.

This is in contrast with the approach adopted by the Parliamentary Assembly to monitoring, which consists of the consecutive opening and closing of successive monitoring exercises, often with regard to the same states, finally resulting in monitoring cycles, as described in Chapter 9. In the course of these monitoring cycles, states receive successive "positive assessments" even when poor state performance, especially in the field of minority protection, persists, regardless of the high political importance given to appropriate state performance, especially in this field at a declaratory level. The open-ended approaches of the Congress, which allow a greater scope for stringency than consecutive "opening and closing" as in the Assembly's case, have been accompanied, like those of the Assembly, by the establishment of fixed terms for subsequent review, thereby providing clear deadlines within which progress in state compliance with Congress recommendations is expected.

Although references to CoM monitoring[232] – as a form of follow-up and guarantee of the implementation of Congress decisions – have started being used by the latter organ, this practice has been less pronounced that in the case of the Parliamentary Assembly. As a constant feature, the Congress has offered continuous direct involvement and the provision of technical assistance to states, both with regard to the overall reform of the system of territorial administration, and/or with regard to concrete aspects of it, including specific problems which affect the fate of minorities in particular.

In another important aspect of its monitoring activity, the Congress has extended its coverage to international instruments other than the European Charter of Local Self-Government and ones which are also of paramount importance for minority protection. This has been the case, for example, with instruments in the field of transfrontier co-operation between territorial communities or authorities. Further, the Congress's position as the Council of Europe organ where the most innovative initiatives for the adoption of international instruments originate, is consolidating. The recent Congress proposals in the field of regionalisation and mountain regions serve as an illustration, and would deserve continued attention in the future. Not all aspects for which the Congress has shown special concern have been reflected in the international instruments adopted so far. Just to mention an example of direct relevance in the international arena, the participation of territorial authorities in the decision-making process at the international level which affect their interests has not been delineated.

The importance of transfrontier co-operation for minority protection has been underscored in recent decisions adopted by the Congress, and even if in practical initiatives undertaken by the Congress in that field minority protection has not become commonplace, minority concerns have been reflected. The Convention on the Participation of Foreigners in Public Life at Local Level has only recently and occasionally been integrated in the monitoring procedures of the Congress. This has often been done in the context of addressing the situation of persons belonging to minorities who do not have the possibility, in practical terms, of access to the citizenship of the state they live in, in spite of their long, often life-time residence in the country, a situation which places them in a particularly vulnerable position.

Although the European Charter of Local Self-Government may be of greater relevance to minorities in general, the text as such does not reflect upon the minority question. Minority considerations are yet to be streamlined in most of the Congress's activities. It has been in early initiatives dealing with the issue of mountain regions where the Congress has shown the greatest awareness of minority questions, and proposed the most advanced yet practical solutions, even if these were later watered down. In recent initiatives concerning the adoption of new treaties relating to regional self-government and mountain regions, the monitoring role of the Congress has been expressly previewed. It remains to be seen, however, how long it will take for these proposals and approaches to be accepted and implemented by the Council of Europe member states.

Finally, an important, practical activity of the Congress is that involving Local Democracy Agencies. LDAs have been the response of the Congress to situations of post-conflict rehabilitation and reconstruction affecting war-torn areas of Europe in recent years. This initiative entails the first – and longest-lasting – Council of Europe presence in the field in the area of minority protection, and it promotes co-operation between member states at the grass-roots level. It requires however, besides the active contribution of European cities, regions and NGOs, strong political and financial support from the Council of Europe and its member states in order to ensure the success of this operational programme, sometimes developing in difficult areas. Again in this respect, the practical commitment of Council of Europe structures and states to minority protection remains to be tested.

Notes

1.   The Congress was for a long time called the Standing Conference of Local and Regional Authorities of Europe.

2.   Statutory Resolution (2000) 1 was adopted by the CoM on 15 March 2000, at the 702nd meeting of the ministers' deputies. For more detailed information on the stages leading to the establishment of the Congress, see P. Thornberry and M.A. Martín Estébanez, *The Council of Europe and Minorities,* Doc. COEMIN, p. 57, note 250. On its present composition and function see the introduction.

3.   See Article 4 of Statutory Resolutions (94) 3 and (2000) 1.

4.   See further, the report submitted by special rapporteur A. Eide to the UN Sub-Commission on Prevention of Discrimination and Protection of Minorities, *Possible Ways and Means of Facilitating the Peaceful and Constructive Solution of Problems Involving Minorities*, UN Doc. E/CN.4/Sub.2/1993/34, Chapter II, B and C. Different perceptions on this matter are discussed in Chapters 2 and 3.

5.   The concept of local democracy is explained by the Congress by reference to the European Charter of Local Self-Government "which lays down the essential characteristics of a genuine system of local democracy". This is stated, for example, in Resolution 3 (1994) of the Congress (see below).

6.   This has been the case, for example, with the European Charter for Regional or Minority Languages (see Chapter 3) and the European Charter of Local Self-Government (see below, and in particular, the explanatory report of the charter, section A. "Origins of the charter").

7.   Resolution 232 was adopted by the Congress on 18 March 1992.

8.   On this resolution, and others adopted by the Congress in the early 1990s relevant to minority protection, see P. Thornberry and M.A. Martín Estébanez, op. cit., pp. 59-62.

9.   See Congress Recommendation 43 (1998), adopted on 27 May 1998.

10.   Paragraph 10 of Resolution 52, adopted by the Congress on 3 June 1997.

11.   For clarification on the content of the concept of cultural autonomy, A. Eide, "Cultural Autonomy: concept, content, history and role in the world order", in M. Suksi (ed.), *Autonomy: Applications and Implications*, pp. 251-76.

12.   Paragraphs 11-12 of Resolution 52 (1997).

13.   Paragraph 16 of the resolution.

14.   Ibid., Appendix, paragraph A.

15.   See further, Chapter 2.

16.   See below.

17.   In Recommendation 90 (2001), the Congress deals with the financial relations between state, regional and local authorities in federal states, on the basis of an international conference held in Moscow on 5-7 October 2000. Resolution 110 (2001) of the Congress is also concerned with the same question.

18.   Ibid., Appendix, paragraph B.*a.*

19.   Paragraph 11 of the recommendation.

20.   Ibid., paragraph 14.

21.   Ibid., paragraph 13.

22.   Ibid., paragraph 18.

23.   Ibid., paragraph 23.

24.   See paragraphs 15 and 20 of the Recommendation, adopted on 28 May 1998.

25.   Paragraph 16 of the Resolution, adopted on 22 May 2003.

26.   Ibid., paragraph 23. The Congress refers in particular to the hearing on inter-cultural and interfaith dialogue held during the spring session of the Chamber of Local Authorities.

27.   The same applies to Resolution 145 (2002) of the same title as the Recommendation and adopted on the same date, 6 June 2002.

28.   Article 2, 3 of Statutory Resolution (2000) 1.

29.   See, for example, Resolution 71 (1998), as quoted below, paragraph 2.

30.   European Treaty Series No. 122. See also the commentary contained in the explanatory report of the charter, a Council of Europe document published in Strasbourg in 1996. For a summary description of the content of those provisions of the charter particularly relevant to minority protection, see P. Thornberry and M.A. Martín Estébanez, op. cit., pp. 58-59.

31.   In contrast with the spurious interpretation of the concept in the EU framework, for example. See further, I. Bullain, "Autonomy and the European Union" in M. Suksi (ed.), *Autonomy, Applications and Implications*, op. cit., pp. 343-56.

32.   Paragraph 1 of Resolution 71, adopted by the congress on 28 May 1998.

33.   The number of signatures and ratifications of the charter has substantially increased as a result of the enlargement of the Council of Europe, as it has become a key requirement for membership of the organisation (see Chapter 9). At the time of writing 37 states have signed and 34 have ratified the charter. France and Belgium are among those states which have not ratified it yet.

34.   The proceedings of this conference were compiled in a voluminous report: "What have you done with the European Charter of Local Self-Government? – Legislation and jurisprudence", Standing Conference of Local and Regional Authorities of Europe, Studies and Texts (Strasbourg: Council of Europe, 1993).

35.   See the recommendations and resolutions enumerated in paragraph 4 of Resolution 71 (1998) on monitoring the application of the European Charter of Local Self-Government. On the remaining content of this resolution, see further below.

36.   Paragraph 6 of Recommendation 2, adopted on 2 June 1994.

37.   Paragraph 9 of Resolution 3 (1994). It should be noted in this connection that the monitoring actually concerns not only states which have ratified the charter, but also states which have signed it, as discussed further below.

38.   Ibid., paragraph 13.

39.   Paragraph 15.b and c of Resolution 34, debated and approved by the Chamber of Local Authorities on 3 July 1996 and adopted by the Standing Committee of the Congress on 5 July 1996.

40.   Paragraph 7.c of Recommendation 39, adopted on 6 March 1998.

41.   Paragraph 3.d.i-ii of the recommendation. On the activities of the CDLR, see further, Chapter 7.

42.   With regard to endeavours to adopt an instrument universal in scope, see Congress Recommendation 98 (2001) on the draft world charter of local self-government: state of discussions, and Resolution 118 (2001) of the same title. For an account of more recent and disheartening developments, see Resolution 138 (2002) on the second draft world charter of local self-government, adopted on 4 June 2002.

43.   According to the explanatory report of the charter, section B, General remarks: "The Charter does not provide for an institutionalised system of control of its application, beyond a requirement for parties to supply all relevant information concerning legislative or other measures taken for the purpose of complying with the Charter ... It was felt possible to dispense with complex supervisory machinery, given that the presence within the Council of Europe of the Congress with direct access to the Committee of Ministers would ensure adequate political control of compliance by the parties."

44.   Paragraph 2.*a*.i and *b* of Resolution 71, adopted on 28 May 1998.

45.   See, in particular, paragraph 2.*c-f* of the resolution.

46.   By way of example, the fourth report, "The financial resources of local authorities in relation to their responsibilities: a litmus test for subsidiarity", has been examining the application of Articles 3.1; 4.1-5; and 9 of the charter and resulted in Congress Recommendation 79 (2000) and Resolution 97 (2000), adopted on 23 May 2000.

47.   These problems identified are summarily presented in Resolution 58 (1997) on the situation of local democracy in member countries, adopted by the congress on 5 June 1997.

48.   This article includes among the aims "the submission of proposals to the Committee of Ministers in order to promote local and regional self-government".

49.   Paragraph 8 of Resolution 31, adopted on 4 July 1996.

50.   Ibid.

51.   Ibid., paragraph 11.

52.   Ibid., paragraph 11.

53.   For some background information on the minority situation in that state before the Congress decisions were adopted, see European Centre for Minority Issues (ed.), *From Ethnopolitical Conflict to Inter-Ethnic Accord in Moldova*, ECMI Report No. 1 (Flensburg: European Centre for Minority Issues, 1998).

54.   Paragraph.10.2 of Recommendation 38, adopted on 6 March 1998.

55.   Ibid., paragraph. 11.1.

56.   This opinion is contained in an appendix to the recommendation.

57.   See paragraphs 7 and 15.e of Recommendation 84, adopted on 25 May 2000.

58.   Ibid., paragraph 8.

59.   See paragraph 8 of Resolution 103 (2000).

60.   Paragraph 8 A.*a*, *b*, of the Recommendation, adopted on 5 June 2002.

61.   Ibid., paragraph 8 F.*e* and *f*.

62.   Ibid., paragraph 10.

63.   Paragraphs 4-6 of the Resolution, adopted on 5 June 2002.

64.   Ibid., paragraph 10.

65.   Paragraph A.3.2 of Recommendation 45, adopted by the Congress on 28 May 1998.

66.   Paragraph 6.6 of Recommendation 46, adopted by the Congress on 28 May 1998.

67.   Ibid., paragraph 6.15.

68.   Paragraph 3 of Resolution 67, adopted by the Congress on 28 May 1998.

69.   Congress Recommendation 47, adopted on 28 May 1998.

70.   Ibid., paragraph 7.*a* and *b*.

71.   Ibid., paragraph 9. For comments in this latter recommendation of the Congress, see further below.

72.   Paragraph 5.*a* of Recommendation 48, adopted by the Congress on 28 May 1998.

73.   Ibid., paragraph 15.*a.*

74.   Paragraph 6 of Resolution 68, adopted on 28 May 1998.

75.   Recommendation 49, adopted by the Congress on 28 May 1998.

76.   Ibid., paragraph 19.

77.   Ibid., paragraph 26.i.

78.   Ibid., paragraph 27.

79.   Ibid., paragraph 57.

80.   Ibid., paragraph 58. On the proposal for a Charter of Regional Self-Government, see further below.

81.   Paragraph 7.9.4 of Recommendation 78.

82.   Ibid., paragraphs 7.10.1; 7.10.4; and 7.10.5. Decision of the *Conseil Constitutionnel* 99-412 DC, 15 June 1999. Some of the arguments which were given in favour of ratification before the decision of the *Conseil Constitutionel* was taken have been cited in B. Poignant, "Prospects for ratification of the charter by France", *Implementation of the European Charter for Regional or Minority Languages, Regional or Minority Languages, No. 2* (Strasbourg: Council of Europe, September 1999, pp. 47-49).

83.   Paragraph 4.*e* of Resolution 94 (2000).

84.   Paragraph 9.*k* of Recommendation 77, adopted on 25 May 2000.

85.   Ibid., at 9.*l* and *n.*

86.   Paragraph 2.*a* of Resolution 93, adopted on 25 May 2000.

87.   Recommendation 81 was adopted on 25 May 2000.

88.   Ibid., paragraph 23.

89.   Ibid., paragraph 34.

90.   Ibid., paragraph 36.

91.   Paragraphs 7-10 of Recommendation 82, adopted on 25 May 2000.

92.   Ibid., paragraphs 44-45.

93.   Ibid., paragraph 26.

94.   Ibid., paragraph 32.

95.   Ibid., paragraphs 57 and 59.*a.*

96.   Ibid., paragraph 17.

97.   Ibid., paragraph 53.

98.   See report of the visit to monitor the trials of Mr Rufi Osmani, Mayor of Gostivar, and Mr Aladjin Demiri, Mayor of Tetovo ("the former Yugoslav Republic of Macedonia") from 15 to 18 June 1998, Congress doc. CG/BUR (5) 75.

99.   Ibid., paragraph 31.

100. On Local Democracy Agencies see further below.

101. Ibid., paragraphs 63 and 64.

102. Paragraph 3 of Resolution 100, adopted also on 24 May 2000.

103. Paragraphs 6 and 7 of Recommendation 87, adopted on 30 May 2001.

104. Ibid., paragraph 11.

105. Ibid., paragraph 13.A.*b*.i.

106. Ibid., B.*c* and *d*.

107. Ibid., C.*b*.iii and E.

108. Ibid., F.

109. Ibid., 14.*b* i and ii.

110. Paragraphs 5 and 6 of Recommendation 88, adopted on 30 May 2001.

111. Ibid., paragraph 9.

112. Ibid., paragraphs 10 and 13.*b*.

113. Ibid., paragraph 13.*n*.

114. Ibid., paragraph l.

115. Paragraph 5 of Resolution 109, adopted on 30 May 2001.

116. Paragraph 4.i, of Recommendation 89, adopted on 30 May 2001.

117. Ibid., paragraph 4.iv.

118. Ibid., paragraph 4.*b*.iii.

119. Ibid., paragraph 4.*c*.ii and iii.

120. Ibid., paragraph 4.vi.

121. Paragraph 8 of Recommendation 96, adopted on 30 May 2001.

122. Recommendation 122 (2002), adopted on 14 November 2002, paragraph 7.*a* and *d*.

123. In the Maltese case, however, the Congress criticises the fact that Malta has remained strongly centralised in practice, and asks the Maltese minister responsible for local self-government to participate in the forthcoming meeting of the Chamber of Local Authorities to present the measures taken and/or envisaged the implement the Congress's recommendations. See, in particular, paragraphs 8.*e, f, g* and 9.*c* of the Recommendation.

124. Ibid., paragraph 14.

125. Ibid., paragraph 18.vi, i and v.

126. Ibid., paragraph 21.

127. Paragraph l of Recommendation 97, adopted on 30 May 2001.

128. Ibid., paragraph 13.

129. Ibid., paragraph 16.*n*.

130. Ibid., paragraph 16.*j*.vi.

131. Ibid., iv.

132. Paragraph 1.c of the Recommendation, adopted on 5 June 2002.

133. Ibid., paragraph 5.*a*.i. and ii.

134. Ibid., paragraph 5.*a*.iii.

135. Paragraph 3.e of the Resolution, adopted on 5 June 2002.

136. See paragraph 9.c of Recommendation 120 (2002).

137. See Resolutions 147 (2002) and 142 (2002) on local and regional democracy in Spain and Hungary, respectively.

138. Paragraph 12 iv. of Recommendation 116 (2002), adopted on 6 June 2002.

139. The fact that Poland is not yet a party to the European Convention on Regional or Minority Languages and the European Convention for the Participation of Foreigners in Public Life at Local Level is also regretted by the Congress. See paragraph 6 of Recommendation 120, adopted on 14 November 2002, in particular.

140. See paragraphs 16 to 19 of Recommendation 121 (2002), adopted on 14 November 2002.

141. On this latter aspect, see paragraphs 8-10 in particular.

142. It should be noted, however, that the charter also enshrines the principles of transfrontier and interterritorial co-operation, without giving this specific name to them. According to Article 10.3 of the charter "local authorities shall be entitled, under such conditions as may be provided for by the law, to co-operate with their counterparts in other States".

143. European Treaty Series, No. 106, and explanatory report. For a brief overview of the convention and the problems initially faced in its implementation, see P. Thornberry and M.A. Martín Estébanez, op. cit., pp. 68-73.

144. See Vienna Summit Declaration of 9 October 1993, Appendix II on national minorities. See further, Chapter 5.

145. European Treaty Series, No. 159.

146. See the explanatory report of the Additional Protocol to the European Outline Convention on Transfrontier Co-operation between Territorial Communities or Authorities, especially section on General comments.

147. European Treaty Series, No. 169.

148. The text of this preliminary draft was appended to Resolution 248 (1993). For an overview of this draft, see P. Thornberry and M.A. Martín Estébanez, op. cit., pp. 76-79.

149. See paragraph 4 of the explanatory report of Protocol No. 2 to the European Outline Convention on Transfrontier Co-operation between Territorial Communities or Authorities concerning interterritorial co-operation.

150. Ibid., paragraph 3.

151. Paragraph 7.*e* of Resolution 119, adopted on 31 May 2001.

152. Ibid., paragraph 8.

153. Ibid., paragraph 10.

154. Ibid., paragraph 11.*d*.

155. Paragraph 3 of Recommendation 85, adopted on 25 May 2000.

156. The conference, co-organised by the Congress and the Parliamentary Assembly, and attended by local, regional and national elected representatives and representatives of European border regions and their associations, was held in Timisoara, Romania, from 28 to 30 October 1999. See the text of the Final Declaration, appended to Congress Recommendation 85 (2000), p. 7.

157. See further, Chapter 5.

158. Recommendation 85, paragraph 16.

159. Ibid., paragraphs 20-23.

160. Paragraph 8 of Resolution 104, adopted by the Congress on 25 May 2000.

161. Ibid., paragraph 6.

162. Ibid., paragraph 9.

163. Ibid., paragraph 13.

164. See below.

165. Paragraph 5 of Recommendation 74, adopted on 24 May 2000.

166. Paragraphs 10.*a, b, f* and 11.*a* of the Recommendation, adopted on 6 June 2002. In paragraph 13 the Congress addresses two recommendations to the EU, including the consideration of transfrontier co-operation in the management of structural funds.

167. Paragraph 7 of the Resolution, adopted also on 6 June 2002.

168. Ibid., paragraph 9.*a, b* and *h*.

169. European Treaty Series No. 144.

170. Status as at 10 October 2003. Charter of treaty signatures and ratifications, Council of Europe Treaty Office.

171. Articles 1 and 12 of the convention. European Treaty Series No. 93. For a discussion on this and some other aspects of the convention relevant for minority protection, see P. Thornberry and M.A. Martín Estébanez, op. cit., pp. 82-85.

172. Status as at 10 October 2003. Charter of treaty signatures and ratifications, Council of Europe Treaty Office.

173. Preamble of the convention.

174. Paragraph 15 of the explanatory report.

175. See the discussion on this and other articles of the text contained in the explanatory report of the convention. For references to this and other aspects of the convention relevant to minority protection, see also P. Thornberry and M.A. Martín Estébanez, op. cit., pp. 62-64.

176. Explanatory report, paragraph 64.

177. Paragraph 17 of the Recommendation, adopted on 6 June 2002.

178. Paragraph 14 of the Resolution, adopted on 6 June 2002.

179. According to Congress Resolution 112 (2001), this study has been published in the Congress's Studies and Text series, No. 69.

180. Adopted by the Congress on 31 May 2001.

181. Ibid., paragraph 2.*b-e.*

182. Ibid., paragraph 2.*h.*

183. Ibid., paragraph *g.*iv-v.

184. Ibid., paragraph *k* and *l.*

185. Ibid., paragraph 4.*a, i* and *c.*

186. Draft explanatory report on the draft European Charter of regional self-government, rapporteur Mr Rabe, Congress Doc. CPR (4) 4 Part II, Addendum revised, 2.

187. Ibid.

188. Note, in particular, the final replacement of the term "autonomy" by "self-government".

189. Section II of Recommendation 34 (1997), paragraphs 1-3.

190. Ibid., Appendix, preambular paragraphs 6 and 8.

191. Ibid., paragraphs 10 and 9.

192. Ibid., Article 14, 3 and 4.

193. Ibid., Article 12, 1.

194. Ibid., Articles 9 and 10.

195. Ibid., Part I, section C.

196. Ibid., Article 25.

197. Ibid., Article 20.

198. The text was adopted on 19 March 1997.

199. See Recommendation 65 (1999) on the current state of, and prospects for, regionalisation in Europe, adopted by the Congress on 17 June 1999, extract from the Official Gazette of the Council of Europe – June 1999, paragraph 7, in particular.

200. Ibid., paragraph 8.*d.*

201. See paragraph 3 of Recommendation 83, adopted by the Congress on 25 May 2000.

202. Ibid., paragraph 8.

203. Ibid., paragraph 7.*a.*

204. Paragraph 6 of Resolution 102 (2000).

205. Decisions taken by the ministers' deputies at their 693rd meeting on 12 January 2000.

206. Especially paragraphs 10 and 12 of the Resolution, adopted on 6 June 2002.

207. Contained in doc. MCL-13 (2002) 8 final.

208. Paragraph 4.*e* of the Resolution, adopted on 22 May 2003.

209. Ibid., paragraph 10.*b.*

210. Following this favourable opinion, the Committee of Ministers of the Council of Europe decided to set up an intergovernmental working party to prepare a convention on mountain regions.

211. See Recommendation 75 (2000) on the draft European outline convention on mountain regions, adopted by the congress on 24 May 2000.

212. Ibid., paragraph 4.

213. Ibid., text of the draft European outline convention on mountain regions, paragraph 10.

214. Ibid., paragraph 14.

215. Part III, Article 5.1 of the draft.

216. Ibid., Article 6.

217. Ibid., para. 9.

218. Resolution 251 (1993) contained a call for territorial authorities to play a role in the preservation of democracy at the grass-roots level. On the origins of the Local Democracy Embassies and the evolution of this concept into that of Local Democracy Agencies, see the appendix to Resolution 73 (1998), quoted below. See also P. Thornberry and M.A. Martín Estébanez, op. cit., p. 80. See Document CG (10) 8 of the Congress, also available on the website of the LDA Association (www.ldaaonline.org).

219. This was highlighted at the Plenary Session of the Congress (May 2003) on the occasion of the 10th Anniversary of the LDA programme (see below).

220. See Resolution 73 (1998) on local democracy agencies, adopted by the Congress on 28 May 1998, paragraph 10.

221. Ibid., Appendix, foreword.

222. Ibid., Appendix, 1.B. On confidence-building measures, see Chapter 7.

223. Ibid., Appendix 3.D. The duties of the delegate, a word which denominates the person mainly responsible for the LDA's operation in the field, are also described in the appendix, section 3.E.

224. Ibid., Appendix 3.A.2.

225. Ibid., Appendix 2.

226. Ibid., paragraph 2.

227. See Recommendation 58 (1999), adopted on 17 June 1999, paragraph 21.

228. See Chapter 7.

229. See Recommendation 24 (1996), on local democracy embassies – a contribution to democratic security adopted on 5 July 1996, paragraphs 3-4.

230. Ibid., paragraphs 9-12. See also Resolution 73 (1998), paragraph 14.

231. See Chapter 6.

Chapter 11

The European Commission against Racism and Intolerance (ECRI)

Introduction

Discrimination on the ground of "race" is prohibited by contemporary international law, commencing with the proscription of discrimination based on "race, sex, language or religion" in the Charter of the United Nations.[1] International law has outlawed racial discrimination through a series of instruments, some allied to the international struggle against apartheid and colonialism, and the prohibition of racial discrimination is now widely regarded as part of *jus cogens.*[2]

In general international law, the most influential definition of racial discrimination is that contained in the International Convention on the Elimination of All Forms of Racial Discrimination [ICERD],[3] Article 1.1 of which defines racial discrimination as: "[a]ny distinction, exclusion, restriction or preference based on race, colour, descent, or national or ethnic origin which has the purpose or effect of nullifying or impairing the recognition, enjoyment or exercise, on an equal footing, of human rights and fundamental freedoms in the political, economic, social, cultural or any other field of public life".[4] The scope of the convention is thus broader than most folkloric or "scientific" notions of race or the "idiom of race as a way of defining ... otherness"[5] – though it may be observed that "race" as such is not defined by the convention, and neither is "racism", which is only referred to in terms of condemning "racist doctrines and practices", and "racist activities".[6]

The Political Declaration adopted in 2000 by Ministers of Council of Europe member states at the concluding session of the European Conference against Racism reaffirmed that "Racism and racial discrimination are serious violations of human rights in the contemporary world and must be combated by all lawful means."[7] The various bodies within the Council of Europe – including the European Court of Human Rights and the European Commission of Human Rights – have sought to address the problem of racism, racial discrimination and related phenomena over several decades.[8] The Political Declaration noted with satisfaction the "key role" of the Council of Europe in combating racism and related problems:

> as affirmed at the highest political level and demonstrated by
>
> - the European Convention on Human Rights and its additional Protocols, as well as the European Court of Human Rights and its case-law;[9]
> - the adoption by the Committee of Ministers of Protocol No. 12 to the Convention, which introduces a general prohibition of discrimination;[10]
> - the Organisation's other human rights and legal instruments providing for equality and non-discrimination, including the Framework Convention for the Protection of National Minorities;[11]
> - the action of the European Commission against Racism and Intolerance (ECRI);
> - the contribution of the Commissioner for Human Rights.[12]

The 1993 decision, by the first (Vienna) Summit of Heads of State and Government of the Council of Europe, to set up the European Commission against Racism and Intolerance (ECRI) is recalled in the introduction to the present work and in Chapter 5;[13] the second summit of Heads of State and Government, held in Strasbourg in 1997 "confirmed the priority given by the Council of Europe to combating racism, xenophobia, anti-semitism and intolerance".[14] The ECRI has been in operation since March 1994.

As a follow-up to the European Conference against Racism, the Committee of Ministers (CoM) of the Council of Europe adopted on 13 June 2002 a resolution containing a new statute for ECRI, which builds upon and extends earlier practice.[15] The statute describes the task of ECRI as "combating racism, racial discrimination, xenophobia, anti-semitism and intolerance in greater Europe from the perspective of the protection of human rights, in the light of the European Convention on Human Rights".[16] The objectives of this "body of the Council of Europe"[17] are drafted in wide terms: ECRI is to review member states' legislation, policies and other measures in the above fields, propose further action at local, national and European level, formulate general policy recommendations to member states, and "to study international legal instruments applicable in the matter with a view to their reinforcement where appropriate".[18]

One member of ECRI per member state is to be appointed, and the members shall have "high moral authority and recognised expertise"[19] in the above-described fields. The statute provides that members of ECRI "shall serve in their individual capacity [and] shall be independent and impartial in fulfilling their mandate"; it is specifically mentioned that members "shall not receive instructions from their government".[20] Accordingly, the statute makes it very clear that members of ECRI are to fulfil the role of "independent experts"; it is further provided that the CoM may request a member state to appoint another person where the qualifications envisaged in the statute would not be fulfilled.[21] Membership is for a fixed and renewable term of five years, subject to the provisions on change of circumstances and the like.[22]

The statute makes various provisions concerning the modus operandi of ECRI. In addition to provision for the organisation of consultations, and the assistance of rapporteurs or consultants, it is provided that "ECRI may be seized directly by non-governmental organisations on any questions covered by its terms of reference".[23] ECRI is also authorised to seek the opinions of Council of Europe bodies concerned with its work.[24] The ECRI programme, which may be modified, shall include, inter alia, three aspects: the country-by-country approach; work on general themes; and relations with civil society.[25] It is also provided that ECRI shall, as appropriate, integrate a gender perspective into its programme.

Article 11 of the statute elaborates the programme outline: the country-by-country approach involves the monitoring of racism and allied phenomena "by closely examining the situation in each of the member states of the Council of Europe", in the context of which "ECRI shall draw up reports containing its factual analyses as well as suggestions and proposals" as to how each country "might deal with any problems identified".[26] The country reports are to be published following transmission to the national authorities, "unless the latter expressly oppose such publication".[27] ECRI's work on general themes typically consists of policy recommendations to national governments and the collection and dissemination of "good practices" in combating racism and allied problems.[28] Article 13 of the statute envisages the development of relations with civil society, the promotion of dialogue, and awareness-raising and information activities. The potential for further development of the work of ECRI is appraised in the conclusion to the present chapter. The ECRI strategy for constantly enhancing its activities has been described as taking "a step-by-step approach, building on the work it has already accomplished by evaluating, consolidating and extending its action".[29]

Basic terms

ECRI's overall task has been summarised as:

> to combat racism, xenophobia, anti-semitism and intolerance at the level of greater Europe and from the perspective of the protection of human rights. ECRI's action covers all necessary measures to combat

violence, discrimination and prejudice faced by persons or groups of persons notably on grounds of race, colour, language, religion, nationality and national or ethnic origin.[30]

The reference to discrimination based on religion – as well as race and analogous notions – extends the work of ECRI beyond, for example, that of the UN Committee on the Elimination of Racial Discrimination (CERD) working under the Convention on the Elimination of All Forms of Racial Discrimination. Under the terms of the latter convention, CERD would only be concerned with discrimination on grounds of religion if such discrimination overlapped with discrimination on racial/ethnic grounds.[31] ECRI does not appear to regard itself as similarly limited and has for example issued a general recommendation on Islamophobia:[32] while many Muslims in Europe are of a different ethnicity from the majority in the society in question, this is not always the case.

ECRI's General Policy Recommendation No. 7 on National Legislation to Combat Racism and Racial Discrimination[33] defines "racism" in wide terms as meaning "the belief that a ground such as race, colour, language, religion, nationality or national or ethnic origin justified contempt for a person or a group of persons, or the notion of superiority of a person or a group of persons";[34] the definitions of "direct" and "indirect" discrimination employ the same broad catalogue of "grounds" including "religion".

The definitions in this text of direct and indirect discrimination are explicit and illuminating: "direct racial discrimination" means "differential treatment" based on the above grounds "which has no objective and reasonable justification"; and there is no such justification when treatment "does not pursue a legitimate aim or if there is not a reasonable relationship of proportionality between the means employed and the aim sought to be realised". "Indirect racial discrimination" is taken to mean "cases where an apparently neutral factor such as a provision, criterion or practice cannot be as easily complied with by, or disadvantages, persons belonging to a group designated by a ground such as [above list of grounds] unless this factor has an objective and reasonable justification. This latter would be the case if it pursues a legitimate aim and if there is a reasonable relationship of proportionality between the means employed and the aim sought to be realised".[35]

In all this, it may be commented that the definition of "racism" is innovative – the term is used but not defined in the Political Declaration or the General Conclusions of the European Conference against Racism, nor in the final documents of the Durban World Conference against Racism. The definitions of direct and indirect racial discrimination are stated to draw their inspiration from key directives of the European Union[36] and the case-law of the European Court of Human Rights. In the case of the ECHR, it may be noted that the concept of indirect discrimination has not undergone a great deal of development,[37] so that in turn the ECRI account of this concept may be of service to the Court, and in the interpretation of ICERD, Article 1 of which refers to discrimination as "purpose or effect", but without further elaboration.

The country-by-country approach[38]

i. *Basic procedures*

The idea behind the reports is to study the country situation in each of the member states of the Council of Europe in detail before drawing up specific proposals for the solution of problems. The annual report for 2000 summarises the procedure:

> The first aspect of ECRI's activities concerns its country-by-country approach. This is a method whereby ECRI closely examines the situation in each of the member states of the Council of Europe and draws up, following this analysis, suggestions and proposals as to how the problems of racism and intolerance identified in each country might be dealt with. The aim of this exercise is to formulate helpful and well-founded proposals which may assist governments in taking practical steps to counter racism and intolerance.[39]

It may be observed that, in common with the majority of human rights monitoring bodies at the Council of Europe and the United Nations, the objective of ECRI is essentially to present a constructive critique of the efforts of the state in question to address the particular human rights problem. However, unlike the analogous body at the United Nations – CERD – the ECRI reports are authored by ECRI itself, and not by the country examined.

The preparation of country reports for discussion by ECRI is entrusted to country-by-country working groups (CBC groups), consisting of four or five ECRI members,[40] none of whom is a national of any country being examined.[41] In practice, the CBC group will not have among its membership nationals of states neighbouring those being examined.[42] The sources of information for compiling reports are wide-ranging, and include state reports to other treaty-bodies and observations made by such bodies, international and national NGO reports, media reports, information on legislation and country visits. ECRI tries to finalise draft country-specific texts through consensus; where this is not possible, decisions are taken by vote to adopt the analysis and proposals by consensus. If this is not achieved, a vote is taken.[43]

There follows a dialogue with the relevant national authorities, after which ECRI discusses and adopts the final report – again by consensus if possible.[44] ECRI country reports contain appendices containing the viewpoints of the national authorities, where the latter deem it necessary.[45] Once adopted in their final form, ECRI's country reports are transmitted to the governments of the countries in question through the CoM,[46] and may be made public two months after the transmission "unless the governments in question are expressly against making the texts public".[47]

ECRI's country-by-country approach concerns all Council of Europe member states on an equal footing. Reports for the first cycle, Round 1, were completed in late 1998. At the beginning of 1999, ECRI started its second stage, Round 2, of country-by-country work. Ten countries were to be examined each year over a four-year period (1999-2002). In Round 2 reports, ECRI seeks to follow-up CBC proposals and general recommendations, update information, and provide greater in-depth analysis.[48] In other words, the first round of reports provides a platform for continuing dialogue.

For the second round, contact visits to states and joint meetings with governments and NGOs take place and are viewed as part of the regular procedure.[49] National authorities co-operate in the organisation of visits, although ECRI itself selects and contacts relevant NGOs with which it sets up meetings during the visit.[50] ECRI summarises the reporting activity as:

> a stage in the development of an ongoing, active dialogue between ECRI and the authorities of member states with a view to identifying solutions to the problems of racism and intolerance with which the latter are confronted. The input of non-governmental organisations and other bodies or individuals active in this field is a welcome part of this process.[51]

In term of raising national awareness of issues, ECRI arranges for translation of reports into the main national languages, and encourages national events around the publication of a report.[52]

ii. *Structure of reports*

The structure of the Round 1 country reports is fairly standard.[53] A typical report starts with a fairly brief introduction, which sets out the basic structure of the state, incidence of minorities, and so on, and identifies "key areas meriting particular attention". This is followed by a section on "legal aspects", including a list or account of relevant international instruments (relevant to discrimination and intolerance) ratified by the state and instruments which ECRI considers should be ratified. The instruments are not confined to those of the Council of Europe, but include texts of the United Nations, encompassing agencies such as the United Nations Educational, Scientific and Cultural Organisation (UNESCO) and the International Labour Organisation (ILO).

This section is typically completed by an analysis of relevant constitutional law, criminal, civil and administrative law provisions, as well as provisions on citizenship, minorities, relevant specialised bodies, and the like. The third section is designated "policy aspects" and is wide-ranging, with many variations depending on the specific practices, demography and political organisation of the state in question. Among policy aspects regularly included are those on:

- reception and status of non-citizens;
- the judiciary;
- inter-community relations;
- police and policing;
- media;
- education and awareness-raising on racism and related phenomena in the society in general;
- education of minority groups;
- linguistic issues;
- racial violence and harassment;
- employment and immigration;
- the question of political leadership;
- asylum-seekers and refugees;
- the need for statistics and monitoring;
- the associational life of minority groups;
- and, where relevant, a section on vulnerable groups such as the Roma or other specific groups such as the Saami.

Problems in particular areas of the state can also be identified, and statistics assessed. A bibliography lists the main published sources consulted during the preparation of the report. ECRI's proposals, recommendations and critique tend to be distributed throughout the narrative, rather than being grouped into positive and negative aspects, and recommendations, at the end of the documents or in a separate set of observations. Comments can relate to any aspect of issues raised by racism and intolerance, and are not confined to suggestions to ratify more human rights instruments. Criticism will not usually include condemnation of the state for violations – this is regarded as not being the mandate of ECRI.[54]

Round 1 reports are compiled in four volumes, encompassing a tremendous amount of information and critique on the state of racism and racial discrimination in the countries of the Council of Europe. In the space available, it is possibly only to highlight the kinds of issues on which ECRI has expressed concern – the "key areas meriting particular attention". These include but are not limited to:

- activities of racist groups (including neo-Nazi and "skinhead" groups in some countries) and the need to address violence on the part of such groups;
- questions of the effectiveness of legislation in force;
- the lack of appropriate structures and policies to address issues of racism and the like;
- the need to address indirect as well as direct discrimination;
- the general climate of opinion towards immigrants, asylum-seekers and refugees;
- problems faced by young people from immigrant backgrounds;
- the need to improve inter-agency co-ordination for persons of immigrant origin;
- the need for police education in questions concerning immigrants and minority groups;
- racist incidents and public hostility towards Roma/Gypsies;
- the need to promote tolerance and understanding for those who are different, including religious tolerance;
- the need to improve statistical records on the areas of discrimination, the size of minority groups, and so on.

Round 2 reports are divided into Section I: "Overview of the situation", and Section II: "Issues of particular concern". In Section I, issues are regularly grouped under headings such as:

- international legal instruments;
- constitutional provisions and other basic provisions;
- criminal law provisions;
- civil and administrative law provisions;
- administration of justice;
- specialised bodies and other institutions;
- education and awareness-raising;
- reception and status of non-citizens;
- access to public services – including health care, welfare, housing, and education
- access to employment;
- monitoring the situation in the country;

- monitoring the news media;
- conduct of law enforcement officials;
- vulnerable groups.[55]

Section II – "Issues of particular concern", concentrates on the particularities of the country in question, augmenting the critique. In most cases, the section constitutes a significant element in the narrative as a whole. As with Round 1, critical observations and recommendations pervade ECRI reports as a whole. Issues of particular concern have included:

- the existence and practice of indirect or hidden discrimination;
- the non-application of legislation against racial discrimination;
- discrimination in access to public services;
- discrimination in access to public places;
- discrimination in employment;
- a range of problems concerning the reception and treatment of asylum-seekers and refugees;
- the difficult position of categories of non-citizens – such as undocumented immigrants;
- the negative climate of public opinion towards immigrants and "others";
- limitations in or lack of education and public awareness of issues of racism and discrimination;
- the existence of racial harassment and anti-semitism in certain countries;
- discrimination against Roma/Gypsies;
- the role of local authorities in addressing racism and discrimination;
- the need for intercommunity confidence-building;
- the exploitation of racism in politics;
- reflection on political contexts such as official acceptance of ethnic or other pluralism in the country concerned, and consequent difficulties for members of minority groups to express their identity;
- the strained state of interethnic relations in particular countries and its potential for engendering conflict.

The ensemble of reports paints a sometimes dramatic picture of the state of interethnic relations throughout the membership of the Council of Europe. The incidence of any or all of the above varies with the country on which the report is based. It will be observed that many of the issues addressed in Round 1 reports continue to be addressed in Round 2, suggesting the persistence of key problems. There are also many positive elements in national attempts to address these issues. Particular sensitivity to questions of racism is displayed by a large number of countries; ECRI finds pertinent legislation throughout most countries examined, and well-developed and structured approaches to tackling problems.

Most countries exhibit a generally tolerant approach towards minority groups, though the globalisation-induced speeding-up of migration flows has produced strains in the social fabric. A number of countries have developed specialised bodies to address racism, and such developments are regularly commended by ECRI. Democratic reforms are also regularly commended and proceed apace in states recovering from totalitarian government. The situation of Roma/Gypsies in many countries also varies – there are laudable and innovative attempts to address discrimination against Roma/Gypsy communities.[56]

Some issues of minority rights

Some of the reports are of special interest in the context of a work devoted to issues concerning minorities – in terms of ECRI's approach and that of the state concerned. In the Round 2 report on France, the non-recognition issue was present throughout,[57] wherein ECRI reiterates its call for ratifications,[58] and observes again that rights of individuals connected with their identity suffer from the non-recognition approach.[59] The position of vulnerable groups is postulated as another consequence of non-recognition. Following ECRI's Round 2 reports, observations from the French authorities amount to a spirited attempt to rebut some accusations and defend the "French republican model",[60] noting that the government "is obviously not unaware of the limits of the France model for integration, but it considers that the fight against racism and intolerance must be waged according to this model".[61]

ECRI's Round 2 report[62] on Greece welcomes this country's ratification of the ICCPR (a recommendation of ECRI) and notes that signature and ratification of Council of Europe instruments on minority rights (Greece has signed the Framework Convention) are under consideration.[63] In the report, the situation of a number of "vulnerable groups" is assessed – religious groups in general, Jewish communities and Macedonians.

The report contains a substantial section on issues of particular concern with headings on "The challenge of a multicultural society", "Roma/ Gypsies", "Albanians" and "Members of the Muslim minority of western Thrace". The sections of the ECRI make use of the case-law before the European Court of Human Rights.[64] The observations of the Greek authorities note that Greek laws and policies "do not stem from any theoretical/ideological position as to the compositional character of ... Greek society", but on the other hand "do not imply adherence by the Greek Government to the notion of a multicultural character of ... Greek society"[65], a position which, in itself, possesses ideological significance.

Two observations by ECRI stand out in the Round 2 report[66] on Turkey. The first concerns elements of Turkish law which:

> stipulate that it is forbidden to form associations which: work against the unity of the Turkish State; involve in activities based on the principle of region, social class, religion or sect; claim that there are minorities based on the same principles, or 'create' minorities by promoting languages other than Turkish. Although some of these provisions provide grounds for the prevention of the establishment of associations with racist or discriminatory aims, ECRI is concerned that they also excessively restrict the possibilities for different groups within Turkey to express their ethnocultural and linguistic identity through the establishment of associations.[67]

The second observation (listed among issues of particular concern) is made in the context of some amelioration of the long-running conflict in south-east Turkey. Commencing with an appraisal of the "Republican model" which, *inter alia*, "does not give any official recognition to ethnic background at the level of the State",[68] ECRI concludes that:

> this new context of reduced tension constitutes an ideal opportunity for a more open attitude towards cultural and linguistic plurality within Turkey, allowing more space for non-violent public as well as private expression of cultural and ethnic identity to the benefit of members of all groups who are part of the Turkish society.[69]

The above examples are included precisely because they echo arguments that run throughout the present work. It is clear that ECRI allies itself with basic propositions of international law concerning the existence of minorities and the role of the state in making "determinations" of various kinds. ECRI is also aware of the increased recognition of minority rights in the international canon, and of the inter-relationship between practices of discrimination and refusal to recognise the presence of particular groups. Notions of pluralism and diversity are diffused throughout ECRI's assessments – including its appreciation of the positive effect on interethnic relations of state policies that welcome and embrace diversity. These questions are not tangential to combating racism; on the contrary they are "the heart of the matter" for many societies.

In Round 2, the "observations" appended by states look as if they will become a regular aspect, if not a formalised aspect, of the ECRI process – a development which has analogues elsewhere in the field of human rights. By the end of 2002, State observations on Round 2 reports had been made by Austria, Belgium, Bulgaria, Croatia, Denmark, Estonia, France, Georgia, Germany, Greece, Hungary, Italy, Latvia, Norway, Poland, Portugal, Romania, the Russian Federation, Turkey, the United Kingdom and "the former Yugoslav Republic of Macedonia".[70]

Most of these do not "challenge" the conceptual basis of ECRI action; nor do they delineate a specific citizenship concept. The government responses in general seek to express and where necessary challenge the Commission on points of law and fact, provide updates of developments in the field of racism and racial discrimination, and provide further, detailed information. Minority rights "issues" surface only occasionally – such as for example in the government argumentation on the rights and status of non-citizens in Estonia and Latvia, which should be understood against the background of vibrant arguments on the definition of the concept of "minority", and its application in the Baltic States.[71]

Work on general themes

i. *General policy recommendations*

As part of its activity on general themes, ECRI works on a series of general policy recommendations addressed to the governments of all member states.[72] They cover the main areas of racism and intolerance and provide basic guidelines for the development of comprehensive national policies. The first recommendation, entitled "Combating racism, xenophobia, anti-semitism and intolerance" divides into a lengthy pre-amble, section A "Concerning law, enforcement and judicial remedies", and section B "Concerning policies in a number of areas".

The preamble recites ECRI's conviction that "effectively countering racism, xenophobia, anti-semitism and intolerance requires a sustained and comprehensive approach reflected in a broad range of measures which complement and reinforce one another, covering all aspects of life". The recommendation also emphasises that legal measures alone are not enough, but are nevertheless of paramount importance "and that non-enforcement of relevant existing legislation discredits action against racism and intolerance in general".

Section A contains a raft of recommendations, including defining common offences that have a racist or xenophobic nature as specific offences, and enabling racist or xenophobic motives of offenders to be taken into account. It is also proposed that incitement to hatred against racial, ethnic, national or religious groups should be legally categorised as criminal offences, and that measures should be taken to combat racist organisations (banning them if necessary) "bearing in mind the fact that they can pose a threat to the human rights of minority groups". Awareness of anti-racist legislation, consistent prosecution of racist offences, and adequate remedies for victims of discrimination are also called for.

582

Section B focuses on information, education and training, and calls for school curricula to enhance the appreciation of cultural diversity. Special training is envisaged for police, criminal justice personnel and prison staff, as well as personnel dealing with non-citizens, in particular, refugees and asylum seekers. Among other points, minority group recruitment into public services is to be encouraged, and there should be non-discriminatory delivery of public services to all members of the public. The state is also encouraged to engage in research in the racism area, and collect data which will assist in evaluating the situation and experiences of groups suffering discrimination. Finally, a list of international legal instruments which the state is invited to ratify is included in an appendix.

Recommendation 2 deals with the particular question of "Specialised bodies to combat racism, xenophobia, anti-semitism and intolerance at national level". The preamble takes into account work done at the United Nations and the Council of Europe on national institutions for the promotion and protection of human rights,[73] observing that a number of states have set up specialised bodies in the racism field. Accordingly, ECRI invites states "to consider carefully the possibility of setting up a specialised body to combat racism ... at national level, if such a body does not already exist". The ECRI position is that the regular judicial and administrative system alone is not adequate to deal with racism and allied phenomena and that specialised bodies are required for an effective policy.

The appendix to the recommendation sets out basic principles, suggesting as alternatives the creation of national commissions for racial equality, discrimination ombudsmen, centres for combating racism, and so on.[74] Considerable emphasis is laid on the independence of such institutions and the provision of clear terms of reference.[75] It is suggested that the composition of specialised bodies "should reflect society at large and its diversity";[76] accessibility is also a desideratum.[77] On their powers (states should provide as many as possible of the following list), the spectrum of possibilities includes expression of opinion to state organs, working for friendly settlements, initiation of proposals for better laws and practice, and provision of aid and assistance to victims. Further ECRI work on the theme of institutions has developed the concepts of Recommendation 2.[78]

Recommendation 3 deals with the substantive question of "Combating racism and intolerance against Roma/Gypsies".[79] The recommendation was drafted in consultation with European Roma organisations.[80] The preamble in this case is substantial and, besides referring to work elsewhere in the Council of Europe, incorporates statements on the community of shared values that is Europe, and of which the Council of

Europe is "the embodiment and guardian". The horrors of war visited on the Roma community are recalled, in particular their suffering and deaths from policies of "racist persecution and extermination". The focus on a particular minority is justified in the light of the fact that

> Roma/Gypsies suffer throughout Europe from persisting prejudices, are victims of a racism which is deeply-rooted in society, are the target of sometimes violent demonstrations of racism and intolerance and their fundamental rights are regularly violated or threatened.

Recommendations to address discrimination and related phenomena against Roma include the important point, from a minority rights perspective, that states ensure that "the name used officially for the various Roma/Gypsy communities should be the name by which the community in question wishes to be known". This applies the principle of self-identification discussed elsewhere in the present work to the level of the community.

Further, states are recommended to ensure legal aid for Roma victims of racism, and to deny impunity to those who commit crimes against the Roma. This is coupled with a provision that lack of impunity should be known to the general public. Training for justice personnel is envisaged, and dialogue between police, Roma and local authorities encouraged. Other recommendations resonate with themes explored in the present work. The collision between Roma travelling practices and settled communities in the jurisprudence of the ECHR is recalled in the demand to ensure that "the questions relating to 'travelling' ... in particular regulations concerning residence and town planning, are solved in a way which does not hinder the way of life of the persons concerned".

Respect for the Roma way of life is built in to the ECHR, but may be placed in the context of other considerations relating to public order and town planning. The ECRI recommendation in effect makes the point that this is a freedom-of-movement question with clear cultural implications. Minority rights to participation in decision-making processes are reflected in the injunction to develop appropriate institutional arrangements to facilitate participation. The recommendation recalls the plight of Roma/Gypsy women, suffering from double discrimination, calls upon states to combat educational segregation, and looks to a place for the history and culture of Roma in the educational curricula of all schools.

Recommendation 4 focuses on "National surveys on the experience and perception of discrimination and racism from the point of view of potential victims" – from minorities and other vulnerable groups. The idea is to contribute to a more comprehensive understanding of discrimination. Surveys are envisaged as highlighting areas for remedial action, and increase public understanding and awareness of problems as seen from victim perspectives. An extensive set of guidelines for the organisation and design of surveys is appended to the recommendation.

The preamble to General Policy Recommendation 5, on "Combating intolerance and discrimination against Muslims",[81] recalls key articles of the ECHR (9 and 14), the work of the Parliamentary Assembly[82] and the European Committee on Migration,[83] and "Islam's positive contribution to the continuing development of European societies of which it is an integral part". The preamble also observes that intolerance towards Islam and Muslim communities is increasing in countries where Muslims are in a minority,[84] sometimes on the basis of stereotypical images of Islam which do not reflect "the great diversity intrinsic in the practice of this religion". Preambular reflections are followed by a string of recommendations on ensuring non-discrimination and imposing sanctions for violations, raising awareness in public institutions,[85] taking the necessary measures to end discrimination on the ground of religious belief in connection with access to citizenship, education, employment, assessing "whether Muslim communities suffer from discrimination associated with social exclusion" and if they do, taking measures to combat the phenomenon.

A particular point is made on the need to guarantee freedom of religious practice, including removal of "unnecessary legal or administrative obstacles to the construction of sufficient numbers of appropriate places of worship for the practice of Islam". The recommendation adverts to "double discrimination" against Muslim women, and – as elsewhere – to the issue of the school curriculum. On the latter, states should

> ensure that curricula in schools and higher education, especially in the field of history teaching, do not present distorted interpretations of religious and cultural history and do not base their portrayal of Islam on perceptions of hostility and menace.

The recommendation concludes with a series of proposals directed to the facilitation and encouragement of local and national dialogue, and media responsibility "to avoid perpetuating prejudice and biased information". States are also urged to monitor and evaluate the effectiveness of measures in the various spheres above.

A sixth General Policy Recommendation entitled "Combating the dissemination of racist, xenophobic and anti-Semitic material via the Internet" was adopted on 15 December 2000.[86] The recommendation recalls, *inter alia*, Article 4 of the Convention on the Elimination of All Forms of Racial Discrimination, and Recommendation R (97) 20 of the CoM on hate speech, as well as elements of ECRI General Policy Recommendation 1, and the general conclusions of the European

Conference against Racism. The work of the Council of Europe in processing a convention on cybercrime is also referred to.[87] The recommendation stresses the positive as well as the negative uses of the Internet, the need for international solutions to address the negative aspects, and the importance of incorporating the dimensions of racism and xenophobia, and the like, in developing international and national legislation, international co-operation programmes, and so on. A clarification of responsibilities under Internet law is also recommended, and the development of public awareness (including awareness-raising among children) of the uses of the Internet for racist purposes.

Elements of ECRI's seventh general policy recommendation, on national legislation to combat racism and racial discrimination, adopted on 13 December 2002, have been the subject of comment above. Following the section on definitions, the recommendation includes paragraphs on constitutional law, civil and administrative law, criminal law, and "common provisions".[88] According to the explanatory report, the ensemble of recommendations "focuses on the key elements of national legislation to combat racism and racial discrimination", adding that although ECRI "is aware that legal means alone are not sufficient to this end, it believes that national legislation against racism and racial discrimination is necessary to combat these phenomena effectively".[89]

The message that laws are essential but not enough is contained in the preamble to the recommendation, together with the notion that legislating against racism and racial discrimination also plays an educative function within society, "transmitting the powerful message that no attempts to legitimise racism and racial discrimination will be tolerated in a society ruled by law".[90] The overall thrust of the recommendation is towards enacting new legislation or completing existing legislation, ensuring that key components set out in the text are provided for by law.

The section on constitutional law recommends that the principle of equal treatment, the promotion of equality and the prohibition of discrimination should all be enshrined in the constitution, and that exceptions to the principle of equal treatment may be established by law provided they do not constitute discrimination. The second element in this section goes to another key question in the area of racism, in that it recommends that freedom of speech, assembly and association "may be restricted with a view to combating racism".[91]

The recommendations on civil and administrative law envisage states making clear legislative definitions and prohibitions of direct and indirect discrimination; making provision for exempting – from the prohibition of discrimination – temporary special measures for disadvantaged persons;[92] listing acts such as segregation and "announced intention to discriminate"[93] as forms of discrimination; prohibiting both public and private discrimination; placing public authorities under a duty to promote equality, and ensuring that public contracts are awarded on a non-discriminatory basis; providing remedies and sanctions for racial discrimination; reviewing legislation and administrative provisions at all levels for discriminatory elements; prohibiting racial harassment; and making provision for suppression of any public financing of racist organisations, as well as for the dissolution of organisations promoting racism. The section also addresses the question of burden of proof, recommending that it be placed upon the respondent if the plaintiff establishes facts from which the discrimination may be presumed.[94]

The section on criminal law, besides listing basic criminal acts which should be penalised, and suggesting that racist motivation for criminal offences should constitute an aggravating factor, recommends also the penalisation, when committed intentionally, of "the public expression, with a racist aim, of an ideology which claims the superiority of, or which depreciates or denigrates, a grouping of persons on the grounds of their race".[95] This is followed by a recommendation for penalisation under the same condition of "the public denial, trivialisation, justification or condoning, with a racist aim, of crimes of genocide, crimes against humanity or war crimes."[96] Although, in this context, the explanatory report confines itself to a mention of the Convention against Genocide and the Statute of the International Criminal Court,[97] the recommendation would also be appropriate to address issues of "Holocaust denial".

Finally, the section on "common provisions" looks to national establishment of an independent, specialised body to combat racism and racial discrimination with wide powers including powers related to court proceedings, and awareness-raising,[98] as well as one or more independent bodies to investigate discrimination in the army, police, prisons and similar organisations.[99]

ii. *Collection and dissemination of examples of good practices*

In the course of its work, ECRI commenced building up a collection of positive examples from member states in dealing with racism, and decided to make these good practices known.[100] These do not amount to ECRI recommendations, and are not accompanied by explicit value judgements.[101] Examples from the first compilation include those dealing with areas such as education and training,[102] specialised bodies,[103] awareness-raising,[104] police training, cultural life,[105] vulnerable groups,[106] employment, media,[107] statistics and research – including scientific conferences and the suggestion from Austria that xenophobia be designated as a focal area in the social sciences – and mediation. A further twenty-one examples of mostly media-orientated good practices are set out in a second compilation of April 2000,[108] relating to the press, radio, television, training, trades unions and associations, and prizes.[109] As noted, the most recent compilation – not explicitly styled "good practices" – relates to combating racism against Roma/Gypsies.[110]

iii. *Protocol No. 12 to the European Convention on Human Rights*

ECRI has also made a major contribution to the development of Protocol No. 12 of the ECHR, initially through findings submitted to the CoM, findings which proposed a new protocol. In proposing the protocol, ECRI recognised that law alone cannot eliminate racism in its many forms, but that the achievement of racial justice cannot succeed without the law. ECRI closely followed the process of developing the text, and, following its adoption, continues to promote the prompt ratification of the protocol by member states.

iv. *Relations with civil society*

ECRI has also issued a policy statement on relations with NGOs,[111] which deals with the issues in general and the contribution of NGOs to the country-by-country work and other activity. In particular, ECRI seeks to enhance the NGO role in its reporting, and welcomes NGO assistance in disseminating them. The focus is primarily on national NGOs within the ECRI areas of competence. The annual report for 2000 states that:

> Specific co-operation between ECRI and NGOs in 2000 focused above all on developing relations and exchanging information during the contact visits prior to the drawing up of the second stage country-by-country reports. ECRI also provided active support for a number of NGO-organised events ... ECRI Secretariat's involvement in the European preparations for the World Conference against Racism ... also provided an opportunity for increased co-operation with NGOs working to combat racism and intolerance.[112]

The European Conference against Racism

A comprehensive raft of recommendations emerged from the European Conference against Racism in October 2000, called to address the changing manifestations of racism under the impact of globalisation. The conference was prepared by governmental experts within a technical working group at which ECRI was represented. The conference focused on four main themes:

- legal protection against racism and related discrimination at sub-national, national, regional and international levels;

- policies and practices to combat racism at sub-national and national level;
- education and awareness-raising to combat racism at local, national, regional and international levels;
- information, communication and the media.

ECRI drafted position papers on all four themes.[113] Participants adopted general conclusions, and ministers adopted a Political Declaration at the close of the conference. The general conclusions draw on ECRI general policy recommendations and, *inter alia*, invite states to take fully into account the recommendations of monitoring mechanisms at national, European and international levels, "including the country-specific approach of the European Commission against Racism and Intolerance",[114] and also call on participating states, as appropriate, to "consider how best to reinforce the action of [ECRI]".[115]

The Political Declaration expresses a commitment to "consider how best to reinforce European bodies active in combating racism, discrimination and related intolerance, in particular the European Commission against Racism and Intolerance".[116] ECRI's "stream of discourse" is reflected in many provisions of the final text of the World Conference against Racism, notably in paragraphs of the declaration and programme of action dealing with "Roma/Gypsies/Sinti/Travellers", Islamophobia, the uses of the Internet, the need for specialised national institutions to combat racism, and the need for accurate statistics as an indispensable aspect of social policies in the area of race relations.[117]

Concise assessment

Annual reports attempt to draw up an inventory of the main trends encountered by ECRI in its work. Among others, the trends demonstrate the magnitude of ECRI's tasks. The annual report for 1999 identifies "persistent racial and ethnic discrimination in such areas as employment, housing and the provision of services"[118] as features recurring in its country analyses, as well as the lack of effective and comprehensive anti-discrimination legal provisions. This may be summarised as the gap between rhetoric and reality. ECRI finds racism and prejudice prevalent in public institutions, an increase in complaints of racism against the police, an increasing use of mass communication technologies for racist purposes, intensification of the spread of anti-Semitic ideas, hostility towards persons of immigrant origin – often stoked up by politicians and the media – and moves by otherwise democratic parties towards extreme views in order to win votes.

On the positive side, there are trends towards an increasing commitment on the part of states and civil society to combat negative phenomena, as well as new legislation and increasing recognition and public debate about racism and allied phenomena, so that it is possible to say that; "racism, xenophobia, anti-semitism and intolerance and the need to counter these phenomena are beginning to be seen as issues that are crucial to the survival of democracy in European societies". The trends implicitly set out a formidable challenge to ECRI and analogous bodies in the anti-racism field. The annual report for 2000, which identified a range of similar issues, cited the Commissioner for Human Rights for the statement that "[c]ompleting anti-discrimination legislation at national level remains a priority. It is incredible – but true – that in the year 2000 not all countries possess such legislation".[119]

The same report notes the recrudescence of racist violence in many countries, and the use of racist and xenophobic propaganda in politics. On this[120]

> ECRI believes that there is, unfortunately, insufficient opposition at present to extremism – particularly that of political parties. The line crossed by certain democratic parties when entering into coalition with extremist, racist and xenophobic political parties in order to exercise power is a real danger; such coalitions gradually trivialise the use of racist and xenophobic arguments in the day-to-day life of countries.[121]

The report for 2000 also observes that "[p]rejudice against Muslim communities (Islamophobia) is a disturbing trend, manifested in violence, harassment, discrimination, general negative attitudes and stereotypes".[122] Nevertheless, on the positive side, there is new legislation in a number of countries, as well as good practice, the renewed commitment of European states through the European Conference against Racism, the adoption and opening for signature of Protocol No. 12 to the European Convention on Human Rights, and perhaps most important, an increasing acknowledgement within European society of the problems of racism, xenophobia, anti-semitism and intolerance.

The main lines of ECRI concern, and the recognition of positive developments, are further adumbrated in the reports for 2001 and 2002. A fresh note is struck by the Commission concerning the events of 11 September 2001 – the "attack on America". In the 2001 report, ECRI recalls the "ignominious" attack of 11 September as a demonstration of how terrorist activities, irrespective of their origins, threaten democratic values. In line with other human rights bodies,[123] ECRI states that it is "convinced that effective measures must be taken to combat terrorism, but strongly believes that this combat must not become a pretext under which discrimination and intolerance are allowed to flourish. The response to the threat of terrorism should not weaken the protection and promotion of human rights".[124]

The report for 2002 notes, in the context of an observation on the unsatisfactory implementation of anti-racist provisions, the adoption by ECRI of General Policy Recommendation No. 7. The report restates the main themes of previous reports, and adds to its previous expressions of concern at the phenomenon of Islamophobia the observation that this phenomenon became more acute in several countries following the terrorist attacks of 11 September 2001.[125] In terms of legislation addressing racism and racial discrimination, ECRI welcomes the fact that most member states are in the process of revising legislation, and that implementation is receiving increased attention at the national level. The adoption of the additional protocol to the Convention on Cybercrime, and of Protocol 12, and of the ECRI Statute, were all to be welcomed – in the last case as an expression of "the determination of the member states to continue to co-operate in combating racism ... within the framework of the Council of Europe."[126]

ECRI recognises that the challenges faced by institutions dedicated to transforming thought and practice in the field of racism and intolerance are formidable. ECRI's position paper for the European Conference against Racism[127] envisages further contributions which it could make in its field "subject to the granting of adequate resources", including production of anti-racist educational materials, perhaps co-operating in this with the EU European Monitoring Centre on Racism and Xenophobia; supplying expertise to governments; meeting with NGOs for exchanges of ideas and experiences; and developing flexible machinery for co-operating with CERD at European level on specific topics.

ECRI adds to the battery of international instruments and bodies which address fundamental questions of discrimination and intolerance. Its effectiveness will be measured by what it adds to the whole, by the nature and distinctiveness of its contribution; otherwise the exercise could be judged superfluous. The institution may be open to criticism for appearing unduly intergovernmental; while the performance of the individual members of ECRI may carry through ECRI's mandate in an objective and professional manner, the nature of the appointment process could give cause for concern, though the new statute enhances the independence of the members.[128] The transparency of processes is not enhanced by the emphasis on private meetings.

On the other hand, judged by output to date, ECRI would rank as one of the stronger bodies in the fight against racism and intolerance. The recommendations appear comprehensive and competent, and address questions of substantial importance. The active programme of country visits suggests strongly that ECRI is a "hands-on", pro-active institution. The potential consciousness-raising and galvanising effect of recommendations in the cases of Roma/Gypsies and Muslims is considerable.

Although ECRI is only one of many bodies addressing the latter issues, it is in a position to integrate the prescriptions in its general recommendations with practical action. The focus on Islamophobia is more relevant than ever in the post-September 11 world, and particularly in view of the high levels of immigration to Council of Europe states from North Africa and elsewhere in the Muslim world. ECRI combines concern for traditional minorities with concern for immigrants, and its work is infused with awareness of currents of thought and practice deriving from the UN and other intergovernment bodies.

ECRI's reports mount a sustained critique of principle as well as practice in the states examined. Their effectiveness many be gauged in part by the responses they elicit – they have clearly provided food for thought for authorities in the respondent states, who have sometimes been minded to reply in strong terms. ECRI's approach to minority rights is very much in line with the instruments in that sphere which they regularly encourage the states to sign and ratify. Reports have interpreted the underlying philosophy of minority rights as well as making a raft of specific suggestions and focusing on issues of particular concern. A cardinal virtue of the approach is the even-handedness between states of the east and west of Europe: this is ECRI's effort to address the historic problem of double standards in the application of minority rights which plagued international law even before the League of Nations.

On the whole, ECRI's work does not dig deep into sociology, social psychology and related disciplines in order to explain and address racism. Nor is there detailed reflection on the scope of international norms concerning the basic phenomena which the institution is dedicated to combat. However, the definitions of racism, and of direct and indirect discrimination, in General Policy Recommendation No. 7 make a distinctive contribution to the understanding of the international normative framework, and further clarifications of key concepts are likely in the ongoing process of combating discrimination. Besides its clarifying definitions, ECRI's treatment of minority rights, Roma issues and Islamophobia in the elaboration of its mandate means that it is drawn inexorably into a function properly described as the "development of discourse", which will, in the longer run, add to our readings of troubling conceptual and practical issues, and how to address them.

Notes

1.	The phrase is used four times in the charter, commencing with Article 1, paragraph 3.

2.	Peremptory norms of general international law from which no derogation is permitted – see P. Thornberry, *International Law and the Rights of Minorities* (Oxford: Clarendon Press, 1991), Chapters 29-37.

3.	Adopted by the General Assembly of the United Nations in Resolution 2106 A, 21 December 1965. The convention is described by ECRI as "the cornerstone of the fight against racism at the global level" – ECRI position paper for the European Conference against Racism, 2000, text in *European Conference against Racism, Proceedings* (Secretariat of ECRI and Directorate General of Human Rights – DG II, Council of Europe, Strasbourg), pp. 267-84, at p. 269.

4.	A definition influenced by the ILO Discrimination (Employment and Occupation) Convention 1958.

5.	M. Banton, *International Action against Racial Discrimination* (Oxford: Clarendon Press, 1996), p. 76. For a synopsis of the work of UNESCO in deconstructing "race", see K. Boyle and A. Baldaccini, "A critical evaluation of international human rights approaches to racism", in S. Fredman (ed.), *Discrimination and Human Rights: the Case of Racism* (Oxford: Oxford University Press, 2001), p. 152, No. 77. For an extended account of the problematique of "race", see M. Banton, *Racial Theories* (Cambridge University Press, 2nd edition 1998); and "The historical context of racial classification", *1984 UNESCO Yearbook of Peace and Conflict Studies* (Westport, Conn: Greenwood Press, 1986), pp. 79-127. The UNESCO Declaration on Race and Racial Prejudice 1978 is discussed in P. Thornberry, *International Law and the Rights of Minorities*, ch. 33. See also the illuminating collection of essays in B. Boxill (ed.), *Race and Racism* (Oxford: Oxford University Press, 2001) and J. Rex, *Race and Ethnicity* (Milton Keynes: Open University Press, 1986).

6.	In the preamble and Article 4, respectively. See below on ECRI General Policy Recommendation No. 7, which offers a definition of "racism". The recommendation also comments on "race": a footnote to paragraph 1 on its use makes the point that: "Since all human beings belong to the same species, ECRI rejects theories based on the existence of different 'races'. However, in this recommendation ECRI uses this term in order to ensure that those persons who are generally and erroneously perceived as belonging to 'another race' are not excluded from the protection provided for by the legislation".

7.	Political Declaration of 13 October 2000, adopted by the ministers of Council of Europe member states at the concluding session of the European Conference against Racism: text in *European Conference against Racism: Proceedings*, p. 13. The European Conference against Racism was a contribution to the World Conference against Racism, Racial Discrimination, Xenophobia and Related Intolerance which took place in Durban, South Africa in August/September 2001.

8.	There is extensive reference to the work of such bodies in two ECRI compilations: Recommendations adopted by the Parliamentary Assembly of the Council of Europe in the field of Combating Racism and Intolerance, CRI (98) 28 (Strasbourg, 1998); and Recommendations adopted by the Committee of Ministers, CRI (98) 16 (Strasbourg, 1998).

9.	Chapter 1 above.

10.	Ibid.

11.	Chapter 2 above.

12.	*European Conference against Racism: Proceedings*, p. 15. For the work of the Commissioner, see Chapter 12 of the present work.

13.   Introduction. The initial terms of reference are to review legislation and policies in the fields of racism, etc.; to propose further action at local, national and European level; to formulate general policy recommendations to member states; and to study applicable international legal instruments with a view to their reinforcement where appropriate. Updated terms of reference are incorporated in the ECRI statute – below.

14.   ECRI position paper, p. 268. See further, Chapter 5.

15.   Resolution Res(2002)8, adopted at the 799th meeting of the Ministers' Deputies. The preamble to the resolution recites elements in the history and motivation for the strengthening of the position of ECRI; the statute is contained in the appendix to the resolution.

16.   Article 1.

17.   Ibid.

18.   Article 1.

19.   Article 2.2.

20.   Article 2.3.

21.   Article 3.3; cf. Article 3.4. relating to change in a member's situation.

22.   Provisions on deputies are set out in Article 4. For provisions on representation in ECRI without the right to vote for various bodies, including the Management Board of the European Monitoring Centre on Racism and Xenophobia, see Article 5.

23.   Article 6.4.

24.   Article 6.5. Meetings of ECRI are held in camera "unless ECRI decides otherwise" – Article 8.1.

25.   Article 10.

26.   Article 11.1.

27.   Article 11.3. The reports shall also include appendices with the viewpoints of the national authorities "where the latter deem it necessary". These national viewpoints do not form part of ECRI's analysis.

28.   Article 12.

29.   CRI (2001) 20, p. 5. See also the preamble to Res(2002)8 – above.

30.   "ECRI and its programme of activities" – from CRI (99) 53 rev 2, on ECRI website http://www.coe.int/ecri

31.   On the other hand, this situation arises frequently in the vast span of groups addressed in state reports to CERD. It is a reasonable supposition that CERD will take up this issue in future.

32.   Discussed below.

33.   Adopted on 13 December 2002, CRI (2003) 8.

34.   Paragraph 1 of the Recommendation. The explanatory report adds (paragraph 7) that "For racism to have taken place, it is not necessary that one or more of the grounds listed should constitute the only factor or the determining factor leading to contempt or the notion of superiority; it suffices that these grounds are among the factors leading to contempt or the notion of superiority." The definition relates in part to Article 4 of ICERD which explicitly prohibits "all dissemination of ideas based on racial superiority or hatred". Concerning the "grounds" of discrimination, the phrase "such as" (used also for direct and indirect discrimination) indicates that these are not exhaustive, though the explanatory report suggests (paragraph 6) that "in criminal law, an exhaustive list of grounds could be established in order to respect the principle of foreseeability which governs this branch of the law".

594

35. The explanatory report adds (paragraph 8) that "differential treatment based on race, colour or ethnic origin may have an objective and reasonable justification only in an extremely limited number of cases ... More generally, the notion of objective and reasonable justification should be interpreted as restrictively as possible with respect to differential treatment based on any of the enumerated grounds".

36. Directive 2000/43/CE of the Council of the European Union implementing the principle of equal treatment between persons irrespective of racial or ethnic origin; Directive 2000/78/CE establishing a general framework for equal treatment in employment and occupation.

37. See Chapter 1.

38. See "ECRI's country-by-country procedure" and related documents, in Procedural Documents, CRI (98) 18, pp. 19-24. By the end of 2002, second-round reports were available for Albania, Austria, Belgium, Bulgaria, Croatia, Cyprus, the Czech Republic, Denmark, Estonia, Finland, France, Georgia, Germany, Greece, Hungary, Ireland, Italy, Latvia, Malta, the Netherlands, Norway, Poland, Portugal, Romania, the Russian Federation, Slovakia, Switzerland, "the former Yugoslav Republic of Macedonia", Turkey, Ukraine and the United Kingdom: information from ECRI website: http://www.coe.int/ecri

39. Annual report for 2000, (CRI (2001) 20, p. 11.

40. In practice assisted by the ECRI Secretariat.

41. The ECRI member from the state concerned is invited to provide comments before the draft country-specific texts are transmitted to ECRI: Procedure; Modalities of implementation, adopted by ECRI at its 7th Plenary Meeting, 5-8 March 1996, Procedural Documents, p. 19. Hannikainen comments that the national member "should avoid becoming an advocate of his/her country and should act in accordance with his/her proper role as an independent member" – ibid., p. 187.

42. L. Hannikainen, "The European Commission against Racism and Intolerance (ECRI)", in L. Hannikainen and E. Nykanen (eds.), *New Trends in Discrimination Law: International Perspectives* (Turku: Turku Law School, 1999), pp. 177-220, at pp. 186-87.

43. Procedural Documents, p. 19.

44. Ibid.

45. Recall Article 11.3. of the Statute – above.

46. Decisions adopted by the ministers' deputies at their 598th meeting, 1-3 July 1997, Procedural Documents, p. 20. At this meeting, the ministers' deputies stated their understanding that "as regards the transmission of country-by-country texts to the governments concerned, the Committee of Ministers will not take a stand on the content of these texts."

47. Ibid.

48. Docs. CRI (98) 59, CRI (98) 71, Addendum 1, CRI (98) 72. For reports to the beginning of 2001, see above.

49. In 1999, contact visits were made to Belgium, Bulgaria, the Czech Republic, France, Greece, Hungary, Norway, Poland, Slovakia and Switzerland: Annual Report for 1999, section 10. In 2000, visits were made to Albania, Austria, Croatia, Cyprus, Denmark, Germany, the Netherlands, the Russian Federation, "the former Yugoslav Republic of Macedonia", Turkey and the United Kingdom – Annual Report for 2000, paragraph 12. In 2001, visits were made to Estonia, Finland, Georgia, Ireland, Italy, Latvia, Malta, Portugal, Romania and Ukraine: Annual Report for 2001, Appendix III. In 2002, the programme continued with contact visits to Andorra, Armenia, Azerbaijan, Iceland, Liechtenstein, Lithuania, Luxembourg, Moldova, San Marino, Slovenia, Spain and Sweden: Annual Report for 2002 (CRI (2002) 23, Appendix III.

50.   The "national liaison officer "is the person nominated by the government in question to act as contact person of the authorities with ECRI.

51.   Annual report for 1999, section 5, paragraph 12.

52.   Ibid., paragraphs 14 and 15.

53.   For the reports see Docs. CRI (97) 48 – Vol. I; CRI (98) 21 – Vol. II; CRI (98) 54 – Vol. III; CRI (99) 6 – Vol. IV.

54.   Hannikainen, op. cit., p. 189.

55.   In all cases, this is preceded by the explanation that "This section covers certain minority groups which may be vulnerable to particular problems of racism, discrimination and intolerance in the country in question. It is not intended to provide an exhaustive overview of the situation of all minority groups in the county, or to imply that groups not mentioned face no problems of racism and discrimination".

56.   See ECRI, "Practical examples in combating racism and intolerance against Roma/Gypsies", CRI (2001) 28 (Strasbourg, October 2001).

57.   CRI (2000) 31, adopted 10 December 1999.

58.   Round 2 report, paragraphs 1-3.

59.   Paragraph 4.

60.   Observations, paragraph 1.

61.   Ibid.

62.   CRI (2000) 32, adopted 10 December 1999.

63.   Paragraph 1. Ratification of other Council of Europe instruments is recommended, and ECRI reiterates the recommendation to allow individual communications under the International Convention on the Elimination of All Forms of Racial Discrimination – Greece is a party to this convention.

64.   See Chapter 1 of the present work, especially *Ahmet Sadik v. Greece* and *Sidiropoulos v. Greece.* paragraph 44 of the report is relevant to the ECHR case of *Serif v. Greece*, which is not cited.

65.   CRI (2000) 32, p. 25.

66.   CRI (2001) 37, 3 July 2001.

67.   Ibid., paragraph 8.

68.   Ibid., paragraph 53.

69.   Second-round report, paragraph 56.

70.   For later reports, see the ECRI website: http://www.coe.int/ecri

71.   See, in particular, Chapter 2 of the present work.

72.   All the general policy recommendations may now be found on the ECRI website.

73.   Including UN General Assembly Resolution 48/134, 20 December 1993 on national institutions for the promotion and protection of human rights, and the Paris Principles (1991) of the first international meeting of national institutions for ... human rights. The preamble also refers, among others, to Committee of Ministers Recommendation R (85) 13 on the institution of the ombudsman, and the work of the CDDH on independent human rights institutions.

74.   Principle 2.

75.   Principles 1 and 5.

76.   Principle 4.

77.   Principle 6.

78.   According to ECRI's *Annual Report for 1999*, holding regional meetings to encourage and assist the setting up of specialised bodies to combat racism and intolerance in member states is one of ECRI's future priorities: section 6, paragraph 21.

79.   The recommendation is referred to briefly in Chapter 13 below. Compare the ECRI recommendation with the General Recommendation XXVII (2000), adopted by the UN Committee on the Elimination of Racial Discrimination.

80.   Hannikainen, op. cit., p. 193.

81.   Text in *Annual Report for 1999*, p. 20.

82.   Recommendation 1162 on the contribution of Islamic civilisation to European culture, 19 September 1991. See further, Chapter 8.

83.   Strasbourg seminar on religion and the integration of immigrants, 24-26 November 1998. On the work of the CDMG, see further, Chapter 7.

84.   Notwithstanding this, "one of the characteristics of present-day Europe is a trend towards diversity of beliefs within pluralistic societies".

85.   Which should be made aware of "the need to make provision in their everyday practice for legitimate cultural and other requirements arising from the multi-faith nature of society".

86.   CRI (2001) 1. For this general policy recommendation, ECRI drew on a study of *Legal Instruments to Combat Racism on the Internet,* prepared by the Swiss Institute of Comparative Law – CRI (2000) 37, Strasbourg, August 2000. Drawing further on the results of the study, ECRI adopted a number of conclusions which it submitted to the European Conference against Racism – Annual Report for 2000, paragraph 22.

87.   See further, Chapter 5.

88.   The range of international instruments drawn on in the preamble includes, besides the basic texts of international law (ICERD, etc.), more recent developments such as Protocol No. 12 of the ECHR, the Charter of Fundamental Rights of the European Union, the two European Council Directives referred to above, No. 7, the Political Declaration of the European Conference against Racism, and the Declaration and Programme of Action of the Durban World Conference against Racism.

89.   Explanatory report, paragraph 1.

90.   Preamble, penultimate paragraph.

91.   The explanatory report refers in this context to permissible restrictions under articles 10 (2) and 11 (2) of the ECHR. Limitations on these freedoms may also be derived from Article 4 of ICERD.

92.   Compare Article 1.4. and 2.2. of ICERD.

93.   Paragraph 6.

94.   Paragraph 11.

95.   Paragraph 18 (d).

96.   Paragraph 18 (e). Paragraph 19 recommends the penalisation of genocide: on this, the explanatory report observes in paragraph 45 that what is referred to is "penalisation of genocide and not of war crimes and crimes against humanity since these are not necessarily of a racist nature."

97.   Paragraph 41.

98.   Paragraph 24.

99.   Paragraph 28.

100. The first of these collections is entitled "Combating racism and intolerance: a basket of good practices", CRI (96) 38, p. 5.

101. Ibid. The compilation is on the basis of entries from ECRI members from countries concerned, and summaries from the ECRI Secretariat of examples presented particularly in the context of the CDMG.

102. See, in particular, the entry (15) on the Gandhi Secondary School in Budapest, which was established as a school for the Roma/Gypsy population. The relevant page contains the note that: "Although experience has often shown that segregation may lead to a worsening of ethnic problems, the establishment of the Roma/Gypsy secondary school has been accepted as an effective method to help this population integrate into ... Hungarian society". This suggests a certain tension in elaborating an appropriate policy, in view of the general opprobrium attached to the term "segregation" – the report is careful to point out that the project follows a civil initiative by the Roma/Gypsy population, supported by the government. The school is envisaged as having a life of thirty to fifty years, since the purpose of the segregated education is to make higher education accessible to Roma/Gypsies. Lessons are given by Roma/Gypsy and Hungarian teachers, and two languages and cultures are conveyed in a pluralist ethos.

103. Including presidential round tables, mediation bodies, anti-racism units, anti-discrimination centres, and federal commissions against racism.

104. Through drama, solidarity statements, exhibitions, television programmes, etc.

105. Through story-telling, dialogue groups, festivals and suchlike.

106. Concerning immigrant groups, and various Roma projects.

107. Including multicultural radio stations.

108. CRI (2000) 19.

109. The foreword states (6) that the examples have been compiled by a consultant journalist and that the publication "does not fall under the responsibility of ECRI, the Council of Europe or its member states. The examples which follow should in no respect be regarded as recommendations to the member states of the Council of Europe".

110. Cited above. See also the *Annual Report for 2001*, paragraph 20; *Annual Report for 2002*, paragraph 22.

111. CRI (98) 32.

112. *Annual Report for 2000*, paragraph 29. See also the *Annual Report for 2001*, p. 16; *Annual Report for 2002*, p. 19.

113. *European Conference against Racism*, Proceedings, pp. 267-84.

114. General Conclusions of the European Conference against Racism, in *European Conference against Racism, Proceedings*, pp. 19-38, paragraph 48.

115. Ibid., paragraph 58.

116. *European Conference against Racism, Proceedings*, p. 18.

117. The report of the World Conference against Racism, etc., is contained in UN Doc. A/CONF.189/12.

118. *Annual Report for 1999*, p. 4.

119. *Annual Report for 2000*, p. 7. See discussion above of General Policy Recommendation No. 7.

120. Ibid., pp. 7-10.

121. Ibid., pp. 7-8.

122. *Annual Report for 2000*, p. 8.

123. See, for example, the "Statement on racial discrimination and measures to combat terrorism" adopted by CERD in March 2002: UN Doc. A/57/18, pp. 106-07.

124. *Annual Report for 2001*, paragraph 3. See also the ECRI Declaration of 11 December 2001 endorsing the content of the communique adopted by the Committee of Ministers at its 109th session on 8 November 2001: *Annual Report for 2001*, paragraphs 4 and 5.

125. Paragraph 7.

126. Paragraph 20.

127. *European Conference against Racism, Proceedings*, pp. 267-84.

128. See in particular Articles 2.2, 2.3 and 3.5 of the Statute.

Chapter 12

The Commissioner for Human Rights

Introduction

In the "Budapest Declaration for a greater Europe without dividing lines", and more concretely with the adoption of CoM Resolution (99) 50 contained in Appendix II of the declaration, the Council of Europe Commissioner for Human Rights was instituted, and its terms of reference established.[1] Álvaro Gil-Robles, a former Spanish ombudsman, has been the first person appointed to this position.

Neither the full title of the Commissioner nor his terms of reference mention minority or any other particular area of human rights protection, but refer to human rights generally. Minority issues, however, have become a prominent aspect of the activities of this institution. The mandate given to the Commissioner and the possibilities for minority protection which can be drawn from it are discussed below. Also an overview of the implementation of this mandate, since the first incumbent to the post took up his position in October 1999, is provided.

The mandate of the Commissioner[2]

The character of the institution

The character of the Commissioner's office and his general tasks are established mainly in Article 1 of the resolution. This article refers to the Commissioner as a "non-judicial institution to promote education in, awareness of and respect for human rights, as embodied in the human rights instruments of the Council of Europe". It also indicates that "the Commissioner shall respect the competence of, and perform functions other than those fulfilled by the supervisory bodies set up under" the ECHR "or under other human rights instruments of the Council of Europe", in a clear reference to the need for the Commissioner to avoid overlapping with already existing institutions. Although in Article 1 the reference to the need to avoid duplication of activities focuses on the supervisory bodies of the Council of Europe, in Article 3.i a wider reference to "other international institutions for the promotion and protection of human rights" is also made in conjunction with a reference to the need for the Commissioner to co-operate with existing institutions.

The second part of Article 1 insists once more on denying the judicial or quasi-judicial character of the office by stating that "the Commissioner shall not take up individual complaints". It should be noted, however, that as Article 5.1 of the resolution indicates, and the Commissioner has soon started to underscore, the Commissioner "may act on any information" relevant to his functions. The article also mentions expressly information addressed to him by governments, national parliaments, national ombudsmen or similar institutions in the field of human rights, individuals and organisations. Thus, individual claims, in as far as they may serve as illustrations of a more general pattern of human rights violations, would be relevant to the Commissioner's mandate, and constitute a legitimate object of concern for the Commissioner under Article 5, like any other information provided by individuals and organisations.

In interpreting this aspect of his mandate, the Commissioner himself has indicated that:

> he may act, within the context of the Commissioner's function of promoting human rights, on any relevant information concerning general aspects of the protection of human rights, as enshrined in Council of Europe instruments.
>
> This information and requests may be addressed to the Commissioner by governments, national parliaments, national Ombudsmen or similar institutions, as well as by individuals and organisations.[3]

In this connection it should be noted that at a meeting of the Commissioner with western European ombudsmen held in Paris, particular attention was devoted to how the Commissioner should handle individual complaints, the possibility being discussed that individual complaints received by the Commissioner be forwarded directly, and without prior consultation of the applicant to the national ombudsmen.[4] This measure was justified on grounds of timesaving, although arguments were put forward that this infringed upon the rights of the complainants. However, according to the first annual report of the Commissioner, an agreement was reached that the Commissioner might transfer to the state ombudsmen "individual complaints he believes fall within their competence".[5]

Another, related aspect of the "definition by exclusion" of the Commissioner's role is given in Article 5.2 of the resolution, according to which "the gathering of information relevant to the Commissioner's functions shall not give rise to any general reporting system for member states". This limitation to the Commissioner's competencies may have been built on the argument of the "reporting overburden" to which states are often appealing in recent times, as they complain of having to report on their human rights performance to a plurality of human rights treaty bodies and mechanisms at the universal and regional level. However, this limitation has deprived the Commissioner of a periodical, structured and formal means of dialogue with states on human rights issues, which makes the fulfilment of his duties more difficult.[6] This is especially so in view of the fact that this limitation acts in conjunction with other shortcomings, discussed below.

No exclusions have been established as to the type of human rights protection situations the Commissioner can deal with. Thus, certain limitations – which exist, for example, in the mandate of the OSCE High Commissioner on National Minorities (HCNM) with regard to situations involving organised acts of terrorism – do not apply to the Council of Europe Commissioner for Human Rights.[7] This has allowed the Commissioner to deal with situations in regions where, according to the official position of states, acts of terrorism are carried out. Actually, as discussed below, these types of situations have become the first objective of the Commissioner's activities.

Promotion of human rights

Following the definition by exclusion of the role of the Commissioner in Article 1, Article 3 defines in a positive manner the scope of his duties, which can all be considered as relevant for minority protection. The activities envisaged by this article, in the area of information, advice and promotion, seem to open the door for the Commissioner to acquire the role of a mediator with the state authorities in situations in which the human rights of minorities are violated, although the role of "negotiator or political mediator" between state authorities and the leadership of secessionist regions has been expressly ruled out by the Commissioner.[8]

Nevertheless, mediating attempts cannot be excluded in the case of some initiatives for the organisation of seminars taken by the Commissioner. This seems to have been the case of the seminars organised in connection with the Abkhazian conflict in Georgia (see below). In the seminars organised in relation to the Chechen conflict in the Russian Federation, the Chechen opposition has not been represented so far.

An attempt to curtail the possibility of direct contacts with persons belonging to minorities or minority representatives could possibly be read in the requirement, included in the mandate, that the Commissioner "when dealing with the public ... wherever possible, make use of and co-operate with human rights structures in the member states. Where such structures do not exist, the Commissioner will encourage their establishment".[9] This demand could seem to be geared to the Commissioner prioritising the channelling of his inquiries through "official" human rights structures, rather than freely choosing his inter-locutors. Nothing in the text would seem, however, to prevent the interpretation of the wording of this provision in its wider sense, to include also non-governmental actors, and comprise support for their establishment and effective operation.[10] Article 3.*d* is also a reference point in this connection, as indicated below.[11]

The practical implications of this requirement largely depend on the level of stringency with which the words "wherever possible", are inter-preted by the Commissioner. Those words as such do not define a clear threshold as to a level of difficulty which the Commissioner should encounter and which could undermine the Commissioner's capacity of assessment in this respect, especially in view of the need for the Commissioner to fulfil the remaining duties under his mandate in an efficient manner. The request that states facilitate the Commissioner's contacts, including travel, in the context of his mission and provide information requested by him in good time, would seem to reinforce the Commissioner's discretion as to which structures to engage in contacts, to co-operate with and from which to seek information and advice. It should be emphasised, that the duty of the Commissioner to seek the co-operation of the state concerned would remain unabated, and it undoubtedly constitutes an essential element of the successful develop-ment of his functions.

Another duty of the Commissioner, to "facilitate the activities of national ombudsmen or similar institutions in the field of human rights",[12] is closely connected with his role indicated in Article 3.*d* in establishing human rights structures in those member states where they do not exist. These articles emphasise the role that the Commissioner should play in connection with the establishment and proper functioning of human rights institutions in the Council of Europe member states. The reference to "similar institutions" opens the door for the creation of institutions especially devoted to minority questions, among others.[13] So far, the Commissioner seems to have adopted a positive stance with regard to minority protection in this area of his competence.

During the first meeting of ombudsmen of central and eastern Europe with the Commissioner, held in Budapest, the need for the ombudsmen to devote special attention to minorities and aliens, considered as some of the most vulnerable groups of the population, was underscored.[14] During the second meeting, held in Warsaw, Roma issues were one of the two specific subjects discussed by the ombudsmen. National ombuds-men or "similar institutions" are specifically mentioned as sources of information relevant to the Commissioner's functions.[15] Thus, a close link is established between these institutions and the Commissioner, the former becoming special interlocutors for the dialogue between the Commissioner and the states.

At the second meeting of the Commissioner with ombudsmen of central and eastern Europe, the participants "considered it extremely useful for the Commissioner, when visiting their countries, to call in at their offices to take heed of the information and opinions they put forward".[16] Further, at meetings of the Commissioner both with western ombudsmen on the one hand, and with central and eastern European ombudsmen on the other, it has been agreed that liaison officers should be appointed both at the Commissioner's and the ombudsmen's offices, in order to facilitate co-operation.

In the Commissioner's mandate a clear emphasis has been placed on human rights "promotion" and "assistance" rather than on "assessment" or "evaluation", as can be deduced from the content of the provisions of Article 3. This is further emphasised by the exclusion of the establishment by the Commissioner of any general reporting mechanism. The Commissioner has himself indicated that: "as I see my mandate, I am strictly speaking neither an 'expert rapporteur' nor 'a public prosecutor', nor do I have a specific part to play in your [the CoM's] monitoring procedure".[17]

In spite of the limitations in the Commissioner's mandate – given that references to "promotion" are linked to those of "effective observance", "effective implementation" and "full enjoyment" of human rights – the mandate given to the Commissioner offers possibilities for thorough and in-depth examination of the performance of states in this area, and opens the door to targeted intervention and follow-up by the Commissioner, especially given his capacity for issuing recommendations, opinions and reports, as discussed below. In this framework, individual cases have already been object of the Commissioner's attention.[18] As to the involvement of the Commissioner in the monitoring by the CoM[19] and by the Assembly,[20] the Commissioner, in a recent communication to the Assembly, seems not to have excluded the possibility.[21]

Identification of shortcomings

The emphasis placed on "promotion" in the Commissioner's mandate is reinforced by the wording used in the only reference to his role in examining the performance of the states in the field of human rights. The Commissioner shall "identify possible shortcomings" in the law and practice of member states concerning their compliance with human rights.[22] This activity is further tied up with the qualification "human rights as embodied in the instruments of the Council of Europe". Minority rights find themselves in a relatively good position in this respect, given the progress achieved by the Council of Europe with regard to standards in this field during recent years. No specific instruments are earmarked for the Commissioner to achieve this, leaving a wide variety of options open.

The follow-up action previewed for this identification of shortcomings is that the Commissioner "promote the effective implementation of these standards by member states". The only constraint – and, at the same time, gateway – for the Commissioner is the additional duty to "assist" states, "with their agreement, in their efforts to remedy such short-comings".[23] Thus, the competence given to the Commissioner seems to be geared to encouraging states' efforts, and making proposals for the direction those efforts should follow, possibly taking initiatives within the states concerned with their consent. An important instrument of the Commissioner in this connection is the duty established in Article 6 for states to provide in good time information requested by the Commissioner. Another important instrument is the possibility pre-viewed in Article 9 that the Commissioner "may issue recommendations, opinions and reports".

The competence for the Commissioner to address recommendations to states (whether included in "formal" recommendations, opinions or reports) on the basis of any shortcomings he may have identified – a competence also available to political organs of the Council of Europe – is of the utmost importance for the success of his work. Such recom-mendations, however named, constitute an essential element of his pro-motional function as well as a powerful tool to prevent human rights violations and respond to their occurrence. Whereas other forms of assis-tance provided to states would seem to require the states' agreement, in accordance with Article 3.e the issuing of recommendations, opinions and reports is not subject to this or any other type of constraint.

Besides those country-specific recommendations contained in the visit reports issued by the Commissioner after his missions to states, the con-tent of which is discussed in detail below, two formal recommendations have been adopted by the Commissioner so far. The first, "concerning the right of aliens wishing to enter a Council of Europe member state and the enforcement of expulsion orders" does not aim at addressing a specific country situation directly, but existing practice of Council of Europe states generally.[24] Although the second – the "Recommendation of the Commissioner for Human Rights concerning certain rights that must be guaranteed during the arrest and detention of persons following 'cleansing' operations in the Chechen Republic of the Russian Federation"[25] – aims at addressing a specific state, it touches on aspects of minority protection directly and its formulation also aims at drawing general principles, which could be applicable to situations which might occur elsewhere.

This latter recommendation addresses the issue of the protection of the rights of civilian persons detained and transferred to military areas, determination of the responsibility to ensure respect for their constitutional rights, and measures to improve respect for their rights. This recommendation has been adopted by the Commissioner in the context of his on-going efforts, which began when he took up office, to stop human rights violations in Chechnya. It includes specific recommendations addressed to the Russian authorities, which adopt a formal, international-instrument type of format and an emphatic tone, aiming at its reinforcement.

As to the formal opinions adopted by the Commissioner so far, the first "Opinion of the Commissioner for Human Rights on Recommendation 1492 (2001) of the Parliamentary Assembly on the rights of national minorities" served for him to endorse the Assembly's perception of the need to increase efforts aimed at protection for national minorities, including through the allocation of an additional person at the Commissioner's office to deal with this issue. The Commissioner, however, in indicating the need for such a person to deal with other aspects of the work of his office, indirectly indicated the lack of resources of his office (see below). Two subsequent opinions have been devoted to replying to requests by various institutions (see above).

The first dealt with the formal inquiry addressed by the Joint Committee on Human Rights of the Parliament of the United Kingdom on the measures derogatory of Article 5 of the ECHR contained in the 2001 United Kingdom Anti-terrorism, Crime and Security Act.[26] The second was addressed to the Commissioner during the year 2002 by the Northern Ireland Human Rights Commission, following an invitation by the Northern Ireland Office to comment on the Government's draft response to the Commission's own report on the adequacy and effectiveness of the functions conferred on it under the Northern Ireland Act of 1998.[27]

Drawing in particular on the Paris "Principles relating to the status and functioning of national institutions for the protection and promotion of human rights" and other relevant standards,[28] the Commissioner's opinion focuses on certain aspects of the competencies of the Northern Ireland Human Rights Commission, raised by the latter in its report – especially, the questions of the funding, financial independence, and autonomy of action of the Commission; its powers of investigation, including access to places of detention, its competence to compel the production of relevant information, documentation and material proof; its competence to have referred to it draft legislation and policies that affect human rights enjoyment, with sufficient notice to provide appropriate advice; and its powers to initiate proceedings in its own name, particularly before the Courts.

Other tools, which have expressly been made available to the Commissioner in following up his identification of shortcomings, are discussed below. It is interesting to note here that in order to "identify shortcomings", the Commissioner has started to organise "seminars" in the course of his activity. Some of these seminars have been "country-based" and organised in relation to specific situations, mainly in relation to interethnic conflicts (see below). Others have been thematic and yet others have been undertaken in connection with "specific actors": ombudsmen, the leaders of the main monotheistic religions in Europe, the armed forces and NGOs (the so-called "meetings"). Increasingly, pre-selected themes have also been object of discussion at each meeting. Relevant aspects of the meetings convened so far by the Commissioner with the ombudsmen are discussed elsewhere in this chapter.

The fact that the first seminar on Human Rights and the Armed Forces was held in Moscow in December 2002, after the adoption of the Commissioner's recommendation "concerning certain rights that must be guaranteed during the arrest and detention of persons following 'cleansing' operations in the Chechen Republic of the Russian Federation", points to an endorsement and broadening of the process to which the recommendation contributed (see above), in order to deal with the issue of the respect of human rights by the armed forces more generally.[29]

As to the seminars organised with leaders of the main monotheistic religions in Europe, which have become an annual event, the first was on the topic "The role of monotheistic religions vis-à-vis armed conflict", and was held in Siracusa on December 2000 almost one year before the 11 September attacks in the USA. The conclusions of the meeting emphasised that: "fanaticism is a perversion of religion. Religious beliefs must not be used to justify armed conflicts, just as armed conflicts must not be used to suppress the exercise of religious freedom". The conclusions highlighted the question of minority protection, and called "for respect for religious convictions and ideas, for holy places and for the religious lifestyles chosen freely by believers, both at national and international level". The participants undertook to "continue developing education in mutual respect and human rights, as opposed to the teaching of contempt, while also fostering understanding of other people and groups".[30]

The second seminar dealt with "Church–State relations in the light of the exercise of the right to freedom of religion", and was held in Strasbourg in December 2001. Its conclusions emphasised the importance of registration of religious denominations for the effective exercise of the right of association and to freedom of religion. They also emphasised the belief that Council of Europe member states must grant religious communities the necessary rights to enable them to fully enjoy the rights set out in Article 9 of the ECHR, and to guarantee equal treatment "without any distinction based on historical traditions or the number of believers".[31]

Finally, the conclusions state the acknowledgement by the participants of the special status of certain religious communities and the fact that this does not constitute discrimination, "provided that co-operation between these communities and the state is based on objective and reasonable criteria such as their historical or cultural relevance, representativeness of usefulness to society as a whole or to a large or specific sector of the population".[32] The positive obligation of the state to help preserve the religious, cultural or historical heritage of religious communities is also asserted. Thus, while especial protection of majority religions is upheld, so is the possibility for minority religions to receive adequate support.

The third and most recent seminar, held in Louvain-la-Neuve in December 2002, dealt with the more philosophical issue of the extent to which the values of respect and tolerance at the centre of human rights discourse meet with analogous values in the doctrines and requirements of the leading "monotheistic faiths". It does not seem to have addressed aspects of minority protection or endorsed this protection, but instead promoted education within the school system "of the beliefs and histories of all the leading faiths in Europe".[33] This is an element not necessarily beneficial for minority protection, given that "leading" is normally identified with "majoritarian".

Finally, the "meeting between the Commissioner for Human Rights and NGOs" organised in Paris on 18 and 19 December 2000 deserves special consideration, since, although it did not address questions of minority protection, it established a basis for structured dialogue between the Commissioner and NGOs. At the meeting it was decided to create a network of correspondents to liaise between the NGOs and the Commissioner's office. It was also decided to hold an annual meeting for exchanging views and improving the co-ordination of activities.[34] The NGOs expressed their views on the Commissioner's work, and among the conclusions reached was that the Commissioner's role "should continue to be that of an institution complementing other Council of Europe bodies, capable of a rapid, public response and able to call member state authorities to account for blatant violations of human rights". The participants encouraged the Commissioner "to alert the press whenever human rights were in danger". They emphasised the need for the Commissioner's visits to states to "give rise to reports publicly and force-fully speaking out against violations of human rights".[35]

The NGOs offered their assistance to the Commissioner, and it was agreed that:

> NGOs would be consulted by the Commissioner's office ahead of visits, and would forward to the Commissioner any information which they deemed necessary to clarify the national situation. In addition, at the start of each visit the Commissioner would attempt to arrange meetings with local NGOs for a clearer picture of the situation on the spot. Once a report had been published, the Commissioner would do his utmost to ensure that it was made available to the NGOs that had helped with preparations for the visit.
>
> For their part, the NGOs could address information to the Commissioner at any time, asking him to visit a member state in the event of serious problems or a threat of human rights violations.[36]

The NGO representatives further suggested that the Commissioner should adopt a thematic approach, which "might relate to groups of countries and also focus primarily on the countries in western Europe".[37] Several specific topics were suggested. In connection with the former aspect it should be noted that visits by the Commissioner to states in western Europe started early in the year 2001, that is, soon after the meeting.

"Controls and tools" for the Commissioner

The follow-up activities of the Commissioner, after his identification of shortcomings in state performance, are reinforced (in fact he is provided with a "stick") in the text of Article 3.*f.* According to this provision, the Commissioner, if he "deems it appropriate" shall address "a report concerning a specific matter to the Committee of Ministers or to the Parliamentary Assembly 'and' the Committee of Ministers".[38] The CoM thus becomes a necessary interlocutor for the Commissioner when it comes to this reporting activity. It should be noted, however, that besides this the Commissioner has made presentations "to different parliamentary commissions on specific issues".[39]

The formula "concerning a specific matter" in the mandate of the Commissioner does not seem to reduce the choice as to the issues on which the Commissioner may report in a substantial way. Actually the reports to the CoM and Parliamentary Assembly have become a constant feature of the Commissioner's engagement in specific states, as the Commissioner has elaborated a so-called mission report after his return from each of the visits to states that he has carried out in implementing his mandate. These reports have covered so far a variety of aspects of human rights protection, according to an ad hoc selection of themes by the Commissioner.

An essential safeguard of the Commissioner's independent choice and action is Article 6. Member states not only have a duty to respect the independent and impartial function of the Commissioner, which they have themselves mandated[40] and aimed to guarantee,[41] but in accordance with Article 6 they "shall facilitate the independent and effective performance by the Commissioner of his or her functions". The independence requirements of the mandate have not been interpreted as preventing the involvement of the Commissioner in his country of origin.[42] No formal requirements are imposed on the Commissioner as to engaging in direct contact with the member states[43] or undertaking visits, since states are given the specific duty to assist the Commissioner, facilitating contacts (with no limitations being established as to which type of contacts), including travel. Normally, however, the Commissioner has carried out visits to states following invitations by the state authorities. The duty to provide information in good time, introduced in Article 6, is particularly relevant in connection with the organisation of the Commissioner's visits.

The duty for the Commissioner to respond to requests made by the CoM or the Parliamentary Assembly, in the context of their task of ensuring compliance with the human rights standards of the Council of Europe, introduced in Article 3.*g,* could be considered to put a strain on his independence[44] and facilitate the manipulation of his role for political ends. However, the possibility for the Commissioner to respond in the manner he "deems appropriate" to such requests, also offers him the escape route of following-up those requests in whichever way he considers most suitable, thus contributing to avoiding political manipulation of his function.

The requests made by these organs also provide any follow-up action which the Commissioner may decide to undertake with additional endorsement and political weight. Thus the provisions of Article 3.*g* may actually be deemed an additional tool for effective action by the Commissioner. The Commissioner has so far evaluated positively the co-operation with the CoM, referring in particular to "frank and clear dialogue" and considering the support received "in general" important in enabling him "to broach" various subjects after his visits. He also qualified the support of the Assembly as "vital" when talking with governments in moments of crisis.[45]

The obligation of the Commissioner to submit an annual report to the CoM and the Parliamentary Assembly, in accordance with Article 3.*h* provides the Commissioner with a window of opportunity to bring human rights violations to the highest political instances and to obtain political support for his activities, rather than just representing an exertion of political control by these organs. This duty gives the Commissioner a chance to inform the political bodies of the difficulties he encounters in the development of his duties, and to propose adequate solutions. In the first annual report of the Commissioner, which covered the period 15 October 1999 to 1 April 2001, he gave an account of his work, and his approaches so far, to the CoM and the Parliamentary Assembly, and provided information on the resources he relied on.[46] To the credit of the Commissioner, his dialogue with the parliamentarians (following the presentation of his first annual report to the Assembly) has been published as a constituent part of the report.

Although Article 4 of his mandate would seem a restriction on the Commissioner's independence – it says he "shall take into account views expressed by the Committee of Ministers and the Parliamentary Assembly of the Council of Europe concerning the Commissioner's activities" – an open dialogue with both political organs can be a useful tool in the hands of the Commissioner and facilitate the development of his mandate. It should be noted, however, that dialogue with the Assembly in particular has not always fulfilled the expectations of the Commissioner, as illustrated by their intercourse in connection with the situation of the refugees and internally displaced persons in the Federal Republic of Yugoslavia in connection with the conflict in Kosovo.[47]

The duty of the Commissioner to co-operate with other international institutions, established in Article 3.*i* can also provide the Commissioner with a useful tool in carrying out his duties. Good communication, synergy of approaches and mutual reinforcement would seem essential, in particular with regard to the OSCE High Commissioner on National Minorities, who in his role as an instrument of conflict prevention has strongly contributed to minority protection.[48] Also, co-operation with Council of Europe expert bodies, such as the Advisory Committee under the Framework Convention is very important,[49] not only because of the need for coherence within the Organisation, but also because of the benefits which can be derived from the close interaction of both institutions with the political organs of the Council of Europe, especially the CoM. This should encourage both institutions to synchronise their efforts and approaches.

Similarly ECRI's activities and recommendations to states should be very much in the Commissioner's eye, to avoid duplication of roles, and for mutual reinforcement in advancing suggestions made.[50] In accordance with Article 12, an office of the Commissioner for Human Rights has been established within the General Secretariat of the Council of Europe.

This and other aspects of the implementation of the Commissioner's mandate are further discussed in the next section.

The implementation of the Commissioner's mandate

A fluid dialogue with the CoM has characterised the implementation of the mandate of the Commissioner from the start. Little over a month after Alvaro Gil-Robles had taken up his position, he exchanged views with the CoM, expressing his preliminary intentions in carrying out his mandate.[51] At this time, the Commissioner shared an awareness of the need to avoid duplication of activities, and to act prudently to avoid being perceived as a trespasser "on the preserve of other long-standing occupants", especially within the Council of Europe itself.

The Commissioner mentioned the minority issue and the combating of discrimination as "questions which are likely to be of primary interest to us". Nevertheless he indicated that only after visiting the member states – to establish contact with the respective national structures dealing with human rights, as well as with NGOs active in the promotion and protection of human rights – would he be in a position to establish priorities for his office. Since then, the Commissioner has undertaken missions to member states having secessionist regions within their territory, illustrating that this type of minority situation has become an object of particular concern for the Commissioner.

During his first exchange of views with the CoM, the Commissioner also put forward the problems he was encountering in the implementation of his mandate, namely the lack of personnel in his office.[52] He also pointed out the lack of resources in his operational budget, which curtailed even possibilities for travel and the hiring of consultants. These problems seem to have been partially overcome, as in his first annual report the Commissioner pointed to increases in his staff and support received from the Secretary General and voluntary contributions by states as having reduced his organisational difficulties.[53]

The missions of the Commissioner

Russia

Soon after his first exchange of views with the CoM, the Commissioner undertook his first mission, in connection with the armed, ethnic conflict in Chechnya. The so-called "mission to the Northern Caucasus region" was undertaken without mediating a formal request from the CoM or the Parliamentary Assembly in accordance with Article 3.*g* of the Commissioner's mandate, but on the basis of Articles 3.*e* and 5 instead. Nonetheless, the Commissioner reported to the CoM on his visit upon his return. The visit to the region, which developed within areas controlled by the authorities of the Russian Federation, was preceded by a trip to Moscow, during which the Commissioner contacted several NGOs concerned with the situation in the region.

The visit to the region itself, which lasted forty-eight hours, was organised by the Russian federal authorities, and the Commissioner was accompanied throughout the visit by the Vice-Prime Minister of the government of the Russian Federation and official representative of that government for Chechnya. The Commissioner referred to the fact that the federal authorities "demonstrated a remarkable effort of co-operation and openness in respect of all questions of specific information and requests for on-site visits: within the limits of the time available". The Commissioner pointed to the approach and high-level status given by the authorities to his visit as an illustration of their willingness to co-operate with the Council of Europe.

The report by the Commissioner to the CoM contained a detailed account of the visits made (including to camps of internally displaced persons [IDPs] and one detention centre), the antecedents of the current conflict and the stage of the hostilities. The Commissioner pointed to human rights violations by the Chechen regime before the conflict, and by the Russian military forces during hostilities, although references to abuses by the latter forces during acts not directly connected with the conduct of the hostilities were minimal.[54] Concerning recommendations made by the Commissioner to the Russian authorities as presented in his report, besides requesting that the federal authorities close down the detention centre visited,[55] the Commissioner:

> proposed that the Office of a Chechen Commissioner for Human Rights be set up for the territories recently liberated from the Chechen regime, which would, among other things, have the task, for as long as there are neither native police forces nor courts nor similar supervisory bodies, of serving as an intermediary between the local community and the federal forces of occupation.[56]

It should be advanced here that, after the endorsement of this recommendation by the CoM on 15 December 1999,[57] Mr Vladimir Kalamanov was appointed "Special Representative of the President of the Russian Federation for ensuring human rights and freedom of people and citizens in the Chechen Republic", by means of a Russian presidential decree adopted two months later.

Following a positive assessment of the findings of the first visit, the main recommendation of the Commissioner to the CoM concerned the support of Russia's status "as a fully fledged member of the European Family" without questioning the status of this state as a member of the Council of Europe. The importance of the Russian Federation as a member state was also emphasised by the Commissioner in connection with the role which the Organisation could play "to better resolve certain domestic problems touching on human rights protection". As discussed in Chapters 5, 6, 8 and 9, this has been in contrast with some of the approaches adopted by the Parliamentary Assembly and the Secretary General, although it has been in line with the approaches of the CoM (see Chapters 5 and 6 in particular).

The Commissioner agreed with the Russian minister of justice, seconded by the minister of foreign affairs, to hold a seminar in the Northern Caucasus "on the role of democratic institutions in the construction of a state founded on the principles of the rule of law and respect of human rights". Following the endorsement of the initiative by the CoM,[58] a seminar was co-organised in Vladikavkaz, by the government of the Russian Federation, the government and president of North Ossetia-Alania (one of the subjects of the Federation) and the Council of Europe Secretariat, on 30 and 31 May 2000.[59] Although emphasis was made during the seminar on the need for the restoration and effective operation of civilian authority in the region and the need to engage in every effort to achieve reconciliation between Chechens, the seminar as such did not entail any type of "political mediation" attempt, as the Chechen opposition was not represented at the meeting.[60] At the time of writing, no public record of contacts between the Commissioner and the Chechen opposition seems to exist.

A second visit to the Northern Caucasus, called the "Second visit to the Russian Federation, in particular Ingushetia and Chechnya-Grozni", was undertaken by the Commissioner at the end of February 2000. This was done, as in the case of the first visit, without mediating a formal request by the CoM or the Parliamentary Assembly. In contrast with the previous visit of the Commissioner, this one was agreed with the Russian authorities at short notice, during the Commissioner's visit to Moscow on 25 February. The visit to the Northern Caucasus concluded on 28 February.[61] During discussions in Moscow, the Russian authorities agreed to the Commissioner's proposals for co-operation between the Council of Europe and the recently appointed Mr Kalamanov.[62]

On this occasion, and following the Commissioner's own request, he was accompanied on his visit to the Northern Caucasus by Mr Kalamanov, as well as a group of Russian and foreign journalists.[63] Following a visit to Ingushetia, including IDP camps, the Commissioner visited Grozny, "to see for myself, in so far as possible, whether reports alleging that the Russian army had set out to completely destroy the town were correct".[64] During a visit to a food distribution centre, the Commissioner was able to discuss with some locals the problems they were facing, which mainly concerned basic material needs, and restrictions to freedom of movement. As to the hostilities, the Commissioner indicated among other things that "we saw a large number of large buildings destroyed not by bombs dropped from the air but by explosions originating in cellars or basements".[65]

In the conclusions of his report on this mission, the Commissioner emphasised the need for the Council of Europe to co-operate with the office of Mr Kalamanov, in the belief:

> that the mere establishment of his office will already have considerable preventive effect and that its effective operation will depend in particular on the free co-operation with this office of Russian NGOs and a number of intergovernmental organisations such as the Council of Europe and the OSCE. If foreigners could effectively collaborate, with full authority and recognition, with the Russian officials responsible for registering and processing the complaints received, the value and indeed the credibility of this office would be all the more enhanced, at the very least from the point of view of those bringing to it complaints of all sorts of abuses alleged against members of the armed forces, the police and even the federal civilian administration. This office would be the focus for complaints against what took place under the 'Chechen regime' and in this regard it seems to me to be perfectly appropriate and necessary for collaboration between foreign specialists and Russian officials.[66]

In fact, the mandate given to Mr Kalamanov by the Acting President of the Russian Federation is worded in rather general terms, and places much emphasis on co-operation with international actors. It consists of i. the safeguarding of the conditions for the implementation by the president of his constitutional powers in relation to human rights and freedoms of the people and citizens of the Chechen Republic, and ii. the co-ordination of Mr Kalamanov's activities, by officially recognised means, with international organisations and NGOs, in order to elaborate a coherent approach to the safeguarding of human rights and freedoms of the citizens of the Chechen Republic.[67]

In accordance with the previous recommendation, the Commissioner proposed that the Council of Europe send two or three staff members to assist Mr Kalamanov's team in their task of receiving and processing complaints of human rights violations in Chechnya as well as the financing of the infrastructure and logistics of his offices. The main office of Mr Kalamanov was to be established in Znamenskoye (in Chechnya) close to two large IDP camps and was to be staffed with fifteen persons, including five human-rights specialists. The second one was to be established in Moscow, "to follow up the action taken by the federal authorities with regard to the complaints transmitted".[68]

As already indicated in Chapter 5, the Council of Europe experts do not work under the responsibility of the Commissioner for Human Rights, but under that of the Secretary General of the Council of Europe, to whom they have a duty to report. This points to the limited capacity of the Commissioner to influence their activities, delimited in the Memorandum of Understanding agreed on by the Secretary General and the Russian Minister for Foreign Affairs.[69]

The team of three Council of Europe experts arrived in Znamenskoye on 21 June 2000, two months after Minister Ivanov and the Secretary General of the Council of Europe reached an agreement on the presence of Council of Europe experts in Mr Kalamanov's office, due to security considerations.[70] According to a report of the Secretary General, the 3 500 applications filed at Mr Kalamanov's office before 5 September 2000:

> contain allegations about illegally detained or missing relatives, illegal restrictions on freedom of movement, non-compensation for damaged or confiscated property, lack of administrative or judicial remedies as well as about some serious crimes. So far, the competent Russian authorities provide very little feedback to the Office as to the follow-up given to the registered applications. Our experts continue their efforts to obtain such information.[71]

According to the same report:

> the biggest number of registered applications concern illegally detained or missing relatives. The Council of Europe presence in Znamenskoye has encouraged Russian authorities to move towards more transparency as regards persons detained during mop-up operations or other checks. However, still not all law-enforcing agencies have agreed to provide full information concerning detained persons. Under amnesty regulations, but also under pressure from the Office, the Russian authorities have released a number of illegally detained people.[72]

The third mission of the Commissioner to Chechnya, from 25 February to 4 March 2001, was made at the request of the CoM, and included visits to Moscow and Chechnya. The purpose of the mission was to "gain an accurate overview of the situation in general and, in particular, of the respect for human rights and the follow-up to the Commissioner's earlier recommendations resulting from his two previous visits".[73] Its two main objectives were for the Commissioner to become directly acquainted with the activities of Mr Kalamanov's office and the examination of the judicial machinery in place.

The Commissioner referred to environmental problems, health care in the IDP (and refugee) camps in particular, access to food, forced disappearances and lack of guarantees for personal safety (which the Commissioner attributed both to federal forces and to Chechen combatants). He also referred to NGO accusations that the Russian military forces committed other crimes against the civilian population: "most notably of summary executions, torture, unauthorised detentions, and extortion", and that none of these offences were being adequately investigated by either the civilian or military *prokuraturas*.[74] He also referred to reports about brutality against soldiers within the Russian armed forces, ill-treatment during detention of a journalist reporting those abuses (the Ms Anna Politovskaya case), and to the recent discovery of a mass grave.

The Commissioner identified three main areas of priority action: material reconstruction; re-establishment of political and representative institutions; and the end of the climate of impunity surrounding crimes committed.[75] With regard to the first aspect, the Commissioner referred to the Russian government reconstruction programmes and emphasised the need for international humanitarian and reconstruction aid to be internationally monitored, so that it reached its intended recipients. He proposed the establishment of a joint Russian and international body responsible for financial co-ordination and supervision of aid distribution, and supported the Assembly's initiative for the Russian Federation's membership of the Council of Europe Development Bank.[76]

With regard to the restoration of political and administrative institutions, the Commissioner referred to the "normalisation plan" of the chief of the Chechen Administration appointed by the Russian Federal authorities, A. Kadyrov.[77] This included the creation of a consultative organ attached to Mr Kadyrov's administration, composed of representatives of the civil society, elders and religious minorities, the deployment of Chechen policemen and reduction of the number of federal armed forces, and the formation of a provisional Chechen government responsible for the supervision of the reconstruction of Chechnya.[78]

The Commissioner proposed the holding of a seminar on institutional reconstruction on Chechen soil, envisaged as a follow-up of the seminar held in Vladikavkaz in May 2000 (see above). Finally a meeting on "the protection and respect for human rights as a basis for the democratic reconstruction of the Republic of Chechnya" was held on 26-27 November – in Strasbourg, due to the difficult security situation in Chechnya. Members of the public authorities present in Chechnya and also of a section of the opposition as well as representatives of NGOs present in Chechnya (such as "Memorial") attended this meeting.[79]

Finally, with regard to the restoration of the judicial system, the Commissioner referred to accounts by NGO representatives and international observers of the little progress made on the question of accountability, including in relation to those initiatives undertaken by Mr Kalamanov's office.[80] The Commissioner referred to his first talks with representatives of the civil and military *prokuraturas*, who highlighted problems regarding judicial investigations, especially security-related ones.[81]

The Commissioner also referred to his declining an offer to visit the military base on which the journalist Ms Anna Politovskaya had reported, favouring a visit by Mr Kalamanov in his place.[82] Instead, the Commissioner insisted on a visit to a military base outside Grozny to meet the Commander of the Federal Military Forces, General Baranov. This points to an increasingly self-assertive role of the Commissioner in determining his own agenda. General Baranov strongly denounced the treatment of Russian soldiers kept captive by the Chechen militia, while the Commissioner insisted "that a democratic state adhering to the rule of law ... cannot use the same methods as criminals".[83]

The Commissioner made a statement to the media denouncing the prevailing impunity.[84] He proposed the establishment of a "collaborative" commission composed of representatives from the *prokuratura* and Mr Kalamanov's office, which could keep track, during monthly meetings, of the progress made by the files transferred from the latter to the former.[85] This would result in the creation of a Consultative Commission, which would meet on a periodic basis. In the final considerations of the Commissioner, he identified positive developments, such as the beginning of the re-establishment of the judiciary, including the Supreme Court of Chechnya, and the trial of a Russian colonel.[86]

The most recent mission of the Commissioner in relation to the conflict in Chechnya, from 10 to 16 February 2003,[87] was prompted by the Commissioner's perception of the lack of an adequate reply to his recommendation "concerning certain rights that must be guaranteed during the arrest an detention of persons following 'cleansing' operations in the Chechen Republic of the Russian Federation" (see above). In the Commissioner's report on his visit, which included travelling to Moscow, Chechnya and Ingushetia, he denounces the worsening of the security situation and the growing number of disappearances,[88] usually in the context of identity checks at so-called block-posts or during so-called "targeted anti-terrorist operations".[89]

The Commissioner points at progress made with regard to administrative provisions (such as the adoption of Order 80 by General Moltenskoy, requiring the clear identification of military units operating in Chechnya at night,[90] which the Commissioner relates to the Strasbourg meeting on 26-27 November); the co-operation between the *prokuratura* and the office of the special representative of the President of the Russian Federation for the defence of human rights and freedoms in the Chechen Republic, currently held by Mr A.-K. Sultygov (who replaced Mr Kalamanov following President Putin's appointment on 12 July 2002); the *prokuratura's* stand for strict compliance with the law when present during arrests by the federal authorities; and the establishment of a new interior ministry, which should help to reduce the activity of the federal army.

Nevertheless, the Commissioner also points out that General Moltenskoy's order is largely being ignored; co-operation between the *prokuratura* and the office of the special representative of the President of the Russian Federation remains sporadic; the *prokuratura* lacks the resources for effective inquiries, and legislation does not allow for comprehensive supervision of the army operations; and investigations carried out rarely lead to charges or to the guilty being sentenced, while co-operation with NGOs is undermined by mutual lack of trust.

Curiously, the Commissioner fails to comment on the advisability or timing of the forthcoming (constitutional) referendum,[91] probably due to the fact that this was a matter being addressed by the Assembly and possibly in order to avoid further controversy with the Russian authorities. Nevertheless, he points at the difficulties hampering its fairness, especially those encountered by internally displaced persons wishing to vote, and those affecting the free exercise of rights to freedom of expression, association and public debate in Chechnya generally.

Probably unaware of the reservations later to be expressed by the Assembly,[92] the Commissioner welcomes the idea of an amnesty. He finally addresses some aspects of the prevailing material living conditions, referring in particular to those of internally displaced persons being compelled to abandon their camps and to the problem of widespread corruption preventing reconstruction aid from reaching its intended beneficiaries. The Commissioner concludes by making a general recommendation asking for action on three fronts: i. personal security, rule of law and human rights protection; ii. the establishment of institutions allowing for political dialogue; and iii. the improvement of material living conditions, so that the population has a prospect of development in the medium term

Georgia

In June 2000, the Commissioner accepted an invitation from the Georgian minister for foreign affairs, I. Menagarishvili, "to visit his country in order to provide the Council of Europe with exhaustive, up-to-date information on the human rights situation in Georgia".[93] The programme of the visit was drawn up by the Georgian ministry of foreign affairs, and the Commissioner was also able to add – as emphasised by the Commissioner, "sometimes at the last minute" – meetings with the local representatives of international organisations. Ambassador D. Boden, special representative of the Secretary General of the UN, was in charge of the programme for the Commissioner's visit to the secessionist region of Abkhazia,[94] where on this occasion the Commissioner met with the highest representatives of the secessionist authorities in the region.

As the report of the visit to Georgia made by the Commissioner to the CoM illustrates, the Commissioner focused this time on identifying the issues of concern affecting the country generally, rather than just concentrating on the situation in the secessionist regions, in this case Abkhazia and South Ossetia (the latter was not visited by the Commissioner). The situation within these regions, especially in Abkhazia, and its overall effects on the situation of human rights in the state, did, however, occupy a prominent place in the considerations of the Commissioner. Other minority protection issues affecting the state also received preferential attention, particularly those in relation to the situation of refugees. This included the activities of the Kists and Chechen refugees living in the Pankisi Valley, discussed in connection with the conflict in Chechnya, and the problems of South Ossetian refugees and deported Meskhetians wishing to return to Georgia.

The issue most thoroughly addressed by the Commissioner, that on the present situation in Abkhazia, covered also living conditions of the ethnic Georgian IDPs who wished to return there, in particular to the Gali district. In relation to the latter, in the section of his report entitled "Conclusions and recommendations", the Commissioner stated the need for a closer monitoring of the government bodies and agencies which deal with them, as well as the need

> to resume and speed up the negotiations with a view to the return of the IDPs to Abkhazia, even if this would mean discussing, in the first instance, the return of IDPs to Gali only. As I have already emphasised several times, the right of these IDPs to return to Abkhazia will not be called into question by anyone and the exercise of this right will be obviously very much facilitated if their personal safety could be genuinely guaranteed if they return, for example, regarding the particular situation in the Gali region, by effective supervision of human rights by the competent international organisations.[95]

With regard to the minority situation in the country generally, "and the less numerous minorities such as the Abkhazians and Ossetians ... [who] have had or have conflictual relationships with the 'privileged' Georgian majority with respect to their language and religion", the Commissioner indicated:

> that the solution to these complicated and often highly emotional problems would consist in new legislation settling 'once for all' the rights of persons belonging to national minorities, including the more or less autonomous status of the regions of Georgia where these minorities are in the majority. In this connection, however, no one is in a position to

'sell to the Georgians' a tried and tested model of a federal state, nor indeed detailed model regulations governing the rights of minorities. It is for the Georgian authorities to take up these issues ... and to find an overall solution to them at national level, taking account of their own traditions, characteristics and national imperatives, without, however, completely overlooking the European standards which already exist in this field. It is reassuring to know that part of this work has already begun ... To this end, a fertile imagination and constructive proposals will be needed in order to rapidly achieve political compromises which are viable in the long term and which respect the rights of all Georgian citizens and of everyone living in Georgia.[96]

The Commissioner did not give an indication of his possible contribution to such a process, although he was later to take the initiative to hold a seminar on the legal aspects or the solution to the Abkhaz-Georgian conflict, the seminar being held from 12 to 13 February 2001 and co-organised by the Council of Europe and the United Nations Observer Mission in Georgia (UNOMIG), in Pitsunda (within Abkhazia). This "provided an opportunity for dialogue between representatives of the Georgian Government and the Abkhazian side of the conflict".[97] A follow-up seminar was organised in Tbilisi on 16 and 18 July 2001.

Moldova

From 16 to 20 October 2000 the Commissioner undertook a visit to another state having, once again, a secessionist situation within its territory: Moldova. The visit, which took place "at the repeated request of Moldova's Ministry of Foreign Affairs" included the secessionist region of Transnistria.[98] During this visit, the Commissioner was assisted by two members of his office, and he was accompanied, during all meetings and on-site visits made in Chisinau, by the permanent representative of the Republic of Moldova to the Council of Europe. During the visit of the Commissioner to Transnistria, he was assisted by a member of the OSCE Mission to Moldova.[99]

In the Commissioner's report, he expressed awareness of the Moldovan authorities' expectations concerning his visit. He stated his understanding "of the Moldovan authorities' concerns regarding developments in Transnistria (where the secessionist authorities continue to consolidate their actual independence) and the Moldovan desire to win the support of intergovernmental organisations, including the Council of Europe, for the purpose of finding a durable and equitable solution to the 'Transnistrian conflict'". At the same time, he expressed his disappointment with the approach to his visit by the president of the state.[100] The Commissioner relied largely on non-governmental sources of information in giving an account of the deficiencies in the human rights record of the state, both in adopting relevant laws,[101] and in their implementation.

The fact that Moldova has a national ombudsman for national minorities, M. S. Ostaf, proved of invaluable assistance in providing the Commissioner with relevant information concerning the situation of minorities in the state. Among the specific problems regarding the observance of human rights in Moldova, the Commissioner devoted special attention to "linguistic problems". This concerned mainly the issue of discrimination against minority languages in Moldova, "in terms of teaching of these languages in schools, their use in public or in dealings with public authorities and their use in private relations, including business relationships", as well as the imposition of a linguistic quota in the broadcasting field.[102] The Commissioner pointed to problems concerning the attitude of public authorities towards the approach of private schools to language teaching, as well as towards minorities having schools where the teaching is done in the mother tongue.[103]

The Commissioner concluded that the Moldovan authorities are following "a policy of 'forced' use" of the Moldovan language. He indicated that a similar practice takes place in the secessionist region of Transnistria with regard to the Russian language. The Commissioner referred to the issue of language discrimination in this territory, and in particular to policies of forced education in the Russian language, Moldovan being officially taught only in Cyrillic script.[104] The Commissioner indicated that schools using the Latin script and other than Russian out-dated textbooks were blacklisted, so that they did not receive funding from the de facto authorities in the region. They were also subject to discriminatory and arbitrary local rules with regard to their material survival and short-term operations.[105]

The Commissioner concluded his report by pointing to the harmful effects of the continued conflict in the region of Transnistria for the overall situation in Moldova, indicating among other things that

> the greatest need is to encourage the relevant Moldovan authorities to pursue their legislative work, beginning with cleared and more realistic legislation on the rights of persons belonging to national minorities and laws on the status of asylum seekers, refugees and displaced persons.[106]

Andorra

Soon after the start of the year 2001, the Commissioner made his first visit to a state in western Europe, Andorra, following an invitation from the Andorran government.[107] As pointed out by the Commissioner, a peculiarity of this state is that Andorran citizens are actually in a minority, as compared with the foreign population, which is double the number of citizens. This is why one of the specific questions addressed by the Commissioner was the situation and rights of foreigners, who face draconian conditions for acquiring the citizenship of the state, such as a residence requirement of twenty-five years and "sufficient integration and participation in the Andorran society", assessed by a "committee on nationality". This includes passing a test on knowledge and understanding of the Catalan language.[108]

The Commissioner stressed that foreigners are not entitled to vote in municipal or parliamentary elections, and while recognising that the situation as regards to the latter is similar in other European states, he indicated that "there are fewer restrictions elsewhere on the participation of foreigners in municipal elections, particularly in the member States of the European Union".[109] He also referred to the limitations to the exercise of economic rights, especially the right to set up a private company, for long-term residents.[110] The Commissioner recommended that the periods of residence required to apply for naturalisation and the acquisition of full economic rights be reduced as much as possible.[111]

Spain

In February 2001, and for the first time without mediating an invitation from the state authorities since the Commissioners' visits to the Russian Federation, the Commissioner carried out a mission to Spain: to Madrid and to the Basque Country.[112] The argument given by the Commissioner for the visit was "the continuing violations of human rights in this autonomous community caused by terrorist action". According to the Commissioner the situation there "has deteriorated to such point that it affects not only the fundamental rights of individuals but also the free exercise of certain civil and political rights which are the basis and foundation of every democracy".[113] In the course of his visit, the Commissioner met with state authorities, the authorities of the Autonomous Community, organisations representing the victims of terrorism, citizens' organisations denouncing terrorism, organisations representing the families of those imprisoned for terrorist offences, representatives of political parties, spokespersons of parliamentary groups, the Basque ombudsman, the Bishop of San Sebastian, representatives of a police trade union, academics and the media.[114]

The Commissioner does not seem to have met representatives of the armed group ETA, or representatives of Batasuna, the political party endorsing the use of violence – which, although subsequently declared illegal (in 2003), enjoys the support of a substantial part of the population in the Autonomous Community, and was at the time of the Commissioner's visit represented in parliament and holding office in a substantial number of municipalities. The Commissioner did, however, maintain contacts with ETA prisoners with regard to their treatment by the authorities.

In the Commissioner's report, much attention is devoted to discussing the situation of the oppression of the population living in the Autonomous Community that does not hold pro-independence ideas, by ETA and by the groups of *kale borroka* (street bands) allegedly connected with it. In a section of the report entitled "General approach", the Commissioner denounces the situation of tension and terror experienced by a large section of the population who do not share pro-independence ideas, and the prevailing climate of impunity, responsibility for which is attributed to the Basque police force.[115]

The Commissioner places this against the background of the high level of self-government of the Autonomous Community, including exclusive powers in areas such as education, health, transport, roads, industry, culture and other matters, mentioning also the existing competencies to levy taxes and the autonomous police force. To illustrate the high level of self-government, the Commissioner indicates that the levels of powers are comparable to and broader than those of a German *Land*.[116]

In a section of the report entitled "on the practical causes of human rights violations in the Basque Country", the Commissioner refers to two major causes: the direct action taken by the terrorist group ETA and the urban violence carried out by groups close to ETA. The Commissioner gives an account of the activities of murder and extortion in connection with terrorist action, directed towards those who do not support independence. He refers to the creation of a climate of fear in which freedom of thought and expression, or the possibility to develop political activity, are threatened, leading a part of the population to leave. The Commissioner states that the free exercise of the right to vote in electoral processes is jeopardised in small towns where radical nationalists are in control of municipalities.[117]

In connection with urban violence by organised groups, the Commissioner denounces the passivity of the Basque police force, for which the Basque authorities are allegedly responsible.[118] The Commissioner states that:

> it is clear that the Basque government bears some responsibility for the failure to provide sufficient and effective protection of citizens' fundamental rights, but it must not be forgotten either that, in pursuance of Article 1 of the ECHR, the Spanish state is responsible for securing 'to everyone within their jurisdiction the rights and freedoms defined in Section 1 of this Convention', so it is also under an obligation to adopt or strengthen the measures needed to guarantee the fundamental rights of all Basque citizens.[119]

In a section of the report dealing with human rights issues raised by the organisations representing the families of detainees and prisoners accused in connection with acts of terrorism or their legal representatives, the Commissioner indicates that no response has been given to the Commissioner's requests to provide concrete facts and specific information on human rights violations of detainees and prisoners. The Commissioner also indicates that he has not received complaints of ill treatment or torture from the detainees he met in his visit to a prison, while he received complaints from prison wardens, who are being subjected to threats and attempts on their lives.[120]

The Commissioner backs recommendations made by the European Committee for the Prevention of Torture and Inhuman or Degrading Treatment of Punishment (CPT) with regard to the reduction of the periods of detention and the practice of involving forensic medical examiners.[121] Similarly, the Commissioner supports a policy of approximation of detainees to their places of origin or family's residence by the Spanish authorities. In connection with administrative handovers of detainees to the Spanish authorities by other EU states, which circumvent extradition procedures, the Commissioner points to the need to provide a sound legal basis to the existing mechanisms through an EU regulation,[122] without maintaining their illegality.

The Commissioner's final considerations cover aspects of culture and education. He pointed to the need to examine the content of some textbooks, which run against the promotion of mutual understanding and co-existence, as well as programmes shown on the Basque public television in which children sing songs showing disrespect for people who are pro-Spanish.[123]

The Commissioner's report was the object of heated discussion, during the presentation of the first annual report by the Commissioner to the Parliamentary Assembly of the Council of Europe, only comparable to that held in relation to the situation in Chechnya, mainly as a result of the intervention of Spanish parliamentarians. Questions regarding the role of the media, education and the role of the Assembly in taking initiatives to combat terrorism were made. While the report was widely supported, an indirect accusation was made by a parliamentarian that the Commissioner's report was being used as a political instrument in the context of the electoral campaign taking place in the Autonomous Community at the time the report was made public.[124]

Norway

In April 2001, the Commissioner visited Norway. Of the three specific issues of concern identified by the Commissioner, one was the treatment of aliens and another that of national minorities. Under the latter category, the Commissioner referred to the Saami, the Kven, the Skogfinn, the Roma/Gypsies, the Travellers and the Jews. However, the only minority representative that the Commissioner seems to have met was one of the Kven.[125] The latter referred to the danger of extinction of the culture and language of the Kven in spite of recent efforts of the authorities, which he qualified as inadequate, but according to the Commissioner: "he did not allege any human rights violations".[126]

The Commissioner met with several NGOs representing immigrants and refugees, who pointed to discrimination in access to employment and housing. The Commissioner referred to the anti-immigrant and anti-refugee discourse used by the second largest party in the country during the last local elections as a cause of concern. He also expressed his hope that the law in preparation on the prohibition of ethnic discrimination "will be effectively reinforced".[127]

The Slovak Republic

The Commissioner was invited by the Slovak state authorities to visit the Slovak Republic from 10 to 16 May 2001, in the context of the efforts initiated in 1998 and acknowledged by the Commissioner,[128] to bring the country out of isolation and to integrate it into the EU and NATO. Following the visit, the Commissioner referred to recent institutional and legislative achievements, including those concerning minority protection and representation in government and parliament,[129] but he also pointed to persisting difficulties, referring among others to the situation of ethnic minorities, and the Roma/Gypsy community in particular. As to the minority situation generally, the Commissioner just referred to the recent Opinion adopted by the Advisory Committee under the Framework Convention, calling for a better legal framework to be rapidly introduced so that constitutional rights granted to national minorities and ethnic groups be implemented.[130]

The Commissioner focused on the situation of the Roma/Gypsy community, underscoring that prejudices prevent the pursuance of a policy of integration and participation, and calling for the authorities and the civil society to facilitate Roma/Gyspy integration. The Commissioner cited a concrete example in the field of employment in the city of Kosice (illustrating discrimination in this field) and called for the Slovak authorities to "be encouraged to set up concrete projects, even if only on a small scale, and submit them to the Council of Europe's Development Bank for funding".[131]

Finally the Commissioner referred to the fact that the 1991 population census did not reflect accurately the proportion of the Roma population in the state, due to the Roma being fearful of suffering discrimination as a result of indicating their ethnic identity. This placed the Roma in a situation of disadvantage in the reception of public funding. The

Commissioner pointed at minimal involvement of Roma as census officers or commissioners in the process of census elaboration, and although taking note of the funding of an awareness-raising campaign by the government, he also dealt with claims that this funding was clearly insufficient.[132]

The Commissioner dismissed claims by the government relating to the fact that the selection of census commissioners had been the responsibility of the local rather than the central level of government, pointing out that it is the ultimate responsibility of the central government to ensure that legislation is complied with.[133] In his final recommendations, the Commissioner called for the government "to take all necessary measures to ensure" the integration of the Roma in the Slovak society and on the authorities to devise practical projects along the lines mentioned above, while indicating that the Roma "must devote a great deal of effort into training and educating the members of their community to play an active part in the relevant institutions".[134]

Finland

In the Commissioner's report of his visit to Finland in June 2001, the Commissioner dealt first of all with the question of national minorities, referring to the Saami, the Roma, the Jews, the Tatars and the Russians, in view of the special status enjoyed by the Swedish-speaking minority. According to the Commissioner the latter group did not present any complaints to him vis-à-vis the authorities,[135] while the other groups complained about negative stereotyping regarding minorities in the media, particularly of the Roma, Russians, Somalis "and other minority groups which arrived more recently".[136] The Commissioner indicated the need to continue the efforts of the government to educate journalists concerning minorities, without providing details of their nature and content.[137]

Nevertheless, in addressing the issue of discrimination and xenophobia in his report, the Commissioner referred to the action plan – adopted by the government three months before the Commissioner's visit – to combat ethnic discrimination and racism, intended to last until the year 2003, which covers new immigrants, immigrants with several years of residence in the state, "second generation" migrants and Roma/Gypsies. The programme includes national, regional and local measures to promote ethnic equality and diversity, and was due to be subjected to an evaluation report to be presented by the Government to the Parliament in 2002. Similarly, the creation of an anti-discrimination ombudsman institution is previewed.

With regard to the Saami, the Commissioner referred to tensions in the Saami territory resulting from the delay on the settlement of land rights and on the definition of those entitled to enjoy Saami status. The Commissioner advocated the arrival "to the earliest possible solution, one which should take due account of the Saami culture and of all the interests at stake". The recommendation was made that Finland ratifies ILO Convention No. 169.

With regard to the Roma/Gypsies, the Commissioner referred to the efforts of the authorities in outlawing discrimination, improving access to housing and teaching of the Roma language, and referred to a government report: "Strategies of the policy on Roma in 2000" which indicates the low education level of the Roma and identifies prejudice and discrimination, as well as a lower socio-economic position than the majority population. According to the Commissioner, the Roma representative asserted that the Roma are subject to discrimination particularly as regards access to private housing and employment. He also referred to discrimination regarding access to private businesses open to the public including restaurants and shops, due to inappropriate implementation of existing anti-discrimination legislation.

The Commissioner addressed recent cases of use of violence against the Roma in prison by other inmates, resulting in the need for the isolation of the former. The Commissioner pointed to the fact that few local authorities have availed themselves of the possibility to provide the teaching of the Roma language in primary and secondary schools, resulting in a low percentage of Romani children receiving this education. Furthermore, the Commissioner indicated that large numbers of children are reportedly placed in special education units. He advised that thought should be given to measures enabling Roma pupils to attend normal classes.[138]

Regarding the Russian minority living in Finland, the Commissioner made a recommendation with important conceptual connotations from the minority protection perspective: the need for the authorities to reassess the distinction they have established between the "old" minority living in Finland and recent immigrants. As the Commissioner indicated, the latter have been excluded from the protection provided under the Framework Convention.[139] The Commissioner also raised another interesting aspect. He referred to the majority population profiting from minority language education facilities, wanting to learn the minority language as a foreign language, and resulting in the needs of the minority community's own language students being neglected.

Turkey

On 3 to 6 December 2001, the Commissioner visited Turkey, without mediating an invitation by the Turkish authorities. The visit had the stated purpose of initiating contacts both with these authorities and with representatives of Turkish civil society during the period of legislative reform, following the amendment of the Turkish constitution – in particular, with regard to "the arrangements and timetable envisaged for passing of the necessary implementing legislation".[140] The Commissioner's main concern was the timetable and "spirit" of the constitutional amendments designed to strengthen the protection and improve the exercise of human rights in Turkey. The public use of languages other than Turkish was specifically mentioned in this context.

The Commissioner informed the Turkish authorities before his visit that he "had no intention of making an in-depth assessment of the general situation regarding respect for human rights in Turkey",[141] referring to the activities of other Council of Europe organs in this regard, and possibly with the intention of facilitating a climate of dialogue with the authorities. During the visit, the Commissioner met representatives of the three officially recognised, non-Muslim religious minorities under the 1923 Treaty of Lausanne (Jewish, Armenian and Christian). They raised the problem of the lack of legal personality of their communities, which prevents them from having bank accounts or accepting gifts of land or buildings.[142] Although the Commissioner seemingly did not meet with Kurdish representatives or refer to the Kurdish question during his visit, he generally called for a rapid transition from a period of violence to one of normality, and the speedy implementation of the constitutional amendments.

In order to facilitate this implementation, he proposed the organisation of two seminars: one on the role and working methods of ombudsmen in several western countries, to contribute to the public discussion on the adoption of a bill concerning the ombudsman institution in Turkey, and the other on improving co-operation between the authorities and civil society for the purpose of protecting human rights in practice.[143] With regard to the latter aspect, a seminar on "the role of civil society in the consolidation of modern democracy" was subsequently organised in Ankara on 6-7 May 2002, which was attended by state authorities, Turkish and international NGOs, and the head of the EU Commission Representation in Turkey. Minority groups do not seem to have been represented at the meeting.[144]

Bulgaria

As in the case of the Slovak Republic, the invitation by the Bulgarian ministry for foreign affairs for the Commissioner to visit Bulgaria from 17 to 20 December 2001, "to take stock" of the process of complex institutional reform and transition undergone by this state, was placed against the background of the state candidacy to join western European institutions, the EU in particular.[145] In addressing the situation of minority protection in the state generally, the Commissioner took note of the ratification of a significant number of relevant international instruments, but pointed to the lack of a genuine government strategy for their implementation. He referred to NGO claims of the existence of aggressive nationalism and xenophobia, and of the treatment of the Roma/Gypsy community as a matter of prime concern, and also to parliamentary claims of delay on the adoption of relevant legislation, particularly in the field of discrimination, undue treatment of the Roma minority by the police, insufficient representation of the Turkish minority in the civil service, and the infrequency of events highlighting cultural diversity.[146]

The Commissioner visited a Roma neighbourhood in Sofia, during which he met community representatives. Pointing to the high rate of unemployment among the Roma, and increasing slightly the level of precision of the recommendations made with regard to the Slovak Republic for example, he pointed to the need for schemes to assist this community to gain access to the labour market and to combat all possible forms of discrimination in employment matters. In referring to the particular situation in a school he visited, he also pointed more generally to the situation of Roma segregation in schools with a lower level of education and state finance, resulting "in unacceptable discrimination".[147]

He also referred to the commitment to reform, and efforts to keep children at school in spite of the prevailing socio-economic conditions, on the part of a number of Roma representatives; and he suggested the advisability of applying for a loan from the Council of Europe Development Bank as a way of solving the problem of building and maintenance of schools throughout Bulgaria.[148] The Commissioner emphasised that the non-implementation of the "Bulgarian framework programme for equal integration for Roma: participation in the policy-making process" was due to lack of political will rather than lack of resources and support from donor countries and international organisations, as argued by the government.[149] He insisted on the need of passing laws on combating racial discrimination, equal opportunities and on the ombudsman institution to create a situation conducive to the implementation of the programme.

The Commissioner also met with religious leaders and civil society representatives, who voiced their concerns in relation to restrictions of religious freedom resulting from the state refusal to register certain religious groups, and bans that prevented non-registered groups from holding public religious services. See the comments on the Case *Church of Bessarabia v. Moldova* in Chapter 1. He referred to the non-restitution of Church property confiscated during the Communist period, while pointing at recent governmental steps to broaden the debate on the adopted Denominations Act. He also referred to the questions of "allow-ing Islamic education in schools for those pupils who so wish" and the "licensing of religious broadcasts on radio and television".[150] In his final recommendations, the Commissioner insisted on some of the points mentioned above, while calling for the introduction of a co-ordinated policy in respect of all minorities.[151]

Greece

Following a visit to Greece on 2-5 June 2002, the Commissioner issued a report in which the question of minority groups in Greece received specific consideration.[152] Questions relevant to minority protection, how-ever, were raised by the Commissioner also in dealing with the issue of "Freedom of thought, conscience and religion" and "Measures to prevent violence against foreigners". With regard to the latter aspect, the Commissioner referred to ECRI's second report on Greece, according to which it is necessary to strengthen the range of criminal law measures against offences of a racist or xenophobic character and criminal sanc-tions should take account of the culprits' possible racist or xenophobic motives.[153]

With regard to freedom of thought, conscience and religion, problems concerning the catholic community (in relation to the recognition of legal personality to some of its institutions), the scientology community (in relation to proposals for sect legislation), as well as more generally the questions of the persistent criminalisation of proselytism; Orthodox Church intervention in the granting of permissions for the building of places of non-Orthodox worship; and lack of an officially recognised mosque and Muslim cemetery in Athens, were raised by the Com-missioner.[154] In dealing specifically with the Muslim minority in Thrace, the question of the state appointment of the muftis, as opposed to their direct election by the minority without official intervention, and the arguments in support of this state intervention were presented by the Commissioner.[155]

In dealing with the situation of the Roma/Gypsy community, the Commissioner echoed the difficulties expressed by government officials in involving local authorities in action plans for the benefit of the Roma population. He pointed at the role of education in this connection, while referring to the ultimate responsibility of the central government in ensuring that obstacles to state policy are overcome.[156] Also in connection with the Roma, the Commissioner referred to the appalling conditions in which Roma families settled on the outskirts of Athens live, lacking water supplies and other essential services.

The Commissioner noted allegations of the NGO "Organisation Mondiale Contre la Torture" condemning the eviction of Roma communities from their dwellings in Athens ahead of the 2004 Olympic Games and criticising the International Olympic Committee for its silence.[157] He also referred to the Greek authorities' denial of this allegation, and their assurances that all families needing to be moved because of the games would be relocated on state-owned land. The Commissioner noted, however, that through his direct contacts with the Roma community, he had discovered that the Olympic games argument was being used by local authorities as a pretext for refusing to take in Roma communities or hastening their departure.

Finally, the Commissioner addressed the question of the right of persons belonging to minorities to self-identification by reference to ECRI's report, pointing to its denial to the Turkish-speaking community in Thrace, as well as to a recent suspended prison sentence for distributing a brochure of the European Bureau for Lesser Used Languages about minority languages in Greece "on the ground of disseminating false information".[158] In this connection, the Commissioner called for the ratification of the Framework Convention and the signature and ratification of the Languages Charter by Greece. The latter was reiterated by the Commissioner in the framework of the final remarks and recommendations he included in his report, together with other advice in connection with some of the issues raised above.

It is interesting to note that following the presentation of the report to the CoM on 11 September 2002, and in view of the comments brought by the permanent representative of Greece to the Council of Europe, the Commissioner proceeded to incorporate additional comments in his report, consisting of "precise details concerning measures taken by the Greek authorities following his visit". This practice would be repeated in subsequent reports adopted by the Commissioner following his visits to states.

Hungary

In the Commissioner's report on his visit to Hungary, he devoted a particular section to dealing with "rights of minorities and of the Roma/Gypsy community.[159] In this section he addressed the issue of the lack of appropriate legislation implementing the constitutional requirement of appropriate representation of minorities in Parliament, in accordance with the demands of the Hungarian constitutional court. He also echoed minority complaints about their representation at local level, amounting to the demand for quotas of representation, and parliamentary calls for the reform of the 1993 Law on National Minorities to overcome persistent problems. The Commissioner referred to the state authorities' request that he comment on the draft law on the fight against discrimination presented by the ombudsman for minorities.[160]

The Commissioner referred to the difficulties encountered by the Roma in their access to employment as a result of "prejudices" (a term which, as already noted, the Commissioner frequently prefers to a straight reference to "discrimination") and the resulting difficulties in their access to appropriate housing.[161] He stated the community's representatives' call for an assistance plan in the field of employment, aimed at the encouragement of the creation of small enterprises by Roma, facilitating their access to loans, both through direct financial assistance and governmental guarantees for loans contracted between Roma enterprises and banking institutions.[162]

In his final Recommendations, the Commissioner includes a general call for the adoption of an assistance plan for the Roma community, to combat discrimination in the field of employment through the adoption of legislative measures and targeted financial help.[163] The Commissioner refers to the need to set up vocational training programmes for the Roma to facilitate access to work. Also in dealing with the question of education, the Commissioner refers to the systematic practice of including Roma children in classes providing for a lower level of education and following a simplified curriculum, without experienced teachers and with poor facilities. The Commissioner calls for the disappearance of this type of distinction, and the provision of resources for academic support and assistance to the most disadvantaged children, to halt discrimination.[164]

Romania

The report of the Commissioner on his visit to Romania, on 5-9 October 2002, devotes one of its sections to the question of "Minorities and the special situation of the Roma/Gypsy community".[165] Besides reporting on progress with regard to the treatment of specific minorities and pointing to the uniform treatment of various minority groups as a source of discontent for some of them, the Commissioner invites the state authorities to ratify the Languages Charter and Protocol 12 to the ECHR. In dealing with the "special situation of the Roma/Gypsy community", the Commissioner refers to its poor socio-economic conditions, including in fields such as employment, education, health care and justice, and its suffering from all forms of discrimination.

In his final recommendations, the Commissioner indicates the need to address the serious public-health problem afflicting the Ferentari, the particular area he visited. With regard to the field of health care, the Commissioner points in particular to the fact that the Roma do not have the identity documents required for access to health care, and recommends that it should be made easier to obtain the necessary documents through a reduction of the prices of birth certificates. With regard to employment, he refers to the failure to apply equal-opportunity legislation in practice, and calls for the start of legal proceedings against employers explicitly excluding Roma applications for job vacancies in job advertisements, as well as against the publishers of such (newspaper) advertisements.

The Commissioner asks for the allocation of the necessary resources for the development of the national strategy for the Roma initiated by the state, and points to the absence of representatives of vulnerable groups in the National Council against Discrimination, which is responsible for monitoring the application of the principle of equality. Further, in addressing aspects of the implementation of the rule of law and access to justice, the Commissioner calls for the investigation and prosecution of members of the police who have committed abuses, and the intensification of the training programmes launched by the authorities to improve the attitudes of police officers towards vulnerable groups, and in particular the Roma community.[166]

Poland

The Commissioner dedicates one of the sections of the report on his visit to Poland, on 18-22 November 2002, to the question of "non-discrimination and the situation of minorities".[167] With regard to the former aspect, the Commissioner points out that Poland has little specific anti-discrimination legislation – in areas such as housing, contractual relations between individuals and access to public places – by reference to ECRI's assessment. The need to adopt specific legislation is extended by the Commissioner to the field of minority protection, in areas such as the right to use minority languages with the administrative authorities, in order to meet the concerns of minority representatives. The Commissioner echoes the concern expressed by the latter that xenophobia, anti-semitism and negative stereotyping of minorities are common phenomena, and that there are difficulties for some minorities to preserve their culture and language, or to access the media, and their situation is one of disadvantage in areas such as housing and employment.

He also points to the lack of a coherent foundation for the protection of minorities, as a result of its regulation mainly through bilateral agreements on good neighbourliness and friendly co-operation with individual countries, agreements which do not cover all minorities. It should be noted in the latter connection that in the "final remarks and recommendations" contained in the report, the Commissioner calls for the ratification by Poland of the Languages Charter and Protocol 12 to the ECHR. The Commissioner supports the views of the Ombudsman for Children, noting "that efforts should be strengthened to ensure that all Roma children can attend integrated classes, instead of special Roma classes". Seemingly, this indirectly points to the existence of a situation of actual segregation, and not to the existence of education especially geared to meet the particular needs of Roma children in the educational field.

Concluding remarks

Some preliminary remarks can be made concerning the Commissioner's initial involvement in Chechnya, in the light of information available, including that provided by the Council of Europe officers who have been present in the region. Official, high-level, short, fact-finding missions to conflict zones do not necessarily provide the most detailed and accurate account of the "real" human rights situation in a state, especially during an on-going situation of virulent armed conflict.

There is a high risk that the government's perceptions of the conflict will permeate the results of the mission, especially when the personal security situation is volatile and the organisation of the programme of the visit relies largely on the state authorities. Similarly, the possibilities for human rights institutions to influence the actual situation on the ground on a significant scale during situations of long-term developing conflict is very limited, especially if there is a lack of active political support for the cause they are upholding from the international community and from particular states.

Although the present Commissioner has stated his intention to visit all Council of Europe member states before the end of his term in office, the missions of the Commissioner during the first year of his mandate were centred on states recently affected by interethnic conflict, and having secessionist regions within their territory. A consideration relating to the missions undertaken by the Commissioner up to the end of the year 2000 is that states with secessionist regions may try to use high-level, international involvement in the human rights field as an instrument to justify their activities concerning those regions. This has not escaped the attention of the Commissioner, as the report of his visit to Moldova illustrates. In the latter country, as well as in Georgia, the Commissioner has taken the opportunity to present the issues negatively affecting human rights protection in the state overall, and especially those concerning minority protection, rather than concentrating on those arising from the situation in the secessionist region, as the state authorities inviting the Commissioner would have preferred.

The activities of the Commissioner have focused mainly on reporting on some of the deficiencies – of state legislation and practice in relation to various aspects of human rights protection – identified by the Commissioner as still outstanding. These aspects have varied, although minority protection has been a constant one, in particular with regard to the country-specific activity of the Commissioner. For example, the situation of persons imprisoned has received particular attention by the Commissioner in the reports on his visits to states, which have often referred to the findings of the European Committee for the Prevention of Torture and Inhuman or Degrading Treatment or Punishment (CPT). This has often included the treatment of persons belonging to minorities who are in prison.

The questions of minority protection raised have varied, depending on the situation in the state considered. The attention given by the Commissioner to the minority question, even if constant, has not been systematic. The latter contention also applies to other aspects of human rights protection, and can be explained by the limited resources available to the Commissioner and his consequent inability to engage in a formal reporting mechanism.

The level of attention paid to particular aspects of minority protection has also varied, although an increasing effort by the Commissioner to systematise his analysis of this issue can be detected. Some aspects of minority protection have started to become a constant feature in his recommendations to specific states, such as the need to accede to relevant Council of Europe instruments relevant to minority protection. Similarly, aspects of discrimination and the situation of the Roma community have become the object of constant attention. This comes as no surprise, given the momentum gained by this human rights question in Europe and the especial concern of the Commissioner for the more disadvantaged groups in society.

An important aspect of the Commissioner's approach to the minority question in the respective countries is that he has strongly relied on information directly provided by members of the minority communities, in trying to identify their problems through direct contacts, even if exceptionally in some states these direct contacts have not taken place or have been limited to specific groups. This has allowed him to detect some problems and needs largely unnoticed by other monitoring bodies.

The "identification of possible shortcomings" function, indicated in the Commissioner's mandate, thus seems to have taken up most of his attention. At the same time, the very limited human and material resources which the Commissioner has at his disposal have seriously curtailed his ability to engage in thorough, systematic and independent fact-finding of the "real" human rights situation in over forty Council of Europe member states. This has made the implementation of this part of his mandate particularly difficult.

The Commissioner has had to rely mainly on external sources of information to identify the human rights concerns in member states and find appropriate solutions to them. Until this problem is overcome, the need for the Commissioner to concentrate mainly on the "promotional" aspect of his mandate will continue. On the basis of the information already available, which the Commissioner will need to sort out as best his limited resources allow, he may need to make increasing use of targeted recommendations, as thorough as possible, proposing specific solutions to existing human rights violations and trying, as far as these resources permit, to follow up their implementation.

In this connection, the importance of a fluid dialogue with the political organs of the Council of Europe cannot be overstated. Through a continuous dialogue with these organs, the Commissioner may get further support for his recommendations and activities. The role of the Parliamentary Assembly in this connection cannot be exaggerated either. Also, the Congress of Local and Regional Authorities can play an important political role, even if no reference is made to this organ in the Commissioner's mandate. Especially with regard to aspects of minority protection for which the local authorities are directly responsible. Increasing references by the Commissioner to ECRI's reports, in particular, point to an effort on the Commissioner's side to pursue the work of other monitoring mechanisms. The annual reports of the Commissioner are becoming an increasingly useful instrument of dialogue, and provide additional opportunities to make recommendations to states, and follow up those already made.

This political dialogue may also contribute to consolidating the position of the Commissioner in relation to the structures of the Council of Europe Secretariat that deal with human rights protection. Dialogue with the other expert bodies within the Organisation can also help to push forward the Commissioner's recommendations, especially those in relation to setting up mechanisms of minority protection within individual states. Through co-operation with other international organisations, the UN, the OSCE, and increasingly the EU, the Commissioner may be able to obtain both political and logistic support for his initiatives.

Finally, non-governmental actors are called upon to become an essential pillar of the Commissioner's activities. He has increasingly relied on them in identifying shortcomings in the practice of particular states. Even if the resources of the office of the Commissioner were to be substantially increased, non-governmental actors would remain an essential source. In addition, it is very important that the Commissioner meets the high expectations created by the establishment of his office within civil society. The high level of openness and transparency with which the Commissioner has developed his activities so far can only facilitate relations with the NGO community. A very positive step was taken by the Commissioner in convening a meeting with NGOs, a meeting which established the basis for structured dialogue. Efforts should not be spared to ensure that the Commissioner is not perceived as simply a tool used by states to improve their human rights record (as the mandate of the Commissioner tends to portray) but also as an interlocutor for civil society, and for minorities in particular. The activities of the Commissioner are increasingly pointing in that direction.

Notes

1.   The resolution on the Council of Europe Commissioner for Human Rights was adopted by the Committee of Ministers at its 104th Session, held on 7 May 1999 in Budapest (henceforth, "the resolution"). On the remaining content of the Budapest Declaration relevant to minority protection and the previous endeavours aiming at the establishment of the Office of the High Commissioner, see Chapter 5.

2.   The mandate of the Commissioner for Human Rights and other public information concerning the exercise of his functions are available on the Commissioner's website http://www.commissioner.coe.int

3.   Council of Europe Internet website, Commissioner for Human Rights home page, presentation of the Commissioner for Human Rights, section on "Role and activities".

4.   See annual report, 15 October 1999 to 1 April 2001, op. cit., p. 122.

5.   Ibid., p. 12.

6.   Among the initial concerns expressed by the Commissioner, in relation to the implementation of his mandate, was that of "how to obtain rapidly a brief overview of the 'human rights' structures in forty-one member states and co-operate efficiently with them, in addition to the indispensable co-operation with international governmental organisations and national and international NGOs". See "Council of Europe Commissioner for Human Rights – exchange of views", speech delivered at the 687th meeting of the Committee of Ministers, Item 4.3 on the agenda, 16 November 1999, Commissioner's home page, Council of Europe website.

7.   This has not prevented the HCNM's involvement in relation to situations of violence, including in post-conflict situations. See R. Zaagman and H. Zaal, "The CSCE High Commissioner on National Minorities: prehistory and negotiations" in A. Bloed (ed), *The Challenges of Change: The Helsinki Summit of the CSCE and its Aftermath* (Dordrecht: Kluwer, 1994), p. 108. See also M.A. Martín Estébanez, "The High Commissioner on National Minorities: development of the mandate" in *The OSCE in the Maintenance of Peace and Security*, op. cit., pp. 129-30. For an analysis of the involvement of the HCNM in a situation which illustrates this, see J. Packer, "The role of the OSCE High Commissioner on National Minorities in the former Yugoslavia" in *Cambridge Review of International Affairs*, Vol. XII/2, spring/summer 1999, pp. 169-84.

8.   See the Commissioner's statement in connection with his mission to Moldova and the situation in Transnistria, contained in the "Report by Mr Alvaro Gil-Robles, Commissioner for Human Rights, on his visit to Moldova (16 to 20 October 2000) for the Committee of Ministers and the Parliamentary Assembly", Section I, paragraph 3. See also "Report by Mr Alvaro Gil-Robles, Commissioner for Human Rights on his visit to Spain and the Basque Country (5-8 February 2001) for the Committee of Ministers and the Parliamentary Assembly", section I, paragraph 1. On the content of these missions of the Commissioner, see further below.

9.   Article 3, paragraph *c* of the resolution.

10.   The importance of the role of the Commissioner in establishing ombudsman institutions in central and eastern Europe has been acknowledged at the meeting with western European ombudsmen organised by the Commissioner in Paris, 1 December 2000. See annual report, 15 October 1999 to 1 April 2001, op. cit., p. 122.

11.   In this regard it should be noted that, at a meeting between the Commissioner and NGOs held in Paris on 18 and 19 December 2000, mechanisms of co-operation were agreed upon, including that NGOs would be consulted by the Commissioner ahead of visits, and the Commissioner would attempt to arrange meetings with local NGOs at the start of his visits to states. See further, annual report, 15 October 1999 to 1 April 2001, op. cit, p. 126.

12.   Ibid., Article 3, paragraph *d.*

13.   In this connection it should be noted that in the "Conclusions of the meeting between the ombudsmen of central and eastern Europe and the Council of Europe Commissioner for Human Rights", organised by the Commissioner in Warsaw, 28-29 May 2001, the participants stated that "at present the priority was to foster the national ombudsman institution rather than to set up specialist or sectoral ombudsmen, who tended to dilute the effort to protect human rights without offering any guarantee of efficacy". See the conclusions, paragraph A.a. In the account of the meeting included in the first annual report of the Commissioner it is further specified that: "The appointment of specialised or sectoral ombudsmen, independent of those that already existed, might weaken the position of the latter. In particular, in a period of transition and financial insecurity, it would be more rational to concentrate all available resources on the office of the existing national ombudsman and, where appropriate, appoint deputies to deal with specific issues". See annual report, 15 October 1999 to 1 April 2001, op. cit., pp. 113-14.

14.   See "Conclusions of the meeting between the ombudsmen of central and eastern Europe and the Council of Europe Commissioner for Human Rights", Budapest, 23-24 June 2000, paragraph 3, Internet, Commissioner's home page, Council of Europe website.

15.   Article 5 of the resolution.

16.   See "Conclusions of the meeting between the ombudsmen of central and eastern Europe and the Council of Europe Commissioner for Human Rights", Warsaw, 28-29 May 2001, paragraph A.*d.*

17.   See "Statement by Mr Alvaro Gil-Robles, Commissioner for Human Rights, on his visit to Georgia (1-10 June 2000)", document published 13 July 2000, section I, paragraph 5. On the CoM monitoring procedure, see Chapter 6.

18.   See the reference to the case of the Russian journalist Ms Anna Politkovskaya, in the report of his latest visit to Chechnya: "Report by Mr Alvaro Gil-Robles, Commissioner for Human Rights, on his visit to the Russian Federation and the Republic of Chechnya (25 February to 4 March 2001) for the Committee of Ministers and the Parliamentary Assembly", p. 3, section I, paragraph 5.

19.   See Chapter 6.

20.   See Chapter 9.

21.   See reply by Commissioner Mr Alvaro Gil-Robles to Mr Jaskiernia, parliamentarian, following the presentation by the Commissioner of his first annual report to the Assembly, 15 October 1999 to 1 April 2001, op. cit., p. 23.

22.   Article 3.*e* of the resolution. The Commissioner has interpreted his promotional role both, it seems, in a broad and in a narrow sense, to include "effective observance" on the one hand, and, apparently, comprising education and awareness raising as separate and complementary, on the other. See foreword to the annual report, 15 October 1999 to 1 April 2001, op. cit., p. 5, paragraph 2.

23.   Ibid.

24.   Doc. Comm DH/Rec (2001) 1, Strasbourg 19 September 2001.

25.   Doc. Comm DH/Rec (2002) 1, Strasbourg 30 May 2002.

26.   See "Opinion 1/2002 of the Commissioner for Human Rights, Mr Alvaro Gil-Robles, on certain aspects of the United Kingdom 2001 derogation from Article 5, para. 1, of the European Convention on Human Rights", doc. Comm DH (2002) 7.

27.   See "Opinion 2/2002 of the Commissioner for Human Rights, Mr Alvaro Gil-Robles, on certain aspects of the review of powers of the Northern Ireland Human Rights Commission", 13 November 2002, doc. Comm DH (2002) 16.

28. The Commissioner refers, among other things, to the Vienna Declaration and Programme of Action, Part I, paragraph 36, Resolution 2002/83 of the UN Human Rights Commission, and to the content of a UN handbook: "National human rights institutions: a handbook on the establishment and strengthening of national institutions for the promotion and protection of human rights".

29. See "Conclusions of the seminar on human rights and the armed forces, Moscow, 5-6 December 2002", doc. Comm DH (2002) 22 and "Conclusions of the 2nd seminar on human rights and the armed forces, Madrid, 15-16 September 2003", doc. Comm DH (2003) 9.

30. See annual report, 15 October 1999 to 1 April 2001, op. cit., p. 124.

31. See "Conclusions by Mr Alvaro Gil-Robles, Commissioner for Human Rights, on the Seminar concerning Church–State relations in the light of the exercise of the right to freedom of religion", Strasbourg, 10-11 December 2001, doc. Comm DH (2001) 15, 12 December 2001, paragraph 4.

32. Ibid., paragraph 6.

33. See the Commissioner for Human Rights, "3rd Annual Report, January to December 2002, to the Committee of Ministers and the Parliamentary Assembly", Strasbourg 19 June 2003, doc. Comm DH (2003) 7, p. 36.

34. Ibid., p. 125.

35. Ibid., pp. 2-5.

36. Ibid., p. 126, paragraphs 5-6.

37. Ibid., p. 7.

38. Article 3.*f* of the resolution. Present authors' emphasis.

39. See foreword, in the annual report, 15 October 1999 to 1 April 2001, op. cit., p. 5, paragraph 1.

40. Article 2 of the resolution.

41. Ibid., Articles 10 and 11.

42. As an exception to what has become the usual practice of the Commissioner, he became involved in the situation in Spain concerning the Pais Vasco at his own initiative, rather than as a result of an invitation by the state. See "Report by Mr Alvaro Gil-Robles, Commissioner of Human Rights, on his visit to Spain and the Basque Country (5-8 February 2001) for the Committee of Ministers and the Parliamentary Assembly", p. 1, section 1, paragraph 1.

43. Under Article 7, "the Commissioner may directly contact governments of member States of the Council of Europe".

44. According to Article 2 of the resolution: "the Commissioner shall function independently and impartially".

45. See reply by Commissioner A. Gil-Robles to Mr Jaskiernia, Parliamentarian, following the presentation by the Commissioner of his first annual report to the Assembly, 15 October 1999 to 1 April 2001, op. cit., p. 23.

46. See ibid.

47. See the Commissioner for Human Rights "3rd Annual Report, January to December 2002, to the Committee of Ministers and the Parliamentary Assembly", p. 20.

48. See M.A. Martín Estébanez, "The High Commissioner on National Minorities: development of the mandate", op. cit., pp. 123-65, especially pp. 151-64.

49. See Chapter 2.

50. The Commissioner included only a short reference to ECRI's work in his speech to the European Conference held in preparation for the World Conference against Racism, Racial Discrimination, Xenophobia and Related Intolerance held in Strasbourg on 11-13 October 2000, Doc. EUROCONF (2000) 9. On the European conference, see further, Chapter 5.

51. "Council of Europe Commissioner for Human Rights – exchange of views", 687th meeting of the Committee of Ministers, Item 4.3, 16 November 1999.

52. He mentioned specifically that he was only receiving the assistance of one secretary, as well as the director of his office and his respective secretary, while waiting for two additional professional posts and an additional secretarial one, which had been assigned to his office, to materialise.

53. See annual report, 15 October 1999 to 1 April 2001, op. cit., p. 6.

54. This was confined to a reference to the implementation of the curfew established by the federal authorities at a border crossing point between Chechnya and Ingushetia, included in section II, paragraph 3 of the speech. See also the references to abuses of authority reported by individuals, NGOs and journalists after he left the city of Gudermes, section II, paragraph 4.

55. Ibid., section II, paragraph 4.

56. Ibid.

57. "Follow-up to the exchange of views with the Council of Europe Human Rights Commissioner", Committee of Ministers 692nd meeting, 15 December 1999, Item 4.6, Council of Europe website, Committee of Ministers home page.

58. Ibid.

59. See "Conclusions presented by Mr Alvaro Gil-Robles, Commissioner for Human Rights of the Council of Europe" at the seminar on Democracy, the rule of law and human rights, held in Vladikavkaz in May 2000.

60. This seems to have resulted from the conditions established by the minister for foreign affairs of the Russian Federation, Mr I. Ivanov, for organising the seminar. During the talks held by Mr I. Ivanov with the Commissioner on 24 and 25 February 2000, Mr I. Ivanov agreed to the organisation of the seminar "provided that only persons prepared to discuss Chechnya's future under the Constitution of the Russian Federation were invited". See "Report by Mr Alvaro Gil-Robles, Commissioner for Human Rights to the Committee of Ministers and the Parliamentary Assembly of the Council of Europe on the second visit to the Russian Federation, in particular Ingushetia and Chechnya-Grozny, 1 March 2000 – second report", paragraph 7.

61. Ibid., paragraph 4.

62. Ibid., paragraph 7.

63. Ibid.

64. Ibid., paragraph 9.

65. Ibid.

66. Ibid., paragraph 10. Present author's emphasis.

67. See "Rapport de M Alvaro Gil-Robles, Commissaire aux Droits de l'Homme, Au Comité des Ministres, le 1er mars 2000", Annex 1, paragraph 2.

68. See "Report by Mr Alvaro Gil-Robles, Commissioner for Human Rights to the Committee of Ministers and the Parliamentary Assembly of the Council of Europe on the second visit to the Russian Federation, in particular Ingushetia and Chechnya-Grozny, 1 March 2000 – second report", paragraph 10.

69.   See "Letter from the Secretary General to Mr Igor Ivanov, Minister for Foreign Affairs of the Russian Federation", *Activities of the Council of Europe: 2000 Report*, pp. 370-71.

70.   See "Secretary General's Interim Report on the presence of Council of Europe Experts in the Office of the Russian President's Special Representative for Human Rights in Chechnya", Doc. SG/Inf (2000) 27 revised, 5 September 2000, paragraph 1.

71.   Ibid., paragraph 6.

72.   Ibid., paragraphs 8-9.

73.   See "Report by Mr Alvaro Gil-Robles, Commissioner for Human Rights, on his visit to the Russian Federation and the Republic of Chechnya (25 February to 4 March 2001) for the Committee of Ministers and the Parliamentary Assembly", p. 1, paragraph 1.

74.   Ibid., paragraph 3.

75.   Ibid., paragraph 6.

76.   Ibid., section II, paragraphs 3-6.

77.   With this the Commissioner was referring to the Chechen administration supported by the Russian authorities.

78.   Ibid., section III, paragraph 1.

79.   See "2nd Annual Report April 2001 to December 2001, to the Committee of Ministers and the Parliamentary Assembly", doc. Comm DH (2002) 2, paragraph 15.

80.   Ibid., section IV, paragraphs 3-4.

81.   Ibid., paragraph 6.

82.   Ibid., paragraph 5.

83.   Ibid., paragraph 8.

84.   Ibid.

85.   Ibid., paragraph 11.

86.   Ibid., paragraph 2.

87.   See "Report by the Commissioner for Human Rights, Mr Alvaro Gil-Robles on his visit to the Russian Federation (Chechnya and Ingushetia) from 10 to 16 February 2002 for the attention of the Committee of Ministers and the Parliamentary Assembly", doc. Comm DH (2003) 5, Strasbourg, 4 March 2003.

88.   The Commissioner refers both to data provided by the *prokuratura*, according to which 1500 persons have disappeared over the last three years, and by the NGO Memorial, according to which the number rises to 2000 over the same period.

89.   See "Report by the Commissioner for Human Rights, Mr Alvaro Gil-Robles on his visit to the Russian Federation (Chechnya and Ingushetia) from 10 to 16 February 2002 for the attention of the Committee of Ministers and the Parliamentary Assembly", paragraph 4.

90.   This is Order No. 80 of Lt Gen. V. Moltenskoy, Commander of the Joint Troops Group in the North-Caucasus Region, "On measures to enhance the activity of local authorities, the population and the law-enforcement organs of the Russian Federation in combating violations of lawfulness and to increase official responsibility for violations of lawfulness and legal order in the course of special operations and targeted measures in the settlements in Chechnya".

91.   See Chapters 5, 7 and 8.

92.   Chapter 8.

93.   See "Statement by Mr Alvaro Gil-Robles, Commissioner for Human Rights, on his visit to Georgia (1-10 June 2000)", document published 13 July 2000.

94. Ibid., paragraph 2.

95. Ibid., section IV, paragraph ii.

96. Ibid., section IV, paragraph iii.

97. See annual report, 15 October 1999 to 1 April 2001, op. cit., p. 10.

98. See "Report by Mr Alvaro Gil-Robles, Commissioner for Human Rights, on his visit to Moldova (16 to 20 October 2000) for the Committee of Ministers and the Parliamentary Assembly", section I, paragraph 1.

99. Ibid.

100. Ibid., section I, paragraph 4.

101. Ibid., section I, paragraph 5 in particular.

102. Ibid., section II.B.c, paragraph 9. On this issue consult the Guidelines on the Use of Minority Languages in the Broadcast Media, recently adopted under the aegis of the OSCE High Commissioner on National Minorities (The Hague: High Commissioner on National Minorities, 2003, available on www.hcnm.org).

103. Ibid., section II.B.c, paragraph 12. On this, and specific aspects discussed below, see the The Hague and Oslo Recommendations also.

104. Ibid., section II.B.c, paragraph 13.

105. Ibid., section II.C.c, paragraph 3.

106. Ibid., section III.

107. See "Report by Mr Alvaro Gil-Robles, Commissioner for Human Rights, on his visit to Andorra (10-12 January 2001) for the Committee of Ministers and the Parliamentary Assembly", p. 1, Introduction, paragraph 1.

108. Ibid., section III.A, paragraphs 1-2.

109. Ibid., section III.A, paragraph 4.

110. Ibid., section III.A, paragraph 5.

111. Ibid., section III.A, paragraph 7.

112. See "Report by Mr Alvaro Gil-Robles, Commissioner for Human Rights, on his visit to Spain and the Basque Country (5-8 February 2001) for the Committee of Ministers and the Parliamentary Assembly", p. 1, Introduction, paragraph 1.

113. Ibid.

114. Ibid., p. 1, Introduction, paragraph 3.

115. Ibid., section II, paragraphs 1-2.

116. Ibid., section II, paragraph 4.

117. Ibid., section III, paragraph 3.

118. Ibid., section III, paragraphs 5-6.

119. Ibid., section III, paragraph 8.

120. Ibid., section IV, paragraph 1.

121. Ibid., section IV, paragraph 3.

122. Ibid., section IV, paragraph 4.

123. Ibid., section V.

124. See question by Mr Guardans, in annual report, 15 October 1999 to 1 April 2001, op. cit., p. 20.

125. According to the programme of the Commissioner's visit, the only formal meeting held with NGOs was restricted to that held with two human-rights experts.

126. See "Report by Mr Alvaro Gil-Robles, Commissioner for Human Rights, on his visit to Norway, 2-4 April 2001, for the Committee of Ministers and the Parliamentary Assembly", p. 5, section 3, paragraph a.

127. Ibid., section 3, paragraph *b*.

128. See "Report by Mr Alvaro Gil-Robles, Commissioner for Human Rights, on his visit to the Slovak Republic, 14-16 May 2001", doc. Comm DH (2001) 5, Strasbourg, 19 September 2001, section I.

129. Ibid., section II.

130. Ibid., section III.1.

131. Ibid., section III.1.a.

132. Ibid., section III.1.b.

133. Ibid.

134. Ibid., section v.

135. See "Report by Mr Alvaro Gil-Robles, Commissioner for Human Rights, on his visit to Finland, 4-7 June 2001, for the Committee of Ministers and the Parliamentary Assembly", p. 1.

136. Ibid.

137. Ibid.

138. Ibid., section I, paragraph 2.

139. Ibid., section I, paragraph 3.

140. See "Report by Mr Alvaro Gil-Robles, Commissioner for Human Rights, on his visit to Turkey, 3-6 December 2001, for the Committee of Ministers and the Parliamentary Assembly", doc. Comm DH (2001) 14, Strasbourg, 12 December 2001, paragraph 2.

141. Ibid., paragraph 1.

142. Ibid., paragraph 5.

143. Ibid., paragraph 7.

144. See doc. Comm DH (2002) 4, Strasbourg, 14 May 2002, Appendix II.

145. See "Report by Mr Alvaro Gil-Robles, Commissioner for Human Rights, on his visit to Bulgaria, 17-20 December 2001, for the Committee of Ministers and the Parliamentary Assembly", doc. Comm DH (2002) 1, Strasbourg, 10 April 2002, section I.

146. Ibid., section II.3.1.

147. Ibid., section II.3.2.a.

148. Ibid.

149. Ibid., section II.3.2.b.

150. Ibid. section II.4.

151. See section V. at ibid.

152. See "Report by Mr Alvaro Gil-Robles, Commissioner for Human Rights, on his visit to the Hellenic Republic, 2-5 June 2002, for the attention of the Committee of Ministers and the Parliamentary Assembly", doc. Comm DH (2002) 5, Strasbourg, 17 July 2002, section III.

153. Ibid., section IV.

154. Ibid., section II.

155. Ibid., section III.A. For a discussion on jurisprudence under the ECHR in this connection, see further, Chapter 1.

156. Ibid., section III.B.

157. Ibid.

158. Ibid., section III.C.

159. Section I of the "Report by Mr Alvaro Gil-Robles, Commissioner for Human Rights, on his visit to Hungary, 11-14 June 2002, for the Committee of Ministers and the Parliamentary Assembly", doc. Comm DH (2002) 6, Strasbourg 2 September 2002, section I.

160. Ibid. section I, paragraph 6.

161. Ibid, paragraphs 11-12.

162. Ibid., paragraph 13.

163. Ibid., paragraph 55.2.

164. Ibid., paragraph 16.

165. See "Report by Mr Alvaro Gil-Robles, Commissioner for Human Rights, on his visit to Romania, 5-9 October 2002", doc. Comm DH (2002) 13, Strasbourg, 27 November 2002, section III

166. See, at ibid., final remarks and recommendations.

167. See "Report by Mr Alvaro Gil-Robles, Commissioner for Human Rights, on his visit to Poland, 18-22 November 2002", doc. Comm DH (2003) 4, Strasbourg, 19 March 2003, section II.

Concluding reflections

Minorities and minority rights in the work of the Council of Europe: a concluding assessment

The nature of the challenge to the peoples of Europe arising from the minorities issue was discussed in the Introduction. To recapitulate, it essentially resulted from a sea change in awareness of minority questions in theory and practice, resulting from the influence of globalisation, the upsurge in minority-related conflict and the effect of the eastward expansion of European horizons. The present assessment focuses on the response of the Council of Europe in terms of standards, mechanisms and practice in the area of minorities and minority rights.

A set of criteria for gauging the work of the Council appear in the General Course on Human Rights given at the Academy of European Law by T. van Boven, who writes (elaborating on a point by M. Nowak) that:

> It may at least be expected that European systems for the promotion and protection of human rights represent an additional value as compared with the global system. In this connection the three criteria mentioned by Nowak provide useful advice and guidance. The first criterion is that through the regional system a pioneering or innovative effort is made. The second criterion relates to the introduction of a higher level of protection. The third criterion corresponds to clearly established needs of a particular region.[1]

The author points to possible contradictions between the various elements in that, for example, restrictively interpreting 'the needs of the region' might result in a lowering of levels of protection. This takes us back to earlier reflections, and again invites consideration of the broader international and European context in which the developments are set. The criteria of "innovation, protection and needs"[2] suggest that we should offer a critical account of standards, mechanisms and practice, including consideration of the resources devoted to the issue in question, consistency in the distribution of praise and blame for human rights, the "performance" of states, and the growth of public knowledge and awareness of rights.

On standards and practice

Standard-setting is legitimated and demanded by the Statute of the Council of Europe, which refers to "safeguarding and realising" the ideals and principles which are the common heritage of member states and "the maintenance and further realisation of human rights and fundamental freedoms".[3] In terms of the Nowak/van Boven criteria, it is important to remember that standards continue to develop.

Since the report version of this work in 1994, we have witnessed the emergence of the Framework Convention and its coming into force, and that of Protocol No. 12 of the ECHR, as well as an increased awareness of ethnic issues in the practice of the ECHR capable of further development, but also the "failure" of initiatives, such as the additional protocol to the ECHR on minority rights.[4] To this must be added an increase in attention to minority protection by the principal organs and the Secretariat of the Council of Europe, and an ever-sharper focus on particularly disadvantaged or "targeted"[5] groups such as the Roma/Gypsies. In view of the emergence of a number of focal points, the possibility of further standards emerging should not be discounted, even if the "vocation of the age"[6] is to make existing standards work better in practice.

The European Convention on Human Rights

It is abundantly clear that minority rights are fully integrated into the contemporary canon of human rights at the Council of Europe, as well as in the United Nations, the OSCE, the Central European Initiative and the Council of Baltic Sea States, and in a multitude of bilateral arrangements in Europe. The European Union has proclaimed respect for cultural and linguistic diversity.[7]

In the Council of Europe in particular, the ECHR has been assessed for its strengths and limitations on minority issues. The results are mixed. The "indirect" approach of the ECHR to minority protection has produced an indispensable matrix of rights for the basic freedoms of citizens, and a broad commitment to pluralist democracy essential for minorities to thrive. The contribution of the ECHR to the democratic protection of European citizens is enormous. Although the text is relatively "light" on key questions such as non-discrimination, because of the subsidiary character of that principle in the text of the Convention, possibilities of development are present.[8]

Some early decisions of the organs of the Convention, such as the *Belgian Linguistics* case, have tended to inhibit normative movement. However, the greater sensitivity to minority questions in the Council of Europe and beyond should gradually produce effects on the inter-pretation of norms: in particular, the advent of Protocol No. 12 inter-relates the convention system with broader developments in international law and their rich content of minority rights. The influx of judges to the Court from parts of Europe where minority issues are well understood will also have its effects. The emergence of complementary norms such as those in the Framework Convention should not inhibit the develop-ment of the Court's jurisprudence: the potential synergy between the two instruments, working within their frames of reference, is capable of having positive systemic effects on the minority question.

The innovative potential of the ECHR is reflected in its global reputation as a major depositary of justiciable human rights norms.[9] While the level of its standards on minority rights could be compared unfavourably with analogous instruments, such as the ICCPR, this stems primarily from textual limitations, strongly suggesting that further possibilities of elaboration of additional protocols in the minority/ethnic/cultural diversity field should not be abandoned.[10]

The Framework Convention and a note on "autonomy"

The Framework Convention for the Protection of National Minorities is now the Council of Europe's "flagship" in the sphere of minority rights. Critics, including the Parliamentary Assembly,[11] had a field day when the text emerged, comparing it unfavourably with the UN declaration, the OSCE Copenhagen Document, and other documents. The text is marked by a trenchant "individualisation" of norms, and an extreme caution in its language. On the other hand, compared with the ICCPR, it innovates in the field of languages, education, participation, and the "defence" of the integrity of minority areas. It does not approach the uplands of autonomy.

Besides the important conceptual contribution made by the Congress, in establishing the connection between minority protection and "autonomy" and in developing the substance and practice of territorial autonomy generally,[12] the most explicit employment of "autonomy" in connection with minorities in the corpus of instruments of the Council of Europe appears in Recommendation 1201 (1993) of the Parliamentary Assembly, Article 11 of which provides:

> In the regions where they are in a majority the persons belonging to a national minority shall have the right to have at their disposal appropriate local or autonomous authorities or to have a special status, matching the specific historical and territorial situation and in accordance with the domestic legislation of the State.[13]

651

Recommendation 1201 itself is peculiar, since it is a recommendation for an additional protocol to the European Convention on Human Rights, a protocol which has never emerged.[14] As noted, the recommendation has gained a high political profile by being used as a reference document by the Parliamentary Assembly when it examines applications for membership of the Council of Europe and in its post-accession monitoring procedure.[15]

The controversy surrounding the proposed article relates to its qualified endorsement of a right to territorial autonomy for persons belonging to national minorities. The polemics and public expressions of concern surrounding Recommendation 1201 reached such a pitch that the proposed Article 11 became the subject of an opinion by the Venice Commission.[16] The reference to autonomy in the proposed article is tentative and qualified. The "local" is contrasted with the "autonomous" (authority) and there is the additional possibility of a "special status". Any of the three alternatives must "match" the "specific historical and territorial situation" and be "in accordance with ... domestic legislation" of the state.

The qualifications are such as to make it unlikely that a particular autonomy pattern could be "forced" upon an unwilling state. This reading coheres with the views of the Venice Commission, for whom the proposed Article 11 does not have the mandate for "acceptance of an organised ethnic entity within their territories",[17] although "being allowed to have local or autonomous authorities represents the most consummate fulfilment of the demands of concentrated minorities within unitary States".[18]

On the phrase "in accordance with the domestic legislation of the State", the Venice Commission observes that it "is the State that prescribes the legal framework within which the right may be exercised", while the phrase also "contains a guarantee that a legal framework will exist for the exercise of the right".[19] It is instructive that the opinion of the Venice Commission on Article 11 comments on the existence of a right to participation rather than autonomy in the Framework Convention, implying that one language can to some extent remedy the lack of another. The Venice Commission observes that "participation in public affairs is above all a question of personal autonomy, not of local autonomy".[20]

Instead of the discourse on autonomy, what the Framework Convention reveals – its ruling idea – is the demarcation of local space, analogously to the cultural/spatial/use concepts deployed by the Human Rights Committee in relation to indigenous groups. The minorities do not own the space in public law, but their presence is to be manifested through a series of public permissions and possibilities set out in the convention. The concepts recognise attachment, historical presence, tradition, force of numbers, needs and spatial integrity. The minorities do not have explicit control, but rights to defend and resist any forced alterations of character, to print their names and make their mark on the territory, along with the names and marks of their non-minority neighbours.[21]

The Framework Convention is an enormously important instrument for the Council of Europe, and deserves a generous appropriation of resources to fulfil its vocation in volatile political spaces. As suggested in Chapter 2, the balance between the political body (the Committee of Ministers) and the expert body (the Advisory Committee), is crucial to success. As far as possible, the Framework Convention should be "managed" by the experts, engaging with governments and civil society in transparent processes of dialogue that give as little space as possible to insinuations of political compromise and fix. Experience from the ECHR and UN expert bodies suggests that the greater the insulation from the vagaries of politics, the greater the prestige of the instrument.

It is instructive that experience with the ECHR moved it towards a rigid (judicial) as opposed to a flexible (political) system. One may hope to see a similar practice for the Framework Convention. The balance achieved between the political and the expert will prove or disprove the theses of the convention's many critics. On the basis of the evidence in Chapter 2 of the present work, the omens are favourable for the entrenchment of the Framework Convention at the heart of European minority policy.

The Languages Charter

The Languages Charter is an innovative instrument. There are no real equivalents in the canon of international law. The principles it elaborates are synthesised with other texts in the Oslo recommendations regarding the linguistic rights of national minorities, and the guidelines on the use of minority languages in the broadcast media prepared under the auspices of the OSCE High Commissioner on National Minorities, suggesting the emergence of a new canon of human rights in the field of languages. The language question has been of cardinal importance in the development of minority rights in Europe and has frequently been the cause of tension and conflict. As has been observed, the language issue was a staple of the League of Nations system. UN endeavours focused on the question of discrimination in the area of languages, rather than the promotion of positive linguistic rights, although the ICCPR[22] and the UN Declaration on Minorities have developed the concept, as has the OSCE. The ECHR has not developed a canon of language rights with any great clarity. Language in the Framework Convention is addressed in key articles.

The difference between the Languages Charter and the other cited instruments is that the charter is about the languages, rather than the rights of speakers. This "deflection" facilitated the emergence of the text at a time when the Council of Europe arguably represented an unfavourable institutional environment for minority rights. The situation has changed to a considerable extent since minority rights were brought into the mainstream of human rights and into the work of the Organisation as a whole. As an example of innovation, the charter possesses admirable technical qualities, and if its potential is truly unleashed, it can achieve a great deal for the preservation and strengthening of linguistic and cultural diversity in Europe.

A number of countries have recognised this in ratifying the charter, and/or building charter prescriptions into other documents – the UK-Ireland Good Friday Agreement, for example.[23] In the EU Charter of Fundamental Freedoms, the recognition of respect for cultural and linguistic diversity has great potential for synergy for European states. Countries that have difficulty with the minority concept may have less trouble with the charter. On the other hand, van Boven's criterion of adding to international standards requires careful reflection. In particular, it is suggested that the implementing bodies of the Languages Charter and the Framework Convention should keep a "watching brief" on each other's work. Ideally, the charter can function as a detailed, technically appropriate application of Framework Convention principles within its own sphere. Any effect on rights standards requires careful attention to general principles of non-discrimination and minority rights in the application of the charter. In all this, background "universal" rights standards should not be forgotten.[24]

The Roma/Gypsies

The situation of the Roma/Gypsies[25] represents a kind of testing-ground for international standards and mechanisms, as well as domestic law and practice. The situation of the Roma figures prominently in virtually all reports of states under the Framework Convention, and in the jurisprudence of the ECHR. Landmark documents emanating from the Council of Europe include Recommendation 1203 (1993) of the Parliamentary Assembly and the ECRI General Recommendation No. 3 (1998), on combating racism and intolerance against Roma/Gypsies. This document was drafted in consultation with Roma organisations, representatives of a people who wish to be called by their own name. Many difficulties experienced by Roma can be addressed by conscientious application of equality and non-discrimination principles.

However, the contribution of positive cultural rights should not be underestimated.[26] For example, many applications of "development" policy include attempts to eliminate poverty by programmes that neglect the cultural dimension and do not go to the root causes – which may be precisely those neglected and under-appreciated cultural dimensions. In the case of the Roma, insistence that there is only a "social" issue to be unravelled may be similarly blind. The work of ECRI assists in developing awareness that the practice of "travelling" may have important cultural dimensions; and there are others. The settled state has difficulties with this practice, but the difficulties are not insurmountable with goodwill and effort, including efforts at mutual understanding. As ECRI notes, legal measures will not be enough; education is key. Failure to improve the lot of the Roma will be taken as symptomatic of a wider failure to cope with the reality of diversity, so often celebrated in theory, if not in practice. As the Political Declaration of the European Conference on Racism put it:

> Europe is a community of shared values, multicultural in its past, present and future; tolerance guarantees Europe's pluralist and open society, in which cultural diversity is promoted.

The treatment of Roma through international effort and local practice tests this hypothesis to the full.

On minorities

In the introduction to the present work, A. Eide's definition of "minority" was offered as a working hypothesis. The practice of the various bodies/institutions of the Council of Europe does not offer much further clarification. Restrictive readings of "national minority" found directly in texts such as Parliamentary Assembly Recommendation 1201 (1993), and indirectly in the Languages Charter, are not followed through with any consistency. By way of example, the Parliamentary Assembly, as observed, has dealt with non-citizens in the course of its work on minorities, and the drafters of the Framework Convention found themselves unable to arrive at a consensus about the meaning of "national minority": restrictive approaches adopted by some states under the convention are open to challenge by the Advisory Committee and to critical comment by other states.[27]

In such cases, the background criterion presented by international law in general – recalled in the introduction to the present work – should be borne in mind: the existence of minorities is a question of fact, not of law. The principle of "fact, not law" does not prohibit states from determining how many and which minorities exist on their territory, but indicates that they should "tell it how it is", and not report to treaty-bodies and others through an ideological fog. The rich variety of European minorities is not suited to the application of reductionist, norm-avoiding characterisations. Definitions, it many be noted, abound at the domestic and community levels. Their absence at the level of international law is partly accounted for by the nature of the system, which remains essentially dynamic and fluid, allowing for development, change and adaptation. Another reason is the capacity of people to define themselves, to say who they are as persons and collectives.

The legal point is that all definitions are open to international scrutiny, and that the "resolution" of a definition puzzle is ultimately conceived as a dialogic exercise in which individuals, communities and states should play a part, as can international bodies. In this last respect, the bodies of the Council of Europe have adopted a range of stances towards the "existence" of minorities: by defining (above), by encouraging states to keep the questions open (the Advisory Committee), or by applying criteria in a manner approaching the parameters of a definition (the Venice Commission).

On the related question of indigenous peoples, we have not advanced a characterisation of these groups – apart from an initial reference to ILO Convention No. 169 – but have observed their presence through the lenses of undifferentiated human rights and of minority rights: references to the Saami and to the Inuit of Greenland appear in various chapters; the position of the Roma under ILO Convention No. 169 has been the subject of comment by the ILO.[28] This omission of a specific account of indigenous rights is not in any way to demean their claim to the status of peoples in international law, but suggests only that at least some of their claims can be advanced through the rights practice and instruments set out in this volume.[29] Perhaps it is time that "Europe" elaborated a treaty on indigenous rights: especially in view of the considerable enlargement of the number of indigenous and "tribal" groups in the Council's sphere as a result of the accession of the Russian Federation and other states of the CIS.

Mainly on mechanisms

Council of Europe summits, the Committee of Ministers and its monitoring procedure

The intergovernmental bodies of the Council of Europe have not always been active pursuers of minority issues. Only when confronted with situations of massive conflict involving the fate of minorities in Europe after the fall of the Berlin Wall did they become actively engaged in finding a role for the Organisation, and then only after initiatives by other organisations, such as the OSCE, were well under way. The minority issue began to be addressed in the context of the process of enlargement towards the east after the end of the cold war. Since 1993, two Council of Europe summits have highlighted this issue as one of the top priorities, and the Vienna Summit, in particular, devoted a large share of its decisions to concrete steps facilitating minority protection. This has brought the Organisation to the forefront of minority protection in Europe, in both standards and monitoring mechanisms.

It should be noted, however, that the procedure to monitor the implementation of commitments by the member states, recently established at the level of the Committee of Ministers (CoM), has not paid specific attention to the minority question. The principle of "non-discrimination" among states characteristic of thematic monitoring – along which lines this monitoring mechanism has been mainly developed, implying that a specific issue of concern under the procedure should be approached in all member states simultaneously – may have contributed to the minority issue not being firmly brought under the monitoring agenda.

The high level of sensitivity of the minority question for interstate relations seems to favour a CoM preference for leaving the minority question to the separate, voluntarily undertaken monitoring machinery, endowed with legal parameters and expert filters, provided under the Framework Convention. As a result, a substantial number of states, especially those which have not signed or ratified the Framework Convention, may remain shielded against addressing the minority questions within their borders. Whether the political consensus will be reached to overcome this fencing-off of minority issues – by means of the CoM monitoring mechanism – remains an open question.

The CoM's thematic monitoring procedure will most probably continue to address topics that are relevant to minority protection, even without dealing with that issue expressly, but in its own slow-moving, isolationist and formalised ways. Whether the minority question is ever brought under the CoM's monitoring procedure will probably depend on the assessment of its performance in addressing connected topics. Results under thematic monitoring so far seem to have reflected underachievement rather than success, especially in tackling issues concerning West European states.

Urgent human rights situations in specific states need prompt and high-profile political action. The failure to incorporate that kind of flexibility into the mainstream of thematic monitoring possibly resulted from fears by Western states that any new tools could be used against them in the future, but that inflexibility has been the cause of lost opportunities to address specific country situations under the CoM's monitoring mechanism.

That difficulty of adapting has also determined the need to develop parallel, country-specific procedures whereby the non-discriminatory criterion is abandoned. These alternative, more intrusive country-specific forms of monitoring under the CoM's monitoring mechanism, developed since 2000, have been instrumental in dealing with outstanding aspects of human rights protection and democratic performance in some states, selected on the basis of realpolitik considerations. Aspects of minority protection have been touched upon as a result.

However, the non-discriminatory spirit of the CoM monitoring mechanism overall may, ironically, act as a deterrent to prevent this country-specific monitoring being applied to an ever growing number of states, due to fears – by western European states, in particular – that assessment of their own performance could be next in line. This fear may spread to the "new democracies", which, in the aftermath of membership of western organisations may no longer feel compelled to show a higher level of performance, especially in the field of minority protection. They may also lose the incentive to engage in monitoring exercises that go beyond the light, non-intrusive kind which thematic monitoring provides, and which still allows wide scope for selective consideration..

It will be up to the CoM to opt for continued low, slow performance in isolation – keeping its monitoring mechanism fenced off even from interaction with other institutions (originally perceived as useful) and from any direct input from civil society – or to make a choice for progress and the benefits derived from external contribution instead. The latter would seem to serve better the "spirit of our time", which perceives such interaction as an essential element of international co-operation, especially in view of the growing weight of the non-governmental sector and societal dialogue. From this perspective it would seem that a substantial effort lies ahead and challenges the CoM and its present approaches.

It remains to be seen whether the high level of concern for minority protection that the Council of Europe has declared in recent times will endure, once conflicts involving minorities – conflicts that have devastated Europe – have reduced in intensity. There may now be an emerging interest, for an ever-growing majority of Council of Europe member states, in sweeping the minority issue under the carpet once again.

On the basis of non-discriminatory treatment among states, there will be no reason to continue to address the minority question in central and eastern European member states of the Organisation and not to do so in the western ones. Therefore, much will depend on the level of political support that the Committee of Ministers is ready to give to the standards and mechanisms recently set up at its own initiative. If minority protection really becomes a shared concern for European states in practice and if the will to engage in active co-operation in order to address it is finally proved, it will show that the lessons from the past have finally been learnt.

Intergovernmental co-operation activities

Several intergovernmental committees operating under the authority of the Committee of Ministers are responsible for developing co-operation between member states in areas relevant to minority protection. An important aspect of the work of these committees, in which they have achieved varying success, has been their promotion of international instruments relevant to minority protection. This has concerned not only their conceptual work of standard-setting but also their work to promote accession by states to existing international instruments.. Insufficient attention and follow-up seems to be frequently given to the policy recommendations resulting from the – often very thorough – analysis in which these committees engage, analysis which occasionally involves consultation processes that extend into civil society. As illustrated by the recent suspension of the very valuable work so far of DH-MIN in particular, progress achieved in the framework of these committees may be easily jeopardised by changing priorities.

In spite of the general lack of transparency and public information about the concrete activities of these committees, the information available indicates that DH-MIN in particular had become an important instrument of interstate dialogue and exchange of experience among states on minority questions, undertaking activities highly relevant for the definition of minority protection. It had undertaken important initiatives concerning minority groups that are in an especially vulnerable position, possibly falling beyond the scope of current minority protection regimes, and it increasingly engaged in dialogue with civil society on minority questions. In the absence of the DH-MIN however, expert committees, such as the Advisory Committee of the Framework Convention, have taken up part of this activity. In considering the restoration of the DH-MIN, it would be important to guarantee that its activities do not overlap or interfere with existing expert work, but serve to support and complement it, by reaching out to aspects of minority protection which are not covered by existing international instruments and expert bodies.

Similarly, the activities of the European Committee on Migration (CDMG) seem to have contributed to the development of new conceptual approaches to integration policies, applicable in many cases to all types of minorities, including the new minorities resulting from migration flows. In recent times, the CDMG has increasingly focused its activities in identifying concrete problems that make the integration of these minorities especially difficult and finding the avenues to overcome them.

While some of the achievements of the work done under the aegis of the Council for Cultural Co-operation (CDCC) were of high relevance for minority protection, they were not followed up by the CDCC itself as a result of lack of political support. On the other hand, some of its activities, which have been continued under the GR-C, such as the cultural policy reviews, have shown increasing awareness of minority protection aspects. However, a much higher degree of awareness of and attention to these aspects, as well as the provision of practical guidelines for their effective redress at the domestic level, still need to be provided, if the protection of cultural diversity is to acquire any real meaning.

Cultural protection is an area where much still needs to be achieved; and this applies also at the level of the Organisation generally, as recent regulatory attempts illustrate. Progress in this field could provide a very useful channel by which to address minority concerns in the future, so practical work in this area by the Organisation remains of the utmost importance, and the standard-setting objective, especially under the ECHR, should remain a priority.

The European Population Committee (CDPO/CAHP) has made a very important contribution in carrying out an assessment of the objective conditions of minorities in the member states. This will be highly relevant in the approaches to be taken by the international community towards the development of concrete policies in the area of minority protection in the member states, and in determining the adequate content such policies should have. It is to be hoped that the committee's findings will be taken into consideration.

Finally, the CDLR's work has started to take an interesting path, given its recent engagement in direct dialogue with territorial authorities in states on practical aspects of territorial self-government. This can contribute to facilitate improvements in state practice in areas of particular relevance for minorities, such as transfrontier co-operation. With the support of the Congress of Local and Regional Authorities of Europe a debate has been opened on the establishment of the legal and other mechanisms needed to allow territorial self-government to develop in practice, both within individual states and in the framework of the Organisation overall. However, in view of the follow-up provided to the activities of the intergovernmental committees generally the existence of a real and continuing commitment of Council of Europe governmental structures to co-operative and effective action in the field of minority protection remains in the balance.

Activities of the secretariat

The former Council of Europe Secretariat activities concerning minority protection, under the ADACS programme, were mostly limited to those carried out under the joint programmes on minorities with the EU Commission. The joint programme on minorities constituted the first thorough attempt to promote effective co-operation between representatives of government offices responsible for minority questions. The programme lacked a built-in system for continuity, and was discontinued despite its very positive results and the positive assessments received by the governments voluntarily involved, with an increasing number of western European states participating.

Coincidentally, the joint programme was discontinued when the initiative for the expansion of the programme to states in western Europe generally and the more active involvement of civil society were both gaining momentum. The groundwork and achievements of the joint programme on minorities should not be abandoned and allowed to decay, but should be built on and developed instead. This is especially so since it proved suited to assisting states to address practical aspects of minority protection and existing gaps in it under international instruments, including the Framework Convention. The continuation of the programme, or the start of a similar one, allowing for interstate dialogue on practical concerns and an adequate degree of NGO input, could strongly contribute to the positive redress of minority questions by Council of Europe states.

Other important activities of the Secretariat have concerned the provision of legal assistance in addressing minority questions, and the promotion of recently adopted legal instruments relevant to minority protection. The work presently carried out by the departments dealing with implementation of the Languages Charter and the Framework Convention require especial consideration. It is in the context of their activity – in support of the work of their corresponding expert bodies – that some of the most interesting Council of Europe initiatives involving dialogue between governments and civil society on minority issues within states are currently being developed. Similarly, Secretariat activities in the cultural policy field remain highly important, and support for cultural policy reform recently under way in several Council of Europe states should pay a higher degree of attention to minority concerns.

Finally, under the confidence-building measures in civil society programme, a rapidly increasing number of projects aimed at grass-roots level have been supported. There has also been a simultaneous increase in the level of direct governmental control over the programme. It would benefit from a higher level of transparency, especially as regards the acceptance or refusal of specific projects and their output, which could set an example for better practice at the domestic level. The role of the Secretariat in ensuring that its activities concerning minority questions are promoted also in western Europe, rather than simply concentrating on central and eastern European states as has been the case so far, will help to maintain the Organisation as a relevant actor in connection with this aspect of human rights protection.

The Parliamentary Assembly and its monitoring procedures

The Parliamentary Assembly is the Council of Europe organ with the longest and most active record in dealing with minorities in Europe and in searching for avenues of improvement. Often, the Assembly's prioritisation of specific minority questions has responded mainly to political concerns and its approaches have been affected by a geo-political bias. However, the Assembly has also increasingly paid attention to minority situations which do not attract political attention or which are of little relevance to the friction between geo-political blocs.

Human rights considerations in a more strict sense seem to be progressively gaining ground over political ones. This is a line of thinking and action which should be pursued in the future; it is important also from the perspective of long-term conflict prevention. The Assembly has played an essential role in developing a conceptual framework for minority protection, singling out aspects of political and social life which deserve consideration in relation to this protection, and promoting the adoption of international standards applicable to minorities. The role of the Assembly will remain of paramount importance in keeping the minority question on the agenda of the Council of Europe's intergovernmental bodies in the future, particularly in view of the possible trends towards dilution and decay identified above.

Even if various important Assembly proposals in the field of standard-setting and the establishment of monitoring mechanisms in relation to minorities have been neglected by member states, the Assembly's constant and persistent work in examining and determining relevant aspects, and appropriate levels of protection and commitment to, minority questions has had an important impact. The search for effective solutions to minority questions within the Organisation has largely been due to the Assembly's initiative. The Assembly has shown the flexibility necessary to adapt its approaches to developments resulting from inter-governmental initiatives and activities, or the lack of them, and persevered in advancing its own projects dealing with either standard-setting or implementation.

At the same time the Assembly has followed rather consistent approaches, without losing sight of the need to achieve recognition of appropriate minority rights matched with optimal guarantees for their implementation. The Assembly has placed emphasis on the justiciability of the rights of minorities. This explains the insistence of the Assembly in bringing the question of minority protection under the aegis of the ECHR, via the adoption of an additional protocol to the Convention, dealing specifically with minority concerns.

As to the assessment of state performance, the Assembly's approaches have also been generally consistent, but often undermined by geopolitical considerations. Probably the greatest missed opportunity of the Assembly in recent years regarding minorities was its role in the Council of Europe enlargement process. The possibility of obtaining adequate guarantees for the implementation of minority rights, in connection with the requirements for membership, was not sufficiently used by the Assembly.

The Assembly's part in the assessment of state compliance with accession requirements has undoubtedly contributed to the prominent place occupied by minority protection in the process. Nevertheless, the Assembly's endeavours in this regard have been overshadowed by political imperatives for rapid enlargement. Hence, the Assembly has needed to keep adapting its own monitoring procedures, and creating new ones after closing previous ones, in order to keep responding to situations of inadequate state performance, particularly in relation to minority protection. So from this perspective a "flexibility excess" has been the rule.

On the positive side, this continued process of adaptation has been instrumental in opening new doors for engagement of the "old" or Western democracies in the implementation of minority rights. Whether these states will agree to enter these doors, so that they also actively engage in minority protection, remains an open question. The reputation – and subsequently the acceptability – of the Assembly's procedures will remain in the balance until they do. It is to be hoped that the Parliamentary Assembly will continue to play its important role in keeping the minority question on the agenda of the political bodies of the Council of Europe. Given the possibility that it may now be in the interest of the majority of member states to de-emphasise the minority issue, the activity of the Assembly to prevent such a development will be of paramount importance.

It is likely that specific minority situations, and questions of minority protection, will continue to attract the attention of the members of the Assembly. This may remain true even if the impetus which the minority question has received in recent years – and which has resulted in the mobilisation of the intergovernmental organs of the Council of Europe and the increasing activities of the Secretariat – were to recede in the medium or the long term, especially in the absence of interethnic conflicts. Similarly, it is likely, and to be hoped for, that the Assembly will remain as a source of developments in standard-setting, and will continue to bring the lack of adequate implementation and justiciability of minority rights to the attention of the political bodies.

The Congress of Local and Regional Authorities of Europe and its monitoring procedures

In spite of the consolidation of the Congress as a fully fledged Council of Europe organ only recently, and the parallel development of its monitoring capabilities, the Congress has been responsible, in recent years, for a large share of the most relevant initiatives for the protection of minorities adopted within the framework of the Organisation. The Congress is also primed to become a major focus of daily activity in minority protection within the Organisation. The basic aims of the Congress, such as the achievement of local and regional self-government, are fundamental for minorities.

The Congress quickly grasped the relevance of its activities for minority protection, and has been able to conceptualise this relation, bringing it into the mainstream of its work. The Congress repeatedly succeeds in bringing and incorporating into Council of Europe discourse such concepts as territorial autonomy, which had previously been the source of considerable controversy when raised by the Parliamentary Assembly, and was considered taboo by intergovernmental bodies of the Organisation.

The Congress's monitoring of local and regional democracy in member states has centred mainly on the implementation of the European Charter of Local Self-Government. This has highlighted a series of long-standing issues concerning minorities in various member states. Nevertheless, other instruments of great importance for minority protection, such as the European Outline Convention on Transfrontier Co-operation between Territorial Communities or Authorities, together with its additional protocols, and the Convention on the Participation of Foreigners in Public Life at Local Level, have started to attract the Congress's attention.

The adoption of these instruments by an increasing number of states and their appropriate implementation will be an important pointer for minority protection in the future. The last-named instrument in particular relates to the development of democratic practices within the territorial (particularly local) authorities and communities themselves, and is an aspect of minority protection which will need a higher degree of attention by the Congress. Only through the assurance of minority protection at the local level will it be possible to ensure that genuine democracy becomes a reality at all levels of government.

In the same light, the international initiatives undertaken by the Congress in connection with its Local Democracy Agencies need to be praised. It seems, however, that they have not been receiving enough intergovernmental financial and other support, in spite of the validity of the local authorities' aims and efforts. The will to remedy this situation seems to be increasingly present, especially through the medium of EU finance.

The Commissioner for Human Rights

The recently-established Commissioner for Human Rights is consolidating a role as a flexible mechanism for the protection of human rights. In spite of the lack of specific references to minority protection in his mandate, minority issues have become one of the main targets of the Commissioner's activities. His attention initially focused on the situation of states undergoing conflict or post-conflict situations involving secessionist regions. Initial invitations for the Commissioner to visit states enmeshed in this type of conflict, following the Commissioner's visit to Russia in relation to the situation in the Chechen Republic, may have raised doubts about the perception by Council of Europe states of the Commissioner's role.

However, the Commissioner has progressively reaffirmed his standing as a monitor of states' general performance in the area of human rights, and especially minority protection, rather than as an instrument to advance the state's position in connection with a particular conflict. Further, the Commissioner has taken the important step of starting to monitor the human rights situation in the states of western Europe, occasionally without mediating a formal invitation of the authorities concerned, adopting a non-discriminatory approach to the implementation of his mandate.

The performance of the Commissioner has been marked by a high level of transparency, openness towards the media and direct contact with civil society. He has established broad channels of communication with Council of Europe organs, as well as dialogue with other international organisations. In contrast to the approach of the High Commissioner on National Minorities of the OSCE, the Commissioner has not seen his role as one of quiet diplomacy.

Although his formal mediation attempts have obtained mixed results, by increasingly relying on information from NGOs and civil society and forwarding their assessment on the human rights situation in the states to the Council of Europe political organs, the Commissioner is contributing to open lines of contact between civil society and governmental authorities under international and public scrutiny. The Commissioner has contributed to highlighting aspects of state performance of which little general knowledge existed, raising international awareness.

The Commissioner's activities concerning specific member states have mainly centred on pointing to existing problems, although the

Commissioner has also made some recommendations as to their solution, and this latter aspect has acquired a growing importance in the development of his activities. It should be highlighted in this connection that the large gap between the extent of the duties given to the Commissioner and the highly questionable level of resources presently at his disposal remains a source of concern. It does not contribute to the making of targeted recommendations, and especially to pursuing and following up their implementation, in spite of the Commissioner's efforts, which are increasingly reflected in the results of his monitoring work. Finally, reference should be made to the conceptual development and standard-definition activity with regard to aspects of human rights in which the Commissioner has engaged. This work has concerned issues that the Commissioner has perceived as being of particular importance to the implementation of his mandate, and related to the fate of minorities in particular.

Governments, citizens and the ownership of human rights

To outsiders, the Council of Europe may appear highly intergovernmental in its approach to human rights, including minority rights. However, the position varies, and the input of NGOs is significant in some areas of activity: for example, the alternative reports under the Framework Convention are capable of having significant influence in practice. The point of all human rights instruments is that they are not in the possession or ownership of governments or the intergovernmental bodies which produced them. In the drafting of the Universal Declaration of Human Rights, attention was switched from the authors of the declaration to the readers by changing the title from the "International Declaration" to the "Universal Declaration", a move designed to shift attention away from the authors of texts to their readers or addressees: all human beings.[30]

Too much intergovernmentalism is bad for human rights and does not reflect their essence. Thus, the growth of expert committees in the service of human rights in the Council of Europe is to be welcomed. Leading on from the example of the organs of the ECHR, the development of bodies such as the Advisory Committee under the Framework Convention and ECRI is an important pointer to a methodological balance between the demands of governments and the demands of the instruments in question. It is important in practice that expert committees are not regarded as secondary to government imperatives.

In the slow development of human rights since the Charter of the United Nations, the notion that human rights were a deviation from principles of classical international law has lost ground, to be replaced by the perception that human rights are a new note in the system, with their own validity and independent grounding. It follows that they are not at the mercy of states. They belong to the peoples of Europe and elsewhere. This cardinal principle should and must inform the efforts of inter-governmental organisations, and all those dedicated to the service of human rights.

Coda: on the importance of minority rights

Many practical problems of minority rights can be "solved" (in a technical sense) by the application of principles of non-discrimination. But there are cases where groups ask for explicit "recognition" in law and practice, for increased sensitivity to their voices, and for opportunities to promote their character and culture – not merely tolerance by others.[31] These demands and desiderata are the stuff of minority rights, symbols of that recognition and care.

While minorities may need more of the Council of Europe's attention than those who are comfortable, oppression is not unique to minorities. Derrida paints a dramatic picture:

> Never have violence, inequality, exclusion, famine, and ... economic oppression affected as many human beings in the history of the earth and humanity ... let us never neglect this macroscopic fact, made up of innumerable singular sites of suffering: no degree of progress allows one to ignore that never before, in absolute figures, have so many men, women and children been subjugated, starved or exterminated.[32]

In this theatre of cruelty, the provision of minority rights instruments can appear "light", frothy, superficial, dealing with superstructural questions of culture and language. Derrida's macroscopic drama can be set alongside Eagleton who writes that

> Culture is not only what we live by. It is also, in great measure, what we live for. Affection, relationship, memory, kinship, place, community, emotional fulfilment, intellectual enjoyment, a sense of ultimate meaning.[33]

There is also the point that ethnicity may not be a "light" matter to others. Ethnicity and the perception of "otherness" are distinctive bases of oppression and under-privilege. Poverty results from cultural disintegration. Cultural assertion and self-determination, in negotiation with the norms of the broader community, form a mode of resistance to the narratives and stereotyping of others.

It may be that in time the intense contemporary focus on minorities and their rights will diminish. If the forces of "one state: one nation" and other totalising ideologies become weaker, then oppressed cultures will flourish again. If threats to minorities emanate from the state, then minority groups and a supportive civil society will appeal and resist. If threats emanate from transnational corporations, the continuing support of the state is vital. In the working through of international standards on minority rights, governments have modified their behaviour, if some-what unevenly: the glass is half-empty and half-full.

The same could be said of the work of the Council of Europe in this field. On our three criteria, outlined in the Introduction, the work of the Council (in various degrees, depending on its organs) has certainly been pioneering and innovative, exploring areas of minority rights where others feared to tread. A higher level of protection than the global norm has not always resulted from such endeavours, though often it has. With serious if not always flawless strategies, the Council of Europe has attended to the needs of the region and bestowed an example to the world at large.

Notes

1.   T. van Boven, "General course on human rights" in *IV: Collected Courses of the Academy of European Law,* Book 2 (1995), pp. 1-106, at p. 18. The citation of M. Nowak is from "The contribution of intergovernmental organisations to an all-European system of human rights protection" in *All-European Rights Yearbook* (1991), pp. 211-20.

2.   Present author's emphasis.

3.   Article 1 (present author's emphasis).

4.   Discussed in detail in Chapter 8.

5.   The term is prominent in *the General Conclusions of the European Conference Against Racism,* EUROCONF (2000) 7 Final, 16 October 2000, p. 4 – the category includes persons identified – "targeted" – on grounds of language, religion, national or ethnic origin, migrants, refugees and asylum-seekers, non-nationals, indigenous peoples, etc.

6.   Cf. F.K. von Savigny, *On the Vocation of Our Age for Legislation and Jurisprudence* (1831).

7.   Charter of Fundamental Rights of the European Union, especially Article 22: "The Union shall respect cultural, religious and linguistic diversity".

8.   See references in Chapter 1 to *Thlimennos v. Greece.*

9.   See works cited in Chapter 1, and J.G. Merrills and A.H. Robertson, *Human Rights in Europe: A Study of the European Convention on Human Rights* (Manchester University Press, 4th edition 2001).

10.   Hence the disappointment expressed in Chapter 1 on the outcome of the UK cases of *Chapman et al.*

11.   Notably in Recommendation 1255 (1995).

12.   See Chapter 10.

13.   Compare Congress Recommendation 43 (1998) on territorial autonomy and national minorities, adopted on 27 May 1998; and the Congress Declaration on federalism, local autonomy and minorities, 26 October 1997. The recommendation links subsidiarity and autonomy, and the preamble affirms that "the use of the subsidiarity principle to assist in solving the problem of national minorities is not detrimental to the unity of the State, but should be an opportunity to strengthen that State's cohesion and solidarity". See the comment below on the legitimisation of the autonomy discourse by the Congress.

14.   See Chapter 8.

15.   See Chapter 9.

16.   Doc. CDL-INF (96) 4, 22 March 1996.

17.   Ibid., p. 5.

18.   Ibid., p. 7.

19.   Ibid., p. 9.

20.   Ibid., p. 4.

21.   P. Thornberry, "Images of autonomy and collective rights in international instruments on the rights of minorities" in M. Suksi (ed.), *Autonomy: Applications and Implications* (The Hague: Kluwer Law International, 1998), pp. 97-124.

22.   Notably in *Ballantyne, Davidson and McIntyre v. Canada.*

23.   The Belfast Agreement: Agreement reached in the multi-party negotiations in Northern Ireland, Cm. 3883 (1998).

24. Various remarks in *From Theory to Practice: The European Charter for Regional or Minority Languages* (Strasbourg: Council of Europe, 2002). See also contributions in *International Journal of Minority and Group Rights*, Vol. 6, No. 3 (1999), passim.

25. See Chapter 4 in particular.

26. The strategies of some Roma organisations are moving in the direction of claims to peoples' rights, including self-determination, and the proclamation of a Roma nation: a nation without territory. We may also bear in mind the "Halonen initiative" – a Roma representative body at the pan-European level. For a summary of the original initiative and animated discussion on proposals, see *Roma and the Question of Self-Determination: Fiction and Reality* (Project on Ethnic Relations (PER): Princeton, 2003); and *Leadership, Representation and the Status of the Roma* (Project on Ethnic Relations: Princeton, 2001). For an update of the current state of the initiative, see "Joint French and Finnish contribution on the European Forum of Roma and Travellers, GT-ROMS (2003) 6, 3 July 2003.

27. Discussed in Chapter 2.

28. Introduction.

29. The strategic possibilities for indigenous peoples of various human rights "pathways" are elaborated at length in P. Thornberry, *Indigenous Peoples and Human Rights*, op. cit.

30. J. Morsink, *The Universal Declaration of Human Rights: Origins, Drafting and Intent* (Philadelphia: University of Pennsylvania Press, 1999), p. 33.

31. Hence the recent initiative by some Roma groups declaring themselves a nation, rather than simply relying on rules against discrimination by others against them.

32. J. Derrida (trans. P. Kamuf), *Spectres of Marx* (1994), p. 85, cited in S. Marks, "The end of history? Reflections on some international legal theses", *European Journal of International Law*, Vol. 3 (1997), pp. 449-77, at p. 457.

33. T. Eagleton, *The Idea of Culture* (Oxford: Blackwell Publishers, 2000), p. 131.

Select bibliography

Alston, P., Bustelo, M., and Heenan, J., eds., *The EU and Human Rights*, Oxford University Press, Oxford, 1999.

Anderson, Benedict, *Imagined Communities*, Verso, London, 1991.

Arquint, R., "Regional or minority languages and education problems", *International Conference on the European Charter for Regional or Minority Languages 1*, Council of Europe Publishing, Strasbourg, 1998.

Azcarate, P. de, *The League of Nations and National Minorities*, The Carnegie Endowment, Washington, 1945.

Banton, M., *International Action against Racial Discrimination*, Clarendon Press, Oxford, 1996.

Barnes, C., and Olsthoorn, M., *The Framework Convention for the Protection of National Minorities: a guide for non-governmental organisations*, Minority Rights Group, London, 1999.

Benoît-Rohmer, F., *The Minority Question in Europe: texts and commentary*, Council of Europe Publishing, Strasbourg, 1996.

Benoît-Rohmer, F., *The Minority Question in Europe: towards a coherent system of protection for national minorities*, Council of Europe Publishing, Strasbourg, 1996.

Bloed, A., and de Jonge W., eds., *Legal Aspects of a New European Infrastructure*, Europa Institute and Netherlands Helsinki Committee, Utrecht, 1992.

Bloed, A., Leicht, L., Nowak, M., and Rosas, A., eds., *Monitoring Human Rights in Europe*, Martinus Nijhoff, Dordrecht/Boston/London, 1993.

Bloed, A., ed., *The Conference on Security and Co-operation in Europe: analysis and basic documents, 1972-1993*, Kluwer Law International, Dordrecht/Boston/London, 1993.

Bloed, A., ed., *The Challenges of Change: the Helsinki Summit of the CSCE and its aftermath*, Martinus Nijhoff, Dordrecht, 1994.

Bloed, A., and van Dijk, P., eds., *Protection of Minority Rights through Bilateral Treaties: the case of central and eastern Europe*, Kluwer Law International, The Hague, 1999.

671

Bothe, M., Ronzitti, N., and Rosas, A., eds., *The OSCE in the Maintenance of Peace and Security*, Kluwer Law International, The Hague/London/ Boston, 1997.

Boven, T. van, "General course on human rights", *Collected Courses of the Academy of European Law*, Vol. IV, No. 2, Martinus Nijhoff, Dordrecht/Boston, 1993, pp. 1-106.

Boxill, B., ed., *Race and Racism*, Oxford University Press, Oxford, 2001.

Boyle, K., and Sheen, J., eds., *Freedom of Religion and Belief: a world report*, Routledge, London/New York, 1997.

Brandtner B., and Rosas, A., "Human Rights and the External Relations of the European Community: an Analysis of Doctrine and Practice", *European Journal of International Law*, Vol. 9, No. 3, 1998.

Brölmann, C., Lefeber, R., and Zieck, M., eds., *Peoples and Minorities in International Law*, Martinus Nijhoff, Dordrecht, 1993.

Burchill, R., Harris, D., and Owers, A., eds., *Economic, Social and Cultural Rights: their implementation in United Kingdom law*, University of Nottingham Human Rights Law Centre, Nottingham, 1999.

Byers, M., ed., *The Role of Law in International Politics: essays in international relations and international law*, Oxford University Press, Oxford, 2000.

Cassese, A., *Self-Determination of Peoples: a legal reappraisal*, Cambridge University Press, New York/Cambridge, 1995.

Charter of Fundamental Rights of the European Union, Office for Official Publications of the European Communities, Luxembourg, 2001, can also be accessed at www.eu.int

Clements, L., Thomas, P.A, and Thomas, R., "The rights of minorities: a Romany perspective", *Patrin Web Journal*, 02 May 2000, www.geocities.com

Cohen, C.P., ed., *Human rights of indigenous peoples*, Transnational, Ardsley/New York, 1998.

Conforti, B., and Francioni, F., eds., *Enforcing International Human Rights in Domestic Courts*, Martinus Nijhoff, The Hague, 1997.

Council of Europe, *Collected Edition of the "Travaux Préparatoires"*, Vol. 1, Martinus Nijhoff, The Hague, 1975-85.

Council of Europe, *Framework Convention for the Protection of National Minorities: collected texts*, Council of Europe, Strasbourg, 1999 and 2001.

Coussey, M., *Framework for Integration Policies*, Council of Europe, Strasbourg, July 2000, p. 5.

Cumper, P., and Wheatley, S., eds., *Minority Rights in the "New" Europe*, Martinus Nijhoff, The Hague, 1999.

Derrida, J. (trans. P. Kamuf), *Spectres of Marx*, Routledge, New York, London, 1994.

De Witte, B., "Politics versus Law in the EU's approach to Ethnic Minorities", *European University Institute Working Paper* No. 4, RSCAS-Law, Florence, 2000.

De Witte, B., ed., *Linguistic Diversity and European Law*, Intersentia, Antwerp, forthcoming.

Dijk, P. van, and Hoof, G.J.H. van, *Theory and Practice of the European Convention on Human Rights*, 3rd edn, Kluwer Law International, The Hague, 1998.

Dimitrov, N., *The Framework Convention for the Protection of National Minorities: historical background and theoretical implications*, Matica Makedonska, Skopje/Melbourne, 1999.

Dinstein,Y., and Tabory, M., eds., *The Protection of Minorities and Human Rights*, Martinus Nijhoff, The Hague,1999.

Drzewicki, K., "The future relations between eastern Europe and the Council of Europe" in Bloed, A. and de Jonge, W., eds., *Legal Aspects of a New European Infrastructure*, Europa Institute and Netherlands Helsinki Committee, Utrecht, 1992.

Duerr, K., Spajic-Vrkaš, V., and Ferreira Martins, I., *Strategies for Learning Democratic Citizenship*, CDCC, DECS/EDU/CIT, 2000.

Eagleton, T., *The Idea of Culture*, Blackwell, Oxford, 2000.

European Centre for Minority Issues, ed., *From Ethnopolitical Conflict to Inter-Ethnic Accord in Moldova*, ECMI Report No.1, European Centre for Minority Issues, Flensburg, 1998.

Fauconnier, J.-L., "Statement from CROMBEL on the Poignant report", *Contact Bulletin*, Vol. 15, No. 2, European Bureau for Lesser Used Languages, 1999.

Field Update on Chechnya, Human Rights Watch, Brussels, 22 January 2001.

Gal, K., and Martín Estébanez, M.A., *Implementing the Framework Convention for the Protection of National Minorities*, European Centre for Minority Issues, Flensburg, 1998.

Gayim, E., *The Concept of Minority in International Law: a critical study of the vital elements,* University of Lapland, Rovaniemi, 2001.

Geertz, C., *Local Knowledge*, Fontana Press, London, 1993.

Ghai, Yash, *Public Participation and Minorities*, Minority Rights Group, London, 2001.

Ghebali, V.-Y., "The protection of minorities at the CSCE – a greater European approach", paper presented to the Athens Colloquy on the rights of minorities and peoples, December 1992.

Ghebali, V.-Y, *L'OSCE dans l'Europe Post-Communiste 1990-1996: vers une identité paneuropéenne de sécurité*, Bruylant, Brussels, 1996.

Gilbert, G., "The Council of Europe and minority rights", *Human Rights Quarterly*, Vol. 18, No. 1, Feb. 1996.

Greco, E., *L'Europa Senza Muri: la sfide della pace freda*, Stampa Tipomonza, Milan, 1995.

Gurr, T.R., and Harff, B., *Ethnic Conflict in World Politics*, Westview Press, Boulder/San Francisco/Oxford, 1994.

Gutmann, A., ed., *Multiculturalism and the "Politics of Recognition"*, Princeton University Press, Princeton, New Jersey, 1992.

Hampson, F., "Recent Turkish cases: their contribution to the case-law of the European Court of Human Rights", *Human Rights Law Review*, Vol. 4, No. 3, Nottingham University Human Rights Law Centre, Nottingham, December 1999.

Hannikainen, L., *Cultural, Linguistic and Educational Rights in the Åland Islands: an analysis in international law*, Advisory Board for International Human Rights Affairs, Helsinki, 1993.

Hannum, H., *Autonomy, Sovereignty, and Self-Determination*, University of Pennsylvania Press, Philadelphia, 1990.

Hannum, H., ed., *Documents on Autonomy and Minority Rights*, Martinus Nijhoff, Dordrecht, 1993.

Harris, D.J., O'Boyle, M., and Warbrick, C., *Law of the European Convention on Human Rights*, Butterworths, London/Dublin/Edinburgh, 1995.

Hillgruber, C., and Jestaedt, M., *The European Convention on Human Rights and the Protection of National Minorities*, Verlag Wissenschaft und Politik, Cologne, 1994.

Huber, K.J., and Zaagman, R., "Towards the prevention of ethnic conflict in CSCE: the High Commissioner on national minorities and other developments", *International Journal on Group Rights*, No. 1, Dordrecht, 1993.

Huntington, S., " The clash of civilisations", *Foreign Affairs: an American quarterly review*, Vol. 72, No. 3, Council on Foreign Relations, New York, 1999.

Hutchinson, J., and Smith, A.D., eds., *Ethnicity*, Oxford University Press, Oxford, 1996.

Henrard, K., *Devising an Adequate System of Minority Protection: Individual Human Rights, Minority Rights and the Right to Self-Determination*, Kluwer, London, 2000.

Jacobs, F.G., and White, R.C.A., *The European Convention on Human Rights*, 2nd edition, Clarendon Press, Oxford, 1996.

Jonge, W. de, ed., *Legal Aspects of a New European Infrastructure*, Netherlands Helsinki Committee and Europa Institute, Utrecht, 1992.

Kemp, W.A., ed., *Quiet Diplomacy in Action: the OSCE High Commissioner on national minorities*, Kluwer Law International, The Hague/London/Boston, 2001.

Koh, H.H., and Shue, R.C., *Deliberative Democracy and Human Rights*, Yale University Press, New Haven/London, 1999.

Kuhl, J., *The Schleswig Experience: the national minorities in the Danish-German border area*, Institut for Graenseregionsforskning, Åbenrå, 1998.

Kymlicka, W., *Multicultural Citizenship: a liberal theory of minority rights*, Clarendon Press, Oxford, 1995.

Kymlicka, W., ed., *The Rights of Minority Cultures*, Oxford University Press, Oxford, 1995.

Kymlicka, W., and Norman, W., eds., *Citizenship in Diverse Societies*, Oxford University Press, Oxford, 2000.

Lerner, N., *Group Rights and Discrimination in International Law*, Martinus Nijhoff, Dordrecht, 1991.

Liebich, A., and Regler, A., eds., *L' Europe Centrale et Ses Minorités: vers une solution Européenne?*, Presses Universitaires de France, Paris, 1993, pp. 51-72.

Macartney, C.A., *National States and National Minorities*, Oxford University Press, London, 1934.

Marks, S., "The end of history? reflections on some international legal theses", *European Journal on International Law*, Vol. 8, No. 3, 1997. Can also be accessed at www.ejil.org.

Martín Estébanez, M.A., *International Organisations and Minority Protection in Europe*, Åbo Akademi University, Åbo/Turku, 1996.

McKean, W.A., *Equality and Discrimination under International Law*, Clarendon Press, Oxford, 1983.

675

McDonald, R.St J., et al., eds., *The European System for the Protection of Human Rights*, Kluwer Law International, Dordrecht, 1993.

Mélanges Offerts à Polys Modinos. Problèmes de droits de l'homme et de l'unification européenne, Editions A. Pedone, Paris, 1968.

Memorandum on Domestic Prosecutions for Violations of International Human Rights and Humanitarian Law in Chechnya, Human Rights Watch, Brussels, February 2001, can also be accessed at www.hrw.org.

Mickiewicz, H., "A human right to the native spelling of a personal name?", *Journal of International Relations and Development*, Vol. 4, Nos. 1-4, Centre for International Relations, Ljubljana, 1997.

Minority Rights Group, ed., *Minorities and Autonomy in Western Europe*, Minority Rights Group, London, 1991.

Minority Rights Group, ed., *World Directory of Minorities*, Minority Rights Group, London, 1997.

Monitoring the EU Accession Process: minority protection, Central European University Press, Budapest/New York, 2001.

Morsink, J., *The Universal Declaration of Human Rights: origins, drafting and intent*, University of Pennsylvania Press, Philadelphia, 1999.

Neuwahl, N., and Rosas, A., eds., *The European Union and Human Rights*, Kluwer Law International, The Hague/London/Boston, 1995.

Niessen, J., and the European Cultural Foundation: *Diversity and Cohesion: new challenges for the integration of immigrants and minorities*, Council of Europe, Strasbourg, July 2000.

Nowak, M., "Is Bosnia and Herzegovina ready for membership in the Council of Europe? The responsibility of the Committee of Ministers and of the Parliamentary Assembly", *Human Rights Law Journal*, Vol. 20, No. 70-11, 30 November 1999.

Nykanen; E., ed., *New Trends in Discrimination Law – international perspectives*, Turku Law School Publications, Åbo/Turku, 1999, pp. 177-220.

Packer, J., "The role of the OSCE High Commissioner on National Minorities in the former Yugoslavia", *Cambridge Review of International Affairs*, No. 2, Centre of International Studies Cambridge University, Cambridge, 1999, pp. 169-84.

Packer, J., and Myntti, K., eds., *The Protection of Ethnic and Linguistic Minorities in Europe*, Åbo Akademi University, Åbo/Turku, 1993.

Pellet, A., "The opinions of the Badinter Arbitration Committee – a second breath for the self-determination of peoples", *European Journal of International Law*, Vol. 3, European Journal of International Law, Firenze, 1992, pp. 178-81.

Pentassuglia, G., *Minorities in International Law*, Council of Europe Publishing, Strasbourg, 2002.

Pettit, P., *Republicanism: a theory of freedom and government*, Clarendon Press, Oxford, 1997.

Phillips, A., and Rosas, A., eds., *Universal Minority Rights*, Minority Rights Group and Åbo Akademi University, London/Åbo, 1995.

Poignant, B., "Prospects for ratification of the Charter by France", in *Implementation of the European Charter for Regional or Minority Languages*, Council of Europe, Strasbourg, 1999.

Polakiewicz, J., *Treaty Making in the Council of Europe*, Council of Europe, Strasbourg, 1999.

Rex, J., *Race and Ethnicity*, Open University Press, Milton Keynes, 1986.

Robertson, A.H., and Merrills, J., *Human Rights in the World*, 4th edn, Manchester University Press, Manchester, 1996.

Robinson, J., et al., *Were the Minorities Treaties a Failure?*, Institute of Jewish Affairs, New York, 1943.

Rosas, A., and Helgesen, J., eds., *The Strength of Diversity*, Kluwer Academic, Dordrecht/London, 1992.

Sanders, D., "Collective rights", *Human Rights Quarterly*, No. 13, Johns Hopkins University Press, Baltimore, 1991.

Savigny, F.K. von, *Of the Vocation of Our Age for Legislation and Jurisprudence* (1831), The Lawbook Exchange, 2002.

Shuibhne, N., *EC Law and Minority Language Policy: Culture, Citizenship and Fundamental Rights*, Kluwer, The Hague, 2002.

Shute, S., and Hurley, S., eds., *On Human Rights: the Oxford amnesty lectures*, 1993, Basik Books, New York, 1994.

Sicilianos, L.-A., ed., and Bouloyannis-Vrailas, C.B., assoc. ed., *The Prevention of Human Rights Violations*, Kluwer Law International and Ant. N. Sakkoulas, The Hague/New York/London/Athens, 2001.

Skutnabb-Kangas, T., *Linguistic Genocide in Education – or worldwide diversity and human rights*, Lawrence Erlbaum Associates, Mahwah/New Jersey/London, 2000.

Spiliopoulou-Åkermark, A., *Justifications of Minority Protection in International Law*, Kluwer Law International, London, 1997, pp. 244-45.

Suksi, M., ed., *Autonomy: applications and implications*, Kluwer Law International, The Hague, 1998, pp. 97-124.

Swepston, L., and Tomei, M., *Indigenous and Tribal Peoples: a guide to ILO Convention No. 169*, International Labour Office, Geneva, 1996.

Taylor, C., *The Ethics of Authenticity*, Harvard University Press, Cambridge, Mass./London, 1991.

The Human Rights Watch World Report 2000: Events of 1999, Human Rights Watch, New York/Washington/London/Brussels, 2000.

Thornberry, P., *Minorities and Human Rights Law*, Minority Rights Group, 1991.

Thornberry, P., *International Law and the Rights of Minorities*, Clarendon Press, Oxford, 1991.

Thornberry, P., *Indigenous Peoples and Human Rights*, Manchester University Press, 2002.

Thornberry, P., and Martín Estébanez, M. A., *The Council of Europe and Minorities*, Council of Europe, Strasbourg, 1994.

Tomuschat, C., ed., *Modern Law of Self-Determination*, Martinus Nijhoff, The Hague, 1993.

Vel, G. de, The Committee of Ministers of the Council of Europe, Council of Europe, Strasbourg, 1995.

Webster's Encyclopaedic Unabridged Dictionary of the English Language, Dilithium Press, New York/Toronto/London/Sydney/Auckland, 1989.

Williams, Jr., R.A., *The American Indian in Western Legal Thought: the discourses of conquest*, Oxford University Press, New York/Oxford, 1990.

Cases[1]

in chronological order

X v. Federal Republic of Germany, No. 6742/74, D.R. 3 (1975), p. 98.

X v. Netherlands, No. 7230/75, D.R. 7 (1976), p. 109.

Kalderas Gypsies v. Federal Republic of Germany and Netherlands, 6 July 1977 (Commission decision).

X and Church of Scientology v. Sweden, No. 7805/77, D.R. 16 (1979), p. 68.

Christians against Racism and Fascism v. the UK, No. 8440/78, 21 D.R. (1980), p. 138 at 152.

Church of Scientology v. Sweden, D.R. 21 (1980).

Liberal Party v. UK, D.R. 21, p. 211 18 December 1980 (Commission decision).

Young, James and Webster v. the UK (1981), Ser. A, No. 44, paragraph 64.

X v. Ireland (1983).

Abdulaziz, Cabales and Balkandali v. UK, Series A 94 (1985).

Kitok v. Sweden, UN Doc. CCPR/C/33/D/197/1985.

Bideaut v. France, No. 11261/84, D.R. 48 (1986).

Mathieu-Mohin and Clerfayt v. Belgium, Series A, No. 113 (1987).

Rothenthurm Commune v. Switzerland, D.R. 59 (1988).

Asociación de Aviadores de la República v. Spain, D.R. 41 (1988), p. 211.

Smith Kline and French Laboratories v. the Netherlands, D.R. 66 (1990), p. 70.

Powell and Rayner v. the United Kingdom, Series A, No. 172, (1990).

Pine Valley Developments Ltd. and Others v. Ireland, Series A, No. 222, (1991).

Beckers v. Netherlands (1991).

---

1. For more information on cases see HUDOC at http://hudoc.echr.coe.int/hudoc

Van De Vin v. Netherlands (1992).

Ballantyne et al. v. Canada, UN Doc. A/48/40 (1993).

Kokkinakis v. Greece, Series A, No. 260-A, judgment of 25 May 1993.

Hoffmann v. Austria, Series A 255-C (1993).

Coeriel and Aurik v. Netherlands, UN Doc. A/50/40, Vol. I (1994).

Manoussakis and Others v. Greece, judgment of 26 September 1996, Reports of Judgments and Decisions 1996-IV.

Buckley v. the United Kingdom, judgment of 25 September 1996, Reports of Judgments and Decisions 1996-IV.

Ahmet Sadik v. Greece, 15 November 1996.

Zana v. Turkey, 69/1996/688/880, judgment of 25 November 1997.

Canea Catholic Church v. Greece, judgment of 16 December 1997, Reports of Judgments and Decisions 1997-IV.

National and Provincial Building Society, Leeds Permanent Building Society and Yorkshire Building Society v. UK, Nos. 21319/93, 21449/93 and 21675/93, judgment of 23 October 1997.

Chapman v. UK, No. 27238.

Socialist Party and Others v. Turkey, 20/1997/804/1007, judgment of 25 May 1998.

Twalib v. Greece, No. 24294/94, judgment of 9 June 1998.

Sidiropoulos and Others v. Greece, 10 July 1998.

Assenov and others v. Bulgaria, judgment of 28 October 1998, Reports of Judgments and Decisions 1998-VIII.

Arslan v. Turkey, No. 23462/94, 8 July 1999.

Başkaya and Okçuoğlu v. Turkey, Nos. 23536/94 and 24408/94, ECHR 1999-IV.

Ceylan v. Turkey, No. 23556/94, ECHR 1999-IV.

Erdoğdu and İnce v. Turkey, Nos. 25067/94 and 25068/94, ECHR 1999-IV.

Gerger v. Turkey, No. 24919/94, 8 July 1999.

Karataş v. Turkey, No. 23168/94, ECHR 1999-IV.

Polat v. Turkey, No. 23500/94, 8 July 1999.

Sürek and Özdemir v. Turkey, Nos. 23927/94 and 24277/94, 8 July 1999.

Oglu v. Greece, No. 33738/96, decision of 16 March 1999.

Öztürk v. Turkey, No. 22479/93, judgment of 28 September 1999.

Giustiniani v. Italy, No. 35972/97, 21 October 1999.

Grande Oriente D'Italia di Palazzo Giustiniani v. Italy, No. 35972/97, 21 October 1999, ECHR 2001-VIII.

Thlimennos v. Greece, appl. No. 34369/97, ECHR 2000-IV.

Cha'Are Shalom Ve Tsedek v. France, 27 June 2000.

Sener v. Turkey, No. 26680/95, judgment of 18 July 2000.

Hasan and Chaus v. Bulgaria, No. 30985/96, judgment of 26 October 2000.

Varey v. UK, No. 26662/95, 21 December 2000.

Coster v. UK, No. 24876/94, 18 January 2001.

Beard v. UK, No. 24882/94, 18 January 2001.

Lee v. UK, No. 25289/94, 18 January 2001.

Jane Smith v. UK, No. 25154/94, 18 January 2001.

Cyprus v. Turkey, No. 25781/94, ZCHR 2001-IV.

Association Ekin v. France, judgment of 17 July 2001.

Grande Oriente D'Italia di Palazzo Liberal Party v. Italy, D.R. 21, p. 211, 2 August 2001.

Useful websites

Minority rights in Europe

Council of Europe

http://www.coe.int/ (Council of Europe)

http://www.echr.coe.int/ (Human Rights Court)

http://www.humanrights.coe.int (Human Rights Directorate, Council of Europe)

http://www..coe.int/T/E/human_rights/minorities (Framework Convention for the Protection of National minorities)

http://www.coe.int/minlang (European Charter for Regional or National Minorities)

http://www.coe.int/T/E/Social_Cohesion/Roma_Gypsies/ (Roma/Gypsies)

https://wcm.coe.int/rsi/cm/index.jsp (Committee of Ministers)

http://assembly.coe.int/ (Parliamentary Assembly)

http://www.coe.int/t/e/CLRAE/ (Congress of Loal and Regional Authorities of Europe)

http://www.ecri.coe.int (European Commission against Racism and Intolerance)

http://www.commissioner.coe.int (Commissioner for Human Rights)

http://www.venice.coe.int (Venice Commission)

http://conventions.coe.int

Other interesting sites

http://www.osce.org (OSCE)

http://www.unhchr.ch (UN High Commissioner on Human Rights)

http://www.abc.net.au/rn/talks/lnl/stories/s61928.htm

http://www.romnews.com/ (RomNews Network, Hamburg)

http://www.memo.ru/eng/hr/

http://www.osce.org/hcnm/documents/recommendations

Sales agents for publications of the Council of Europe
Agents de vente des publications du Conseil de l'Europe

AUSTRALIA/AUSTRALIE
Hunter Publications, 58A, Gipps Street
AUS-3066 COLLINGWOOD, Victoria
Tel.: (61) 3 9417 5361
Fax: (61) 3 9419 7154
E-mail: Sales@hunter-pubs.com.au
http://www.hunter-pubs.com.au

BELGIUM/BELGIQUE
La Librairie européenne SA
50, avenue A. Jonnart
B-1200 BRUXELLES 20
Tel.: (32) 2 734 0281
Fax: (32) 2 735 0860
E-mail: info@libeurop.be
http://www.libeurop.be

Jean de Lannoy
202, avenue du Roi
B-1190 BRUXELLES
Tel.: (32) 2 538 4308
Fax: (32) 2 538 0841
E-mail: jean.de.lannoy@euronet.be
http://www.jean-de-lannoy.be

CANADA
Renouf Publishing Company Limited
5369 Chemin Canotek Road
CDN-OTTAWA, Ontario, K1J 9J3
Tel.: (1) 613 745 2665
Fax: (1) 613 745 7660
E-mail: order.dept@renoufbooks.com
http://www.renoufbooks.com

CZECH REPUBLIC/
RÉPUBLIQUE TCHÈQUE
Suweco Cz Dovoz Tisku Praha
Ceskomoravska 21
CZ-18021 PRAHA 9
Tel.: (420) 2 660 35 364
Fax: (420) 2 683 30 42
E-mail: import@suweco.cz

DENMARK/DANEMARK
GAD Direct
Fiolstaede 31-33
DK-1171 COPENHAGEN K
Tel.: (45) 33 13 72 33
Fax: (45) 33 12 54 94
E-mail: info@gaddirect.dk

FINLAND/FINLANDE
Akateeminen Kirjakauppa
Keskuskatu 1, PO Box 218
FIN-00381 HELSINKI
Tel.: (358) 9 121 41
Fax: (358) 9 121 4450
E-mail: akatilaus@stockmann.fi
http://www.akatilaus.akateeminen.com

FRANCE
La Documentation française
(Diffusion/Vente France entière)
124, rue H. Barbusse
F-93308 AUBERVILLIERS Cedex
Tel.: (33) 01 40 15 70 00
Fax: (33) 01 40 15 68 00
E-mail: commandes.vel@ladocfrancaise.gouv.fr
http://www.ladocfrancaise.gouv.fr

Librairie Kléber (Vente Strasbourg)
Palais de l'Europe
F-67075 STRASBOURG Cedex
Fax: (33) 03 88 52 91 21
E-mail: librairie.kleber@coe.int

GERMANY/ALLEMAGNE
AUSTRIA/AUTRICHE
UNO Verlag
Am Hofgarten 10
D-53113 BONN
Tel.: (49) 2 28 94 90 20
Fax: (49) 2 28 94 90 222
E-mail: bestellung@uno-verlag.de
http://www.uno-verlag.de

GREECE/GRÈCE
Librairie Kauffmann
28, rue Stadiou
GR-ATHINAI 10564
Tel.: (30) 1 32 22 160
Fax: (30) 1 32 30 320
E-mail: ord@otenet.gr

HUNGARY/HONGRIE
Euro Info Service
Hungexpo Europa Kozpont ter 1
H-1101 BUDAPEST
Tel.: (361) 264 8270
Fax: (361) 264 8271
E-mail: euroinfo@euroinfo.hu
http://www.euroinfo.hu

ITALY/ITALIE
Libreria Commissionaria Sansoni
Via Duca di Calabria 1/1, CP 552
I-50125 FIRENZE
Tel.: (39) 556 4831
Fax: (39) 556 41257
E-mail: licosa@licosa.com
http://www.licosa.com

NETHERLANDS/PAYS-BAS
De Lindeboom Internationale Publikaties
PO Box 202, MA de Ruyterstraat 20 A
NL-7480 AE HAAKSBERGEN
Tel.: (31) 53 574 0004
Fax: (31) 53 572 9296
E-mail: books@delindeboom.com
http://home-1-worldonline.nl/~lindeboo/

NORWAY/NORVÈGE
Akademika, A/S Universitetsbokhandel
PO Box 84, Blindern
N-0314 OSLO
Tel.: (47) 22 85 30 30
Fax: (47) 23 12 24 20

POLAND/POLOGNE
Główna Księgarnia Naukowa
im. B. Prusa
Krakowskie Przedmiescie 7
PL-00-068 WARSZAWA
Tel.: (48) 29 22 66
Fax: (48) 22 26 64 49
E-mail: inter@internews.com.pl
http://www.internews.com.pl

PORTUGAL
Livraria Portugal
Rua do Carmo, 70
P-1200 LISBOA
Tel.: (351) 13 47 49 82
Fax: (351) 13 47 02 64
E-mail: liv.portugal@mail.telepac.pt

SPAIN/ESPAGNE
Mundi-Prensa Libros SA
Castelló 37
E-28001 MADRID
Tel.: (34) 914 36 37 00
Fax: (34) 915 75 39 98
E-mail: libreria@mundiprensa.es
http://www.mundiprensa.com

SWITZERLAND/SUISSE
BERSY
Route de Monteiller
CH-1965 SAVIESE
Tel.: (41) 27 395 53 33
Fax: (41) 27 395 53 34
E-mail: bersy@bluewin.ch

Adeco – Van Diermen
Chemin du Lacuez 41
CH-1807 BLONAY
Tel.: (41) 21 943 26 73
Fax: (41) 21 943 36 05
E-mail: info@adeco.org

UNITED KINGDOM/ROYAUME-UNI
TSO (formerly HMSO)
51 Nine Elms Lane
GB-LONDON SW8 5DR
Tel.: (44) 207 873 8372
Fax: (44) 207 873 8200
E-mail: customer.services@theso.co.uk
http://www.the-stationery-office.co.uk
http://www.itsofficial.net

UNITED STATES and CANADA/
ÉTATS-UNIS et CANADA
Manhattan Publishing Company
468 Albany Post Road, PO Box 850
CROTON-ON-HUDSON,
NY 10520, USA
Tel.: (1) 914 271 5194
Fax: (1) 914 271 5856
E-mail: Info@manhattanpublishing.com
http://www.manhattanpublishing.com

Council of Europe Publishing/Editions du Conseil de l'Europe
F-67075 Strasbourg Cedex
Tel.: (33) 03 88 41 25 81 – Fax: (33) 03 88 41 39 10 – E-mail: publishing@coe.int – Website: http://book.coe.int